The Mighty Endeavor

The Mighty Endeavor

CHARLES B. MACDONALD

LUME BOOKS

LUME BOOKS

This edition published in 2021 by Lume Books
30 Great Guildford Street,
Borough, SE1 0HS

ISBN 987-1-83901-337-9

Typeset using Atomik ePublisher from Easypress Technologies

www.lumebooks.co.uk

For Mary MacQueen MacDonald,
who had four in it

'Almighty God — Our sons, pride of our nation, this day have set upon a mighty endeavor, a struggle to preserve our Republic, our religion, and our civilization and to set free a suffering humanity...'

from President Franklin D. Roosevelt's statement on D Day, 6 June, 1944

Table of Contents

Chapter One – The Path to Decision

It was not in the American image to plan for war when there was no war.[1] Spontaneity and improvisation, the record would show, were virtues in the American way of waging war. Not longer ago than 1915, when responsible officials in the War Department had dared to plan for the possibility of war with Germany and let word of it reach the press, President Woodrow Wilson, "trembling and white with passion,"[2] had threatened to relieve and order out of Washington every officer of the General Staff.

Hiding behind the illusion that the world had seen the last of warfare on a grand scale, Americans in the twenties and much of the thirties had comfortably donned the blinders of isolationism. They read their Sinclair Lewis, their Dreiser, their Fitzgerald, their Civil War romances. They idolized a new species of talking, singing film stars; persecuted and then lamented Saeeo and Vanzetti; made a millionaire out of Henry Ford, a demigod of Charles A. Lindbergh, Jr. They rode in the rumble seat; outlawed the liquor they drank; applauded the naval limitation

---

[1] For the first chapter, I have relied primarily on Louis Morton's excellent essay, "Germany First: The Basic Concept of Allied Strategy in World War II," in Greenfield, ed., *Command Decisions*, but a number of the U.S. Army's World War II volumes provide additional material, including Morton's own, *Strategy and Command: The First Two Years* (1962), and Watson, *Chief of Staff*. Morton's bibliographical note to his essay affords a guide to other published material, and his footnotes provide full identification of original documents. See also Pogue, *Ordeal and Hope*. For home-front events in this and subsequent chapters, I have consulted files of *The New York Times*, *The Washington Post*, *The Chicago Tribune*, and *Time* Magazine. Also useful were: David Hinshaw, *The Home Front* (New York, 1943); Jack Goodman, ed., *While You Were Away* (New York, 1946); and A. A. Hoehling, *Home Front, USA* (New York, 1966).

[2] Frederick Palmer, *Newton D. Baker — America at War* (New York, 1931), pp. 40-41. Unpublished material in OCMH reveals that much of Wilson's fury was directed at the leak to the press.

1

conferences and the Kellogg-Briand Pact while reserving the League of Nations for the immoral European states that needed it. Having added one teetering building block after another to their economy until it inevitably came tumbling down, they drove Hoover carts, played Monopoly, and went to bank night at the movies. Half in desperation, to set their little insular world right again, they unwittingly voted in a kind of socialism they earlier had disdained.

As for a military establishment, that was a necessary evil, good for an honor guard, for chasing bonus marchers off the Anacostia flats, or for an occasional headline, as when airman Billy Mitchell, who claimed to have had a vision that would dispense with warfare on ground and sea, challenged the traditionalists—and to hell with the consequences! Yet in general the sign reputedly found in a Texas café caught the prevailing mood: DOGS AND SOLDIERS NOT ALLOWED[3]

The Navy, of course, was different, made up as it was of a composite Dick Powell-Fred Astaire who came crooning and dancing into port to an Irving Berlin score into the waiting aims of Ruby Keeler-Ginger Rogers. Nor was there concern, in view of the restrictions imposed by the naval conferences with Great Britain and Japan, that the Navy might grow so large as to invite war. In 1933 the Navy had only 91,000 men and 1,186,000 tons of ships.

As for the Army, the National Defense Act of 1920 had decreed that at maximum strength it should be a hard, lean force of 280,000. It was actually a neglected, spavined, meager force of only 135,000, little more than the Versailles Treaty allowed defeated Germany. That left it in seventeenth place among the armies of the world.

Incredible that within those skeletal and impoverished organizations, and with the scorn in which they were held, there were men who could do more than play at the game of soldier or sailor. More remarkable still, in view of the national determination to outlaw war by ignoring war, there were men in those establishments who had the heart to plan for war. Yet there were such men. There was, too, the apparatus by means of which they could engage in strategic planning, however theoretical, even abstract.

That was the Joint Board, which was composed of equal numbers of Army and Navy officers, including the Army's Chief of Staff and the Chief

---

[3] A personal recollection

of Naval Operations, and was charged with handling all matters requiring cooperation between the two services. To the original Joint Board of the World War had been added a joint Planning Committee, composed of four officers each from the War Plans divisions of the Army and the Navy. Neither this committee nor the Joint Board itself had the power of command or ultimate decision, which was reserved, in the end, to the President; but decisions would be made on the basis of the deliberations of the Joint Board. If spontaneity and improvisation ceased to be virtues in the war to come, these men, in large measure, would be responsible.

During the twenties and early thirties it was difficult to find likely enemies upon which the joint planners might legitimately focus. Yet the planners dutifully catalogued several and gave a color code name to the war plan dealing with each—even Great Britain (RED). This was nevertheless little more than theoretical, for the Great War had left most European nations destitute. The only likely enemy meriting serious consideration was in the Pacific. There Japan (ORANGE), strengthened by emerging industrialization and by a peripheral, opportunistic engagement in the war, had long displayed expansionist tendencies.

So long as no European power emerged as a real threat to peace, no disagreement would arise between Army and Navy planners over the priority to be accorded war in the Pacific. Although the ORANGE plan as adopted in 1924 foresaw primarily a naval war, with the Army's role distinctly secondary, no ugly interservice jealousy arose. Not even consideration of a combined RED-ORANGE plan based on the possibility of a two-front war with Britain and Japan could turn the Army's head toward the Atlantic, possibly because the likelihood of any war with Britain appeared, if not impossible, at least immoral.

However unrealistic the thought of war with Britain, there emerged from the RED-ORANGE planning a theory, a concept, however tentative, bearing—though no one knew it at the time—tremendous import for the future. In a war with Japan, the planners believed, the chance of the Japanese seizing Hawaii, Panama, and certainly any part of the continental United States was remote; but in a war with Britain the threat of invasion would be real. Since the United States in a combined RED-ORANGE war would lack the resources to fight offensively at the same time in both Pacific and Atlantic, the more serious threat posed in the Atlantic might have to be eliminated first.

3

"It is not unreasonable to hope," the planners noted more prophetically still, "that the situation at the end of the struggle with RED may be such as to induce ORANGE to yield rather than face a war carried to the Western Pacific."[4]

Despite a past record of British naval intransigence, war with Britain nevertheless remained so improbable that no combined RED-ORANGE plan was officially adopted. Well past the midpoint of the thirties, the ORANGE plan, with its focus on the Pacific and Japan, drew most attention. Growing Japanese militarism, as exemplified by invasion of Manchuria in 1931 and full-scale war with China in 1937, along with bombing of the American gunboat *Panay*, was sufficient justification for continuing concern.

Yet in the meantime, threats and actual aggression had emerged in Europe as well. In 1935, Benito Mussolini's Italy, virtually egged on by the impotence of the League of Nations, attacked Ethiopia; and in 1936, while civil war ravaged Spain, Adolf Hitler sent a revived German army into a demilitarized Rhineland.

Late in 1937, in recognition of world developments, the Joint Board directed the planners to re-examine the ORANGE plan. Explicit was the continuing belief that Japan still posed the principal threat; but the planners also were to consider the possibility that the United States might become involved at the same time in a war with some European power.

A schism quickly developed between Army and Navy planners. The men trained at Annapolis remained firmly wedded to the idea of far-ranging offensives in the Pacific, while those from West Point cast their eyes toward the Atlantic. Army planners insisted that, with the threat of a coalition of Italy and Germany, bound to one another as the Rome-Berlin Axis and to Japan by the Anti-Comintern Pact, it would be foolhardy to undertake offensive operations in the Pacific beyond those necessary to protect the strategic triangle formed by Alaska, Hawaii, and Panama. On the other hand, countered the Navy theorists, even if the Axis nations should help Japan, Britain could be depended upon to offset that help.

So deep was the split that the Joint Board eventually had to turn to a rank-heavy *ad hoc* committee for compromise. As finally determined, a new ORANGE plan maintained the traditional offensive strategy for the

---

[4] Proposed Joint Estimate and Plan — RED-ORANGE, prepared in War Plans Division and approved by the Chief of Staff, June 3, 1940, as cited by Morton, "Germany First."

Pacific but sharply modified it. No offensive was to begin in the Pacific until it was certain that no attack would be forthcoming against the United States in the Atlantic.

That was vague enough to please everybody.

The Army planners had nevertheless come close to scoring a point and, in the process, had nourished those first seeds of strategic reorientation that had emerged in the earlier RED-ORANGE discussions. Even the Navy, for all its preoccupation with the offensive in the Pacific, was not unimpressed. As if to shore up its dependence on Britain, the Navy had sent the head of its War Plans Division to London, even as the planners disagreed, to confer with the Admiralty on new construction programs and on the cooperation that might be expected should both countries become involved in a war with Japan.

Yet all planning in those years took place against a backdrop of unreality. All through the years when the ORANGE plan constituted the nation's basic strategic design, Army officers, in particular, were acutely conscious that a parsimonious Congress had made it impossible for the Army to do what was expected of it under almost any plan. Reassured by the presence in the White House of a former Assistant Secretary of the Navy, Franklin D. Roosevelt, the Navy could more understandably flirt with the attractive image of the offensive. In mid-decade Roosevelt even managed to push through a modest naval expansion program, though in the guise of making work to alleviate unemployment.

Until 1938 there was little in the national attitude as reflected by Congressional action to encourage even the Navy. In 1934, for example, a Senate committee, headed by North Dakota's Gerald Nye, was investigating the munitions industry and the bankers of the World War; it underscored the convictions already held by millions of Americans that the nation had been bamboozled into the war, and that the only way to escape another was to eliminate the profit motive and to legislate strict neutrality. The fervor stirred by Nye's investigations led directly to neutrality legislation enacted piecemeal from 1935 through 1937. There were to be no loans or credits to belligerents, no arms shipments, no travel by Americans on the ships of belligerents, no weapons on American merchant vessels. If the United States—the theory went—put itself in an isolation ward, it would effectively seal out the disease of war. Few observers remarked that the nation might so weaken itself by self-imposed regulation as to facilitate the entry of persistent germs.

Whether because of the depression or of isolationism, neither Army nor Navy flourished during the first four years of Roosevelt's New Deal. Despite a growing Congressional concern about inadequate defenses in the nation's outposts—the Philippines, Alaska, Hawaii, Panama—Army appropriations in 1936 totaled less than $578,000,000, while the Navy got just under $489,000,000. The Army had slightly less than 138,000 men; the Navy, 96,000. Many of the naval craft were obsolete; the hard core of battleships, for example, had fought the Kaiser. The Army's basic artillery piece still was the French 75, mostly mounted on wooden, steel-rimmed wheels; if towed by modern trucks instead of horses, the piece would have fallen apart.

Ever wary of moving too fast for the mood of the people, Franklin Roosevelt nevertheless tried to point up the fallacy of unpreparedness and inaction. In Chicago, heart of isolationist sentiment, he warned in the fall of 1937, soon after Japan moved against China, that aggressor nations should be quarantined by mutual action of peace-loving peoples, else "let no one imagine that America will escape, that America may expect mercy, that this Western Hemisphere will not be attacked."[5]

In theatrical parlance, Roosevelt laid an egg.

"War-mongering," domestic critics called it; and abroad no tangible support for interaction developed. How could a nation drawn and quartered by the Neutrality Acts have the effrontery even to suggest that other powers join in action that would violate that nation's own restrictions?

The next year, 1938, marked a turning point—no dramatic awakening of the sleeping giant, but a turning point nonetheless. Spurred by Hitler's bloodless coup against Austria in March and by the start of German agitation against Czechoslovakia over the Sudetenland, Congress in May voted funds for some 659,000 tons of new naval construction. When the European democracies capitulated in late September at Munich, Roosevelt called on his military leaders to come up with a plan to produce 10,000 planes over the next two years.

[5] Samuel Rosenman, ed., *The Public Papers and Addresses of Franklin D. Roosevelt*, 13 vols. (New York, 1939 — 1950). Unless otherwise noted, all subsequent quotations from Roosevelt's speeches are from the same source.

War Department leaders were upset by what appeared undue preoccupation with aerial warfare, and countered with a plan for a buildup instead of balanced ground and air forces. That in turn led the Joint Board to ask its planners for a completely new approach to war planning. They were to devise courses of action in the event of simultaneous war in both the Pacific and the Atlantic. Under this concept the planners prepared five new basic war plans. Since the plans envisaged war against more than one enemy and in more than one theater of operations, the planners gave them the collective code name: RAINBOW.

Two of the new plans—RAINBOW 1 and RAINBOW 4—dealt primarily with action to be taken in event of enemy aggression within the Western Hemisphere. RAINBOW 2 assumed European allies who would free the United States to make its major commitment in the Pacific, while RAINBOW 3 advanced the premise of moving into the Pacific once defense of the Western Hemisphere was assured. Only RAINBOW 5 reiterated the tentative idea, first advanced in the RED-ORANGE discussions, that the United States might have to assume the strategic defensive in the Pacific until the enemy in Europe could be beaten. It seemed to all concerned in mid-1939 that, of the five plans, the one most likely to be used was RAINBOW 2: European allies to handle Germany and Italy, while the United States concentrated on defeating Japan.

Events in Europe in September reinforced that view.

The crisis had been building for months. Through much of the typically hot summer the air had been filled with tension and dread, seemingly climaxed in August with disclosure of the Nazi-Soviet Non-aggression Pact.

On the last day of August, the Gallup Poll revealed that 87 per cent of Americans believed Hitler's claims on Poland unjustified; but only a day earlier a St. Lôuis radio station had cut news commentator Dorothy Thompson off the air when she criticized the German dictator. Crowds swarmed the World's Fair in New York, displaying an almost morbid curiosity in the Polish pavilion. Twenty-one passengers returning on Pan American Airways' *American Clipper* told of "feverish" defense preparations abroad. The President's mother, Mrs. Sara Roosevelt, her European tour cut short, arrived on the liner *Washington*; while at Newport News, the President's wife, Eleanor, christened the *America*, largest merchant ship ever built in the United States.

Behind the bat of a gentleman with the lyrical name of Joe DiMaggio, the New York Yankees held the attention of the baseball world. Fun shows like *Hellzapoppin* did the best business with summer visitors to Broadway. Judy Garland and friends—the Tin Woodman, the Scarecrow, the Cowardly Lion, and the Wizard of Oz—were on display in movie houses over the country. For 35 cents one could buy the 78 rpm record of the nation's number one song hit, Judy singing "Over the Rainbow." New houses in a Washington suburb were priced at $6,250, with payments as low as $29 a month. A 1939 Plymouth with "very low mileage" was going for $625.

In Boston, delegates to the annual encampment of the Veterans of Foreign Wars cheered Senator Henry Cabot Lodge and Major General Smedley Butler, U.S. Marine Corps, when they called for a neutrality policy strong enough to keep the nation out of any European war. Americans should be "permitted" to fight, Butler shouted, for only two things: "defense of home and the Bill of Rights."

On the next day, Friday, the first of September, before daylight, the nation learned of the Nazi blitzkrieg in Poland.

"It's come at last," said the President into the telephone that had awakened and informed him. "God help us all."[6]

Three days later, with declaration of war by France and Britain, the Great War had become World War I, and World War II had begun. That night the President took to the radio networks for a fireside chat. Two days later, on September 6, he proclaimed the nation's neutrality, as required by the Neutrality Acts, and thereby placed an embargo on arms and munitions. Three days after that he declared a limited national emergency. Armed with the powers inherent in that proclamation, he authorized by executive order modest increases in the armed forces: for the Navy, 58,000 men; for the Army, 17,000.

An ambiguity expressed by the President in his fireside chat reflected the mixed emotions and conflicting anxieties that the explosion in Europe caused the entire nation. War anywhere, Roosevelt said, endangers the peace everywhere; but, he added, "Let no man or woman falsely talk of America sending its armies to European fields." Unlike Wilson, he declined

---

[6] Joseph Alsop and Robert Kintner, *American White Paper: The Story of American Diplomacy and the Second World War* (New York, 1940), p. 1.

to ask Americans to remain neutral in thought; but America, he insisted, still had to maintain neutrality. "I have said not once but many times," he said, turning a phrase that was grist to his satirists, "that I have seen war and that I hate war."

Ambiguity was one more obstacle to the nation's rearmament, already hampered by the fact that the military and naval establishments had for two decades been beaten down physically and to a great extent morally by the deadening influences of excessive economies and the naval limitation treaties. The nation was to remain neutral, but it had to prepare for war. ("National Defense" was the euphemism coined to cover the discrepancy.) This it had to do in an antimilitarist atmosphere of which the military leaders were acutely conscious. As often as not they were content to let the impetus for expansion come from some source other than their own. Even the original drive for rearmament, which dated from November 1938, was touched off not by the military but by the President himself with his call for 10,000 planes. In that igniting spark there was ambiguity, for the President was thinking not so much of planes for his own forces as of planes for France and Britain.

When war came that September 1939, the Navy was well along on its limited expansion program as authorized the preceding year; but the Army, in the words of its Chief of Staff, still was "that of a third-rate power."[7] The Army was up to a strength of 185,000, but none of its units had a full complement of men. The Army theoretically had nine infantry divisions; but only three were genuinely organized as divisions, and even those were at less than half-strength. None had enough transport for field maneuvers. In armor the Army had little more than one mechanized cavalry brigade at half-strength. Although the Air Corps was scheduled for limited expansion as a result of the President's action the preceding November, it actually had only 17,000 men organized in 62 understrength, ill-equipped squadrons. The National Guard, totaling 199,000 men, had not enough even of obsolete equipment for its 18 skeletonized, poorly trained divisions.

Despite the outbreak of war, the President saw no hope that the Congress would support any increase in the armed forces greater than

[7] *Biennial Report of the Chief of Staff of the United States Army, July 1, 1939, to June 30, 1941, to the Secretary of War* (Washington, 1941).

the modest expansion authorized in his executive order. Had not Lindbergh, espousing an isolationist neutrality, commanded a radio audience on September 15 as great as the President himself had for his fireside chat?

Roosevelt concentrated instead on a second try (he had failed in July) to repeal the arms embargo provision of the Neutrality Acts. Calling a special session of Congress, he asked in forceful terms for a cash-and-carry provision that would eliminate the advantage inherent in the embargo to the land power, already prepared for war, for whom imports were nonessential. Since the cash-and-carry plan was clearly aimed at helping France and Britain (and, incidentally, though unintentionally, Japan), it fell far short of strict neutrality; yet the Congress failed to bridle so long as the risk was confined to the belligerents. On November 4, with obvious relief the President signed the new bill into law.

As Europe's armies glowered at each other through a winter of what became known as the "phony war," military and naval leaders preparing their budget estimates for the new fiscal year beginning July 1, 1940, revised and juggled them in response to every new development in the world situation (the Soviet Union attacked Finland on November 30) and to every apparent indication of the mood of the Congress and the public. At the same time, the joint Board's Planning Committee was continuing to work on its RAINBOW plans, paying particular attention to defining details to meet the possibility of RAINBOW 2, with its emphasis on the Pacific. In the process the planners soon realized that all planning for American action in the Pacific was unrealistic without coordination with the potential allies in Europe. Early in April 1940 they asked authority to consult with the three main Pacific colonial powers: Britain, France, and the Netherlands.

Also in early April the Army's appropriations bill came to the House of Representatives. It was a large budget of $853,000,000—approximately $2,000,000 more than that of the previous year—with its provisions for the Air Corps and the limited emergency measures; yet even before it went to the House committee, it had been scaled down sharply by Presidential directive and failed by a long way to meet the Army's requirements. While obviously warm to the Army's new Chief of Staff, General George C. Marshall, the committee nevertheless cut the request by almost 10 per cent—despite George Marshall's striking appeal: "If Europe blazes in the late spring or early summer, we must put our house in order before the sparks reach the Western Hemisphere."[8]

Before the Senate could take up the bill, before the Navy put in its budget request, and before the planners could arrange their consultations on RAINBOW 2, everything changed. Europe did blaze.

Already, on March 12, Finland had capitulated to the great Russian foe. Then, on April 9, Germany moved against Denmark and Norway. A violent onslaught against the Low Countries and the Western Allies followed, before dawn on May 10. Five days was all it took to conquer the Dutch. For the Belgians, despite the help of Britain and France, it took only nineteen days. On May 27 the British began to withdraw from the Continent at Dunkirk. On June 10, Italy hit France from the rear. In the early minutes of June 25, France lay prostrate, beaten in a forty-two-day campaign that stunned the world. Britain, standing alone, obviously was next.

Speaking at graduation exercises at the University of Virginia in Charlottesville, hours after Mussolini had announced his intention of attacking France, President Roosevelt decried the diabolical act of "the hand that held the dagger." He went on to declare for the first time his and his nation's outright support for the Allies. "We will extend to the opponents of force," he said, "the material resources of this nation." Then he expounded a determination to rearm to a point "equal to the task of any emergency and every defense." To many a listener that presaged a call for something that was anathema to Americans in peacetime: compulsory universal military training—the draft. Yet as the President neared the end of his speech, cheering from his audience became general. Members of the faculty abandoned academic decorum to stamp their feet as they applauded.

Congress, too, applauded, but not unanimously. "I would have liked it better," said Senator Burton K. Wheeler of Montana, "if he had added that he was going to keep this country out of war." Yet that was about as far as all but the most virulent critics would go. Even many diehard isolationists were at that point committed to aid for the Allies short of war and to a realistic rearmament program. Although the Committee

---

[8] House Appropriations Subcommittee, *Military Estimate Appropriations Bill 1941*, February 23, 1940, p. 3.

to Defend America by Aiding the Allies soon had a counterpart in the America First Committee, even that band of isolationists rejected the support of groups as extreme as Fritz Kuhn's German-American Bund and, while decrying "aid short of war," called for building an impregnable American defense.

A candidate for the Republican presidential nomination, Wendell Willkie, could criticize only the Administration's handling of the defense program, not its intent. "Homespun old words like 'democracy' and 'liberty,'" said *Time* Magazine, "had become respectable again." On Broadway, Robert Sherwood in *There Shall Be No Night* presented a grim warning to the unprepared. The poet, Edna St. Vincent Millay, put her caveat in verse:

> *Dear Islander, I envy you;*
> *I'm very fond of islands, too;*
> *And few the pleasures I have known*
> *Which equaled being left alone.*
> *Yet matters from without intrude*
> *At times upon my solitude;*
> *A forest fire, a dog run mad,*
> *A neighbor stripped of all he had*
> *By swindlers, or the shrieking plea*
> *For help of stabbed Democracy.*[9]

So persistent were the demands of public, Senate, and President for new estimates of budget outlays that military men could hardly keep up. In late May the Senate, moved not only by events abroad but also by obvious shortcomings of the Army as displayed on maneuvers in Louisiana for a scorning world to see, passed without dissent a War Department appropriations bill that almost doubled the earlier House-approved version; and the House in turn retreated entirely from its April position. Even before the expanded bill could clear the Congress, a supplemental bill was in the making and was approved before June was out. The total of both bills provided the War Department with authority for 375,000 men and nearly three billion dollars.

---

[9] "There Are No Islands, Any More," *Lines written in passion and in deep concern for England, France, and my own country* (New York, 1940).

Meanwhile, the Chief of Naval Operations, Admiral Harold R. Stark, with perfect timing, submitted to the Congress on June 17, the day France asked for armistice terms, a request for four billion dollars to begin building a two-ocean navy. In little more than a month he had the funds for 1,325,000 tons of new construction.

Responding to secret cables signed "Former Naval Person" (the Prime Minister of Great Britain, Winston Churchill), President Roosevelt concluded in September a destroyers-for-bases deal, exchanging fifty overage destroyers for air and naval bases in the Caribbean. Linking transfer of the destroyers with bases nipped most isolationist criticism in advance, for this was ostensibly only a way to improve hemisphere defense.

Both the President and his military and naval advisers understood that the public and the Congress had come a long way since the day in 1937 when the President had made his quarantine speech in Chicago—but just how far none in authority was fully sure. When members of the Civilian Military Training Camps Association, an outgrowth of the businessmen's training camps of World War I—the "Plattsburgh idea"—proposed pushing legislation for a draft, the Army's Chief of Staff, General Marshall, deemed it best to let civilians lead the way. Marshall lent support behind the scenes.

Once introduced in the Congress in mid-June 1940, the Burke-Wadsworth bill, calling for the nation's first peacetime draft, promptly gained surprising support. The President himself remained aloof, lest his endorsement also tend to compromise the bill's chances. Authority to call the National Guard and Army reservists passed on August 27, and close behind it the draft. The bill had some restrictive provisions—a limit of one year's service, a proviso against posting outside the country, a limit on numbers to be called in any one year of 900,000; but more important, for the first time in the nations history the United States had a selective service act more than a year before war was to come.

Strategic planning by the Joint Board had in the meantime undergone just as striking a shift in response to the eruption in Europe as had public and Congressional opinion. With France down and Britain reeling, RAINBOW 2, which depended on the Western Allies to handle the Atlantic, was no longer applicable. Nor was RAINBOW 3 with its similar orientation toward the Pacific. Nor even RAINBOW 5 with its division of responsibilities with the European allies. Only plans 1 and 4, both focusing on the likelihood of direct aggression against the Western Hemisphere in the absence of major allies, appeared relevant; and of those two, RAINBOW 4 more nearly approximated the situation apparently posed by the powerful Axis nations.

When, in mid-June, President Roosevelt called on the intelligence chiefs of the Army and the Navy for an evaluation of the situation, the planners and their chiefs were convinced that not only would the French fleet pass into Axis hands, but that Britain, if not the British Empire, might fall. Both General Marshall and Admiral Stark approved in principle Staff recommendations that the United States adopt a purely defensive position in the Pacific, make no further commitments for aid to the Allies, and mobilize immediately for hemisphere defense.

The President, for his part, refused to accept that view. American action, Roosevelt asserted, should be based on the theory that Britain would survive, that a small amount of American aid might see the British through without materially affecting American preparations. Although the planners went along, they did so tentatively until both the War and the Navy departments could send observers to London to gauge for themselves Britain's chances.

The first fury of the *Luftwaffe's* attempt to drive the Royal Air Force from the skies was raging when in August those observers reached London. Pragmatic as they were, it still took little time for them to become swept up in the determination and long-range optimism that pervaded the British Isles. Churchill's England, they could report, was not the England of Neville Chamberlain, the man of Munich.

Having come around to the President's contention that Britain somehow would stick it out, Army and Navy planners faced a situation radically different from that presumed in RAINBOW 4, which had presupposed no major allies. It remained for the Navy, which had been slow to adopt the reorientation toward the Atlantic, to articulate the new direction the planning should take. In November 1940, on the eve of Roosevelt's election to a third term, Admiral Stark submitted a memorandum designed to elicit a firm statement of American policy and to provide a basis for coordinated planning with the British.

Because the recommended course of action in the event of war was contained in Paragraph D, which came out DOG in the military's phonetic

14

alphabet, it became known as the "Plan DOG" memorandum. It was, in effect, a return to the precepts of RAINBOW 5.[10]

"Shall we direct our efforts," Stark asked in Paragraph DOG, "toward an eventual strong offensive in the Atlantic as an ally of the British, and a defensive in the Pacific?"

Yes, said Stark for the Navy.

Yes, said Marshall for the Army.

When representatives of the British services came secretly to Washington in late January 1941 for exploratory Staff conversations, they, too, predictably, said yes.

Following fourteen sessions ending late in March, military planners representing the two nations laid down basic guidelines for coordination of war effort and aims "should the United States be compelled to resort to war." In essence, their report, known as "ABC-1," was an enlarged restatement of RAINBOW 5: a strategic defensive in the Pacific while the major effort of both powers, in conjunction with Canada, was directed toward defeat of Germany and its allies in the Atlantic and Europe, "the decisive theater."

By April the Army and Navy joint planners were back at work on a refinement of RAINBOW 5. The Joint Board approved their plan in May. Although the President withheld formal approval—ostensibly because the British government had yet formally to accept ABC-1, but possibly as a gesture toward maintaining a myth of continued neutrality—nobody questioned either his general concurrence or that of the British.

The broad outline of how the United States was to fight World War II was down on paper.

Europe First.

---

[10] All quotations relating to the "Plan Dog" memorandum are from Morton, "Germany First."

Chapter Two – Growing Pains of the High Command

Like most easterners who had the means, Franklin Delano Roosevelt had traveled and studied in Europe during his youth. (The attack of poliomyelitis that crippled him did not strike until he was thirty-eight.) Although he early understood the historical and cultural heritage that binds the United States of America to Europe, it is hard to say precisely when, in the crisis years 1938-1940, Roosevelt accepted the fact that Europe's cause against fascism was inescapably America's cause. Possibly as early as Munich, which he tried to forestall and subsequently deplored. "Peace by fear has no higher or more enduring quality," he warned, "than peace by the sword."[11]

It was definitely at the time of Munich, the autumn of 1938, that Roosevelt first became alarmed that the European democracies might prove incapable of carrying freedom's cause alone; but like millions of other Americans who felt conscience-heavy sympathy for Britain and France,

[11] For this chapter, basic sources were: Watson, *Chief of Staff*; Matloff and Snell, *Strategic Planning: 1941-1942*; Craven and Cate, eds., *Plans and Early Operations*; Leighton and Coakley, *Global Logistics and Strategy*; Pogue, *Ordeal and Hope*; Morison, Vol. Ill, *The Rising Sun in the Pacific* (Boston, 1948), and *The Battle of the Atlantic*. See also Alfred Goldberg, ed., A *History of the United States Air Force* (Princeton, 1957). Raymond G. O'Connor, "Did FDR Want War in 1941?" in Raymond G. O'Connor, ed., *American Defense Policy in Perspective from Colonial Times to the Present* (New York, 1965), provides a provocative essay on the President's early wartime attitudes. For a guide to the published material on lend-lease, see Davis, *The Experience of War*, and to the civilian governmental agencies, The National Archives, *Federal Records of World War II*, Vol. I, *Civilian Agencies* (Washington, 1950), and Bureau of the Budget, Committee of Records of War Administration by the War Records Section, *The United States at War, Development and Administration of the War Program by the Federal Government* (Washington, 1946).

the President for a long time shrank from the prospect of Americans dying again on European battlefields. Despite the stunning blow of impending French collapse, he pledged at Charlottesville only the nation's material resources. He appeared to have convinced himself that with that aid Britain could stand alone.

Yet in his heart Roosevelt probably recognized as France fell that America eventually would have to join Britain if Nazism was ever to be extirpated. That he failed to pledge more than the materials of his nation may well have been but another gesture to public opinion. Surely by late summer he knew from his correspondence with Winston Churchill that even though the British might stand with American aid, they alone lacked the strength to return to the Continent to abolish a Nazi terror nourished by the enslaved industry and population of all Europe.

If by the end of 1940, Roosevelt had not yet accepted the inevitability of eventual American intervention, then he was kidding himself. At least a form of war was in his mind that day in December 1940 when he posed a kind of parable to press correspondents in the Oval Study at the White House.[12]

Suppose a neighbor's house caught fire, the President said, and he had a length of garden hose that his neighbor might connect to a hydrant to help put out the fire. "Now what do I do?" he asked. "I don't say to him, 'Neighbor, my garden hose cost me fifteen dollars; you have to pay me fifteen dollars for it.'" He did not want fifteen dollars, Roosevelt said; he only wanted his garden hose back after the fire was out.

An undeclared war began for Mr. Roosevelt and the nation in those closing days of 1940. The President put it forthrightly one night in late December before a battery of microphones and newsreel cameras in another fireside chat. "If Britain should go down," he said, "all of us in all the Americas would be living at the point of a gun, a gun loaded with explosive bullets, economic as well as military. We must produce arms and ships with every energy and resource we can command…We must be the great arsenal of Democracy."

A few days later Roosevelt appealed to the Congress to provide for what he called the Four Freedoms—freedom of speech, freedom of religion, freedom from want, freedom from fear. In the second week of January 1941, House and Senate majority leaders introduced the bill the President

---

[12] Davis, *The Experience of War*, pp. 48-49.

wanted: a bill designed to make the United States a true arsenal of democracy. The Clerk of the House of Representatives stamped it "HB 1776," giving it a connotation lost on no one.

The fight was bitter. On the one side, strong support from the Committee to Defend America by Aiding the Allies; on the other, unstinting opposition from the America First Committee. Burton K. Wheeler said it would "plough under every fourth American boy." Although Charles Lindbergh testified against the bill, the Republican whom Roosevelt had defeated for the presidency the preceding November lined up in support. "If aid to Britain is what is going to get us into war," said Wendell Willkie, then the United States already was in it.[13]

With large majorities, House and Senate passed the bill. On March 11 the President signed it. The Congress had bestowed upon him broad powers "to sell, transfer title to, exchange, lease, lend, or otherwise dispose" of war goods to "the government of any country whose defenses the President deems vital to the defense of the United States."

It was momentous legislation.[14] By means of it Britain, China, and later the Soviet Union would be sustained through some of history's darkest hours.

They called it at the time "lease-lend." It would gradually come to be known in the reverse, "lend-lease."

Had Germany or Italy been ready to ignite a war with the United States in early 1941, lend-lease would have provided an ample spark. Neither nation, it turned out, was of a mind to take that step.

For Italy there was no real choice, tied as Mussolini was to the power of the senior Axis partner. Furthermore, events the preceding autumn, when Mussolini had moved unilaterally against Greece, had underscored the basic impotence of the Italian legions.

In view of British assistance to Greece, Hitler would have to go to the aid of his headstrong ally, not so much for the sake of prestige as for the effect an unquenched fire in the Balkans might have on a momentous task the *Fuehrer* had assigned his armed forces for late spring of 1941. Playing accepted at least temporary repulse in the aerial war over Britain, Adolf

---

[13] The quotes from Wheeler and Willkie are from contemporary newspaper accounts.

[14] The Lend-Lease Act is quoted in several secondary sources; I have used Buchanan, *The United States and World War II*, p. 26.

Hitler had decided to get on with the clash that, with malice aforethought, he had postponed only temporarily in negotiating the Nazi-Soviet Pact: the clash with bolshevism. Even though his timetable for the new conquest was short, he had no wish to invite a new opponent in the west until he had achieved security in the east.

As for Japan, which since the summer of 1940 had been tied intimately to Rome and Berlin by the anti-American Tripartite Pact, the United States was an inevitable foe. The start of a Japanese study for a surprise attack on the naval base at Pearl Harbor in Hawaii actually coincided with the first Congressional consideration of lend-lease; but before that, moves were to be made against crumbling British, French, and Dutch empires in southeast Asia. The Japanese were not ready to take on the United States—not yet.

Nor was there, from the viewpoint of the United States, any rationale for openly entering the war. Reasons that earlier had prompted Roosevelt to deny appeals from Churchill to join the fight as France was failing, still were valid. Although a sizable majority of Americans was at last conscious of the threat the Axis posed, the opposition to war still was loud and influential. If war had to come, Roosevelt wanted a united nation behind him. Even more important, the nation's armed forces and its industry still were egregiously unprepared. Better to wait, if the enemy so permitted, and in the meantime to do everything possible to sustain embattled Britain and thereby keep alive the chance of avoiding a shooting war. Even were war declared, it would be long months before the United States could do more than what was already proposed under lend-lease.

The state of the armed forces was proof enough of that.

Even Congressmen had discovered that it would take more than a wave of the magic wand of appropriations to undo the neglect of twenty years. Nor could legislation to call up the National Guard and begin the draft—however welcome to military leaders—set everything right. Indeed, the timing of the legislation added sharply to the Army's problems, for it meant a sudden expansion with little time to construct proper housing and training facilities before winter weather closed in.

That added to a problem of morale already inherent in the fact that peacetime draftees are, at best, reluctant warriors. Unlike the Navy and its ground adjunct, the Marine Corps, which were experiencing a more gradual growth, and which until 1912 met manpower needs by draft-stimulated recruitment, the Army was a villain. A critical press and sensitive Congressmen appeared unable to comprehend that the Army had no wish to deny guns and equipment to its soldiers, but that today's shortages were yesterday's legacy. Nor could they understand that it would take time to replace those overage and incompetent officers that the years and politicians had foisted on the National Guard; that bases were located in godforsaken places like Centreville, Mississippi, not out of spite but because land was cheaper, the climate was warm enough for year-round training, and long-term Southern senators and congressmen held the chairmanships of the military affairs committees. Encouraged by a press that fed on controversy, malcontents by midsummer of 1941 were bombarding Congress with protests and petitions, and on walls and sidewalks appeared crude letters urging mass desertions. "OHIO," the signs read, meaning "Over the hill in October."

For the Navy, once its leaders had settled on the requirements of a two-ocean force and had gained approval for it—including full commitment to a new class of capital ship, the aircraft carrier—problems of procurement were relatively simple; for governmental and civilian shipyards could gear themselves to a firm program. Not so for the Army and its ambitious subsidiary, the Air Corps. Given the rapid pace of world events, appropriations requests were out of date long before the Congress acted on them, and one estimate after another failed to match the dark shade of the threats from abroad. In May 1940, for example, the Air Corps had projected a 41-group program, but only two months later the goal had been raised to 54 groups, which would provide an air arm of 5,000 combat aircraft and over 200,000 officers and men. In the autumn of 1941 that would again be expanded to a goal of 84 groups with 7,800 combat planes.

The Congress, fortunately, still had no inclination to close the public purse. In June 1941 the House Appropriations Committee recommended a record $9,800,000,000 for the War Department, including in it an unprecedented blank check for the Chief of Staff to order the tanks and other equipment for an armored force and hang the cost. Further to demonstrate its largesse, the committee recommended a sinking fund, another $25,000,000 for any outlay of an emergency nature.

Yet blank checks and even sinking funds were useless if there was nothing and no place to buy. Hampered by budget restrictions, the Ordnance Department, the Air Corps, and other procurement agencies of the Army had been slow to develop the prototypes that would be needed for winning World War II. Even where those had been decided, it was difficult to anticipate appropriations and needs with a firmness that would prompt manufacturers to retool and build new plants far enough in advance to meet demands. Add to that the competition for arms by Britain, China, the South American countries, and later the Soviet Union; and the equation of demand versus supply became shockingly unbalanced. The Army, for example, early settled on a 105-mm. howitzer to replace the 75-mm. gun, but so slow and imprecise were indications of production on the new piece that only under heavy pressure would military leaders release their outmoded World War I weapons to the potential allies.

As the senior and larger service and the one more vitally concerned with the problem of procurement in all its ramifications, the War Department had prepared between the wars a comprehensive industrial mobilization plan providing for a civilian review board with broad, firm powers of decision. At the first signs of crisis in arms production the Army had recommended activating the board; but the President would agree to nothing more than a seven-man committee, the War Resources Board, from which he wanted no more than advice on the kind of emergency organization to establish. Headed by Edward R. Stettinius, Jr., of United States Steel, the War Resources Board tried to accommodate itself to the President's wishes—but to no avail.

Roosevelt, who was both ever mindful of the delicate temper of the people in regard to rearming and opposed to business running the presidency, was determined to relinquish no part of his executive authority in the all-important field of industrial mobilization. He tabled the recommendations of the War Resources Board, thanked each member, and let them know their job was finished.

Not until mid-1940, when Europe blazed, did the President create any kind of industrial authority. Even then he declined to give up any of his personal emergency powers. He chose instead to reactivate the Council of National Defense, composed of the secretaries of the six major government departments, and the Advisory Commission to that council, which had served in World War I under an act never repealed. Once the council had approved the Advisory Commission, composed of seven prominent leaders in management, labor, agriculture, and the like, Roosevelt was content to let the council die. Even to the Advisory Commission he gave no real authority. He appointed no chairman and, as events would show, planned to use it as little more than a rubber stamp for various emergency agencies he intended to create. Whereupon this committee, too, might be allowed to wither away.

For lack of authority and timely, firm decision, little had been accomplished during 1940 toward regulating industry for arms production, even after the President in the fall of the year established within the National Defense Advisory Commission the Priorities Board headed by Donald M. Nelson, an executive of the mail-order house, Sears, Roebuck and Company. Only in the early days of 1941 did Roosevelt act to create an agency that could do the job, and even then, for fear of alienating labor, he was reluctant to appoint a real czar over production. He settled instead for the Office of Production Management, headed by a policy council composed of a director, William S. Knudsen of General Motors, representing management; an associate director, Sidney Hillman of the Congress of Industrial Organizations (CIO), representing labor; and two members, the Secretaries of War and Navy, Henry L. Stimson and Frank Knox.

There followed, throughout 1941 and 1942 and well into the next year, a veritable proliferation of emergency agencies with diverse ancestry, genesis, duties, and duration. Almost every aspect of the national life and economy came under one agency or another, sometimes more than one—National War Labor Board, War Production Board, War Shipping Administration, the Offices of Alien Property Custodian, Civilian Defense, Economic Stabilization, and numerous others, many of which evolved out of earlier organizations or through mergers. Until 1943, when the President at last created a virtual czar—the Supreme Court Justice James F. Byrnes, heading the Office of War Mobilization—all agencies were subordinate to the Office of Emergency Management, a device whereby the President himself could coordinate, supervise, and even personally direct the work of any agency involved in emergency activities.

As events in December 1941 would demonstrate, Mr. Roosevelt had waited dangerously long before taking steps to regulate the nations resources for war. In the end, the same goals that had been set for the War Department's rejected industrial mobilization plan were met; but because the wartime organization evolved piece by piece, it lacked centralized lines of coordination and control, which in large measure explained the evolution and change that characterized it throughout. It would remain problematical whether the mood of the nation would have accepted the Army's all-embracing plan in 1940 or at any time before December 1941. What was certain was that without that plan the nation came dangerously close to catastrophe.

Only with creation of the Office of Production Management—just eleven months to the day before war came—and, within it, of the War Production Board, was any real regulation applied to the nation's material and industrial resources. Now, the word "priorities" became a commonplace, mainly in regard to materials but extending also into related fields. Although a tourist-hungry Florida Chamber of Commerce could advertise, "There are no priorities on sunshine," the ways of getting to it could be regulated and allocated. Many a traveler found himself "bumped" from a scheduled air flight because he lacked a government "priority."

For all the impact of priorities, the late start meant that gaping holes in the armaments of both Army and Navy would long despoil the entire fabric of defense preparations. Despoiling it, too, were other blemishes, equally disturbing: the end of the draft and the relief of National Guard units from federal service. (They had gone to camp to the country-music strains of "Goodbye, Dear, I'll Be Back in a Year, Little Darling.") Depressing was the outcome of a new series of maneuvers in the summer of 1941: again iron pipes served as cannon, commercial trucks as tanks, and light sport planes as bombers. The likelihood of losing the Guard and the draftees was even more upsetting, because their brief period of service had coincided with vast changes taking place within the Army. The units, for example, had yet to be reorganized into the new triangular division that was to replace the heavy square division. They had had time to learn little more than the new, simplified platoon drill that was replacing World War I's complex "squads rights, squads left."

Since the summons of National Guard, reserve officers, and draftees had of necessity been staggered, some units and individuals would complete their scheduled year of service well before others, beginning in mid-September 1941. That would leave an ill-balanced force and at the same time, with deactivation of Guard units, would cripple the training mechanism for the new draftees still to come.

Hardly had the first recruits completed their AGCT (Army General Classification Test) before the prospect prompted the Army to consider extending the period of service. In view of a worsening world situation,

General Marshall in June 1941 deemed he had no choice but to ask for extension. When accused of breach of faith, Marshall cited the original Selective Service Act. By its terms, he noted, the Congress was free to extend the twelve-month period if "the national interest is imperiled."

"The question is," said Marshall, "do you think the national interests are imperiled? I do, most decidedly."[15]

Marshall went on to point out the problems of fulfilling the Army's commitments when it was shackled by restrictions of time and overseas service on its soldiers. A regiment sent to reinforce the garrison in Hawaii, he noted, would have to be disbanded, because most of its men had to be returned at the end of their year of service. Much the same situation, he might have added, had hobbled the nation in the Civil War and in the wars with Mexico and Spain. For other commitments special task forces had to be formed of volunteers and regular officers—a process that so stripped some units that they had to be rebuilt entirely, and at the same time cut into the ranks of regulars who should have been training draftees.

Sensing that isolationist Congressmen were particularly opposed to any but volunteers serving outside the United States and its territories, Marshall decided to postpone pressing that measure until the fight for extending the period of service could be won. Even so, every forecast of how the vote might go in the House of Representatives was marginal, if not downright pessimistic.

Well they might have been. When the matter came to a vote in August 1941—less than three months before the Japanese were to attack Pearl Harbor—it passed, amid extraordinary excitement, by an incredibly thin margin: 203 to 202.

George Marshall's vision and persistence indicated that a military leader of impressive stature was emerging to guide the destiny of the War Department in World War II.

George Catlett Marshall was more than soldier, he was politician and statesman as well. Not a handsome man, he was nevertheless, even in his early sixties, a striking figure. In bearing and demeanor obviously a soldier, a determined but self-disciplined soldier, eschewing the volatile, embracing the tranquil, but demanding of his subordinates. With

[15] Watson, *Chief of Staff*, p. 220, citing records of the Senate Committee on Military Affairs, 77th Congress, 1st Session.

patience, tolerance, and an acute sense of the role of the professional soldier in American democracy, Marshall built up a support in Congress that served him and the Army well during the war. In the appropriations battles, for example, Marshall calmly and astutely resisted pressures to ask, once the purse strings were loosened, for more than the Army could effectively expend, lest, as he himself put it, he "choke the patient" and incite overconfidence in the public.

Marshall early gained the respect of his President. ("I could not sleep at night," Roosevelt was to tell him later, "with you out of the country."[16]) Marshall himself worked hard at the relationship. At White House social functions he refused to crack a smile at the President's jokes on the theory that he wanted to maintain a strictly official association, lest some day some War Department strategic plan might be dismissed "with a wave of a cigarette holder."[17] The two men could never have been close in any case, for each in his own right was too much a strong, dominant personality. In Marshall's view, Roosevelt was a masterful politician and a great leader but he had to be restrained so that, in his ignorance of logistics, he did not scatter the Army's resources so widely that no campaign could ever be terminated successfully.

If, as numbers of his contemporaries believed, Marshall had talent close to genius, it was probably best revealed in his ability to select worthwhile subordinates. With notably rare exceptions, the generals he chose for high command measured up to expectations. He always kept close at hand a little black notebook for recording his impressions of officers.

George Marshall assumed the position of Chief of Staff the day Germany invaded Poland. The Army and the nation would have strong reason to be grateful that the position found the man when it did.

Although George Marshall had outstanding qualities as an administrator, his command post as war approached was far from organized for war. (It

---

[16] Robert E. Sherwood, *Roosevelt and Hopkins* (New York, 1948), p. 803. See also Maurice Matloff, *Mr. Roosevelt's Three Wars: FDR as War Leader* (1964 Harmon Memorial Lecture, U.S. Air Force Academy), for a definitive examination of the President's role in high command. Marshall is analyzed by his authorized biographer, Forrest C. Pogue, in *George C. Marshall: Global Commander* (1968 Harmon Memorial Lecture).

[17] Interviews with Marshall by Riley Sunderland and Charles F. Romanus in OCMH files.

was, he himself admitted, "the poorest command post in the Army."[18]) No matter how demanding the myriad requirements of rearmament, both he and the Army had been slow to adjust the headquarters organization to the new strategic concept of a two-front or global war. As the last year of pre-war preparations began, the high command remained organized in terms of refighting World War I.

That involved a so-called GHQ (General Headquarters) plan of 1921, which had established the War Plans Division as a fifth increment of the General Staff, intended in wartime to provide officers as a nucleus of GHQ, a headquarters analogous to "Black Jack" Pershing's field headquarters in France. The Chief of Staff himself was supposed to assume command of the headquarters once active fighting began.

In July 1940, GHQ had actually come into existence with Brigadier General Lesley J. McNair—another stalwart, though crusty, personality— serving as its Chief of Staff. The belief was the GHQ eventually would whip into shape some new American Expeditionary Force like Pershing's, but its role at first was only to administer training.

Trouble arose a year later, in mid-1941, as officers moved from the War Plans Division to McNair's Staff to prepare GHQ for its functions in a theater of operations. It rapidly developed that the whole theory of GHQ ran counter to two incontrovertible facts.

First, splitting the War Plans Division left the Chief of Staff with no single agency responsible both for formulating strategy and for control- ling overseas operations; and once the Chief of Stall himself assumed command of GHQ, no single person would be left to coordinate all the diverse Army commands and agencies. Second, the War Department had a child that was growing up and wanting to leave home to seek its fortune. The child's size and the responsibilities it had assumed afforded strong argument that the time had come. The child was the Air Corps.

For all the vehemence of air advocates in the fledgling years following World War I—possibly because of it—air leaders before 1931 had achieved little of the autonomy they sought, other than a change of name from Air Service to Air Corps. In that year the Navy, under pressure, had conceded to the Army responsibility for air defense of the nation's coasts. The move had given weight to the contention of air partisans that in a new war the

---

[18] Pogue, *Ordeal and Hope*, p. 289.

role of the air forces would go beyond mere tactical support of the ground armies. It also provided impetus to development of a long-range bomber and led in 1935 to the prototype of the B-17 Flying Fortress with a range of 2,000 miles.

By 1935 ground-oriented Army leaders had tacitly accepted the fact that air forces would conduct some operations independent of the ground arms, but they still insisted that even those operations should fall under the direction of the theater or GHQ commander. That was still the situation, with little gain apparent for the advocates of a separate air arm, when the *Luftwaffe* scored awesome successes in Poland, the Low Countries, and France.

Press and public then joined the clamor for a separate air force. The Germans, it appeared to the layman, had demonstrated that a separate air force meant a more powerful air force.

Although General Marshall was more sympathetic to the airmen's cause than any of his predecessors had been, he was nevertheless unprepared to support autonomy, or even, at that time (late 1940), equality. Fundamental to his and to all Army opposition to an autonomous air arm was a conviction that the purpose of air operations, including strategic bombing, was to support or prepare the way for the ground arms. While the *Luftwaffe* admittedly was a separate service, it had scored its successes under a unified command. Other than to create a Department of National Defense, a ponderous undertaking in the shadow of crisis, the best way to ensure unified command was to retain the air arm within the Army. As for giving the airmen equality with the ground forces, Marshall believed that the Air Corps had for so long been dependent on the Army for Staff functions that it lacked sufficient depth in its officer corps to handle those matters alone.

But Marshall took steps in the direction the airmen wanted to go. In the spring of 1941 he arranged to fill an existing but long vacant office of Assistant Secretary of Air and made Major General Henry H. Arnold his Deputy Chief of Staff for Air with authority to coordinate all strictly air matters. After becoming convinced over the next few weeks that the Air Corps was having genuine difficulty arranging its sudden expansion through the General Staff, he took a bigger step. In June 1941 he created a new entity, the Army Air Forces, with two increments, the Air Corps itself and the Air Force Combat Command. The latter, encompassing all air combat units, nevertheless remained subject to the direction of a ground commander, the head of GHQ; and even though the regulation did not specifically say so, the Air Staff remained subordinate to the General Staff.

To the more partisan airmen those reservations left the situation as onerous as ever. Although they launched a new campaign for a separate arm, the Deputy Chief for Air, General Arnold maintained his position that the time for change was not in midstream. Yet Arnold continued to insist that GHQ was alien to the organization, and that air and ground forces should be reconstituted on a level of genuine equality.

Arnold's thesis drew an assist late in 1941 from ground officers themselves. By that time several commitments imposed on the Army by the President made it apparent that World War II, when it came to America, would be a multitheater war requiring a number of theater commanders. Many in the War Department questioned the value of imposing an additional headquarters—GHQ—between the Chief of Staff and the theaters.

As the year 1941 neared an end, there the matter stood, to be resolved only under the impetus of Japanese bombs on Pearl Harbor. Yet even as a decision remained in abeyance, an admirable absence of rancor existed—a radical change from the fire and brimstone days of Billy Mitchell, and a testament to the reason of men who with discipline and objectivity approached the common goal of what was best for their country.

As for the Navy, no major upheaval in command appeared in the making, though there, too, an incipient revolution by airmen had to be squelched. Despite two attempts by Congressional committees early in the expansion period to engineer a major change in naval organization, naval leaders held onto their time-tested headquarters system of a Chief of Naval Operations served by a substructure of bureaus. The only adjustment that appeared at first necessary was to arrange for unified operational command should two or all of three inchoate fleets—Asiatic, Pacific, and Atlantic—operate together. The decision was that overall command was to rest with the admiral of the Pacific Fleet. Since that arrangement was a bow to the then superior size of the Pacific Fleet, it proved tentative.

Chapter Three – Mr. Roosevelt's Undeclared War

As these internal arguments and accommodations took place, Mr. Roosevelt's undeclared war, implicit under lend-lease, was heating up. That was inevitable; for once the United States had contracted to provide Britain and others with the tools of war, the nation assumed an unwritten but certain responsibility to flirt with belligerency, if that was required, to see that the tools got into the hands of those who would use them.[19]

Although conducted in secret, ostensibly shunned by the President, and masked by the euphemistic phrase, "should the United States be compelled to resort to war,"[20] the ABC conversations between American and British military Staffs in Washington in the late winter of 1940-1941 actually marked the start of American participation in World War II. Even before the United States formally entered the war, its armed forces had begun to take steps under the consensus of those talks that to many observers seemed to be outright belligerency; and the President himself had begun to act and make commitments that touched at least the outer fringe of his constitutional authority.

Although the American and British military staffs were destined to spend long months, even years, in spirited debate over the proper strategy to employ in defeating Germany, they quickly came to terms on such

---

[19] For this chapter, basic sources were: Morison, *The Battle of the Atlantic*; Watson, *Chief of Staff*; Conn, Engelman, and Fairchild, *Guarding the United States*; and Langer and Gleason, *The Undeclared War*. See also Fairchild, "The Decision to Land United States Forces in Iceland," in Greenfield, ed., *Command Decisions*.

[20] Watson, *Chief of Staff*, p. 373.

matters as allocating aircraft from American production and arranging a continuous exchange of views on military matters by means of permanent military missions. Most important of all, harmony existed on the vital questions of getting war supplies to Britain and relieving the British of some of their widespread responsibilities. The Americans were to take over as fast as possible most defenses in the North and South Atlantic except for the British Isles themselves, thereby releasing British troops and naval vessels for duty elsewhere; and if war came, the United States Navy was to assume as soon as possible the task of protecting transatlantic convoys.

As the ABC conversations drew to a close, the threat to British survival had shifted from the *Luftwaffe* and invasion to submarine, air, and surface attacks on British shipping. Strikes by German submarines, or U-boats, operating in groups called "wolfpacks," were particularly deadly. By March of 1941 the British were losing ships five times faster than they could build them. Unless those losses could be reduced or construction radically increased, Britain soon would face a crisis more critical than that following Dunkirk.

Having assisted in the earlier crisis by allowing British pilots to be trained at American fields and British merchant vessels to be repaired in American ports, President Roosevelt moved quickly to make lend-lease funds available for building merchant vessels and convoy escort ships for the British and for repairing both merchant vessels and warships in American yards. At the end of March the United States seized sixty-nine Axis and Danish ships in American ports and turned them over to the British. (In the process 875 Axis seamen were jailed for "attempted sabotage.") A few days later the President declared the Red Sea no longer a combat zone, and thus circumvented the Neutrality Acts to enable American ships to carry supplies to hard-pressed British troops in the Near East. In May the United States with nominal tribute took over French shipping caught in its ports, including, in New York Harbor, the luxury liner *Normandie.*

The Germans, meanwhile, had announced that the war zone in which U-boats would sink belligerent and neutral vessels alike was being extended to waters off Iceland and the east coast of Greenland. In keeping with one of the Navy's war plans, the Chief of Naval Operations, Admiral Stark, responded with a shift from Pacific to Atlantic of three battleships, an aircraft carrier, four light cruisers, and two squadrons of destroyers. He also urged the President to draw a line down the middle of the Atlantic and declare that belligerent vessels crossing it would be presumed intent on attack.

Guided by a troubled personal adviser, Harry Hopkins, whose sensitive ear picked up disturbing rumblings from the isolationists, and by a knowledge of how feeble America's armed forces still were, Roosevelt declined to go that far. He drew the line, but he sanctioned a warning so softened that it would have frightened few foes, least of all a Germany that had yet to incur any reverse other than that in the air over Britain. Passing the line by belligerent ships was "to be viewed as possibly actuated by an unfriendly interest toward shipping or territory in the Western Hemisphere."

By that edict Roosevelt did nothing more than extend the radius of the "neutrality patrol." Maintained ostensibly to protect American "neutral rights," the patrol had begun in American waters soon after war first erupted in Europe. A month later, upon joint declaration by the United States and other countries of North and South America, it had been extended to a line up to a thousand miles deep around the Western Hemisphere. The patrol was to report the approach of belligerent vessels, thereby presumably demonstrating American determination to defend the Western Hemisphere; but more and more, American ships had begun to signal the location of Axis ships to the British.

The German proclamation extending the war zone also focused new attention on Iceland and Greenland. At the invitation of the Icelandic government, after Germany had overrun Denmark and Norway, the British army had occupied Iceland; and the United States had assumed, as American newspapers put it, "an unofficial protectorate" over Greenland. That amounted to little more than Coast Guard surveillance until the War Department early in 1941 decided that airfields in Greenland would be a help in delivering planes to Britain. In April the Danish Minister to the United States signed an agreement whereby the United States became protector of Greenland, responsible for its supply and defense until Denmark was free. Two months later engineer and anti-aircraft units from the U.S. Army began to land.

Events at sea meanwhile had taken a sharp turn toward a shooting war. The first incident—bloodless, as it turned out—occurred on April 10 off Iceland. As the destroyer U.S.S. *Niblack* was pulling aboard the last of three boatloads of survivors from a torpedoed Dutch freighter, her detection gear picked up the sound of an approaching submarine. The *Niblack* dropped depth charges. The submarine retired.

Two other incidents followed in May. Early in the month a German raider in the South Atlantic sank a neutral passenger ship of Egyptian registry carrying 150 American passengers. A few days later a German submarine in nearby waters sank the S. S. *Robin Moor*, an American freighter carrying general cargo.

Although in neither case were American lives lost, the incidents were disturbing, demonstrating to many that the Neutrality Acts provided no foolproof formula for keeping the United States out of war. Yet the attacks lacked the effrontery and terror of the unrestricted submarine warfare that had pulled the United States into World War I. Nevertheless, on May 27, the President cited the incidents in a warning to the nation that the war was "approaching the brink of the Western Hemisphere itself." Before finishing his radio broadcast, he declared an unlimited national emergency.

Many people felt that the President was either overreacting or groping for justifications; but there were broader considerations behind his move. He may have hoped the declaration would boost war production, and he obviously coveted the additional powers of executive decision the declaration afforded. More likely he acted from genuinely increased concern over the crisis in British shipping and, specifically, from alarming indications of a possible German move in the direction of South America.

A move against South America was a nightmare that had haunted American leaders since the start of Hitler's rise, a concern that had grown with each new revelation of German power. With the aid of a "fifth column" of internal subversion, Hitler might gain a foothold in one or more of the volatile South American countries or one of the Caribbean islands, perhaps French-owned Martinique. Only the critically impoverished United States armed forces could pose any opposition.

Suppose the Germans moved against South America, noted an obscure Army major, Walter Bedell Smith, after one of several periodic decisions to transfer a big cache of obsolescent but usable weapons to Britain: "Everyone who was a party to the deal might hope to be found hanging from a lamp post."[21]

In May 1941 all intelligence gleaned by both Americans and British pointed to Spain and Portugal as next on the German schedule of conquest.

---

[21] Ibid., p. 312.

That meant a direct threat to the Azores, the Cape Verde Islands, and the western bulge of French West Africa at Dakar, only a relatively short leap from the eastern bulge of Brazil. When on May 24 the great new German battleship *Bismarck* came out of hiding to sink the British battle cruiser *Hood* with a single salvo, then to disappear somewhere in the Atlantic, the predictions took on added substance.

That had triggered President Roosevelt's emergency declaration. Even when the Royal Navy and Air Force at last found and sank the *Bismarck*, only hours before the President went on the air, fears were only partially allayed; for a sister ship, the *Tirpitz*, still was afloat somewhere, and Harold Stark's Navy had no vessel capable of trading blows on anything like equal terms.

United States Marines were training to occupy the Azores, the Army was trying to get enough material together to equip a task force to assist, and the President had frozen Axis assets in the United States and closed Axis consulates when, in early June, the crisis finally passed. New intelligence, Winston Churchill revealed personally to Roosevelt, indicated that the next German move would be not southward but eastward, against Soviet Russia. Churchill urged that the Marines go instead to Iceland, there to relieve part of the British garrison and set up a base useful both for covering the northern convoy route to Britain and for expediting aid to Russia by way of the Arctic port of Archangel.

The new intelligence was right.

It happened before dawn on Sunday, June 22.

"I have today decided," Hitler proclaimed, "to give the fate of the German people and the Reich and of Europe again into the hands of our soldiers."[22]

For all the long-standing enmity between democracy and communism, for all the distrust and fear of a predatory bolshevism, Churchill promptly pledged help for the Russians. "No one has been a more consistent opponent of Communism than I have for the past twenty-five years," he intoned. "I will unsay no word that I have spoken about it. But...any man or state who fights on against Nazidom will have our aid."[23]

[22] Contemporary newspaper accounts

[23] Churchill, *The Grand Alliance*, pp. 371-73

To the American ambassador he confided: "If Hitler invaded Hell, I would make at least a favourable reference to the Devil in the House of Commons."[24]

Two days later Roosevelt set the same policy for the United States, though less precisely, and stretched his constitutional authority again to declare that it would be unnecessary to invoke the Neutrality Acts against Russia.

It was in this atmosphere of renewed world crisis and of partial belligerency for the United States that Roosevelt a month later, in July, called on the Secretaries of War and the Navy to prepare a "Victory Program." He wanted detailed estimates of the men and equipment that would be required for ultimate victory against the likely enemies. This, the President believed, would help in allocating production among the conflicting demands and in gearing industry for long-range requirements. It served also, as it turned out, as a forum for airing two divergent concepts of how the war should be fought.

To the Navy, the way to victory was to exploit the air and sea power of the United States and Britain and to employ land forces only in regions where the Germans would be unable to bring their own powerful land armies to bear—a kind of "peripheral strategy" not unlike that to be championed by the British. Although the Navy admitted that Germany could be finally defeated only by land armies on the European continent, the planners envisaged deploying no more than one million American troops to Europe, considerably fewer than in World War I.

Nor did the Navy contemplate particularly large increases in its own manpower. Naval planners anticipated a total strength of 1,300,000 men, including not quite 162,000 marines—figures that would contrast sharply with the strength actually reached during the war: 3,400,000, including 485,000 marines. In formulating its Victory Program, the Navy looked toward something well short of maximum national effort, relying instead on foreign manpower backed by the output of American industry.

The Army, on the other hand, saw no substitute for directly confronting the enemy's armies on the ground. The Army and the Army Air Forces would require, War Department planners estimated, 8,795,000 men.

[24] Ibid, p. 370.

That was strikingly close to the actual peak strength reached during the war—8,291,000—but the estimate erred markedly in the composition of the force. Instead of a projected 215 ground divisions, only 91 actually were formed, and far more air and service troops than estimated proved to be needed.

The Navy's program with its lesser sacrifices was easily the more attractive; it was Roosevelt's "arsenal of democracy" transplanted to a shooting war. Politicians clearly favored it, as did for the moment equipment-hungry Britain and the Soviet Union. Indeed, pressure began to mount even to reduce the current army, grown to 1,500,000 men, in order to make more material available for lend-lease, particularly for the hard-pressed Russians. The President himself appeared to favor the Navy's plan and in late September called General Marshall to the White House to defend the Army's program. All a disturbed Marshall would venture as he came away was that the President probably would order no immediate cut.

Through the summer and fall of 1941 sentiment for the Navy's brand of war grew, to the marked detriment of the preparedness program, particularly that of the War Department. Under a policy laid down in September, for example, the bulk of new American munitions was to be allotted to lend-lease. It was a policy that would leave the Army almost stagnant at the existing strength of one and one-half million men lacking most of the tools of modern warfare.

Paradoxically, the slowdown began and continued even as the President openly embraced the British cause for all the world to see, even as the undeclared war in the Atlantic expanded into a *de facto* shooting war, and even as events in the Pacific appeared to be fast approaching a climax.

By August, having conspicuously failed to take public notice of the ABC Staff conversations in Washington earlier in the year, President Roosevelt deemed public opinion far enough advanced to warrant open collaboration with the British. In view of continuing British defeats—Greece and Crete were lost, British troops in North Africa were driven back on Egypt—he also sought an opportunity to bolster British morale. Meeting with Churchill aboard ship in Argentia Bay, Newfoundland, he helped draft, then signed and proclaimed, a declaration of war aims, even though his nation was not at war. This was the Atlantic Charter, forerunner of the Declaration of the United Nations, which was to be signed a little over four months later.

Even to Churchill, Roosevelt's participation in the Atlantic Conference while still professing neutrality was "astonishing." The United States was a maiden who had gone so far down the path of seduction that it appeared to her seducer a bit foolish not to go the rest of the way. Churchill and his military Staff pleaded and cajoled, but the maiden still demurred. Until rearmament progressed further, Roosevelt and his military and naval advisers believed they could contribute more by refraining from openly entering the war.

If events in the Atlantic continued on the course they then were following, the time would be short, in any case, before the United States became involved in a shooting war. For with acceptance of the British proposal that Americans relieve the British in Iceland, the United States was committed within waters that the Germans already had declared to be a war zone.

Although U.S. Marines failed to get an "invitation" from a reluctant Icelandic government until they were practically ashore, a brigade had landed in Iceland in July, whereupon the Navy began to convoy supply ships back and forth to the new base. This the Germans well might have ignored, except that the United States extended the protection of the convoy to ships of any nationality that chose to join. When British ships took advantage of the invitation—which was why it was issued—the U.S. Navy for all practical purposes began to escort British vessels more than halfway across the Atlantic, where British convoys picked them up for the rest of the voyage. They followed the same practice, in reverse, going the other way.

Nobody bothered at first, possibly intentionally, to say whether American ships were to engage German and Italian submarines unless fired on first. The question still was unanswered when in early September the destroyer U.S.S. *Greer* encountered a submerged U-boat. Although the *Greer* tracked the submarine, she attacked only after the U-boat fired a torpedo. Evading the missile, the *Greer* dropped depth charges. After firing a second torpedo that also missed its mark, the submarine retired.

An indignant President called the attack an "act of piracy." From that point, he announced, ending all speculation, German or Italian vessels of war entering waters that the United States deemed vital for its own defense "do so at their own risk." That meant "Shoot on sight."

With the declaration the United States was at war in the Atlantic, although neither side appeared anxious to step up the pace of the shooting. Before the United States formally entered the war, only two more incidents would occur. The first was in mid-October when the U.S.S. *Kearny*, one of five destroyers that came to the aid of a British-escorted convoy under attack by a wolfpack, took a torpedo in her side. Eleven men were killed, seven wounded, but the *Kearny* made it to port under her own power. A fortnight later, the U.S.S. *Reuben James* was far less lucky. When she took a torpedo, the explosion ignited a forward magazine, blowing the vessel in two. One hundred men went down with her.

These incidents contributed to the President's success in November in persuading the Congress to repeal the remaining restrictive provisions of the Neutrality Acts, including that against arming merchant vessels; but the incidents produced no cry of outrage from the American public. Here was no *Athenia*, no *Lusitania*. Besides, the people these days were more sophisticated, reconciled to the fact that incidents were bound to occur, that when playing with inflammable toys, somebody might get hurt.

The only real outcry came from the isolationists. A minority, the isolationists nevertheless still were powerful, as evidenced by the close vote in the House of Representatives on extending selective service. They greeted each new Presidential decree, each new incident in any way related to the possibility of war, with increased recalcitrance.

Senator Wheeler publicly announced the landing of U.S. Marines in Iceland while the operation was in progress. Gerald Nye investigated the motion picture industry on the theory that anti-Nazi films were leading the nation down a primrose path to war. As the Army worked on its ultrasecret Victory Program, Robert McCormick's Chicago *Tribune*, Anglophobe house organ of the isolationists, speculated that the Army was preparing an expeditionary force to help the British in Africa. When General Marshall personally denied it, the *Tribune* called him a liar. To buttress its case, the *Tribune* published for all eyes to see the complete text of the Victory Program.

That was on December 4, 1941, only three days before a "date which will live in infamy."

The fact that crisis was approaching between the United States and Japan had been partly concealed from public attention by the size of the headlines from the Atlantic and Europe. Yet for all the efforts of the Secretary of State,

Cordell Hull, to reach a *modus vivendi* with Japan, official Washington suspected that a day of reckoning was close.

In response to an ill-disguised Japanese conquest of French Indo-China, Roosevelt froze Japanese assets in the United States. He also imposed an oil embargo—a move, Marshall and Stark believed, that might impel Japan to launch an early expansionist drive to capture new sources of oil. Despite some gradual reinforcement of the garrison in the Philippines, a United States dedicated to a policy of Europe First was in no position yet, the military and naval chiefs believed, to stand up to Japan.

In reality nothing the United States could have done or not done at that point could have deterred Japan from a collision course for war.

Despite having broken the Japanese diplomatic code, Washington had no specific knowledge that the Japanese were about to strike. By counting ships, intelligence experts nevertheless reckoned that before long the Japanese would start some move toward the south. On November 27, on the basis of that deduction, alert warnings went out to Army and Navy commanders at all Pacific stations, but nothing in them indicated that the Japanese had decided to eliminate—or at least to neutralize—in one bold stroke the principal instrument of American action in the Pacific: the Pacific Fleet.

It was unseasonably warm all over the United States that first week in December. Along the eastern seaboard, fog at night, burned away by an Indian-summerlike sun in the daytime. Flowers bloomed incongruously in New York parks.

It had been an autumn of peace amid disquieting indications of war. People were still collecting "Bundles for Britain." That awful word "priorities" meant a cutback in production of automobiles. Despite new taxes on luxury items, people were hurrying to buy radio-phonographs, electrical kitchen appliances. A government-imposed embargo on silk for ladies' hose and underwear sent women scrambling to sales counters. Since August, in the eastern states, in an effort to forestall a gasoline shortage that might follow transfer of great numbers of tankers to the transatlantic run, service stations had been forced by government decree to close by 7 P.M. Across the Potomac from Washington work had begun on a new five-sided building to house a burgeoning War Department. Newsreel audiences had changed from hissing to applauding the Russian dictator, Josef Stalin.

Bars and nightclubs were jammed with servicemen and newly affluent defense workers. On Broadway one marquee provided a grim reminder of the times—Paul Lukas in *Watch on the Rhine*. A remake of World War I's *Smilin' Through*, this time with Jeanette Macdonald, was playing in the first-run movies, along with some of the anti-Nazi films that disturbed Senator Nye. In between historical novels people read Ernest Hemingway's *For Whom the Bell Tolls*.

That first week in December the America First Committee announced support for any antiwar candidate for Congress, regardless of party; William L. Shirer's *Berlin Diary* headed the non-fiction bestseller list; maneuvers were ending again, this time in the Carolinas. P-38 Lightning fighter-bombers were coming off assembly lines; production of merchant ships soon would reach one a day; six new 35,000-ton battleships had slid down the ways in the course of the year. Duke and Oregon State were scheduled for the Rose Bowl in Pasadena (no one knew yet that the game would be transferred to Duke's stadium in Durham, North Carolina). "Big name bands" were luring dreamy young crowds—Glenn Miller, Harry James, the Dorsey brothers, Glen Gray. Kate Smith sang her big heart out on the radio, rallying the nation with Irving Berlin's "God Bless America."

Few knew, and few would have understood the portent anyhow, that on Saturday, December 6, the Harvard educator, James B. Conant, met in an office on P Street in Washington with a small group of scientists awaiting special word from the White House. The Government of the United States, the word came at last from the President, had decided to make an all-out effort to produce an atomic bomb.

The next day, Sunday, December 7, a strong northwest wind had begun to sweep away the unseasonable mild.

It was then that word came about Pearl Harbor.

Chapter Four – Reorganization and the War at Sea

With one blow the Japanese had achieved marked advantage in naval power in the Pacific. Of eight American battleships at Pearl Harbor, one was destroyed, one capsized, another was heavily damaged, and three were damaged but able to proceed under their own power. Three cruisers were damaged, 2 destroyers heavily damaged, 2 auxiliaries sunk and 2 damaged, 161 planes destroyed on the ground, 5 in the air. In the first moments of the war 2,345 American soldiers and sailors were killed.[25]

For the United States, an abysmal intelligence failure and a disgraceful tragedy. For the Japanese, a brilliant tactical victory, even a temporary strategic success; but in the end, a colossal political blunder, for it unified the United States as few other acts could have done.

While Britain decorously delayed, an eager United States Congress the

---

[25] For this chapter in matters of reorganization, I have relied primarily on Watson, *Chief of Staff*; Cline, *The Operations Division*; and Pogue, *Ordeal and Hope*. For statistics on Pearl Harbor, I rely on Conn, Engelman, and Fairchild, *Guarding the United States*. The Historical Division of the Department of the Navy has furnished statistics on American naval strength after Pearl Harbor. For the naval war, I have used almost exclusively Morison, *The Battle of the Atlantic*. See also Theodore Roscoe, *United States Submarine Operations in World War II* (Annapolis, 1949) and *United States Destroyer Operations in World War II* (Annapolis, 1953), and S. E. Smith, ed., *The United States Navy in World War II* (New York, 1968). David Mason, *U-boat: The Secret Menace* (New York, 1968) appeared too late to be of real assistance in my study but is an excellent treatment of the Atlantic battle, one of a growing number of impressive war studies in a new series by Ballantine Books. I have found no definitive studies on the merchant marine, but for a flavor of what it was like, see John Mason Brown, *To All Hands* (New York, 1943) and *Many a Watchful Night* (New York, 1944); also Lieutenant Bob Berry and Lloyd Wendy, *Gunners Get Glory* (Indianapolis, 1943). Scientific advances in the naval war are treated in the Morison work and in James Phinney Baxter, *Scientists Against Time* (Boston, 1952).

next day hastened to declare war. Only a female pacifist in the House of Representatives, who had voted against entering World War I, kept the vote from being unanimous.

Armed with decoded intercepts of Japanese messages to Berlin, the President postponed asking a declaration of war against the European members of the Tripartite Pact in order to let the onus of making war fall on them. Three days passed, tense days, for as Roosevelt publicly pointed out, what did freedom stand to gain by the defeat of Japan if the Nazi colossus still stood unchecked astride Europe and Africa? Yet there were reasons for Hitler to demur: the Japanese had acted without consulting Germany, and Hitler had no burning desire for a confrontation with the United States until the Russian campaign was finished. On the other hand, he had actually encouraged a unilateral Japanese attack by promising to enter the fight even if the Japanese attacked first.

On December 11 the waiting ended. Both Hitler's Germany and Mussolini's Italy at last declared war on the United States.

In light of the catastrophe at Pearl Harbor and the inability of the United States and Britain to defend more than a few of their possessions in the Pacific and the Far East, the outlook for the Allies was dismal.

Although sinkings in the Atlantic had decreased in the summer and fall of 1941—a reflection both of improved British anti-submarine methods and of German transfer of planes and submarines to the war against Russia—they still averaged about 160,000 tons a month, a figure too high for complacency. With the exception of tiny Switzerland and Portugal, all of continental Europe was under either direct or indirect Axis domination; and the prospect of totalitarian Spain either moving against Gibraltar to block the Mediterranean to Allied shipping or allowing the Germans to do so was depressingly real. While not actively allied with the Axis, France's associated states in Africa were loyal to a collaborationist government in Vichy and were pledged to resist any Allied attempt to bring them into the war; and dangerous remnants of the French fleet were still afloat. In the latest phase of a seesaw battle waged along the North African littoral, British forces defending Egypt, the Suez Canal, and the oil resources of the Near East had been driven back inside the Egyptian frontier. Despite what would prove to be the start of a major counteroffensive in front of Moscow on December 6, the Soviet Union still fought for its life.

Furthermore, neither the United States Army nor the Navy was anywhere near ready to wage war.

On the day after Pearl Harbor the Navy had only 9 battleships fit to fight, plus 29 seaworthy cruisers and 6 aircraft carriers. Some 325,000 men were in the Navy, plus 70,000 in the Marine Corps and 25,000 in the Coast Guard.

Although the Army had grown to almost 1,750,000 men, that was far from the 4,000,000 that responsible officials deemed necessary even to defend the Western Hemisphere. Continuing equipment and ammunition shortages meant that at the time of Pearl Harbor only one division was fully trained and equipped to fight, although 37 others were in some stage of training. Even had more divisions been ready, so limited was shipping that few could have been transported overseas.

Within the Army, only 348,535 men were in the Air Forces. Once the surprise Japanese strike against Hawaii and others against the Philippines were over, the number of ready combat planes was down by 350 to a distressing nadir of 807, of which only 159 were four-engined bombers.

The real accomplishment of the preparedness program thus would have to be sought not in what had been completed but in what had been started. Keels had been laid and substantial work accomplished on eight new battleships, while construction was so far along on new aircraft carriers that within two years the Navy would have ten, plus thirty-five of a new class, a small escort carrier. Eleven government shipyards and over a hundred private yards were working three eight-hour shifts a day, including Sundays. The Marine Corps had experimented at length with techniques of amphibious landings and, along with the Army, had settled on prototypes of landing craft that were going into production. Some of the planes that would prove to be the workhorses of the air war were already in production: pursuit planes (or fighter-bombers) like the P-38 Lightning, the P-47 Thunderbolt, and the P-51 Mustang; medium bombers like the A-20 Havoc; and the first of the big bombers, the B-17 Flying Fortress and the B-24 Liberator. Others were coming off the drawing boards, including the B-29 Superfortress, destined for use against Japan. More than 425,000 people were working in aircraft plants, and already the industry had expanded to the point that almost 3,000 planes would come off the assembly lines during the first month of 1942.

As for the equipment and munitions shortages of the ground arms, most plants had nearly completed the tedious process of retooling for war production; this, plus the impetus provided by actual war, would speed output dramatically. In 1941, for example, the automobile industry had produced over 5,000,000 civilian automobiles and trucks; the facilities that had done that would be turned swiftly to making machines of war. The Maritime Commission had developed the Liberty ship, an emergency freighter that could be constructed in sections, then welded together.

Before the Congress in January, the President set production goals for 1942 of 60,000 planes, 45,000 tanks, and 8,000,000 tons of merchant shipping. The figures sounded incredible, even to those intimately involved in achieving them; but most would be met. At the time of Pearl Harbor the United States still was unprepared for war, but it stood much nearer the threshold of preparedness than it had at the start of any previous war.

As with production, the command and organizational changes that would carry the nation to victory had yet to be made, but two years of emergency planning and expansion had produced a fairly firm idea of what the changes would be. They would go into effect early in the first year of the war.

Only two weeks after Pearl Harbor the President eliminated the equivocal arrangement whereby the commander of the largest of the Navy's three fleets also acted as overall fleet commander. Making the position of Commander-in-Chief a separate post, he named the former Atlantic Fleet commander, Admiral Ernest J. King, to fill it.

In theory, the Commander-in-Chief assumed authority for plans and operations, while the Chief of Naval Operations retained responsibility for logistics, procurement, and housekeeping. It was, in a way, a division of authority not unlike that inherent in the relationship between the Army's Chief of Staff and the head of GHQ, and it contained just as many conflicts and ambiguities. To solve them, in March of 1942 the President put one man in both positions, Admiral King, while sending Admiral Stark to Britain as commander of U.S. Naval Forces in Europe.

With the addition of King, the President's wartime operational command post was almost filled. There were, in addition, the stalwart Marshall, the two Republicans Roosevelt had enlisted in quest of bipartisan political support—the Secretaries of War and the Navy, Henry L. Stimson and Frank Knox—and the head of the Army Air Forces, General Arnold. Conspicuously missing from the war council—indeed, specifically excluded—was the Secretary of State, Cordell Hull; for Roosevelt, like Wilson, liked to be his own Secretary of State. To the list would have to be added one who ostensibly had no place but one who had been living in the White House in a special relationship with the President since the day Hitler invaded the Low Countries. Crony and confidant, adviser, personal envoy, at once hatchet man and conscience, one forced by disease to serve under sedation, Harry L. Hopkins.

In March, too, the War Department completed the reorganization sparked originally by the airmen's drive for autonomy and by the incongruity of GHQ's location between the Chief of Staff and theater commanders. GHQ was out. In its place were three separate arms: Army Air Forces—Arnold; Army Ground Forces—McNair; and Army Service Forces—Lt. Gen. Brehon B. Somervell.

Roosevelt's choice of Admiral King over Admiral Stark represented no summary relief in the sense that the Army and Navy commanders in Hawaii were relieved as scapegoats in the Pearl Harbor disaster; there were good and valid reasons for upgrading King, a dynamic, relentless man of vast experience and an immense capacity for command and work, a true "old salt." (King was so tough, Roosevelt liked to say, that he shaved with a blow torch.) Yet it was, in a sense, an casing out, part of a response to Pearl Harbor that affected many who held top command and Staff positions in the two services. Both the head of Army intelligence and the chief of the Army's War Plans Division also were transferred. Few in top positions other than General Marshall, whom the President already had come to look upon as indispensable, retained their posts.

In the meantime, machinery had been created for joint Army-Navy direction of the war and for combined direction with the British. In place of the old Joint Board gradually emerged the Joint Chiefs of Staff, made up of the Chief of Naval Operations, Admiral King, and the Army's Chief of Staff, General Marshall, plus—in recognition of the upgrading of the air arm and in accommodation to Britain's separate air force—the commanding general of the Army Air Forces, General Arnold. There remained only to add in the summer of 1942, as personal Chief of Staff, the trusted Fleet Admiral William D. Leahy, a World War I associate and former Chief of Naval Operations, whom Mr. Roosevelt called from his post as ambassador to Vichy France. (Marshall encouraged the addition of Leahy as a counter to the pro-Pacific and almost Anglophobe views of Admiral King.)

These four merged with their opposites on the British side—Field Marshal Sir Alan Brooke, Chief of the Imperial General Staff; Admiral of the Fleet Sir Dudley Pound, the First Sea Lord; and Air Chief Marshal Sir Charles Portal, Chief of the Air Staff—to form the Combined Chiefs of Staff. Since Washington became the permanent seat of the Combined Chiefs' organization, a subordinate Staff headed by a personal envoy of Mr. Churchill, Field Marshal Sir John Dill, represented the British Chiefs in the intervals between formal conferences. A tall, sinewy man, a former Chief of the Imperial General Staff, Sir John had some of the attributes of George Marshall—sincere, frank, self-disciplined—an admirable choice as permanent liaison between British an Americans.

With this machinery, plus several combined civilian and paramilitary agencies such as the Munitions Assignments Board, the Shipping Board, and the Production and Resources Board, the United States and Great Britain fused their war efforts in a manner previously unknown among allies. About all that was missing was an equal sharing of the hardships—an accident of geography—and joint citizenship. The arrangements provided a central planning and direction in no way matched on the Axis side.

Most of the men making up the Combined Chiefs actually had held their first meeting the preceding August aboard ship in Argentia Bay. The first meeting after the United States entered the war was in late December of 1941 in Washington. Known as the ARCADIA conference, it created the apparatus of the Combined Chiefs while setting a pattern of several top-level conferences to follow.

Despite a general predilection in some quarters to get on with the war against the nation that had attacked Pearl Harbor, neither the President nor his military advisers wavered at first in their dedication to the principle of beating Germany and Italy first. In practice, nevertheless, the war against Japan would for long months draw a preponderance of American resources, simply because so few resources in relation to the breadth of the Japanese effort had been deployed in the Pacific when war came. While it was early recognized that the Philippines might not be saved, Washington was determined at whatever cost to hold open a line of communications through Hawaii to Australia. That required men and that most critical of all commodities at the moment, shipping, leaving little for troop movements in the Atlantic.

45

Reaffirming the principle of Europe First and creating the apparatus of the Combined Chiefs were the two main decisions affecting the war against Germany and Italy to emerge from the ARCADIA conference. The representatives of the two Allied powers also reiterated their desire to relieve remaining British troops in Iceland and noted the possible necessity of sending American troops to the British Isles early in 1942; but ARCADIA was primarily a sounding-out on both sides, with American military men sharply conscious of their nation's weaknesses and continually concerned lest the eloquent Churchill in private moments with Roosevelt obtain concessions beyond their capacity to implement.

It was Mr. Churchill who introduced the conference's most controversial subject. Encouraged by recent victories that had carried the British from Egypt into Libya, the Prime Minister raised the possibility of a British drive on to the west to the border of Tunisia. That accomplished, Churchill suggested, Vichy France might agree to let the Allies enter the associated North African states in order to bring them back into the war and clear the entire south shore of the Mediterranean Sea. The British, he revealed, had accumulated enough troops and shipping to occupy Algeria and Tunisia, but French Morocco would have to be an American assignment.

Eager for some early offensive operation to give the American people a feeling that they were started on the way to victory, President Roosevelt warmed to the idea.

His military advisers did not. Some questioned the strategic value of North Africa and wondered how much occupation of it would contribute toward the eventual defeat of Germany, but in the main the objections were practical. Where was the shipping to mount the assault and to sustain it? A subcommittee appointed to study the project produced figures showing that if the operation were attempted, no other major movement could be made in the Atlantic until well into the next year. That meant no more United States troops for Iceland and none for the British Isles, neither of which Mr. Churchill was willing to forgo.

In January enough shipping was at last assembled to send 3,000 soldiers in sardine-like accommodations to Iceland, a first step in relieving British and marines, and 4,000 to Northern Ireland. Not until the last day of April would enough be available to send sufficient numbers to relieve all the marines and the bulk of the British and to put a sizable contingent of 19,000 men in Northern Ireland.

The shipping shortage failed to kill the North African venture, but it put it on the shelf.

As the Combined Chiefs talked, entry of the United States into the war greatly accelerated action in the Atlantic. Even with no increase in German submarines, the number of sinkings rose simply because the number of unrestricted targets more than doubled, now that all American shipping was legitimate prey. So many were the targets that German U-boat captains began to ignore convoys, even those with only scant protection, to concentrate their wrath on unescorted vessels, particularly in the Caribbean and in United States and Canadian coastal waters.

Short of submarines since the war began, unaware of the Japanese intention to force war, and already committed to a campaign against British shipping in the Mediterranean, the Germans failed to send submarines to the Western Atlantic until a month after Pearl Harbor. It was early in January, as Hitler declared the Atlantic Coast and the Caribbean to be "blockaded" in order to justify sinking neutral ships, that three U-boats manned by veteran crews arrived in American waters.

With new construction and shifts from the Mediterranean, that figure rose rapidly to approximately forty by June, though the need to refuel and provision meant that probably no more than half of them were actively preying on shipping at any one time. Even so, in the first six months of 1942, submarines in the Atlantic sank 506 Allied vessels, representing 2,250,000 tons of shipping. At that stage of the war the shipbuilding industry could come nowhere near replacing losses on such a scale.

So unprepared were America's defenders against the submarine during that period that they sank only six U-boats in American and Caribbean waters. The fault was the Navy's. Despite explicit warnings from the President himself, the Navy had concentrated its rebuilding program almost exclusively on bigness, leaving little room in the program for smaller, less spectacular craft needed against the submarine.

Since the Navy at first had no land-based planes capable of searching far out to sea, that task fell during the first few weeks to the Army Air Forces. Yet the Air Forces could make available only a pitiful six short-range bombers for the assignment. By the first of April the air weapon had grown to 84 Army and 86 Navy planes based from Maine to Florida, still far from enough. Many of the planes lacked radar, a radio-wave device developed by the British for tracking a surface or an aerial object on a screen; and crews were inexperienced and only perfunctorily trained for this specialist warfare. The number of surface vessels to fight the U-boats remained meager: only 23 large and 42 small Coast Guard cutters, plus 29 miscellaneous craft and 22 converted trawlers, the latter lent with crews by the Royal Navy.

Although government officials early appealed to coastal residents to dim their waterfront lights in order to diminish the sky glow silhouetting offshore vessels, the plea produced little more than cries of anguish from coastal resorts. A dimout, the Chambers of Commerce railed, would ruin the tourist trade.

So vehement was the outcry that timid Army and Navy officials failed to insist on the measure until losses became too heavy to ignore. In mid-April the Navy at last ordered waterfront lights and big neon signs doused; a month later the Army directed a stringent dimout to include coastal cities like New York and Miami. Close to the waterfront, residents had to use blackout curtains and drive their cars with parking lights.

It was a grim war, the war at sea. Clad in civilian clothes, merchant seamen ashore drew taunts of "draft dodger" or "4-F"; but the moment their vessels left harbor, their lives were in deadly peril. They earned big money—their unions saw to that—but during the war thousands perished.

Once a torpedo hit a vessel, often without warning, chances of survival were few. Death might come with the first explosion, or a man might be trapped belowdecks. Burning oil often extended hundreds of yards from the stricken ship, cruelly weighting the odds of death. If there was time to man lifeboats before the last convulsive shudder of the vessel, survivors might find themselves face to face with the U-boat that had damned them, as it surfaced to survey the agony and sometimes to add to it by machine-gunning lifeboats and floating survivors. So few rescue craft were available in the early days that survivors often were prostrate from hunger, blistered by a merciless sun, or stiff from an icy sea before rescue came—if it came at all. Although many merchant vessels carried machine guns and 20-mm. cannon manned by Navy crews, they might as well have thrown spitballs, so ineffectual were the guns against the armament of the U-boats.

The main weapon against the submarine during the first months was the inaccurate depth charge, inherited with few refinements from World

War I. Not until 1943 would appreciable improvements in the depth charge and the means of expelling it be achieved, including a new plastic explosive more powerful than TNT. To find the U-boats, naval engineers had developed an improvement over World War I's listening devices—a supersonic echo-ranging sound detector called "sonar." Yet in order to operate sonar successfully, long weeks of complex schooling were required to teach a man to distinguish among the sounds of a submarine, of the sea itself, and of a German defensive device that shot out small gas bubbles to return false echoes.

Scientists provided yet other aids: they early applied the techniques of operational research; they produced an expendable sonobuoy to be dropped from aircraft to do much the same kind of eavesdropping for planes that sonar did for ships; they developed high-frequency radio direction finders ("Huffduff," they called it) to be located ashore or on convoy escort vessels to pinpoint a U-boat from its own radio transmissions; and when German submarines rendered radar innocuous with search receivers that let the captain know when he was under surveillance, scientists countered with a new microwave radar that German receivers were unable to detect. Yet World War II ended with no definitive answer to the U-boat.

Particularly during the crisis days of 1942, winning the battle of the Atlantic was less a question of science than of adapting old methods to the means at hand. So heavy was the toll of unescorted oil tankers (375,000 tons in March 1942) that the government forbade them to ply the coastal route—a ban that led in May to gasoline rationing in seventeen eastern states. The Navy, meanwhile, created a special anti-submarine command, set up new schools for anti-submarine training, and worked against time to install radar in all its planes and ships. The Navy also canvassed private shipyards for small craft readily convertible to submarine chasers and belatedly placed contracts for destroyer escorts and other small, fast vessels useful on killer patrols. Hundreds of private yachts and cabin cruisers were soon performing picket duty off the coast, reporting U-boat sightings to naval headquarters ashore and rescuing drifting survivors of torpedoed merchant vessels. The Civil Air Patrol similarly performed reconnaissance duty.

The Navy early directed shipping to stick as close as possible to the coast and, where draft permitted, to use the Delaware-Chesapeake and Cape Cod canals. Still too short of escorts to institute a true convoy system along the coast, the Navy in April stationed craft on anti-submarine duty outside harbors and directed merchant vessels to travel only in daytime in bounds of just over one hundred miles from one protected harbor to another. Off Cape Hatteras, where no adequate harbor was available for the long run from Norfolk to Charleston, the Navy set up a net-protected anchorage. This leapfrog system was a help, but over the next four months submarines still sank eighty-two merchant ships along the coast, some within view of bathers at Virginia Beach and Atlantic City.

In early May enough escort craft at last were assembled to start a convoy system from Norfolk to Key West and later in the month to add a northern link. The Germans in June still sank thirteen ships in coastal waters; but with increasing protection, the number in July fell to three.

That was the end of the crisis. Not a single ship succumbed to the U-boat terror off the Atlantic coast during the remaining months of 1942.

It was an end to the terror in one spot, a beginning in another. Confronted with protective measures off the coast, the U-boats merely transferred operations to the Caribbean. There they sank an average of one and one-half ships a day until finally, in September, with notable help from the Brazilian navy, convoy protection was extended to those waters. To spread available escorts, the U.S. Navy established "local" convoys in the Caribbean to feed into "express" convoys plying between Key West and New York, where they connected with others making the North Atlantic run.

By the end of 1942 the submarine had been beaten in both Caribbean and American coastal waters, primarily by a time-worn convoy system which naval officers deplored for its cost in escort craft but for which nobody had devised a substitute. Nevertheless the battle of the Atlantic went on, for already the U-boats had turned their fury on the transatlantic routes they had been neglecting for the easy pickings in American waters, and on perhaps the most difficult run of all for Allied ships, that through icy Arctic waters to the Russian ports of Murmansk and Archangel.

The shift to the North Atlantic began in August, and with it came new tactics by the submarines. As their underseas fleet was constantly increased by new construction against few losses, the Germans were able to strike not with single wolfpacks but with echelons, each preceded by one or two U-boats whose primary job was to find the convoy, then to serve as decoy if any of the escort dropped off for a killer hunt. The wolfpacks also struck by day as well as by night, and in the fall the Germans doubled the effectiveness of their fleet with "milch cows"—big 1,600-ton submarines that delivered fuel, provisions, water, and torpedoes to the wolfpacks.

For their main killing ground the Germans chose the mid-Atlantic north of the Azores, beyond range of Allied planes based in Newfoundland, Greenland, Iceland, and the British Isles. They struck, too, in the South Atlantic, particularly off Trinidad, where convoys were only gradually introduced as escort craft became available, and in the Atlantic narrows between Brazil and Africa. An average of 91 U-boats plied the Atlantic during the last half of 1942, sinking as many as 106 Allied ships in one month—November, the worst of the war.

The task of escorting most transatlantic merchant convoys fell at the time to the British and Canadian navies, since in addition to convoy duties along the United States coast, in the Carribean, and in the Pacific, the U.S. Navy had to concentrate on protecting faster troop convoys feeding an increasing buildup of American troops in Britain. Only one loaded troopship was lost during the war on the transatlantic run.

As dangerous as was the transatlantic route, it was the run to North Russia for which most merchant seamen reserved the label of Hell. There to the threat of the wolfpacks was added that of German planes based within easy range in Norway and of the remains of the German surface fleet sallying forth from Norwegian fjords and harbors. There, too, was the additional peril of high seas, cold, ice, snow, and fog, though at times the seamen would bless the screen afforded by snow and fog. There, too, even after a ship gained harbor, safety was only relative. German planes were within ten minutes, flying time of Murmansk and could sneak onto their target over the rim of mountains that encase the port as in a saucer. Those who fought their way through to Murmansk and Archangel to keep Russian resistance alive engaged in one of World War II's more savage battles, for which fat paychecks and big bonuses could be only partial compensation.

Most American merchant ships bound for North Russia accompanied a transatlantic convoy as far as Iceland, there to pick up a British-escorted convoy for the twelve-to fourteen-day run to Murmansk and Archangel. To stay as far as possible from German airfields, the convoys hugged the fringe of the Arctic ice pack. The Russians, who had no naval air arm, provided little aerial protection; they also treated requests to base British planes in Russia with suspicion. Losses on the North Russian run, in terms of number of ships involved, were greater than on any other route. In the months of March through May 1942, for example, out of four convoys each way, 27 of 162 ships were lost.

The grimmest convoy battle of the entire war occurred on that run in July of 1942—Convoy PQ 17. Paradoxically, PQ 17 was also one of the most heavily escorted, at least at the start.

The convoy contained 33 merchantmen, 22 of them American, with an escort of 6 destroyers and 16 other vessels. There was also a support force of 2 American and 2 British cruisers and a total of 9 destroyers and corvettes. To guard against forays of German surface ships, the Admiralty also provided a covering force that included the American battleship, U.S.S. *Washington*, a British battleship and aircraft carrier, and 14 other ships. As the covering force was also designed to see a westbound convoy safely through, it was to provide assistance for just over half the distance from Iceland to Murmansk.

Although the Admiralty had provided the extra protection merely as a precaution through an area where an eastbound and a westbound convoy were to pass, the Germans actually were planning a major operation against the next convoy to be sighted. They intended attacks by the battleship *Tirpitz*, two cruisers, and a fleet of destroyers.

The next convoy turned out to be PQ 17.

A harbinger of trouble appeared the third day out of Iceland with the appearance of German reconnaissance planes. The next day the convoy beat off 8 torpedo planes and a pack of U-boats; and the next, 26 German planes. The Germans reserved their strongest strikes for the American holiday, the Fourth of July, after the convoy had already passed beyond the range of protection of the big covering force. All day torpedo planes and dive bombers pestered the ships, sinking two merchant craft and damaging five others; but the *Tirpitz* and the other German surface vessels failed to show.

Confused by the presence of two convoys and the heavy collection of protective vessels, the Germans had called back their surface fleet, but not before British reconnaissance planes had detected their sortie. Unaware of the reversed orders and of no mind to give battle to the powerful *Tirpitz*, the Admiralty ordered the naval covering and support forces to retire, the convoy to scatter. Although the escorting screen was not included in the order, its commander thought he would be needed to help deal with the *Tirpitz* and pulled away. That left it up to each merchant ship to make the last 450 miles on her own, defenseless except for .30- and .50-caliber machine guns and an occasional 3-inch piece.

As the merchantmen scattered, German planes swooped to the attack. One by one they sought out the hapless ships. The surviving crewmen of those that were sunk endured cruel rigors of cold and hunger before reaching another ship or land, where they faced long treks through snow and ice to find help in those sparsely populated northern reaches. Some ships escaped by painting their starboard sides white, covering their hatches and decks with bed and table linen, and hiding in the Arctic ice pack, starboard to the enemy, for as long as two weeks until the fury of the German attack subsided.

Out of 22 American merchantmen, only 7 got through. Of the entire total of 33 merchant ships, 22 were sunk, plus a rescue ship and a fleet oiler. Out of 188,000 tons of precious cargo, 123,000 tons were lost. On the basis of that experience the Admiralty canceled further convoys along the route until September, when the days grew shorter.

As the first anniversary of Pearl Harbor passed, the shipping problem still loomed large and real as a critical obstacle to victory and in the game of death between submarine and convoy, the rays of hope were faint. The faster troop convoys were getting through, and as older pre-war merchant vessels were sunk—some might rationalize—all convoys were speeding up. Also, during the last quarter of 1942, new construction for the first time exceeded losses, except in tankers; but that was more a reflection of rising construction than of declining losses. Another gloomy fact was that the Allies still were destroying only a few U-boats—sixty-four in the last half of the year, only eleven by American forces—while a fairly steady average of about twenty new submarines slipped off German ways each month. Allied production of escort vessels would require another year to catch up with demand.

In the matter of troop transports, so critically short at the time of Pearl Harbor, the year had begun inauspiciously when the French luxury liner *Normandie*, which was being converted to a troop carrier, caught fire at a New York pier from a workmans acetylene torch, burned, and capsized, a total loss. As disaster followed disaster in the Pacific (Guam, Wake, and Hong Kong fell before 1941 was out; the British at Singapore capitulated on February 15, the Dutch East Indies on March 9, American forces on Bataan a month later, the fortress of Corregidor on May 6), there was faint hope for an early shift of transports from the Pacific.

Because the British were preoccupied with buildup in the Near East and Egypt, the first assistance they could provide had come only at the end of April when the venerable liner *Aquitainia* transported American troops to Iceland and Northern Ireland. The proud *Queen Mary* made her first voyage with American troops in mid-May, carrying much of an armored division; while two smaller British transports managed to accommodate the rest of the division by "double loading," whereby the troops ate and slept in shifts. The *Queen Elizabeth*, carrying 11,000 men, mostly airmen, sailed in early June. Yet not until August or September were regular voyages established for these big vessels, which were fast enough to sail the Atlantic without convoy.

Faced with the shipping shortage, American leaders and planners could but fret in frustration. Not only did they have to assemble shipping to get the troops, their tanks, their artillery, across the Atlantic, but enough shipping had to be found to move material for building bases, canton-ments, airfields, and to keep the men in rations, clothing, ammunition, fuel. Air squadrons and ground divisions were at last emerging trained and equipped, but how to get them overseas?

At the end of 1942, a year after America's entrance into the war, the outcome of the merciless duel between Allied shipping and German submarines was still in doubt.

Chapter Five – A Decision for North Africa

Pressures developed early in America's first year at war to reverse the strategic decision only recently reaffirmed at the ARCADIA conference—Europe First. To many who received the dreaded pale yellow messages announcing that next-of-kin were dead, wounded, missing, it seemed only right to get on as rapidly as possible with defeating those who were actually killing American "boys" and stealing United States possessions.[26]

The former isolationists rallied to this cause, for even they could rationalize a fight against a people who had actually fired the first shots. For the racists among them, many of whom through the years had accorded at least tacit approval to Hitler's persecution of the Jews, the fight against the "Yellow Peril" had many of the earmarks of a crusade. To others, Anglophobes like Gerald Nye, to go after Hitler first, rather than Hirohito, was to fall into a cunning trap the British had been baiting since 1938.

Joining in, too, were thousands of nervous people from the west coast who thought a Japanese invasion was just over the horizon. So jittery was the population in the west, particularly in southern California, so vehement the demands of their representatives in the Congress, that in mid-February the President and the Army bowed to their fears and agreed to evacuate more than 110,000 Japanese aliens and Americans of Japanese ancestry from the coastal states to inland internment camps. It was a repressive step impossible to justify even under the guise of military

---

[26] Most helpful for this chapter were: Matloff and Snell, *Strategic Planning, 1941-1942*; Leighton and Coakley, *Global Logistics and Strategy*; Pogue, *Ordeal and Hope*; and (for the Churchill visit) Davis, *The Experience of War*. See also Leo J. Meyer, "The Decision to Invade North Africa," in Greenfield, ed., *Command Decisions*. For the definitive work on evacuating Japanese-Americans, see Stetson Conn, "The Decision to Evacuate the Japanese from the Pacific Coast," in the same volume.

necessity in a nation ostensibly fighting a war for human freedom.

The U.S. Army commander in the Pacific, General Douglas Mac-Arthur—alternately pleading, cajoling, demanding additional resources—heard these voices sympathetically even if he did not encourage them openly. Admiral King, too, the new Chief of Naval Operations and Commander-in-Chief, United States Fleet—no devotee of the global strategy hammered out in large measure by his predecessor, Admiral Stark, and as jealous as the next naval officer of sea-oriented Britain—heard them as voices of reason.

In mid-February and again in early March, King specifically proposed that the Army broaden its effort in the Pacific. In view of the unscheduled priorities already accorded the Pacific, many a result of the unanticipated speed of Japanese conquest but many also a result of pressures from King himself, this new demand was to George Marshall downright upsetting. So it was, too, to Marshall's new Chief of War Plans (called at this point the Operations Division), Major General Dwight D. Eisenhower. While the United States continued to spread its slender resources thinly around the globe, Hitler might any day subdue the Soviet Union and turn all his power against the Western Allies.

Both Marshall and Eisenhower considered that the time had come to reaffirm the strategy of Europe First; no repetition of the broad generalities of the ARCADIA conference but a specific commitment to include a time and place for striking a major blow—a goal to which all training, production, and allocation of men and shipping might be directed.

"We've got to go to Europe and fight," was the way Eisenhower put it, succinctly if less than brilliantly, "and we've got to quit wasting resources all over the world—and still worse—wasting time."[27]

With single-minded determination, General Marshall pushed that view to formal acceptance in the Joint Chiefs of Staff; then on the first day of April he presented to the President a War Department plan for an invasion of Europe. The Allied goal, Marshall proposed, should be a buildup in Britain (code-named BOLERO) to support an invasion (ROUNDUP) by forty-eight divisions supported by almost six thousand planes. Two-thirds of the divisions and more than half the planes were to be American. The invasion should be launched within a year, around the first of April 1943; but should the Soviet Union show signs of collapse,

---

[27] Matloff and Snell, *Strategic Planning, 1941-1942*, p. 156, citing an Eisenhower memorandum of January 22, 1942.

an emergency invasion (SLEDGEHAMMER) might have to be mounted before 1942 came to an end.

Mr. Roosevelt approved the plan the same day, and within the week an American delegation headed by Marshall and Hopkins left for London to sell it to the British.

That was no easy assignment. To Churchill and his military leaders, the forbidding memories of an earlier generation of Englishmen wiped out at the Somme, Ypres, Passchendaele, Gallipoli, and of the more recent experience of bleeding expeditionary forces recoiling before Hitler's might at Dunkirk and in Norway and Greece, were all too vivid. Given the manpower available to the Germans, the way to beat them was to blast them with air and sea power while nibbling away at the periphery of their conquests—North Africa, Norway, possibly elsewhere. Only when they were near collapse should the Allies confront them directly on the Continent. These arguments and more the British raised: their precarious position in Egypt, in the Indian Ocean, the appeals of invasion-scared Australia. Yet Marshall and his colleagues refused to relent.

Fearing that the American allies would abandon them and concentrate on the Pacific, Churchill and the British Chiefs of Staff on April 14 at last accepted the proposal. Although they accepted without formal qualification, it was clear to Marshall that they had agreed only "in principle," that almost all the conferees had "reservations regarding this or that."[28] A myriad of arguments would rage in many another Allied conference before the outlines of Allied strategy in Europe were finally defined.

Thus the strategy of Europe First remained in effect, but that did not mean the decision was inviolate. Indeed, in little more than two months it was to face its severest test.

The coming of war, meanwhile, had been doing much to alter life in the United States. On Monday, December 8, 1941, the country's first full day as a belligerent, the Chicago *Tribune* shifted a flyer from editorial page to front, a quote from Stephen Decatur: "Our Country! In her intercourse with foreign nations, may she always be in the right, but our country, right or wrong." In Washington, noted a writer for *The New York Times*, one could almost hear national unity click into place.

---

[28] Matloff and Snell, p. 189.

In Philadelphia, Cleveland, Detroit, New York, some merchants taped their display windows and erected sandbag barricades, as they had seen British shopkeepers do in the newsreels. Art galleries moved priceless treasures to vaults. Many people who had yet to buy new automobile tires or electrical appliances rushed to the markets. All the armed services noted a sharp upswing in recruits.

Rationing more than anything else quickly brought a taste of war to almost everybody—gasoline, tires, sugar, coffee, fuel oil; but in most cases it was more inconvenience than hardship. Various campaigns to salvage scarce materials—scrap iron, fats, silk, paper, rubber, tin, aluminum—did less to alleviate shortages than to give people a sense of participating. The entire nation went on daylight saving time. The Congress levied a special "victory tax" on income; raised taxes on tobacco, liquor, travel, theaters, nightclubs; and passed a strict price control bill. Colleges speeded up their schedules to allow men to complete degrees before going to war, while the Navy took the lead among the services in utilizing college facilities by creating a preflight training program. Apparently everybody read Marion Hargrove's short spoof of Army life, *See Here, Private Hargrove*; and Irving Berlin and the Army collaborated on a hit musical with soldier performers, *This Is the Army*.

By midyear more than 12,500,000 people were engaged in war production work; many of them were women ("Rosie, the Riveter," took a position, however fleeting, as a national heroine beside Molly Pitcher and Barbara Fritchie). Kaiser and Higgins became big names in shipbuilding. To boost morale and production, the Navy awarded a pennant and badges bearing an "E" (for Excellence) to plants and workers achieving exceptional records.

The armed services continued their unprecedented growth. The Congress readily passed a record $42,000,000,000 appropriations bill for the Army, and for the Navy authorized an expansion to more than 5,500,000 tons, largest in the world. The Congress also authorized the services to enlist women for noncombatant jobs: the WAAC (later WAC) for the Army, WAVES for the Navy, WAAF for the Air Forces, SPARS for the Coast Guard, and for the Marine Corps, women who, like men, would be known simply as marines. Servicemen got a pay raise and free mailing privileges, plus National Service Life Insurance. An ubiquitous little military vehicle with four-wheel drive, the Willys Jeep, captured the imagination of the nation. Soldiers ceased to be "dogfaces" or even "doughboys"; now everybody called them "GIs" for "Government Issue." To expedite identification in case of fatality, all servicemen wore about their necks twin metal plates, providing name, serial number, next of kin, and religion—"dog tags," they called them. The Congress quickly extended the draft to apply "for the duration and six months" and later in the year lowered the age from twenty-one to eighteen.

Neon-lit "victory towns" sprang up outside every post: uniform and insignia emporiums, beer parlors, greasy short-order restaurants featuring "home cooking," souvenir stands selling satin pillows reading "Mother." Landlords the country over gouged the serviceman's family for high rents. Thousands in uniform jammed the little towns around camps and bases on Saturday nights, mainly to walk the dull streets in boredom. Some patronized the USO (United Services Organization).

In early June four Germans landed from a submarine on a lonely stretch of Long Island beach; four others, a few days later in Florida near Jacksonville. Although bent on sabotage they accomplished none, for in a matter of days Federal agents apprehended the lot. A special military tribunal convened on order of the President and sentenced two to prison, the others to death. A firing squad did the job early in August.

From the fiehting fronts and the war at sea, the news was in most cases depressing—the surrenders in the Pacific, the sinking of the *Prince of Wales* and the *Repulse*, the siege of Leningrad—but bright spots did emerge. In an exploit specifically staged to bolster American morale, sixteen B-25 bombers took off in April from aircraft carriers to raid Tokyo. Early in June the Navy in the battle of Midway scored a signal success—indeed, it would eventually be known as the turning point in the war in the Pacific. In Europe, on Independence Day, planes of the Eighth Air Force made the first American raid against Nazi-occupied Europe. In the first week of August, U.S. Marines landed on Tulagi and Guadalcanal in the Pacific to start the first American ground offensive of the war.

In April, under pressure from American leaders, Winston Churchill had agreed to work toward a large-scale invasion of the European continent in the spring of 1943. He had agreed, too, if circumstances dictated, to SLEDGEHAMMER, an emergency invasion designed to stave off Russian defeat. He had put his heart in neither plan. Nor did he consider either agreement final or binding.

Churchill came to the United States that oppressively hot June a disturbed man. A few weeks earlier President Roosevelt had, in effect, promised the visiting Soviet Foreign Minister, Vyacheslav Molotov, that the Allies would open a "second front" in 1942. To Churchill, whose own government had gone only so far as to assure Molotov that honest preparations for a landing were under way, the promise was shocking. Although the President had not said so specifically, the words "second front" connoted a cross-Channel attack, a landing in France.

His American friends, it seemed to Churchill, were naive. That they looked on the landing as in all probability a sacrifice operation mattered little. If the Russians were truly near collapse, what hope that a minuscule foothold on the Continent would draw any German strength away from the Red Army? Assuming even that Allied troops got ashore, what would happen should the Russians collapse and the Germans turn everything against the Allied beachhead and then against Britain? Under the circumstances, Churchill believed, a failure would be worse than doing nothing at all.

He had come to the United States with the specific goal of preventing Allied sacrifice on French beaches in 1942—"the only way," he was convinced, "in which we could possibly lose this war."[29] Going first to the President's estate at Hyde Park, he found it difficult to restrain himself from broaching the topic at once, even though he knew the arena for fighting the battle was not Hyde Park but Washington, where his military chiefs had preceded him to begin discussions with their American opposites. The subject he and the President discussed that afternoon of June 20—the possibility of splitting the atom and the advisability of British-American cooperation on the project—was so obviously one that had to be answered affirmatively, however uncertain the likelihood of success, that he wanted to settle it swiftly and get on with the more mundane but more immediately pressing problem of SLEDGEHAMMER.

As the day waned and time neared to board the President's private railroad car for the overnight trip to Washington, the Prime Minister handed the President a note.[30] Did the Americans have a plan for SLEDGEHAMMER? What troops would be used? Where? What shipping

[29] Sherwood, *Roosevelt and Hopkins*, p. 591.

[30] Churchill, *The Hinge of Fate*, pp. 381-82.

and landing craft? Who was to command? What British help was required? For all the concern for the Russians, which he himself fully shared, no responsible British military authority saw any hope for a cross-Channel attack in 1942 unless the Germans were at a point of collapse.

What alternative, then, but a peripheral operation, perhaps North Africa?

Churchill's sense of relief upon delivering himself of this heretical catechism would have been heightened had he known that before his host joined him for the journey to the capital, he had telephoned George C. Marshall and Ernest J. King. Assuming dire happenings in late summer on the Russian front, the President postulated, what did Marshall and King have in mind?

The question spoiled the sleep of both Marshall and King, but of Marshall especially. Wary, as always, of the influence of the Prime Minister on the President, sharply conscious of the lack of a unanimous, pre-established American position vis-à-vis British proposals, Marshall had to approach the question with the knowledge that a U.S. Navy intent on building capital ships had so sorely neglected developing the means of putting the Army ashore that SLEDGEHAMMER, North Africa, or anything else was almost hypothetical. Landing craft, naval leaders maintained, were an untried weapon, unworthy of a speculative diversion of resources from capital construction. It was a reaffirmation of the Navy's concept of a Victory Program, of its fear of repeating the failure at Gallipoli in World War I, of its belief that an invasion of hostile shores could succeed only after seaborne guns and airborne bombs had reduced the enemy to the point of submission.

Only with the threat of developing his own landing craft and the crews to man them—in effect, of creating the Army's own navy—had Marshall at last, only days before Churchill was due in Washington, persuaded his opposite, Admiral King, to make landing craft a priority project. A Britisher, Lord Louis Mountbatten, who had preceded Churchill as an emissary of understanding, had provided the telling argument. Speaking as one naval man to another, he told King: "You are selling the birthright of the Navy. We can't stop the invasion of Europe...The Army puts itself ashore, and in the long run you don't need the Navy."[31]

---

[31] Pogue, *Ordeal and Hope*, p. 331.

Delighted with the triumph, Marshall was nonetheless keenly aware that deciding on a program of production was one thing, getting landing craft off the assembly line was another. The legacy of the Navy's reluctance to develop landing craft would complicate many an Allied decision as the war progressed. Marshall had to face Churchill with the disturbing knowledge that landing craft adequate for almost any amphibious venture were a thing of the future.

The news that greeted Prime Minister Churchill the morning of June 21, soon after he joined the President in the Oval Study of the White House, might have thrown all awry the prepared strategy of a lesser man. He learned that as a climactic blow to a new Axis offensive that had driven the British Eighth Army back on Egypt, Tobruk had fallen—Tobruk, the coastal fortress that theretofore had held when all else failed, Tobruk with thirty-three thousand men and enough supplies to withstand a three-month siege.

Churchill was staggered. The British in Africa were back where they had been two years before. A continued Axis drive might destroy all British forces in Egypt, gain the Suez Canal, the Near East and its vital oil, even link up with German armies driving down from Russia or through the Balkans.

Roosevelt was movingly sympathetic. With George Marshall's support, he promptly offered help: first an American armored division; then, instead, upon fuller consideration, 300 medium tanks and 100 self-propelled guns. Knowing something of the shortages that still plagued his allies, Churchill was touched. He would be further gratified later when the Americans promptly replaced 70 tanks that went down when the ship carrying them was sunk.

Yet however staggered by the news, however moved by the American reaction, Churchill had no inclination to deviate from his charted course. If the Americans had a feasible plan for SLEDGEHAMMER, he said, or could come up with one, His Majesty's Government would welcome it cordially and "share to the full with their American comrades the risks and sacrifices."[32] Otherwise, the intimation was clear: there could be no cross-Channel invasion in 1942.

To Churchill's relief, he could see that preliminary maneuvers he had

---

[32] Matloff and Snell, *Strategic Planning: 1941-1942*, p. 239, citing a memorandum from the Prime Minister to the President.

conducted before coming to Washington had produced results. First by letter, then by Mountbatten's visit, then by the note at Hyde Park, he had revived in advance his earlier proposal to invade French North Africa. That had been enough, he discovered, to divert Roosevelt from SLEDGEHAMMER. Although Marshall and his colleagues were prepared to fight the proposal for North Africa, they would do so, not in terms of a SLEDGEHAMMER that was precarious at best, but in terms of the threat invading North Africa posed to BOLERO, the buildup in the United Kingdom for an invasion of the Continent in 1943.

For that, too, Churchill was ready. "Can we afford to stand idle in the Atlantic theater during the whole of 1942?" he asked. "Ought we not to be preparing within the general structure of BOLERO some other operation by which we might gain positions of advantage, and also directly or indirectly take some of the weight off Russia?"[33]

Working for him, Churchill knew, was the President's previously expressed predilection for the North African proposal, his desire to give his newly raised troops battle experience, his wish for some kind of ground offensive against the Axis to raise morale and end the frustration of inaction, to keep the people—as Marshall later put it—"entertained."[34] Churchill would have to beware nevertheless lest too persistent an espousal should so antagonize Marshall, Arnold, and Leahy that they would swing around to the Pacific orientation of that crusty man of the sea, Admiral King, and to the arguments of one almost as eloquent as Churchill himself, Douglas MacArthur.

Working against him, Churchill recognized with some irritation, was the opinion of his own Chiefs of Staff, particularly that of Field Marshal Brooke. In conversations with their American opposites, the British Chiefs seemingly had agreed that invading North Africa was inadvisable. Like the American Navy, the Royal Navy felt there were commitments enough already in the Atlantic; and all agreed that North Africa would provide scant relief for the Russians while it would slow BOLERO considerably. No major operation should be attempted in the Atlantic in 1942, said the British Chiefs in conjunction with the American Chiefs, unless "an exceptionally favorable opportunity presented itself."[35]

---

[33] Matloff and Snell, p. 240, citing the same memorandum.

[34] Pogue, *Ordeal and Hope*, p. 330.

[35] Matloff and Snell, *Strategic Planning: 1941-1942*, p. 239, citing a paper of the Combined Chiefs of Staff.

The Combined Chiefs had yet to present their ideas formally to their heads of state when the meeting that began with the discomfiting news of Tobruk took place in the White House. In sometimes heated phrases the Prime Minister and General Marshall argued their cases to the President. To Marshall, the basic issue was to deny anything that would delay BOLERO and an invasion early in 1943 and at the same time lead the Allies so far down the path of peripheral strategy as to afford no return. To Churchill, it was to make a solid use of available resources to further the Allied cause, however peripheral the approach. North Africa would help the British retain the Near East, would bring the French states back into the war, and would open the Mediterranean as a southern route to Russia.

In the end there emerged a statement of principles designed to please all hands but one that still cried for decision:

1. Push preparations for an invasion in 1943 but also prepare to act offensively in 1942.

2. Press plans for an operation against the Continent in 1942, but if no sound plan could be contrived, be ready with an alternative.

3. The best alternative: North Africa.[36]

Although General Marshall would succeed later in watering down the third point, Mr. Churchill could leave Washington with some satisfaction. The Americans, he might note, still thought in terms of Europe First, and he could be fairly well assured that SLEDGEHAMMER was faltering. He had also reinstated North Africa as the leading proposal to satisfy Roosevelt's hunger for early action. As for BOLERO, even if he did have reservations—as the Americans believed—about any invasion of the Continent until the Germans were at the point of collapse, the buildup would assist other operations that might later be proposed. Furthermore, the American troops who came to the United Kingdom under BOLERO also represented a means—even a man with the conviction of a Churchill would have to consider, perhaps with a shudder—to augment a last-ditch defense of his revered isle should the Russians, after all, collapse.

Back in London the British Chiefs of Staff remarked that they had authority to launch an operation (SLEDGEHAMMER) that their

---

[36] Matloff and Snell, p. 243.

government (Churchill) did not want. Restudying its possibilities, they noted the vast amount of vital shipping and landing craft that preparing for SLEDGHAMMER would tie up, thereby slowing and jeopardizing plans for the bigger landings in 1943. They also noted the thin chances of success, the dismal repercussions of failure.

Armed with this restudy, Churchill decided that the risk of allowing continued talk and preparations for SLEDGHAMMER had passed the point he could accept. The idea of any operation against the Continent in 1942 had to be put down forcefully and finally, even if the decision should send George Marshall into the eager arms of King and MacArthur.

Washington got the news on July 8, and it threw George Marshall into a rare but awesome rage. A measure of fury still was with him two days later when he reported the British decision to the Joint Chiefs of Staff. Ignoring the British reasons, he noted only that the British would not mount SLEDGEHAMMER and hoped the Americans would go along with the invasion of North Africa.

This, said Marshall, full of ire, raised two questions: First, should the United States agree to invade North Africa? Second, did the British really intend to invade the Continent in 1943?

An invasion of North Africa, Marshall said, would be "expensive and ineffectual" That answered the first question. The fact that the British again raised the issue of North Africa, he went on, revealed a lack of dedication to BOLERO; and "without full aggressive British support" it would be impossible to mount either SLEDGEHAMMER or an invasion of Europe in 1943. That answered the second question.

George Catlett Marshall, one of the architects of the policy of Europe First and, on the American side of the Atlantic, its most ardent champion, was prepared to deliver words that would electrify his colleagues, even Admiral King, whose tenets he at this point ostensibly embraced.

"If the British position must be accepted," Marshall continued, he proposed that the United States "should turn to the Pacific for decisive action against Japan."[37]

Although Marshall, unlike King, still favored Europe First, he did not propose to be tied to a purely British strategy in Europe. With the encouragement of Secretary of War Stimson, who was equally disenchanted with

[37] All quotations on this page Matloff and Snell, p. 268, citing minutes of the Joint Chiefs of Staff.

Churchill's obstinacy, Marshall and King put their proposal in writing to the President.

It was, Marshall claimed later, largely bluff. It appeared, on the surface at least, an ultimatum.

Whatever it was, the President would have none of it. There was room in Allied councils for honest disagreement leading to workable compromise, he believed, but no room for "taking up your dishes and going away." He quickly put Marshall and King on the defensive with a telephone call from Hyde Park asking that a full outline of "your Pacific Ocean alternative" be sent that afternoon by plane.

They had to admit, of course, that they had no detailed plan. They had to admit also, in response to questioning, that distances and lack of bases in the Pacific would more than halve the number of American troops to be deployed each month, and that a shift to the Pacific would have at least a temporarily unfavorable effect on the Russian front.

Roosevelt telegraphed Marshall the next day. He intended, he said, to send Marshall, King, and Hopkins to London immediately.

"I want you to know," he added, "that I do not approve the Pacific proposal."[38]

As the two service chiefs and the ailing Hopkins prepared to leave National Airport for London on Thursday, July 16, Mr. Roosevelt spelled out his views on their mission. In the process he stated clearly and simply the reasoning behind the concept of Europe First:

It is of the utmost importance that we appreciate that defeat of Japan does not defeat Germany and that American concentration against Japan this year or in 1943 increases the chance of complete German domination of Europe and Africa. On the other hand, it is obvious that defeat of Germany, or the holding of Germany in 1942 or in 1943, means probable, eventual defeat of Germany in the European and African theatres and in the Near East. Defeat of Germany means the defeat of Japan, probably without firing a shot or losing a life.

[38] Henry L. Stimson and McGeorge Bundy, *On Active Service in Peace and War* (New York, 1948), p. 424. Although Stimson went along with Marshall on the proposed shift to the Pacific, he later regretted his concurrence. Pogue, in *Ordeal and Hope*, pp. 340-41, says Marshall's switch was "well laced with bluff." See also Matloff and Snell, *Strategic Planning, 1941-1942*, p. 272.

Roosevelt was willing, his instructions revealed, to give his representatives one more chance to persuade the British to undertake a cross-Channel attack in 1942 or at least early in 1943; but should the Prime Minister hold his ground, they were to insist on an alternative, which probably would be either the Near East or North Africa, possibly Norway (which was what Churchill personally wanted in any case). Roosevelt himself agreed with Mr. Churchill that to stage a diversion in the Mediterranean in 1942 was not, as Marshall claimed, to rule out a cross-Channel attack in 1943. In any event, he was willing to take a chance on that in return for early action.

"It is of the highest importance," he noted, "that U.S. ground troops be brought into action against the enemy in 1942."[39]

The delegation was beaten even before the plane made a weather-imposed landing at Prestwick, Scotland, for the British were aware that their visitors' views were split. Hopkins, reflecting Roosevelt, was for North Africa, King for the Pacific, Marshall for Europe.

For three days, from July 20 through much of July 22, Marshall nevertheless argued with fervor for SLEDGEHAMMER as an emergency operation for which preparations would contribute to ROUNDUP in 1943 even if an improved Russian situation made launching it unnecessary. Point by point he lost the battle until, late on the twenty-second, he as much as admitted defeat.

Even then Marshall went down fighting. Accepting North Africa, which Marshall admitted was the best of the proposed alternatives, also meant, he said, abandoning any invasion of the Continent during 1943. To invade North Africa thus was to adopt a new strategy for the war in Europe, a defensive, encircling strategy—the strategy that the British, in the American view, had espoused all along. The question thus became not SLEDGEHAMMER versus North Africa but whether to stay with ROUNDUP or to abandon ROUNDUP. A decision should be delayed, he urged further, as long as possible consistent with launching the North African invasion during 1942, so that the final say might reflect the last possible appraisal of the situation in Russia. The latest practicable date, he ventured, was September 15.

Sure in the ways of the conference table, the British gradually but

---

[39] Matloff and Snell, pp. 273 and 277, citing a memorandum from the President.

effectively blurred the sharp line Marshall had drawn to pose North Africa as the killer of ROUNDUP, a reversal of strategy. That left Marshall with no lever more powerful than the date for final decision on abandoning ROUNDUP, September 15.

Marshall's own colleague, Harry Hopkins, was soon to take that lever from him. The decision for North Africa was no more than tentative, Hopkins noted, yet the President had charged the delegation with obtaining a clear-cut decision to guide operations in 1942. In a hastily dispatched personal message he urged the President to circumvent "procrastinations and delay"[40] by insisting on a target date for the invasion no later than October 30.

The President promptly obliged. He further clarified his view by asking Hopkins to tell the Prime Minister he was "delighted" the decision had been made. Orders were, he said, "Full speed ahead."[41]

Still sincerely convinced that to invade North Africa was to abandon a cross-Channel attack in 1943, which was a mistake, General Marshall and Admiral King would continue to insist that the decision for North Africa was the same as that against ROUNDUP and should not be taken before September 15. Even that futile device soon was denied them when logistical considerations made it imperative to come to a decision right away.

Any doubt that still remained dissipated on the evening of July 30 at the White House. As Commander-in-Chief, Mr. Roosevelt stated plainly, he had made the decision. The principal objective of American forces, to take precedence over all other operations, was Operation TORCH, the invasion of French North Africa.

---

[40] Sherwood, *Roosevelt and Hopkins*, p. 611.

[41] Matloff and Snell, *Strategic Planning: 1941-1942*, p. 282, citing a message from the President.

Chapter Six – North Africa: Intrigue

French North Africa was vast, stretching from the Atlantic coast across barren mountains and desert wastelands of Morocco, Algeria, and Tunisia more than thirteen hundred miles to the border of Italian Libya, roughly halfway across the sprawling continent. Almost all the 16,700,000 population—mostly Berbers and Arab Moslems—clustered in relatively fertile maritime regions along the Atlantic or the Mediterranean, principally in the ports. Of some one and one-half million who were French either by birth or naturalization, more than three-fourths lived in Algeria, where the coastal settlements formed three of the departments of metropolitan France. A French governor and a military administration ruled the rest of Algeria, while Morocco and Tunisia nominally were subject to native potentates, the Sultan of Morocco and the Bey of Tunis, though a French resident-general in both states supervised civil affairs.[42]

The French through the years had carried out a substantial program of public works, constructing several artificial harbors against a heavy swell

---

[42] Most of the sources useful for this chapter were also important for the two following chapters. I have depended in large measure on the following: Howe, *Northwest Africa*; Morison, *Operations in North African Waters*; Craven and Cate, eds., *Europe — TORCH to POINTBLANK*; Peter Tompkins, *The Murder of Admiral Darlan* (New York, 1965); Martin Blumenson, *Kasserine Pass* (Boston, 1967); and William L. Langer, *Our Vichy Gamble* (New York, 1947). Also useful are some of the war memoirs: Robert D. Murphy, *Diplomat Among Warriors* (New York, 1964); Dwight D. Eisenhower, *Crusade in Europe* (New York, 1948); Omar N. Bradley, *A Soldier's Story* (New York, 1951); Mark W. Clark, *Calculated Risk* (New York, 1950); William D. Leahy, *I Was There* (New York, 1950); and Lucian K. Truscott, Jr., *Command Missions* (New York, 1954). (The memoirs of Eisenhower, Bradley, Truscott, and Clark are valuable for many subsequent chapters. Although I have used them where applicable, I shall in most cases avoid the repetition of continuing citation unless a direct quote is involved.) See also Vigneras, *Rearming the French*.

and surf on the Atlantic coast of Morocco, the largest of which was at Casablanca, and either improving natural harbors or creating new ones in Algeria at Oran, Algiers, Bougie, Philippeville, and Bône and in Tunisia, notably at Bizerte and Tunis. A standard-gauge railway connected most of the ports in Morocco and Algeria with a narrow-gauge route traversing the Tunisian littoral. Two hard-surfaced highways ran either along the coast or a few miles inland, but at many points there existed bottlenecks, one-way bridges and tunnels and sharp curves at dizzying heights. Each territory had several good airfields.

French North Africa was a land of contrasts. Fertile coastal strip, but inland, bare, eroded mountain crags and glistening, trackless desert. In the cities a high European civilization; in the native quarters and in the countryside Arabs in rags making an existence with the help of half-starved camels and donkeys. In the ports white-washed, palm-shaded tourist hotels; in the countryside mud hovels alongside crumbled ruins of old civilizations.

In the warring world of 1942, French North Africa was also an anomaly. By much the same strange logic that had prompted the French government to capitulate rather than to continue the war in exile, the colonials in North Africa and the war refugees who lived among them put their faith in strict adherence to the terms of the armistice of 1940, dutiful obeisance to an aging Marshal of France, Henri Philippe Pétain, who ruled from Vichy that portion of France not occupied by the Germans with a curious blend of autocracy and collaboration. So firm was the conviction that that was the proper course that clandestine Resistance groups, already proliferating in metropolitan France and beginning to coalesce around a formerly obscure *général de division*, Charles de Gaulle, found few converts in North Africa.

A lightly equipped, 135,000-man army, made up mainly of territorials but with regular French officers, was permitted by the armistice for the defense of North Africa; it kept the native tribes in order, took the traditional two-hour noontime siesta, held retreat parades as if nothing in the world had changed. An air force of some 350 dated combat planes was there to fight whoever might come, Germans, Italians, or British alike. The navy manned coastal defenses and such warships as had not been incarcerated at Toulon under terms of the armistice or sunk or seized that tragic day when the embattled British, fearful that the powerful French navy might be turned against them, had opened fire on the vessels of their defeated ally.

That attack, which cost the French more than thirteen hundred killed and missing, had dealt a smashing blow to a Franco-British amity already suffering from mutual recriminations accompanying defeat in Flanders. That London gave shelter to Charles de Gaulle and his French National Committee, challengers of the duly constituted Pétain government, did further damage to the British image. The army that de Gaulle was creating—called at first the "Free French," later the "Fighting French"—had even borne arms in Syria and at Dakar against other Frenchmen. Those who had rallied to de Gaulle were at best renegades and rebels.

As in metropolitan France, the catastrophe of 1940 had done little to unify the French in North Africa. Although most were firmly anti-Axis, they remained divided as to how best to serve France under the excruciating circumstances of defeat. There were avid monarchists in North Africa and left-wingers, too; but by far the greatest number, particularly among the officer corps, believed in Pétain, if not because they reckoned the old marshal to be handling the Germans shrewdly, then from the certain knowledge that to cross the Germans was to invite total subjugation of all of France and of the protectorates and colonies as well.

Pragmatism in the American approach to the defeated nation furthered the anomaly of French North Africa. While paying lip service—and little enough of that—to the Fighting French, the United States maintained diplomatic ties with Pétain in Vichy and provided an envoy, Robert D. Murphy, to Algiers.

Once the British and the Americans had decided to invade North Africa, the peculiar political climate posed special problems for an operation cursed in advance by vast distances. If they were to gain French North Africa without heavy cost and with the speed essential to prevent a counter landing by Germans and Italians, they needed to forestall French resistance. Yet how to achieve that when the Frenchman in their camp was Charles de Gaulle, a man who apparently had little following in North Africa, to whom President Roosevelt was pointedly cold, and with whom they dared not even trust advance knowledge of the invasion? To rely on the loosely organized Fighting French to guard a secret was to expect a sieve to hold water.

In deference to the tarnished British image among the French, British and Americans from the first agreed that the invasion force should fly the Stars and Stripes with no evidence of the Union Jack. That led, inevitably, to the choice of an American commander. The British nominated George Marshall. As his deputy, they suggested the man who, since Pearl Harbor, had headed Marshall's War Plans (Operations) Division, Dwight D. Eisenhower. In the last weeks before the decision to invade North Africa, the British had come to know Eisenhower, now a lieutenant general, since Marshall in May had sent him to London to survey a growing American establishment, then in late June had sent him back to stay as commander of the European Theater of Operations.

Yet Franklin D. Roosevelt was not about to part with Marshall's services at home, though he did ask Marshall if he wanted the assignment. He named instead Eisenhower, who was Marshall's choice as well. Although naming Eisenhower meant selecting one considerably junior to many British commanders, the British raised no objection.

As his deputy, Eisenhower himself named the man he had brought with him to Britain, a tall, spare, hawklike soldier, a man of infinite energy and ambition, impatient sometimes to the point of fault but a man so anxious to get on with the job of beating the enemy that he would knock heads together to gain his goals: Major General Mark Wayne Clark. To Eisenhower's own affable, optimistic personality, Clark afforded an abrasive complement.

It was not so easy to settle on an outline plan for Operation TORCH. Now that the Americans bore the primary responsibility for the invasion, some of the impatience and bravado they had brought to the rejected cross-Channel attack evaporated; while the British, who would have borne the burden of SLEDGEHAMMER and thus had been acutely conscious of the hazards, now endorsed risks as essential if the Allies were to occupy all French North Africa before the Axis could intervene.

Unlike the Americans, who insisted on landings on the Atlantic coast of Morocco to ensure a line of communications to the United States, the British Chiefs of Staff wanted the entire expeditionary force to land inside the Mediterranean basin, at Oran, Algiers, and Bône. While aware that Bône lay within easy range of Axis planes in Sicily, which was the reason for forgoing landings in Tunisia, they were willing to accept the risk in exchange for a landing close enough to Tunisia to enable a mobile column to strike swiftly overland for Bizerte and Tunis.

Like the Americans, the British thought it possible that Francisco Franco's pro-Axis Spain would enter the war, either seizing Gibraltar or affording the Germans passage to do so, and thereby trapping the convoys inside the Mediterranean; but the British deemed swift victory the best way to forestall Franco. The British insisted, too, on an early date for the invasion, even if that meant no rehearsals, lest the Germans fathom Allied intentions and counter with troops released by a winter lull on the Russian front.

To the American Joint Chiefs, still obsessed with a now unspoken but continuing doubt whether the North African venture was worth doing, the British concept involved risks they could hardly accept. Better to flirt with a prolonged struggle, they reasoned, than openly to court failure. They insisted on an invasion date far enough advanced to permit amphibious rehearsals and conversion of ocean liners to assault transports, which meant no earlier than the first week in November.

They insisted, too, despite the hazards of high surf in late autumn, on a landing on the Atlantic coast. In company with simultaneous landings inside the Mediterranean, they suggested, that would impress both Franco and the French with Allied power and would provide an escape route should Franco act.

By late August the discussions had reached a virtual impasse, not without acrimony. It was then that the political heads of state intervened.

They might have acted sooner had not Churchill been on a visit to Moscow, there to absorb Soviet invective over the decision to forgo a second front in Europe. (The Russians were particularly edgy: the Germans were massing outside the gates of Stalingrad.) Upon returning to London, Churchill quickly sensed the depth of the dispute and began a series of transatlantic exchanges with Roosevelt.

As agreed by the President and the Prime Minister, Operation TORCH was to involve an American landing on the Atlantic coast to take Casablanca, another American landing inside the Mediterranean at Oran, and a third, to be followed by British reinforcement, at Algiers. Once Algiers had fallen, additional British troops were to land at eastern Algerian ports for the drive into Tunisia.

Control of French North Africa assured, the Allies were to push into Italian Libya to hit from the rear those Axis forces that by that time were to be under attack by the British Eighth Army in a new offensive staged from Egypt. The Axis thus might be eliminated from all of North Africa, enabling land-based Allied aircraft to open the Mediterranean to Allied shipping, including lend-lease supplies for Russia, and to relieve a beleaguered British outpost off the coast, the island of Malta.

As Commander-in-Chief, Eisenhower set the date for the invasion—November 8. Even though that date followed the 1942 Congressional elections, Mr. Roosevelt, while wishing it otherwise, raised no issue.

These arrangements brought purpose and direction at last to the vast apparatus being hurriedly fabricated for the invasion, but their cautious nature appeared to obviate the chances for a speedy conquest. Assuming the Axis would make a fight of it, even the most optimistic Allied planners could see no end to the campaign until the spring of 1943, five months after the invasion.

As George Marshall had insisted back in July, a decision for North Africa was a decision against a cross-Channel attack in 1943.

Early in September, from the Allied Force Headquarters set up in Norfolk House on St. James's Square in London, General Eisenhower plunged into detailed planning and filled out his Staff and roster of tactical commanders. Organized on the principle of balanced national participation, the Staff included equal numbers of British and American officers. If the chief of a section was American, his deputy was British, and vice versa; and their subordinates operated in teams composed of one officer of each nationality.

Eisenhower himself set the tone for this headquarters and the other Allied commands that were to follow in the Mediterranean and European theaters. It was, Eisenhower insisted, an *allied* command, a unified command, no loosely linked war council made up of purveyors of national interests. To act or even to think on purely nationalistic grounds was to invite stern discipline from a man who ordinarily chose to command by persuasion. (Oft repeated was the story that he sent one officer home, not because he called a colleague a son of a bitch but because he called him a *British* son of a bitch.)

Born in Texas, raised in humble circumstances in Kansas, educated at West Point, this fifty-two-year-old soldier had few immediately apparent attributes, other than an infectious smile, to account for a meteoric rise from relative anonymity. Yet a clear study of his earlier career (he had worked for both Pershing and MacArthur) would reveal that he did possess qualities ably fitting him for the unprecedented assignment to create a workable

Allied command. He had a degree of flexibility anchored favorably just at the boundary of inconsistency and rigidity. He had, too, a sensitivity to others and a warmly human personality that made men like him, want to please him, to serve him. There would be those who wished through long months ahead for more evidence of quick, firm decision, but the majority in the coalition command would readily concede that Dwight D. Eisenhower—"Ike," they called him—was suited to his job.

As commander of a 35,000-man Western Task Force to land on the Atlantic coast of Morocco, General Eisenhower chose an associate of long standing, Major General George S. Patton, Jr., whom George Marshall had nominated for the assignment. A fifty-six-year-old cavalryman who had early (World War I) transferred his affections to armor, Patton became one of the wars more colorful and controversial figures.

With his opposite, Rear Admiral Henry Kent Hewitt, a naval officer whom others than Patton later would extoll for ability and cooperation, Patton shared responsibility for an amphibious attack to be mounted on one side of the Atlantic and executed on the other, a rare and awesome undertaking. In 107 ships, including escort vessels, men of the Western Task Force were to sail from east coast ports, mainly Norfolk, to dodge submarines in the South Atlantic, and to go ashore in frail plywood Higgins boats at three minor ports on the Moroccan coast. After moving quickly by land to open the major port of Casablanca, Patton was to drive almost 500 airline miles eastward to link with the Center Task Force at Oran.

The command of some 39,000 American troops of the Center Task Force fell to Major General Lloyd R. Fredendall, whose name Eisenhower chose from a list suggested by Marshall. Fredendall was a stocky, belligerent infantryman about whom Eisenhower had early doubts which were soon dispelled but were destined to rise again. Transported from the United Kingdom almost entirely in British ships, Fredendall's force was to go ashore on beaches near Oran, then seize the port.

The commander of the Eastern Task Force—some 10,000 Americans, 23,000 British—was a Britisher, Lieutenant General Kenneth A. N. Anderson, an experienced but dour officer whom his own colleagues described as "difficult." As part of the scheme to give an American complexion to the landings, Anderson was to remain at first at Gibraltar, while Major General Charles L. Ryder, commander of the 34th U.S. Infantry Division, directed the assault force—two-thirds American, one-third British—at Algiers. Like the Center Task Force, Ryders troops were to be transported from the United Kingdom mainly in British ships.

Since the bulk of the ships involved were from the Royal Navy, the job of Naval Commander-in-Chief under Eisenhower went to a Britisher, Admiral Sir Andrew Browne Cunningham.

No such centralized authority was present at first for aerial units. Instead, the British furnished an Eastern Air Command composed of 454 Royal Air Force planes, while Brigadier General James H. Doolittle, who had led the carrier-borne strike against Tokyo in April, headed a separate Western Air Command composed of the newly created Twelfth Air Force with 1,244 American aircraft. That arrangement would work satisfactorily so long as the two air commands were engaged on separate missions connected with the assault landings, but later would require the addition of an overall air commander.

Assembling and training enough American air and ground units for a major invasion less than a year after the United States went to war was a task fraught at times with frustration, often with exasperation, and always with doubts. American air commanders in Britain had to part with much of the resources they had been laboriously assembling for the air offensive against Germany. In the United States the Army Ground Forces pirated officers and men from as many as nine divisions in order to bring the selected assault divisions up to strength, and "scalped" (Marshall's word) units all over the country to raise sufficient equipment. As the vanguard of United States troops going to France to join Pershing had gained the first view of some of their weapons aboard ship, so many sailing for North Africa would get their first glimpse of a recently developed anti-tank rocket called the "bazooka." The difference was that Pershing's men landed behind friendly lines; Eisenhower's were facing a shore likely to prove hostile.

The landings promised little innovation in amphibious techniques over those employed a quarter-century before at Gallipoli, except that military men had long since learned that soldiers and equipment to be unloaded first should be put aboard last. Most landing craft to be used on the Atlantic coast were Higgins boats—36-foot plywood craft, some without a landing ramp, so that the men had to clamber over the sides to get out—and all were vulnerable to goring by rocks or beach obstacles. A few of the first models of a steel LCM (Landing Craft, Mechanized), capable of carrying a 30-ton tank, would also be used. For landings inside the Mediterranean the British furnished the bulk of the landing craft—a variety of models, many makeshift, such as oilers converted to carry light tanks, and some more closely resembling the lifeboats of the *Titanic* than the sophisticated ship-to-shore vessels the Allies were to use later in the war.

Staff and command positions filled, tactical and logistical planning under way, units brought to strength and equipped by one expedient or another, there remained the enigma of the French. Would the French fight?

What the French might do at Algiers was particularly crucial, for if they either passively accepted or actively aided the operation, General Anderson might move swiftly to land British troops in eastern Algerian ports and speed the drive into Tunisia. If the French fought, it might take three weeks to occupy the easternmost port of Bône. That would guarantee meeting Germans and Italians in strength in Tunisia.

Disguised as a field-grade Army officer, the State Department's man in Algiers, Robert Murphy, conferred in September with General Eisenhower in a rural retreat near London. The size of the invasion force, Murphy said, was about what trusted French contacts in North Africa deemed necessary. As to the choice of a leader around whom the French might rally, his associates suggested General Henri Honoré Giraud, a respected senior officer who had attracted attention earlier in the year by escaping, as he had during World War I, from a German prison. Living at the time in unoccupied France, Ciraud was in contact with General de Corps d'Armée Charles E. Mast, the anti-Vichy Chief of Staff of French forces in Algiers, who with four civilians (they were to become known collectively as the "Five") comprised the anti-Vichy leadership in Algiers.

Hardly had Murphy returned to Algiers when an emissary approached him on behalf of Admiral Jean Francis Darlan, next in succession in the Vichy government to Marshal Pétain and Commander-in-Chief of all French armed forces. Considered by many to be irretrievably tainted by collaboration, hated by millions of Frenchmen as a betrayer of French patriots, strongly Anglophobe, Darlan had confided to an American official late the year before that he might be persuaded to lead his countrymen back to the Allied side. Now Darlan's representative told Murphy that he was rapidly being driven to make a choice: collaborate much more closely with the Germans or join the Allies. If he were afforded guarantees of American aid, Darlan might switch, bringing with him the French fleet.

Darlan's choice, it seemed to Murphy, could hardly be more difficult than the one Darlan himself posed for the Allies. A man as schooled in the intricacies and intrigues of French politics as Murphy was could scarcely have ignored the problems and criticisms any traffic with Darlan would generate; he nevertheless recommended that the Allies work out some kind of cooperation between Giraud and Darlan.

Even as the trusted General Mast and others of the Five protested collusion with Darlan, General Eisenhower posed a recommendation. Giraud, he suggested, might be named civil and military governor-general of French North Africa and be encouraged to accept Darlan in a military position that was mutually agreeable. Although Eisenhower had in mind elevating Giraud to become his deputy, once Mark Clark moved on to command an American army, the British pointed out that a governor-general—as Giraud would be—could not properly serve in such a position. Only Darlan—the untouchable—would be available for the post. Yet for all Darlan's taint, the arrangement proved acceptable not only to Eisenhower but to the Combined Chiefs of Staff, to Churchill, and to Roosevelt. As Churchill put it: "Kiss Darlan's stern if you have to, but get the French Navy."[43]

Even without Darlan, Giraud himself posed problems, not the least of which was whether his name provided the magic essential to rally the French. Although Murphy's contacts in Algiers swore as much, they also revealed that Giraud thought in terms of an invasion not of North Africa but of unoccupied France. Giraud thus had no concept either of the timetable or of Allied capabilities. Furthermore, Giraud looked to liberation not by the Allies but by French forces with Allied help and insisted that in joint operations involving France he himself was to be Commander-in-Chief.

The time had come, the Five confided to Murphy in mid-October, both to reach agreement with General Giraud and to discuss specific military plans. They proposed a rendezvous five nights later in a seaside villa ninety miles west of Algiers.

By air to Gibraltar, thence by submarine, Mark Clark (unlike history, his contemporaries knew him as Wayne) and four other members of

---

[43] Tompkins, *The Murder of Admiral Darlan*, p. 59.

Eisenhower's Staff arrived at the rendezvous point off the Algerian coast too near daylight on October 21 to hazard a landing. It was almost dawn the next morning before Mast and Clark at last sat down to talk.

True to instructions from London, Clark made no mention of Darlan, nor was he free to reveal to the French that the landings were less than a fortnight away. The French, for their part, produced valuable information—coastal defenses, troop concentrations, and the like. On Giraud and supreme command they agreed that that should be handled directly between the Allies and Giraud. If the French general should elect to participate, he was to be brought out of France by an American submarine.

The officers were still poring over maps when, in mid-afternoon, an accomplice in the local police station telephoned. French police, he warned, were on their way to the villa.

While most of the French scurried like rabbits for their cars or the under-brush, Clark and his companions hid in a wine cellar. To the gendarmes Murphy and the owner of the villa insisted that nothing more was going on than old friends getting away from wives and stuffy officialdom in Algiers for a little masculine fun. Upon approach of the police, they lied, the ladies in their party had hidden upstairs. Since the gendarmes knew who Murphy was, they pursued the matter no further.

A high surf that night made it difficult for Clark and his party to get back to the submarine. Time after time breakers crashed against their frail boats, either swamping them or hurling them back toward shore. Although the officers finally made it, Clark left behind a bankroll he had carried to ease negotiations, his trousers, and whatever dignity the latter loss entailed.

Nobody in Eisenhower's headquarters could be sure how much the Germans, the Italians, and the Vichy French knew about Allied plans to invade North Africa. There had been several flurries of excitement: a plane carrying a British courier with a letter containing an outline of Operation TORCH was shot down off the coast of Spain; a TOP SECRET message was dropped by a secretary on a London street; a package of maps of North Africa was lost from a truck, and the finder queried de Gaulle's porous headquarters to ask if they belonged to the French.

Had the Axis caught on?

Vichy France knew nothing. As for the Germans and Italians, they were merely suspicious. Hitler was concerned that the Allies would strike somewhere during 1942. Although various indications in early autumn pointed to the Mediterranean, most analysts leaned toward Dakar. If the Allies entered the Mediterranean basin, most Germans believed, they would bypass French North Africa to hit the rear of the Axis troops in Libya or perhaps try to seize a beachhead on the southern coast of Europe. Although the Italians suggested that the Axis move into Tunisia—not to beat the Allies to it but to get better ports for supporting the war in Libya—the Germans disagreed, lest the move impel the French to join the Allies. In any event, as winter approached, the Germans decided there would be no Allied strike until the spring of 1943.

The Axis forces in the Mediterranean area were in no position in any case to take protective countermeasures. Francisco Franco had put such a price on his assistance that Hitler had forbade his name to be mentioned; and in Libya the combined Italian-German army—headed by a German, Field Marshal Erwin Rommel, but subject to control of the *Comando Supremo*[44] (Italian High Command) in Rome—had pushed the British to the point of defeat during the summer but had had to stop short of victory for lack of supplies. (The Russian front ate up almost everything, and British planes on Malta harried all Axis shipping.) A renewed effort in August to deliver the *coup de grâce* also had failed, partly because of scanty resources, partly because of an obdurate British defense.

Then on October 23, behind such a thunderclap of artillery fire as was never before heard in the desert, the British Eighth Army under a new general, Bernard L. Montgomery, had struck back at Rommel at a place called El Alamein.

On November 5, as time ticked inexorably toward the eighth, the date for the landings, General Eisenhower moved into an advance headquarters deep inside the rock of Gibraltar. On an airfield outside stood row upon row of Allied planes, plainly visible to any Axis agent who stood beyond the wire fence separating the British enclave from Spain. The harbor, too, spoke of frenzied activity in support of something big; and through the narrow strait, silent but in full view, steamed the first transports bound for Algiers.

[44] To simplify identification, Axis headquarters and tactical units are italicized.

Doubt still crowded upon doubt in Eisenhower's mind. Appraised at last of the date of the invasion, General Mast and his group in Algiers—so Robert Murphy had reported—insisted on a three-week postponement. Although uninvolved in Mast's machinations and thus unaware of the impending assault, the Commander-in-Chief of French forces in North Africa, General Pierre Alphonse Juin, in effect also counseled delay. On a recent visit Juin had told Murphy that Admiral Darlan had reiterated his standing instructions that North Africa was to fight back against any invader, Axis or Allied; but, Juin confided, if the Axis moved first, as appeared likely on the basis of threats developing against Tunisia, the French would welcome the Allies.

Yet delay, Eisenhower knew, was out of the question. Allied convoys already were on their way: vessels from the United States had departed as many as seventeen days before.

And what of the Germans? Were they even then readying planes and U-boats to despoil the vulnerable convoys entering the Mediterranean? Would Spain act? How about the French? Was Montgomery's resounding victory at El Alamein enough to deter them? There had been no further word from the Vichyite, Admiral Darlan, and precious little from General Giraud.

It was well into the day of November 7, the eve of the invasion, when word came at last that Giraud had indeed boarded the submarine sent to fetch him from a rowboat off the French coast. In mid-afternoon the French general strode ashore at Gibraltar, but Eisenhower's concern about him was far from over.

He had arrived, Giraud announced grandly, ready to assume command. Many hours of testy argument later, even as Allied troops were departing their transports for the little landing craft that were to take them under French guns, a fatigued Eisenhower turned a seemingly futile task of persuasion over to Mark Clark. Giraud, it appeared, was playing for time, delaying his participation until the first French blood had been shed, and nobody could accuse him of spilling it.

Typically, Clark's patience was short. Tell him, Clark said finally to the interpreter, "I hope you know that from now on your ass is out in the snow."[45]

* * *

---

[45] Captain Harry C. Butcher, *My Three Years with Eisenhower* (New York, 1946), p. 171. Clark in *Calculated Risk* sanitizes the remark.

As the Allied convoys headed for the Moroccan and Algerian coasts, nobody—neither French nor Axis—spotted the armada of the Western Task Force in the Atlantic, but Axis spies quickly reported the naval movements past Gibraltar. Possibly because almost all ships entering the Mediterranean were British, the logical explanation to Germans and Italians was that the British were trying to run a convoy to Malta. Even when reports came in of troop transports carrying landing craft, the finger pointed not to French North Africa but toward the rear of Rommel's army in Libya. To forestall the move, Hitler ordered an ambush in the narrow Sicilian straits, with submarines forming a screen and land-based German planes readying a kill that might offset Rommel's discouraging losses on land.

The tragi-comic Italian dictator, Benito Mussolini, foresaw landings in French North Africa; but nobody listened to him.

Among the Vichy French, there were some who, like Mussolini, feared the worst. Several in authority urged Pétain to go to North Africa to spare Vichy commanders the dilemma that would confront them when Allied troops came ashore, but the old marshal refused. One did not defend France, Pétain said, by leaving France.

As the convoys passed on beyond Oran and Algiers during the night of November 6 and the morning of the seventh, most French commanders in Algeria relaxed. Not so the local naval commander in Algiers, Vice-Admiral d'Escadre Moreau. While agreeing that the position and course of the ships could place them off the coast of Sicily before dawn on the eighth, he also deduced that they had but to reverse course at nightfall to return to waters off Algeria.

Moreau hastened to tell his concern to one whom none on the Allied side other than Robert Murphy conceived to be in Algiers—Jean François Darlan. Admiral Darlan and his wife had flown to Algiers on November 5 to the bedside of a son whom they believed to be dying of infantile paralysis. Although his son's condition had begun to improve, Darlan had stayed on to make arrangements for taking him back to France.

Yet Darlan would not listen even to Moreau's alarm. He had the word of Robert Murphy himself, Darlan insisted, that the Allies would come to French territory only when invited by the French.

Having recovered from the first shock of learning that the landings were to come so soon, General Mast and the civilian members of the Five began last-minute preparations that they hoped would put the Allies in control in Algiers without opposition. There was hope, too, in Morocco, but at Oran plans had collapsed. Leader of pro-Allied forces there, the Chief of Staff of the Oran Division had prematurely alerted his division commander in the mistaken belief that the general was sympathetic. When the general ridiculed the whole idea, the Chief of Staff, fearful of arrest, had canceled the plans.

The general, fortunately, had spread no alarm, so that the apparatus of an uprising remained intact in Algiers. Only two real concerns existed there. First, nobody from the Navy was in on it, but the hope was that by seizing the Navy's communications system the conspirators might paralyze the coastal batteries. Second, Mast and his companions expected that their small bands might hold the critical points in the city for two hours. If Allied troops failed to arrive in that time, all might be lost.

The conspirators in Algiers numbered almost a thousand, but in the interests of security few other than top officials were let in on the secret until late on Saturday, November 7. By that time many conspirators had left the city to take advantage of a warm autumn weekend. When the startling message came over the British radio—"*Allo, Robert, Franklin arrive!*"—fewer than four hundred men responded. Few of those had weapons more formidable than rifles left over from the Franco-Prussian War of 1870.

Half an hour after midnight Mast and small groups of men wearing white armbands nevertheless struck. Using mainly civilian groups led by junior army officers, they seized control of the telephone service, police headquarters and substations, and the Algiers radio station, where despite an alarming absence of word from General Giraud, they prepared to broadcast an appeal in Giraud's name for all French troops to rally to the cause. Others cut telephone wires leading to naval headquarters and the big coastal batteries. Placing his superior, Général d'Armée Louis-Marie Koeltz, in protective custody, General Mast himself ordered the main body of French troops, the Algiers Division, to assist the landings. Guides headed toward nearby beaches where they expected the invaders to come ashore, while an army detachment seized control of an airfield closer in.

Robert Murphy and a State Department colleague meanwhile proceeded to the Villa des Oliviers in a western suburb of Algiers, the official residence of the French Army commander, General Juin. Awakening Juin,

Murphy explained that American troops were landing. The general, he trusted, would join the cause.

Juin paced up and down in pink-striped pajamas. Only four days earlier, he reminded Murphy, he had told of Admiral Darlan's reiterated orders to defend North Africa against all comers. Murphy had promised then that the Americans would act only on express invitation of the French.

They had been invited, said Murphy, a strapping man whose Irish countenance invited trust.

By whom?

By General Giraud.

Giraud had no authority, said Juin. In any case, he went on, the decision was not his to make since his superior, Admiral Darlan, was at hand.

Despairing of a decision from Juin, Murphy agreed to a telephone call to Darlan. Told that the matter was urgent, the admiral volunteered to await Murphy's car and come to Juin's residence.

When Murphy told his story, Darlan purpled with rage. Like General Juin, he insisted that Murphy had given his word that the Americans would come only on invitation, and Giraud was in no position to invite them. Furthermore, a commando type of raid like that at Dieppe was just the excuse the Germans wanted to occupy all French North Africa and the south of France as well.

Although Murphy insisted that the landings were in no sense a raid, Darlan remained unconvinced, and the silence of the night outside appeared to give the lie to Murphy's word that landings already were under way. On that point Murphy himself was growing restless.

Insisting on some word from French sources, Darlan directed an officer to go to the naval commander, Admiral Moreau, but outside the villa young men wearing white armbands barred the way. Darlan was at that point a prisoner, which upset him more than ever.

Despairing finally of getting help from the admiral in any other way, Murphy agreed to a message from Darlan to Marshal Pétain in Vichy, telling him of the landings and asking freedom of action. Although Murphy's State Department colleague headed toward the cable office with the message, he stopped off at the headquarters of the conspirators. Opening the message, they learned that Darlan had merely apprised the marshal of the situation and told him he was following government orders. For the moment the message would not be sent.

It was past two o'clock in the morning when the conspirators could report that all critical points in Algiers were in hand, not a shot fired in the process; but the guides sent to bring Allied troops from the beaches had yet to return. Out there in the darkness, only silence, no sound of an invasion.

In the Villa des Oliviers, Robert Murphy also was lamenting the silence of the night when outside a brief commotion arose. A detachment of *gardes mobiles* drove off the cordon of young Frenchmen wearing white armbands.

Murphy, not Juin and Darlan, became the prisoner.

A few hours earlier, in Casablanca, a secret radio station set up on the roof of a building near the port had provided word to the U.S. Consul General that landings of the Western Task Force were imminent. He promptly dispatched messages from President Roosevelt addressed to the Sultan of Morocco and the French resident-general, Auguste Paul Noguès.

At the same time the anti-Vichy man in Morocco, Général de Corps d'Armée Emile Béthouart, commander of the Casablanca Division, sent a courier with a letter to the home of General Noguès in the capital of Rabat. With American help, the letter explained, General Giraud was assuming command of all French North Africa and had designated Béthouart to take over in Morocco. A group of Béthouart's soldiers surrounded Noguès' residence to await his decision.

General Béthouart himself headed for the headquarters of the French army's Commander-in-Chief in Rabat, where an infantry battalion already was arrayed to protect him. Béthouart placed the Commander-in-Chief and the head of the air forces in custody and himself assumed command.

A letter from Béthouart similar to that handed General Noguès also went to the French naval Commander-in-Chief in Casablanca, Vice-Admiral François Michelier. As neither French air nor submarine patrols had reported the approach of an American convoy, Admiral Michelier found it hard to believe Béthouart's story. The general, he decided, was the victim of a hoax, a trick to give the Germans an excuse to occupy French North Africa.

Michelier assured General Noguès by telephone that no invasion force was offshore. He also telephoned General Béthouart's assistant division commander and ordered him to countermand Béthouart's orders to the

Casablanca Division. If, as appeared unlikely, landings were to take place, the division, like the naval forces, was to fight.

Noguès, for his part, vacillated.

Admiral Michelier's assurance that no invasion force stood offshore was compelling; for even if Michelier were wrong, the invaders, to remain undetected, could hardly be in strength sufficient to prevent Axis reprisals or—a consideration that seemed to influence many a French commander—to assure the safety of his own neck. The fact that the landings had failed to begin at the hour specified by General Béthouart reinforced Michelier's prognosis, as did telephone calls to outlying military districts, which revealed that there had been no landings and that commanders there were not swinging to Béthouart's side. Nobody in authority, including Noguès, had heard a recorded appeal from President Roosevelt broadcast from London. The letter to Noguès from the President, while delivered, remained unopened and unrecognized in the confusion.

Yet a man like Béthouart, Noguès knew, would hardly be taken in by a ruse. Besides, Noguès wanted to believe. He decided to reserve judgment until later.

Béthouart himself, in the meantime, had been growing increasingly concerned. It was well past 2 A.M., the hour the landings were to have begun; yet there was no sign anywhere of the Americans.

Chapter Seven – North Africa: Invasion

Since French North Africa technically was at peace, lights ashore were shining brightly as troops of the 1st Infantry and the 1st Armored Divisions scrambled into assault boats off beaches east and west of Oran. A blare of ship public address systems transmitting a short-wave radio broadcast of the Army-Notre Dame football game in New York added to the incongruity.[46]

Fortunate it was that an aura of peace prevailed on the beaches as well, for the men making the assault were unpracticed in their tasks, and fate, as always, was capricious. Guides failed to arrive at the expected points, entire companies and battalions drifted off course, ships carrying tanks ran aground well offshore, and at one spot vehicles that were disgorged on a sand bar foundered in deep water between the bar and the beach. Nobody got ashore at the appointed hour of 1 A.M. (0100 in military parlance). A battalion of paratroopers, scheduled to take an airfield, came to earth all over the landscape.

Some coastal batteries opened random fire, but the crews of most guns awoke to what was happening only as infantrymen came upon them from the rear. Even the units of the Oran Division were not deployed to oppose the landings. Although the Commander-in-Chief had been forewarned by his Chief of Staff's futile quest for collaboration, he did nothing until he heard the first fire from coastal batteries. Since the navy was fighting, he ordered his men to join in.

The delay meant that the first genuine resistance to most of the invading troops developed only after daylight, as small columns headed for Oran and nearby airfields. From behind stone walls and buildings French troops

---

[46] With three exceptions (see next three notes), the direct quotations in this chapter are from Tompkins, *The Murder of Admiral Darlan*. Tompkins made wide use of published French material

fought, but it was a dilatory resistance that obviously could be eliminated once artillery and tanks got ashore.

The only serious fight developed in the harbor of Oran. There 477 soldiers in two small British cutters were to thrust directly into the harbor, seize the wharves, and board French vessels to forestall scuttling. It was, as the men themselves quickly deduced once they learned details of their task, a suicide mission.

As the two cutters approached the entrance to the harbor, sirens in the city screamed and lights went out. A searchlight focused on the bow of the first cutter, the *Walney*. Over an amplifying system an officer cried frantically in French that the vessel was friendly, but a big shell ripping into the side gave the French answer. A crippled *Walney* raced forward, broke the boom barring the harbor, and slipped inside while searchlights, coastal batteries, and machine guns turned on the companion vessel, the *Hartland*.

The men aboard the *Walney* had begun to launch canoes as a first step in boarding the ships in the harbor, when a French destroyer came out of the night head on and raked the decks with fire. The British skipper had no choice but to order abandon ship.

Aboard the *Hartland*, at this point drawing the brunt of French fire, most gun crews and many of the troops crouching belowdecks were killed; the skipper was blinded by a shell fragment. The vessel nevertheless raced into the harbor but in the darkness drew alongside a French destroyer moored to a wharf. The destroyer poured fire into her insides. Amunition exploded. The cutter burst into flames. Again the order: abandon ship.

The toll of Navy crews and Army troops: 307 killed, 350 wounded. Only 47 soldiers landed unhurt, and all of them were quickly captured.

At Algiers one reason Robert Murphy, Admiral Darlan, and others could detect no sign of invasion was an absence of gunfire. No French troops defended the beaches, and the Royal Navy had mistakenly put the invaders ashore much farther from the city than insurgent leaders expected. Also, coastal batteries were slow to open fire. At Cap Sidi Ferruch, west of Algiers, where Frenchmen themselves had come ashore in 1830 to avenge an affront from a Moslem ruler, the only battery that could have shelled two of the three invasion beaches capitulated, a victory for the French conspirators.

Although the Americans had intended moving quickly to the city, the landings were too scattered and confused for that. Landings of both the

34th Division near Cap Sidi Ferruch and the 9th Division east of Algiers suffered from the inexperience of boat crews and troops alike. Men of one battalion were strewn along fifteen miles of coast. It was almost daylight before either of the two American forces could send a column toward Algiers, and even then the men had only light infantry weapons and no way to move except on foot.

The first indication anybody in Algiers had that an invasion might be under way developed close to 4 A.M. On a daring antiscuttling mission like that at Oran, two British destroyers, the *Broke* and the *Malcolm*, headed for the harbor to put 739 men, mostly Americans, ashore. The two vessels still were outside the harbor when the city's lights went out, searchlights swept the water, and coastal batteries opened fire. A hit set the *Malcolm*'s deck afire, forcing withdrawal.

Trying it alone, the *Broke* ran a gauntlet of fire, berthed, and discharged its troops, close to three hundred men, including the overall commander of the operation, Lieutenant Colonel Edwin T. Swenson. The men scattered quickly, seized an electric power station, and began to fan out along a street parallel to the shore. French rifle and machine-gun fire, fierce at first, gradually subsided. As dawn came, all was quiet except for a persistent ringing of church bells in the city.

Unfortunately for Swenson and his men and for the entire scheme to deliver Algiers, the heavy cannonade of the coastal batteries had awakened the city. Officials and soldiers began to report to their posts. The little groups of Frenchmen wearing white armbands knew that they could not long hold against this tide.

Even as General Juin's adjutant was commandeering a force of *gardes mobiles* to rescue Juin and Darlan at the Villa des Oliviers, General Mast's superior, General Koeltz, in custody in his own headquarters, threw a written message from a window calling on his soldiers to come to his aid. A few minutes later, freed, he relieved Mast of command of the Algiers Division and issued strict orders to fight.

At the harbor, soon after daylight, Colonel Swenson's little force became aware of hostile Senegalese troops taking up positions nearby. As coastal batteries suddenly renewed their fire against the destroyer *Broke*, the skipper signaled recall, but Swenson decided to stay, confident that he could hold out until other American troops arrived overland.

Swenson succeeded against the Senegalese; but about noon, faced with

French light tanks, he had to surrender. At roughly the same time the last of the little bands of conspirators, whose rifles, *circa* 1870, were no match for the weapons and numbers of the French regulars, also gave in.

Even as the conspiracy collapsed, American soldiers were at last approaching the western outskirts of Algiers, not far from the Villa des Oliviers; but they were too late. Barring some change in the stalemated negotiations with Darlan and Juin, the Allies faced a fight for Algiers.

In Morocco the Americans were to land, General Béthouart believed, at 2 A.M. The landings actually were scheduled to begin two hours later, and for one reason or another they were later than that.

As 5 A.M. approached, still with no news of landings, General Béthouart himself seriously doubted that the Americans were coming. Intermittent rain squalls outside the headquarters in Rabat, where Béthouart waited, added to his depression.

The telephone rang. It was the resident-general, Noguès.

"Where are they?" Noguès asked, "your Americans?"

General Béthouart had no way of knowing that the first wave of American landing craft was at last churning toward the Moroccan coast—at the little port of Safi, 140 miles southwest of Casablanca; at Fedala, 15 miles northeast of Casablanca; and at Port Lyautey, 70 miles farther up the coast. What he did know, for this Noguès told him, was that a force of French armored cavalry was on the way to Rabat to rescue Noguès and, unless Béthouart buckled, to quell Béthouart's infantry guard.

If he capitulated, Béthouart well knew, the Americans—assuming they arrived—probably would have to fight; and if the invasion failed, he himself would be shot. The alternative was internecine warfare among the French.

Béthouart gave himself up.

In the meantime, at Safi, the first shots had been fired.

Weighted with sixty-pound packs, plus weapons, the American troops were slow to descend the landing nets along the sides of the transports and to take their places in the landing craft. Although the sea was miraculously calm (four out of five days in November it would have been otherwise), heavy swells made the little boats pitch and roll against the sides of the mother ships. Delays in loading forced postponement of the start of the run from transports to beaches from 4 A.M. to 4:30.

Fifteen minutes later the landings began as two old destroyers, shorn of much of their superstructures to accommodate 450 men of the 9th Division, dashed for the mouth of the harbor. Nine French artillery pieces and two coastal guns opened fire, but the troops got ashore to make quick work of strategic points inside the town. Landing craft meanwhile brought other troops to nearby beaches, and the big guns of American battleships silenced the French pieces.

A French garrison of fewer than five hundred men continued to fight at isolated points in Safi through much of the day of November 8, but awed crowds of native Arabs posed the bigger problem. They milled among the troops, picking and poking at the wounded, disdainful of all fire. Heads turning in unison, they watched shooting exchanges between Americans and French as if they were spectators at a tennis match.

Early the second morning, while carrier-based planes patrolled against French reinforcement from the interior, a combat command of the 2d Armored Division would head north along the coast toward Casablanca, 140 miles away. The natives then might turn to a new *divertissement*—filching ammunition, fuel, and rations from stores brought ashore.

At Fedala, within range of the formidable guns of the French battleship *Jean Bart*, which had been under construction at the time of the armistice and was moored in the harbor at Casablanca, troops of the 3d Division had much the same difficulty getting into their landing craft as did those off Safi. They headed for shore only at 4:45.

As the landing craft neared the beaches, their motors drumming, lights ashore went out. Searchlights probed first the sky, then the sea, but machine guns on close-support craft quickly forced the French to turn those off. The landing craft touched down against the backdrop of nothing more noisy than the surf crashing against rock-strewn beaches, nothing more deplorable than infantrymen drowned because they were too heavily laden to swim for it when their boats capsized or to get up again when a wave knocked them down. Those men who made it pushed quickly into Fedala, there to take a company of Senegalese by surprise.

The fight started as dawn was breaking.

Coastal batteries opened fire, only to be silenced by bigger guns on the American battleships. Then at nearby Casablanca, French anti-aircraft batteries fired at naval observation planes, and four French submarines started a run for open water. That was all that watchful pilots of planes flying off escort carriers needed. They began to bomb and strafe the harbor, while American warships took on a powerful coastal battery on a promontory and the big guns of the *Jean Bart*.

As the bombardment turned the harbor into a shambles, a squadron of French destroyers aided by a cruiser emerged to attack the transports off Fedala and, if that failed, to lure American battleships into range of the guns of the *Jean Bart*. Unfortunately for the French, a freak hit by an American shell quickly put the *Jean Bart's* powerful battery out of commission. Deprived of that support, the destroyers were no match for the 6-inch guns of the *Brooklyn*, the 8-inch pieces of the *Augusta*, and droves of pesky naval aircraft. Through the morning the battle raged while wives and children of the French crews watched in horror from high buildings in Casablanca.

The battle ended with four French destroyers and the cruiser finished off. A hit by a coastal battery on the U.S. cruiser *Wichita* killed three men and wounded twenty-five—the only American losses. The French lost more than a thousand men.

At Port Lyautey the objective was an airfield several miles inland along the Sebou River, whence P-40 fighter-bombers flying in from Gibraltar might either assist the campaign to the south or fight back should the Germans or the Spanish bring the adjacent territory of Spanish Morocco into the fray. There were two serious problems: a marsh, canalizing advance of invading infantry and armor; and the Kasba, a many-gunned fortress commanding the mouth of the river.

From the first a garrison of more than thirty-five hundred Moroccans and Foreign Legionnaires fought back at Port Lyautey, coming close to pushing equal numbers of the 9th Division and the 2d Armored Division into the sea. A combination of tilings finally carried the day: tenacity on the part of the American soldiers, growing indecision on the part of the French, and sheer daring on the part of the crew of a destroyer, the *Dallas*, which negotiated the shallow, meandering Sebou River under the guns of the Kasba to land a task force almost atop the airfield.

The absurd battle between former allies who—save for false honor, multiple misunderstandings, and human frailty—might have been turning their combined resources against a real enemy, went on, not only in Morocco, but also at Oran and for a time at Algiers. Yet except at Oran, the issue would be decided, not by the continuing blasts of naval guns, rifles, machine guns, cannon, and aircraft, but by the arguments and interpretations of soldiers and sailors playing at the game of diplomacy. It would be decided in Algiers, Rabat, and Vichy, troubled capitals of defeat.

A decision came first at Algiers.

By mid-afternoon of the first embattled day in French North Africa, precious few American troops had penetrated Algiers. Bypassing resistance that held up the main body in a western suburb, a captain and twenty-five men had gained the vicinity of Fort l'Empereur, an old fortress serving as General Juin's headquarters; but without reinforcement they dared not attack. Since Colonel Swenson and his little band on the docks had surrendered, there was nothing they could do.

Yet to the French leaders it was apparent that, for all the lack of American troops in Algiers, the Allies were staging no Dieppe-like raid. Almost constant flights of aircraft overhead, heavy naval bombardment and air strikes against coastal batteries that still held out, and the awesome presence of the British fleet offshore were proof enough of that. Reports of heavy fighting in Morocco and at Oran further confirmed Robert Murphy's insistent claim that this was something big.

Even Admiral Darlan had reached that conclusion, though he was in no rush to do anything about it. He had received a message in secret code from Pétain in Vichy affirming the old marshal's trust. "You may act and inform me," the message said. "You know you have my full confidence." Thus reassured, Darlan was prepared to make full use of both sides. Whether the Allied landings succeeded or not, French resistance would afford Vichy an advantage in dealing with the Germans. As for the Americans, Darlan early in his deliberations with Murphy had decided that they would do almost anything for a ceasefire. The more Darlan could demonstrate that French resistance or acquiescence depended upon him, the stronger would be his hand with the invaders.

Later in the afternoon, after notifying Vichy that Algiers might be taken by nightfall, and after removing General Juin's authority over Morocco and Tunisia, Darlan telephoned Juin to stop the fight. Juin was to arrange a ceasefire for Algiers alone.

It was close to six o'clock when Juin's adjutant found the commander of the Eastern Task Force, General Ryder, alongside a hedge on the western fringe of the city. The sooner the fighting stopped, said Ryder, the more lenient would be the terms. Within minutes French buglers at various points around the city began to trumpet a ceasefire.

The shooting was over in Algiers, but a conference that night between Ryder and Darlan revealed that a political settlement and a ceasefire throughout French North Africa would be less easy to come by. About all Darlan would agree to immediately was that Allied ships might seek shelter in the harbor of Algiers against Axis submarines.

In political matters Darlan clearly intended to retain his and Vichy's power, and the devil take those Frenchmen who had connived to bring the Allies to North Africa.

The only other hope for an overall ceasefire, Henri Giraud, the man to whom the Allies had pinned their label, arrived by air the next afternoon, the ninth. Instead of a flower-bedecked motorcade from the airfield which he had expected, he got only a furtive ride in Murphy's car through back streets to headquarters of the conspirators.

With most of the young supporters of the insurrection already in prison, General Mast and the civilian members of the Five were understandably concerned about what would happen to them if Darlan remained in power. To Giraud they insisted that he had to act swiftly, to make up for lost time. Giraud shook his head. Darlan was his superior. As long as Darlan was in charge, he could do nothing without Darlan's approval. Close to desperation, the conspirators saw that their only hope was to dance with the devil himself. They themselves had in General Giraud the key to Allied cooperation, but only Darlan had the power and the authority to release senior army and navy officers from their oaths of allegiance to Marshal Pétain.

A wary telephone call to Juin's adjutant revealed that Juin, an old friend of Giraud's, had been thinking along the same lines. A meeting before daylight in the Villa des Oliviers completed the agreement. Junior to Giraud, Juin was willing to accept a subordinate command and let Giraud have his position as Commander-in-Chief of French forces in North Africa.

It remained only to persuade Darlan, but that proved to be about as easy as talking a top sergeant out of a fatigue detail.

Admiral Darlan was not about to give up one vestige of his power now that its severest test—a conference with the Allied deputy commander, General Clark—was only hours away. Clark had arrived by plane late on the ninth—the night of the first Axis air raid on Algiers—and had met Darlan briefly at the palm-shrouded Hotel St. George as the latter was conferring with Ryder. Since Clark wanted to talk first with Robert Murphy, he postponed a formal conference until 10 A.M. on the tenth.

Darlan prepared for the meeting by cabling Vichy a summary of mild armistice terms that General Ryder had said would be imposed if an armistice could be quickly arranged. Darlan also knew the details of harsher terms to be used in event of continued resistance, for Ryder had pretended to leave a copy of them inadvertently on the conference table, and Darlan had read them. By secret code Darlan told Vichy that he and his senior officers believed the cause lost and recommended quick acceptance of the more lenient terms.

Marshal Pétain, the reply came back, was "in intimate agreement with Darlan," but he cautioned delay. The Vichy Premier, Pierre Laval, was in Germany for a conference with Hitler on the North African situation, the message revealed, and Darlan should do nothing to compromise Laval's position.

When on the morning of the tenth the diplomatic niceties of the conference were over, Darlan stalled for time by studying the harsher armistice terms as if for the first time. Aware that fighting still went on at Oran, Casablanca, and Port Lyautey, and that German troops had begun to arrive by air in Tunisia without opposition from the French, Clark quickly became impatient.

At his urging, Murphy questioned Darlan bluntly: "Are you ready, Admiral, to have hostilities cease in North Africa?"

Darlan shifted his plump figure in his chair and wiped his bald head with a handkerchief. His own view, he explained, was that it was foolish to continue the fighting, but, he confided, Laval was on his way to Munich to see Hitler. He could do nothing that would—

Since that was the case, said Murphy, General Clark saw no reason to continue the conversation. He would deal instead with Giraud. Darlan would have to be taken—as the euphemism had it—into protective custody.

Distressed, General Juin placed on Clark's sleeve a right hand maimed in the fighting of 1940. In English he begged for five minutes to talk with Darlan. "Give me five minutes," he repeated.

Clark and his entourage retired. Five minutes later they came back. Pale, obviously torn by emotion, Darlan began to draft a directive ordering a ceasefire.

There were, Darlan said to Clark, certain officers with whom he could no longer associate—Mast, Béthouart, others. Intent at this point on no other objective than to obtain a valid ceasefire, Clark agreed that "so long as Admiral Darlan is Commander-in-Chief," these officers would hold no command. What went unsaid was Clark's determination that, if he had his way, Darlan's tenure as Commander-in-Chief would be short.

And Giraud, Darlan wanted to know—what of Giraud?

That, Clark said firmly, was a matter to be settled only after a ceasefire was in effect.

Word of Darlan's order went out to Tunisia, Oran, and Morocco. Nobody heeded it in Tunisia. It was no longer needed at Oran: the French commander there had already ordered a ceasefire during the morning of the tenth when an American armored column penetrated deep into the city. Whether it was needed or even heeded in Morocco was problematical. At Safi the Americans had imposed their will, and at Port Lyautey surrender negotiations already were under way.

As for Casablanca, Noguès, the resident-general, as early as November 9, second day of the invasion, had learned that members of the local German armistice commission deemed that the French had fought well and that their cause had become hopeless. Noguès thus had been free for some time to surrender.

Yet the fight had gone on.

The news of Darlan's ceasefire reached General Noguès in late afternoon on the tenth, but it was an hour before he could get details of the order to his naval opposite, Admiral Michelier. The admiral had in the meantime received a message from Vichy ordering him to continue to fight. There followed news that Darlan in Algiers had canceled his ceasefire order, that he had issued it in the first place only because he was a prisoner of the Americans.

By order of Marshal Pétain, the message continued, General Noguès, not Darlan, was the top man in French North Africa.

The news was basically correct. Hardly had Marshal Pétain learned of

Darlan's ceasefire than the Germans, too, learned of it and confronted Pierre Laval with the news moments before the Vichy Premier was to step before the German *Fuehrer*. Laval was furious. So violent were his protestations to Pétain, so dire his predictions of what the Germans would do to the French, that Pétain had disavowed Darlan to appoint Noguès.

Darlan protested to General Clark that he would have to annul the ceasefire.

"Damned if you do!" said Clark.

The alternative, said Darlan, was to make him a prisoner.

Agreed, said Clark, and put him under house arrest.

General Noguès, who was preparing to go to Algiers on November 12 to take over Darlan's position, raised no question about the Vichy order, yet he continued with plans for an armistice at Casablanca. Admiral Michelier also agreed to an armistice, since another message from Vichy provided him an out by ordering resistance "as long as it is possible." Without a ship left (even the *Jean Bart* had by this time been sunk at her moorings), a ceasefire was hardly difficult to justify.

Getting the word to the Americans was nevertheless a slow process. General Patton's ground forces were arrayed against the eastern fringe of Casablanca—field artillerymen were set to pull their lanyards, planes and the battleship *New York* in position to blast the city into submission—when, shortly after dawn on November 11, word at last got through.

That afternoon Patton, Hewitt, Noguès, Michelier, and several subordinate commanders sat down together to lunch at the Hotel Miramar in Fedala, while Emile Béthouart languished in a prison under likely sentence of death by firing squad.

The fighting in Algeria and Morocco had cost the Allies 1,181 men killed and missing, of which 584 were United States losses. Another 891 American soldiers, sailors, and airmen were wounded; 178 British were wounded. The French lost over 1,600 men (two-thirds of them naval casualties at Casablanca), and another 1,000 were wounded.

It took almost three more days of maneuvering and countermaneuvering, of shift and countershift, of intrigue and counterintrigue to hammer out a workable agreement in Algiers for the North African protectorates. Clark and Murphy first tried to enlist General Giraud in a scheme to double-cross Darlan by installing Giraud in his stead, but the latter showed that

97

he had no penchant for politics, that he wanted only to get on with the fight against the Germans. Next, by secret code, another message arrived from Vichy, this time disavowing Darlan's relief: it had been done under duress. Yet if Noguès insisted on taking over, who would believe Vichy's latest message? Even if Noguès cooperated, French leaders in Tunisia still were operating under Vichy's disavowal of Darlan.

Once news arrived that the Germans and Italians had moved swiftly to occupy Vichy France before daylight of the eleventh, General Juin dusted off a regulation dating from the Franco-Prussian War whereby no French soldier was obligated to take orders from a chief who had fallen into enemy hands—in this case, Pétain. By telephone he ordered the French army commander in Tunisia to resist the Germans, and told General Koeltz to begin moving the Algiers Division to Tunisia.

Koeltz balked. Neither Juin nor Darlan was in charge, he pointed out, but instead Noguès, who had received his orders before the Germans occupied Vichy. Juin backed down and annulled his orders.

When a dapper little General Noguès arrived from Morocco on November 12, he readily agreed that Darlan might remain as political head, but he himself would assume military command and would have nothing to do with Giraud, whom he considered a traitor in the same company as Mast and Béthouart. Only an ultimatum from Clark issued in the name of General Eisenhower—reach agreement quickly or he would either put Giraud in charge or rule himself—brought Noguès around. Even then Noguès would agree to Giraud's assuming no higher command than a corps of volunteers in Tunisia.

With Giraud in a weak position, General Mast and the Five were again in trouble. When they protested to Clark that the prelanding agreement to make Giraud Commander-in-Chief should be honored, Clark replied that it was a matter for the French to work out among themselves.

Juin, the peacemaker, stepped into the breach. At his insistence Noguès at last consented to Giraud's assuming command if he operated under Darlan in the name of Pétain, and if Charles de Gaulle were prevented from setting foot in North Africa.

That afternoon, the thirteenth, General Eisenhower met Darlan, Giraud, Noguès, and Juin at the Hotel St. George to give his blessing to the arrangement. Later, to cement the position with the Americans, Darlan would bring some of General Mast's civilian associates into his cabinet, but by the afternoon of the thirteenth the basic arrangement that the world came to know as the "Darlan Deal" had been made.

The "Darlan Deal" assured stability of a sort for what soon would become Allied rear lines of communication; but it assured precious little else. No promise of resistance to the Germans by French leaders in Tunisia; no French fleet—on November 27, seventy-three ships of the fleet, the world's fourth largest, would be scuttled in the harbor at Toulon. Yet on the other side there was assurance that Vichy's neofascism with its press censorship, subjugation of dissent, and anti-Semitic laws would be perpetuated in North Africa. The situation was particularly disturbing in Morocco, where not until November 17 were General Béthouart and his pro-Allied associates released from prison after having narrowly escaped execution for treason, and where pro-Axis propaganda and sentiment openly flourished. Only relief of General Noguès would have squelched it, and in exchange for Noguès' keeping the natives and the various dissident French elements in hand, George Patton was not about to disavow him.

Like his military leaders, President Roosevelt happily embraced the "Darlan Deal," but four days later, under mounting criticism at home and from Britain, he labeled it a "temporary expedient."[47] Churchill and his Foreign Office detested it from the first but went along, despite sharp criticism from Parliament.

All the while General Eisenhower insisted that he had had no choice. Darlan, he said, was "the source of every bit of practical help we have received."[48] Yet Darlan actually had contributed little. He had sanctioned a ceasefire in Algiers only when military defeat was inevitable, and he had delayed the overall ceasefire until it was no longer needed at Oran; it probably had little to do with an armistice in Morocco; and it accomplished almost nothing in Tunisia. And Darlan did not deliver the French fleet, and on no point had he given in until threatened by prison or another ultimatum or until the military situation reached a point where he had no alternative.

The better rationale for Eisenhower's—and Murphy's—embracing Darlan was the time factor. They courted Darlan when Giraud had failed them, when they were unsure that a 110,000-man invasion force could

---

[47] Churchill, *The Hinge of Fate*, p. 633, quoting a public announcement by Roosevelt.

[48] Churchill, *The Hinge of Fate*, p. 636.

do the job, and when they were trying desperately to beat the Germans and Italians to Tunisia.

Criticism would persist nevertheless. Much of it was legitimate, for as Charles de Gaulle put it to Churchill: "It is a strategic error to place oneself in a situation contradictory to the moral character of this war."[49] Yet what if Murphy and Eisenhower had refused to deal with Darlan, and the French, as a result, had prolonged the conflict long enough to enable Germans, Italians, and perhaps Spaniards to enter Algeria and Morocco?

The cruel realities of war sometimes require compromise.

---

[49] Davis, *The Experience of War*, p. 343, quoting Charles de Gaulle, *War Memoirs: Unity, 1942-44*, pp. 56-57.

Chapter Eight – The Campaign in Tunisia

To French leaders in Tunisia, as to those in Algeria and Morocco, the Allied landings had brought trepidation and moral anguish, made all the more disturbing by the proximity of Axis aircraft and warships in Sicily. Almost five days of indecision, vacillation, and quandary followed.[50]

On word from Vichy, on November 9 the French let more than 100 German planes land at an airfield near Tunis. French troops, their hostility apparent, ringed the airfield. The next day brought Italian fighters and 150 German troop-carrier aircraft. On November 12 both Germans and Italians came ashore on the docks at Bizerte with heavy equipment, including tanks.

When firm orders to fight finally arrived that night, it was too late for the French navy in Tunisia. The Axis strength in Bizerte and Tunis was too great to challenge.

The French army was in much better position because the commander, Général d'Armée Georges Barré, had made up his mind early that out of all the indecision and confusion eventually would emerge an order to fight the Axis. Even before receiving that order, he had begun to deploy his troops in the mountains forty-five miles west of Tunis astride highways leading into Algeria. The men faced east, whence would come the Germans.

Refusing even to confer with a German emissary sent to enlist his cooperation, Barré as much as invited attack. Within a few hours German

---

[50] Among those sources cited for **Chapter Six**, I have made particular use in this chapter of Howe, *Northwest Africa*, and Blumenson, *Kasserine Pass*. Howe provides an especially comprehensive account of the German side, derived primarily from captured German records. See also B. H. Liddell-Hart, ed., *The Rommel Papers* (London, 1953), and H. A. Jacobsen and J. Roliwer, eds., *The Decisive Battles of World War II: The German Side* (New York, 1965).

planes bombed his position, German artillery opened fire, and infantry attacked. Although Barré's troops eventually fell back to secondary positions, what mattered most was that they had taken the crucial step of actually fighting. Theirs was the first active commitment of the French army in North Africa on the side of the Allies.

Adolf Hitler was traveling in his special train on the way to Munich when news came of Allied landings in North Africa. He reacted almost instinctively. First, calm the Italians. Second, move troops to Tunisia. When his *Luftwaffe* commander in Italy, Field Marshal Albert Kesselring, asked authority to intervene, Hitler promptly approved.

Kesselring's plan was simply to pour Germans and Italians into Tunisia quickly and array them as far to the west as possible in order to check the anticipated Allied drive from Algeria and to provide depth and maneuver room for a German beachhead. That would protect the rear of Field Marshal Rommel's army in Libya and gain the Tunisian ports for supplying Rommel.

Rommel, who was falling back after the crushing defeat by Montgomery's Eighth Army at El Alamein, considered it absurd, in view of the limited Axis resources and a deep commitment in Russia, to try to hold in North Africa at all. A handsome, talented soldier who early had played the Nazi game but then quit it and who by his deft military maneuvers had earned the nickname "Desert Fox," Rommel could view German involvement in North Africa with professional detachment. At the same time he recognized that for reasons of prestige Hitler and Mussolini would never agree to give up North Africa altogether. Since they had insufficient resources to hold both Libya and Tunisia, Rommel thought it best to abandon Libya and concentrate in Tunisia for an attack westward against the Allies.

Rommel sent an aide to present that view to Hitler but got a slap on the wrist for his trouble: an admonition to hold Libya and leave the security of his rear in Tunisia to steadier and wiser heads. Yet the incident did prompt Hitler and Mussolini to formulate a strategy for North Africa more positive than that inherent in Kesselring's defensive deployment. While Rommel erected a new defense in Libya, other Axis forces were to drive westward to seize Algeria and lure Spain into the war on the Axis side.

Although Rommel welcomed the positive aspects of this decision, he was convinced that his seventy thousand men in Libya could hold nowhere short of Gabès at the waist of Tunisia, where a chain of lakes and salt marshes stretching westward almost to the impenetrable desert restricts passage to a narrow twelve-mile coastal corridor. Holding the corridor with minimum strength, he would be able to reinforce the offensive against Algeria. Victory achieved in Algeria, the entire Axis force might turn against Montgomery to drive him back across Libya to Egypt.

Sending first another aide with this proposal, then going himself to see Hitler, Rommel achieved nothing. Hitler apparently believed that El Alamein had left Rommel nervous and defeatist in his thinking. Rommel headed back to Libya, wary lest the Allies seize the Gabès bottleneck themselves and cut him off from the Tunisian beachhead.

Like the Axis, the Allies had begun the race for Tunisia even as the French were still struggling with their consciences. Before daylight on November 11, British troops of the Eastern Task Force under General Anderson went ashore near Bougie and with French connivance quickly took over the port. The next day two British destroyers slipped into the harbor at Bône in early morning darkness to put ashore British commandos.

Some of the British troops moved overland to establish a block on the coastal road just inside the Tunisian frontier, while on the sixteenth a contingent of British paratroopers dropped inside the frontier astride an inland highway and railroad leading through the mountains to Tunis. There they established contact with General Barré's French troops. In the meantime a battalion of American paratroopers landed near the border one hundred miles inland to anchor the Allied southern flank along the edge of an expanse of trackless mountain wasteland stretching away to the south.

The object of these early moves was to capture ports, highways, and the railroad, but especially airfields. The critical nature of airfields was pointed up the afternoon of the eleventh and all day on the twelfth as flight after flight of German fighter-bombers attacked British ships at Bougie. The Germans sank four ships, including three transports. Since the closest Allied airfield was nearly two hundred miles away, Allied planes could provide scant protection.

Almost from the first the race for Tunisia became a contest as much for the air as for the ground, for without close air cover to fend off the enemy's planes foot troops would be hard pressed to hold ground even when they arrived first. In this confrontation the Axis held all the advantages. From established air bases in Sicily, Sardinia, and Italy, they were able to shift planes and maintenance facilities quickly to former French fields at Bizerte and Tunis, scant minutes from the ground fighting that developed. The closest fields the Allies might use were one hundred miles away; and to build up planes, gasoline, and maintenance facilities at those fields, the Allies had to transport everything from Algiers, three hundred miles to the west.

As a British division supported by an American tank battalion began a drive on November 25 to seize Bizerte and Tunis, German planes quickly and forcefully demonstrated their local superiority. Although a contingent of American tanks got as far as an airfield within fifteen miles of Tunis, there to shoot up parked planes before retiring, German aircraft the next day opened a relentless attack on anything Allied that moved. Almost treeless countryside provided little cover or concealment for Allied tanks, trucks, and infantrymen alike.

Although Allied medium and heavy bombers struck at Axis airfields, the blows could not keep the enemy's fighters out of the air. Only Allied fighters based close enough to be able to hover long over the scene of battle could do the job required.

General Anderson on November 29 called off the attack. Although reinforcements were on the way—a British armored brigade and a combat command of the 1st U.S. Armored Division—even those could not alter the situation unless something could be done to balance the equation in the air. The only hope of that was to repair a damaged French airfield at Medjez el Bab, only thirty miles from Tunis.

That the Axis forces would afford Anderson no time to accomplish. Employing portions of a newly arrived panzer division, the Germans counterattacked early on the first day of December. When the fighting subsided three days later, they had taken little ground, but they had inflicted such losses on already thin Allied ranks that all hope of renewing the drive on Bizerte and Tunis immediately had passed.

"We have gone beyond the sustainable limit of air capabilities in supporting ground forces in a pell-mell race for Tunisia," General Eisenhower reported to the Combined Chiefs of Staff on the third.[51] He saw no alternative but to pause, replenish the fighter squadrons, improve

---

[51] Howe, *Northwest Africa*, p. 320, quoting an Eisenhower message to the Combined Chiefs of Staff.

runways and other facilities at the airfields, speed equipment and supplies over the long line of communications from Algiers, and regroup the ground units to forestall a German strike into the rear of the troops facing Tunis by way of mountain passes to the south.

Weather permitting, Eisenhower hoped to renew the attack within about ten days, but the weather, he soon discovered, would work against him for a long time to come. The rains came, and with the rains, mud of an incredibly gooey consistency. Rain and more rain. Mud and more mud.

On Christmas Eve, Eisenhower admitted the inevitable. Not until the end of the rainy season, more than two months away, would he be able to make a major attack.

The Allies had lost the race for Tunisia.

In Algiers, in the meantime, the stability that the Darlan Deal presumably had achieved among the French had begun to erode. To the civilians among the Five who had conspired to bring the Allies to North Africa, the presumably temporary expedient of Darlan looked more and more as if it might become permanent. What point in driving German fascism from France if it was to be replaced by a Darlan version of the same evil?

The civilian leaders agreed that Darlan had to go, but who would succeed him? Giraud wanted to be no more than military chief; Noguès would represent little change from Darlan; and hardly anyone else could command a following.

The antipathy of Darlan and the other French in North Africa to General de Gaulle and his Fighting French in London complicated the problem. The Allies found themselves in the ambiguous position of supporting two French leaders, each of whom apparently would delight in cutting the other's throat, and each of whom had his own French fighting force dependent in large measure on Allied arms and equipment.

The matter stood unresolved until the afternoon of December 24— Christmas Eve—when Admiral Darlan returned to his office from a luncheon where he had discussed, among other matters, the possibility of retiring from office. There was a shot. Then a second. Darlan fell to the floor in the doorway, bleeding from the mouth. A short while later he was dead.

The assassin was a youth of twenty, Fernand Eugene Bonnier de la Chapelle, who had been active in the prelandings resistance movement and on the night of the landings had been among those who surrounded the Villa des Oliviers. He was caught by a guard before he could leave the scene of the murder, tried by a hastily convened court-martial, and executed early on the twenty-sixth by a firing squad.

As for Darlan's successor, the Allied command and the Five could breathe easier when Noguès revealed that he had no desire for the job. The Five wanted the Count of Paris, pretender to the French throne. The Allied command wanted Giraud. The latter was summoned to the Hotel St. George and, for all his dislike of politics, agreed to serve.

Meanwhile, many people recognized that Bonnier de la Chapelle had not acted alone, but such was the turbulence of the political scene in Algiers that he alone paid for the crime.

Faced with a protracted struggle—a "logistical marathon," General Eisenhower called it—the Allies had to adjust to the changed complexion of the campaign. The original plan of smashing Rommel's army in Libya between Montgomery's Eighth Army pushing west from Egypt and an Allied force driving east from Tunisia, had to be jettisoned. Instead, General Montgomery would have to continue fighting Rommel alone until Eisenhower could build up enough strength to challenge the Axis forces in Tunisia. Since Montgomery hoped to push Rommel back into Tunisia by late January of 1943, and Eisenhower might be unable to attack until March, the final campaign would be fought not against Rommel alone but against a united Axis force in the Tunisian beachhead.

Reorganizing his troops, General Eisenhower tried to keep units of one nationality together. General Anderson's British, which constituted no more than a corps with the equivalent of three divisions but was redesignated the First British Army, continued to hold in the north and still posed a threat to Bizerte and Tunis. The French, under the overall command of General Juin but with General Koeltz as corps commander, held the center with three weak divisions, still lightly gunned and ill equipped. Commanding headquarters of the II Corps, General Fredendall assumed responsibility for American forces in the south. Only one United States division was as yet present—the 1st Armored. A buildup would take time, and General Eisenhower felt impelled to hold divisions in Morocco and at Oran to guard lines of communications and to counter any possible Axis move from Spanish Morocco. Farther south, in the almost trackless desert, an occasional patrol of the French Camel Corps kept watch.

Despite Eisenhower's aim, considerable intermingling of troops of different nationalities would continue until additional British and American strength could be accumulated, and until the French could be provided enough modern arms and equipment to enable them to stand alone. Problems of command would continue as well. The French refused to serve under a British commander; French strength hardly justified giving a Frenchman overall command; and United States officers were far too junior to the Britisher, General Anderson. Although much of Eisenhower's time was pre-empted by duties far from the front in Algiers, he had to exercise direct command over the Tunisian front at the same time. Eisenhower set up a forward headquarters where Major General Lucian K. Truscott, Jr., served as his deputy to coordinate the three Allied commands in Tunisia—but coordination is not the same as command.

In the brown land of central Tunisia, mountains that in the north are one solid mass divide into two chains, like an inverted "Y." Along the eastern chain, known as the Eastern Dorsal, French and American troops established their defensive line overlooking a fertile coastal plain. Rising abruptly from the plain to craggy, eroded heights reaching 4,500 feet and called "djebels," the Eastern Dorsal can be crossed at only five gaps and passes or around the southern end along a road leading northwest from Gabès. French troops held all the passes, while American troops began to concentrate behind those in the center and south to back them up.

A semi-arid plateau some thirty-five miles wide—the plain of Sbeitla—separates Eastern and Western dorsals. Sharply eroded, the plain supports little growth other than patches of bunch grass, some scrub trees along seasonal streams, occasional cactus patches, and here and there a palm-fringed oasis, usually the site of a town or a village. Rain falls only in the winter months; at other times the stream beds, called "wadis," are dry, giving an air of incongruity to the bridges spanning them. In all the towns stand ruins of earlier civilizations—Christian catacombs, Roman arches and baths, fortifications of the Byzantine era. Tarmac roads run generally straight as a ruler from one town to the next.

Through the Western Dorsal pass five main roads, all leading northwest into Algeria toward the coast around Bône or to Constantine, some fifty miles inland. Those in the south near the towns of Fériana and Kasserine lead first to the Algerian town of Tébessa, headquarters site for Fredendall's II Corps. Near Fériana and Tébessa the Americans took over French airfields as bases for fighter planes of the XII Air Support Command and started building new ones.

Into the Axis beachhead the Germans moved a senior commander from the Russian front, Generaloberst Juergen von Arnim, a sullen, ambitious officer who had a reputation for getting things done, ruthlessly if need be. With hooked nose and Hitler-like mustache, Arnim was perfectly cast to play the heavy opposite Rommel's hero. Although the Italian *Comando Supremo* ostensibly exercised supreme command over Arnim as over Rommel, the Germans looked for direction more to their own commander, Field Marshal Kesselring, whose headquarters was in Italy.

With Rommel still retreating in Libya, General von Arnim became the new court favorite. Reinforcements went not to Rommel's 70,000-man *Italian-German Panzer Army* but Arnim's *Fifth Panzer Army*, so that by the end of January, Arnim would have more than 100,000 men, three-fourths of them first-rate German troops.

Since the Russian front—the battle of Stalingrad in particular—made unstinting demands on German resources, Hitler recognized at last that Rommel had been right. The only hope of gaining sufficient superiority for decision in North Africa lay in joining Rommel's and Arnim's troops in Tunisia, then striking before the British Eighth Army could follow Rommel in strength. At the end of December he authorized Rommel to fall back within the southern border of Tunisia to a series of old French fortifications known as the "Mareth Line," but Rommel was to take two months to do it, in order to allow Arnim time to build up in Tunisia.

Beginning on Christmas Day, Arnim moved against the Allied positions on the barren djebels of the Eastern Dorsal that overlooked his troops on the coastal plain. Against French troops, armed in most cases with weapons left over from World War I, the Germans quickly gobbled up two of the five passes, struck two weeks later at the seam between British and French, and finally took a third opening through the Eastern Dorsal far to the south, the Faid Pass. Only swift intervention by contingents of American and British armor prevented Arnim from cutting off all French troops in the Eastern Dorsal.

Arnim's successes had a salutary effect on the Allied command. So weak were the French that the British to the north, the Americans to the south, would have to be prepared at all times to go to their rescue. That situation prevailed until Eisenhower could afford to pull French units from the line to refit them with modern gear. General Juin had to swallow his pride to admit that under the circumstances one commander for the three national forces was essential. Eisenhower ordered General Anderson to take over, and Juin acquiesced.

As newly arrived contingents of the U.S. 1st and 34th Infantry Divisions provided new strength, the new command arrangement was bound to improve the Allied position. Unfortunately, the personality traits of some of the commanders was to rob the arrangement of much of its potential.

The problem began with Anderson himself. Although personally bold and fearless, he was dour and reserved and appeared to American officers unduly pessimistic. He disagreed with Eisenhower's decision to concentrate American units in central Tunisia. That detracted, Anderson believed, from the more important task of reinforcing the British First Army for the offensive that really mattered, the drive on Tunis.

General Fredendall of the U.S. II Corps aggravated the situation. A man of bombast and bravado in speech and manner, Fredendall failed to live up to the image he tried to create. He had come off his command ship at Oran only after the city was ready for an armistice. He had set up his headquarters near Tébessa, over seventy miles behind the front, in an almost inaccessible gulch adequately screened by trees, then had insisted on underground quarters for himself and his Staff. He turned out to be Anglophobe in general, anti-Anderson in particular, and he had little patience for the French and their pathetic mule-drawn carts, charcoal-burning trucks, obsolete guns, and pitifully inadequate light tanks.

Between Fredendall and the commander of the 1st Armored Division, Major General Orlando Ward, whose red-tinged hair prompted the nickname "Pinky," existed what one associate called a "most unusual" antipathy. Fredendall openly detested Ward, as he demonstrated by his practice of bypassing the division commander to issue orders direct to his combat commands. A competent commander, methodical, thorough, Ward for his part had no use in his quiet, calm way for Fredendall.

February 1943 ushered in a period that Allied commanders had been dreading, and that Axis commanders had been anticipating with some relish.

Having succeeded in delaying the British Eighth Army for only one month rather than for the two Hitler had specified, Rommel and his *Italian-German Panzer Army* crossed the border into southern Tunisia and moved into the Mareth Line. Over 1,400 miles from bases in Egypt, the pursuing British were temporarily spent, unable to pressure Rommel until the demolished Libyan port of Tripoli could be refurbished. The combined Axis forces, numbering more than 150,000 men, might turn with impunity against the weaker Allied troops in central and northern Tunisia.

General Anderson's intelligence Staff diagnosed that the Axis would strike in the north to try to cut off the British First Army. To help counter the threat, Anderson attached the 1st Armored Division's Combat Command B (CCB) to the British.

If the Axis should launch a subsidiary drive' farther south, Anderson ordered, both the French and Fredendall's II Corps were to fall back to the Western Dorsal. Although that meant that the II Corps then would have to stand at Fériana and Kasserine, disturbingly close to the airfields and supply complex at Tébessa, no other choice appeared open with the limited means available. The last of the 1st and 34th Infantry Divisions had arrived by this time, but only a regiment of each was available; the rest were in the line farther north with French and British. With CCB of the 1st Armored Division also detached, Fredendall had only the rest of the armored division, a regiment each of the two infantry divisions, some additional artillery, tank destroyers, and a Ranger battalion, dangerously few troops for holding more than a hundred miles of front.

There was no hope of further reinforcement. Although Spain's failure to act had convinced General Eisenhower that he might release the divisions held in Morocco, the long supply line from Algiers would support no greater strength in Tunisia until trucks and vital spare parts arrived from the United States.

General Fredendall, for his part, doubted Anderson's diagnosis of Axis plans. His own intelligence Staff had been amassing evidence pointing to an enemy buildup in the south rather than the north. Arab laborers had suddenly vanished. Reconnaissance patrols met stiffened opposition. Outposts reported increasing noise of vehicular traffic. Pilots noted large troop concentrations.

Convinced the strike would come in the south, Fredendall was just as sure that he could hold along the Eastern Dorsal. Determined to stand despite Anderson's order to fall back if attacked, he drew a detailed plan of defense for the 1st Armored Division's Combat Command A behind the Faid Pass. General Ward, Fredendall directed, was to base his defense on two isolated djebels flanking the highway, these to be held by attached troops of the 34th Division's 168th Infantry. A mobile reserve of CCA was to be at hand in the nearby village of Sidi Bou Zid.

These djebels, "Pinky" Ward noted, looked better on a map in Fredendall's underground headquarters than they did on the ground. An aggressive enemy might readily encircle them, then reduce them one at a time, since they were too far apart for mutual support, and the mobile reserve in Sidi Bou Zid was too small to be decisive. Because CCB was attached to the British and another part of the 1st Armored Division was backing up the French, Ward had at his disposal, once Fredendall directed the dispositions on the djebcls and at Sidi Bou Zid, only a battalion each of tanks and infantry and a few self-propelled but thin-skinned tank destroyers mounting 75 mm. guns.

Yet Fredendall would listen to none of Ward's objections; and even General Eisenhower, after touring the front on February 13 and going as far forward as Sidi Bou Zid, ordered no change in the defense. By failing to direct otherwise, he also tacitly accepted Fredendall's defiance of Anderson's order to retire to the Western Dorsal.

It had long been Erwin Rommel's idea to unite with Axis troops in the Tunisian beachhead and strike to the northwest to reach the coast near Bône and trap all Allied troops in Tunisia. In early February, as he pulled into the Mareth Line, he posed the plan to General von Arnim and Field Marshal Kesselring. It had to be done, said Rommel, else American troops might hit the rear of the Mareth Line.

Arnim objected. Since Rommel had come back to Tunisia a month ahead of schedule, the Axis buildup had yet to progress far enough to support so ambitious an operation. He proposed instead a limited strike from two of the passes in the northern end of the Eastern Dorsal to break onto the plain of Sbeitla and force French and Americans to withdraw to the Western Dorsal.

Although Kesselring regretfully admitted that Arnim was right about resources, he still looked wistfully on the larger opportunity. He settled on a third scheme: two thrusts with limited objectives which would put the Axis in excellent position—Rommel and Kesselring both noted with sly satisfaction—for mounting later the drive to the coast. Arnim was to attack with two German panzer divisions in a two-pronged thrust on Sidi Bou Zid by way of the Faid Pass and the Maizila Pass farther south. Using a mixed Italian-German force, Rommel was to drive up the road from Gabès to take the town of Gafsa, southern gateway to the plain of Sbeitla.

Kesselring wanted to put Rommel in overall command of the two strikes—as a field marshal, he was senior to Arnim—but the Italians disagreed. Disenchanted with Rommel's conduct of the retreat through Libya, Mussolini wanted to replace Rommel with an Italian general. The Italians would sanction no arrangement whereby Rommel might become established as Arnim's superior.

Accepting that the two operations would have to be launched independently, Kesselring nevertheless confided to Rommel that if they attained sufficient success to justify going further, he would see to it that Rommel got the command. That was all Rommel needed. He was determined to wring every advantage from the attacks.

Arnim, on the contrary, saw only limited ambition in the two drives. To him they were basically defensive, designed to spare Rommel a threat against the narrow neck at Gabès and the rear of the Mareth Line. Once the threat was out of the way, he might then get on with the real offensive he planned against the British in the north.

The American soldiers on the two craggy, eroded hill masses behind the Faid Pass and at Sidi Bou Zid had scarcely a chance. Aside from inexperience and limited numbers, the men lacked the resources of their foe. To counter the enemy's powerful tanks, the infantrymen had a towed 37-mm. anti-tank gun, little better against the German armor of the period than a peashooter and in sharp contrast to the German 88-mm. high-velocity piece, which deserved to be called the French 75 of World War II. Although the tank destroyer—"TD," the men called it—that backed up the American infantryman had an advantage in being self-propelled, even its 75-mm. gun was inferior to the 88.

The infantryman had also the 2.36-inch bazooka—named for the rustic musical instrument of a hillbilly radio comedian, Bob Burns. This the Germans lacked and later copied, but the bazooka was effective only at such short ranges that the infantryman had difficulty getting close enough to a tank for a telling shot, particularly in open country like Tunisia. Not a single verified instance of a tank knocked out by a bazooka was to emerge from the Tunisian campaign.

The American light tank, the Stuart, was so lightly armored and its 37-mm. piece so lacked armor-piercing qualities that it had no place on a battlefield where mediums might be employed. Even the German light tank, the Mark III, with heavier armor and a 50-mm. gun, was superior. The American medium, the Grant, could stand up to the German medium, the Mark IV, in armor and firepower, but in design the Grant was an aberration. Its 75-mm. gun was sponson-mounted—off to one side of the turret—and had such limited traverse that, in effect, the crew had to aim the tank rather than the gun.

Like the Americans, the Germans had seen the tank at first only as an offensive weapon, not in an anti-tank role. Thus they had yet to put their powerful 88-mm. gun on the battlefield on a mobile armored platform, but the day was coming: General von Arnim had received for battle-testing nineteen experimental Mark VI tanks, the Tiger, a behemoth mounting the 88. Even the American Sherman, soon to replace the Grant and destined to become the Allied mainstay for the rest of the war, would be no match for the Tiger.

Only in artillery had American troops no need for concern. American 105-mm. and 155-mm. howitzers played a subordinate role to none; and American fire direction procedures were excellent, even as early as the Tunisian fighting. Yet in the early fighting they did lack numbers—only divisional artillery, and none of the guns that operated normally under corps control, had yet made the long trek from Algiers.

In biting cold made more bitter by a relentless wind that whipped sand about with stinging force, German tanks and infantry came out of the dawn on Valentine's Day—February 14—to sweep swiftly around the two djebels behind the Faid Pass. The commander on the northern djebel, Lieutenant Colonel John K. Waters, sent a company of supporting tanks to counterattack, but with no success. Spared from direct attack by the German armor because of the rugged nature of the high ground, the American troops could but try to hide from the dive bombers and wait for the German infantry, led by Arab guides, to move against them.

Only once during the day did American fighter planes appear, and they retreated quickly. It was an all too common example of a lack of coordination between forces that fought on the ground and those that fought in the air. American airmen at this stage in the war saw their role in only one dimension: they had a calling to defeat the enemy's air forces, a strategic assignment; the tactical mission of supporting their own troops on the ground inspired little consideration.

Composed basically of just over fifty Grant tanks and a few tank destroyers, the mobile reserve in Sidi Bou Zid rushed toward the djebels to help, but the tanks had yet to give battle when the enormity of the task facing them became apparent. On the flat, treeless plain the crewmen could count more than eighty German tanks, and word came that another large armored force was approaching Sidi Bou Zid from the southeast, the direction of the Maizila Pass. They would discern eventually that a panzer division was debouching from each of the passes with well over two hundred tanks, including twelve of the new breed of 63-ton Mark VI Tigers.

Word went back early by radio and telephone of how mammoth was the German assault, but it was almost noon before General Ward in Sbeitla began to realize the true scope. More than half the tanks from the mobile reseive, he learned, already had been knocked out. Still unconvinced of the German power, the II Corps commander, General Fredendall, refused a request by the infantry commanders on the two djebels for permission to withdraw.

While the infantrymen stayed, the other troops with or without orders fell back—a feeble seven tanks that had escaped destruction, artillerymen, command post clerks, infantry stragglers, engineers. Harassed by German planes, chased by long-range fire from tanks and artillery, they poured across the sandy plain, up and over the folds, down and across the wadis, back toward Sbeitla, twenty miles to the rear.

Convinced at last that matters were serious. Fredendall prevailed upon the Britisher, General Anderson, to release a tank battalion from the 1st Armored's CCB, but Anderson refused to send the full combat command. The fight at Sidi Bou Zid, he said, was no more than a diversion for the bigger attack still to come in the north.

In view of reports that other Axis troops were massing against Gafsa, Anderson did agree to abandon that town on the Allied south flank and to fall back on the Western Dorsal behind Fériana. As French and American troops pulled out that night in a rainstorm, hordes of natives joined them, herding goats, jackasses, sheep, camels, crying children. At the airfields near Fériana, airmen hurriedly flew out serviceable planes, destroyed others, set gasoline afire, tried to blow up those other supplies they were unable to carry away.

At Sbeitla, Ward mustered a task force composed of a battalion of infantry, a battalion of self-propelled artillery, and the tank battalion of CCB. Soon after midday on February 15 the task force headed toward Sidi Bou Zid. Tormented by dive bombers, taken in flank by enemy guns, the task force marched to its destruction. Only four of the tank battalion's Grants survived.

That ended any chance of rescuing the infantry on the djebels. Before dusk on the fifteenth a plane managed to drop a message to those on the northern djebel telling them to withdraw, and a radio operator finally got through to those on the other. Only some three hundred men succeeded in working past the Germans in the darkness and back over the long miles to Sbeitla. Some were still trudging across the open plain when daylight exposed them and a motorized German force machine-gunned them down. Arabs stripped dead and wounded alike of clothing and weapons.

Over 2,000 officers and men were lost on the two hills, 1,400 of them captured. Among the prisoners was Colonel Waters, who was General Patton's son-in-law. John Waters, POW, was for a long two years to drop out of sight in the kaleidoscope of the war, only to reappear in the spring of 1945 at a place in Germany called Hammelburg.

In Sbeitla that second night General Ward rallied everybody he could find while an infantry battalion screened to the east. In equipment alone, Ward learned, he had lost some sixty halftracks, twenty-six self-propelled artillery pieces, and—most critical of all—ninety-four tanks.

At higher levels of command, recognition came at last that this was in reality the major Axis blow. With Eisenhower's approval, General Anderson insisted on early withdrawal of all Allied troops from the Eastern to the Western Dorsal. Given a presumably critical Axis supply situation and the possibility of an early attack by Montgomery against the Mareth Line, Anderson deduced that the Germans had to succeed quickly or not at all. By giving ground slowly while preparing the passes of the Western Dorsal for defense, the Allies might wear the enemy down in a matter of days.

General Ward was to continue to hold Sbeitla to allow time for shifting troops to other critical points, for Sbeitla was a key to three of the five roads leading through the Western Dorsal. One heads almost due north from Sbeitla through the Sbiba Pass to the road center of Le Kef, vital to protection of British positions in the north. Two other roads emerging from Sbeitla lead to the Kasserine Pass, whence one proceeds northward through the village of Thala to Le Kef, the other northwest toward Tébessa. Two other roads farther south, also leading to Tébessa, were to be guarded by the troops that had withdrawn from Gafsa.

The Sbiba Pass, Anderson believed, was the most sensitive spot, for the concentration of German effort at Sidi Bou Zid appeared to point to a turn north from Sbeitla. To help Ward hold and thus delay a thrust through the Sbiba Pass, Anderson released the remainder of the 1st Armored Division's CCB, while to Sbiba he rushed a British armored brigade. The British armor was to hold the pass until portions of the U.S. 1st and 34th Divisions and some French units might withdraw from northern reaches of the Eastern Dorsal.

As far away as Morocco the Allies began moves they hoped would ease the crisis in Tunisia—a provisional force of twenty-five new Churchill tanks, another of thirty-five Shermans. At Oran, men of a regiment of the 9th Division got orders to strike their tents in the midst of a pelting rainstorm and to head for Tunisia. West of Oran, a giant of a man who took his nickname from the auburn color of his hair, Brigadier General S. Leroy Irwin, also got orders to move the units he commanded, the four field artillery battalions of the 9th Division, plus two attached cannon companies (short-nosed 105's). Five hours later "Red" Irwin and his men set out on a schedule of forced marches that left little time for eating or sleeping. Over fog-shrouded, rain-slick roads, they were to cover at least 180 miles a day.

While the Allies began these adjustments, the Germans dallied. Under the original arrangement with Field Marshal Kesselring, General von Arnim was to have released the *21st Panzer Division* to Field Marshal Rommel once Sidi Bou Zid had fallen. This Arnim declined to do. He intended using the *21st Panzer Division* to contain or eliminate the Americans at Sbeitla, thereby freeing the *10th Panzer Division* to turn north and cut off those Allied troops still holding in the Eastern Dorsal.

Having overestimated Allied strength in Gafsa, Rommel had delayed starting his attack until he could get the *21st Panzer Division*. Fuming with frustration when Arnim refused, Rommel followed up the Allied withdrawal from Gafsa and sent patrols toward Fériana, but he saw no hope of exploiting toward the coast unless Arnim backed down.

The commander in a position to resolve the issue was Field Marshal Kesselring. Uninformed by his subordinates of the timetable for their attacks, Kesselring had flown to Germany to confer with Hitler. Learning on the evening of February 15 of Arnim's success, he immediately ordered his Chief of Staff to direct that Arnim and Rommel, under the latter's overall command, drive vigorously for the coast by way of Tébessa after the manner of the grand maneuver he and Rommel had envisioned.

Because Arnim and Rommel technically were under *Comando Supremo*, the order had to be cleared first with the Italians. Lacking Kesselring's powerful presence to support the plan, the Italians received it apathetically and gave every indication of taking their time in making a decision.

Under no pressure, Arnim delayed an attack on Sbeitla while eliminating the American infantry from the djebels near Sidi Bou Zid. Not until after nightfall of the sixteenth did he move against Sbeitla.

In the darkness amid gnarled and misshapen olive trees on the fringe of Sbeitla, the first surge of German shells and machine-gun fire sent some of General Ward's men fleeing in panic. "We just lost our heads," one soldier later sheepishly admitted. To Arnim it appeared that little more than a show of force might prompt the Americans to abandon Sbeitla, and to many on the American side the entire defense appeared to be breaking up. Yet the coming of daylight revealed that only a few men had pulled out, that most had held, and that German tanks had yet to penetrate the olive groves.

Under orders to hold Sbeitla at least until 11 A.M. on the seventeenth, Ward was relieved when that hour passed with no renewal of the German attack. Having failed to carry the town in one swift rush, it was afternoon before Arnim's tanks were ready to try again.

Through much of the afternoon the battle raged, but the men and tanks of the 1st Armored Division held fast, while inside Sbeitla vehicles of supply and support units formed a heavy stream of traffic pouring west toward Kasserine. As the day faded, CCB skillfully broke off one segment after another from the battle to retire to the west, while CCA fell back to the north on the Sbiba Pass. It was 5 P.M. before Arnim's tanks at last entered Sbeitla.

Learning of Arnim's latest success, Field Marshal Rommel was more than ever convinced that the time had come to strike deep into the Allied rear—if not to the coast, at least as far as the American supply base at Tébessa. Late on February 17 he telephoned Arnim, but the commander of the *Fifth Panzer Army* stuck to his position. He had already directed the *10th Panzer Division*, he said, to turn north and cut off Allied troops still in the Eastern Dorsal. He needed the *21st Panzer Division* to protect his rear at Sbeitla. Furthermore, neither men nor supplies were sufficient to sustain a deep thrust.

After another failure on the eighteenth to convince Arnim, Rommel in desperation cabled *Comando Supremo*, begging authority to make an immediate attack on Tébessa, then to drive on to the coast. When a few hours later a message from Kesselring revealed that the field marshal had just returned to Rome and would try to sell the project to the Italians, Rommel grew excited and impatient.

He had to wait until midnight for news of the Italian decision—and then, crushing disappointment. Although *Comando Supremo* gave him command of both the *10th* and *21st Panzer Divisions*, he was to use them not for an attack west on Tébessa but for one north on Le Kef. To Rommel it was a timid, unimaginative solution, a shallow rather than a deep envelopment, tactical rather than strategic.

Field Marshal Kesselring, for his part, was satisfied. The directive was so worded, he believed, that a daring, imaginative commander like Rommel might interpret it to make the main effort of his attack wherever he wished. Rommel, he reasoned, would provide enough of a show in the direction of Le Kef to satisfy *Comando Supremo* while striking in strength toward the coast by way of Tébessa, the goal Rommel and Kesselring both were after.

The 1st Armored Divisions stand at Sbei'tla and the Axis indecision had gained for the Allies invaluable time. By daylight on February 19, General Anderson and General Fredendall had managed to erect a semblance of defense at each of the four passes through the Western Dorsal. In keeping with the expectation of a German turn to the north, the strongest was in the Sbiba Pass, while at Kasserine stood a battalion of the 1st Divisions infantry supported by contingents of engineers, tank destroyers, and artillery—two thousand men at most. A few miles to the north, at Thala, stood a British armored brigade—a fancy name for a task force of infantry and outmoded tanks. The battered 1st Armored Division, assembling near Tébessa, might be used as a reserve either at the Kasserine Pass or at the other passes to the south.

The Allies also had taken a big step toward unified command with the arrival of General Sir Harold R. L. G. Alexander, a tall, mustached Englishman, the epitome of the stalwart British professional, who had been overall commander in Egypt. Alexander assumed command of the 18th Army Group, signifying a projected linking of Montgomery's Eighth Army with the Allied troops in Tunisia.

Alexander toured the American defenses in the rain and mist of February 18 and disliked what he saw: stragglers, confusion, uncertainty among subordinate commanders, lack of information and decision at Fredendall's headquarters. In the process, he gained an unfavorable impression of the American soldier that was to last a long time.

It was a strange battle that began on February 19—the battle of the Kasserine Pass—for it looked so distinctly different as it unfolded to the troops and commanders on the two sides fighting it. To the Allies, it was a succession of crises; to the Germans, one frustration after another.

Contrary to Kesselring's expectation, Erwin Rommel, the "Desert Fox," scourge of the British until chastened at El Alamein, was playing it strictly according to the stage directions. *Comando Supremo* had said the goal was Le Kef, so Le Kef it was. The only latitude left him, Rommel reasoned, was whether to make his main effort through the Kasserine Pass, thence north through Thala on Le Kef, or directly north through the Sbiba Pass. The more direct route appeared to him to pose the better opportunity. While probing the Kasserine Pass with the weak units he had brought from the Mareth Line, he might send the *21st Panzer Division* against the Sbiba Pass. When General von Arnim released the *10th Panzer Division* later in the day, he would be free to decide on the basis of the day's results through which pass to commit the second panzer force.

Secondary effort or not, the German attack at the Kasserine Pass appeared to American defenders to be powerful in its own right. Although they repulsed the first direct probes, they became conscious as the day waned that the Germans were changing their tactics and infiltrating small groups up wadis and around crags to take the defenders in rear. American commanders took heart from the arrival of a second battalion of infantry during the afternoon and the promise of another during the night, but they still deemed their strength insufficient.

The commander of the British armored brigade at Thala, Brigadier Charles A. L. Dunphie, agreed and asked authority to move his troops into closer backup positions. Although defense at the Sbiba Pass had held well during the day against what was apparently the larger German force, General Anderson was still concerned lest he have need of the armor at Sbiba. He granted permission for Dunphie to shift only a small portion of the brigade.

For Rommel the day of the nineteenth had started the parade of frustrations. Neither at the Sbiba Pass nor at Kasserine had he achieved the penetration he had to have, and he saw that he had erred in sending greater strength to Sbiba. Although he intended now to commit the *10th Panzer Division* at Kasserine, General von Arnim held onto the division so long that it arrived too late to join an attack early the next day. Furthermore, Arnim had retained a portion of the division, including the new Tiger tanks, under the pretense of being too closely engaged to break contact. The renewed attack at Kasserine thus again would be weak. Rommel had only three battalions of German infantry that had been used the first day, plus a battalion each of Italian tanks and motorized infantry.

To the American defenders, that again seemed strength enough. During the night, part of the defense had disintegrated when some of the engineers, unaccustomed to fighting as infantry, got "night fever" and melted away toward some nebulous place of refuge called "the rear." German shelling constantly knocked out telephone wires, a condition all the more serious because a river swollen by rain split the American position. Shortly before noon the remaining engineers gave way. That afforded the Germans an entrée through the pass into a vast elliptical basin behind it and a road junction where one road branches north toward Thala, the other west toward Tébessa.

To Rommel the gain was nothing more than a start. He needed maneuver room behind the pass before committing the *10th Panzer Division*, and he needed it quickly, for word had come that the British Eighth Army had begun attacking outposts of the Mareth Line. Since Rommel did not know the British attack was but a feint, he deemed that he had to pierce the Western Dorsal quickly or else give up and attend the Mareth Line.

Field Marshal Kesselring lunched with Rommel that day. Agreeing that speed was vital, Kesselring asked where his host intended turning once he had secured the pass—north on Thala and Le Kef, or west on Tébessa? Rommel said he was undecided. To drive on Tébessa would take him away from the *21st Panzer Division*, which was still trying to get through the Sbiba Pass. Kesselring failed to press the issue. Some of the enthusiasm both men had felt originally for a drive to the coast had faded.

Still without the maneuver room he wanted, Rommel nevertheless committed a portion of the panzer division in mid-afternoon of February 20. Behind a barrage fired by five battalions of artillery and *Nebelwerfer* rocket launchers ("Screaming Meemies," the Americans called them), the Germans destroyed the little British task force that had come down from Thala.

The defenses were collapsing. Stragglers crowded the road toward Thala or melted into the hills along the south rim of the basin. Allied commanders believed the only hope was to block the Tébessa and Thala roads and to build a line of infantry on the south rim of the basin so that the enemy would be unable to turn against the rear of the passes to the south. Prospects were best along the rim of the basin and on the Tébessa road, since during the night of the nineteenth General Fredendall had started infantry of the 1st Division moving onto the south rim and the 1st Armored Division's CCB astride the road to Tébessa. On the Thala road General Anderson hurriedly committed the rest of the little British armored brigade to hold as long as possible midway between Kasserine and Thala, while he improvised a force of stragglers, tank destroyers, anti-tank guns, artillery, anything at hand to set up a new position a mile south of Thala.

Through February 21, CCB frustrated every Axis effort to drive up the road toward Tébessa. On the Thala road, where Rommel intended his heavier strike, the British armor gained a respite through the morning as the Germans regrouped, but at noon a task force of the *10th Panzer Division*, including fifty tanks and self-propelled assault guns (the equivalent of the American tank destroyer), attacked with a fury.

Taking cover in wadis and behind crags and hummocks, lighter and less powerfully gunned British tanks lured the bigger Mark IV's into close range, then opened a deadly fire. In mid-afternoon Rommel himself, despairing of a breakthrough, took personal command. For an hour an exercise in violence raged. In late afternoon, with fifteen of his outgunned tanks destroyed, Brigadier Dunphie decided at last that he had bought all the time he could. He ordered surviving troops to fall back on the new line just short of Thala.

Behind a smokescreen and in gathering darkness Dunphie's tanks moved through the new line to apparent safety, but as the last of the British vehicles passed, still others continued to come. Too late the British discovered what had happened. Following close on Dunphie's column, the Germans had put a captured British tank at the head of their own tanks. Without challenge from the defenders, they had followed that iron Trojan horse full into the British position.

The night erupted in a blaze of tank and machine-gun fire. Tanks went up in flames. Ammunition exploded. Bursts of tracer bullets split the darkness. For three hours a brutal mêlée raged, a struggle without quarter, a battle for survival.

Like a storm that blows itself out from its own fury, it at last subsided. The British fell back a half-mile to the very edge of the village of Thala. The Germans, temporarily spent, pulled back a similar distance to the south. A strange stillness took the place of the turmoil.

As the worn, dispirited British infantrymen and a few surviving tank crews retired, there seemed to them to be nothing to set matters right between Thala and the sea. A few hours earlier that had been the case; but like cavalrymen in a movie about the Old West, new hope strode onto the scene.

All the way from Oran they had come by forced march to arrive at a critical moment: "Red" Irwin and four battalions of 9th Division artillery.

While General Irwin took command of all surviving artillery and anti-tank pieces at Thala and directed them to enfilading positions to stop the Germans on the morrow, Brigadier Dunphie rallied a small covey of tanks around midnight to launch a diversionary sortie to the south. The weakness of the thrust belied its importance. To the night-blind Germans, fatigued and bloody from the day's fight, it appeared to be the opening blow of an Allied counterattack.

The next morning, the twenty-second, fourth day of the battle, the Germans south of Thala held in place, watching warily for the counterattack they were sure was to come. Thundering fires from "Red" Irwin's hastily emplaced artillery seemed a prelude, and an appearance in strength of American fighter-bombers, heretofore only rarely seen, furthered the impression. Again, too, Brigadier Dunphie sent a little band of tanks on a diversionary foray. Although the Germans quickly knocked out five tanks, the diversion reinforced the belief that a spirited counterattack was soon to begin.

Field Marshal Rommel still had ordered no renewal of the assault on Thala when soon after midday Kesselring arrived at his headquarters. Kesselring found Rommel depressed, counting the negative factors. Fuel for the tanks was running low. Fog and rain denied help from the *Luftwaffe*. The attack had forced no shift of British and French reserves. Rommel had taken too many casualties. Montgomery soon would hit the Mareth Line.

Bowing to the inevitable, Kesselring agreed to call off the attack. Apprehensive Allied commanders had no way of knowing it, but the battle of the Kasserine Pass was over, and with it any chance of Axis victory in Tunisia had passed.

That night the Germans began to withdraw back to the Eastern Dorsal. Stunned when their adversary turned at the apparent moment of triumph, the Allied troops were slow to follow. The Germans got away undeterred.

The fighting that began at Sidi Bou Zid and ended at Thala cost the Germans not quite 1,000 casualties, half of them killed or missing, plus 20 tanks. The Americans alone lost more than 6,000 men, 300 of them killed, another 3,000 missing (mostly captured), and 183 tanks, two-thirds of the tank strength of the 1st Armored Division.

Except for General Fredendall, most American commanders who had been tried by fire at Sidi Bou Zid and Kasserine retained their commands. To replace Fredendall as head of the II Corps, General Eisenhower brought in George Patton with orders to cast the American troops in his own hard-bitten, swashbuckling mold.

A major change of command occurred on the Axis side as well. Convinced that trying to hold Tunisia could lead only to futile sacrifice of troops, Field Marshal Rommel flew to Rome, then to Hitler's head-quarters in an attempt to obtain permission to evacuate the beachhead. Hitler told him instead to go on extended sick leave. General von Arnim moved up to command *Army Group Afrika*, containing the *Fifth Panzer Army* and Rommel's old command, the *Italian-German Panzer Army*.

As part of a process of getting ready to resume the offensive, the new Allied commander, General Alexander, directed a realignment of forces, returning to parent units the hodgepodge of battalions, task forces, and combat teams that had grown out of the defensive battles. The British First Army with 120,000 men remained in the north; the French with 50,000 concentrated in the center; and the U.S. II Corps with 90,000 men, including the 1st, 9th, and 34th Infantry Divisions and the 1st Armored Division, assembled in the south.

As the time neared for General Montgomery to assault the Mareth Line, General Patton's II Corps launched a diversionary attack that in eight days took Gafsa and lured the *10th Panzer Division* away from the Mareth Line. Montgomery struck the line on March 20 and nine days later entered Gabès. On April 6 the British attacked a new Axis line at the twelve-mile land bridge between the sea and the salt marshes near Gabès. The next day patrols of the Eighth Army and the II Corps met.

As Axis forces began a precipitate withdrawal up the coast, the followup by the Eighth Army pinched out the II Corps, and Alexander shifted the Americans to the extreme north to part of the British sector along the coastal road leading from Algeria to Bizerte. To release Patton to head a new American force for the next Allied operation to follow victory in North Africa, Major General Omar N. Bradley, a bespectacled, mild-mannered classmate of Eisenhower's at the United States Military Academy, colorless but highly respected by his colleagues, took command of the II Corps.

The big Allied drive began on April 19. On May 7, British armor entered Tunis, while American infantry moved into Bizerte. Six days later the last Axis resistance collapsed. A human wave of more than 250,000 men filled prisoner-of-war enclosures, more men than the Russians had taken at Stalingrad. In all of the fighting in North Africa, the Axis had lost 340,000 men, an entire army group.

Six months after the landings in Morocco and Algiers, the Allies controlled the entire North African coast at a cost of 70,341 British, French, and American casualties, 10,290 of them killed, including 2,715 Americans. A few days later, on May 24, the first unopposed British convoy since 1940 reached beleaguered Malta.

It was a turning point in the war. The initiative no longer belonged to the Axis but to the Allies. It was a turning point for American troops as well. At Sidi Bou Zid, on the djebels at the Faid Pass, and at Kasserine the test of battle had found them wanting. Despite numerous incidents of individual and group heroism, they had failed to measure up in training, equipment, and leadership. Moreover, their commanders had not done right by them in committing them to battle in driblets, which negated the effect of the divisional system of combined arms and, in the process, dealt a heavy blow to the soldier's will to fight.

By the time victory came in Tunisia, many defects had been corrected. "Even though they didn't do too well in the beginning," wrote the folksy newspaper columnist Ernie Pyle, "there was never at any time any question about the American bravery. It is a matter of being hardened and practiced by going through the flames."[52]

The troops did not know it, but they could be grateful that the flames were less searing than they might have been, because German commanders, like those on the Allied side, had human failings—jealousy, overambition, indecision, despair. And they and a lot of other Americans could be grateful in the end for a Winston Churchill who saw that they got a tryout in the brown land of North Africa rather than a disastrous opening performance on the green shores of France.

---

[52] Blumenson, *Kasserine Pass*, p. 312, quoting a column by Ernie Pyle.

Chapter Nine – Prelude to Sicily

When, in November 1942, Franklin D. Roosevelt invited Winston Churchill and the Russian head of state, Josef Stalin, to join him in a strategy conference somewhere in Africa early in the new year, he had assumed that all French North Africa, including Tunisia, would have by then been won. That would have fixed the Allies favorably for confronting the suspicious head of world communism and his embarrassing demands for a second front.[53]

In view of the fitful campaign that actually remained before victory in Tunisia, it was just as well that Stalin declined every overture. Behind a veil of various excuses Stalin indicated that he had nothing to talk about. The only course for the Western Allies, he believed, was clear: to fulfill the promise to open a second front in Europe.

Stalin's declining failed to deter Roosevelt and Churchill. Even though they soon discerned that Tunisia probably would be cleared only in the spring of 1943, it was important to decide in advance where the Allies were to go next.

The two Allied leaders opened their conference on January 14 in the Hotel Anfa in a suburb of Casablanca. The setting was delightful: palm trees, orange trees, bougainvillea, azure skies, a backdrop of Casablanca's white-washed buildings framed against the blue Atlantic. Roosevelt and Churchill themselves met frequently in private villas assigned them on

---

[53] For this chapter, basic sources were: Matloff and Snell, *Strategic Planning, 1941-1942*; Matloff, *Strategic Planning, 1943-1944*; Garland and Smyth, *Sicily and the Surrender of Italy*; Cline, *Washington Command Post*; Craven and Cate, eds., *Europe — TORCH to POINTBLANK*; and Davis, *The Experience of War*. See also Churchill, *The Hinge of Fate*; Sherwood, *Roosevelt and Hopkins*; Morison, *Sicily — Salerno — Anzio*; Herbert Feis, *Churchill, Roosevelt, Stalin* (Princeton, 1957); and Arthur Bryant, *The Turn of the Tide* (New York, 1957).

grounds of the hotel, while plenary sessions and meetings of the military chiefs took place in the hotel itself.

The American Joint Chiefs of Staff went to Casablanca thinking their British counterparts were going to insist on invading Sardinia, probably as a first step toward invading Italy. General Marshall and his colleagues wanted no part of it. They wanted to get on with the cross-Channel invasion in 1943. Yet they had to recognize that the delay in Tunisia, the worldwide shipping shortage, and the continuing struggle against the U-boat might force postponement—as Marshall had predicted in opposing TORCH—until 1944. In that case the alternative was some operation in the Mediterranean region to utilize the forces that soon would become idle in Tunisia.

Sardinia, the Americans believed, would provide air bases for hitting Germany, but it led nowhere except possibly to northern Italy. While aware of the military maxim that one enters Italy from the top as one does any other boot, they had no wish to go into Italy from either top or bottom.

A better choice, the American Chiefs believed, would be Sicily. Control of Sicily would afford almost unrestricted use of the Mediterranean, thus obviating the long voyages around the African continent to reach the oil of the Near East and to carry supplies to Russia. Taking Sicily also might be enough to force Italy out of the war without invading the Italian mainland.

The British Chiefs, ironically, had been concerned that the Americans would choose not Sicily but the softer target of Sardinia. Pleased to learn otherwise, they agreed, in exchange for postponing a cross-Channel invasion, to honor forceful demands promoted by Admiral King for increased resources to exploit a limited initiative recently achieved in the Pacific. The atmosphere of the conference soon became as harmonious as the surroundings at the Hotel Anfa.

Decision came on the fourth day. To use the troops available in Tunisia, to secure the Mediterranean sea lanes, to divert Axis forces from the Russian front (a euphemism for saying they were as yet unable to launch a true second front), and so to pressure the Italians that in the face of increased bombardment from the air, they might be persuaded to forsake the war, the Allies agreed on an operation with the code name HUSKY: the invasion of Sicily, perhaps as early as July 1943.

Beyond that, the conferees agreed to give top priority to ridding the Atlantic of the U-boat, continuing the buildup in the United Kingdom for an eventual cross-Channel invasion, and launching a stepped-up aerial offensive against Germany to be known as the "Combined Bomber Offensive." They made no decision on what to do after Sicily. Were they then to continue into Italy, as Winston Churchill clearly wanted, to take advantage of what Churchill called the "soft underbelly" of Europe, perhaps even to continue into the Balkans to come at the Germans through the back door?

To General Marshall, the presence of one towering mountain range after another made Europe's underbelly look less like sponge than armor plate. Why fight up the readily defended rocky spine of Italy to a dead end at the Alps and the incredibly difficult Ljubljana Gap, a circuitous route at best to the heart of German power? Why dissipate the resources essential to a successful cross-Channel attack?

Apparently enjoying the moment of accord at Casablanca, neither side pressed the issue.

Political considerations, meanwhile, were the province of Churchill and Roosevelt in the informal meetings in their villas. The main political goal Roosevelt had set for himself, and one in which Churchill concurred, was to force a marriage of two antipathetic Frenchmen, Charles de Gaulle and Henri Giraud.

The conference was nearly over before de Gaulle even consented to come to Casablanca; he had delayed not because he objected to meeting Giraud, but because he wanted neither to share any power with him nor to give any impression of collaborating with the tarnished men of Vichy, with whom Giraud had dealt. De Gaulle arrived at last on January 22. Although he engaged in private discussions with Giraud that were amicable enough, he resisted at length all efforts to bring him to a public conciliation. Even a Churchillian threat to withdraw British support of the Fighting French failed to move him. He gave in finally only to Roosevelt's calculated but nonetheless earnest pleading that he needed de Gaulle's public endorsement of Giraud to counter rumblings back home against the policy of dealing with Vichyites in North Africa.

De Gaulle condescended at last, "I will do it for you."[54]

In the garden outside Roosevelt's villa, before reporters and cameramen

---

[54] Davis, *The Experience of War*, p. 377, quoting de Gaulle, *Unity*, p. 89.

assembled for a final pronouncement by the Allied leaders on achievements of the conference, he did it. Unsmiling, unbending, Charles de Gaulle shook hands with Henri Giraud.

Roosevelt and Churchill had brought off their wedding. Making it a successful marriage would be another matter.

Responding to the presence of press and camera, Roosevelt supplemented the little pantomime with apparently extemporaneous remarks. To assure the peace of the world, he said, German and Japanese war power had to be totally eliminated. That meant the "unconditional surrender" of Germany, Italy, and Japan.[55]

It was a catchy term, tested years before by Ulysses S. Grant, a rallying slogan for the Allied nations and Allied sympathizers everywhere, an assurance that there would be no negotiations with the traitor of Munich, no repetition of the compromises with fascism practiced in North Africa. Although Roosevelt appeared to have invented the term in an off-the-cuff remark, the policy and the specific term itself had earlier been discussed with Churchill, cleared with the British Cabinet, and recommended by a State-Army-Navy committee in the United States.

Many critics later would label the formula a mistake. They claimed that it left the Germans and the Japanese no out, thus unnecessarily prolonging the war. Yet that attitude ignored the context in which Roosevelt put it: not, he had said, "the destruction of the population," but "the destruction of the philosophies…which are based on conquest and the subjugation of other people." To argue that this prolonged the war was to grope for an apologia for a people and a military who had so prostrated themselves before the idol of National Socialism that they were powerless to rise.

At Casablanca the Allies had kept the question of what they were to do after Sicily hidden in a closet, an unwanted guest at a banquet of accord. Well they might have, for the question was intricately tied to an issue that the American Chiefs had come to see by this time in stark shades of black and white. What to do after Sicily meant taking a stand on a peripheral strategy versus a direct strike at the Germans with great masses of men across the Channel.

---

[55] A good discussion of Roosevelt's unconditional surrender formula is in Smyth and Garland, *Sicily and the Surrender of Italy*, pp. 11-12.

Yet the question could no longer be ignored when next the Allies met, this time in the less romantic surroundings of Washington. TRIDENT, they called the conference. It opened in May 1943, in an aura of victory at last in Tunisia, amid a touching outpouring of American affection for Winston Churchill, the bald, rotund, indomitable warrior, his two fingers upraised in the "V" sign for "victory."

Churchill and the British, it became clear at the first plenary session in the White House, wanted to devote all available Allied resources during 1943 to the Mediterranean and the task of eliminating Italy from the war. They readily admitted that this meant relegating a cross-Channel attack to the indefinite future.

For Marshall, King, Arnold, and Leahy, this was like waving a red flag before a bull. Defeating Germany first, to which they were still dedicated, meant a direct, determined attack on the European continent at the earliest possible date. Nibbling away at the outer fringes of German power was equivalent to repudiating the strategy of Europe First. Rather than abandon that strategy indirectly, they were prepared, they intimated, to transfer the bulk of their resources to the Pacific.

Either this old spook retained considerable power to frighten, or Churchill and his Chiefs of Staff were less in favor of peripheral strategy and less opposed to a cross-Channel invasion than the American Chiefs believed. Probably the latter. In any case the British accepted the principle that all proposed operations were to be aimed toward a cross-Channel attack with a target date of May 1944, but in return they insisted on assurance that the main task for 1943 was to force Italy from the war.

When the TRIDENT conference ended on May 19, those points were agreed to, but the matter of *how* to eliminate Italy remained. The British wanted to invade the Italian mainland, but the Americans resisted on the theory that an invasion would siphon too much strength from the buildup for the cross-Channel attack. Marshall and his colleagues would agree to nothing more ambitious after Sicily than to invade Sardinia and possible Corsica—steps that might lead eventually to an invasion of southern France to assist the cross-Channel attack.

In lieu of a decision, the Combined Chiefs tossed the problem to the man who would be charged with executing whichever approach was eventually chosen, Dwight D. Eisenhower. General Eisenhower, they directed, was "to plan such operations in exploitation of HUSKY [the invasion of

Sicily] as are best calculated to eliminate Italy from the war and to contain the maximum number of German forces." He was to employ only those forces already available in the Mediterranean less seven divisions that were to be transferred late in 1943 to the buildup in the United Kingdom.

Although Churchill accepted the indecision of TRIDENT, he was visibly disappointed. For all the concessions made to a cross-Channel attack, Churchill—unlike his Chiefs of Staff—still believed firmly that only the massive Soviet armies could be decisive on the European continent, and that the Allies should confine their contribution to air and naval power, plus relatively small ground actions in peripheral places like Italy and Norway until such time as the Germans were so beaten down that a cross-Channel attack would constitute a *coup de grace*. (He was, his personal physician would note years later, haunted by the crippling losses on the western front a quarter-century earlier—"fighting the ghosts of the Somme."[56])

Hardly had the conference concluded before Churchill announced his intention to fly to Algiers to press his case before General Eisenhower. So that he would not appear to exert undue influence, he begged the President to send General Marshall with him.

In meetings that began in Eisenhower's villa on May 29, Churchill found cause to regret his dogged insistence on bringing along the U.S. Army's Chief of Staff. Although Eisenhower's own planners looked beyond Sicily to Sardinia and Corsica on the theory that those objectives would tie the Allies less irretrievably to the Mediterranean, Eisenhower himself favored going directly to the mainland. Had Marshall not been present, Churchill would have won his point. Ever watchful of anything that might interfere with a cross-Channel attack, Marshall responded that any decision before the nature of Axis resistance became clear in Sicily, would be premature. When he suggested that Eisenhower set up two planning Staffs—one for Sardinia and Corsica, another for Italy—Eisenhower agreed.

Although Churchill would have preferred a definite decision for Italy, he was so convinced that conquering Sicily would take less than a month that he looked on these terms as equivalent to saying go on to the mainland. He began to talk enthusiastically of achieving revenge on Mussolini, a man whom he once had admired, and of capturing Rome.

[56] Pogue, *Ordeal and Hope*, p. 317. See also *Taken from the Diaries of Lord Moran* (Churchill's physician), *The Struggle for Survival 1940-1965* (Boston, 1966), p. 34.

Whether conquering Sicily or even capturing Rome would produce Italian capitulation, no one, of course, could say; but to lack agreed surrender terms should the Italians falter would be imprudent. Unfortunately the first exchange of ideas on how the Italians might surrender revealed a split as great as that on post-Sicily operations. The British thought in terms of maintaining the monarchy as an Italian government pledged to put the nations facilities at the disposal of the Allies for prosecuting the war against Germany. To the Americans the formula of unconditional surrender meant more: it meant an Allied military government.

Even as Allied soldiers boarded landing craft for the invasion of Sicily, the terms for Italian surrender remained as vague as where the Allies were to go next.

Unlike the meshed machinery of the Combined Chiefs of Staff on the Allied side, the Axis way of directing the war was to invest everything essentially in two men, the Fascist and Nazi dictators, Benito Mussolini and Adolf Hitler, neither of whom had approached World War II with any concept of overall strategy. How strained the relations between them had become under the impact of Russian blows in the east and of Allied victory in North Africa could be fully apparent only to those on the inside.

As an absolute dictator—both Chancellor and President of the Third Reich—Hitler exercised supreme command of the German armed forces through the Armed Forces High Command (*Oberkommando der Wehrmacht*, or OKW). Under OKW each military service had its own commander: the navy, Grossadmiral Karl Doenitz; the *Luftwaffe,* Reichsmarschall Hermann Goering; the army (*Oberkommando des Heeres*, or OKU), Hitler himself. Wearing two command hats, Hitler used one, OKH, to direct the war in Russia; the other, OKW, to command all other German forces elsewhere. The only organ of unified command was the person of Hitler himself, whose megalomaniacal belief in his own infallibility made him more and more convinced that German failures were the fault of untrustworthy generals. As time passed, it had become increasingly difficult for any other than sycophants to advise or serve him.

As *Duce* of the ruling Fascist party in Italy, Mussolini was the head of the government, though the King, Victor Emmanuel III, remained as head of state. Mussolini obtained his powers as commander of the armed forces by delegation from the King. Unlike Hitler, who had no peer, Mussolini remained technically submissive to the head of state, who presumably could withdraw his delegated authority over the armed forces or even depose Mussolini as head of the government. Whether because of those possibilities or by personal preference, Mussolini, unlike Hitler, chose to leave military details to his military subordinates.

The Armed Forces General Staff, the *Comando Supremo*, acted as Mussolini's military Staff and directed operations in the various theaters of war. Yet on matters affecting both Italy and Germany the *Comando Supremo*, like OKW, had no authority: decision came only at the top, from Mussolini and Hitler.

Although Hitler genuinely admired Mussolini as a leader and friend, Mussolini rarely reciprocated. As German predominance in the alliance had grown, Mussolini, the new Caesar, had found his ally increasingly hard to take. While Mussolini had needed Hitler's help in Greece and North Africa, he had found it galling. When increased German strength in North Africa prompted Hitler to upgrade Field Marshal Kesselring and his headquarters in Italy from a *Luftwaffe* liaison Staff to an operational command post—*Oberkommando* (OB) SUEDWEST—Mussolini had a disturbing example of growing German influence within his own homeland.

The Allied invasion of North Africa had done much to nourish a suspicion in Mussolini's mind that the Axis could win the war only if Hitler made a separate peace with the Soviet Union. To his son-in-law and Minister of Foreign Affairs, Count Galeazzo Ciano, he had entrusted the mission, in December 1942, of persuading Hitler to take that step.

Ciano might have saved his breath. Hitler was convinced the Russians eventually would bleed to death. He had but to continue pressure on them while holding all prior Axis gains, and victory would be his.

Rebuffed, Mussolini saw no course remaining except to stand up to the Germans. To do so, he dismissed the head of the *Comando Supremo* on the grounds that he was servile to the Germans, and replaced him with Generale d'Armata Vittorio Ambrosio, Chief of the Army General Staff, who thoroughly disliked them. When Ambrosio proposed both to stand up to the Germans and to bring Italian troops from other theaters to defend the homeland, Mussolini cried: "*Benissimo!*"[57]

That same month—February 1943—when General Ambrosio insisted

---

[57] Smyth and Garland, *Sicily and the Surrender of Italy*, p. 36.

on withdrawing Italian troops from Yugoslavia, despite increasing insurrection by Yugoslav partisans, Hitler grew suspicious. When Mussolini continued to press for peace with the Russians, tensions multiplied. A top-level conference called in April to heal the breach only widened it. Hitler vehemently protested any thought of peace with the Soviet Union. Mussolini, who had been in poor health since early the preceding winter and was thus not the forceful debater he had once been, failed even to convince him that the Italians would have to have German help if they were successfully to defend their own homeland.

From the conference General Ambrosio emerged certain that a separate peace in the east was no longer possible, that no hope remained for Italy unless Mussolini broke the alliance with Germany. Although Mussolini, too, came home believing the Axis had lost the war, breaking the alliance was another matter. Only with victory could his Fascist regime survive, and the only hope of victory, however uncertain, lay with German power.

Mussolini could see no way out. If the Italians were to sever the alliance and forsake the war, the initiative would have to come from someone else. Yet who? By this time—the spring of 1943—three separate groups were trying to find a way out of the war: dissident Fascists, military officers, and underground anti-Fascist parties; but not one of the three would presume to act without authority from the King.

Although a diminutive, retiring Victor Emmanuel permitted audiences with all the groups and listened apathetically to their appeals to dismiss Mussolini, he maintained a stolid silence. He disliked the Germans and wanted out of the alliance, but he feared a German takeover if he ousted Mussolini or terminated the alliance without German consent. Deeming no one else as capable as the clever *Duce* at ending the alliance, getting out of the war, and keeping the unpleasant business of government out of the monarchy's unwilling hands, he saw no point in replacing Mussolini.

As for the defense of Italy and the islands of Sicily and Sardinia, all were agreed that the Italians desperately needed German help. The people were war-weary. The combined German and Italian air forces in the Mediterranean had fewer than a thousand planes, and the Germans would send more only if the Italians improved their airfields and provided better anti-aircraft protection, which they were unable to do. The navy had not enough surface vessels to justify any hope of defeating an invasion fleet, and the ground forces—drained of their best men and equipment by the fighting in Russia and North Africa—were patently incapable of repelling an invasion.

Yet Mussolini—and to a slightly lesser degree, Ambrosio—was reluctant to ask for more German ground forces. Once Mussolini admitted dependence on the Germans, he would cease to be, as Kesselring put it in a platitude, "master of his own house." If the Germans were present in Italy in strength, he might never be able to wriggle out of the alliance.

So dismal were the prospects of defense without German help that early in May, Ambrosio and Mussolini nevertheless finally accepted a German offer of three divisions. When Hitler raised this to five, Mussolini, at Ambrosio's urging, declined.

The refusal increased Hitler's suspicions. While Kesselring continued in good faith to cooperate with the Italians and persuaded them to accept a fourth division, Hitler and OKW devised a plan to be implemented should Mussolini try to defect: when the alarm came, six or seven German divisions were to speed into Italy to occupy the northern part of the country.

Those developments pointed up Mussolinis quandary. Wanting out of the war, he nevertheless felt impelled to accept the German help that would make it more difficult for him to get out. Fascist Italy was unable either to make war or to choose peace.

The invasion of Sicily—a Vermont-sized island which the Greeks had called Trinacria, "three-cornered"—provided a severe test for the theories and machinery of Allied command. The basic question was whether to opt for a close-knit assault that was sure to hold against the inevitable early counterattack, or to spread available resources in a series of stabs to eliminate a dozen Axis airfields and seize essential harbors. Although the ideal plan would have been a direct blow against the northeastern port of Messina, which—owing to its location on the narrow sea moat between Sicily and the mainland—provided the only escape hatch for Axis troops, powerful coastal batteries and the distance from Allied fighter bases prompted the planners to rule this out. Forced to land elsewhere, the invaders would be able to reach Messina only by means of shallow coastal shelves on either flank of gargantuan, volcanic Mount Etna, over 11,000 feet high and 400 miles around at the base.

Busy with the campaign in Tunisia, neither General Eisenhower (promoted now to four-star rank) nor three of the other principals—General

Alexander, who was to be overall ground commander; General Montgomery, who was to command the British; and General Patton, who was to lead the Americans—could give much attention to the early planning. A special headquarters, called "Force 141" from the number of the room in the Hotel St. George in Algiers which served as the main office, worked out a plan, subject to approval by the principals, including air and naval commanders. The target date of July 10 was but six weeks off before agreement came, mainly on the basis of what General Montgomery wanted.

The plan represented a sharp compromise between the optimum requirements of concentrating the invasion force and of seizing airfields and ports. All landings were to be made in the southeastern corner of the island. Montgomery's Eighth Army was to come ashore on the southeastern coast near Catania, eliminate nearby airfields on the Catanian plain, then drive up the narrow shelf along the east coast to Messina. Patton's American command, the Seventh U.S. Army, was to land on the southwestern coast near the fishing port of Gela, take close-in airfields, then block to the northwest to prevent Axis interference with the British drive on Messina.

Although the Americans would have no major port, Patton agreed, on the basis of advice from logistical experts, to accept the handicap. The theory was that new types of landing and supply craft—in particular, the DUKW, an amphibious truck—could sustain the troops over the beaches.

What irked Patton was the proviso that once ashore the Seventh Army was to have no more than a passive role protecting a British flank. Unfamiliar as he was with the British concept that an early plan is nothing if not a basis for argument, he declined to protest. Since the overall commander, General Alexander, retained the low opinion of American troops he had formed at Kasserine, it is doubtful in any case whether Patton could have engineered a change. He had to content himself with devising stratagems—at which he was more than able—designed to expand the American role once the troops were ashore.

Patton and his American naval opposite, Admiral Hewitt, were similarly disturbed over the matter of air support. The problem was no longer a unified air command, for that had by this time been achieved under Eisenhower in the Mediterranean Air Command headed by a Britisher, Air Chief Marshal Sir Arthur Tedder, whose authority embraced British and American air units in the Near East, Malta, and North Africa. By far the largest of three subordinate commands was the Northwest African

Air Forces, commanded by an American, Lieutenant General Carl Spaatz, and including American and British tactical, strategic, and troop carrier aircraft. Under Spaatz were units headed by those who had commanded in the North African invasion: both the American, General Doolittle, and the Britisher, Air Vice Marshal Sir Arthur Coningham.

Yet for all the new unity, air commanders would earmark no planes specifically for direct support of ground troops. That was a result partly of the British principle of a separate air arm, partly of the fascination of American airmen with the equation of air versus air. American airmen in particular had yet to accept the fact that direct tactical support of ground troops was important enough to justify a consciously planned effort to provide it.

"You can get your Navy planes to do anything you want," said Patton to Hewitt; "but we can't get the Air Force to do a goddam thing!"[58]

The fault was not entirely that of the airmen. In Tunisia, American ground commanders had seen air power in strictly a ground-support role, as a new form of fire power available at their beckoning to hit targets that in many cases were more the province of artillery than of aircraft. So the airmen had resisted as any misused specialist would resist. They believed that they themselves understood better than the ground commanders their own capabilities. These included the ability to cripple the enemy's air arm and also to strike with effect against enemy troop movements and concentrations of which ground commanders often were unaware. Yet how to do those things when they were constantly harangued by ground commanders demanding strikes against this tank or that machine-gun nest?

There were points for and against on both sides which would be resolved only in the course of more experience against the foe.

To deceive the Axis about the target of the invasion, Allied intelligence specialists planted fictitious credentials and a counterfeit letter on the corpse of a British serviceman who had died of pneumonia, a death that has many of the same characteristics as death by drowning. The letter specified that the Allies were to make feints against Sicily and the Greek islands in order to conceal real thrusts against Sardinia and the Greek mainland.

The body was set adrift off the Spanish coast in early May with a courier's briefcase realistically chained to one wrist, in the expectation that it would

---

58 Morison, *Sicily — Salerno — Anzio*, p. 22.

wash ashore and come to the attention of Axis agents. Three days later Spanish authorities notified the British that they had found the body of Major William Martin, believed to be a British courier. The body was duly transferred to British authorities, and intelligence specialists ascertained that the letter had indeed been opened, then resealed.

Hitler and his top-level advisers accepted as authentic the news carried by Major Martin—"a man who never was," as a book about the episode called him. In early May OKW directed that defensive measures on Sardinia and the Greek mainland receive top priority.[59]

Yet not all Axis commanders or intelligence Staffs were deceived. Italian intelligence discounted Major Martin from the first, and Kesselring shared the Italian view that Sicily remained a likely target. The head of the *Comando Supremo*, General Ambrosio, reluctantly concluded that at least two German divisions were essential for defending Sicily. Although that meant allowing a fifth division to come into Italy, the pitiful state of all Italian defenses gradually took precedence over concern about the obstacle the Germans might pose to Italian surrender.

The extent of Italian weakness was underscored starkly early in June after Allied planes began a devastating bombardment of the tiny island of Pantelleria, midway between the North African coast and Sicily. During the first ten days of June, more than thirty-five hundred planes bombed the island relentlessly, then dropped leaflets demanding surrender. On the eleventh, as the bombers struck again, an invasion fleet carrying a British division took position offshore. As landing craft headed toward the island, the Italian commander raised a white flag.

The seizure of Pantelleria, which gave the Allies a valuable way station on the road to Sicily and eliminated a dangerous Axis airfield, shook the Axis command. To the Italians, it was depressing, a shockingly dismal start to the defense of the homeland. To the Germans, it demonstrated all too clearly what they might expect in the future from their Italian allies.

General Ambrosio called on the Germans to send two more divisions to Italy, a sixth and a seventh. Italy began to take on the look of an occupied nation.

One of those unpredictable mistrals, the bane of voyagers on the

---

[59] The story of the man who never was is from Ewen Montagu, *The Man Who Never Was* (Philadelphia, 1954).

Mediterranean Sea, blew up shortly after dawn on the ninth of July, changing the usually placid sea into a gyrating mass topped with foam which angrily battered some three thousand Allied ships ranging from big battle wagons to landing craft. Looking like open shoeboxes, the new landing craft, which had only recently come off production lines, plunged, heaved, rolled. Everything and everybody in them were drenched with spray.

There were big LST's (Landing Ship, Tank) and smaller LCT's (Landing Craft, Tank), plus LCI's (Landing Craft, Infantry); all had slanting bows that could be lowered to provide a runway onto a hostile beach. Alongside some of the LST's or wallowing in their wakes were steel ponton causeways, designed to bridge the water gap between shifting false beaches and the true beach. On the davits of the attack transports, 36-foot plywood LCVP's (Landing Craft, Vehicle and Personnel) tore at their hangings.

Inside the poorly ventilated guts of the transports, soldiers miserable with their lot braced themselves against bulkheads and tried not to vomit. Many wondered why their commanders did not call the whole thing off. How could they hope to lower the landing craft? How could they find the right beaches? How could they even find Sicily in such a gale?

Aboard one of the ships, Ernie Pyle, the GI's Boswell, bemoaned his fate and the fate of those around him. Never in his life, he wrote later, had he been so depressed.[60]

The man who had to make the decision to continue, General Eisenhower, had gone to Malta to await first reports of the invasion. Although he seriously considered delay, meteorological experts predicted that the storm soon would abate. Rubbing seven coins together for luck, Eisenhower made up his mind. The decision was to go.

---

[60] *Brave Men* (New York, 1944), p. 20.

Chapter Ten – The Invasion of Sicily

The invasion began in the early minutes of July 10 with an airborne assault. A brigade of British glider troops set out to seize a vital bridge behind the British invasion beaches, while thirty-five hundred paratroopers of America's new and first airborne division, the 82d, tried to take high ground behind the beaches near Gela. An airborne attack on such a scale was unprecedented for the Allies. It was also, to all early appearances, a dismal failure.[61]

The wind and inexperienced pilots did it. Of 144 gliders, only 54 landed in Sicily; most of the rest in the turbulent sea. Something less than a hundred British airborne troops made their way toward the critical bridge, while the American paratroopers scattered all over southeastern Sicily. Only one battalion came to earth anywhere near intact, and it was twenty-five miles from the designated drop zone.

The greatest achievement of the airborne attack appeared at first to be to alert the Axis defenders. Soon after midnight the island's commander, Generale d'Armata Alfredo Guzzoni, issued a proclamation exhorting soldiers and civilians alike to repel the invaders. Yet that took a long time to get down to the lonely outposts by the sea, where Italian sentries, tired from long nights on the alert, rested, secure in the belief that nobody would try to come ashore in such a storm.

Even those who might have sounded the alarm did little to spread it. As

---

[61] The definitive account of the Italian surrender and the Sicilian campaign is Smyth and Garland, *Sicily and the Surrender of Italy*. I have used also: Morison, *Sicily — Salerno — Anzio*; Craven and Cate, eds., *Europe — TORCH to POINTBLANK*; and Churchill, *Closing the Ring*. Three other memoirs are important for this and subsequent chapters: George S. Patton, Jr., *War as I Knew It* (Boston, 1947); Matthew B. Ridgway, *Soldier: The Memoirs of Matthew B. Ridgway* (New York, 1956); and James M. Gavin, *Airborne Warfare* (Washington, 1947).

the U.S. flagship *Biscayne* anchored two and one-half miles off the coast more than an hour before curtain time, first one Italian searchlight, then five focused on her. For a full twenty minutes it was light enough on deck to read a book. Then the lights went out; not a sound had emerged from Italian guns. The explanation was that Italian guns lacked the range to take the *Biscay ne* under fire. Elsewhere, Germans manning radar search stations refused to believe the enormous blips that showed up on their screens. Only after daylight made it clear they were no fools did they report their sensings.

Eschewing a preliminary naval bombardment in the hope of maintaining surprise, the seaborne invaders began to land at 2:45 on the morning of July 10. Although the worst of the storm had passed, heavy swells and surf persisted.

On the more sheltered southeast coast the British had little trouble getting ashore. Italian coastal defense units mustered only feeble resistance, and big naval guns quickly silenced those coastal batteries and artillery pieces that dared open fire. By the end of the first day the British (including a division of Canadians) held thirty-five miles of the southeastern coast of Sicily, including the port of Syracuse.

American landings on the southwestern coast went less smoothly. Many ships were late, thrown off schedule and in some cases out of formation by the gale. Fully exposed to a diminishing yet still powerful west wind, some had trouble launching the LCVP's to take the assault waves of infantrymen to the beaches. One davit gave way, dumping a boatload of men into the water. Nine drowned. Thrown off course in the darkness by the heavy sea, several landing craft crashed broadside against rocks at the foot of a precipitous promontory. Weighted by equipment and pounded against submerged rocks, twenty-seven men drowned.

Determined fire from the Italian defenders would have made matters infinitely worse. As it was, whenever a coastal searchlight focused on the incoming craft, a gun from some warship quickly scored a hit. Only after most of the first wave of troops had touched down did machine-gunners and artillerymen in coastal fortifications open fire. The second wave caught most of the venom, but much of the fire was inaccurate in the darkness, and those troops already ashore were generally able to silence it quickly. A war correspondent landing with the first wave answered a ringing telephone in an abandoned Italian command post and in faultless Italian assured a worried general that he should go back to bed, that all was quiet at the beaches.

By the time the sun of July 10 was out in force, infantrymen of three divisions—1st, 3d, and 45th—were pushing forward into another brown land. Except on the 1st Division's beaches around Gela, where enemy shelling was a hazard all day, supporting artillery was coming ashore with few problems, mainly because of the trucks with amphibian skirts, the DUKW's. Supplies, too, swiftly accumulated. The big difficulty was getting tanks ashore, again particularly on the 1st Division's beaches. There were too many false beaches for tanks to land directly from landing craft, and but one of the ponton causeways so laboriously towed from North Africa arrived with the 1st Division.

The lack of tanks worried commander and common soldier alike. To fight tanks without tanks, every foot soldier knew, was like pitting a man empty-handed against a lion.

Dawn was tinting the sea when the first Axis aircraft roared over the assault beaches. A Stuka dive bomber caught the destroyer *Maddox* with a bomb on her stern, sending her down within minutes with most of her crew. Moments later another German plane got a mine sweeper.

Less apparent than those first Axis counterblows, but in the long run more meaningful, were the efforts of Axis commanders to muster a counterattack to throw the invaders into the sea. For such a task General Guzzoni and his German "liaison officer," Generalleutnant Fridolin von Senger und Etterlin, lacked considerable resources and were slow to discern the pattern of the Allied assault.

Guzzoni had in Sicily six Italian coastal divisions (made up primarily of Sicilian reservists), four regular Italian divisions, and two excellent German divisions—the *15th Panzer Grenadier* (mechanized) *Division* and the *Hermann Goering Panzer Division*—all together over 300,000 men. In anticipation of several widespread landings, Guzzoni had sent the panzer grenadiers to the western part of the island. Although he ordered them back well before dawn on the tenth, it was doubtful whether they would be able to return before the invaders were solidly established ashore.

The critical time for counterattack against a seaborne invasion, Axis commanders knew, was within hours after the first troops debarked, before the invaders could organize on high ground and link their landings into a single beachhead. According to plan, an Italian division and a German armored task force were to counterattack swiftly against landings on the southeast coast, while another Italian division and the *Hermann Goering* tanks hit landings on the southwest coast.

Yet that was reckoning without the damage Allied pre-assault bombing and scattered but determined paratroopers could do to telephone lines, plus that which Allied planes and naval guns could inflict once daylight exposed Axis troops moving to the attack. A counterattack against the British never got started on the first day. The Italian division and the German tanks were able to strike against the Americans; but because of the lack of communications and the weight of Allied fire, they hit separately, without the power a coordinated assault might have achieved.

That was fortunate for the Americans, particularly since the Axis columns struck the most impoverished of the invading forces, the 1st Division at Gela. The Italians came first, aiming for the high ground near Gela which had been the objective of the American paratroopers. Because of the scattered drop, no paratroopers had gained that objective; but a small band had gathered at an isolated villa that the Italian infantry and obsolete light tanks had to pass to reach the high ground. They were so delayed by this band that a reinforced battalion of the 1st Division got to the high ground first. With the help of accurate naval shelling, the battalion turned back the main Italian force. Although some of the light tanks penetrated into Gela, Rangers and combat engineers played such a determined game of hide-and-seek among the drab buildings, fighting the tanks with grenades and bazookas, that the surviving tanks finally fled.

In early afternoon a more serious threat developed with arrival of the *Hermann Goering Panzer Division.* In two columns the Germans attacked, employing just over 100 tanks, 17 of them the new Mark VI Tigers. Since Axis shelling was still slowing unloadings on the 1st Division's beaches, the American defenders had few anti-tank guns, precious little artillery, and no tanks, with scant hope of getting any soon. In mid-morni ng a German bomb had hit an LST that was disgorging its vital cargo onto the lone ponton causeway, and blew it up and the causeway with it.

The first German thrust aimed at the same infantrymen on the high ground who had borne the brunt of the Italian strike. Halting the German infantry with small arms and artillery fire, the defenders called for naval gunfire against the tanks. As 5-inch and 6-inch shells cascaded in from the sea, the tanks slowed, sputtered, and finally stopped.

A second German column, including the big Tigers, struck an adjacent battalion of the 45th Division. The defenders at that spot lacked the coordination with the ships that the 1st Division had achieved at Gela. The German tanks quickly broke through, capturing the infantry commander and many of his men and sending the others scurrying back to the beaches.

All might have been lost had not another battalion of the 45th Division rushed into the breach. The fire of those men drove off the German infantry, sending them reeling back in panic. Without infantry support, the tanks, too, retired.

As night approached, the crisis had been temporarily averted, but none doubted that Italians and Germans both would be back. On General Patton's order, the floating reserve, which included the bulk of the 2d Armored Division, began to disembark; but the problem of putting tanks ashore was still formidable. Only ten Shermans made it during the night, and they soon bogged helplessly in the soft sand of the beaches.

Daylight had barely come the second morning, July 11, before the Germans and Italians returned, this time together. Although the infantry near Gela and the Rangers and the engineers in the town took care of the Italians with the help of naval gunfire, the German tanks rumbled inexorably toward the beaches east of Gela. The great plain around the town became an inferno of exploding shells, smoke, fire, death. Reaching the coastal highway just over a mile from the sea, the tanks raked supply dumps and landing craft with cruel fire. Some jubilant German Staff officer at headquarters of the panzer division reported that the Americans had given the order to re-embark.

The report was premature.

Coming ashore in DUKW's at the height of the crisis, big guns of a field artillery battalion moved straight into firing positions along the edge of the sand dunes and opened direct fire on the German tanks. A regimental cannon company also raced with its snub-nosed 105-mm. howitzers to the dunes; and four of the ten Shermans which earlier had gotten ashore only to bog in the sand, at last churned free. Infantrymen, engineer shore parties, everybody hastened to build a line for a last-ditch stand among the dunes.

They had no need for it. The artillery and the four tanks did the job.

The German thrust ground to a halt at the coastal highway. Milling in confusion, the Mark VI Tigers began to fall back. As they turned, naval guns that had been unable to participate in the fight while the combatants were closely locked, added a special fury to the scene.

Even as this main thrust withered so close to victory, the German commander refused to admit defeat. He desperately summoned another column forward, but he did not know that that force had come under attack from the rear by about three hundred American paratroopers, who had banded together following their abortive drop and had followed the age-old maxim of marching to the sound of the cannon. Joined by infantrymen of the 45th Division and by tanks that had come ashore over that divisions beaches, the reinforced paratroopers, like angry hornets, so pestered the second German column that all hope of reviving the dying counterattack at Gela soon passed.

As the fighting lapsed into the inevitable calm that follows violent battle, twenty German tanks lay burning on the Gela plain. In the two-day fight the *Hermann Goering Panzer Division* had lost half its committed armor—fifty-five tanks, ten of them the awe-inspiring Tigers.

One who watched the battle that day from a hill a few miles inland was the senior German officer in Sicily—a bony, uninspiring figure whose appearance belied his imposing name, General von Senger und Etterlin. As he saw the panzers crumble before the American fire and looked beyond them to the spectacle of hundreds of ships lining the horizon, multitudes of landing craft plying back and forth from ship to beach, Senger acknowledged to himself that Sicily was lost. The anticipated arrival the next day of the panzer grenadier division from western Sicily would be too late to do more than assist the delaying action that would precede the inevitable end.

Conspicuously missing during the two days of crisis was direct support from American planes. Although they continued their campaigns against Axis airfields and engaged targets of opportunity over the entire island—and in the process fired on many Axis tanks and troops—no planes were available on call from the hard-pressed men on the ground and in the ships. Under the procedure specified by the airmen, all requests for direct support had to be funneled through headquarters in North Africa or Malta, both for approval and then for dispatch of planes, by which time the need or the crisis almost always had passed. Although the planes in the long run made major contributions to victory in Sicily by their strategic and armed reconnaissance programs, that was scant consolation to sailors beleaguered by Axis planes or to riflemen begging for help as Axis tanks and infantry poured toward them.

The paratroopers who had landed in advance of the seaborne invasion had been scheduled for airborne reinforcement the next night, but in view of the confusion created by the first Axis counterattacks, their commanders had called it off. On June 11, needing help from any quarter, General Patton ordered the reinforcement that night.

Unknowingly Patton invited tragedy. Although the word went to ships off the coast and to anti-aircraft units ashore that slow, low-flying C-47 transport planes carrying paratroopers strapped in their aluminum bucket seats would be arriving close to midnight, that did little to forestall the catastrophe that followed.

After the two-day crisis in the beachhead, the troops ashore could hardly have been other than jumpy. And the sailors supporting them could have been no less nervous, for through the day of the eleventh they endured one Axis air attack after another. In mid-afternoon a bomb had struck the Liberty ship *Robert Rowan*, turning her load of ammunition into spectacular fireworks. Sinking in shallow water, the *Robert Rowan* for long hours belched smoke into the sky, a beacon for the Axis planes that followed.

Just two hours before midnight the *Luftwaffe* staged a massive strike. Since the ships weighed anchor and dispersed, the damage was slight, but an hour's mêlée did nothing to salve the nerves of anti-aircraft gunners aboard the vessels.

Into the uneasy calm following that last raid flew the planes carrying the two thousand paratroopers. The first wave made it without incident, the paratroopers dropping as scheduled; but as the second flight approached, somewhere a lone machine gun opened fire. That signal set off almost every anti-aircraft gun on and off the shore.

"Planes dropped out of formation and crashed into the sea," a surviving paratrooper recalled later. "Others, like clumsy whales, wheeled and attempted to get beyond the flak, which rose in fountains of fire, lighting the stricken faces of men as they stared through the windows."[62]

---

[62] Smyth and Garland, *Sicily and the Surrender of Italy*, p. 180, quoting Captain Adam A. Komosa.

Some men died in the planes. Others drowned in the sea. Troops on the ground cut down others as they floated helplessly in their harness. Nervous sentries killed still others after they had come to earth.

Of 144 planes that had departed Tunisia, 23 never returned, and 37 were severely damaged. A total of 81 men died; 16 were missing and presumed dead; and 132 were wounded.

It was hard to fix the blame. Many anti-aircraft gunners on land and sea had failed to get the word that American planes were due. Others, already excited by the recent Axis raid, got caught up in the contagion of the firing. The important tiling from the standpoint of Allied victory was that it not happen again.

Yet it did happen again.

Two nights later British paratroopers winged toward Sicily to seize a bridge over a river and speed a British attack on the port of Catania. Scarcely had the transport planes passed Malta when Allied ships off the Sicilian coast began to raise a heavy curtain of anti-aircraft fire. The fire cut down two transports and forced nine others to turn back after pilots were wounded or planes badly damaged.

Those that made it through the fire of their own forces encountered an even more deadly barrage from alerted enemy guns. Ten more planes turned back; thirty-seven went down in flames or crashed into the sea. Only eighty-seven made it through, and those scattered their human cargo up and down the coastal strip like windblown confetti. Only about two hundred men landed near the bridge, there to discover that they had dropped almost on top of a battalion of German parachutists that had dropped only a few hours earlier. Incredibly, this little band managed to seize the bridge and either hold it or keep it under controlling fire until British ground troops arrived.

By nightfall of the second day, in spite of the crisis at Gela and the disasters in the air, the Allies clearly had staged a successful invasion, whose amphibious phase would not be exceeded in size by even the cross-Channel attack to come. Although Hitler early decided to fly in a German parachute division and later to commit another panzer grenadier division and a German corps headquarters, those were insufficient to alter the fact, diagnosed early by General von Senger und Etterlin and later concurred in by Kesselring, that the Axis had no hope in Sicily but to delay the Allied conquest as long as possible.

By building a strong line along the foothills of massive Mount Etna, the Germans and their faltering Italian allies nevertheless proved strong enough to thwart a quick British drive up the east coast on Messina. Looking for a way to break the impasse, General Montgomery persuaded General Alexander to allow the British Eighth Army to launch a second thrust on Messina around the other side of Mount Etna.

This plan seemed logical to Alexander, who believed the inexperienced American divisions could best be nursed along with limited assignments that gradually would build their morale. It was sharply disappointing to an ambitious Patton and his subordinates, who had long feared just such a passive role. When Alexander granted authority for limited American reconnaissance moves to the west, Patton determined to expand the permission into something big. Denied participation in the drive for the main objective, Patton made up his mind to take a consolation prize, the islands largest city near the western tip, the port of Palermo. A swift drive to Palermo, he reasoned, would bring some glory to American arms and provide a start toward achieving his personal ambition of exceeding the reputation of Erwin Rommel as a master of armor.

"Palermo," one of Patton's division commanders noted, "drew Patton like a lodestar."

Without asking General Alexander's approval, Patton directed General Bradley to send part of his II Corps north to cut the island in two. That accomplished, Patton was determined to unleash his main strength toward Palermo.

Hardly had Patton devised the stratagem when General Alexander issued a new directive that foiled it, specifically restraining further American advance until the British could reach the north coast and swing east toward Messina. To Alexander, that was but a precaution in case the Americans got too involved in their own operations to protect the British flank adequately. To a sensitive Patton and to some other top American commanders, it was a direct affront, an attempt to deny them even the consolation prize.

This time Patton was too incensed to accept the order without protest. On July 17 he flew to Tunisia to argue his case before the overall ground commander. So forceful was he that Alexander deemed he had no choice but to acquiesce, for even if he disapproved, Patton probably still would head for Palermo.

No sooner had Patton returned to his command and issued his orders than a new directive arrived from Alexander. He had reconsidered. Although he still granted approval for a drive on Palermo, Patton was to launch it only after reaching the north coast in such strength that the British flank would be unquestionably safe.

The Seventh Army's Chief of Staff, Brigadier General Hobart R. Gay, who was dedicated to his commander and to his concept of operations, saw the message first. Patton never got a look at it. Gay himself made sure of that.

On July 19 a corps-sized force headed by Major General Geoffrey Keyes began the drive for Palermo. From the first the attack was little more than a road march. In the lead, men of the 82d Airborne Division gained twenty-five miles the first day, twenty the second. They found no Germans, only Italians who usually required but a few rounds of small arms or artillery fire to induce them to throw hands high in surrender. On the twenty-first Keyes committed the 2d Armored Division. The next day, as the tanks approached Palermo, the Italians fell over themselves surrendering the city. By nightfall on the twenty-third all of the western end of Sicily was under American control.

Disregarding the emptiness of the victory—what glory in racing through scattered, demoralized Italian units?—newspapers in the United States trumpeted the accomplishment. More than sixty miles in four days while the British got nowhere. The nation had a new hero, Georgie Patton, "Old Blood and Guts." Patton loved it. The drive, he said, was "a classic example of the use of tanks."[63]

In Rome, two days before Palermo fell, Benito Mussolini returned from northern Italy, where he had conferred with Hitler. Mussolini had gone determined to stand up to the *Fuehrer*, to find a way out of the war. He had come back revealed as a spineless wretch, who had abjectly acquiesced in every German demand. That same day American planes for the first time bombed Rome.

Under the impact of the two events Victor Emmanuel made up his mind to act. The opportunity came on July 24 when dissidents in the Fascist Grand Council passed a resolution calling upon the King to resume

---

[63] Harry H. Semmes, *Portrait of Patton* (New York, 1955), p. 163.

command of the armed forces. This vote, the King told Mussolini coldly, required Mussolini's resignation, not only as head of the armed forces but as head of the government.

As Mussolini left the palace, an officer of the *carabinieri* escorted him to a waiting ambulance, which whisked him away. Mussolini was under arrest.

The news turned the streets of Rome into a carnival. People danced, embraced, tore down Fascist symbols, confident that the house of Savoy would achieve immediate peace.

They reckoned without the strain of indecision that ran deep in the characters of both their king and the aging soldier he chose to replace Mussolini. They reckoned, too, without the Germans.

The political chicanery in Rome had little repercussion on the fighting in Sicily. In the first rush of anger over Mussolini's dismissal, Hitler raged that all German troops would have to evacuate Sicily immediately and fall back on the mountain passes in northern Italy; but second thoughts, coupled with one assurance after another that the Italians would continue to fight, brought a return to normality. The only change among Axis forces on the island was a shift from Italian to German command, but that was going on over General Guzzoni's objections even before Mussolini's fall.

On the Allied side, General Alexander decided to reward rather than censure George Patton for his insubordination. By July 23, the day after the capture of Palermo, Alexander had concluded that Montgomery's Eighth Army lacked sufficient strength to advance on Messina around both sides of Mount Etna; indeed, Montgomery had yet to break into Catania, the gateway to the east coast road (he made it only on August 5). To Patton and his Seventh Army, Alexander assigned two roads to Messina—one along the northern base of Mount Etna, one along the narrow northern coastal shelf.

Patton was ecstatic. Messina was no longer strictly a British objective. Having taken the consolation prize, he also had a chance at the grand prize.

Patton set about the task of beating the British to Messina with a vengeance, sanctioning no delays, no equivocations, no arguments with his plans. He was seemingly everywhere at once, exhorting his commanders, threatening, cajoling, roaring up and down dusty Sicilian roads in a jeep with three stars of rank prominently displayed, pistols with flashy ivory-encrusted handles strapped at either side (pearl-handled, the press erroneously reported). His was a conscious effort to create an image that would instill in the soldiers under him courage, speed, audacity.

Many detested him for it. From the viewpoint of the individual soldier, the drive for Messina achieved less momentum from Patton's histrionics than from the alleged remarks of a commentator of the British Broadcasting Company. The spokesman, word had it, contrasted heavy fighting on the British front with a soft life in the American sector—soldiers eating figs and grapes, swimming in the sea, gamboling among the olive orchards and the lemon trees. The story angered men who were drenched with the sweat of a Sicilian summer (100 to 110 degrees before noon), perpetually thirsty, dog-tired from clambering up one cliff-like mountainside after another, sick to the teeth of dust, death, garlic smells and sewage smells and animal smells, the sunbaked land. As the story spread, the men, like their commander, became wholly determined to beat the British into Messina.

The American soldier in Sicily was different from the man who had fought at the Kasserine Pass. He had met the enemy and knew he could beat him. Like his adversaries, he was impressed with the sophisticated fighting equipment, machines, and landing craft his people had provided him in a short span of months. Gone was the ungainly Grant tank; in its place, the sleek Sherman with 360-degree power-operated traverse for a turret-mounted 75-mm. gun. The semiautomatic M-1 Garand rifle was a trusted friend. While he still wore hot, uncomfortable leggings and envied the dapper boots of the paratroopers (not to mention the extra pay), he had many of the amenities that mattered: free cigarettes, mail from home, a soldier newspaper, *The Stars & Stripes*, a magazine called *Yank*, hot food when kitchen crews could get it to him, at other times monotonous but ample C-rations and K-rations. No liquor, lest the ladies' clubs back home be scandalized, but Sicilian *vino* on those few occasions when he was off the fighting line.

There might be snafus (sanitized, that meant "situation normal, all fouled up"), as when the anti-aircraft gunners had gone after the transport planes or when American fighter-bombers twice mistakenly strafed columns of the 2d Armored Division; but in general he had ample evidence of the efficiency of his army. His artillery, he was aware, could give as good or better than the enemy's (frail little spotter aircraft called "grasshoppers" gave a new dimension to artillery observation). He knew that if wounded he would get good care (blood plasma and the anti-infection drugs, sulfanilamide and penicillin, increased his chances to survive). He was aware, too, that specialists backed him up: engineers, stevedores, launderers, bakers, signalmen, military police, chaplains—the essentials of civilian life dressed in olive drab and transported half across the world.

He had evidence, too—as he had not in the early days in Tunisia—that the commanders who held his destiny in their hands knew what they were doing. Patton he might dislike, but he did not doubt him. Bradley of the high-pitched voice was obviously competent in a calm, reassuring way. Division commanders, too, seemed to know their business: a university dean (Louisiana State) turned soldier, Troy Middleton of the 45th; steady Manton Eddy of the 9th; dashing Terry de la Mesa Allen of the 1st; imperturbable Lucian Truscott of the 3d; one of the pioneers of armor, Hugh Gaffey of the 2d Armored; and handsome Matthew Ridgway of the 82d Airborne.

They used divisions as entities, not in small parcels scattered and intermingled with other units. The infantry divisions had the support of attached separate tank and tank destroyer battalions, and the concept of the regimental combat team composed of an infantry regiment supported always by the same 105-mm. howitzer battalion and increments of division support troops, was firmly proven. A new division, the 45th, made up originally of National Guardsmen from the southwestern states, had demonstrated that the new units were better trained, more nearly ready for the crucible of combat.

He hated Sicily, this soldier—the hot, dry brownness; the malaria; the dysentery; the tragic people who applauded him in one voice, then begged of him in their plaintive tongue, "*Mangiare, caramelli, sigaretto.*" He hated the dust and wished to hell it was mud, in the same way he later would hate the mud and wish to hell it was dust.

He wished to hell he was someplace else.

On the two roads to Messina—one mountainous, one clinging to cliffs by the sea—the Germans stood in the way with two panzer grenadier divisions. Although on August 8, Field Marshal Kesselring gave the order for the Axis troops to evacuate Sicily, they were to do it in planned stages; nowhere was the fight to be lessened until they were forced to retire to the next prepared line.

Unlike Montgomery, who persisted with unimaginative frontal assaults, Patton launched a series of end runs, small amphibious sorties to get behind the German line either to trap Germans dependent for withdrawal on the road along the coastal shelf or to hasten their departure. Three times Patton launched the runs. The idea was good enough to contribute to a Patton legend, but the size of the forces and the depths of the penetrations were too minor to achieve dramatic results.

To the delight of the infantry, American aircraft at last joined the close-in war. Having exhausted strategic targets, including Axis planes, the fighter-bombers roamed almost at will in the skies over Sicily. There was an excitement, a derring-do, the pilots discovered, in direct support of the men on the ground.

Although the massive collection of ships that had put the troops ashore had dispersed to other tasks, enough remained at Palermo to provide support from the sea whenever Patton needed it. As proof of the efficacy of Allied air attacks against Axis planes, seldom after the first two days had German aircraft attacked Allied shipping.

By the end of the second week of August, Germans and Italians had pulled back well behind the crest of Mount Etna to a line only twenty miles from Messina, while ferries plied across the narrow strait to the mainland with men and equipment already withdrawn from the line. Despite a preponderance of air and sea power, the Allies did little to interfere with the evacuation. Naval commanders did not care to pit their vessels in the narrow waters against Italian coastal batteries. When Allied air commanders based their attacks on the theory that the ferries would operate only at night, Axis commanders responded by resorting to daylight operations. By the time Allied commanders appreciated the extent of the change, it was too late.

In the land war General Montgomery finally elected to speed the British advance on Messina by an end run like the runs staged by Patton. Before daylight on August 16 about four hundred Tommies with tank support came ashore on the east coast in an effort to trap a portion of the *Hermann Goering Division*. They missed. They hit only the tail of the panzer divisions rear guard, which turned and fought back all day.

That resistance gave the race for Messina to the late-starting American Seventh Army. During the night of the sixteenth a reinforced platoon of the 3d Division pushed deep into the city. Just at daylight the next morning the last Axis troops crossed to the mainland.

Although Messina's civilian dignitaries offered a formal surrender to the 3d Division commander, General Truscott, he had his orders to await the arrival of General Patton. At ten o'clock on the seventeenth Patton joined Truscott on a ridge overlooking the city. "What in hell are you all standing around for?" he roared. Taking his place at the head of a motorcade, he raced downhill into Messina—the grand prize—while enemy artillery registered protest from the other side of the strait.

Blocked first by a German rear guard, then by a demolished bridge, the first British troops reached Messina only after Patton had accepted the formal surrender. Rising above Patton's slight in staging the ceremony without British representation, the senior British officer shook Patton's hand.

"It was a jolly good race," he said. "I congratulate you."[64]

The Allied conquest of Sicily was another stepping stone successfully in place for the seven-league hike to the Continent, and with it came valuable airfields and ports. Some 164,000 Axis troops—only one-fifth of them German—had been killed or captured at a cost to the Allies of just over 22,000 casualties, including 1,030 American naval losses (half of them dead) and 2,237 men of the Seventh Army killed. The campaign also further undermined Germany's already faltering Italian ally.

Faced at the time of Mussolini's fall with the prospect of abandoning Sicily, the Germans nevertheless had held for just over a month, with little help from the Italians, against overwhelmingly superior Allied forces (at peak strength, 217,000 Americans, 250,000 British). Once the landings had succeeded, the Germans, rather than the Allies, had dictated how the campaign was to evolve. They had also escaped with the bulk of their forces—40,000 men, 10,000 vehicles—while the Italians had brought out 70,000 men.

Greater daring and imagination on the part of Allied commanders might have shortened the campaign or even have trapped the foe. One word describes the victory: methodical.

---

[64] Richard Tregaskis, *Invasion Diary* (New York, 1944), p. 89.

Based on the theory that the Italians would fight—actually they were, as many an American G-2 (military intelligence) predicted, "filled with sawdust"—the plan of invasion was conservative and took scant advantage of Allied naval and aerial superiority. Once the troops were ashore, an opportunity for a swift push on Messina still existed, but General Alexander had forfeited it by relying almost entirely on an Eighth Army that lacked the strength for two thrusts. Even at the end greater damage might have been done the enemy had Allied air and naval forces brought more initiative, power, and flexibility to bear on the retreat across the Strait of Messina.

Yet for all the might-have-beens, Sicily was another victory at acceptable cost, and it had helped bring closer to maturity the American soldier, his commanders, and the services that supported him. When compared with North Africa, the seaborne assault was a marvel of amphibious sophistication. Although the outcome of the airborne phase so depressed some leaders that they talked of abandoning the concept, it impressed others (as it did the Germans) and impelled them to greater effort to make it succeed. For all the early preoccupation with strategic attack, the fledgling American air arm had obtained in the end such experience in the art of close support of ground troops that air commanders would eventually come to accept its importance. More than anything else, Sicily had proved that the supplies for an invasion could effectively be brought in over the beaches. (God bless the DUKW's and the new landing craft!)

From the campaign had emerged two American field commanders of impressive stature. One was Omar Bradley, so self-effacing that the general public had yet to discover his true worth, but his military superiors and colleagues knew it. The other was George Patton, a man so dedicated to the job of soldiering that in his quest for victory and personal glory (the two in apparently equal proportions) he overlooked the fact that some methods are inimical to the American way.

Patton had performed well in Sicily, as he had briefly in North Africa; he was a thoroughly capable field commander, but hardly brilliant. As the sweep to Palermo had been empty, his only real accomplishment exceeding that of a man he looked on as personal rival—Montgomery—was to get to Messina first, and that was only by a matter of hours, despite the end runs.

Yet Patton had impressed his superiors and, of equal importance, many people back home who were in search of a man astride a white horse. He had woven the first threads of a legend; and as Patton, the student of history, knew, many a military man has graduated to glory on the basis of less.

Yet in pursuit of a legend in Sicily, Patton had come close to destroying himself.

Visiting a field hospital just over a fortnight before the campaign ended, Patton approached a patient whose preliminary diagnosis indicated "psychoneuroses anxiety state—moderate severe." He asked the soldier, a private, what was troubling him.

"I guess I can't take it," the man replied.

Patton flew into a rage, cursed the soldier, slapped him across the face with his gloves, grabbed him, and threw him out of the tent.

Slightly more than a week later, visiting another hospital, Patton came upon another soldier whose condition attracted his attention. The man lay huddled, shivering, on his cot. Again Patton asked the trouble.

"It's my nerves," the man replied.

"What did you say?" Patton roared.

"It's my nerves," the man repeated. "I can hear the shells come over, but I can't hear them burst."

"Your nerves, hell, you are just a goddamned coward, you yellow son of a bitch!" Patton raged. "You're a disgrace to the Army and you're going right back to the front to fight, although that's too good for you. You ought to be lined up against a wall and shot. In fact, I ought to shoot you myself right now, goddamn you!"

Patton reached for one of his pistols and waved it in the soldier's face. As the man quivered on his cot, Patton struck him sharply across the face with his free hand. He insisted to the commander of the hospital that he get the soldier out of the tent. "I won't have these other brave boys seeing such a bastard babied."

As Patton turned to leave, he noted that the soldier was openly crying. Rushing back to him, he struck him again, this time with such force that he knocked off the man's helmet liner, sending it crashing to the floor of the tent. The commander of the hospital put himself between Patton and the man. Patton stormed out.[65]

News of the incident and of the one that preceded it swept the island. One war correspondent said he believed there were fifty thousand men

---

[65] The account of the slapping incidents and the direct quotations are from Smyth and Garland, *Sicily and the Surrender of Italy*, pp. 426-31.

in the Seventh Army who would shoot their commander if they had the chance.

When word of the incidents reached General Eisenhower, he sent a personal letter to Patton, offering him an opportunity to deny the allegations, but stating that if they were true, they raised serious doubts of Patton's future usefulness as a commander. In a notably cruel manner Patton had violated an unwritten but strict law that an American officer lays no hand on an enlisted man.

Chastened, Patton begged forgiveness, apologized to the two soldiers and to the medics who had witnessed the outbursts, and addressed the men of every division in the Seventh Army to express his regrets (though many who heard the speeches deemed them less apology than justification). Considering Patton too valuable, his remorse sincere, Eisenhower closed the book on the incidents.

There the matter might have stood (war correspondents—knowing whence all blessings flowed—acceded to Eisenhower's request to hush it up) had not a keyhole columnist new to the theater reported it four months later. In the furor that ensued Eisenhower stuck to his decision, but to General Marshall he reported: "In no event will I ever advance Patton beyond army command."

Patton, like Montgomery, had come along at that opportune moment in the war when the people back home—and to a lesser extent, the troops in the field—demanded a hero. Both Patton and Montgomery might at one time or another overplay their hands, but so anxious were many on the Allied side to find a hero, that all would in the end be forgiven or explained away.

Chapter Eleven – The Surrender of Italy

The Allies were so surprised by Mussolini's ouster that they were slow to capitalize on Italy's desire to get out of the war. Although General Eisenhower promptly proposed a radio broadcast offering peace under honorable conditions, in exchange for which the Italians would rid their country of the Germans and grant the Allies unrestricted use of Italian territory, Roosevelt and Churchill vetoed the idea. They were too wary of the odium of another "Darlan Deal."[66]

"We should let the Italians…stew in their own juice for a bit," Churchill told the House of Commons on the twenty-seventh, two days after Mussolini's fall, until they were amenable to unconditional surrender. In a public address the next day Roosevelt declared, "We will have no truck with Fascism in any way, shape, or manner." Having delivered themselves of those banalities, the two heads of state agreed three days later to a broadcast asking Italians surrender on much the same reasonable terms Eisenhower had proposed six days earlier.

To replace Mussolini as head of the Italian government, King Victor Emmanuel had chosen aging Marshal Pietro Badoglio, a shrunken little man almost as diminutive as the King himself; as chief of the *Comando Supremo*, he had led Italy's rape of Ethiopia. In keeping with the King's wishes, Badoglio intended to avoid conflict with the Germans by ending the war jointly with them. If that proved impossible, he hoped at least to terminate the alliance and Italian participation in the war with German consent.

---

[66] Dr. Smyth's excellent account in Smyth and Garland, *Sicily and the Surrender of Italy*, was the primary source for this chapter. The texts of both the "short" and "long" terms are included in that volume as appendices. All direct quotations are from Smyth and Garland with one exception, noted below.

Hitler's first febrile impulse upon the ouster of his friend was to seize Rome, kidnap the King and the government, and restore Mussolini, but his military commanders persuaded him to wait. To move precipitately, they insisted, was to invite the Allies to enter Italy; better first to infiltrate the country with substantial German strength and so be prepared to take over if the Italians gave signs of defecting.

Even as Eisenhower's headquarters was broadcasting the delayed invitation to the Italians to surrender, Hitler was ordering the first of several additional divisions to Italy, the vanguard of an entire army group under Field Marshal Rommel. Once the army group was in place in the industrial north, Kesselring was to withdraw German troops from Sicily and southern Italy, while two divisions already positioned near Rome seized the capital and the government. Hitler personally chose an SS officer, Captain Otto Skorzeny, to find and liberate Mussolini.

Ever wary of allowing more German troops into Italy, the Italians resisted by using the subterfuge that railroads were too congested to accommodate more German traffic. As a precaution General Ambrosio ordered Italian divisions to Rome to guard against any German attempt at a *coup d'état*, and instructed commanders on the frontiers to place demolition charges along rail lines. If the Germans insisted on bringing in additional divisions, the Italians were to fight.

Although the stage was set for a direct confrontation, Marshal Badoglio lacked the nerve to bring it off. Hiding behind the argument that he needed time to enroll the Germans in a joint effort to end the war, he approved part of an infantry division crossing the northern frontier by road—a gesture aimed at showing Italian good faith.

That was all Hitler required. Having gained consent for a slight concession, he went on to ravish his victim. Once the infantrymen had entered the country, they spread out along the railroad to assure passage of other German units. The Germans insisted that they had to reinforce Italy's defenses lest the Allies mount an invasion to capitalize on the change of government. By mid-August they had eleven divisions in Italy, including four panzer divisions, plus another in Sardinia and the four that were withdrawing from Sicily—a total of sixteen.

Through it all the wizened, aging marshal in whose uncertain hands the King had entrusted the government continued to insist on his loyalty to the Axis. "This," declared Hitler at one point, "is the biggest impudence in history. Does the man imagine that I will believe him?"

Yet the man was genuinely serious until the Germans themselves foiled him. They did it by denying him a top-level conference with Hitler at which he intended to press his ideas for jointly ending the war. They sealed it by sending so many German troops into Italy that Badoglio's government became a virtual prisoner of its partner in the alliance.

The Italians made their first effort to contact the Allies at the end of July through American and British envoys to the Vatican, but their communications were not secure enough to risk a highly secret transmission. A few days later representatives left to contact British diplomats at Lisbon and Tangier, but their approach had little to do with surrender. What the Italians wanted was Allied help, possibly an invasion of the Balkans to draw off German strength and enable them either to break with the Germans or turn against them. Although they wanted to change sides, they would have to be rescued first.

That Allied armies were to go into Italy after conquering Sicily had been fairly well determined once it became clear that the Axis would make no prolonged fight for Sicily: that was the essence of the agreement reached in Eisenhower's villa in Algiers six weeks before the invasion. Mussolini's downfall and the likelihood of Italian surrender served merely to confirm what had already been tacitly accepted. On July 26, the day after Mussolini's arrest, the Combined Chiefs formally authorized General Eisenhower to invade Italy.

As Allied leaders in mid-August assembled for another top-level conference—in the imposing Château Frontenac in Quebec (code name: QUADRANT)—the issue in the Mediterranean had ceased to be where to go. Because of differences on strategy still existing between Churchill and Marshall, the issue had become in what strength they were to go.

To Marshall, the stipulation of the TRIDENT conference that Eisenhower was to use in the Mediterranean only the resources already there, and that seven divisions were to be shifted to the United Kingdom by November 1943, was foolproof insurance that Mediterranean operations were to be subordinate to the cross-Channel attack. It failed to disturb him that the stipulation might permit no more than a holding attack in Italy.

To Churchill, whose secret passion was to go at Germany first by way of the Balkans and Norway, the minimum acceptable objective in Italy was to seize Rome, the capital; and his Chiefs of Staff were convinced that the elimination of Italy from the war was prerequisite to a successful cross-Channel attack. If Eisenhower required additional resources to achieve those ends, he should, in the British view, have them.

Sensing British attitudes in advance of the QUADRANT conference, and seeing in them flagging support for the direct-thrust strategy, the Joint Chiefs and the President formulated a unanimous position for the conference—a unanimity, all had noted with regret, that had been missing at Casablanca and TRIDENT. The essence of American strategy, the Americans told the British in Quebec, was the cross-Channel attack, synchronized with the bombing campaign against Germany. The Mediterranean was to be a subordinate theater employing only those resources already there. For the Mediterranean they would agree to objectives no more ambitious than establishing air bases as far north as Rome, seizing Sardinia and Corsica, and later invading southern France as a diversion for the cross-Channel attack.

The British responded that they agreed in principle, but they saw no point in restrictions that might obviate Mediterranean achievements essential to success of the cross-Channel attack. In the British view, the Allies should aim not only for Rome but also for northern Italy, whence Allied planes could strike Germany without passing through the deadly belt of anti-aircraft guns on the run from the west.

In the end the Americans finally emerged with a written reaffirmation of Allied faith in a cross-Channel attack in the spring of 1944. They also obtained confirmation of the Mediterranean as a subordinate theater and agreement against operations in the Balkans, but they failed to get the categorical restriction on forces for the Mediterranean that they desired.

It was, even Marshall would agree, about all they could have hoped for; but it failed to eliminate the recurring concern that the Mediterranean might draw off resources that, in the American view, could be more profit-ably employed in the main attack. Rome and its environs, the conferees had agreed, was the minimum territorial objective to be gained in Italy, and "unremitting pressure" was to be maintained against German forces that might make a stand farther north.

Yet what if—as appeared unlikely at the moment, of course—the Italians refused to surrender, and the Germans joined them in a deter-mined defense of the peninsula? Or if the Italians surrendered, but the

Germans stayed in Italy? Under those circumstances how much effort and how many men was the Italian capital worth?

QUADRANT failed to provide the answer.

The fact that Churchill was aboard ship en route to Quebec when the first Italian emissaries showed up at Lisbon and Tangier slowed the Allied response, but it hardly would have been swift in any case. The Allies knew, as the Italians did not, that they simply had insufficient resources to invade the Balkans immediately, or even Italy; and in that case, why hurry to reply? Furthermore, Churchill noted, Badoglio seemed determined to doublecross somebody, and the Prime Minister wanted to make sure it was somebody else, not him.

As top officials in Rome awaited response, some of them chafed at the failure of Badoglio and the King to break openly with the Germans. That would lead inevitably to armed conflict but just as inevitably, they believed, to Allied intervention on the Italian side. Others, among them Badoglio, deemed breaking the alliance inconsistent with honor, but they would have welcomed the Germans' making the break. "If the Germans would only attack us," Badoglio moaned, "the situation would have a solution."

Still others, including a protégé of General Ambrosio's in the *Comando Supremo*, Generale di Brigata Giuseppe Castellano, who had led the military dissidents in opposing Mussolini, believed that the Italians themselves should act but only after reaching accord with the Allies for military cooperation. Yet that accord should be expedited. It could best be achieved by a military emissary, Castellano himself.

On August 12, the day before the Allies responded to the first Italian overtures with a terse insistence on unconditional surrender, General Castellano departed in disguise for Madrid, there to pour out to the British ambassador a troubled account of Italy's agony. The Italians were in no position to seek any terms, he said; they asked only that the Allies find some way to enable them to join the fight against the Germans.

The Allies fortunately had at last reached some agreement on conditions for Italian surrender on the basis of what they called "short terms," essentially a military capitulation. They had yet to approve British-proposed "long terms," involving political, economic, and financial provisions. In Quebec they agreed that General Eisenhower should send two Staff officers to communicate the short terms to Castellano and inform him that the long terms would be submitted later. The Allies, the Combined Chiefs specified, were to relax none of their demands in respect to Italy's changing sides, but the Italians could soften the long-range surrender terms in proportion to the scale of assistance they rendered after capitulating under the short terms.

To Lisbon on August 19 to meet Castellano went General Eisenhower's Chief of Staff, tough, brusque Major General Walter Bedell ("Beetle") Smith, and his British Chief of Intelligence, quiet, scholarly Brigadier Kenneth W. D. Strong. He was authorized, Smith said, to communicate terms of a military armistice that would have to be accepted unconditionally. He had no authority to arrange for Italian participation on the Allied side. To avoid further fighting between Allied and Italian troops, General Eisenhower would announce the armistice a few hours before the main Allied landing on the Italian peninsula.

Poor Castellano! He had come to discuss how his government, prisoner of the Germans, might join the Allies in expelling the Germans from his country. He learned instead that the government had to surrender in advance, that to avoid a fight with Italian troops the surrender would be announced before the Allied landings, that he would not be told when or where the landings were to be. That was tantamount to giving the Germans advance notice to move against the capital, to seize the fleet, to occupy key points all over the country, to wreak brutal revenge on their erstwhile ally.

If Castellano's government accepted the armistice, Smith continued, word was to be conveyed by a seemingly innocuous radio message about Italian prisoners of war, whereupon Castellano himself was to fly to Sicily on August 31 for final negotiations. If the Allies had received no message by the thirtieth, they would assume that the Italians had rejected the terms.

The situation, Castellano reflected, was far different from that imagined in Rome. There they believed Italy was still in a position to bargain.

In Italy relations between Germans and Italians were becoming increasingly acrimonious. At a conference of senior commanders the Germans deployed a detachment of SS troops as an obvious guard against Italian treachery. "From the outset," Kesselring later noted, "a palpable tension brooded over the proceedings."[67] When Italian officers insisted on returning

---

[67] Albert Kesselring, A *Soldier's Record* (New York, 1954), p. 209.

Italian divisions from France to defend their homeland, a German asked sarcastically whence they expected attack—from the sea or from Germany?

The brusque, bitter German attitude prompted several ranking Italian officers, who knew nothing of Castellano's mission, to urge the government to send an emissary to the Allies. Even when told that General Castellano had departed, they insisted in their concern on sending someone else as well. When more than a week passed with no word from Castellano, Badoglio agreed.

On August 24, General Giacoma Zanussi, a firm believer in the stratagem of changing sides, left for Lisbon. Having just gotten rid of one Italian general, the British ambassador was of a mind to dismiss this one, when word came that Roosevelt and Churchill at last had agreed on the long surrender terms. Zanussi might transmit those to the Italians.

News of the development alarmed General Eisenhower. Beset already with doubts whether Castellano could persuade his government to surrender on the basis of the less severe short terms, he saw the long terms (they had a harsh preamble accenting unconditional surrender) as a threat to both the surrender and the invasion. With approval of the Joint Chiefs, he invited Zanussi to his headquarters in Algiers, there to busy him with discussions and deliberations pending further word from General Castellano.

Eisenhower actually had no need to worry. With the Italians it was a question not of terms but of method—not *which*? but, in heavens name, *how*?

General Castellano arrived in Sicily as scheduled early on the last day of August, but he had no authority, he revealed, to sign an armistice. While nobody in Rome seriously objected to the general terms of the armistice, it was impossible for the Italian government, in the interest of its very existence, to agree to announcing the armistice before the Allied landings. The Italians, Castellano pleaded impassionately, were virtual prisoners. If the Allies should land in insufficient strength or too far away to ensure immediate security for Rome and the government, the Germans would crush the Italians swiftly. Unless the Allies could delay the announcement until they had landed at least fifteen divisions north of Rome, the Italian government could sign no armistice.

"Beetle" Smith responded that if the Allies were in a position to land fifteen divisions, why bother with an armistice? The Italians, he said, had no choice but to accept all conditions or refuse the armistice.

If the latter, all chance of military collaboration would pass, leaving Italy to the mercy of Allied bombing, invasion, and an unsympathetic peace conference.

Although General Smith declined repeatedly to divulge any indication of the size, place, or approximate date of the Allied landing, General Castellano deduced from various remarks that the Allies would commit no more than fifteen divisions to the entire campaign in Italy. He discerned also, from a continuing denial of guarantees for security of the government, that the Allies would land well south of Rome.

Castellano insisted that it was in the Allied interest to gain Rome and asserted that Italian troops alone would be unable to save the city. In the hope of some solution, even if not ideal, he begged for at least a subsidiary landing close to Rome—an armored division by sea, another division by air.

Smith telephoned General Eisenhower in Algiers that he was convinced that the Italians genuinely wanted to surrender, but that they would be unable to muster the courage without some concession in regard to Rome. So meager was the Allied shipping left in the Mediterranean that the success of the invasion, Eisenhower believed, might well hinge upon obtaining Italian assistance. The man who would command the invasion—General Alexander—agreed. Moreover, there was, in view of the Allied schedule, no time to dally.

As General Smith returned to the conference with Castellano, he was prepared to make a concession. All roads, Allied commanders knew, still led to Rome, and holding Rome might well force the Germans out of southern Italy. Since the 82d Airborne Division had been earmarked to protect the north flank in the pending invasion, the division might be diverted to Rome. With that in mind, Smith told Castellano that while he could make no commitment on an armored division, the Allies were prepared to send an airborne division to Rome.

As these deliberations took place, military and government leaders in Rome still were non-plussed over Allied insistence on announcing the armistice in advance; and the officer who would command Italian troops in Rome complained bitterly that one airborne division was hardly enough. Yet most were convinced (Marshal Badoglio, Italy's Pétain, still vacillated) that they had no choice at that point but to surrender. Should they refuse, the Allies had enough evidence in any case to expose their perfidy and precipitate a fight with the Germans.

While deploring the onus of decision, Victor Emmanuel nevertheless made it. In a message that reached General Eisenhower's headquarters before midnight on the first of September, the answer was yes.

How far up the peninsula of Italy the Allies were to strike depended almost entirely on the range of fighter aircraft based in Sicily, for to sustain a growing momentum in the Pacific, aircraft carriers were used almost exclusively for the Pacific war. On that basis Rome or any other spot north of Naples was out of the question. Because Naples was at the extreme range of fighter aircraft, and because so much shipping in the Mediterranean had to be shifted elsewhere, even Naples seemed out of reach until the day Victor Emmanuel relieved Mussolini. Less than twenty-four hours later the Combined Chiefs, in approving an invasion of Italy, directed General Eisenhower to plan Operation AVALANCHE—landings in the vicinity of Naples.

There was, of course, the logical move of jumping the Strait of Messina onto the toe of the Italian boot. That General Eisenhower planned from the start, for no matter what operation followed farther up the boot, control of the narrow channel between the toe and Sicily was essential in order to shorten shipping routes. When AVALANCHE, the landings near Naples, entered the considerations, crossing the strait assumed added importance in order to tie down Axis forces that might move against AVALANCHE.

The job of crossing fell to General Montgomery's Eighth Army with a target date of the first day or so of September. Because some of the assault and supply shipping needed for crossing to the toe would also have to be used at Naples, the main assault would have to follow some days later, on September 9.

For all the Italian expectations of more audacious landings near Rome, Operation AVALANCHE was, to Allied leaders, "the riskiest one that we have yet undertaken," primarily because of the lack of ships to put followup forces quickly ashore. If both Italians and Germans fought for southern Italy, Allied intelligence speculated, they could field thirty-five divisions, far more than Eisenhower had any hope of committing. On the other hand, Italian surrender would remove more than half of those and might prompt the Germans to retire north of Rome. That gave overriding importance to Italian surrender.

After weighing carefully the advantages and the disadvantages of beaches on either side of Naples, Allied planners settled on a third sector, a twenty-mile sandy crescent along the Gulf of Salerno. Although the beaches were ideal for landing craft and were within acceptable range of fighter planes, the coastal plain is narrow and split by a river, mountains dominate the plain, and a towering, rocky mountain mass extending inland from the rugged Sorrento peninsula blocks the way to Naples, twenty-five miles to the north, and to Rome.

With General Alexander serving as army group commander, a tactically inexperienced American army headquarters, the Fifth, was to go ashore in the Gulf of Salerno under command of Mark Clark. The Fifth Army was to have two corps—one American, one British—with a total of seven divisions.

In the course of the surrender negotiations with General Castellano, the Italians offered to open to the Allies the port of Taranto, inside the heel. Since few Germans were in that part of Italy, Eisenhower decided to move a British division directly into the port on warships and later to put additional forces ashore to seize ports on the east coast.

The Allied invasion of Italy thus encompassed three assaults: the toe, the heel, and the main assault in the Gulf of Salerno. The concession to Italian surrender raised the possibility of a fourth, an airborne division at Rome.

In keeping with previous agreement, General Castellano returned to Sicily on September 2: to complete arrangements for the airborne division, he thought; to sign the short terms of surrender, Allied commanders insisted. Operation AVALANCHE was too risky, General Eisenhower believed, to chance the Italians' reneging.

The Italian government took more than twenty-four hours to authorize Castellano to sign. By that time everyone on the Allied side had nevertheless begun to breathe more easily. Behind a tremendous air and artillery bombardment that few except General Montgomery deemed necessary, contingents of the British Eighth Army had gone ashore on the toe of Italy against scarcely any resistance, Italian or German.

After signing the terms of surrender, Castellano helped plan the airborne landing, then suggested that two Allied officers go to Rome to complete the arrangements. To his ardent entreaties for some idea of the date of the invasion, General Smith at last allowed that it might come within two weeks. Since he was staying on in Sicily to begin setting up a permanent

Italian mission to Eisenhower's headquarters, Castellano sent back to Rome such information on Allied plans as he had obtained, including his deduction that the Allied landing probably would take place on September 12. Italian officials in Rome, unfortunately, took the twelfth as definite.

In Rome a curious lethargy had settled over military and government officials alike, as if the orgasm of decision had left them spent. They did little to prepare for what Allied commanders and Castellano considered the Italian commitment—a general uprising against the Germans upon announcement of the armistice. Such plans as they did propose were purely defensive, and all were predicated on an Allied invasion no earlier than the twelfth. The commander responsible for defending Rome was more than ever convinced that his assignment was impossible. On September 6 the head of the *Comando Supremo*, General Ambrosio, displaying peculiar detachment, left for the north of Italy on personal business.

Those in charge in Rome obviously had yet to purge themselves of the expectation not of collaboration but of deliverance.

By way of a British patrol boat, then an Italian corvette, Brigadier General Maxwell D. Taylor, the 82d Airborne Division's artillery commander, and a colonel from the troop carrier command that was to fly the airborne troops to Rome, reached the Italian coast near the capital before daylight on September 7. Their uniforms splashed with water as if they were aviators plucked from the sea, they entered Rome in a Red Cross ambulance just at nightfall.

Only after an elaborate dinner, which the two officers ate with impatience, did the commander charged with defending Rome, Generale di Corpo d'Armata Giacomo Carboni, at last arrive. The most pessimistic of all the Italian Staff, Carboni painted a distressing picture of German strength and his inability to counteract it. When General Taylor told him Eisenhower intended to announce the armistice the next day, the eighth, and that the airborne division would begin to arrive that evening, Carboni was appalled. The armistice, he insisted, would have to be postponed, the airborne operation canceled.

At Taylors urging, Carboni took the two men to see Marshal Badoglio, but only after Carboni had had a private audience with the old marshal first. By the time the Americans saw Badoglio, Carboni had swung him to his point of view. No matter that General Castellano had already signed the armistice terms, the Italians would have to renege. Badoglio pleaded plaintively and emotionally for acceptance, for help, for understanding, but under existing arrangements he simply was unable to go through with the armistice. That would invite German occupation and revenge.

To pin Badoglio down, Taylor insisted that the marshal explain his position in a message to General Eisenhower to be sent by a secret radio. Taylor himself also prepared a message of explanation and a request for instructions. As for the airborne landing, Taylor believed that in view of the situation in Rome, it would be a catastrophe. Since he feared that a message canceling it might be so delayed by the laborious process of encoding and decoding that the airborne troops would have already left Sicily, he used a prearranged signal to cancel the operation.

"Situation innocuous," he radioed.

Sixty-two planes carrying paratroopers were already airborne, circling the airfield to get into formation, when the message reached them.

By the time General Taylor returned by plane to North Africa late on the eighth, General Eisenhower had taken steps to force Badoglio and the Italian government to honor their commitment. The ships carrying Allied soldiers to the beaches of Salerno were too close to their destination to turn back, and the gears of amphibious attack were too complex to shift into reverse on short notice.

"I intend to broadcast the existence of the armistice at the hour originally planned," Eisenhower notified Badoglio. "If you or any part of your armed forces fail to cooperate as previously agreed, I will publish to the world the full record of this affair." A few hours later an outwardly calm Commander-in-Chief of the Allied forces went on the air from Radio Algiers to announce the armistice.

In the Quirinal Palace in Rome, meanwhile, consternation reigned. The pessimistic Carboni, who more than anybody was responsible for the canceling of the airborne landing, maintained that by announcing the armistice on the eighth instead of the twelfth, the Allies had betrayed the Italians. The King, he urged, should disavow Castellano's negotiations. Little effect that would have on the Germans, others with greater realism replied.

As Marshal Badoglio again vacillated, it remained for the King who hated decision again to decide. A little less than two hours after General

Eisenhower's pronouncement, Marshal Badoglio went to the microphones of Radio Rome to confirm Italy's surrender.

Indecisive to the end, neither Italian government nor military officials issued firm orders to the troops in the field. They were no longer to fight the Allies, the order went, and they were not to attack the Germans. They were, in effect, simply to pretend that the war had gone away.

Amid increasing indications that the Germans were moving on Rome, the royal family, Marshal Badoglio, General Ambrosio, and assorted others sneaked out of Rome by automobile before daylight on September 9, and headed for Brindisi on the heel of the boot, leaving their underlings and their people to the whim of their former ally, their new enemy. Ironically, the one officer remaining behind who insisted on fighting was the pessimistic Carboni, but he was unable to counteract clever German promises to the Italian soldiers that if they laid down their arms, they could go home. Rome and almost all of Italy went to the Germans by default.

About all the Allies got out of the surrender of Italy was a pompous little monarch and an irresolute old marshal not a whit more popular with the people than the deposed Mussolini; the Italian fleet (minus the battleship *Roma*, which German planes sank); assurance that the Italian army—feeble in any case—would not fight at Salerno or elsewhere (a British division entered Taranto with no trouble on the ninth); and the psychological boost that came with eliminating one of the three major enemy powers.

The Germans, for their part, no longer had to bother even to consult an ally of dubious value. They also gained a battleground with terrain so inhospitable as to be worth more than hundreds of man-made fortifications. They even got back Mussolini. A persistent Otto Skorzeny found him in a mountaintop ski lodge in the northern Apennines and on September 12 went after him with glider troops and took him off the mountain in a light observation plane. Hitler then set him up in a satrapy in northern Italy.

Had it been handled some other way, the Italian surrender might have forestalled a long, tedious, depressing campaign up the spine of the Italian peninsula. Given Italian cooperation, an airborne landing on Rome could have secured the city against the limited numbers of Germans actually at hand—no more than two divisions, both well outside the city. With

Rome and its roads denied, the Germans in southern Italy would have been compelled to retreat hastily to the north, which was their plan in the event of Allied invasion anyway.

Ironic it was that, had the Allies delayed announcing Italian surrender a few days, they might have precipitated a German withdrawal. On the eighth, the very day of the announcement, Hitler had prepared—in order to force the hand of his Italian ally—an ultimatum that demanded virtual German control of Italy. If the Italians had refused to submit—which they would have to do, since they had signed the surrender—Hitler planned to withdraw German forces immediately to the northern Apennines.

Learning of the Italian surrender, Hitler never delivered the ultimatum.

Chapter Twelve – From Salerno to the Rapido

The German commander in Italy, Field Marshal Kesselring, was genuinely surprised by the Italian defection; and he deduced from the nature of the announcement of the armistice that the Allied invasion would be closely coordinated with the Italians. That would mean landings near Rome, possibly an airborne assault as well, designed to cut the roads that were essential to the German troops in southern Italy. Although Kesselring recognized that Rome was beyond the range of fighter planes based in Sicily, he assumed that the Allies might accept that handicap, so much did they stand to gain by seizing Rome. Besides, given Italian help, they soon might use Italian airfields, and in any case they had full command of the sea and the air.[68]

The one consoling thought was that heretofore the Allies had been conservative, methodical, in going from one operation to the next. Were it not for the Italian defection, they obviously would follow the script and land near Naples, probably in the Gulf of Salerno. For that Kesselring was ready. A panzer division was moving into coastal defenses there,

---

[68] The basic source for this chapter was Blumenson, *Salerno to Cassino*. See also Martin Blumenson, *Anzio: The Gamble That Failed* (Philadelphia, 1963); *Fifth Army History* (written by members of the Fifth Army Historical Section and published in Italy); two volumes in the official U.S. Army *American Forces in Action* series: *Salerno: American Operations from the Beaches to the Volturno* (1944) and *From the Volturno to the Winter Line* (1944); Lieutenant Colonel G. W. L. Nicholson, *The Canadians in Italy, 1943- 1945*, in the Official History of the Canadian Army in the Second World War (Ottawa, 1956); Matloff, *Strategic Planning: 1943-1944*; Morison, *Sicily — Salerno — Anzio*; Chester G. Starr, *From Salerno to the Alps* (Washington, 1948); and William G. F. Jackson, *The Battle of Italy* (New York, 1967). In addition to memoir literature previously cited, see Field Marshal Sir Bernard L. Montgomery, *El Alamein to the River Sangro* (published in Germany by the British Army of the Rhine, 1946), and Admiral H. Kent Hewitt, "The Allied Navies at Salerno," in *U.S. Naval Institute Proceedings* (September, 1953).

and two others were assembled near Naples. Should those fail to defeat the invasion, they still would be able to delay the Allied advance and to withdraw, in conformity with the overall German plan, to the line to be held north of Rome in the Apennines.

Not so if the Allies landed near Rome. Those three divisions, plus two others withdrawing before the British Eighth Army in the toe of Italy, another in the heel, and two others near Rome—all eight grouped together to form the *Tenth Army*—well might be trapped.

It was with immense relief that Kesselring heard the news early on September 9 that Allied troops were coming ashore, not near Rome, but on the crescent of beaches ringing the Gulf of Salerno.

Nothing in war is more complex than an amphibious invasion. Assembling hundreds of ships and landing craft, thousands of troops, and countless items of equipment at the designated ports; securing the necessary mix of troops—infantry, artillery, armor, engineers, signalmen, truck drivers, medics—and assigning them to vessels and later to landing craft; arranging proper loading so that troops and supplies needed first will be unloaded first; scheduling rendezvous at sea so that all vessels arrive off the right beaches at the right time; reconnoitering enemy positions, spotting them for naval gun crews, and assigning them as objectives for ground units, each man of which must know his individual role; designating objectives for fighter aircraft and scheduling flights to assure continuous air cover despite the brief periods each plane can remain over the beaches; assuring early landing of engineer shore regiments and naval beach parties to organize the flow of men and supplies over the beaches; providing special equipment like steel mesh to enable vehicles to move inland over soft beach sand; positioning marker boats; arranging communications, followup supply, followup troops—these and myriad other tasks, any one of which in the presence of enemy fire may spell the difference between success and failure for the man who plunges into the surf with nothing between him and a hostile shore but the rifle he clutches.

Fortunately for those who were to execute the complex amphibious invasion at Salerno, nature cooperated: the sea was a pond, the weather clear. Often perverse man-made things cooperated, too: the ships' showers worked; the food was good. Except for a few incidentals like olive drab uniforms, crowded quarters and decks, guns and other paraphernalia of war, escorting planes overhead, many men might have imagined themselves on a Mediterranean cruise. When at 6:30 P.M. on September 8, ships' loudspeakers carried to the passengers General Eisenhower's announcement of Italian surrender, the hope that it might be just a cruise surged in many a breast.

"I never again expect to witness such scenes of sheer joy," one man recalled. "We would dock in Naples harbor unopposed, with an olive branch in one hand and an opera ticket in the other."[69]

For Allied commanders, no such elation, for the surrender well could mean increased resistance as determined Germans took over coastal defenses from dispirited Italians. A question that had been troubling both British and American commanders also remained: whether to precede the landings with a naval bombardment or to hope for surprise. A British corps, comprising the left element of Mark Clark's Fifth Army and scheduled to land close to the port of Salerno, opted for a preliminary bombardment on the theory that German planes that had attacked the convoy had spread the alarm. Having seen no Axis planes, and hoping that the bombardment on the British front might lull the Germans elsewhere, American commanders shunned the advice of their naval colleagues and decided to try for surprise.

In the early minutes of September 9, as darkness unrelieved by moonlight cloaked the waters of the Gulf of Salerno, apprehensive GI's and Tommies climbed awkwardly down landing nets to take their places in assault boats. When filled, the boats pulled away from the mother ships to circle like disciplined water bugs until joined by others for the run to the beaches in a giant V formation. Wearing the usual olive drab wool uniforms, the Americans carried on their backs light packs with toilet articles and mess kit, two bitter-tasting chocolate bars called "D-rations," and a K-ration consisting of a can of meat, egg-and-ham, or cheese, cellophane-wrapped crackers, a fruit bar, a portion of soluble coffee or lemon powder, two cigarettes, and a parcel of toilet tissue. Attached to cartridge belts were a canteen of water and a first-aid packet containing sulfanilamide powder. Slung over their shoulders were canvas bandoliers of ammunition arranged in eight-round clips for semiautomatic M-1 rifles.

At 3:10 A.M., twenty minutes before the main assault, two battalions

---

[69] Blumenson, *Salerno to Cassino*, p. 55, quoting Major Warren A. Thrasher.

of U.S. Rangers and two of British Commandos touched down on narrow spits of sand alongside towering cliffs of the Sorrento peninsula. Not until the first wave was solidly ashore did any German fire fall. Pushing rapidly inland, the Rangers quickly secured rocky peaks commanding passes leading across the Sorrento mountain mass toward Naples, while the Commandos established a precarious hold on the northern fringe of Salerno.

Guided by colored beacons flashed seaward by scout boats, two regiments of the 36th "Texas" Division headed toward shore at the ancient settlement of Paestum, fifteen miles down the coast from Salerno, a site still marked by remains of a Greek colony established in the sixth century B.C. Close by the sea stand well-preserved ruins of two imposing Greek temples and crumbled remains of a third; their Doric columns form massive landmarks on a narrow coastal plain. Surrounding them are the ramparts of a decaying city wall, almost three miles around and in some places fifty feet high, dominated at one spot by a stone tower.

All was quiet on the gently sloping sands near the temples as leading assault boats dropped their bows, and riflemen stepped out into warm, waist-deep surf. The gamble for surprise appeared wise; the only shooting was in the north at Salerno, whence rose a steady thunder of naval gunfire accompanying what looked from a distance like the play of hundreds of giant lightning bugs.

Then suddenly, over the beaches, bursting flares, illuminating the water with a ghostlike radiance. Just as suddenly, a rain of machine-gun and mortar fire.

Some men dropped to the beach, scrambling to build little parapets of sand with their hands. Bobbing and weaving, others raced headlong for the protection of a line of dunes, while still others plunged on to take cover behind the ancient city wall, some at the base of the Greek temples.

On the flare-lit beaches confusion took charge. Flashes of German guns firing from mountains beyond the coastal plain presaged big explosions along the shore or geysers of water among the landing craft. Some boats turned back, others darted to right or left trying to put their passengers ashore at some calmer spot. Direct shell hits turned some landing craft into pyres, adding another eerie light to the scene. With all hope of surprise lost, landing craft mounting rockets pulled in close to shore to loose one salvo after another. Offshore, naval guns began to belch noisily toward the mountains.

For all the noise and confusion, most men made it ashore and somehow, units intermingled, worked their way toward a railroad parallel to the beach a mile and a half inland. Here and there sergeants or officers organized whomever they found around them and led them, rifles blazing, against flashes of light and noise revealing German positions.

Only some four hundred panzer grenadiers manned scattered positions along the American beaches, yet to the invaders they seemed a small army. As daylight came, those Germans were falling back, awed by a confusion that appeared to them to be a skillful, well-organized maneuver. Having moved to the shore positions only after learning of the Italian surrender, they had had little opportunity to lay mines or create interlocking lanes of fire. Once they had done what damage they deemed they could, they pulled back to join roving groups of tanks that soon after dawn began to strike at various points against American troops pushing slowly inland.

Although the German fire thoroughly disrupted landing schedules, it failed to prevent subsequent waves of infantrymen and tanks and artillery from coming ashore in some fashion. When one shell set a tank afire in an LCT, another tank pushed the burning vehicle over the ramp into the water. Some DUKW's carrying artillery pieces sank. Some tanks and artillery pieces set off mines on the beaches. Despite a constant cover of at least eight Allied planes overhead, several flights of German planes bombed and strafed the beaches. Yet by noon sizable numbers of supporting weapons were in firing positions or were moving forward to help clumps of infantrymen turn back German tanks. By noon, too, beach control parties were creating some order out of incipient chaos. They directed incoming craft with loudspeakers, thus probably giving rise to the long-persistent myth that the Germans had greeted the first assault wave with loudspeakers blaring, "Come on in and give up. We have you covered."[70]

Resistance decreased markedly during the afternoon, so that as night came, men of the 36th Division had pushed inland as far as the first foothills surrounding the plain, though they had yet to reach the little Sele River on their north flank, which was their point of contact with the British. The division's reserve regiment landed at dusk, and portions of another division began to come ashore after dark.

[70] Morison, *Sicily — Salerno — Anzio*, p. 265.

British troops meanwhile had found less opposition on their beaches, possibly because of the preliminary naval bombardment; but ashore the fight was harder. Although some troops got into a village marking a critical road junction near the Sele River, tank-led German infantry forced them out. As night came, the British beachhead was nowhere deeper than two miles. Like the Americans, the British had yet to reach the Sele River, so that the two beachheads still were six to seven miles apart. Except for a little enclave held by Commandos, the British had failed, too, to get into Salerno. A nearby airfield also remained under German control.

All in all, Mark Clark could still judge the first day of Operation AVALANCHE a success. Although the lone German panzer division defending the beaches had fought with determination, its troops had been overextended and hastily deployed. They were in the end no match for the invaders and their powerful fire support from the sea. For all the sound and fury at the start of the landings, casualties for an opposed amphibious assault had been light: for the Americans, about five hundred, one-fifth of them dead.

From the German viewpoint, the panzer division had done a creditable job. That help had been slow to come was attributable to several matters of chance.

The corps commander charged with defense of the Naples-Salerno region happened to be on leave in Germany, and his deputy experienced the natural reluctance of a subordinate to make major decisions without checking with his superiors. Since the Italian surrender had removed Italian communications facilities from German use, other than an untrustworthy civilian telephone system, coordination with headquarters of the *Tenth Army* was slow. The *Tenth Army*'s commander, General Heinrich von Vietinghoff, was reluctant to shift everything to Salerno, lest the Allies stage another landing, or lest Hitler order immediate withdrawal northward; and so preoccupied with events in Rome connected with the Italian surrender was his superior, Field Marshal Kesselring, that Vietinghoff received little guidance.

Fearing that the Allies might stage another landing, General von Vietinghoff did no more on the ninth than order one of the two divisions retreating before the British Eighth Army to hurry north to fight at Salerno. In the expectation that the division would arrive during the night, he told the panzer division that had fought the invaders, to withdraw before the Americans and concentrate against the British, who represented the most direct threat to Naples. Not until the next day, the tenth, did he order any part of the two panzer divisions near Naples to move south, and then, still wary of another landing, he ordered only reconnaissance troops.

As things turned out, only the commander of the division that was supposed to hurry north, arrived during the night of the ninth, and he had bad news. His division was out of gasoline. Instead of arriving as a cohesive force ready to counterattack early on September 10, the division trickled onto the battlefield over the next several days in relatively ineffective portions.

It is largely to these accidents that the final outcome of the invasion at Salerno can be attributed. Since the Allies were almost two hundred miles by sea and air from their bases in Sicily and lacked sufficient shipping to move reinforcements until ships participating in the invasion could return for a second load, they were slow to build up strength in their beachhead. They could be grateful for the German fumbling.

Crisis began to develop in the beachhead only on the third day, September 11. So strong did German pressure become against the British that General Clark sent a newly arrived American regiment north of the Sele River to assume responsibility for linking the two beachheads. To help the Rangers at the passes on the Sorrento *massif*, he sent an infantry battalion by landing craft across the gulf. Meanwhile, against the ships offshore, German planes made their heaviest strikes. Using new radio-controlled glider and rocket bombs, the planes sank four transports, a Liberty Ship, a hospital ship, and eight landing craft. They damaged the cruiser *Philadelphia* and put the *Savannah* out of action.

The next day, as the first Germans from the toe of Italy arrived to oppose the American beachhead, Clark became increasingly concerned about the continuing gap between the two beachheads; yet he had no more troops to commit along the Sele River to close it. The 36th Division was strung out over a thirty-five-mile front, manning less a line than a series of outposts. Not all of a second division, the 45th, had yet arrived, and the British still had only two divisions. To faciliate control of the battle, Clark moved his command post from ship to shore, making camp in an old mansion close to the Sele River.

The German *Tenth Army* commander, General von Vietinghoff, became aware of the gap between the Allied beachheads on the thirteenth. Having committed the two panzer divisions from Naples to attack Salerno from the north, he ordered the division that had first opposed the landings to join newcomers from the toe and drive through the gap to the sea.

The German attack began in mid-afternoon of the thirteenth. First an infantry battalion gave way; then the Germans overran another, capturing five hundred men. Elated German commanders reported the Americans falling back.

As dusk approached, nothing stood between the Germans and the sea but two American artillery battalions and Mark Clark's headquarters. Telephone operators, clerks, cooks, anybody who could be spared from the command post began to dig to create a last-ditch defense line behind the artillery.

Clark himself feared the American beachhead might be lost, and laid plans for shifting a skeleton Staff by sea into the British beachhead. To Admiral Hewitt in his flagship offshore he sent word to prepare a plan for evacuating the beachhead, possibly to shift American troops to the British sector.

Vietinghoff at the same time was sending a jubilant message to Kesselring, and a clerk at the *Tenth Army's* headquarters was putting a laconic but triumphant end to the day's war diary: "The battle of Salerno appears to be over."[71]

How were Allied commanders to meet the crisis?

Although General Alexander ordered General Montgomery to speed his advance from the toe, Montgomery's Eighth Army was still a discouraging 150 miles from Paestum, moving at such a pace that the Germans were having no difficulty disengaging in order to shift to Salerno. British warships that had put troops ashore at Taranto set sail for Salerno, but at best they could reach the scene only in a matter of days. While engineers rushed work on an improvised air strip near Paestum, the strip could accommodate only a few planes; and engineers, planes, and all were subject to German shelling. Although General Eisenhower ordered another American division to leave Sicily in improvised shipping, the voyage would take at least two days. Not until well into September 14 was the

---

[71] Blumenson, *Salerno to Cassino*, p. 136, quoting the *Tenth Army's* War Diary.

45th Division's third regiment to land, along with the first contingents of a British armored division. That might be too late.

As night fell, adding to the confusion in the gap along the Sele River where German tanks and infantry milled about, hope for quick reinforcement at last came. Before midnight—the word was from Sicily—thirteen hundred paratroopers of the 82d Airborne Division were to drop into the beachhead.

All that time the fight was still raging along the Sele River. Laying their artillery pieces for direct fire against the German tanks—while every fourth and fifth gunner took to foxholes to fight off the German infantry—the American artillerymen fired round after round until barrels were hot. Straight from the maws of LCT's, a covey of tank destroyers rushed to the scene. A few minutes later a battery of self-propelled artillery pieces also arrived. In the course of three hours, twenty-eight artillery pieces fired an exceptional 3,650 rounds.

The effort paid off. The Germans fell back.

Through the night, as the paratroopers arrived on schedule (every Allied anti-aircraft gunner on ship and shore was under strict orders not to fire under any circumstances against any plane, German or Allied), General Clark pulled units back from forward positions to shorten the lines and release troops to move to the Sele River. All unloading at the beaches ceased as supply troops rushed forward to help the infantrymen dig in, to create a lane of fire down which the Germans would have to move if they renewed their assault the next day. Nobody slept in the beachhead that night.

Renew the attack the Germans did, but the steam was gone. As five hundred heavy bombers struck road junctions daringly close to the periphery of the beachhead, naval gunners stepped up their fire. In rapid succession American tanks and tank destroyers knocked out thirty German tanks.

As the day waned, the crisis appeared to be over; but for good measure the 45th Division's third regiment began to come ashore, and during the night twenty-one hundred more paratroopers dropped from the sky into the beachhead. The only discouraging event occurred when a battalion of six hundred American paratroopers were committed in a hastily planned operation beyond the periphery of the British beachhead in an effort to disrupt German communications. The men scattered in the darkness, never to get together as a battalion, although about four hundred eventually made their way back to American lines.

The crisis was over, but the Germans displayed no acceptance of it. Again on September 15 they tried to break through, both along the Sele River and against the north rim of British defenses at Salerno, but to no avail. A day later General von Vietinghoff reached the conclusion that time had run out. He asked Kesselring for permission to break off the battle, to begin the withdrawal to the north.

Although the Germans had failed to drive the Allies into the sea, they had saved their troops from the toe and the heel of Italy. They had also inflicted such damage on the invaders that they would have no trouble disengaging for the withdrawal.

"Success has been ours," proclaimed Vietinghoff. "Once again German soldiers have proved their superiority over the enemy."[72]

Since the Allied commanders still lacked firm contact with the British Eighth Army (Montgomery's troops arrived in strength only after the battle was won) and were all too aware that several more days would pass before additional reinforcements might arrive by sea, to say nothing of the shortage of shipping, they could appreciate that had the Germans wished, they could have moved far greater numbers against the beachhead. The result in that event might have been different. Mark Clark, and everybody else, was willing to settle for the way it was.

There was nothing precipitate about the German withdrawal. Taking astute advantage of steep mountain passes, demolishing bridges over streams and gorges, blocking narrow village streets and hairpin turns on mountain roads, German rear guards made Allied columns pay for almost every yard of advance. The Germans relinquished Naples only on October 1, and then only after destroying water and power systems, obstructing the port, planting time bombs in public buildings, looting, burning. On the eastern side of the peninsula, where Montgomery's Eighth Army shifted, the city of Foggia and an important complex of nearby airfields passed into Allied hands the same day. At the end of the first week in October the Fifth Army at last pulled up to the Volturno River, fifteen miles north of Naples.

[72] Ibid., p. 137.

For Field Marshal Kesselring there was method in the slow withdrawal. So successful had been German defense with a minimum of forces that Kesselring determined to change Hitler's mind about withdrawing north of Rome, to persuade him instead to accept a defensive line in harshly rugged terrain some eighty miles south of Rome anchored on Monte Cassino, site of a historic Benedictine monastery. Aside from the advantages of giving up less ground and perhaps forestalling an invasion of the Balkans, Kesselring saw personal advantage. If he held south of Rome, the German troops would remain under his command; north of Rome, they would pass to Field Marshal Rommel.

While accepting withdrawal from Sardinia (a contingent of Allied troops moved to the island on September 18) and Corsica (partisans aided by French regulars—Giraud's, not de Gaulle's—harassed the Germans until they completed withdrawal on October 4), Kesselring urged his views on Hitler at every opportunity. By early October, Hitler was impressed enough with Kesselring's optimism to order Rommel to release two divisions and artillery reinforcements for the south. A month later so pleased was he with the slow pace Kesselring was imposing on his enemies that he went all the way. He ordered Rommel to France and made Kesselring supreme commander of all German troops in Italy.

The Cassino line, Hitler directed, was to "mark the end of withdrawals."

They had left the question unanswered at QUADRANT: what to do if the Germans made a fight for Italy?

Upon the start of German withdrawal from Salerno such a rush of optimism surged in Allied commanders that the question appeared irrelevant. Rome and the country beyond it to the northern Apennines above Florence, perhaps even the Po valley, beckoned. Although the Fifth and Eighth Armies of General Alexander's 15th Army Group could count on but eleven divisions, that number, for a delightful moment, appeared sufficient.

Then early in October intelligence sources began to report German divisions from northern Italy moving south, and by mid-October, General Eisenhower was convinced that the fight up the peninsula would grow increasingly difficult. Yet he also believed that nothing would assist the cross-Channel invasion in the spring of 1944 as much as having Allied forces established in northern Italy. If he was to achieve this with any reasonable celerity, he required additional resources to take advantage of the enemy's lengthy flanks. This meant more troops and more landing craft.

From the vantage point of Washington, thousands of miles away, there seemed little possibility of the Germans' holding anywhere short of the northern Apennines. To the Joint Chiefs of Staff, the strength already at hand in Italy and North Africa appeared adequate for getting that far. Looking at the war in global dimensions with particular emphasis on the forthcoming invasion of France, the Joint Chiefs insisted that Eisenhower do the job with what he had. Eisenhower also was to continue to allow for the release of seven divisions for the cross-Channel attack, although those might gradually be replaced by French divisions as they were trained and equipped with American arms in North Africa. In December, Eisenhower also was to give up 150 strategic bombers and considerable transport aircraft, assault shipping, and landing craft; and eventually he was to furnish troops to invade southern France as a corollary of the cross-Channel attack.

When in the cauldron of creation the world's land masses formed, few regions emerged less conducive to military operations on the ground than the peninsula of Italy. Coastal plains at their widest encompass only a few miles and are everywhere dominated by towering, craggy peaks crossed by only an occasional road or a trail hewn from rocky cliffs. The interior is one range of rugged peaks after another, only here and there creased by the valley of a stream. In villages clinging to hillsides, poverty and the plaintive sadness that is poverty's hand-maiden abide in drab buildings fashioned from native stone and clay. In summer the countryside is hot, dry, dusty, brown. In winter it is cold, wet, muddy, gray. The soldier, at least, sees Italy that way, even if the tourist brochures say otherwise.

Starting at the Volturno River, the Germans delayed from successive positions with the eventual goal of falling back to a line running through Cassino, the Gustav Line (from the symbol for "G" in the German phonetic alphabet). Not until they had imposed every possible casualty and exacted every conceivable delay, not until Allied squads and platoons had maneuvered slowly, painfully into position for the kill, did the Germans withdraw. In the harsh terrain, tanks and tank destroyers counted for little other than to augment artillery, for it was a foot soldier's war.

For the infantryman it was a grim, colorless, almost hopeless existence. There were brief moments to look toward: a day or so out of the line in reserve where life within range of enemy artillery was a foxhole existence but at least was devoid of machine guns; perhaps two days or maybe five at a rest center in Naples, that city of easy virtue. While airmen had a rotation plan whereby after thirty missions a man might go home, the infantryman could get out of it only in two ways—injury or death. That the airman got extra pay for "hazardous duty," while the infantryman, whose casualties were infinitely greater, got none, was particularly galling. A pittance of ten extra dollars a month which the Congress finally voted the infantry enlisted man—though not his officer—made little impression, but a special award that went with it did. This was a rectangular badge of blue with a rifle on it to indicate infantry, a silver laurel wreath to signify combat. The men wore those Combat Infantry Badges with a special pride. They set the wearer apart as one of those who did the fighting, who did the dying.

A four-day advance seven miles up the upper valley of the Volturno cost a regiment of the 34th Division 59 men killed, 148 wounded. In twenty days the entire Fifth Army gained only from fifteen to twenty miles. Up the steep mountains, across yawning gorges and ravines, men of the Fifth Army clawed their way forward, frequently hand over hand. Although pack mules could bring rations and ammunition part of the way, hand-carry details had to take over in the end. Some units cleared enemy minefields by driving herds of sheep and goats across the precipitous slopes before them.

"Wars," one corps commander noted in his diary, "should be fought in better country than this."[73]

From the first, Mark Clark, Alexander, Eisenhower, everybody (including the Germans) saw amphibious end runs as the only solution to counter a steadfast enemy in the cruel terrain. Yet where to get the troops, the landing craft? "If we landed a small force," Eisenhower wrote George Marshall, "it would be quickly eliminated, while a force large enough to sustain itself cannot possibly be mounted for a very considerable period."[74]

As autumn began to turn to winter, where was the alternative?

Although Montgomery's Eighth Army on the east coast reached the Gustav Line, few objectives along that coast would contribute to the primary goal of taking Rome. Clark's Fifth Army, meanwhile, along the

[73] Ibid., p. 234, quoting General Lucas' Diary.

[74] Blumenson, *Anzio*, p. 32.

only logical route to Rome, was still a dozen miles short of the Gustav Line, held up by another formidable delaying position anchored inland in the mountains and along the coastal strip behind the Garigliano River.

In hope of breaking the impasse, General Eisenhower in early November devised a plan predicated on retaining in the Mediterranean until mid-December sixty-eight LST's scheduled for early transfer to Britain. While the Eighth Army broke through the Gustav Line along the east coast, then turned west to threaten Rome, the Fifth Army was to pierce the line near Cassino to enter a relatively wide valley of the Liri River, which was becoming known in Allied circles as the "gateway to Rome." Once the Fifth Army had advanced up that valley some thirty miles beyond Cassino, within fifty miles of Rome, a two-division assault force was to go ashore at Anzio, a little coastal resort thirty-five miles south of Rome. A vital condition of the plan was that the Fifth Army be close enough to Anzio to achieve a rapid linkup.

Although the Combined Chiefs sanctioned holding the LST's, sheer approval could not magically speed the Fifth Army through the defenses in front of Cassino. Battles raged day after day for heights named Camino, la Difensa, Maggiore, for obscure towns called San Pietro, Santa Maria Infante. Always the Germans eventually withdrew; exhausted American, French (two divisions had arrived), and British troops, their ranks thinned by the fight, promptly followed to occupy the rubble or the artillery-scarred peaks. Not that it was easy for the Germans ("Are under heavy artillery fire," a German soldier wrote in his diary. "Had several wounded. Bregenz killed. My morale is gone."[75]); but they fought with a skill and a determination that frustrated any Allied hope for a breakthrough to meet the conditions necessary for an end run to Anzio.

Although General Clark considered that the conditions would not be fulfilled, he urged that an end run be staged anyway. The threat posed by the amphibious strike, he reasoned, might be enough to prompt the Germans to withdraw. Others gave little encouragement to such an assumption. What would happen to a feeble amphibious force if the Germans declined to withdraw?

An end run to Anzio was dying for want of support in high places when a new champion for the project emerged: Winston Churchill.

* * *

---

[75] Blumenson, *Salerno to Cassino*, p. 214.

In late November, Churchill met in Cairo with Roosevelt and the Generalissimo of China—as a preliminary to the conference Roosevelt had long wanted with Josef Stalin—and he felt wholly frustrated. Although committed to a cross-Channel attack, now called Operation OVERLORD, Churchill yearned as always for greater commitment in the Mediterranean.

The target date for OVERLORD of May 1944 was not, Churchill maintained, sacrosanct: OVERLORD should be no tyrant denying all flexibility in Allied operations. What Churchill wanted was to mount various operations in the eastern Mediterranean with already available forces in an effort to bring Turkey into the war, possibly leading to a drive through the Balkans on Vienna. How better to force the Germans to commit almost everything to a decisive eastern front, leaving the Allies to slip into France and march to Berlin by way of the back door?

Dependent, as always—except for North Africa—on the advice of his military chiefs, especially a George Marshall dedicated to OVERLORD, Roosevelt remembered Churchill's espousal a quarter-century before of the disastrous campaign at Gallipoli. Given his head, Churchill might entangle the Allies in indecisive operations, weakening, postponing, perhaps even precluding a cross-Channel attack.

Meeting Stalin in Teheran a few days later, Roosevelt found that the Soviet head of state had no objection to the Allies' assuming the defensive in Italy. What Stalin wanted was a cross-Channel attack at the earliest possible date, and under Roosevelt's coaxing in an effort to offset Churchill, he warmed to the idea of an invasion of southern France, even though that might draw resources from the Italian campaign. Having won at Stalingrad, Stalin had no need and probably no wish for Allied troops to enter a Balkan region he no doubt looked on as a dominion of Communist Russia.

Stopping off again at Cairo for further talks among the Western Allies, Roosevelt sought to smooth over the apparent affront his courting of Stalin had been to his British colleague. His Staff, Roosevelt announced, had determined that those all-important sixty-eight LST's might be retained a little longer in the Mediterranean, until mid-January 1944. That, he hoped, would allow enough time for an amphibious end run to attain what Churchill considered the minimum goal in Italy—seizing Rome.

Yet the conditions for an amphibious end run still had to be met: getting the Fifth Army across the approaches to Cassino and then through the Gustav Line into the Liri valley. Nobody suggested how to accomplish that in the few weeks of desolate, rain-drenched winter remaining before the LST's would have to be relinquished. General Eisenhower himself despaired of it.

After agonizing soul-searching President Roosevelt had decided at Teheran that Eisenhower, not Marshall, was to command OVERLORD, the cross-Channel invasion. Given the choice of remaining in command in the Mediterranean until Rome fell, Eisenhower opted for going to England soon after the turn of the new year. Rome, he reasoned, would for a long time remain out of Allied reach.

There the matter of utilizing the sixty-eight LST's for an end run to Anzio might have rested had not Churchill fallen ill on the way home. Stopping at Tunis to confer with Eisenhower, Churchill took to bed with pneumonia. As he recovered, he determined with typical Churchillian stubbornness to have one more try at rescuing his strategic concepts in the Mediterranean. The key was the end run and Rome (not that Churchill ever used the American football term "end run": he called the stratagem a "cat's claw"). Capturing Rome, Churchill believed, would lead to a rapid sweep into northern Italy and from there possibly to the long-sought drive into the Balkans or westward into France, perhaps eliminating the need for direct confrontation in a cross-Channel attack until the foe was exhausted.

A man of unfaltering resolve, Churchill turned every ounce of it toward the goal of Rome. He played unabashedly on the sympathy of his subordinates for his illness, on General Eisenhower's reluctance to influence a decision for an operation that would take place after he had relinquished command, on the basic unfamiliarity with the situation of Eisenhower's successor, Field Marshal Sir Henry Maitland Wilson, a man so big in height and girth that people called him "Jumbo." And he had no compunction either about asking for even further extension on the LST's or about making the request to Roosevelt on Christmas Day after, he confessed, he already had told Allied commanders to get on with planning the amphibious assault. Only after the decision was firm would he listen to Eisenhower's Chief of Intelligence, General Strong, for what Churchill called "the seamy side of the question."[76]

Anzio was Churchill's new Gallipoli; he would let nothing stand in the way of it.

---

[76] Blumenson, *Anzio*, p. 49.

As planning began in earnest for Anzio, two events bode well for the operation. Re-evaluating Allied global resources, the Combined Chiefs of Staff discovered that by the spring of 1944 several additional American divisions might be sent to Italy, along with more French divisions from North Africa and British forces from the Near East. Also Mark Clark's Fifth Army was at last drawing up to the Gustav Line, across a rain-swollen Rapido River from the town of Cassino and from the monastery that frowned—Argus-eyed, it seemed to Allied troops, and indomitable—from the height of Monte Cassino.

Although one of the conditions for an amphibious attack at Anzio remained unfulfilled—assurance of a rapid linkup with the Fifth Army—Allied thinking turned under the impetus of frustration to the idea earlier advanced by Clark. A landing at Anzio, they thought, might prompt the Germans to withdraw from the Gustav Line. No longer a corollary designed to speed an accomplished breakthrough, Anzio became a vehicle for creating breakthrough.

To prompt the Germans to fall back, General Alexander directed, the invaders at Anzio were to advance immediately on the Alban Hills southeast of Rome, there to cut the enemy's routes of communications running from Rome to the Liri valley and Cassino. Caught off guard at Anzio, with supply lines severed, the Germans would have no alternative but to withdraw from the Gustav Line.

Although General Clark had been the original champion of that concept, he was less sanguine about German reaction to the landing than was Alexander and less sure of a quick linkup with the Fifth Army. Passing on Alexander's directions to the man who was to command the troops at Anzio, Clark distinctly altered the design. Assuming that the Germans would react swiftly and ruthlessly to the invasion, Clark expected the troops to dig in to protect a small beachhead, as at Salerno, and to advance some twenty miles inland to the Alban Hills only after defeating German counterattacks and building strength in the beachhead. Only in the unlikely event of a lightly opposed landing were the troops to move rapidly into the Alban Hills.

By this change Clark unwittingly set the scene for one of World War II's tragic performances. The commander involved was Major General John P. Lucas, an old man—by his own admission—at fifty-four, and one given to confessing to his diary that he thought too often of the soldiers under him, that he was "far too tender-hearted ever to be a success"[77] at his chosen profession. He was a man who had impressed Marshall and others as a training commander in the United States, as Marshall's eyes and ears briefly in North Africa, as Eisenhower's deputy in Sicily; but in those assignments the terrible burden of young American lives had lain directly on someone else.

As the Fifth Army prepared to assault the Gustav Line in mid-January 1944, Clark had eight divisions for the main attack, two for the landings at Anzio, and the equivalent of two more for reinforcing the beachhead. His German adversary, Vietinghoff, had eleven divisions in the *Tenth Army*, two-thirds of them directly opposite the Fifth Army, plus two under Kesselring's control in reserve near Rome. Four more under Kesselring were in northern Italy shoring up Mussolini's new puppet regime. That made a German total of seventeen, slightly less than the overall Allied strength in Italy.

Three rivers that in summer are shallow, placid streams but in winter are swollen torrents relieve the towering mountain terrain over which the Fifth Army was to attack. Rising in mountains inland from Cassino, the Rapido River flows past the foot of Monte Cassino, there to receive from the northwest the waters of the Liri River. Together the two streams flow to the sea as the Garigliano.

Where the Rapido and Liri rivers meet, their valleys create a concourse of relatively flat land that is rare in southern Italy, and the valley of the Liri, some five to seven miles wide, beckons enticingly toward Rome. Except on a narrow coastal plain, the course of the Garigliano is more closely confined between mountain ranges. The coastal plain itself, where the ancient Via Appia leads to Rome, Allied commanders had rejected as too confined for a major drive.

French divisions started the Fifth Army's attack along the upper reaches of the Rapido amid a jumbled mass of mountain peaks and were followed five days later, on January 17, by a British attack across the Garigliano. Although the French got a foothold inside the Gustav Line, theirs was but a diversionary attack; and although the British gained a bridgehead over the Garigliano near the coast, they could neither expand it nor achieve a second crossing farther upstream.

---

[77] Blumenson, *Anzio*, p. 60, quoting General Lucas' Diary.

The British fought with disturbing knowledge of the Allied timetable. During the night of the twentieth, American troops were to cross the Rapido in the hope of gaining the Liri valley for the linkup drive to Anzio. Only two days later, on January 22, British and American troops were to go ashore at Anzio, sixty long miles up the coast.

Yet as American troops prepared to challenge a narrow but raging Rapido, the British bridgehead over the Garigliano had caused more alarm in German circles than the Allies knew. Anticipating a broadened assault, the *Tenth Army* commander, General von Vietinghoff, appealed for help from the two divisions in reserve near Rome. That presented Kesserling with a dilemma: whether to hold the divisions in the event of Allied amphibious assault near Rome, or to commit them right away against what appeared to be "the greatest crisis yet encountered" in the campaign.[78]

Weighing the possibilities, Kesselring decided at last in favor of the Gustav Line, for the Germans had detected no Allied preparations for amphibious assault, and to lose the Gustav Line was to be forced to fall back north of Rome. The two divisions already had begun to bolster the defenses when, on the night of January 20, men of the U.S. 36th Division began to file warily down steep mountain slopes and across marshy bottom land to the raging Rapido.

Almost from the first, everything seemed to go wrong.

To the division commander, Major General Fred L. Walker, it was an impossible assignment in any case, though he confided his doubts only to his diary. "I'll swear I do not see how we can possibly succeed," he wrote.[79] British failure to achieve a second crossing of the Garigliano close to the Rapido added to Walker's concern. So did the fact that the ground near the river was so marshy that infantrymen would have to hand-carry bulky 400-pound assault boats more than two miles. So, too, the fact that every inch of the river valley was so exposed to German eyes that not even a field mouse could move over it in daylight undetected.

A dense fog added to the problems that cold January night. Men

---

[78] Blumenson, *Salerno to Cassino*, p. 318.

[79] Blumenson, *Salerno to Cassino* p. 327, quoting General Walker's Diary.

had trouble finding white tape that marked lanes laboriously cleared through minefields on the river flats. As German guns answered preliminary American bombardment, many men scattered, blundering into minefields and setting off deadly explosions. One company lost thirty men, including its commander, to one volley of German shelling. Tired, cold, frightened, many men in ranks heavy with inexperienced replacements simply abandoned the heavy assault boats and melted into the darkness. German fire so damaged some boats that they quickly sank, carrying overloaded infantrymen down with them. A rampaging current seized others, sending them careening downstream or tossing them unceremoniously back to the muddy launching sites.

In one of the assault battalions not a single man, among some seven hundred who tried, made it to the other side of the river. In another only some thirty men made it before midnight, though valiant efforts by infantrymen and engineers finally got most of the battalion across before dawn, either in assault boats or on a slippery footbridge. Most of the riflemen of another battalion also made it in the same way, but neither battalion had contact with the other, and neither had telephone or radio communications to the rear.

In the single night the 36th Division lost a thousand men, but the attack provoked no flurry of concern among the Germans. "Strong enemy assault detachments, which have crossed the river," the defending German division reported, "are annihilated." To General von Vietinghoff, the American effort appeared nothing more than a reconnaissance in force.

American commanders from Clark down to Walker made plans for a second try on the night of the twenty-first. This time the bulk of three battalions got across, and morning fog augmented by a smokescreen took some of the sting from German shelling; but the limited success merely prolonged the agony. Without supporting weapons and adequate communications, the men on the far bank had little hope for survival. As German shells in mid-afternoon knocked out the only footbridge, individuals and small groups began to filter back, defying the churning waters either by swimming or by paddling across on logs or other debris.

Seeing no hope for the bridgehead, commanders on the scene tacitly accepted the inevitable. It was a painful reverse, one that cost the 36th Division 1,681 casualties, including 143 known dead, some 500 captured, and some 375 missing and probably dead, and one that would generate a postwar Congressional investigation in a politically inspired, vindictive, but indecisive effort to fix blame. Yet for all the cost and for all the bitterness that the losses engendered, the attempt to cross the Rapido was a legitimate if difficult operation. As with all military operations, a shift of events, even minor, this way or that might have changed the outcome entirely. If Clark had known that the British crossing of the Garigliano already had lured German reserves from Rome, he might have used the 36th Division to expand the British bridgehead, a slower though surer way to reach the Liri valley.

Yet Clark had not known. War is like that.

Chapter Thirteen – Anzio, Cassino, and Rome

As General Eisenhower left early in the new year of 1944 for a secret two-week leave in the United States (Marshall insisted on it) and then assumed his new duties as supreme commander for OVERLORD, on January 8 "Jumbo" Wilson became supreme commander in the Mediterranean. Since Eisenhower took a number of familiar faces with him, there was a major shakeup of subordinate commanders. While Alexander remained as army group commander and Clark as head of the Fifth Army, General Sir Oliver Leese succeeded Montgomery in command of the Eighth Army. Air Marshal Tedder's successor as head of the Mediterranean Allied Air Forces was an American, Lieutenant General Ira C. Eaker, who had been commanding the Eighth U.S. Air Force in Britain. Eakers command included a mixture of American and British tactical and strategic air units. Admiral Sir John Cunningham succeeded his cousin, Sir Andrew, as overall naval commander, while the reliable Admiral Hewitt stayed as commander of American naval forces.[80]

In the first dark minutes of January 22, ships of another Allied invasion armada dropped anchor off the Italian coast. For John Lucas, the man

---

[80] Blumenson, *Salerno to Cassino* and *Anzio* were again the basic sources for this chapter. I have also used extensively Wynford Vaughn-Thomas, *Anzio, The Massacre at the Beachhead* (New York, 1961); Morison, *Sicily — Salerno — Anzio*; Martin Blumenson, "General Lucas at Anzio," and Sidney T. Mathews, "General Clark's Decision to Drive on Rome," both in Greenfield, ed., *Command Decisions*; Matloff, *Strategic Planning: 1943-1944*; and *Anzio Beachhead* in the *American Forces in Action* series (1947). See also Fred Sheehan, *Anzio, Epic of Bravery* (Norman, Okla., 1964). The official U.S. Army volume covering the breakout from the beachhead and the drive on Rome has yet to appear. On the bombing of Cassino, see also Craven and Cate, eds., *ARGUMENT to V-E Day*; Fred Majdalany, *The Battle of Cassino* (Boston, 1957); and Harold Bond, *Return to Cassino* (Garden City, 1964).

responsible for the young GI's and Tommies waiting to disembark heavy with the paraphernalia of war, one worry piled upon another. Added to all his other fears was the agonizing knowledge that the crossing of the Rapido had failed. Even if he succeeded in establishing a beachhead, what hope was there for a linkup overland with the main Allied forces?

Yet as, shortly before 2 A.M., assault boats headed toward sandy beaches a few hundred yards north and south of the dark outlines of low masonry buildings constituting the little town of Anzio, the shoreline remained strangely silent. Closer and closer churned the assault boats. Still no sound from the shore. Was it a trap?

As the men stumbled onto the sand, they soon learned that it was no trap. What nobody had even dared to hope was true—incredible, but nonetheless true. There were few Germans at Anzio: a detail of eighteen men whose job was to render the harbor useless, and two coastwatching battalions which quickly fled. Before the first day came to an end, some 36,000 Allied troops were ashore along with 3,000 vehicles and great tons of supplies. What was more, they had taken a minor port intact. The cost was astonishingly light: 13 killed, 97 wounded, 44 missing.

Every condition was right, more right than anyone had had any reason to imagine, for pushing out boldly from the beachhead, seizing the Alban Hills, even Rome itself, and cutting the enemy's vital arteries to the Gustav Line. Having sent two divisions and a corps headquarters to reinforce the Gustav Line, Field Marshal Kesselring had almost nothing left for either defense or counterattack.

That John Lucas did not know, and he could imagine it no more than he could have imagined the Germans' making no fight at the beaches. Somewhere out there in what by all the rules should have been defended countryside, there had to be trouble. John Lucas was not about to alter his carefully detailed plan in order to step brazenly into the unknown of the Alban Hills. He would stick to the plan to build a firm beachhead extending some eight miles inland from Anzio, there to get set for the counterattack that was sure to come.

Upon word of the unqualified success of the landing, General Clark and his superior, General Alexander, raced by fast boat to the beachhead. As they toured the beaches, neither revealed any indication that he disagreed with the failure to push out into the brown hills limning the skyline to north and east. They came—some Anzio wit later put it—they saw, they concurred.[81] For Alexander, that could be explained—with charity—because he was dealing with American subordinates, whom he believed in treating gingerly. (Remember how he had given in to Patton over Palermo?) As for Clark, he made his position clear as he bade Lucas goodbye. "Don't stick your neck out, Johnny," Clark reputedly told him. "I did at Salerno and got into trouble."[82]

The first news of Allied troops coming ashore sixty miles behind German lines raised a flurry of uncertainty among Germans in Rome. Some officials began to pack, others to burn papers, but the man who mattered, he who would have to decide if the landing posed such a threat that the Germans would have to abandon the Gustav Line, refused to panic. In the headquarters of Field Marshal Kesselring just north of Rome, there was anxiety enough, chagrin that it had to happen now that the reserves had left Rome for the south, but no panic. Kesselring had not earned his nickname—"Smiling Albert"—by preaching gloom and doom.

Kesselring knew that even if withdrawal should eventually prove his lot, he still would have to hold onto the Alban Hills if the troops in the south were to get away. To block the roads in that strategic high ground, he hurried there every small unit, every individual soldier he could muster, then ordered all available heavy anti-aircraft units to ring the beachhead and aim the deadly fire of their 88-mm. pieces against ground targets.

He turned then to broader measures. Despite the Allied offensive against the Gustav Line, he ordered General von Vietinghoff to release a corps headquarters and the equivalent of two divisions, including part of the *Hermann Goering Panzer Division*. From the other end of the line came another panzer division and part of a parachute division; from northern Italy, southern France, the Balkans, and Germany, the equivalent of five divisions, plus General Eberhard von Mackensen and headquarters of the *Fourteenth Army*. Yet it would take such time, Kesselring knew, to assemble those forces that if the Allies pressed quickly forward from their beachhead, all might be lost.

In the afternoon of the first day, Kesselring himself drove to the hills overlooking the plain around Anzio. The spectacle of Allied power was

[81] Vaughn-Thomas, *Anzio*, p. 51.

[82] Blumenson, *Anzio*, p. 56, quoting General Lucas' Diary.

awesome: hundreds of ships, with barrage balloons above them glistening in the sunlight; countless landing craft plying back and forth; everywhere troops, vehicles, bulldozers, artillery, tanks; and overhead a bristling curtain of aircraft.

It was enough to induce paralysis even in one so given to optimism as Kesselring, except that the vast array of Allied power appeared to be going no place. From all indications, the Allies intended to indulge in the luxury of holding a small beachhead until they could build their strength. That, Kesselring reasoned, would afford him time to ring the beachhead with resolute defenders and end the crisis.

That night when General von Vietinghoff telephoned to protest sending troops to Anzio, to warn that he would be unable to hold the Gustav Line without them, to urge as an alternative immediate withdrawal to concentrate everything against the landing at Anzio, Kesselring turned him down. Hold fast, Kesselring told him; there would be no withdrawal from the Gustav Line.

Six days after Allied troops arrived unopposed at Anzio, General Lucas still deemed his strength insufficient for a major attack from the beachhead. Pressed by Winston Churchill, who saw his dream of a major victory and capture of Rome foundering in inaction and indecision ("I had hoped we were hurling a wildcat onto the shore," Churchill noted later, "but all we got was a stranded whale"[83]), General Alexander pressed Clark, and Clark in turn pressed Lucas—but to little avail.

"Had I been able to rush to the high ground…immediately upon landing," Lucas rationalized to his diary, "nothing would have been accomplished except to weaken my force by that amount because the troops sent, being completely beyond supporting distance, would have been immediately destroyed. The only thing to do was what I did. Get a proper beachhead and prepare to hold it."[84]

Only on January 30, eight days after the landing, was Lucas at last willing to attack, but by that time the Germans, too, were ready. Kesselring was preparing to launch an attack of his own two days later to drive the Allies into the sea.

---

[83] Churchill, *Closing the Ring*, p. 488.

[84] Blumenson, *Anzio*, p. 90, quoting General Lucas' Diary.

Despite a deafening preliminary bombardment by planes, naval guns, and artillery, a three-division Allied attack on January 30 gained little. It began inauspiciously when in a preliminary night attack two Ranger battalions—elite troops specially trained in hit-and-run tactics—fell into an ambush. Of 767 who had started the attack, only 6 returned. Some 500 surrendered. For two days a British division and two American divisions fought, but they were unable even to reach the Via Appia, the main highway running from Rome to Naples along low swells of ground marking the start of the ascent to the Alban Hills.

Particularly disappointing was an attempt to break the battle open with armor—the U.S. 1st Armored Division, commanded now by Major General Ernest Harmon, a man with a barrel chest and a gravel voice. Frustrated by the cruel geography of Italy, tanks thus far had contributed little to the campaign except as infantry support weapons, a job that was anathema to men who believed armor to be the arm of decision. Circuitous mountain roads, bridgeless defiles and streams—Italy had seemed to the men in the tanks to be one endless anti-tank ditch; but the plain at Anzio looked to be different.

The troops manning the Shermans soon discovered that to be an illusion. Like other plains that had seen the destructive tide of battle in years past—Flanders and the valley of the Po, for example—the open ground about Anzio was deceptive. There was that old enemy of armies and particularly of armor—mud. There, too, were small but soft-banked streams and a grid of drainage ditches dug by Mussolini's regime to regain for agriculture what had been a malarial marsh. There, too, on the high ground were hungry 88-mm. pieces awaiting prey.

As the last hours of January ticked away, General Harmon's surviving tanks pulled back, like—some British soldiers noted wryly—the brave old Duke of York in the nursery rhyme, who marched ten thousand up the hill, then marched them down again.[85] The chance of an early breakout from the beachhead had passed. Wary of counterattack, Alexander and Clark told Lucas to dig in.

Although a failure, the Allied offensive had postponed a German-imposed day of reckoning. The fight required to halt the Allied thrust underscored the improvisation that hasty commitment had imposed in

[85] Vaughn-Thomas, *Anzio*, p. 87.

German ranks—a "witch's brew," one observer called it.[86] Renewed Allied attacks against the Gustav Line near Cassino caused additional concern.

Forced to delay his attack, Kesselring called on his artillery and the *Luftwaffe*. Against a beachhead not fifteen miles deep at any point, German artillery could reach every cranny from commanding positions in the hills. Taking advantage of the distance of Allied planes from their bases, twenty to thirty German planes at a time swept low again and again over the beachhead and the supporting fleet. German bombs forced General Lucas to move his command post into an underground wine cellar. A British cruiser, two Liberty ships, and several landing craft burned or sank.

To prepare the way further for an all-out effort to eliminate the beachhead, Kesselring twice hit the British with damaging night attacks, erasing one small salient on the main road into the Alban Hills and taking a strategic nest of red brick farm buildings that British troops called the "Factory." So vicious was the fight for the "Factory" that it left the British soldiers spent and their ranks so depleted that commanders wondered if they could hold against another assault. Elsewhere Kesselring probed, drew back, probed again, all the while rearranging his front to eliminate the improvisation of the early days and bringing up greater strength in men and guns.

The Allies, for their part, were nearing the end of the reinforcements they could afford for Anzio. In the line they had the equivalent of about five divisions, which with supporting troops made a total of 100,000 men; while at least parts of 14 German divisions ringed the beachhead with some 125,000. Hitler himself was taking a hand in finding troops to eliminate what he called the "abscess south of Rome"; to the German *Fuehrer*, driving the Allies into the Tyrrhenian Sea would be a great moral victory which might delay indefinitely a major invasion of Europe and gain the time he needed to recover from reverses on the Russian front.

As General Lucas and his superiors viewed the German buildup with marked concern, they could draw no comfort from the way things had been going sixty miles away in the shadow of Monte Cassino. There in the Gustav Line, General Clark had little alternative but to continue to attack, no matter how unfruitful, even disastrous, the opening blows; for even if unable to break into the Liri valley, he had to pin down German troops to keep them from moving to Anzio.

---

[86] Blumenson, *Anzio*, p. 107.

In exchange for depressing numbers of casualties, Clark's troops made hardly a dent in the Gustav Line. Although the French and an American division got across upper reaches of the Rapido upstream from Cassino, and the Americans fought into the northern fringes of the town, they ground to a halt exhausted. In freezing weather, alternately heavy with rain and snow, the mere process of staying alive in rain-drenched holes in the ground while sustained by such supplies as could be brought forward by pack mules would have been excruciating enough even without omnipresent enemy shells and bullets.

Something the fathers of those men had come to dread a quarter-century before, a malaise called "trench foot," put in an insidious appearance. Caused by prolonged exposure to damp and cold without exercise, trench foot made a man's toes, sometimes his entire foot, purple and swollen. If he was not evacuated in time and treated, amputation might be the only recourse.

Battalions soon were down to the size of companies, companies to platoons. The Germans and the Allies, General Clark noted, were like two boxers in a ring, both about to collapse, neither possessing the reserve to score a victory. Clark's Chief of Staff visited the troops in the line across the rampaging Rapido and came away with the impression that the men were so disheartened as to be almost mutinous.

Over the entire scene towered the baleful psychological presence of Monte Cassino with its historic religious crown, the imposing old abbey of Saint Benedict. Begun around A.D. 529, destroyed or sacked from time to time through the centuries by Lombards, Saracens, and various factions in the emerging Italian nation, the abbey sheltered priceless artifacts of Christendom and constituted one of the world's most renowned historical and religious treasures.

To many in the Allied divisions fighting in the abbey's shadow, it seemed incomprehensible that the Germans were not using the abbey, if not as shelter for men and guns, at least as an observation post. More than one Allied observer was positive he had seen German troops come and go from the abbey or the glint of sun against field glasses atop the walls.

Yet senior American commanders, whose troops were more directly concerned than were the British and the French, were unconvinced. Official Allied policy, as laid down by the Combined Chiefs of Staff and underscored on several occasions by General Eisenhower before his departure from the Mediterranean, was to make every effort to preserve religious, historical, and classical monuments unless destroying them was a "military necessity." Specific instructions had gone to air and artillery commanders to avoid bombing or shelling the Benedictine abbey. American commanders were certain in any case that, even if the Germans were using the abbey, turning it into a mass of rubble would provide them with both a potent propaganda weapon and more formidable defensive positions.

No one seriously considered destroying the abbey until the second week of February when General Clark replaced American units before Monte Cassino with a New Zealand corps commanded by Lieutenant General Sir Bernard Freyberg. As Major General F. S. Tuker, commander of an Indian division in Freyberg's corps, got ready to attack the town of Cassino, he asked Freyberg to prepare the way by destroying the abbey. He deemed it a "military necessity."

Freyberg agreed.

Since General Clark was away from his command post visiting the Anzio beachhead, his Chief of Staff referred the matter to Clark's superior, General Alexander. Although Alexander was aware that American commanders on the ground dissented, as did Clark, he said that if Freyberg wanted it, he should have it.

Hurrying back from Anzio, Clark personally told Alexander that he disagreed with bombing the abbey, that civilians taking refuge there might be killed, that the destruction would avail nothing but to give the Germans an excuse to move into the rubble. Still convinced that if Freyberg and his subordinate wanted the abbey destroyed, it should be done, Alexander decided nevertheless to consult the new theater commander, General Wilson. After the commander of Allied air forces, General Eaker, flew low over the abbey in an observation plane and claimed that he saw German troops inside, General Wilson concurred. Late on February 14, Allied planes dropped leaflets warning that the abbey would soon be bombed.

Inside the abbey, few of the monks usually residing there remained. A few weeks earlier, after Allied artillery fire had inadvertently imposed minor damage, the Germans had removed many of the art treasures to Rome and encouraged the monks to leave. Only an aging abbot, seventy-eight-year-old Bishop Gregorio Diamare, five monks, a few lay brothers, and about 150 civilian refugees stayed. Although the Germans had dug defensive positions about two hundred yards from the abbey, with at least one as close as fifty yards, no Germans were inside the abbey.

The big bombers came in persistent, droning waves early the next morning, the fifteenth, before the abbot had found time to heed the Allied warning. Some 250 bombers dropped almost 600 tons of explosives on the abbey—merciful by the saturation bombing standards developed later but nevertheless high for a single target.

The crown of Monte Cassino appeared to erupt. The abbey was demolished. The Germans promptly moved in to construct formidable defenses within the rubble.

Down on the plain the attack by General Tuker's Indian division got nowhere.

The German counterattack for which John Lucas had waited warily since coming ashore at Anzio struck the next day, February 16.

Behind a crushing artillery bombardment Kesselring employed a first wave of five divisions and an elite unit sent specifically by Hitler to spearhead the assault—a regiment of picked men who had been Hitler's bodyguard but heretofore had seen no combat. Although two divisions penetrated depleted British units near the "Factory" to gain an alarming two miles, that was a subsidiary effort which adroit commitment of a British reserve halted short of backup positions labeled "Final Beachhead Line." In the main attack down a road leading directly from the Alban Hills to Anzio, three other divisions made rapid gains at first; but as supporting tanks bogged in mud, and as Hitler's elite regiment broke and ran, troops of the U.S. 45th Division found time to re-form.

Early on the second day, as a fight for the final beachhead line was apparently developing, General Lucas put a British division in position to back up the 45th, loaned the 45th Division a battalion of tanks from the beachhead reserve, and committed a battalion of 90-mm. anti-aircraft guns to employ direct fire against German tanks. As night fell, Allied troops still held the final beachhead line; but General Lucas was seriously debating whether to commit his last reserve, and in some quarters there was talk of another Dunkirk.

Since the German divisions in the first wave were seriously hurt during the two days of fighting, the *Fourteenth Army* commander, General von Mackensen, decided to commit a second wave he had been withholding to deliver the *coup de grâce*. As dawn came on the third day, a fresh panzer division and a panzer grenadier division moved against the reeling 45th Division.

The new force was close to breaking one of the 45th Division's regiments when in mid-morni ng General von Mackensen suddenly shifted his strike a few hundred yards to the right against the 45th Division's third regiment, which up to that point had been scarcely touched. To Mackensen's adversaries the shift was inexplicable, for the Germans were at the very threshold of a breakthrough; but Mackensen did not know that. When the violent cacophony of combat died that afternoon, the American regiment had held.

Although the Germans tried for two more days to achieve their breakthrough, the chance to penetrate the final beachhead line had passed. More than five thousand men had fallen on each side. Yet for all the sense of crisis pervading the beachhead, General Lucas had stopped the threat even without calling on the armored division that constituted his final reserve.

As in the Gustav Line, a temporary stalemate settled over the front at Anzio. The two sides were too evenly matched, the two boxers in the ring too groggy, for either to force a decision.

In the lull that followed, General Alexander expressed concern to his British superiors and to General Clark about what he termed the negative quality of command in the beachhead and an absence of drive and enthusiasm. It remained for Clark to perform the execution. On the twenty-second he relieved General Lucas of his command—technically, "without prejudice." Lucas was relieved, Clark said, not because he had failed to take the Alban Hills, but because Alexander thought him defeated and Clark himself thought him worn out.

Although Lucas had long feared, as he put it, that his head would "probably fall in the basket," he was shocked when it came. At that stage, he thought, he had been "winning something of a victory."[87] Clark thought so, too. Lucas was right, Clark believed, not to thrust immediately into the Alban Hills—a view that was shared later by, among others, George Marshall. Clark considered that such a move would have been an invitation to the Germans to annihilate the entire beachhead force.

Yet if that was the case, why Anzio at all?

---

[87] Blumenson, *Anzio*, pp. 107 and 139, quoting in both cases General Lucas' Diary.

Clark did think that Lucas should have pushed out as far as the first tier of towns along the swells of ground just short of the Alban Hills, where a secure hold might have persuaded the Germans of the futility of counterattacking the beachhead. Even Alexander did not condemn Lucas for failing to move *to* the Alban Hills; he objected that Lucas had not moved *toward* those hills—a matter of semantics difficult for many to decipher.

Lucas himself thought he had done the job correctly at Anzio. They were disappointed in him, he believed, because he had failed to prompt the Germans to withdraw from the Gustav Line. Yet the whole idea that a beachhead at Anzio might accomplish that was, in his view, wrong, because the Allies lacked the strength to induce the Germans to withdraw.

A nagging question would forever persist, nevertheless, whether a daring thrust from the unopposed landing sites at Anzio might have prompted the Germans to pull back from the Gustav Line. Even the Germans could not say. Yet if fault there was in failing to push out boldly, sensitive John Lucas, who cared so much for the men under him, shared it with his superiors, Mark Clark and Harold Alexander, who failed to order specifically that the job be done. They had been as indecisive as Lucas, yet when the indecision led to Allied rather than to German crisis, it was Lucas alone who had to pay.

For all the lull in fighting within the beachhead, life in the narrow confines of the Anzio plain remained grim. It was as close as warfare came anywhere during World War II to the molelike existence of World War I.

Here is how an infantry replacement new to the beachhead saw it:

The bottom was squashy. It wasn't a very big hole, about chest deep. Part of it was boarded over…All through the night there were flares going up from the Jerry lines…I was scared.

It was just plain hell all through the day, and the nights were worse. The hole got about six inches of water, and you couldn't do anything but try to bail it out with your helmet. We wrapped shelter halves and blankets around us but they didn't do much good. They got soaked with rain and then you sat on a piece of wood or something and shivered and cussed…You couldn't get out of that hole once the sun came up, or even show the top of your head.

At night we got canned C-rations. Toward the last they brought them up warmed a little, and coffee, only a little warm by the time it got to us, and once in a while a beef sandwich or some doughnuts.

You had to get out of the hole when it got dark for several reasons, one of which was to get some circulation back into your feet. A lot of the boys went to the medics with bad cases of trench foot, but I wasn't that lucky.

Jerry threw in a lot of artillery and mortars. The best thing to do was pull in your head and pray. Some of that big stuff would cave in the side of a wet foxhole like it was sand, and a couple of the boys got buried right in their hole fifty yards away from me. We had two or three casualties every day, mostly from artillery and mortars. If you got it at night you were lucky, because they could get you out right away.

God help you if you got hit in the daytime.[88]

Moreover, Anzio lacked the great contrast in comfort and safety that normally existed between men in the forward foxholes and those in a place that front-line soldiers called, with a mixture of envy and disdain, "the rear." For the rear at Anzio had its own special hell.

The men in the rear were almost as distinct as those in the foxholes to German eyes in the hills, and they had to go about their duties in daylight, no matter what the tempo of German shells, the threat of German bombs. Supplies and reinforcements had to be unloaded in the port or along the beaches, then sorted and moved to depots. In a cluster of hospital tents so exposed to enemy shells that troops called it "Hell's Half-Acre," the wounded had to be tended, and those that could be moved transported to landing craft for transfer to hospital ships or for direct run to Naples. Those and countless other tasks—such as burying the dead—could not wait for night.

Around big installations like storage depots and hospitals, bulldozers piled great parapets of earth or engineers erected sandbag revetments—protection against shell or bomb fragments but no defense against a direct hit or against shells bursting in the air. With the exception of the sinking of a British hospital ship early in the fight, the Germans displayed respect for medical installations, but so many were the shells and so close were other legitimate targets that losses among patients, nurses, and surgeons were inevitable. Even the beachhead cemetery, where Italian laborers helped American soldiers dig graves for rigid forms encased in white mattress covers, was often under fire.

In an effort to blur German vision, chemical troops operated smoke

---

88 Donald G. Taggart, ed., *History of the Third Infantry Division in World War II* (Washington, 1947), pp. 125-26.

generators and staked out smoke pots in a great semicircle within the beachhead. The devices produced a light haze that unquestionably cut down on the accuracy of German fire, but the little beachhead was so crowded with troops and installations that even unobserved fire was almost bound to hit somebody or something. The smoke was unpleasant, too. It had a sickly sweet smell—almost like a corpse; it was black and greasy; it coated a man's clothes and skin, his nostrils, his lungs. That and the mud, the cold, the lack of amenities, the constant expectation of German shelling, the gnawing knowledge that the Germans might at any moment try again to shove the beachhead into the sea.

Continuing to take advantage of the distance of Allied fighters from their bases, the *Luftwaffe* made an all-out fight against the beachhead and the ships that kept it alive. Although Allied engineers built an emergency landing strip for planes in the beachhead, German shelling made it useless. The shelling involved guns of various calibers, including one 280-mm. railroad piece whose shells hurtled into the beachhead with such a roar that Allied soldiers named it the "Anzio Express."

The only safe place in the beachhead was a labyrinth of cellars and tunnels dug many years before as wine cellars in the porous subsoil under the buildings of Anzio. There was room there for an occasional headquarters staff, but mainly the dark vaults served as a refuge for Italian civilians caught up intimately and cruelly in the war. There they dwelt in damp squalor amid stifling odors of wine, garlic, stale cooking, unwashed bodies, until finally space became available for them on some ship going to Naples. More than twenty-two thousand civilians eventually were evacuated.

Strange were the two zones of the beachhead. Back near the beaches, around the town, it was Piccadilly Circus or Times Square dressed in olive drab, so intense was the bustle, so jammed the roads, so thick the soldier population. Yet to drive a few miles inland was to enter another world. Signs reading "No vehicles past this point" marked the dividing line. Ahead lay a tortured, convoluted landscape. Ahead lay a dead land where nothing moved on penalty of death. Yet tens of thousands of men lived there—or died.

The coming of night produced a sharp reversal. In the rear the bustle subsided; the DUKW's quit plying their tireless way to and fro between ship and beach; the bulldozers stopped churning; the uniformed stevedores fell silent; only the peculiar rhythmic throb of a German reconnaissance plane filled the air; but at the same time supply trucks, no light to guide them, began inching toward the dead land. There the human moles had come out of the ground, to eat, to drink, to defecate, to replenish their stocks of things that kept them alive—mortar and artillery shells, hand grenades, clips and belts of bullets. A flare might suddenly erupt, bathing the land in a shimmering, unnaturally brilliant light; whereupon the "moles" would freeze. Long moments later the light would fade and go out. A machine gun might chatter. Then the "moles" would move again.

Commanders, concerned that this existence would sap all offensive fervor from the troops, tried to keep them active with patrols and limited objective attacks, which were euphemisms for fear and hardship and death, and to provide them with occasional surcease from the life at the front. They set up a rest center down the shore from Anzio where despite occasional shelling a man could get a bath, write a letter, see a movie. Every four days 750 men left by LST for a recreation center near Naples. There they might listen to the Fifth Army's radio station or to "Axis Sally," whom most men preferred. They liked her throaty voice, her selections of late American popular tunes, her salty language telling how other soldiers or 4F's were seducing the women the Allied troops had left behind. Some of the propaganda leaflets were diverting, too. Graphically illustrating the fate of the women back home whom "Axis Sally" talked about, they made prized foxhole pinups.

When would it ever end—this tormenting, miserable, uncertain, and above all dull life in the beachhead?

February passed with the last German counterattack. March passed, too, bringing only the discouraging news that even a devastating bombardment by five hundred Allied planes had not enabled New Zealand and Indian troops to conquer all the town of Cassino, and that Monte Cassino and the fortresslike ruins of the monastery still dominated the fighting in the Gustav Line. April came, too, blessed with the promise of spring; a bougainvillea bloomed incongruously in an abandoned garden, but little else.

By mid-April 1944, Allies and Germans each had twenty-two divisions in Italy. Two more American divisions had arrived, along with more British Commonwealth troops and more French units; the latter constituted an entire French Expeditionary Corps within Clark's Fifth Army.

As Allied resources had grown worldwide, the increase in divisions posed no particular strain; although Anzio had created a continuing drain on landing craft, shipping, and air support that few leaders would have countenanced had they anticipated it. The Germans attained their total of divisions by withholding troops critically needed not only in Russia but also in France; for Allied preparations in the British Isles clearly pointed to an early invasion of France.

The Germans deemed they had no choice but to continue to fight in Italy, as far to the south as possible to deny airfields close to vital targets in the Balkans and the homeland. Although civilian laborers and para-military forces had begun to build a new line in the northern Apennines, that was a last-ditch position to which Kesselring would withdraw only when forced. The Gustav Line was still basically intact; a new switch position called the "Adolf Hitler Line" backed the sector that the Allies were trying to penetrate; and a third position called the "Caesar Line" was under construction in the Alban Hills. The Germans still might hold for a long time south of Rome.

Allied policy was less clear. Although American and British leaders alike had come to accept the handicap the Italian campaign imposed on the buildup for the cross-Channel attack (Operation OVERLORD), they disagreed on how much the fighting in Italy should be allowed to afFcct the operation designed to supplement OVERLORD—a simultaneous invasion of southern France. In order to be mounted from resources in the Mediterranean, that invasion would require diverting at least two American divisions from Italy, plus French divisions and that critical item, landing craft.

Churchill and some—though not all—of his military advisers had never been reconciled to the invasion of southern France, which Roosevelt and Stalin had imposed on Allied strategy at Teheran, and to the limits that operation placed on carrying the Italian campaign to a logical conclusion in the Balkans; they believed that Italy had more than southern France to contribute to OVERLORD. The fact that Anzio had failed to break open the Italian campaign and deliver Rome worked both for and against Churchill's position. It was a strong argument, General Marshall and the Joint Chiefs believed, for accepting stalemate in Italy. Yet Churchill could argue in return, that in light of the threat Anzio had posed to the Germans, the maintenance of Allied strength in Italy would prevent more

German divisions from opposing OVERLORD than if that strength were reduced in order to mount an invasion of southern France.

As debate persisted, that unlikely arbiter of strategy—landing craft—developed as the focal issue. The planners for Operation OVERLORD wanted more landing craft in order to develop a larger cross-Channel attack; landing craft were still needed to support Anzio; and landing craft would be needed for southern France. In mid-April the American Chiefs of Staff finally agreed to defer indefinitely a decision on southern France, pending the outcome of an effort in Italy to break out of the Anzio beachhead and eliminate the need there for landing craft.

As the debate progressed, the means and the timing of a new offensive in Italy both were in question, but Allied commanders in Italy proceeded with preparations anyway. They included an ambitious six-week aerial campaign to cut the enemy's supply lines leading down the peninsula. Flying almost 50,000 sorties and dropping 26,000 tons of bombs, the airmen made it more than unpleasant for German supply convoys and in some cases wreaked heavy damage; but mountains, bad weather, and German ability to repair roads and bridges quickly and to move at night frustrated their efforts. Neither Mackensen's *Fourteenth Army* around the Anzio beachhead nor Vietinghoff's *Tenth Army* in the Gustav Line ever hurt for lack of rations or ammunition.

A shift of Allied troops to provide greater strength in the beachhead and before the Gustav Line near Cassino meanwhile proceeded with greater success. After withdrawing a British corps from Clark's Fifth Army, General Alexander shifted Clark's remaining American corps to the coastal sector at the mouth of the Garigliano River and put the French Expeditionary Corps immediately inland. Leaving only holding forces on the Adriatic side of Italy, Alexander shifted the British Eighth Army to Cassino, there to take command of British, Commonwealth, Italian, and Polish troops. The Eighth Army was to try its hand at cracking the fortress of Monte Cassino, then make the main drive up the Liri valley.

To strengthen the Anzio beachhead Clark sent in two more American divisions. That made an Allied total of seven, plus a regimental-sized Ranger-like force of Canadian-American volunteers—the First Special Service Force—which had entered the beachhead in February. Under Alexander's plan, once the Eighth Army had entered the Liri valley, the troops from the beachhead were to drive northeast across lower slopes of the Alban Hills to the town of Valmontone. Since Valmontone lies astride the main highway leading into the Liri valley and south to Cassino, the troops from the beachhead might trap enemy troops attempting to escape from the Gustav Line—in effect a replay of the old scenario for the landing at Anzio.

Despite the reinforcements, Clark doubted the ability of the beachhead troops to reach Valmontone in time to trap appreciable German forces. The route to Valmontone ran through Cistema, a pile of rubble on the periphery of the beachhead, which after long weeks of stalemate fairly bristled with German defenses. Clark doubted also that British troops making a frontal attack toward the Liri valley would play a decisive role in breaking the Gustav Line. That would be reserved, Clark believed, for the Fifth Army, specifically the French Expeditionary Corps advancing through mountains west of the Liri to outflank the Germans in the valley.

With those thoughts in mind, Clark told the new commander in the beachhead, General Truscott—who once had served as Eisenhower's deputy in North Africa and had acquired considerable combat experience in command of the 3d Division in Sicily and the beachhead—to draw up alternate plans. What attracted Clark was a glittering prize whose capture would inflict less damage on the enemy than would entrapment at Valmontone but which would make bigger headlines in newspapers back home. That prize was Rome.

Visiting the Anzio beachhead on May 5, six days before the target date for the big offensive against the Gustav Line, Clark's superior, Alexander, got a look at four plans that Truscott had prepared. Only one, said Alexander, interested him: a thrust through Cisterna to trap the Germans at Valmontone.

General Clark visited the beachhead the next day. Irritated that Alexander had bypassed him in the chain of command, he lodged a telephone protest with his superior. As Clark himself put it, he had no intention either of allowing Alexander to "move in and run" his army or of sitting idly while the British denied the Fifth Army, which in Clark's thinking had borne the brunt of the fighting in Italy, the glory of capturing Rome.[89]

While making no objection to the substance of Alexander's orders to Truscott, Clark in effect contravened them. He told Truscott to be prepared

[89] Clark, *Calculated Risk*, p. 342.

to carry out either the attack Alexander wanted to Valmontone or the one Clark clearly preferred—a direct drive on Rome. He told Alexander only that he wanted to avoid being tied to one plan, to be free to react as the development of the battle might demand—which was a way of saying Clark intended to run things himself.

For the third time in the Italian campaign (fourth, if one counted Sicily) General Alexander handled a subordinate of another nationality with soft-gloved hands. Assuring General Clark that he had no intention of interfering, he withdrew gracefully. By declining to deal firmly, Alexander allowed Clark the chance to jeopardize the Allied offensive even before it began.

As Clark had predicted, it was the French who broke the Gustav Line. Despite a furious cannonade before midnight on May 11 by almost fifteen hundred guns, emplaced from Cassino to the sea, a Polish division joined the roll of those that had recoiled before the defenses of Monte Cassino. Although the British got across the Rapido, it took them three days even to reach the pillbox-barricaded entrance to the Liri valley. American troops in the narrow coastal plain could do no better. It remained for the French Expeditionary Corps with a division of North African Goumiers, who reveled in mountain warfare, to provide the key.

Exploiting the fact that the Germans had weakly manned the trackless crags between Cassino and the coastal plain in order to gain strength elsewhere, the French under Alphonse Juin—he who had come so close to embracing the Allies that November night in the Villa des Oliviers in Algiers—plodded irresistibly over and around the rocky peaks. In two days they reached positions on heights southwest of Monte Cassino, overlooking both the coastal plain and the Liri valley. So torn were the German units before them that Field Marshal Kesselring hastily sent south two divisions he had managed during the weeks of stalemate to pull into reserve near Rome.

Kesselring's move delayed the end in the south, yet about all the two divisions could do was fill holes in the backup position, the Adolf Hitler Line, which the Germans expeditiously rechristened the "Dora Line," lest impending loss do damage to the *Fuehrer's* name. Even so, the French Goumiers quickly tore a gaping hole in that line.

The French success dragged British and Americans along. To avoid envelopment, German units on the coastal plain and at the entrance to the Liri valley began grudgingly to withdraw. With the British on the low ground threatening to outflank Monte Cassino, the Poles again tested the fortress on the crest. This time they took it, after a last turbulent combat, on May 18.

Now that a breakthrough in the south was in the offing, the time was approaching for the troops in the Anzio beachhead to violate their confinement and step astride the enemy's line of retreat at Valmontone. Yet again Clark tried to forestall the maneuver by suggesting that it might not prove the decisive blow Alexander contemplated. Unmoved, Alexander insisted on Valmontone.

In the face of Alexander's resolution Clark felt impelled to order General Truscott to make at least his first strike in the direction of Valmontone. That meant Cisterna. It took the better part of three days, but beginning on May 23, infantry of the 3d Division advancing behind the fury of a thousand artillery pieces and waves of fighter-bombers eventually cleared the reeking, fetid ruins of Cisterna. With that hinge of the German line broken, the door leading to Valmontone was ajar: a way was open to cut the incipient German retreat from the Gustav Line, to remove in one blow the bulk of the German forces in Italy and clear a path to the north, perhaps to impel diversion of German forces from France on the eve of OVERLORD, to realize the potential of a heretofore sterile Italian campaign. Indeed, Kesselring already had ordered the *Hermann Goering Panzer Division*, which was assembling north of Rome en route to France, to cancel all plans and head for Valmontone. That was testament enough to the crisis.

Yet Mark Clark had eyes only for Rome.

On the second day of the offensive Clark asked Truscott if he would be able to change the direction of his attack from Valmontone into the Alban Hills toward Rome. Although Truscott said he could, he thought it inadvisable unless there were marked indications of German weakness in the Alban Hills, and unless the Germans should so reinforce Valmontone that Truscott's forces could not seize the town. Nevertheless, without informing Alexander, Clark told Truscott to be ready on short notice to make the shift.

The next day, May 25, was a day of climax. Along the coastal plain a British-American patrol from the Anzio beachhead established contact with American troops advancing north from the Gustav Line. Later in the day the British Eighth Army broke through the last positions of the Hitler Line to enter the Liri valley. That was also the day when Cisterna fell.

On May 25, too, Clark made his decision. Valmontone? Or Rome?

Despite General Alexander's explicit order, Clark deemed he had three choices: to keep Truscott's full strength of five divisions on the road to Valmontone, to turn full strength toward Rome, or to split Truscott's forces between the two.

Disregarding the Caesar Line in the Alban Hills, to which the Germans who had ringed the beachhead were repairing, Clark believed Truscott's troops capable of handling the Germans at any point. He believed, too, that the Eighth Army could advance readily up the Liri valley without any help from Truscott at Valmontone. And he doubted that taking Valmontone would trap sizable German forces, for the Germans might turn other roads, even though they were serpentine mountain routes, into avenues of escape. Indeed, Clark thought that much of the German *Tenth Army* already had escaped from the Liri valley—a consequence, in his opinion, of less than maximum effort by the pursuing British.

Yet all those reasons were secondary to the fact that Clark wanted Rome and wanted it exclusively for his Fifth Army, to provide tangible, dramatic evidence to the people back home of American success in Italy. Clark knew, too, that the Italian campaign—always a stepchild even as the only active Allied front in Europe—was destined in a matter of weeks, even days, to be practically disinherited by events elsewhere. Clark wanted Rome, and he wanted it before the eyes of the world focused on the beaches of Normandy.

In announcing his decision, Clark deigned to confront personally neither his subordinate, Truscott, nor his superior, Alexander. After entrusting the task of telling Truscott to his operations officer, Clark left Anzio for his command post in the south to brief his Chief of Staff, to whom he was transferring the onus of telling Alexander. He thus would be beyond reach of telephone or radio should Truscott object; and the next day, after the decision had become irrevocable and his Chief of Staff had informed Alexander, Clark would be out of contact again, on his way back to Anzio.

Clark's plan paid no more than lip service to Alexander's order to drive on Valmontone. Only one infantry division reinforced by a contingent of armor and the Canadian-American regiment was to continue to Valmontone. The rest of Truscott's force—four divisions—was to turn into the Alban Hills toward Rome.

Having no relish for Clark's change, Truscott tried unsuccessfully to reach Clark to press his objections. Failing that, he dutifully supported the plan when he presented it to his division commanders, but they did not like it either. Yet none had a choice but to do as directed. And Alexander, when he learned of the decision, had little more of a choice, for the new attack toward Rome was under way on the morning of May 26 before Clark's Chief of Staff—as Clark had planned it—told Alexander about it.

As events developed, Clark's decision neither unlocked the door to Rome nor cut the German withdrawal to Valmontone. In the Caesar Line along vine-clad slopes of the Alban Hills, the German *Fourteenth Army*, which had come so close to pushing the Allies into the sea, repulsed one bloody, fruitless attack after another. Through Valmontone for more than a week the *Tenth Army* retired leisurely: its line of withdrawal was held open by a makeshift force that for three days could not have repulsed a strong secondary effort and even for the rest of the time clearly would have been unable to hold off a full-scale attack by all of Truscott's five divisions.

General von Vietinghoff's *Tenth Army* had taken heavy losses and had left behind the sturdy prepared defenses around Monte Cassino, but it still was an army, an organized force capable of withdrawing skillfully to new positions to fight again and not the mauled, disheartened flotsam that Alexander had intended to make of it. A slow pace by the pursuing Eighth Army had something to do with the *Tenth Army*'s escape, but for the most part Kesserling and Vietinghoff owed their gratitude to Rome and the attraction it held for the commanding general of the Fifth U.S. Army.

Only after the last of the *Tenth Army* had passed Valmontone, and after the *Fourteenth Army* in the Alban Hills, its job done, began to retire, did Truscott's drive on Rome gain momentum. By the second day of June only rear guards barred the way, whereupon Truscott's divisions formed flying wedges of tanks, tank destroyers, engineers, and infantry and began to advance toward the city to secure bridges over the Tiber River. As the last Germans departed the northern fringes on June 4—sparing the capital the pillage and destruction visited on Naples—American troops entered Rome.

The 88th Division's Reconnaissance Troop was the first to pass a sign reading ROMA, along the Via Casiliana at 8 A.M. on the fourth. The Canadian-American regiment was the first to penetrate the heart of the city. For them and for others that followed, it was carnival. As Romans entered on a holiday unparalleled in modern times, it was hard to remember that only a few short months before many of the same laughing, cheering Latin faces had been upturned under right arms extended in the Fascist salute, with voices chanting, "*Duce! Duce! Duce!*" Who wanted to remember anyway? Memory held fire-swept beaches at Salerno, muddy death at the Rapido, carnage at Monte Cassino, grim survival at Anzio. Better to succumb to the cheers, the flowers, the tears of joy, the people holding children aloft, others shouting, "*Benvenuto! Grazie! Liberatori!*"

"Hey, Joe! *Sigaretto?*"

Chapter Fourteen – Under the Sea and in the Air

As Allied troops during 1943 and the first five months of 1944 had confronted the Germans on the ground in North Africa, Sicily, and Italy, the rest of the American effort in the war in Europe had largely revolved about a few thousand square miles of sea-bound landscape: "This fortress built by Nature for herself against infection and the hand of war."[90] In less poetic terms American troops called it "the UK."[91]

In the main this period of the war was a sea war and an air war; but for all the cannon, bombs, depth charges, torpedoes, it was also a war waged with other tools—factories, shipyards, troopships, freighters, railroads, bulldozers, trucks. It was a war of logistics, an ancient yet still imprecise term encompassing producing, moving, storing the materials of war, and training, equipping, transporting, housing, and feeding the men who do the fighting.

One phase of this war had to be won first, for without that victory the other phase could progress only feebly at best. This was the war against the submarine.

As 1943 opened, it remained disturbingly uncertain who would win that particular phase. The wolfpacks still were feeding on Allied convoys,

---

[90] John of Gaunt's speech in *The Tragedy of King Richard II*, Act II.

[91] Basic sources for this chapter were: Morison, *The Battle of the Atlantic* and *The Atlantic Battle Won*; Craven and Cate, eds., *ARGUMENT to V-E Day*; Cajus Becker, *The Luftwaffe War Diaries* (Garden City, 1968); and Adolf Gal-land, *The First and the Last: The Rise and Fall of the German Fighter Forces, 1938-1945* (New York, 1954). See also Ladislas Farago, *The Tenth Fleet* (New York, 1962). Gordon Wright, *The Ordeal of Total War*, pp. 180-81, provides a lucid discussion of saturation versus precision bombing

and one of the worst winters on record was lashing the Atlantic, severely restricting the protective cover shore-based Allied aircraft might weave.

By March of 1943 the situation was fast becoming critical. Submarines sank 108 ships that month, totaling 627,000 tons, almost as many as in the preceding black November; and only 15 U-boats went to the bottom in return, still fewer than the Germans each month were building. An average of 116 U-boats roamed the North Atlantic every day—so many that in evading one wolfpack, a convoy often merely fell into the clutches of another.

The situation was alarming in terms not only of the need to supply Allied troops fighting in Tunisia and to accumulate American troops and supplies in Britain, but also of providing the British people with enough supplies to keep them fighting, producing, even eating. The British had tightened their belts sharply: in 1942 they lived on imports of only 23,000,000 tons, as opposed to 50,000,000 tons annually before the war, and they were fighting at the same time. Yet if something were not done soon about the submarines, famine would overtake the land.

In late April 1943 a forty-two-ship convoy bearing the prosaic name "ONS-5" began the homeward voyage from Britain. For eight of the sixteen days of the voyage, tankers, merchantmen, and escort vessels battled heavy seas and fifty-one U-boats, an unprecedented number. Although thirteen merchantmen went down, an escort never numbering more than nine ships sank five submarines, while American and Canadian planes on shore patrol sank two more. A year earlier that many submarines would have spelled death for the entire convoy.

It was scarcely apparent at the time, but the crossing of ONS-5 marked a dramatic turn in the anti-submarine campaign. In that last week of April and the first three weeks of May, twelve more convoys crossed the North Atlantic with the loss of five merchant ships in exchange for thirteen submarines. At the same time British planes based in England opened a new method of warfare against U-boats coming and going from German-occupied French ports on the Bay of Biscay. Picking up the spoor with microwave radar by night, the planes illuminated their prey with a new type of searchlight controlled by the radar set itself, and either moved in for the kill or called in surface vessels to do the job.

The Americans at about the same time—May 1943—also were introducing what was in effect a new weapon. To correlate various anti-submarine commands and to exercise priority control over all ships and naval aircraft engaged in anti-submarine warfare, Admiral King created a new organization called, for no particular reason, the "Tenth Fleet." Not a ship did the new fleet have. It had instead brain power for research and command power for coordinating what up to that time had been a disconnected endeavor.

In a month the British-American campaign scored a kill of thirty-eight U-boats, which was twelve more than the Germans had built and three fewer than the number of merchant vessels lost. It was a milestone in a war that was far from won, but a milestone nevertheless.

This encouraging turn came almost simultaneously with the introduction of two new American weapons into the campaign—fleets of destroyer escorts (DE's), smaller, faster versions of the traditional destroyer, and escort carriers (CVE's), built with merchant-like hulls on which were superimposed flight decks capable of handling short-range naval aircraft. The escort carriers would go a long way toward making up for a lack of big aircraft carriers in the Atlantic. DE's and CVE's perfectly complemented each other, forming a team that by early summer of 1943 was present in sufficient numbers to have a marked impact on the war at sea.

The escort carriers with their screen of destroyer escorts helped fill the void in protection that still existed in what sailors called the "black pit," that area in mid-Atlantic out of range of shore-based aircraft. Yet the mid-Atlantic still remained a source of peril which could be eliminated only by building aircraft of longer range—which time, if nothing else, ruled out—or by acquiring air bases on the nearest land mass, the Azores, Portuguese-owned islands.

Wary of German retaliation, the Portuguese long had resisted American efforts to obtain airfield rights on the islands. By playing on ancient ties with Portugal, the British finally, at the end of 1943, concluded an agreement for use of one airfield, but it was too small for planes of the range required. Only mounting manifestations of Allied power at last persuaded Portugal to grant adequate concessions in the Azores. It was mid-1944 before planes based there finally conquered the "black pit."

Even though the "black pit" remained an obstacle for a long time, the crossing of ONS-5 was nonetheless significant. In the four months from mid-May through mid-September 1943, sixty-two convoys comprising more than thirty-five hundred merchantmen crossed from North America to Britain by the northern route without the loss of a ship, and the amount of new merchant tonnage constructed in the first nine months of 1943 exceeded that lost everywhere by six million tons. These successes brought an end to the food crisis in Britain.

Although the figures on lost tonnage after the spring of 1943 never approached those on new construction, the war at sea still was far from won. Proved masters of underseas warfare in two wars, the Germans were to introduce devices and expedients destined to deal their adversaries many more blows at sea.

They reverted first to an old tactic of shifting operations to less protected waters; but they soon learned that, unlike 1942 and early 1943, chickens chased from the kitchen were no longer free to roam unmolested in some other part of the house. By the fall of 1943 naval commanders were ready almost everywhere with roving bands of killers made up of an escort carrier screened by destroyers and destroyer escorts. Time after time at various points all over the Atlantic the sea erupted with rumblings, belchings, and bubblings to signal the death of another U-boat.

In late summer of 1943 the Germans introduced a new weapon, an acoustical torpedo which homed on the peculiar pitch of an escort's propellers. In the first trial the device helped a wolfpack sink three escort vessels and six merchantmen, but American scientists had anticipated the acoustical torpedo and had long been at work on countermeasures. By the end of September shipyards already were installing on escort vessels a gear that upset the homing mechanism.

In Atlantic waters not far from the European continent, in Arctic waters, and in the Mediterranean, German planes were also active in the war against shipping. Until the *Luftwaffe* could be defeated or its bases overrun by ground troops, the burden of opposing the planes fell on the escort vessels and on naval anti-aircraft gunners riding the merchantmen, for Allied planes could not maintain such a constant cover that swift German air strikes could not penetrate it. For long months anti-aircraft gunners fought the *Luftwaffe* against heavy odds, until American scientists finally came up with at least a partial antidote. By the spring of 1943 American gunners had begun using a variable time (VT) or proximity fuze which triggered an anti-aircraft shell automatically when close to the target. That took much of the sting from the enemy's dive-bombing attacks.

In the Mediterranean through late 1943 and the spring of 1944, the plane more than the submarine nevertheless remained the scourge of the convoys. The Mediterranean was a busy route, for convoys had to pass not only to Sicily and Italy but on to the Near East, where lend-lease supplies flowed by way of Iran to the Soviet Union or through the Suez Canal to India. From bases in southern France, German planes usually attacked at twilight or after dark, using brilliant parachute flares to illuminate their targets. There were inevitable losses—one of the worst was in April 1943 when a bomb exploded an American ship, killing an eighty-man crew and five hundred men of the Army Air Forces; but the situation in the Mediterranean never reached the point of crisis.

So desperate did the Germans become in Arctic waters in late 1943 that they risked against a convoy to Murmansk their sole surviving battle-ship, the *Scharnhorst*, mounting 11-inch guns. Radar enabled the British escort, which included the *Duke of York* with 14-inch guns, to intercept the German vessel and score one hit after another during a ten-hour chase through the twilight of a winter day in the Arctic and into the night. In early evening of the day after Christmas the *Duke of York*'s big guns fell silent to allow cruisers and destroyers to deliver the *coup de grâce* with torpedoes. The *Scharnhorst* exploded and sank to her grave with two thousand Germans on board.

Early in 1944, with the Allied invasion of the Continent apparently close at hand, the Germans introduced a new device that, had it come early in the war, might have sealed the doom of Allied shipping in the Atlantic. This was the snorkel, which enabled the submarines to breathe. A 26-foot steel cylinder with twin intake and exhaust tubes, the snorkel protruded a few feet above the surface of the water and enabled a submarine to run its diesel engines and charge its batteries while submerged. It vastly increased the range of the submarine, while it obviated the dangerous task of resurfacing to renew power.

Although the snorkel rejuvenated a flagging U-boat campaign, it came too late to save it. German submarines operated, sometimes with deadly effect, right up to the end of the war in Europe, but they were no longer a match for the forces and the devices arrayed against them. This was dramatically apparent in that from the start of the war through May 1943 submarines sank more than seven million tons of Allied shipping, but in the two years after that date only one million tons.

The battle of the Atlantic was costly to both sides. The vanquished lost

781 U-boats and 32,000 crewmen. The victors lost 2,828 merchant ships, at least 187 warships, a large though untabulated number of aircraft, and hardly less than 40,000 men. Only three troopships were included in the total: the transport *Dorchester* sunk by a submarine while en route to Greenland early in 1943, with the loss of 605 men; the American vessel that went down with 500 airmen in the Mediterranean; and a Belgian ship sunk by a U-boat in the English Channel in December 1944, with the loss of 802 American infantrymen.

All through the vicious struggle the stakes were high—for Britain, at least, survival. Had the Allies lost the war against the undersea raiders, there could have been no invasion of the Continent; and without that invasion and victory in Europe, as Roosevelt had pointed out soon after Pearl Harbor, what profited a victory over Japan?

Credit for the victory belonged to many: men of the Royal Navy and Air Force, who in the early months bore a disproportionate share of the struggle; the Royal Canadian Navy and Air Force; the U.S. Navy and Army Air Forces; the Coast Guard and amateur auxiliaries; scientists and shipyard workers in Britain and the United States; ships and squadrons of other Allied nations, notably Brazil. They did it with valor and ingenuity seldom equaled or even approached. The time-tested convoy system; fast vessels like the proud British *Queens* that could outrun the wolfpacks; vital air bases in Newfoundland, Iceland, Britain, the Caribbean, and later North Africa and the Azores; radar and plane-mounted microwave radar, sonar, Huffduff, improved depth charges, and many another weapon and device; the command without ships, the Tenth Fleet—all those and more, without any one of which the campaign would have been even more desperate, the outcome even more and longer in doubt.

Yet just as surely, blame for the unpreparedness that enabled the undersea killers to pose extraordinary crises belonged to the between-the-wars professionals of those same navies that deserved so much credit for victory. Having conquered the U-boat in World War I, they had failed to foresee the miracles that would change the U-boat from a lone raider without communication with its fellows or its home command into an able, willing, gregarious puppet which a master named Karl Doenitz could manipulate and maneuver swiftly and ruthlessly at the end of an electronic string. It had been more pleasant to concentrate within limited budgets on proud ships of the line that would fight according to rules originally laid down by illustrious forebears such as Lord Nelson and John Paul Jones, to ignore the dirty, ignominious business of hiding and fighting beneath the surface of the sea. That affinity for the traditional almost did the Allies in.

Just as success at sea was essential to overall Allied victory, so also was superiority in the air. That phase of the war embraced the tactical—close support of the troops on the ground—but more specifically the strategic—long-range bombardment of the enemy's homeland. The latter involved three interrelated campaigns: one to cripple the enemy's industrial power, another to destroy his morale, a third to drive the *Luftwaffe* from the skies.

There were those on both sides of the Atlantic who believed ardently that victory in the air was all that mattered, that Germany could be so devastated by the new arm that the nation would capitulate even without an invasion or, barring that, with little more than an occupation. Those were undoubting disciples of Giuilo Douhet, Italian air theorist of the 1920's, and his American counterpart, Billy Mitchell. For many in the youthful air services of both the United States and Britain who might not qualify as such avid zealots, the main question was whether air should be the sole weapon or simply the most important one.

The fact that British and American Staff planners, in their early conversations in 1941 and during the first weeks of 1942, gave special attention to strategic bombardment appeared at first to afford endorsement to the airmen's tenets. From the British viewpoint this was for a time essentially correct. Cognizant of Britain's traditional role as a sea power that had gotten into trouble in Europe only when violating traditional concepts and committing large land armies to the Continent, the British Chiefs of Staff looked to air power to punish the foe so severely that when finally there was a direct confrontation between ground forces, no repetition of World War I's massed land battles would ensue. "Our two mightiest weapons," said the British Air Minister, "are the Russian Army and the Royal Air Force."[92]

Yet that was never a true reflection of the views of the American Joint Chiefs. Strategic bombardment was important, they believed, but as no more than a preparatory step to the introduction of ground armies. Under

---

[92] Craven and Cate, eds., *Plans and Early Operations*, p. 592.

the spur of their enthusiasm for an early invasion of the Continent, they were even willing to shorten the preliminaries in order to get on with the main task.

As with SLEDGEHAMMER, it was paradoxical that the nation urging what amounted, in the British view, to precipitate action had little at first to contribute to the preliminaries. Despite the decision for Europe First, the critical nature of the early months in the Pacific dictated that the few trained air units be committed there. In those early months, too, priority on strategic bombers from American factories went either to the Pacific or to the British.

At first the Royal Air Force carried the entire burden. By the spring of 1942 it had grown strong enough to shift from small raids against a variety of targets to concentrated attacks of 200 or more planes. On the last day of May 1942 the RAF established a fresh landmark in aerial warfare with an assault on Cologne in strength exceeding a thousand planes, twice the total number the Germans had employed at the peak of the battle of Britain. Although most assaults still involved from 200 to 600 bombers, twice more within the next month the RAF repeated the feat.

Losses in the big raids ran as high as 52 planes—not an excessive percentage but too high for British replacement facilities to sustain more than occasionally. Overall losses soon were running as high as 200 bombers a month. The fact that British numbers still were limited meant also that the RAF dared not risk additional losses by challenging the inclement weather that is common in northwestern Europe. Those factors together made it impossible for the RAF to make large raids on a day-by-day basis and thus afforded the Germans time between raids to repair damage and provide rest for their defending fighter pilots.

Participation by American airmen was minor. On the first Independence Day after the United States entered the war, American crews manned half a dozen RAF Boston light bombers in a raid against German airfields in the Netherlands—a token effort. The first exclusively American raid in B-17 Flying Fortresses occurred in August against targets in occupied France. Although hopeful of getting into the battle in strength later in the year, American airmen saw the prospects crushed by diversions to North Africa.

The invasion of North Africa and the protracted campaign that followed also altered the American air command in Britain. The senior American air officer was Carl ("Tooey") Spaatz, who had been the first and only Chief of the Air Forces Combat Command before the Army Air Forces had achieved their position of equality with the ground and service forces. As Eisenhower's air officer in the early days in Britain, Spaatz also commanded the only American air headquarters, the Eighth Air Force. When the battle for Tunisia developed and forced an amalgamation of the separate American and British air commands in North Africa, General Eisenhower had called Spaatz to Algiers to do the job as his Deputy Commander-in-Chief for Air; and Spaatz later had headed those same forces when they were merged with the British air units from the Near East under the overall command of Air Marshal Tedder. Command of the Eighth Air Force meanwhile passed to one of Spaatz's subordinates, General Eaker.

The Royal Air Force still was bearing almost the total burden of the aerial offensive when in January 1943 the Casablanca conference foreshadowed increased American participation. To defeat Germany, the conferees reiterated, the Allies had to invade the Continent in force, but only after vigorous aerial bombardment. British and American strategic air forces, the leaders decreed, were to pool their resources in the Combined Bomber Offensive under the code name, Operation POINTBLANK, with the objective of destroying and dislocating the German military, industrial, and economic system and of undermining German morale.

The methods of the bomber offensive—whether "saturation" night bombing, as preferred by the British, or "precision" day bombing, as favored by the Americans, or a combination of the two—also had to be decided at Casablanca, since strong disagreement on the score already had arisen. Such pressure was there from Prime Minister Churchill for American planes to supplement the RAF's night bombing campaign that the Air Forces Chief of Staff, General Arnold, summoned the commander of the Eighth Air Force, General Eaker, to defend American doctrine.

Only one convincing argument, General Eaker maintained, had ever been advanced in favor of night over day bombing: that it was safer. Yet losses in the daylight attacks of the Eighth Air Force, he said, had been lower than those of recent RAF night raids, partly because the Germans had developed improved night-fighter tactics, but also partly because the fire power on American bombers provided a powerful weapon against the fighter. Equipped with a simple but accurate bombsight, American bombers by day could hit small but vital targets that could hardly be found at night. Most important, Eaker insisted, was that day and night bombing together would force the enemy to commit his fighters in costly battle around the clock.

Unspoken in the deliberations was the concern of British airmen to undermine German morale. Despite the example of their own people in the battle of Britain—or perhaps because of it—the British laid great stress on the effect of bombardment on civilian morale. While professing a distaste for indiscriminate bombing of nonmilitary targets, they hoped that prolonged interruption of normal patterns of civilian life eventually would disrupt German war industry. Although American airmen would express no disagreement with morale as a target, they gave it a low priority to be exploited only after precision bombing had rent the enemy's industrial fabric.

The chief witness against daylight bombing, British representatives were quick to point out, was the American record itself—only a limited number of missions and none over the German homeland. That record, Eaker insisted, had nothing to do with the practicality of daylight bombing. It reflected instead the unpreparedness of American crews, the bleeding of the Eighth Air Force to sustain the invasion of North Africa, and a lack of long-range fighters for escort over Germany. These difficulties, Eaker said, soon would be overcome.

Although the British appeared satisfied with General Eaker's presentation, some of the American side remained concerned lest they win the battle while losing the war. If, as in North Africa, American air forces were integrated with British units under RAF command, the British might yet shift American planes to night operations. To circumvent that possibility while assuring coordination on target priority and timing of attacks, American leaders suggested that American bombers come under operational direction of the RAF while maintaining the prerogative of procedure and technique. General target priorities were to be the province of the Combined Chiefs of Staff.

With British agreement to this command arrangement, the broad plan for the Combined Bomber Offensive was set—a round-the-clock campaign in mounting intensity. Yet for all General Eaker's optimism about the level of American participation, several months passed before the Eighth Air Force could enter the fight in telling strength—owing to the continuing requirements of the Pacific, the Mediterranean, and the anti-submarine war in the Atlantic, plus a shortage of ships for transporting essential ground crews. It was the middle of 1943 when the Combined Bomber Offensive actually began.

The Eighth Air Force nevertheless made good on Eaker's promise to press operations against the German homeland. On January 27 ninety-one B-17 Flying Fortresses and B-24 Liberators made the first strike, bombing the port of Wilhelmshafen, with a loss of three planes. Nine more times in the next four months American aircraft flew against targets in Germany, but only two of the missions involved more than one hundred planes, and only one more than two hundred.

Reflecting the crisis with the U-boat, the primary targets of both American and British attacks during the first half of 1943 were submarine construction yards in Germany and repair facilities along the Bay of Biscay. The effect on the U-boats was disappointingly minor. Although photographs tended to indicate heavy damage to construction yards, most of it turned out to be superficial. The aerial campaign had even less effect on the repair facilities because the Germans had encased them in mammoth concrete shelters.

The American effort during the first half of 1943 was essentially experimental, a test of techniques and tactics and even of the very doctrine of daylight strategic bombardment. Losses averaged just over 5 per cent, an acceptable figure which airmen predicted would rise only slightly when the size of bomber formations increased. Experience showed that the *Luftwaffe*, rather than anti-aircraft fire, posed the graver threat to daylight bombing. As many a British colleague came to admit, strategic bombing by the light of day had proved tactically feasible; but as many American airmen asserted, the enemy's air force was so formidable that it would have to be defeated before the bomber offensive could achieve its strategic goals.

In mid-1943, with a diminution of the crisis at sea, the bombers shifted emphasis from submarine-related objectives to industrial facilities vital to operations of the *Luftwaffe*. That marked the official start of the Combined Bomber Offensive. Although the newly oriented campaign produced little that was new in aerial tactics, either Allied or German, it pointed up sharply some of the still unsolved problems of the daylight technique and led to several significant advances in aerial warfare.

Weather remained the supreme arbiter of the campaign and more often than not favored the Germans. Even during the better days of summer

American planes were able to fly only about ten major missions a month. It was a problem less of inclement weather at the bases than of overcast and low cloud cover over the targets. Although the Eighth Air Force early experimented with pathfinder planes equipped with a British radar device, British production was hard put to meet even British demands for this item. In a hurry-up program, an American laboratory produced a facsimile. The first tests in late September and early October provided a basis for restrained optimism, but it was well into 1944 before enough sets were available and the tactics and techniques of radar bombing were sufficiently mastered to make a start on breaking the tyranny of weather.

American operations still were sharply restricted also by the number of available bombers and crews. Although the buildup in the United Kingdom had begun in earnest in May 1943, the Eighth Air Force by September possessed a daily average of only 881 heavy bombers and 661 crews. Seldom was General Eaker's command able to put more than 300 bombers over a target at once. For all their enthusiasm for what air power might do, the airmen had to accept the fact that mounting a telling campaign took time: time to assemble planes and crews; to construct bases; to gain experience for pilots, navigators, bombardiers; to modify planes in response to enemy tactics; to build repair facilities that could speedily return damaged planes to the ready line; to provide ground crews in sufficient numbers and experience to keep the bombers flying.

The Royal Air Force meanwhile continued its powerful night bombardment and in the process precipitated one of the wars more devastating holocausts. On the cloudy night of July 24, 740 Halifax and Lancaster bombers using the new radar target-finding device struck the old Hanseatic port of Hamburg, Germany's second largest city. By tossing into the air thousands of strips of aluminum foil—a simple but ingenious device which the British called "window" and the Americans "chaff"—British crews threw askew their enemy's ground radar controlling both fighters and anti-aircraft guns. With almost free access to the skies over the city, the British bombers dealt demoniacal destruction. As they soared away into the night, great fires raged behind them.

For the next two mornings Flying Fortresses took up the assault— sixty-eight one day, fifty-four the next—adding to the carnage in the port sector of the city; but upon them the entire stable of German fighters—Messerschmitt 109 and Focke-Wulf FW 190 single-engine craft, Messerschmitt 110 and 210 twin-engine planes, and Junkers 88 mediums—vented the fury of their nighttime frustration. "Window" could do little for the attackers in daylight. The surviving Fortresses returned to base riddled, broken, bleeding.

At twenty minutes before midnight on July 27 the second RAF attack began: 739 heavy bombers dropped 2,417 tons of bombs and put the old city to the torch. It was a still, dry night—no wind. As the flames from hundreds of fires leaped skyward, they created their own draft to provide the oxygen needed to keep burning. Cooler air began to rush into the vacuum created by rising heat and gases. The rush of air was at first a gentle breeze; then it swelled to gale force; then two hours after it had begun it was hurricane, typhoon, tornado, and cyclone wrapped into one. At speeds exceeding 150 miles an hour, the storm raged, screeching air and crackling flame, sucking people, trees, vehicles, anything on the periphery forcibly into the clutch of a living, writhing ball of fire making up the entire center of the city.

It was a fire storm—Hell on earth.[93]

Yet as if that were not enough, twice more the big bombers returned, the nights of July 29 and August 2. When at last it was over, they had poured 8,261 tons of bombs into Hamburg, half of them incendiaries, leaving the city a rotting, ash-choked desert hiding the fried corpses of more than 30,000 people.

Prior to this holocaust the world had looked upon the British city of Coventry as the ultimate memorial to the inhuman fury of aerial bombardment. Coventry—with 100 acres of destruction. The British in their revenge had gutted more than 6,000 acres of Hamburg.

Hamburg reputedly shook even Adolf Hitler, at least briefly, into the speculation that repeated attacks on such a scale might force Germany from the war. Yet the peculiar circumstances of weather, atmosphere, and combustible target that had existed at Hamburg could not readily be duplicated. There would be other fire storms in Germany and Japan, but man had to conquer the atom before he could be assured of that kind of destruction whenever and wherever he willed it.

* * *

[93] For the fire storm at Hamburg, I have used primarily Martin Caidin, *The Night Hamburg Died* (New York, 1960), but Caidin's estimate of deaths is exaggerated. See instead Becker, *The Luftwaffe War Diaries*.

In few instances in the varied, far-flung combat of World War II were heroism and tragedy more concentrated and starkly interwoven than in the flights of the big bombers. Engaged on missions of death, they fought for their lives against shark-like fighter planes hungry for the kill. The experience of the 544th Heavy Bomber Squadron over Hamburg provided a grim example of what it was sometimes like.[94]

The Flying Fortresses were just making their turn for the bomb run over the Hamburg docks when the last plane in the formation, called *Passes Cancelled*, reeled from the impact of anti-aircraft fire and slipped into a crazily whirling spin. Only three crewmen were able to bail out. Seven others rode the careening ship to their deaths.

The planes had yet to begin to drop their bombs when a swarm of German fighters got another, *April's Fool*. It went to pieces in the air; the body of the dead co-pilot, slumped in his seat, was visible to other crews. Three minutes later *Long Horn* dropped out of formation, its right inboard engine afire, its nose shot to pieces. Few parachutes blossomed from either plane. A man fell from *Long Horn*'s escape hatch, clawed wildly at the air, then plummeted to his death. Moments later another man fell clear of the spiraling wreckage. Although the white silk of a parachute spilled open, two Focke-Wulf 190's riddled the helpless form dangling in the harness with round after round of machine-gun fire.

Five minutes later *Royal Flush* suddenly lost altitude, then exploded with a blinding flash. At almost the same time a companion plane went down with its tail assembly shot away.

Only two planes remained in the ill-fated 544th. One, *Liberty Bell*, escaped with only minor damage. The other, *Weary Willie*, made it out to sea, but the left wingtip was mangled, and three engines were smoking. Sensing another kill, six German-piloted sharks closed in, ripping the nose of the big plane with blast after blast of 20-mm. cannon fire. The explosions wounded both navigator and bombardier and ripped great holes in the Plexiglas covering to let in freezing gales of air.

Unable to elude the tormenting Focke-Wulfs, despite a desperation dive down to five thousand feet, the pilot elected to ditch his crippled craft. As *Weary Willie* hit the cold water, frustrated German pilots pummeled the sea with fire from their cannon. The crew scrambled into life rafts

---

[94] My account of the demise of the 544th Heavy Bomber Squadron is based on Caidin, *The Night Hamburg Died*.

and paddled away as the stricken ship slipped beneath the surface of the water. A small Danish fishing vessel picked up the men that night. Setting westward sail, the skipper promised to take them within fifty miles of the British coast. Two days later air-sea rescue craft picked them up.

If the fate of the 544th had been often repeated, the daylight bombing campaign could not have been sustained. The experience was nevertheless illustrative of the trials the crews of the big bombers endured. Even when crippled ships made their way back to Britain, they often brought dead and wounded crewmen with them, the insides of the planes decorated with the fiery red of human blood and the rubbish of human organs. Any infantryman who saw one of those returning craft well might have agreed that the hazard was deserving of extra pay.

Before the last of the raids on Hamburg the Ninth U.S. Air Force in North Africa joined the Combined Bomber Offensive to strike at a target beyond the reach of planes based in Britain—oil refineries vital to the Nazi war machine at Plocsti in Rumania. On the morning of August 1, 177 B-24 Liberators, some of them borrowed from the Eighth Air Force for the occasion, began the long flight. As the planes neared the target, high clouds destroyed the unity of the formation so that two groups reached Ploesti ahead of the others.

That alerted German defenders.

A lethal cushion of flak rose to meet the attackers. As surviving bombers struggled to resume formation for the return flight, hosts of fighters rose to harass them. Some 42 per cent of Ploesti's total refining capacity was destroyed, but 54 planes and 532 airmen were lost in the process, one of the highest percentages of planes lost in the entire war.

Not quite three weeks later, on August 17, the Eighth Air Force tried a new tactic of shuttle bombing. B-17's hitting Messerschmitt fighter aircraft factories at Regensburg went on to land at bases in North Africa. The tactic worked to the extent that it probably cut losses by taking the enemy's pursuit craft by surprise, but lack of repair and maintenance facilities in North Africa made repetition impractical.

More noteworthy than the introduction of a shuttle was the cost of the raid and of a companion strike against ball-bearing plants at Schweinfurt. The two missions together totaled 516 bombers, the most yet mounted by the Eighth Air Force. German fighters replied with every tactic in the book. Sixty B-17's went down—a shocking loss of more than 11 per cent.

For all the importance of the targets, those losses were oppressive. In deference to them, the American command would not risk another raid against targets inside Germany for three weeks; and then, on September 6, losses were even higher—45 out of 262 bombers. This was in marked contrast to losses in raids over the occupied western countries, where on September 7, for example, 185 bombers struck without losing a plane.

The reason for the difference was painfully obvious—fighter escort. The thinking behind the creation of the big Flying Fortresses and the Liberators was that with their multiple cannon and machine guns they could defend themselves. They had proved capable of doing that in earlier days—at least to the extent that losses were in acceptable numbers—but under mounting pressure of the bomber offensive, the Germans had beefed up their defenses. Recalling planes from Italy and Russia, they soon had over seven hundred first-line fighters rising to defend the Reich. They also altered their tactics by coming at the big bombers from below against their vulnerable under-bellies and hitting them with a powerful new rocket projectile.

Events during the second week of October pointed up just how critical was the situation. Within six days the Eighth Air Force in four strikes lost 148 bombers and crews, including another 60 over Schweinfurt. Such appalling losses forced a reappraisal of the entire daylight bombing program.

Since the British had come to appreciate the complementary value of American precision bombing methods, they were no longer anxious to shift American planes to night attack; but if the heavy losses continued, and if replacements failed to arrive in greater numbers, they saw no alternative. While agreeing to try to speed training and production in the United States, American leaders sought a more positive solution.

In Washington the Chief of the Air Forces, General Arnold, saw a sizable shift of strategic bombing strength to Italy as at least a partial solution, which would enable the planes to avoid the broad belt of anti-aircraft guns guarding the approaches to Germany from the west. That also might overcome some of the problems of weather and tax German fighters by forcing them to face attack from two directions.

Most airmen on the scene, including the British, resisted such a shift lest it drain strength from bases in Britain which provided more ready access to most vital German targets, and lest the necessity to build bases in Italy delay the campaign. Arnold nevertheless obtained the approval of the Combined Chiefs of Staff to create a strategic command in Italy, the Fifteenth Air Force, which was activated in November; but slow advance on the ground in Italy so frustrated the plan for shifting air strength there that the major portion of the American strategic air effort continued to emanate from the United Kingdom.

Having created a strategic air force in Italy, General Arnold insisted on a combined command of all American air forces in Europe. As much as for any other reason, it was designed to give American airmen a voice high in command echelons; for the Combined Chiefs had chosen a Britisher, Air Marshal Sir Trafford Leigh-Mallory, to head the new Allied Expeditionary Air Force serving the Supreme Commander for the invasion. Early in December 1943 the American Joint Chiefs authorized creation of a new command, the U.S. Strategic Air Forces in Europe. The logical choice as commander was the senior American airman in Europe, he who had been heading the top American air command in the Mediterranean, Carl Spaatz.

The return of Spaatz to London coincided with the other major command changes accompanying General Eisenhower's designation as commander for OVERLORD, the invasion of the Continent. Since supreme command in the Mediterranean passed to a Britisher, an American officer was to head Allied air forces there. Arnold and Spaatz insisted on transferring General Eaker from the Eighth Air Force; their decision was based on experience and ability, although speculation persisted for a while about whether dissatisfaction with the pace of American air operations from Britain was involved in it. Eaker himself found it "heartbreaking to leave just before the climax."[95] The former commander of the Twelfth Air Force in North Africa, General Doolittle, went with Spaatz to England to assume command of the Eighth Air Force.

With these changes made, the basic problem facing the big bombers over Germany remained—lack of fighter escort. It was too late in the war to hope for some radical new long-range fighter to set everything right. The Americans would have to do the job with a makeshift solution, the P-51 Mustang, already in production. Yet even the P-51 would be available in appreciable numbers only in early spring of 1944. For the moment the P-47 Thunderbolt had to suffice; and even with jettisonable auxiliary fuel tanks,

---

[95] Craven and Cate, eds, *Europe — TORCH to POINTBLANK*, p. 749.

which were themselves in short supply, the P-47 could provide escort in a radius of only 350 miles, only slightly beyond the Rhine River. Although a few P-38 Lightnings were arriving to extend the radius to just over 500 miles, that was extreme range, leaving no leeway for the maneuvers of aerial combat and still putting little more than half of Germany within range.

On the last day of October, General Arnold took the drastic step of decreeing that no P-38 Lightning or P-51 Mustang be shipped anywhere in the world during the remainder of 1943 except to Britain. The RAF agreed to help by providing at the start of the new year four of their Mustang-equipped squadrons to escort American bombers.

Meanwhile, on November 3 forty-seven planes of a newly arrived group of Lightnings flew escort on a mission to Wilhelmshafen. The addition of even those small numbers made a sharp difference in bomber losses. Ten days later over Bremen, on the longest escorted mission yet for American planes, the Lightnings were outnumbered as much as five to one, seven failed to return, and sixteen came back badly limping—proof enough that their numbers were far too few; but their presence had kept big bomber losses at an acceptable level.

The first of the P-51 Mustang groups entered the fight early in December. On three missions during the month to targets inside Germany, one of which included escorting a record 710 American bombers, they proved conclusively that they were at least a workable answer to the Eighth Air Force's problem. On that evidence General Spaatz ordered all P-51's reaching the theater to continue to serve the Eighth Air Force. Having come from the Mediterranean to be revamped as the American tactical command in support of OVERLORD, the Ninth Air Force was to make do with Thunderbolts and Lightnings.

With the escort difficulty alleviated, Allied air commanders faced the baffling problem that in a campaign designed to defeat the *Luftwaffe*, German air strength was growing. Allied airmen had seriously underestimated the recuperative power of the German aircraft industry and the time it might take a target to recover before they hit it again. They also had sharply overestimated their scores in aerial combat, particularly those of less experienced crews whose claims often were more than eight to ten times greater than actual German losses.

American bombing accuracy was nevertheless increasing. That was particularly important, since the onus of eliminating the specific target of the aircraft industry rested more upon precision daylight bombing than upon the saturation night attacks of the RAF. The fact that a combination of precision and saturation attacks had seriously embarrassed the German aircraft industry was apparent from increasing dispersal of German plants, but dispersal would in the long run make the targets harder to hit.

Well aware that unquestioned air superiority was essential to OVERLORD, General Spaatz and the Staffs of the Eighth and Fifteenth Air Forces drafted a plan they thought would do the job. Aimed at approximately a dozen critical factories of the airframe industry, the concentrated campaign they planned required at least six days of good weather.

All through January and well into February the airmen waited anxiously, while winter snow, fog, haze, and overcast gripped the Continent. At last, on February 19, the weather over Germany began to open up. Spaatz gave the signal to start the intensive, selective attack the next day.

The force flying the first mission was the largest in the history of American strategic bombing, the first American thousand-plane raid, and was supported by all available fighter escort, seventeen groups. Although the plan involved strikes against twelve different airframe factories, the armada flew together most of the way to gain protection from formation and numbers. The tactic also deceived the German defenders into believing the raid was aimed at Berlin. German fighters suffered another handicap in that a big RAF raid the preceding night had exhausted much of the fighter force. While the bombers wreaked havoc on the targets below, the anti-aircraft and fighter defenses could knock down only twenty-one of the big ships.

It was an auspicious beginning. For the next five days and nights before the weather turned bad, the RAF and the Eighth and Fifteenth Air Forces launched a succession of strikes that Allied airmen came to call the "Big Week." The Eighth Air Force flew over 3,300 sorties; the Fifteenth Air Force, 500; the RAF, 2,351. They cost the British 157 bombers; the Americans, 226 bombers, 28 fighters, and some 2,600 crewmen.

Although the "Big Week" promoted consternation in the German aircraft industry, that was a momentary reaction. The industry again displayed remarkable recuperative power, but again the bombings precipitated a program of dispersing factories which delayed production. The

"Big Week" set back German aircraft production only slightly, basically the time entailed in dispersing the industry; but the delay came at a critical moment, when Allied bombing strength was growing rapidly and invasion was approaching.

What Allied air planners had looked upon as a possible added dividend of the "Big Week" turned out to be its most important result. In opposing the concentrated campaign, the Germans lost more than five hundred fighters and pilots. Since the air war was fast moving toward a climax, the Germans were unable to afford such losses, particularly among pilots.

Just how crucial were German losses during the "Big Week" became apparent during the remaining days of February and in early March. In recognition of the jolting experience, German fighters failed for the first time to challenge many Allied missions. Closing in for the kill, Allied airmen switched from soft objectives to targets and routes of approach that would lure the *Luftwaffe* to battle.

One of the new targets was Berlin: if there was any target for which the German air force would fight, surely it was the capital. Although Berlin had been a target for the RAF since late 1941, an American decision to go that deep inside Germany reflected new confidence in long-range escort. At last on hand were more than one hundred P-51 Mustangs equipped with auxiliary fuel tanks that enabled them to fly a previously unheard-of radius of 850 miles, theoretically putting every city within Germany in range.

On the first try at Berlin on March 4, weather forced most bombers to turn back. Only 29 reached the city, promoting little German fighter reaction, but two days later in partially clearing weather 660 B-17's struck the German capital. The fighters rose to the bait in strength, shooting down 69 bombers and 11 escorting fighters. When American crewmen claimed almost 200 German fighters, their superiors in England scoffed: the figure obviously involved much duplication.

In reality the crewmen were right. They had dealt a crippling blow to the *Luftwaffe*'s fighter forces.

Some inkling of the damage inflicted emerged two days later when the Germans rose in sharply reduced numbers in response to another raid on Berlin. When American planes made a fourth attack near the end of the month, German fighters appeared reluctant to accept the challenge.

It came with no dramatic suddenness. Indeed, no one could have said with any certainty at the time that it had happened at all. Yet it had happened. By the end of March—even though German aircraft production continued to increase through much of 1944, reaching a peak only in the fall—the *Luftwaffe* had begun to fail. The Germans no longer had the trained pilots to exploit their production, and the oil that they had so carefully conserved at the expense of pilot training was soon to come under intensive Allied attack. The *Luftwaffe* on occasion still might hit back and hit back hard, as many an Allied bomber formation would discover in the months to come, but the German air force was no longer capable of sustained reaction to the great waves of bombers that darkened the sky. Such fighters as they had left would have to stay at home to challenge the big bombers, thus all but eliminating tactical air support for German armies in the field.

Barring some drastic new development in aerial warfare, the *Luftwaffe* had lost the war in the clouds.

Chapter Fifteen – Buildup for D Day

As the air and naval campaigns proceeded, the United Kingdom was the nerve center for yet another kind of combat—the war of the clandestine soldier in the occupied countries—called variously "underground," "resistance," "guerrilla," or "partisan" fighters. As sole survivor of the original coalition opposing the Nazis, the British early began to parachute or otherwise to provide arms, supplies, and agents to assist secret armies of civilians and ex-soldiers who opposed their conqueror in Norway, the Netherlands, Yugoslavia, Belgium, Greece, Denmark, Czechoslovakia, Poland, France, and later Italy. Because of the help an underground organization might be when Allied armies were put ashore in France, the French underground—known as the *Resistance*—drew the bulk of British resources and later of American resources as well.[96]

Even before the degrading armistice of 1940 was signed, a tall, inscrutable *général de division*, Charles André Joseph Marie de Gaulle, appealed by radio from a refuge in England for Frenchmen everywhere to keep alive the spark of resistance. Not long afterward posters began to appear

---

[96] For the French Resistance, I have used my own study, "France — 1940-1944," in *Challenge and Response in Internal Conflict*, Vol. II, *The Experience in Europe and the Middle East* (Washington, 1965), for which full documentation is included. To that documentation I would add an important work that appeared later, M. R. D. Foot, *SOE in France* (London, 1966), in the official British history series. For the American buildup in Britain, see Huppenthal, *Logistical Support*, Vol. I; Pogue, *The Supreme Command*; and contemporary issues of *The New York Times* and *Time* Magazine. Some of the unofficial American unit histories also are helpful. For the planning and other pre-D Day events, see Pogue, *The Supreme Command*; Ruppenthal, *Logistical Support*, Vol. I; Harrison, *Cross-Channel Attack*; Craven and Cate, eds., *ARGUMENT to V-E Day*; Morison, *The Invasion of France and Germany*; Davis, *The Experience of War*; Churchill, *Closing the Ring*; Sir Frederick E. Morgan, *Overture to OVER-LORD* (New York, 1950); and Wilmot, *The Struggle for Europe*.

on French walls bearing de Gaulle's words: *La France a perdu une bataille! mais la France n'a pas perdu la guerre!*

In spite of the drama of de Gaulle's appeal, it would not produce impressive results for a long time. The same internal conflicts that had helped lead to defeat still beset the French people, and were accentuated by the bitter but ineluctable fact of the armistice and by the existence in the unoccupied southern half of the country of a government that was a creature of the conqueror, yet wore the trappings of legality and the mantle of a beloved military hero, Marshal Pétain. Under those conditions an obscure general who had fled to safety in the moment of France's agony had little appeal.

In the early weeks of the occupation, too, German troops conducted themselves inoffensively enough to provoke few to active opposition; but Adolf Hitler soon changed that. To Hitler, France, like all the occupied countries, existed only to serve the Third Reich. At his order the Germans began systematically to loot the vanquished of military stocks, machinery, vehicles; to impose oppressive levies in order to feed and pay the occupation armies and supply raw materials for German industry; to curtail civilian freedoms; to persecute the Jews.

The oppressions soon triggered the strong tradition of independence and individualism that had marked the French people at least since the Revolution of 1789. It took subtle forms at first: referring to the conquerors as "*Ces messieurs*" passing on bitter little jokes, chalking derisive comments on walls by night or the "V" symbol for "Victory," surreptitiously sounding the first four notes of Beethoven's *Fifth Symphony*, which are like the dot-dot-dot-dash for the letter "V" in Morse code. It gradually evolved into more contrived hostility: letting sloppy work pass in the factories, delaying or even losing train shipments destined for Germany, concealing rotten vegetables among good ones so the rot would spread. As time passed, individuals performing the acts gradually coalesced into small resistance organizations which spread through occupied and unoccupied France alike. The German invasion of the Soviet Union in mid-1941 propelled into the movement the large French Communist party, with its ready-made underground apparatus.

Within a headquarters called the Special Operations Executive, the British set up a French section to recruit and train agents to enter France, to help organize the Resistance, and to feed back intelligence by clandestine radio. De Gaulle himself, on New Year's Day 1941, sent a representative into the unoccupied zone to organize the various groups into one force called the *Armée Secrète*. The fact that de Gaulle had the money and the arms that the Resistance needed to survive—obtained from wealthy Frenchmen and from the British—went a long way toward countering the objections to his leadership.

Outside of the unoccupied zone, the Resistance was still weak and disorganized when de Gaulle's struggle for power with General Giraud began in North Africa. Following President Roosevelt's attempt at Casablanca to effect a *rapproachement*, de Gaulle and Giraud agreed to serve as co-chairmen of a Committee of National Liberation. For over a year the two men shared the leadership, but Giraud's lack of political acumen eventually enabled de Gaulle to gain control in a test of strength over a minor matter. In April 1944, Giraud retired, leaving de Gaulle the undisputed leader of the colonics and associated states, of France-in-exile, and of the internal resistance.

De Gaulle still had to battle for acceptance by many leaders on the Allied side—most notably Franklin Roosevelt, influenced by his Secretary of State, Cordell Hull, to whom de Gaulle was anathema. Many saw de Gaulle's oft-demonstrated pride as arrogance ill-befitting one who aspired to leadership of a supine nation which was dependent upon Allied largesse to rise again. Not until after the invasion, when de Gaulle's careful prior preparations foiled Communist takeover of national and local governments, and when the acclaim of the French people became manifest, would all on the Allied side acquiesce.

As the French in North Africa with American aid built up an external army called the Fighting French, the resistance movement inside France continued to grow, despite ruthless suppression and mass reprisals by a Hydra-headed organization of German secret police which Frenchmen knew as the dreaded Gestapo. At one point in mid-1943 the Gestapo wiped out the entire leadership of the *Armée Secrète* at one swoop; but for every Frenchman who fell before German executioners, died of torture, or rode off defiantly singing "La Marseillaise" on a deportation train bound for the horror of Nazi concentration camps, others took his place. When the Nazis early in 1943 decreed a compulsory labor draft for work in Germany, young men by the thousands took to the hills and organized in bands called "maquis." The maquis began a widespread program of sabotage, preyed on German troops, and, as more arms became available, even seized control of sections of the country.

The United States first joined the program of aiding the Resistance early in 1943 through the Office of Strategic Services (OSS), a cloak-and-dagger force. Aid consisted at first of training and delivering agents, most of them French-speaking Americans. Before the war was over, 375 American-trained agents entered France, along with 393 sent by the British under their own auspices and 868 under de Gaulle's.

When the supply of French-speaking agents began to run out late in 1943, the Allies formed three-man teams called "Jedburgh" after the place in Scotland where they were trained. Composed of one American, one Britisher, and one Frenchman, the Jedburgh, unlike agents, wore uniforms. That was primarily because some of their members lacked facility in the French language and thus were more liable to capture than were agents; if taken in uniform, they could claim full combatant status under international rules of warfare. Again unlike agents, they operated in localities where the maquis had established some measure of general control. The Americans also provided 374 uniformed officers and men in 11 teams, or Special Operations Groups, armed and trained to fight with the maquis.

Both because of doubts about the value of the Resistance and because of the priority of the Combined Bomber Offensive, the Americans began dropping arms and supplies to the Resistance only at the start of 1944. The help sharply increased the effectiveness of the Resistance, but not until after the invasion proved the true worth of the underground movement, and as more planes were available, did aerial supply come anywhere close to meeting the demand. In the interim many a small maquis perished for lack of arms.

In April 1944, to strengthen control over the Resistance, General de Gaulle superimposed on the *Armée Secrète* a new headquarters, *Forces Françaises de l'Intérieur* (FFI), with a commander-in-chief in London. Thenceforth all Resistance fighters were known as the FFI, although the maquis retained their separate identity within the larger organization.

As the target date for the invasion neared, the Germans, for all their program of repression heaped upon repression, terror upon terror, had to face the reality of a cancer in their midst which posed a major threat to their lines of communication. The shadow army was preparing, the Germans knew, to act in concert with the invaders, but the Germans were

239

powerless to prevent it. None could say with any certainty the army's strength: perhaps 100,000, maybe 200,000; many lacked arms, but all were imbued with love of country and of freedom and with hatred for the Nazis who had taken both from them.

Guided by the headquarters of the FFI in London, the Resistance worked out detailed nationwide plans for sabotage to aid the invasion by delaying the movement of German reserves. The plans were to be set in motion on the eve of the invasion by means of coded messages over the BBC. ("Reeds must grow, leaves rustle." "The tomatoes must be picked.") To avoid exposing Resistance fighters to reprisals, the plans were to be implemented in various localities only as the invading Allied armies neared.

The invasion date was near when General Eisenhower decided that to activate the sabotage program piecemeal would pinpoint for the Germans the site of the invasion. If the French were to contribute, they would have to act everywhere at once, even if that exposed them to German reprisals. Although the decision sealed the death warrant for many a Frenchman, de Gaulle and the FFI took it without flinching.

The war in which the Resistance engaged was cruel and bitter: neither side gave any quarter. Hostages shot at the stake for acts with which they had no connection except that they were Frenchmen. German soldiers cut down from ambush for no reason but that they were German soldiers. Explosions in the night. Civilians forced to ride a flatcar ahead of a military train as decoy against demolitions. Frequent and unannounced searches. Knocks on doors by night. Coded messages over the BBC announcing supply drops in lonely fields. Downed aviators passed from one clandestine hand to another. Forged papers and ration cards. "Safe houses." Agents and double agents. Disguised sound detection trucks combing cities and countryside for concealed radio transmitters.

Torture. Denunciations. Deportations. Death.

The people of the island kingdom that served as the nexus of all aspects of the Allied campaign in Europe went to sleep one night masters of their own house, only to awake to find that, in the words of John of Gaunt, "This land...this dear dear land...Is now leased out."[97]

It had begun as a scarcely noticeable trickle back in January 1942.

---

[97] John of Gaunt's speech in *The Tragedy of King Richard II*, Act II.

Then, as if by spontaneous combustion or osmosis, the numbers had increased to more than a million and a half: an alien population dressed in olive drab, superimposing its own odd version of the English tongue, its mass-produced civilization, onto means, mores, and moods that had taken centuries to form. They brought with them more than sixteen million tons of supplies and equipment—everything from locomotives to dental fillings—enough to sink the island, the word was, had not anti-aircraft barrage balloons been holding it up.

Hardly any tiny corner of the land was left untouched. Great rows of bombs and artillery shells lined narrow Cornish lanes. Trucks, halftracks, tanks, artillery pieces changed pastoral hedge-bordered fields of rolling Somerset into bulging armories. Hardly a day passed that lighters did not take from big ships in the mouth of the Clyde more of the olive-drab invaders, great stuffed duffel bags in hand. Valiant, straining little trains ran through the night bearing men and tools of war in a seeming exercise in perpetual motion. At every turn airfields and little cities of half-moon-shaped Niessen huts pimpled what had before been the world's most orderly countryside. Planes—twelve thousand of them American—made of the sky a crowded turnpike. Shipping in assorted shapes and sizes cluttered the ports. On the south coast of Devon, shells burst as men practiced the art of storming a hostile shore. During one of the rehearsals the enemy provided a touch of realism by slipping through a hole in the escort with fast little torpedo boats, sinking two LST's and sending seven hundred men to their deaths.

London was one vast headquarters and leave center, alive with the uniforms of many lands coming and going in a frenetic existence. Grosvenor Square became an American enclave, where the resonant tones of a British voice sounded foreign. On nearby Park Lane in the Great Ball Room of Grosvenor House, American officers ate more than six thousand meals a day in an assembly-line cafeteria they named "Willow Run" after an aircraft plant back home; every meal cost fifty cents, and proctors moved among the diners to censure him who left food uneaten on his plate. To thousands of enlisted men, Rainbow Corner near Piccadilly was a touch of Main Street packaged and shipped overseas by the American Red Cross.

For all the bond of common purpose, two peoples living on top of each other were bound to experience some irritation. Nothing was wrong with the American soldier, the Britisher quipped, except that he was "overpaid, over-sexed, and over here." While admiring the stamina that had brought the British through grim days that might have found others wanting, the American deemed the stolid acceptance of hardship, the unmitigated orderliness, somehow infuriating.

Yet they lived together, worked together, played together with less friction than most would have believed possible. Sometimes the American made love to the native women, married some of them. (Sergeant Bill Thompson became an international *cause célèbre* when he fathered quadruplets by Miss Nora Carpenter but could not marry her because of an unbending wife back home.) In blacked-out pubs Briton and American shared mild and bitter, a meager ration of Scotch and gin, challenged each other at darts, sang songs—a rousing "Beer Barrel Polka," a ribald "Roll Me Over," a plaintive "I'll Be Seeing You."

When General Eisenhower arrived from North Africa on January 14, 1944, to take up his duties as Supreme Commander for the invasion, he brought with him leaders who had become celebrities in North Africa and Sicily—Montgomery, Bradley, Spaatz, Patton. Bringing Patton inevitably brought problems, too, for despite the general's contrition over the slapping incidents, he was not easily tamed. He created another furor when, in dedicating a British-American serviceman's club, he spoke of America and Britain uniting to rule the postwar world. Then on the very eve of the invasion he delivered himself of what became known as his "St. Crispin's Day speech," a remarkable combination of expletives and four-letter vulgarities.[98] Yet having taken a stand on Patton after the slapping incidents, Eisenhower stuck by him.

A brooding tension—intangible, indescribable, yet wholly real—pervaded life in Britain during those last months before the invasion. The long-awaited second front, all knew, might come any day, and on it more than any other single event hung the outcome of the war.

Nervous German radio broadcasts and, despite censorship, an impatient Allied press fed speculation. In April tension increased as the British government imposed a ban on visitors to large segments of southern England. Like news, all mail had to pass the censor, a proviso soon extended to diplomatic correspondence as well. Travel between Britain and neutral Ireland, presumably thick with Axis agents, was banned.

---

[98] Patton's St. Crispin's Day speech has been published in Dwight Macdonald, *Memoirs of a Revolutionist* (New York, 1958), pp. 95-96.

Despite all precautions, an occasional slip in security occurred. The discovery of classified documents pertaining to OVERLORD in a Chicago post office produced a flurry of concern until investigation revealed that a sergeant had inadvertently and innocently mailed them to his sister. Concern arose, too, when someone noticed a succession of words used as code names for the invasion in the crossword puzzle of the London *Daily Telegraph*—OVERLORD, UTAH, OMAHA, NEPTUNE; but investigation revealed nothing more than coincidence.

More serious was the breach of a major general of the Army Air Forces, who remarked over cocktails that the invasion would be launched before June 15. Eisenhower promptly reduced him to the rank of colonel and sent him home. Much the same happened to a Navy captain.

"The mighty host," Eisenhower noted later, "was tense as a coiled spring."[99]

Tension about the invasion passed over the ocean back to the United States to a population already keyed to a high pitch by wartime living.

More than 17,500,000 Americans now were engaged in war work, and scarcely any home lacked a service flag hanging in a window. Many windows had a gold star, meaning a life lost. Housing everywhere was at a premium, from war-swollen Washington to normally placid country crossroad towns where wives waited to spend brief moments with their airman, soldier, or sailor. Trains ran late, obsolete coaches always were depressingly crowded, sleeping cars were seldom available. New automobiles were a prize rigidly reserved for the most essential individual. Typewriters were "frozen." Shoes joined the list of rationed items. Liquor, cloth, toys, batteries, electric motors—long and ever growing was the roll of those that were in short supply or unobtainable. A thriving black market developed in gasoline ration coupons. Housewives formed long, impatient queues for almost everything. The sharp riposte "Don'tcha know there's a war on?" served to excuse everything shoddy, goods and services alike.

It was under these conditions that the summer of 1943 had seen a succession of deplorable race riots, including a near race war in Detroit which left nine Caucasians and twenty-five Negroes dead. Charged was the atmosphere around many a southern town where Negro troops

---

[99] Snyder, *The War*, p. 363.

in segregated units were held in semi-bondage by rigid mores which Southerners were not about to relax simply because their nation was fighting racism abroad. Wartime conditions contributed, too, to a wave of what people called "juvenile delinquency" which included immorality, theft, crime, and civil strife. Los Angeles in particular was torn by incidents involving "zoot-suited" hoodlums wearing absurdly long coats with padded shoulders and trousers that tapered to ridiculously narrow cuffs. The youthful malcontents took such pleasure in attacking servicemen that the Navy for a while declared the city out of bounds. Less troublesome but nonetheless absurd were swarms of teen-aged girls wearing "bobby-sox" who swooned when singer Frank Sinatra crooned, and some of them doubled as "liberty girls" who hung around military and naval bases as men left on evening or week-end pass.

Strikes marred the labor front, baffling the man in uniform who found it difficult to understand how people could act so selfishly when so much was at stake. (Crewmen of an aircraft carrier derisively collected "pennies for strikers" and mailed them to a strikebound aircraft plant.) Wildcat strikes, often over trifling issues, were rampant. John L. Lewis and his United Mine Workers proved so intransigent that the government took over the mines to keep them working. Management made its share of trouble, too, as in the spring of 1944 when Sewell Avery refused to relinquish his post as chairman of the board of Montgomery Ward, the mail order house, when the government moved to seize the company in the wake of continuing labor disputes. A photograph of helmeted soldiers carrying a defiant Avery to a Chicago sidewalk became one of the period's most famous pictures.

Although perhaps not so blatantly as in World War I, management was guilty of many an instance of featherbedding and pyramiding. The unions, for their part, compelled government subcontractors to hire hundreds of unnecessary workers—all in the presumably holy name of the war effort.

Yet for all the mismanagement, for all the faults that developed in hastily designed equipment, the nation's production record was phenomenal. American factories turned out some 275,000 planes in the course of the war, 86,000 tanks, 315,000,000 artillery shells, and 127,255 ships.

As the winter of 1944 turned into spring, and as May gave promise of hot days ahead, tension mounted. A group of clergymen and writers protesting "obliteration bombing" of German cities aroused vast indignation—not against the bombing, but against themselves. Patrons stood six deep at bars. Congress passed an act providing a number of soldier benefits—the "GI Bill of Rights." Pastors and priests prayed for "our boys" who soon would be carrying freedom's cause to the hostile shore. In reference to the three-year pressure by the Russians for a second front, *Time* magazine reported a joke supposedly current in Britain: a sleepy Churchill picks up his phone at 4 A.M. to hear a familiar voice:

"Winston, this is Joe. I'm at Calais. You can come on over now. It's safe."

Late on June 3 in London a girl apprentice in the Associated Press Bureau, who was practicing on her teletype machine with a key mistakenly open, sent to an apprehensive America false word that the invasion had begun:

URGENT PRESS ASSOCIATED NYK FLASH EISENHOWER'S HQ ANNOUNCED ALLIED LANDINGS IN FRANCE.[100]

Shocked, Eisenhower's headquarters hastened to issue a denial.

The Allies first tested German defenses of the French coast across from the British Isles in August 1942, at a modest resort named Dieppe. In a big hit-and-run raid designed to explore air and naval techniques and the process of putting tanks ashore over hostile beaches, a 6,100-man force, composed mainly of Canadians but including 1,000 British Commandos and 50 U.S. Rangers, almost committed suicide. All but 1,500 of the 5,000 who made it ashore were lost.

After studying the tragedy of Dieppe, planners serving the Combined Chiefs of Staff determined that a cross-Channel invasion required, not a number of separate assaults by relatively small units, but immense concentration in a single grand assault. The site would have to be close to at least one major port, to provide a good road network leading inland, and to lie within easy range of fighter planes based in Britain. The latter fairly well limited the choice to the coastline from the Belgian-French border to Cherbourg: the Pas de Calais across the Strait of Dover, the region already tested around Dieppe, or that part of Normandy along the base of the Cotentin peninsula between Caen and Cherbourg. The first two choices presented totally unsheltered beaches which, because

[100] Found in various sources. I have used Cornelius Ryan, *The Longest Day* (New York, 1959), p. 31.

of their proximity to Britain, probably would be most heavily fortified. The early planners chose the beaches of the Cotentin.

In March of 1943 the Combined Chiefs passed on this analysis to Lieutenant General Sir Frederick Morgan, an able, congenial Britisher, whom they appointed in lieu of a supreme commander to begin detailed planning for the invasion. Morgan's title was Chief of Staff to the Supreme Allied Commander, which became known as COSSAC. It was two months later, at the TRIDENT conference in Washington, that the Combined Chiefs set a target date for the invasion of May 1, 1944, a date reaffirmed six months later in conference with the Russians at Teheran.

The Combined Chiefs charged COSSAC with preparing three plans: a deception maneuver designed to pin German forces in France by creating an impression of invasion in 1943; a blueprint for occupying the Continent in case of sudden German collapse; and the invasion itself, Operation OVERLORD. To the latter General Morgan and his Staff devoted most of their energies. By the time General Eisenhower arrived in London, COSSAC had drawn up a detailed plan for an assault along twenty-five miles of coastline extending westward from the mouth of the Orne River near Caen, plus a simultaneous supporting invasion of southern France.

With Eisenhower's arrival COSSAC passed from the scene, giving way to Supreme Headquarters, Allied Expeditionary Force (SHAEF), located in the southern fringe of London at Bushy Park. As Eisenhower, Montgomery, and the Staff at SHAEF examined COSSAC's plan, they agreed in principle but insisted that it be broadened and strengthened. Instead of a twenty-five-mile front, they wanted forty miles; instead of three divisions, five. With supporting troops, that meant 174,320 men and 20,018 vehicles for the assault phase alone. It meant, too, finding landing craft for them—that old problem, which was intensified at the time by the continuing requirements of the embattled men at Anzio.

Few favored postponing the invasion to wait for the shipyards to turn out more craft—at Teheran, Churchill and Roosevelt had promised Stalin explicitly that the invasion would come in May. Although the promise was flexible enough to allow Eisenhower a month's leeway, one month's production would hardly do the job; and even a month's delay afforded that much less good campaigning weather before winter set in, and that much more time for the Germans to strengthen beach defenses and to bring to bear against crowded Britain a new device Allied intelligence had detected. It was some kind of missile, believed to be either a rocket or an aerial torpedo, or both, some form of pilotless aircraft that might provide a deadly substitute for a crumbling *Luftwaffe*.

To delay longer than a month was to risk postponing the invasion another year. Only May and the summer months bring favorable tides, and only three days out of each month promised the moonlight deemed necessary for airborne landings. If the weather acted up on those few days, what then? Given much more time, the Germans might develop a weapon of such awesome power that only those highest in intelligence circles even suspected the possibility of it, and they spoke of it only in whispers: something about heavy water and an explosive force new to man.

Against the arguments opposing delay were the advantages to be gained from another month of good flying weather for an Allied air arm that had been so busy defeating the *Luftwaffe* that little time remained for targets like bridges, railroads, and tactical airfields which had to be destroyed if German reaction to the invasion was to be crippled. A month's delay also would time the invasion closer to the late thaw in Poland and a renewed Russian offensive. Yet in spite of the advantages, there was still the unalterable fact that one month, while helpful, would not do it in terms of landing craft.

At the end of January, Eisenhower nevertheless recommended, and the Combined Chiefs accepted, a month's delay in the invasion—a target date changed from May to June. Even so, if OVERLORD was to be strengthened as Eisenhower deemed essential, landing craft had to be found somewhere else. That necessity prompted the Supreme Commander to turn questioning eyes on the subsidiary plan to invade southern France, that operation which COSSAC had deemed important, and which the conferees at Teheran had endorsed, but which the British—Churchill, in particular—opposed. Operation ANVIL, they called it.

General Eisenhower himself came up with a solution: to stage ANVIL not simultaneously with OVERLORD but later. Landing craft from the Mediterranean thus might be used in the main invasion, then returned for a postponed invasion of southern France.

The compromise failed to remove all doubts about ANVIL, since the subsidiary invasion also involved diverting divisions and supporting troops from Italy. Only a month later the American Joint Chiefs agreed to put ANVIL on the shelf pending the outcome of the new offensive in

Italy aimed at getting Rome. Yet Eisenhower's compromise assured suffi-cient landing craft for the cross-Channel invasion and—as events would prove—removed the really telling argument against ANVIL.

As detailed planning for the invasion and the buildup of men and supplies proceeded, General Eisenhower moved to right what he deemed a critical defect in command arrangements.

Although British and Americans had agreed to pool their tactical air resources under Eisenhower's control in the Allied Expeditionary Air Force headed by Air Marshal Leigh-Mallory, the British Chiefs long had objected to giving Eisenhower control also of the strategic air arm. Arguing that strategic bombardment was specialized and affected all fronts, not just OVERLORD, they insisted that the big bombers remain responsible directly to the Combined Chiefs. That arrangement, of course, would assure a British finger on the pulse of the air campaign and was tantamount to a guarantee that the saturation bombardment directed at German morale would continue, but it carried no assurance of strategic opera-tions in direct support of the invasion. The new head of the U.S. Strategic Air Forces, "Toocy" Spaatz, sided with the British, for he feared that if Eisenhower controlled the big bombers, he would divert resources from the Combined Bomber Offensive and thus obviate the chance, to which Spaatz still clung, of defeating Germany by aerial bombardment without resort to a ground invasion.

Eisenhower, on the other hand, had no wish to halt or curtail any part of the Combined Bomber Offensive. He did want as Supreme Commander to have direct control of all resources, to be in a position if necessary to switch strategic bombers to targets he deemed essential to success of the invasion. One campaign he contemplated was a concerted bombardment of French railroads over an extended period to curtail German troop and supply movements toward the invasion beaches.

Late in February 1944, General Eisenhower took the problem to Prime Minister Churchill. To refrain from providing the Supreme Commander with control of all resources for the invasion, Eisenhower insisted, was to deny all-out commitment to the invasion. It was an echo of the old American fear that the British put something less than heart and soul in the very theory of cross-Channel attack. If that was the case, Eisenhower said, he would have to pack up and go home.

Thus confronted, Churchill promised to go along with whatever plan Eisenhower and the Chief of the Air Staff, Air Marshal Portal, could work out. Although the two quickly agreed that once they had settled on a plan for strategic air support, control was to pass to Eisenhower—subject to intervention at any time by the Combined Chiefs—the path to a mutually acceptable plan ran through a tangle of divergent views.

The scrimmaging teams this time had an unusual lineup: on the one side, Eisenhower, his new deputy—Air Marshal Tedder—and Leigh-Mallory, the head of the Allied Expeditionary Air Force; on the other, Air Marshal Portal, the British Cabinet, and "Tooey" Spaatz.

The real issue was Eisenhower's control of strategic air resources, but it was early obscured by the more immediate issue of a campaign against French railroads. Portal, it developed, had no specific objection to Eisenhower's controlling strategic air, but he deemed an offensive against railroads a waste because he thought it would hurt the Germans little. Spaatz wanted no interference with the possibility of the air arm's winning the war on its own, and he specifically wanted a chance to shift from the campaign against the enemy's airframe industry—which at that point he considered indecisive—to an offensive against the oil industry. Like Portal, the British Cabinet and Churchill objected primarily to the campaign against French railroads but for a different reason: the penalty in dead, maimed, and homeless that the French people would have to pay.

Although Air Marshal Tedder shared Portal's concern that a campaign against the railroads might deal no crippling blow, he saw it as more effective in the time remaining before D Day than a campaign against oil. To Leigh-Mallory, it meant an additional contribution to a program against German military movements to which his tactical aircraft already were committed. Eisenhower himself favored it because he saw it as the most direct and effective contribution the air forces might make to help Allied ground troops get ashore and stay.

In the end Eisenhower's was the decisive argument. Having been assured that every effort would be made to avoid densely populated areas, and that de Gaulle concurred, Churchill and his Cabinet went along.

Once that matter was solved, so was the real issue of Eisenhower's control of strategic air. On the assurance of continued dedication to the goals of the Combined Bomber Offensive—the destruction of the German military, industrial, and economic systems—and of the U.S. Strategic Air

Forces—the destruction of the German air force—which would involve some deference to Spaatz's desire to hit at the oil industry, the Combined Chiefs of Staff approved placing the strategic airforces 'under the *direction* [as opposed to "command"] of the Supreme Commander, in conformity with agreements between him and the Chief of the Air Staff as approved by the Combined Chiefs of Staff."[101]

However complex it might sound to an outsider, it satisfied everybody concerned and, more important, it worked.

Included in the deliberations and made a part of the solution was the matter of knocking out before D Day the launching sites for the enemy's new aerial weapon, whatever it was. The task fell primarily to medium bombers.

Allied intelligence first had detected launching ramps in Belgium and northern France as the Germans began to construct them during the summer of 1943. Although the Allies lacked full information on the new weapon, they pieced together German propaganda boasts and reports from Polish agents of experiments conducted at Peenemuende on the Baltic coast, and came up with a fair idea of what their enemy was about.

The new weapon was a flying bomb. The Germans named it a "V weapon," from *Vergeltung* for "vengeance"—a play in reverse on the Allied use of "V" for "Victory." From the characteristic putt-putt of the motor, the Allies later nicknamed it "buzz-bomb." It was the first of two new weapons; the second, a supersonic rocket, was introduced later, at which time the two became known as "V-1" and "V-2."[102]

The discovery in December 1943 of sixty-nine launching sites close to the French and Belgian coasts produced a rash of concern that the Germans might so bombard the jammed British ports, depots, and assembly areas as to prejudice the invasion. So seriously did Allied commanders view the threat that on occasion they diverted the precious strategic bombers to the sites. They also launched several raids against Peenemuende, but those had little effect beyond forcing the Germans to disperse their facilities.

Some thirty thousand sorties eventually were flown against the launching ramps; but as time passed, sober analysis of the enemy's capabilities eliminated some of the early concern. On the basis of the most generous

---

[101] Pogue, *The Supreme Command*, p. 125.

[102] James McGovern, *CROSSBOW and OVERCAST* (New York, 1964); also, Pogue, *The Supreme Command*; and Craven and Cate, eds., ARGUMENT' *to V-E Day*.

estimates of German production, Allied experts concluded that the foe would be unable to produce enough flying bombs to launch a major offensive before the invasion began.

As early as March, two months before the invasion, General Eisenhower could conclude that German aircraft, with or without pilots, could pose no serious threat to the landings.

Chapter Sixteen – Cross-Channel Attack

Most of the top names assembled for the invasion were comfortingly familiar: Eisenhower himself. "Beetle" Smith, experienced Chief of Staff. As deputy commander, the British airman, Tedder, who had spent 1943 as a close associate of Eisenhower's heading the Mediterranean Allied Air Forces. Commanding the 21st Army Group, General Montgomery was to serve also as overall ground commander. (Although Eisenhower found Montgomery acceptable, he would have preferred Alexander.) Calm, dependable, though unspectacular, Omar Bradley was the top American ground officer—a result both of Bradley's proven ability and of George Patton's choler. Bradley was to head the First U.S. Army under Montgomery but was to move up to command an army group and to become Montgomery's equal once another American army under Patton came ashore. Bradley's counterpart as an army commander under Montgomery was less well known: General Sir Miles Dempsey, commanding the Second British Army. Also new to the east was Leigh-Mallory, head of the tactical air arm, and Lieutenant General Henry R. D. G. Crerar, who would command a follow-up force, the First Canadian Army.[103]

---

[103] The official U.S. Army account is well done: Harrison, *Cross-Channel Attack*. I have also consulted: Pogue, *The Supreme Command*; Ruppenthal, *Logistical Support*, Vol. I; Craven and Cate, eds., *ARGUMENT to V-E Day*; Morison, *The Invasion of France and Germany*; two volumes in the *American Forces in Action* series: [Charles H. Taylor] *OMAHA Beach* (Washington, 1946), and [Roland G. Ruppenthal] *UTAH Beach to Cherbourg* (Washington, 1947); Wilmot, *The Struggle for Europe*; Major L. F. Ellis, *et ah*, *Victory in the West*, Vol. I (British official history); Ryan, *The Longest Day*; David Howarth, *D Day, The Sixth of June, 1944* (New York, 1959); S. L. A. Marshall, *Night Drop* (Boston, 1962); Hanson Baldwin,

A familiar figure as former British naval chief in the Mediterranean, Admiral Bertram H. Ramsay was to be Allied Naval Commander-in-Chief. While Admiral Stark remained in command of U.S. Naval Forces in Europe, the top American under Ramsay was to be Rear Admiral Alan G. Kirk, new to the top hierarchy of command but long experienced in convoy duty and a student of amphibious warfare. Kirk was to command the ships supporting American troops, called the "Western Task Force."

To deceive the Germans into believing the landings were to hit the Pas de Calais, Eisenhower's Staff devised a variety of subterfuges, including a fictitious "Army Group Patton," presumably massed just across the Channel along the coast near Dover. Dummy installations, false radio traffic, dummy landing craft in the Thames estuary, deceptive information fed to known enemy agents, huge tent encampments, and a careful plan of aerial bombardment to concentrate more bombs on the Pas de Calais than anywhere else—all perpetuated a fiction that would be continued well past D Day, even after Patton himself joined the fighting.

Just how successful was the program the Allies did not know for certain until events unfolded on the beaches. In combination with the logical German mind, it was strikingly successful. None among Hitler's military high command in France and the Low Countries doubted that the invasion would strike the Pas de Calais.

Hitler himself, who substituted intuition for the shortcomings of his military education, saw it otherwise. He suddenly announced in March that the Allies were likely to land on the Cotentin and Brittany peninsulas. His naval commander in France soon echoed this appreciation, calling particular attention to the Cotentin; but once having correctly divined Allied intentions, the naval commander relaxed on the theory that, having failed to attack the coastal batteries on the Cotentin, the Allies were not yet ready to invade.

Hitler's ground commanders in France were convinced, on the contrary, that invasion was soon to come. The Commander-in-Chief in the West, Field Marshal Gerd von Rundstedt—venerable, wizened old soldier,

Battles Lost and Won (New York, 1966); Davis, *The Experience of War*; Hans Speidel, *Invasion 1944 — Rommel and the Normandy Campaign* (Chicago, 1950); Walter Bedell Smith, *Eisenhower's Six Great Decisions* (New York, 1950); Colonel C. P. Stacey, *The Canadian Army — An Official Historical Summary* (Ottawa, 1948); Milton Schulman, *Defeat in the West* (rev. ed., New York, 1968); several of the memoirs previously cited; and Field Marshal the Viscount Montgomery of Alamein, *Normandy to the Baltic* (Boston, 1948).

respected paragon of all that was good and right with the German Officer Corps, he who in 1940 had sparked the penetration through the Ardennes that led to Dunkirk—looked toward the Pas de Calais. So did his top field commander, the head of *Army Group B*, the "Desert Fox," Erwin Rommel.

Like Hitler, Rundstedt and Rommel recognized that in the grave danger of invasion also lay the opportunity for turning defeat into victory. If they could thwart the invasion, the Allies would be unlikely to mount another for a long time: that would enable the Germans to shift perhaps fifty divisions to regain the initiative against the Russians and end the war in the east in time to meet a new threat in the west.

Yet there a meeting of minds ended.

Rundstedt had little faith that his troops, even when bolstered by formidable fortifications of what had become known as the "Atlantic Wall," could stop an invasion on the beaches. He believed instead in a powerful mobile reserve to be held well behind the line and rushed forward to counterattack once the Allies had revealed the site of their main landings.

Rommel, for his part, considered Allied aerial superiority too great to warrant any reliance on a mobile reserve. Repel the invaders at the water line, Rommel believed, or fail.

The divergent views might have made little difference, except that, like all holders of a marshal's baton, both Rommel and Rundstedt theoretically had direct access to Hitler, and the former had specific authority to use it. In first sending Rommel to France late in 1943, Hitler had charged him personally to plan for the defeat of the invasion and had made him responsible not to Rundstedt but directly to OKW, the Armed Forces High Command. Even after Rommel and Rundstedt agreed early in 1944 that Rommel could better serve as commander of *Army Group B* under Rundstedt, the onus of direct responsibility for repelling the invasion remained with Rommel and with it something of the special tie to OKW. Rommel, too, was the more forceful personality—energetic, assured, ready to argue with Hitler—whereas Rundstedt was disposed to avoid dispute by giving in to his volatile *Fuehrer*.

The old field marshal nevertheless could turn a trick or two. Convinced that his theory of defeating the invasion by counterattack was right, he created a special headquarters called *Panzer Group West* to command all armored units in France, subject to his command, not to Rommel's.

That prompted Rommel to a ploy of his own. If he was to be responsible for repelling the invasion—he told Hitler at a meeting of senior commanders in March of 1944—he required control not only of the armored units but of artillery reserves as well. In addition to commanding the two armies comprising *Army Group B* along the Channel coast, he required some control over two others along the southwestern and southern French coasts in case he needed to call on them for help. Hitler agreed.

For all the damage to Rundstedt's pride, it would have been better for the German cause had Hitler stuck by that decision, since that would at least have ensured a unified command in France. Yet this time Rundstedt stood up to his *Fuehrer*. The protest he put in writing drew such support from the Armed Forces High Command that Hitler relented, but only partially. He split the armored reserve, giving a portion to Rundstedt as a central reserve, assigning a portion to Rommel. Hitler thus deprived not one but both commanders of all available means for influencing the battle.

While Rundstedt continued to champion his theory of victory through counterattack (but without adequate means to achieve it), Rommel pursued his strategy of do-or-die on the beaches. He withdrew his troops from the training they sorely needed, and put them to erecting underwater obstacles, sowing mines, digging in artillery pieces, planting fields with slanting poles to counter paratroopers and gliders (*Rommelsspargel*, "Rommel's asparagus," the soldiers called them)—trying feverishly in the uncertain time left to create a barrier some four miles deep that would ensure victory by enabling the defenders to hit with full strength at the moment the invaders touched down, that moment when those coming ashore would be most vulnerable.

To a devotee of maneuver, as Rommel had proved himself to be in North Africa, it was galling to rely on a fixed defense. Yet what other choice in the face of Allied planes? The mounting Allied aerial campaign against French railroads, plus sabotage by the French Resistance, was so destructive that by June the German transportation system in France was at the point of collapse. Of two dozen bridges over the Seine River between Paris and the sea, eighteen were destroyed, three more severely damaged. What choice, too, given the quality and the quantity of German troops available in France?

The divisions in France had long served as a replacement pool for the man-eating Russian front. Late in 1943, Hitler decreed that the west was no longer to be cannibalized to succor the east; but in March of 1944, as Hungary appeared about to pull out of the war, and as the Russians plunged forward two hundred miles, he modified his stand. Divisions from occupied countries that had been earmarked to move to France on first word of the invasion, left instead for the east. So did an entire SS panzer corps from France with two SS panzer divisions, plus all the assault guns of four infantry divisions.

As Hungary docilely accepted occupation, and the Soviet armies outran their supply lines, Hitler was able to repair some of the damage. Yet of the fifty-eight divisions available to Rundstedt, many were burned out from fighting in the east, others were training and so-called static divisions which the sound of Allied guns would summarily upgrade to combat status, and still others were newly formed, of which some were of creditable combat value, some only partially equipped and trained. None compared with the conquering legions of the early months of the war. Units that at one time had boasted of their all-German "racial purity," were in the spring of 1944 laced with "racial Germans" from border areas of adjacent countries, with "volunteers" from allied and occupied countries, and with auxiliaries recruited from Russian prisoners of war. Although the west had priority on tanks during the first half of 1944, the defenders who looked warily across the Channel remained far different from the force that had gazed at the same waters four years before. Moreover they could count on nothing like the grandeur they once had known in the air; the *Luftwaffe* in France was down to fewer than two hundred planes, little more than half of which could operate at any one time.

Faced with but one Allied invasion and that against the Pas de Calais, the German forces nevertheless would have been a formidable foe, perhaps superior to men stepping disorganized onto a hostile shore even in vast numbers and with strong fire support. For a long time Rundstedt and the others took comfort in that reckoning, but events in Italy made them doubt. Grossly overestimating Allied resources, they wondered why the Allies tolerated a stalemate in Italy. When late in January there came the landing at Anzio which seemed to have little tactical connection with the main front in Italy, and when John Lucas failed to push out into the Alban Hills, many on the German side were convinced that the Allies intended to attract and pin down German units with a number of subsidiary landings before striking the main blow. German commanders in France became increasingly wary of committing everything to counter an Allied invasion lest more powerful landings follow elsewhere.

That consideration served to color Rundstedt's and Rommel's thinking when in late April, Hitler began to insist that the invasion would hit the Cotentin and demanded that forces there be strengthened. His field commanders at last saw some merit in Hitler's concern, but not much. On the theory that the Allies might make subsidiary landings in the Cotentin, probably airborne landings, they sent there a few battalions and an infantry division. The main landings, they continued to believe, would strike the Pas de Calais. Even the German naval commander, for all his earlier prescience, came around to that view.

As D Day neared, the German order of battle was much as Allied intelligence pictured it. In keeping with an assigned responsibility for the critical Pas de Calais, the *Fifteenth Army*, with nineteen divisions, was the stronger of the two armies along the Channel coast. Charged with defense of the Cotentin and Brittany peninsulas, the *Seventh Army* had thirteen divisions, but only six of them in Normandy. Five panzer divisions stood behind the *Fifteenth Army*, only one behind the *Seventh Army*, and two in southern France.

As May turned into June, the Germans remained ignorant of the time and place of the invasion. An agent in the British Embassy in Ankara had reported the code name—OVERLORD—but nothing more. German intelligence also had learned that the BBC would broadcast the first line of a poem by the nineteenth-century French poet, Paul Verlaine, as a signal to the French Resistance that invasion was imminent, while broadcast of the second line would mean invasion within forty-eight hours. Yet few German commanders had faith in that information. As Field Marshal von Rundstedt's intelligence officer put it, the Allies would be absurd to announce over the radio in advance when they were coming.

One who did believe was the intelligence officer of the *Fifteenth Army* in the Pas de Calais, Lieutenant Colonel Hellmuth Meyer. On the night of June 1 one of Meyer's monitors picked up the first message, the first line of Verlaine's "Chanson d'Automne"—*Les sanglots longs des violons de l'automne*. Meyer was anxiously awaiting the second line when on the night of the third his men monitored the message that the negligent apprentice teletype operator had sent from London:

EISENHOWER'S HQ ANNOUNCED ALLIED LANDINGS

IN FRANCE.[104]

That threw Meyer for a moment, but not for long. His continuing vigil at last paid off when on the night of June 5 the BBC finally came through with the second line of Verlaine's poem: *Blessent mon coeur d'une langueur monotone.*

Meyer burst excitedly with the news into a room where the *Fifteenth Army* commander, Generaloberst Hans von Salmuth, was playing bridge. Salmuth failed to share Meyers excitement but, to be prudent, he ordered his army to the alert. Then he went back to his cards.

Rundstedt's and Rommel's headquarters also got the word, but neither put out a general alert. They considered it unlikely that the messages actually meant anything out of the ordinary, while the weather augury for an invasion was anything but favorable. Rundstedt's staff in a blockhouse in the Paris suburb of St.-Germain-en-Laye continued planning for an inspection trip the Commander-in-Chief was to make to Normandy the next day. Rommel had left his command post in a château at La Roche-Guyon, along the Seine, for a visit with his wife in Germany. Furthermore, the German navy was not worried: with gale-force winds lashing the Channel, nobody would attempt an invasion. Also unperturbed, the *Luftwaffe* in France went on with the process of transferring its feeble fighter squadrons to airfields closer to Germany, where they might help combat the great aerial armadas that were pummeling the Reich.

Only the *Seventh Army* along the coasts of Normandy and Brittany failed to learn of the messages on the BBC. Because of the foul weather the *Seventh Army* commander, Generaloberst Friedrich Dollmann, canceled a practice alert for the night of June 5. At a corps headquarters in St. Lô, only a few miles from the Cotentin coast, the corps Staff readied a surprise midnight birthday party for the commander. They had to celebrate early because their chief was leaving before dawn for Brittany, where he was to join General Dollmann and a number of division commanders in a war game to be fought on maps.

In the concrete bunkers and blockhouses of the Atlantic Wall, looking out on squall-drenched beaches and a raging surf, sentries of the *Seventh Army*'s forward divisions relaxed, as confident as were their commanders that nobody would try to come ashore on a night like that.

---

[104] The story of the intelligence officer, Hellmuth Meyer, and the quotes therein are from Ryan, *The Longest Day,* pp. 30-34.

On the other side of the Channel, General Eisenhower early in May had set the date for June 5: that day when the vanguard of more than four million Allied troops was, as the Combined Chiefs had ordered, to "enter the continent of Europe and…undertake operations aimed at the heart of Germany and the destruction of her armed forces."[105]

Late in May they had begun to brief lower-level commanders and the troops themselves on what they were to do. In the process they sealed them in great barbed-wire enclosures along the southern coast of England and detailed some two thousand counterintelligence agents to guard them. All contact by the men inside was severed with a countryside already cordoned off from the rest of the world.

The vast paraphernalia for staging the most complex military operation of all time was waterproofed and ready. Much of the material had become commonplace—the artillery, anti-aircraft guns, DUKW's, ambulances, jeeps, trucks, halftracks, tanks, bulldozers, observation planes, landing craft, steel mesh mats for footing on sand and for constructing airfields, field kitchens, aid stations, hospital tents. Ready for early followup were such big items as locomotives and rolling stock. To transport and provide fire support for the invaders, the Allies had assembled almost 5,000 ships, the largest armada the world has ever seen: landing craft, troop transports, Liberty ships, coasters, mine sweepers, almost 900 warships ranging from torpedo boats to battle wagons, even midget submarines to guide assault craft through early morning darkness to the beaches. American air strength alone totaled almost 13,000 planes, including more than 4,500 big bombers.

There were special devices as well. Lest the Germans employ gas, all men carried gas masks and wore uniforms impregnated with a malodorous chemical that made the clothing stiff and hot until it got wet; then it became soggy and slimy. Some tanks wore canvas bloomers so they could swim. Ready for laying on the floor of the Channel were great coils of big rubber hose for piping fuel to feed hungry trucks and tanks—PLUTO, for "Pipe Line Under the Ocean." Ready for towing across the Channel was the most revolutionary device of all—two artificial, prefabricated harbors with the code name MULBERRY. They consisted of an inner breakwater constructed of hollow, floating concrete caissons six stories

---

[105] Quoted in several of the U.S. Army's volumes; see, in particular, Pogue, *The Supreme Command*, pp. 49-55.

high, which were to be sunk and anchored in position, and a floating pier which would rise and fall with the tide while fixed on concrete posts resting on the bottom of the sea. Ponton-supported treadway bridging would connect the piers with the shore, while old cargo ships were to be sunk to provide an outer breakwater.

On May 30 the troops began to climb gangways to landing craft and transports in harbors all along the southern and southwestern coasts of England. By the third day of June all who were to go by sea were crammed aboard. Those that were to go by air stood on close alert, reading, writing letters, playing cards or dice, some shaving their heads to look like Indian braves, daubing war paint on their faces.

All was ready but the weather. The prophet upon whom General Eisenhower depended to predict that, Group Captain J. M. Stagg of the Royal Air Force, had been optimistic at first; but the night of Saturday, June 3, all optimism vanished. The day Eisenhower had chosen for the invasion, Stagg revealed, would be overcast and stormy with high winds and a cloud base too low for flying. Furthermore, Stagg went on, conditions were so unsettled that he could venture no forecast more than twenty-four hours ahead.

The first step was to call back convoys that already had put to sea, then to face the terrible dilemma that Stagg's revelation posed. June 5 was out. As Eisenhower pondered the alternatives on Sunday, the fourth (the day the Fifth Army entered Rome), wind and rain swirled around his command trailer. If they were unable to go on Tuesday, the sixth, the next three days still would provide reasonable tidal conditions; but getting off on any of those days was doubtful, since convoys already at sea would have to be recalled and refueled. The next time when tides would be right was June 19, but that date would afford no moonlight for the airborne troops. The nineteenth and the first possible date in July would mean disembarking troops already briefed and keyed up for the invasion. Even if morale might be sustained, what of security? What, too, of the loss of that much more good campaigning weather on the Continent? What of the perils if the enemy brought new, revolutionary weapons to bear? Already a special arm of British intelligence had warned that the Germans might be capable of contaminating the beaches with a curtain of radioactive materials.

As Eisenhower and the other principals gathered that Sunday night in the library of Southwick House—Admiral Ramsay's headquarters near Portsmouth—rain continued to fall, the wind to blow. When Group Captain Stagg began his briefing, faces were tense.[106]

He had no good news, Stagg revealed quickly, but he had encouraging news. His meteorologists, he said, had spotted a new weather front which should move up the Channel the next day. The rains would stop, the winds would decrease but not desist, the cloud cover would rise enough for bombers to operate much of the night of the fifth and the morning of the sixth. The cloud base at H hour on the sixth might be just high enough to enable observers to spot for naval gunfire. Later in the day the clouds would thicken, the weather would deteriorate again.

To the eager questions that followed, Stagg could say only that the weathermen had done their best. They could make no guarantee of even those merely tolerable conditions.

Eisenhower had little time left to decide. If D Day was to be Tuesday, the sixth, convoys carrying American troops from ports in southwestern England would have to get the order within half an hour.

One by one Eisenhower polled his subordinates.

His Chief of Staff, "Beetle" Smith, said without qualification to go. Conscious of their immense responsibility for helping put the ground troops ashore, the airmen were less definite. At best, said Leigh-Mallory and Tedder, an assault on the sixth would be "chancy."

When it came to the ground commander, General Montgomery, he hesitated not a moment. "I would say—go!"

Yet the final decision could only be made by the Supreme Commander himself. At 9:45 P.M., Eisenhower spoke. "I'm quite positive we must give the order. I don't like it, but there it is. I don't see how we can possibly do anything else."

At a final briefing after midnight to review the weather situation in case it had taken a turn for the worse, Eisenhower confirmed the decision. After three and one-half years of waiting, D Day for Operation OVERLORD, the invasion of the Nazi-held Continent, at last was set. Airborne troops would begin dropping before daylight. Seaborne American troops would start arriving on French beaches at 6:30 A.M.;

---

[106] The conference at Southwick House has been told in various works that differ only in details. I have used primarily Pogue, *The Supreme Command*; Harrison, *Cross-Channel Attack*; Davis, *The Experience of War*; and Butcher, *My Three Years with Eisenhower*.

within the next hour, depending upon tidal conditions, British and Canadian troops on beaches farther east.

The decision was irrevocable.

D Day was to be Tuesday, the sixth of June.

A little before 9 P.M. on the fifth, more than a dozen little British and American mine sweepers approached so close to the Norman coast that men aboard could make out scattered villas on the waterfront. Nobody in the big blockhouses on the shore spotted them. Their job done, the little craft moved back to sea—all but one, the U.S.S. *Osprey*, which detonated a mine, caught fire, and sank with OVERLORD's first losses, six American sailors. Out in the Channel the mine sweepers found a gusty wind still blowing at twelve to twenty knots and stirring up waves five feet high.

D Day was fifteen minutes old when the first Allied soldiers came to Normandy. They were pathfinders and special assault teams of three airborne divisions, the vanguard of 18,300 who were to arrive by air. One division was British, ordered to seal off the left flank of the Allied beachhead by seizing bridges over the Orne River near Caen and by destroying others. Two were American—the 82d and the 101st—with the assignment of assuring success on the Allied right flank by capturing exits of causeways leading across two miles of marshland from a sloping stretch of sand that would forever after be known as "UTAH Beach."

As intrepid men and women of the Resistance moved to appointed secret tasks all over France, Allied planes sowed paratroopers broadcast. Trying to evade anti-aircraft fire which rose in ever-increasing volume, pilots shifted and shunted their vulnerable, slow-flying C-47 transport planes this way and that. Black clouds interfered, too; and many a path-finder had failed to reach the drop zone he was to have marked.

The men came down like pollen scattered by the winds, some as much as thirty-five miles from where they were supposed to land. Hundreds plummeted into vast stretches of lowland that the Germans had flooded to augment their defenses; weighted down by their equipment, trapped in their harness, unknown numbers drowned. Many landed full on German positions. Twenty came down in or close to the town square of Ste. Mère-Eglise, behind UTAH Beach. One man dangled by his harness for more than two hours from the church steeple, playing dead, until the

Germans finally cut him down and captured him. Two British troopers landed just beyond the veranda of a house that served as headquarters for a German division. The division commander himself helped capture them. Here, there, and everywhere men played out thousands of intense individual dramas—sometimes living through them, sometimes not. Many an American trooper held his breath time after time while he snapped a toy metal cricket to identify himself. The response might be a reassuring two snaps from another American, or it might be death from German guns.

Through it all Allied fighters and bombers ranged up and down the coast, hitting coastal batteries, radar sites, headquarters towns, traffic choke points. Before the day was out, Allied planes had flown 11,000 sorties and dropped nearly 12,000 tons of bombs. In keeping with the deception plan, a preponderance of the bombs again was reserved for the Pas de Calais.

As in Sicily, the dispersal of the airborne troops had a positive effect which to some degree offset the negative: it added immeasurably to a confusion that plagued the German foe. Excited cries of "*Fallshirmjaeger!* *Fallshirmjaeger!*" early began to pour into various German headquarters in such volume that it was impossible to fit into a pattern the places where the paratroopers were reported to be dropping.

Dummy paratroopers fused with firecrackers served for a time to deceive many German commanders. Others thought the real paratroopers were crewmen bailing out of ailing bombers. For some time that was the view at Rommers headquarters, *Army Group B*. The dummies temporarily persuaded Rundstedt's Staff that all the excitement signified nothing more than a raid or at worst a diversionary attack, certainly not the invasion. At one division headquarters the commander thought it the work of the French Resistance. Sentries in the blockhouses along the coast still could discern no evidence of invasion by sea, and those radar stations that survived Allied bombing reported no unusual traffic in the Channel.

Most of those who from the first were convinced the invasion was upon them were within the *Seventh Army*, those who had least expected to be hit. At the corps headquarters in St. Lô, where members of the Staff were honoring their commanding general's birthday, first reports put a quick end to the revelry. As the corps passed on the word to army headquarters in Brittany, the Chief of Staff promptly ordered the entire *Seventh Army* to full alert. Yet some of those scheduled to engage in the map exercise early the next day already had left their commands or still did so, despite the alert. The commander of the *91st Division*, which had only recently come to Normandy in response to Hitler's concern about the Cotentin, died on the way at the hands of an American paratrooper.

The *Seventh Army*'s Chief of Staff, who was sure that the invasion had begun and correctly pinpointed it from Caen to Ste.-Mère-Eglise, ordered the *91st Division* to counterattack. Since his superiors at *Army Group B* and Rundstedt's headquarters remained unconvinced, that was the only action higher German commanders took for several hours. The only panzer division along the threatened front, the *21st*, located southeast of Caen, stood to its guns and vehicles, but no orders came to move.

Hundreds of confused local combats were raging when shortly before dawn there came again the drone of planes, followed by a strange fluttering of gliders brushing the air. Men in the frail plywood craft closed their eyes, locked arms, and steeled themselves for the impact of landing. Most of the gliders of the British division made it to the proper landing zones, where they crash-landed in incredible disarray but nonetheless deposited the bulk of their passengers intact. Those of the 101st Airborne Division also made it for the most part, though *Rommelsspargel* and hedgerows of thick earth interlaced with trees and brush took an inevitable toll. The gliders bringing men of the 82d Airborne Division were harder hit. Fewer than half made the correct landing zone. The others crashed into hedgerows or buildings or carried their heavily laden occupants to watery deaths in the flooded marshes.

The first of the gliders was yet to come when Field Marshal von Rundstedt, at his headquarters in St.-Germain-en-Laye, became convinced that some kind of Allied assault was under way, probably a diversionary attack in support of larger landings to hit the Pas de Calais. Yet even diversionary attacks had to be defeated. Somewhere around 4 A.M., Rundstedt ordered two panzer divisions from positions behind the south wing of the *Fifteenth Army*—the closest to the threatened sector of the divisions under his as opposed to Rommel's control—to head for Caen and prepare to counterattack.

Having issued the orders, Rundstedt reported what he had done to OKW, the Armed Forces High Command. Two hours later word came back to halt the divisions pending approval from Hitler. That approval would be a long time coming, for members of Hitler's Staff at the retreat in the Bavarian Alps at Berchtesgaden saw no reason yet to disturb their leaders sleep: they might invoke one of those neurotic tantrums they all dreaded. Although Rundstedt as a field marshal and theater commander could have appealed directly to Hitler, he was too unsure himself whether the situation warranted committing the armor to venture a personal call.

At the *Seventh Army*'s headquarters in Brittany, in the meantime, the persistent Chief of Staff had become more certain than ever that the invasion was at hand. A little before 5 A.M. he telephoned Rommel's headquarters to report without qualification that Allied ships were concentrating from the mouth of the Orne River near Caen to the mouth of the Vire River near Ste.-Mère-Eglise. The information prompted Rommel's own Chief of Staff to act in the name of his absent commander and order the waiting *21st Panzer Division* to head for Caen, but the division was destined to encounter crucial delays.

The job of defeating a seaborne invasion thus fell, as with the airborne invasion, primarily to those German soldiers already in position in the fortifications of the Atlantic Wall or in close reserve in coastal villages and towns. Many of them were aware that something was up, that this time the alert was no practice. They had heard the planes, the word that *Fallschirmjaeger* had landed behind them; but looking out into the gusty Channel where Allied ships were assembling, they still could discern no foe.

It was close to 5:30 A.M. when gathering light first began to reveal form in the mist over the sea. As yet more moments passed, men with field glasses glued to their eyes turned to their comrades in shocked incredulity. The sea, the entire horizon, had begun to come alive with ships, more ships than they would have believed possible for man to assemble in one place.

Fifteen minutes later the naval bombardment began: thundering salvos chewed the bluffs, crushed the villas, rocked the blockhouses. Then overhead roared more planes, wave after wave of bombers.

Out in the Channel, off forty miles of beach, organized pandemonium reigned. Men overburdened with ammunition, guns, and gear moved like automatons across slippery decks, then down rope ladders to landing craft bobbing treacherously in the water below. Officers everywhere were yelling commands of one kind or another; others shouted words or slogans meant for encouragement. Public address systems crackled. Men shook hands with companions. Many prayed, some silently, some aloud. Others were vomiting, miserable in a way that only he who has known a rough crossing of the Channel can comprehend.

Amid the seething mass of men and ships, the throb of motors, the clank of landing craft against unyielding steel plates of the mother ships, big naval guns belched with such noise and vehemence toward the hostile shore that the ships appeared to rock deep in the water from the convulsive effort. Here and there angry coastal batteries tried to return the fire, but it was a one-sided duel. From behind a smokescreen three German torpedo boats tried briefly but generally ineffectively to inflict some hurt. Only one found a mark, a Norwegian destroyer; thereupon the torpedo boats scurried back to base, thus ending the German navy's sole contribution to D Day.

Out of the confusion somehow—few could say how—some kind of order emerged. The circles of churning landing craft increased in size as boats newly filled with humanity joined the formations; and amid the tossing waves they formed into rows and headed beneath the curtain of shellfire toward a shore that was but a dim, distant haze, a shore that planning officers long ago had subdivided and accorded peculiar names like "Easy Red," "Fox Green," "Dog White."

At UTAH Beach—that stretch of sloping sand lying between sea and marshes from which causeways led up to Ste.-Mère-Eglise—men of the U.S. 4th Division were lucky. For all the propaganda boasts, the Atlantic Wall was not everywhere the line of steel and concrete Hitler would have had the world believe. UTAH was one of the weak points, and a strong coastal current carried the landing craft over a mile from the planned landing site to a still weaker spot. In less than three hours men of the 4th Division were in full control of UTAH Beach and had begun to push over the causeways toward firm ground where paratroopers and glidermen anxiously awaited their arrival. The day's losses were remarkably low: 197 killed and wounded, plus another 13 dead when shore batteries sank a destroyer, the U.S.S. *Corry*.

Almost ten miles up the coast to the east the story was strikingly different. There on steep scrub-covered bluffs more than 150 feet high, behind a wide stretch of sand and a narrow carpet of stone shingle, the Atlantic Wall was much closer to being what Hitler had boasted it to be everywhere. Embedded in the sand below the high-tide mark was a devil's delight of obstacles designed to wreck landing craft—hedgehogs, tetrahedra, Belgian Gates, concrete cones, slanting poles topped with mines—the whole draped in barbed wire. In the sand, and particularly in narrow draws leading up through the bluffs, there were quilts of anti-tank and anti-personnel mines. At various levels on the bluffs and in the draws there were casemates, bunkers, blockhouses; many were equipped with big field pieces, others with multiple machine guns sighted through narrow slits to cover almost every inch of the sand below.

It was the added misfortune of the men who came ashore along that stretch of sand to find manning the defenses the *352d Infantry Division*, one of the best divisions in Normandy and one that Allied intelligence had failed to detect until the last moment. There, too, were high seas, for no land mass like the tip of the Cotentin peninsula which protected UTAH Beach existed to either left or right.

This was OMAHA Beach, a name destined to become a symbol for all that was risky, for all that was grim and terrible, about coming ashore on a hostile fortified beach on the coast of France that sixth day of June. There landed two regiments of the 1st Division and one of the 29th.

During the ten-mile run from mother ships to shore, misery piled upon misery for the thirty-odd men crammed with their fighting gear into each of the landing craft. The boats pitched and rolled; waves broke over the gunwales. Gagging, nothing left to vomit, some men lay awash on the floor of the boats, too miserable to care what happened to them. At least ten boats sank, too far away for the men to swim ashore; and those in the other boats had strict orders to get on with their task, leaving survivors to be picked up by rescue craft coming later.

As the other boats neared the shore, a rain of machine-gun fire peppered their bows. German field pieces, which nobody had believed could survive the pounding of the big naval guns, also opened fire, sending water skyward in geysers. Mortar shells, too, poured down.

Some landing craft went up in flames, the victims of shells or mines. Men slipped over the sides of others whenever they reached water shallow enough for wading—sometimes, to their regret, before—in order to avoid that agonizing moment when the ramp would drop and expose the guts of the small craft to the enemy's machine guns. Other men somehow found the courage to race down the ramps. Some miraculously lived to plow slowly through the water, weighted down by waterlogged uniforms and equipment. Some made it—perhaps one-third of them, maybe a few more—to gain hazardous cover at the base of a low sea wall or behind a line of dunes. Hundreds of others died—drowned, cut down as they left the landing craft, hit as they plodded through the surf or across the sea-washed sand.

Lest in the smoke and confusion supporting shells hit the men coming ashore, the naval fire had to lift, thus leaving the Germans free to turn full fury on the pathetic but frightening panorama below them. The little knots of infantrymen and engineers struggling like turtles across the sand could return little fire of their own, other than with rifles or an occasional machine gun or a mortar that somebody had managed to lug laboriously through the surf. The tanks with canvas bloomers which were to have provided early fire support were missing. At least half had sunk, victims of the turbulent sea. Only with the second wave of landing craft did any tanks touch down.

A spectator of the fractured formations arriving on OMAHA Beach during the early hours of June 6 would have deduced that the invasion had failed, or was about to fail. The first wave had been so shattered by the German fire that the next wave seemed almost to be making the first run. Most of the men who made it through the surf and across the sand were bunched along the sea wall, the line of dunes, or the fringe of shingle, in no position to neutralize any of the German guns. A strong coastal current had pulled many units from their appointed landing positions, so that there were many stretches of beach on which no American soldier had yet landed. German fire cut down one engineer after another who tried to get on with the task of demolishing the beach obstacles. Even those who managed to fix explosives to the obstacles found that they could not blow them lest they kill wounded infantrymen seeking cover behind them.

Many men had hoped to find an occasional bomb crater for cover, but the weather had disappointed them. Forced to bomb by instrument through the overcast, bombardiers in B-24 Liberators had delayed their bomb release for several seconds for safety's sake. That was too long. Not a single bomb struck either the beaches or the forward German defenses.

Amid the confusion other landing craft continued to arrive, some to take direct shell hits and go up in flame, others to find no path through the obstacles, but still others to grind their metal noses into the sand. Grass fires started by naval rockets or shells obscured German vision along some parts of the beach, enabling occasional boatloads to reach the edge of the shingle unscathed. Other men simply gritted their teeth and dashed through the German fire as fast as they could. While many fell, others made it, surprised at how much small-arms fire a man can pass through without getting hit.

A few tanks made it too: some of those with canvas floats came under their own power; others churned off landing craft that had managed to get close enough to shore to enable the tanks to disembark. An occasional bulldozer also arrived.

Three companies of Rangers meanwhile were attempting a mission deemed vital to successful landings at OMAHA Beach. They were to knock out a battery of six 155-mm. howitzers believed to be in position a few hundred yards to the west atop an almost sheer cliff called Pointe du Hoe, which towered one hundred feet above a narrow stretch of rocky beach. There it was job enough even to reach the beach without being pounded to pieces by the surf against outcroppings of rock. Touching down, the Rangers fired rockets carrying grapnels attached to ropes and rope ladders to hook into the top of the cliff. As the men began to climb, some Germans at the top opened fire, while others tried to cut the ropes. Having spotted the threat, a destroyer hove perilously close to shore to rake the cliff top with fire.

Less than five minutes after reaching shore, the first Rangers were throwing themselves over the lip of the cliff and clearing haggard, shell-shocked Germans from trenches and gun emplacements that proved to be empty of guns. The howitzers they discovered later in a grove of trees a few hundred yards inland, but the crews had fled. Elated, the Rangers spiked the guns; but hardly had they begun to dig to protect their little enclave when counterattacking Germans closed in. Not until two long days later did other American troops arrive to relieve the Rangers, whose strength of 225 was cut by half.

Back at embattled OMAHA Beach, German observers were sending optimistic reports to their superiors. Debarkation, one said, had ceased. Dead and wounded littered the sand. Bodies bobbed in and out with the action of breaking waves. Men were cowering behind beach obstacles, as the advancing tide nipped at their heels. By 11 A.M. the commander of the *352nd Division* was so convinced he had won at OMAHA that he diverted local reserves to the east, where British troops were hitting his division's right flank.

Much of what the Germans reported was true and echoed many of the same fragmentary reports that were reaching American commanders offshore aboard the flagship U.S.S. *Augusta*. The beach was jammed with men, and enemy fire was obviously still highly effective. LCT's were milling around in the water like "a stampeded herd of cattle."[107] Looking anxiously toward a shoreline barely discernible through haze and smoke, a grim-faced Omar Bradley began to lay plans for evacuating the beachhead and diverting subsequent waves to UTAH or British beaches.

But the drama of OMAHA Beach was not yet finished. Among those who crouched for cover along the sea wall and the shingle walked an intrepid few—officers, noncoms, privates, men of all ranks—who rose to the occasion. "They're murdering us here!"[108] shouted a colonel amid the 29th Division's lone assault regiment at the west end of the beach. "Let's move inland and get murdered!" That division's assistant commander strode calmly here and there, encouraging men to rise, to begin the slow, frightening climb up the bluffs.

Near the other end of the beach in the sector of the 1st Division, a colonel exhorted his men with threat and hope. "Two kinds of people are staying on this beach," he yelled, "the dead and those who are going to die. Now let's get the hell out of here."[109] Others tended to even more forthright persuasion. "Get your ass up that hill!" yelled a sergeant.[110]

Here and there grim-faced men began to move. A few naval fire-support parties were ashore now and could bring the big guns to bear again without fear of killing their own men. Some destroyers came so close to shore that they risked grounding, and raked obvious enemy strongpoints. Here a bazooka man knocked out a pillbox; there a machine gunner neutralized another with rattling bursts of fire. In the surf valiant commanders of two circling landing craft decided to end their futile peregrinations and ram a way through the obstacles. Guns blazing, they made it. Seeing it could be done, others did it, too.

---

[107] Harrison, *Cross-Channel Attack*, p. 320, quoting Colonel Benjamin B. Talley.

[108] Sulzberger, *et al.*, *The American Heritage Picture History of World War II*, p. 503, quoting Colonel Charles A. Canham.

[109] *OMAHA Beachhead*, p. 71, quoting Colonel George A. Taylor.

[110] Baldwin, *Battles Lost and Won*, p. 275.

Up the bluffs the men climbed, slowly, painfully, some falling but others continued to inch forward. The more heavily defended draws, vital for getting vehicles off the beach, remained in German hands, but what mattered for the moment was that men were moving, German positions were collapsing. By noon small, disorganized parties were astride a little highway that runs along the bluffs, only a few hundred yards inland, but inland nevertheless.

Crisis still reigned at OMAHA, but defeat no longer mocked the men full in the face: courage, like fear, is contagious.

No such crisis arose up the coast to the east at British and Canadian beaches. There on strips of sand christened GOLD, JUNO, and SWORD, a Canadian and two British divisions operating under General Dempsey's Second British Army stormed ashore from half an hour to an hour later than the landings at UTAH and OMAHA. The men on these beaches benefitted from the additional naval bombardment the delays afforded. They benefitted, too, from the fact that the beaches sloped gently and had no towering bluffs behind, that German defenses were markedly weaker than at OMAHA, and that no top-ranked German division stood in the way. There stood a static division which included in its ranks impressed foreigners from eastern Europe. Early in the fighting, one battalion of foreigners broke, opening a gaping hole in the line.

Men died at all three of these beaches, many in as cruel a way as at OMAHA; but most pressed quickly inland. There, too, almost all the swimming tanks made it ashore early to provide the close, coordinated fire support the infantry required. There also the *Luftwaffe* made its lone strike of the day against ground troops, a single fruitless strafing run by two Focke-Wulf 190s. Some 250 sorties flown against the invasion armada were equally fruitless.

Before the day was out, British and Canadians were several miles inland; they were short of their assigned objectives of Bayeux and Caen, but sturdy tank and artillery support backed them up. Linkup was achieved with the paratroopers and glidermen who had taken and held bridges over the Orne and had knocked out a deadly German battery which might have enfiladed the landing sites. The defending German division was crushed. The commander, who earlier had helped capture two paratroopers at the edge of his veranda, was reduced to tears.

All the while the German *21st Panzer Division* was moving to counterattack the landings, and its commander and his superiors were secure in the knowledge that their predawn decision to send the panzers toward Caen was right. The greater numbers of British and Canadians employed in the assault wave, the depth they had penetrated—those facts were testament enough that here was the Allied main effort, the *Schwerpunkt* that every German officer was trained to search for.

It was noon before the panzer columns reached Caen, there to find streets piled high with debris from the day's bombings. French civilians further clogged the streets, walking, pushing perambulators filled with belongings, riding their omnipresent bicycles, trying somehow to escape a city almost sure to feel again the fury of Allied bombers. Over the Orne in Caen still stood only one bridge. Moving an entire panzer division across it and through the choked streets would take hours, perhaps days. The commander reluctantly ordered his columns to countermarch and bypass the city to the west.

At four o'clock in the afternoon the *21st Panzer Division* was finally in a position to attack. By that time a British division had established a firm hold on commanding ground four miles inland. When the British called in fire support from three of His Majesty's battleships standing offshore, one German column lost ten tanks in a matter of minutes. Although a company of panzer grenadiers slipped between JUNO and SWORD beaches to reach an observation point above the coast, there to gaze in awe at the naval power massed below, the rest of the *21st Panzer Division* ground painfully to a halt.

It was four o'clock in the afternoon, too, when Hitler at long last approved Rundstedt's employing the two other panzer divisions that the Commander-in-Chief in the west had tried to commit early in the day. By that time the clouds and the overcast that might have screened the tanks from Allied planes had blown away, and the tanks would be able to move only after dark. Because Hitler had slept and then vacillated, the power of those two divisions had been denied at a time when it well might have proved decisive.

Also impotently standing aside as Allied troops poured ashore was the rest of the armored reserve in France—five divisions. Just as impotent were the nineteen divisions of the *Fifteenth Army* in the Pas de Calais. These Rundstedt was saving for the main invasion that was yet to come. He who had focused attention on the Cotentin as the site of the invasion—Adolf Hitler—inexplicably agreed that Rundstedt was right.

Returning from Germany by automobile, Erwin Rommel had no part in the proceedings.

As the climactic day came to an end, the Allied beachheads fell far short of what Eisenhower and his associates had hoped for. They had sought holdings averaging six miles deep; yet at only a few points were Allied troops as much as five miles inland. Although seaborne British troops from SWORD Beach had linked with the British airborne division, and Canadians on JUNO and British on GOLD were in firm contact, nowhere else were any of the five beachheads joined. Because of a German pocket on the coastal side of Ste.-Mère-Eglise, the American 4th Division, for all the relative ease of coming ashore, had yet to link with the two American airborne divisions.

So widely scattered in the night drop, the airborne troops had waged a host of separate and small but nonetheless costly fights. Although a few bands of paratroopers had crossed the little Merderet River in hope of holding a bridgehead that might be exploited later to cut the neck of the Cotentin peninsula and isolate the port of Cherbourg, they were under a state of seige from the enemy's *91st Division*, and overall control of the airborne troops was yet to be established. Four thousand of them still had failed to join their units after the drop.

The 1st and 29th Divisions on OMAHA Beach held a precarious toehold on the enemy shore which was nowhere more than a mile and a half deep. Yet even at OMAHA optimism prevailed. Almost all the first tier of coastal villages was in hand: obscure Norman hamlets which in normal times smelled of cow manure, dairy products, new-mown hay but now gave off a brown odor of smoldering rubble and straw, a yellow smell of burned gunpowder, a green smell of death. They had names indelibly stamped into the senses of the men who fought there: Vierville-sur-Mer, Colleville, St. Laurent, les Moulins, le Grand Hameau.

The beach itself was still a shambles and was raked from time to time by German shelling, even occasionally by machine gun and sniper fire from bypassed Germans reluctant to give up. Somewhere out in the surf rested twenty-six big artillery pieces and more than fifty tanks. Bodies still bobbed in the water. Wrecked landing craft, knocked-out tanks, abandoned bulldozers, and assorted residue of war littered the sand and the fringe of the sea. Men and supplies nevertheless continued to get ashore through the carnage, in considerable numbers even if not as many as the planners had envisaged. A regiment of the 29th Division which had been scheduled to land only on D plus 1, pushed in ahead of time to help extend the beachhead line. Much remained to be done if Allied troops were to stay ashore in Normandy, but hardly anybody on the Allied side was talking of failure.

Had the Allies known of the near bankruptcy on the German side, they would have had more cause for encouragement. General Dollmann's *Seventh Army* already had thrown into the battle every major unit that stood in the Cotentin, including the *21st Panzer Division*. Committing units from Brittany and elsewhere would take time and, as Rommel had been so aware, would expose them to the omnipresent *jabos*, the Allied fighter-bombers. Dollmann was reluctant in any case, in the same way Rundstedt and Hitler were reluctant about the Pas de Calais, to move much from Brittany lest the Allies stage a second landing there.

In the critical hour of trial in the west, a German army that had bled in North Africa, Sicily, Italy, and on the plains of Russia, had had to stand alone, with almost no help from the navy and the *Luftwaffe*. Although the adversary had been weak as he moved from sea to land, the German army had been weaker. It was an army that failed the tests of vigilance and of intelligence. Combined with these failures, Allied power in the aggregate had prevailed.

Allied losses in some places were high. Possibly 2,500 men fell at bloody OMAHA. Once all the stragglers had made their way in, the American airborne divisions set their toll at 2,499 (some had predicted airborne losses of 80 per cent; these were losses of 15 per cent). The Canadians lost 1,074 men; the British, approximately 3,000. The Allied total was probably a little more than 9,000 of which probably one-third was killed.

What mattered more at the moment was that as many as 100,000 other Allied troops had made it safely ashore. That turned the casualty figures into something Allied commanders could accept.

Back in England a relieved Dwight D. Eisenhower authorized a message to be broadcast to the world: "Under the command of General Eisenhower, Allied naval forces, supported by strong air forces, began landing Allied armies this morning on the northern coast of France."[111] (He is reputed to have torn up a note he had written to be released if the landings failed.)

Most people in Britain got the news at work. For many it was a relief—confirmation of something they had suspected, what with all the naval activity off the south coast, the steady drone of planes through the preceding night. Some groups burst spontaneously into singing "God Save the King." Others prayed. Church bells pealed. At noon, before a packed House of Commons, a shrewd Winston Churchill fed German apprehension by calling the invasion "the first of a series of landings in force upon the European Continent."[112]

In the United States the news came in the middle of the night—on the east coast at 3:33 A.M.; on the west coast at 12:33 A.M. Here and there in a sleepy town lights nevertheless came on. People turned on their radios, went to the telephone, knelt in prayer. In America, too, church bells rang.

On the evening of June 6 in Britain, George VI spoke over the BBC. "The Lord will give strength unto his people," he quoted from the Book of Psalms; "the Lord will bless his people with peace."[113]

Franklin Roosevelt called his people to prayer. "Almighty God—Our sons, pride of our nation, this day have set upon a mighty endeavor…"

---

[111] Davis, *The Experience of War*, p. 479.

[112] *Vital Speeches of the Day*, Vol. X, No. 17, June 15, 1944, p. 516.

[113] *Vital Speeches of the Day*, Vol. X, No. 17, June 15, 1944, p. 515.

Chapter Seventeen – The Battle of the Hedgerows

The night of D Day, German troops plucked from a boat that drifted ashore a copy of the field order for the invasion issued by headquarters of the VII Corps, which controlled operations at UTAH Beach. The next evening other German soldiers found on the body of a fallen American officer a copy of the field order of the V Corps, whose troops had landed at OMAHA.[115]

Since the Germans by that time knew the location of the American landings, it came as no great revelation that the immediate American goals were St. Lô, provincial capital and road hub, and the port of Cherbourg. The orders gave no indication that General Bradley's further goal was to drive to the base of the Cotentin peninsula and then turn the corner into Brittany to gain additional ports. Also they provided no inkling of British intentions. Since the British near Caen stood on the threshold of open country leading to Paris, Rundstedt and Rommel—the latter had returned to his headquarters at La Roche-Guyon—deemed they had no choice in any case but to continue to build greater strength against the British at Caen.

The Germans might have deduced from the purloined field orders that the American commitment in the Cotentin was so large as to preclude a second landing in the Pas de Calais. The *Seventh Army* commander, General Dollmann, drew that conclusion. Rundstedt, at least, was inclined

---

[115] Basic sources are: Harrison, *Cross-Channel Attack*; Blumenson, *Breakout and Pursuit*; Blumenson, *The Duel for France* (Boston, 1963); and Wilmot, *The Struggle for Europe*. See also McGovern, *CROSSBOW and OVERCAST*; Craven and Cate, eds., *ARGUMENT to V-E Day*; and Ruppenthal, *Logistical Support*, Vol. I.

to agree—but not OKW and Hitler. Since the Germans had estimated before D Day that the Allies had ninety-three divisions in Britain (they actually had thirty-nine), and since "Army Group Patton" had yet to make an appearance, they saw plenty of latitude for a second and larger invasion. Hitler insisted that Rundstedt hold back the bulk of the panzer reserve, and that the divisions of the *Fifteenth Army* in the Pas de Calais remain inviolate.

Rundstedt had trouble bringing even those forces immediately available to him to act decisively against the invasion. Since the attack of the *21st Panzer Division* had bogged down on D Day, he intended to counterattack the British the next day with the two panzer divisions whose early commitment Hitler's indecision had denied. Yet as Rommel had predicted before the invasion, Allied fighter-bombers proved merciless. Such delays and such heavy losses did the planes inflict that Rundstedt postponed the counterattack until June 8, and even then the tank regiment of one of the divisions failed to arrive in time.

While awaiting this regiment, Rundstedt decided to bring in the special headquarters he earlier had created for controlling the armored reserve, *Panzer Group West*; but by the time this Staff and its commander could arrive, others on the scene had felt impelled to use both panzer divisions to fill great gaps in the line. The counterattack died in the process.

Here early in the fighting the Germans displayed a malaise that was to become a permanent affliction. Delayed and disheartened by losses from incessant air attacks, German units would arrive in driblets; whereupon corps commanders, who seldom could afford the luxury of awaiting an entire division, would in desperation throw in small units to plug gaping holes in the line. Emergency took precedence over doctrine; sealing today's threat denied tomorrow's decision.

Not that Allied troops were advancing with seven-league boots. The terrain where the Americans were operating, particularly, precluded speedy advance. It was hedgerow country, and nobody raced through the hedgerows—those walls of earth several feet thick and five feet high surrounding ten thousand irregular tiny fields. For centuries Norman farmers have used the hedgerows to fence their cattle and protect crops from strong ocean winds. Over the years in the rain-fertilized land the earthen walls have grown dense with bramble, hawthorn, vines, and trees—such a verdant growth that the French call the region the *bocage*.

Between some of the fields are wagon trails with steep hedgerows on either side. Erosion and wear through the centuries have turned the trails into sunken lanes covered by an umbrella of growth that leaves them damp, gloomy, hidden. The lanes provided the Germans with a built-in trench system and covered paths for shifting men from one field to another. In the hedgerows themselves the Germans tunneled deep, revealing on their enemy's side nothing more than a small firing slit to afford a clue to the position. In this country a pair of machine guns dug into a corner where hedgerows meet could sweep two fields with fire enough to discourage the bravest of attackers.

The Americans also faced vast stretches of spongy lowland which the French call *prairies marécageuses*. As paratroopers and glidermen early had discovered, the Germans had denied great expanses of these by flooding. Even the ones not flooded were too boggy for vehicles and were so honey-combed by canals, ditches, streams, springs, potholes, and stagnant pools that they were perilous for a man on foot as well.

Only in front of the British and Canadians was the countryside more open and conducive to swift advance. That was one factor in the deeper gains of the British and the Canadians on D Day. Yet once having achieved a foothold, the British commander, General Montgomery, reacted much as had General Lucas at Anzio. Conscious of the strength the Germans quickly built against him, Montgomery determined to hold in place until he could assemble forces sufficient to assure unquestioned victory. He took Bayeux, five miles inland, and alongside the Americans pushed on several miles beyond, but in front of Caen—also a D Day objective—he dug in deep.

Amid the inhospitable hedgerows and *prairies marécageuses* General Bradley had to split his American forces in quest of two objectives— St. Lô and Cherbourg—while at the same time trying to link the two American beachheads. Failure to join the beachheads quickly was all the more disturbing because buildup over wreckage-strewn beaches was distressingly slow. At the end of D plus 1, June 7, no more than one-quarter of the planned supplies was ashore; the troop buildup was 20,000 men short of a two-day goal of 107,000; and so few vehicles, artillery pieces, tanks, machine guns, and mortars had arrived that the 29th Division and another division that began debarking on D plus 1 represented little more than thin lines of unsupported riflemen. Should the Germans mount a sharp counterattack before the two beachheads were joined, they might annihilate first one, then the other; and Allied commanders reckoned that the Germans would be in a position for decisive counterattack any time after D plus 3.

The task of linkup fell to paratroopers and glidermen of the 101st Airborne Division. To do the job, they had to take the town of Carentan on a narrow spit of land between mouths of two little rivers, which involved attacking along a narrow, exposed causeway leading arrow-like across coastal marshes. Elite troops of a German parachute regiment barred the way, while Rommel ordered an SS panzer grenadier division rushed from Brittany to help.

For five days the Americans fought desperately to traverse the causeway. Under normal circumstances the determined German defense would have provided ample time for the reinforcements from Brittany to arrive; but French saboteurs and Allied planes imposed harshly abnormal conditions. They so crippled the railroads that eventually the SS panzer grenadiers had to unload and finish the march by road. Allied planes even then continued to slow the move, both by direct attacks against the columns and by continuing strikes all over Normandy and northern France which sharply reduced German gasoline stocks.

Just before daylight on June 12, as the American paratroopers at last broke into a smoldering Carentan and pushed out into hedgerows beyond, the panzer grenadiers at last arrived. The next day, the thirteenth, they counterattacked, rudely pushing the paratroopers back to the fringe of the town before naval gunfire and a combat command of armor rushed from OMAHA Beach brought them to a halt.

The basted seam joining UTAH and OMAHA Beaches had stood the test, but so strong were the German reinforcements that many days passed before Americans in foxholes outside Carentan could look back and view more than a few hundred yards of shell-pocked ground between them and the sea. All the while other American troops were pushing from OMAHA toward St. Lô and westward from UTAH to cross the narrow neck of the Cotentin and seal off Cherbourg. Progress in both cases was slow—hedgerow by hedgerow—but it was progress nevertheless; and still no powerful German counterattack developed.

The German failure to mount a major effort to wipe out the beachheads was the big surprise of the invasion. The failure was attributable in part to deception, the German fear of bigger landings in the Pas de Calais. It was attributable in part to the disagreement between Rundstedt and Rommel about how best to counter the invasion, and also in part to persistent Allied attacks which kept the Germans off balance, forcing them here, there, and everywhere to throw arriving reinforcements into the line rather than withhold them to build a reserve capable of a crushing blow. Yet more than to any of these causes, the failure was due to the paralysis imposed by Allied air attacks, with an assist from valiant French partisans.

In the most dramatic instance of French help, Resistance fighters began to harass the *2d SS Panzer Division* the moment it started to march from southwestern France to Normandy. The French pestered the Germans at every turn with fleeting hit-and-run attacks, cutting rails, demolishing bridges, and they called in planes of the Royal Air Force to strafe and bomb. It took the panzers twelve days to cover some 350 miles. They lost 400 men captured and 4,000 killed. In frustrated fury the SS troops summarily shot all male occupants of a village, Oradour-sur-Glâne, then herded the women and children into the village church and burned them alive. All together 642 French civilians perished, and what was left of Oradour-sur-Glâne stood as a monument to mans bestiality.[116]

The German high command in France begged, pleaded, cajoled for help from German planes, but the *Luftwaffe* provided only an occasional night strike against Allied shipping. The few aircraft the Germans had left had to remain in the homeland for the continuing struggle against Allied bombers.

Hitler himself took one constructive step: he ordered an SS panzer corps with two SS panzer divisions to move from the Russian front to France; but that move would take days, perhaps weeks, to accomplish—a reaffirmation of the old dilemma the Germans had always faced in a two-front war. To Hitler's field marshals in France in any case, this transfer would provide only a straw to do the work of a sword. The only hope, they believed, lay in a bold revision of strategy. If they were to prevent the Allies from breaking out of their beachhead and sweeping over all of France, Hitler would have to accept the risk of additional landings and concentrate everything in Normandy.

This Hitler refused to do. The *Fifteenth Army*, he decreed, was to stand

---

[116] The story of Oradour-sur-Glâne is from my work, previously cited, "France — 1940-1944."

intact in the Pas de Calais. Yet he did accede to shifting infantry divisions from other sectors to relieve the three armored divisions that had been forced onto the defensive in Normandy. These three, plus the SS panzer division from southwestern France, another from the Netherlands, and the two from Russia—a total of seven—would provide a reserve sufficient, Hitler insisted, to drive the "Anglo-Saxons"—as he called the Allies—into the sea.

To Rundstedt and Rommel, even this was a half-measure. They wanted full freedom of action to cull divisions from any part of the coast and, in particular, to give ground when necessary to avoid encirclement or to shorten the line in order to create local reserves.

The latter was a point of contention dating from the Russian counteroffensive in front of Moscow in the winter of 1941-1942 when Hitler had ordered positions held even when bypassed or surrounded. Since that policy had averted a precipitate German collapse, Hitler had come to believe that to "hold at all costs" was a panacea for every tactical situation. Nowhere, Hitler had ordered, were the Germans to give ground voluntarily, to abandon any position unless forced to do so. Furthermore, German commanders were forbidden to prepare supplementary positions in the rear, since the *Fuehrer*'s experience as a corporal in the first great war had convinced him that a knowledge of rearward positions acted as a magnet on the soldier.

In the hope of gaining freedom of action, Rundstedt and Rommel begged some high representative of OKW to come to France. Hitler chose instead to come himself. On June 16 he flew to Metz, then motored to Soissons, northeast of Paris, where the German advance in 1918 had stalled owing to the German soldiers' proclivity for cellars stacked with champagne. There on the morning of the seventeenth Hitler met with Rundstedt and Rommel in a concrete bunker built in 1940 to serve as his headquarters for an invasion of Britain that had never come.

To Rundstedt and Rommel it was quickly clear that the meeting would prove futile. Hitler looked sick and fatigued. He sat on a high stool while he kept the field marshals standing, and toyed nervously first with his spectacles, then with colored pencils he held in his hand. He railed about the failure to defeat the landings on the beaches, then about the failure to counterattack. Any proposal to withdraw, he declared, was purely and simply defeatism. Not even troops threatened with entrapment, like those before Cherbourg, were to pull out; they were to fight on, creating a "fortress" that would tie down Allied divisions.

The field marshals were to do the job with what they had, which if properly employed—Hitler insinuated—was ample. The tide soon would turn in any case, since the first of the V weapons had been fired against England, and they soon would be fired in sufficient numbers to settle everything.

Before daylight on June 13 the first flying bomb or pilotless aircraft had appeared over England—one of eleven such bombs launched during the night from hidden ramps in the Pas de Calais. The bomb was a miniature plane with orange flame trailing from its exhaust. It flew at about four hundred miles per hour and sounded like an early make of automobile putt-putt-putting along. Minutes after the sound became audible, the bomb dived to earth near Swanscombe, outside London. A ton of TNT exploded like a thunderclap.

Only three more of the first eleven V-1's reached England, an inauspicious beginning for the first of Hitler's secret weapons. Yet few on the Allied side were inclined to view their advent lightly, and two days later a sharp increase in the tempo of the launchings heightened concern. Of 144 V-1's that crossed the Channel in the twenty-four hours beginning at noon on June 15, 77 dived on London to produce alarming civilian casualties. As Churchill met with his War Cabinet, the decision was nevertheless the same as in the blitz: London would have to take it. Fighter planes and anti-aircraft guns might be turned against the new threat, and Eisenhower would be asked to do everything possible to destroy the launching sites, but nothing was to interfere with winning the war in France.

England was in for a hard time from the deadly but inaccurate V-1. Before the last was shot down near the end of March 1945, almost 6,000 British civilians had died from the flying bombs, and another 17,000 had been seriously injured. During this time the Belgian port of Antwerp also came in for a share of the pounding, but neither in Britain nor on the Continent did the new weapon have any decisive effect.

The first of the V-2 rockets struck the London suburb of Chiswick in the early evening of September 8. Because the rocket was supersonic, the first anyone heard was a deafening explosion, then the sound of a heavy body rushing through the air. Before the last of the V-2 bases was captured, a total of 1,115 rockets left 2,754 British civilians dead and another 6,523 seriously injured. Even more of the rockets fell on Antwerp—1,675. Yet like the V-1, this harbinger of future weaponry had little effect on the course of the war. Indeed, Britons found it easier to live with the V-2 than with the V-1. Since the rocket gave no hint of its approach, whether one lived or died was wholly a matter of chance. One could scarcely devote all one's time to worrying about a death as unpredictable as that.

Long after the first flying bomb crossed the Channel that June, Hitler continued to boast of his secret weapons and to exhort his commanders and his people to have faith in them; but the threat, while locally painful, was strategically empty. All the V weapons the Germans expended lacked the impact of one heavy bombing raid. Like the tank in World War I, the rocket in World War II came onto the scene before the technical development and manufacturing procedures were so advanced as to make it decisive.

After returning from the humiliating confrontation with Hitler at Soissons to the grim chore of trying to assemble forces for counterattack, Field Marshals von Rundstedt and Rommel drew an unexpected assist from the weather. On the morning of June 19 strong winds began to blow from the northeast, bringing with them heavy rains that drove the dreaded Allied planes from the skies. By noon of that day all unloading on the Allied beaches was at a standstill. Through the night and the next day the wind increased to a velocity of more than thirty knots, and a wild surf tossed scores of small craft onto the beaches or crushed them against sea walls and rocks. At OMAHA Beach, the artificial port, the MULBERRY, began to break up.

As the inexorable pounding continued for a third day, portions of the port gave way. Giant waves broke the moorings of the inner breakwater, set pierheads adrift, and twisted into gnarled, grotesque shapes the steel treadway bridging leading from pierheads to shore. By dawn of the fourth day, as the winds at last began to abate, the American port was a wreck. Although the British MULBERRY survived with relatively minor damage, British and American beaches were jammed with battered landing craft and other small vessels. Close to five hundred small craft were destroyed, another eight hundred were stranded high above the normal high-tide mark. It looked like D Day all over again.

Had the storm struck a week earlier, it could have been disastrous. As it was, it dealt a serious setback to the unloading program; but in the continuing absence of large-scale counterattack it was a blow the Allied machine was already strong enough to sustain. By the time the storm struck, almost three-quarters of a million men had landed, and although fewer supplies than planned had been unloaded, the fighting was consuming less than predicted.

In the continuing task of mustering a reserve, German commanders drew little help from the four-day respite from Allied air attack, so much havoc had Allied planes already wreaked on the rail network all over France. Although on June 20, OKW specifically ordered Rundstedt to counterattack, only one of six panzer divisions earmarked for the job was available. Some had yet to arrive; others had been pulled irresistibly into the continuing battle.

On the eighteenth, American troops had driven across the narrow neck of the Cotentin peninsula to reach the sea, then had turned against Cherbourg. Although Hitler personally charged the commandant of the Cherbourg garrison "to defend the last bunker and leave to the enemy not a harbor but a field of ruins," the fight for the small port city was from the German viewpoint shockingly inept and brief.[117] A dominating old French fortress of Fort du Roule fell late on the twenty-fifth, and the next day the German commandant himself surrendered. The Germans had so damaged the port that three weeks passed before the first Allied ship could enter, but American troops in the meantime were free to turn full attention to the companion drive on St. Lô. Lest a breakthrough develop at St. Lô, Rundstedt felt impelled to commit some of the troops he was trying to assemble for counterattack in order to strengthen that part of the line.

The front near Caen also erupted briefly, on the twenty-fifth, when General Montgomery launched an attack with two corps. The British attack not only doomed any hope of pulling panzer divisions from the line but prompted Rommel to throw in contingents of newly arrived divisions. An American attack with an armored division which appeared at first to be more than a limited thrust, drew in additional strength from the reserve. As an added blow, the commander of the *Seventh Army*, General Dollmann, dropped dead of a heart attack.

It was the old malaise again, which from the first had sapped all decision

---

[117] Harrison, *Cross-Channel Attack*, p. 430.

from German tactics against the invasion. On June 29 the Germans finally counterattacked the British, but, far from a decisive blow with six divisions, it was a futile strike with the two SS panzer divisions hurried from the Russian front. By nightfall of the first day the counterattack had largely spent its fury.

Rundstedt and Rommel were not even around for this dreary denouement. Summoned to the presence of their *Fuehrer*, they were on their way to Berchtesgaden.

Rundstedt was tired after the long motor trip from France and found the six-hour wait that Hitler imposed galling. It should come as no surprise, he remarked bitterly to Field Marshal Wilhelm Keitel, the chief of OKW, if an old and sick man like himself should fall dead some day like General Dollmann. The venerable soldier was growing weary of the astringent restrictions inherent in serving his *Fuehrer*.

The meeting was long, but it did no more to solve the tactical differences separating Hitler from his field commanders than had the session at Soissons. Although Hitler at last accepted the ineluctable fact that Allied air power and naval gunfire for the moment forestalled decisive counterattack against the beachhead, his solution to the impasse was as divergent as ever from that proposed by Rundstedt and Rommel. Still anticipating another invasion in the Pas de Calais, Hitler decreed that the troops in Normandy were to stand and fight until the reserves capable of winning could be assembled. If the Allied armies gained access to open country, how could the Germans stop them and at the same time repel another invasion?

Acutely conscious that even with the handicap of arriving by sea the Allies had matched the German buildup and soon would exceed it, Rundstedt and Rommel deemed Hitler's solution negative. Aside from suing for peace—which Hitler obviously would refuse to consider—they saw no alternative but to withdraw slowly—perhaps as far as the Seine, possibly to the old lines in northern France that had served the German cause well a quarter-century before—all the while watching for the opportunity to spring against an overextended foe and defeat him with a decisive counterblow.

To Hitler, withdrawal was out of the question. In his book of tactics one withdrawal led inevitably to another, to mammoth losses in troops and equipment, particularly since the Allies with their abundance of motor transport made a mockery of German mobility, which was still heavily dependent on the horse.

The field marshals returned to France so dispirited that they were quick to seize an opportunity to bring their disagreement with Hitler to a test. When their subordinates, the commanders of the *Seventh Army* and *Panzer Group West*, submitted an estimate of the situation essentially the same as they themselves had presented to Hitler, Rommel approved it and rushed it to Rundstedt, who promptly endorsed it and forwarded it to OKW. Lest there be any doubt that they had thrown down the gauntlet, Rundstedt telephoned Keitel to ask him to tell the *Fuehrer* that he, Rundstedt, did not feel up to the "increased demands."[118] Hitler would be free to interpret the ambiguity in the message as he wished.

The estimate by the field commanders reached OKW early on the first day of July. Hitler's answer was back before the day was ended. The old refrain: hold and fight it out in place.

The next day Hitler's personal adjutant appeared unannounced at the command bunker in St.-Germain-en-Laye, presented Rundstedt with the oak leaf cluster to the Knight's Cross, and handed him a note written by Hitler himself. On grounds of age and health, the note revealed in polite language, Hitler was relieving the field marshal of his command.

Before departing, the adjutant also delivered an order removing the commander of *Panzer Group West*. With Dollmann dead, that left, of the high command that had opposed the invasion, only Rommel.

When Rommel learned of the reliefs, he mused out loud, "I will be next."[119] Yet in his own councils the erstwhile "Desert Fox" held out hope. He knew of dealings back in Berlin that still might salvage something from the impending débâcle in France. It was a grim business, conspiracy, which some might call treason. Yet after his experiences in Normandy and at Berchtesgaden and Soissons, Rommel deemed it the only way out.

To those on the Allied side, the German failure to counterattack remained an enigma, and one for which they were grateful, since the enemy's policy of standing and slugging was causing difficulty enough. By the first of July almost a million men had entered France, along with half a million tons

---

[118] Blumenson, *Breakout and Pursuit*, p. 28.

[119] Harrison, *Cross-Channel Attack*, p. 447.

of supplies and 177,000 vehicles. British and Canadians in the Second British Army had four corps, ten infantry and three armored divisions, while the Americans under Bradley had four corps with eleven infantry and two armored divisions. These forces held a beachhead some seventy miles wide. Yet nowhere other than in the extremes of the Cotentin near Cherbourg was the beachhead as much as twenty miles deep. At some spots, like Carentan, it was less than five miles, and the roar of breakers was all but audible to the troops in the line.

To many on the Allied side, the prospect of trench warfare appeared distressingly real. Even to others less pessimistic, including the Supreme Commander, the failure to push out posed real concern. Because the pre-invasion plan was based on at least early gains in the open country around Caen, that concern logically centered on the tactics of the overall ground commander, General Montgomery, whose British-Canadian troops were to have taken Caen, gateway to open country, on the first day. Three weeks later Caen remained out of reach, and Montgomery still had mounted no really concerted effort to get it. While continuing to promise a "blitz attack,"[120] Montgomery had launched only limited thrusts, which were successful enough in helping prevent a decisive German counterattack but achieved little toward expanding the beachhead and gaining the space for maneuver, for additional troops, for airfields and supply depots, which the Allied forces required.

Interpreting the role of Supreme Commander in those days as a voice more of arbitration than of decision, General Eisenhower moved only gingerly to prod his principal British subordinate. "We must use all possible energy in a determined effort," he wrote Montgomery, "to prevent a stalemate."[121] That was a euphemism for "Get cracking!" but Montgomery declined the bait. "I am, myself, quite happy about the situation," Montgomery replied.[122] He had a "very definite plan," and "Of one thing you can be quite sure, there will be no stalemate."

Something of what Montgomery had in mind became manifest the night of July 7 when almost five hundred heavy bombers of the Royal Air Force dropped twenty-three hundred tons of bombs to prepare the

[120] Blumenson, *Duel for France*, p. 14.

[121] Blumenson, *Breakout and Pursuit,* p. 119.

[122] Ibid., p. 120.

way for a ground attack before daylight by British and Canadian troops. Unfortunately a forecast of impending bad weather prompted the planes to go early, and the ground troops were unready for a quick followup. The several hours between bombardment and attack enabled the Germans to recover from the stunning effect of the bombing. Heavy cratering further slowed the advance. On the morning of July 9, nevertheless, British and Canadian troops entered Caen at last and cleared that part of the city that lies west of the Orne River. Yet that was as far as they went.

The Americans of Bradley's First U.S. Army meanwhile had been plodding through the Cotentin swamps and the ubiquitous hedgerows toward St. Lô in a markedly painful exercise. One corps lost more than ten thousand men in less than a fortnight. For a division to lose more than two thousand in a week was all too common. Newly committed divisions lost the most, since they suffered the inevitable consequences of inexperience. Wide-eyed replacements made daily treks to the front, some to come back on stretchers or in mattress-cover shrouds before the day was out.

For days on end a cold, clammy rain fell, chilling the soldiers and denying them the close air support that might have eased their task. Despite the rain, tanks could help but, in the hedgerow country, only as support weapons to assist the infantry to plod slowly forward rather than as instruments of driving, slashing maneuver. When a corps commander tried to exploit an infantry division's bridgehead over a little Norman river by committing a combat command of armor, tanks and infantry soon became inextricably intermingled in the constricted terrain. The Germans, too, tried to employ armor *en masse*, committing an elite force that formerly had been an armored warfare demonstration unit, the *Panzer Lehr Division*—only to lose a third of the tanks quickly to anti-tank weapons and to see the rest bog down amid the hedgerows.

The job of pushing the Germans back remained one for the infantry, but tank platoons and companies could be parceled out to provide the riflemen small increments of mobile fire support. Separate tank battalions attached to each infantry division were used for the assignment.

Working together among the hedgerows and sunken roads was a difficult task that infantrymen and tank crewmen had to learn through trial and error, as each became accustomed to the peculiar ways of the other. Communication between the man on foot and the man in the tank was particularly trying. Their radio frequencies were different, and during the furor of battle it was almost impossible to gain the attention of crewmen tightly buttoned up in their noisy iron mounts. Most units solved the problem eventually by installing a telephone on the back deck of the tank platoon leader's vehicle.

Finding a way to climb across a hedgerow without exposing the thin underside of the tank demanded ingenuity of another sort. A sergeant—Curtis G. Cullin, Jr.—finally came up with the answer: to make huge iron teeth from German beach obstacles and then weld them to the front of the tank so that it could bull a way through the hedgerow.

In the close fighting larger German tanks sometimes awed American troops. Although the basic German tank still was the 23-ton medium Mark IV, a 45-ton Mark V Panther reached the front in increasing numbers, dwarfing the 30-ton Sherman. There was an occasional Tiger, too, which some American troops had encountered as long ago as North Africa. One excited infantryman described the first Tiger he saw this way: "Colonel, that was a great big sonofabitch. It looked like a whole road full of tank. It kept coming on and it seemed like it was going to destroy the whole world!"[123]

From one hedgerow to the next, then always on to another, the men fought. In the process the battle made tested warriors of men and units capable of standing beside the veterans of North Africa, Sicily, and Italy. The 2d Division, the 4th, the 8th, the 83d, the 90th. Leaders, too—men destined to become part of a first team, like Leonard T. Gerow of the V Corps, calm, almost implacable, painstaking, dependable; Troy Middleton of the VIII Corps, the Louisiana educator who had commanded a division in Sicily; J. Lawton Collins of the VII Corps, who as a division commander on Guadalcanal had gained a nickname, "Lightning Joe," young (forty-eight), ebullient, handsome, the very image of the all-American boy. Division commanders, too—men like Charles Gerhardt of the 29th, flamboyant, fussy, no detail too minor for his attention; and Leland Hobbs of the 30th, always either bragging or complaining.

The fresh-cut-hay lanolin-like smell of Normandy mingled with the acrid odor of decaying flesh. Bloated cows lay upended in the fields, victims of the artillery fires of one side or the other. Because masonry houses afford ready-made forts, the fight for villages always raged fiercely:

[123] Ibid., p. 205.

Montmartin-en-Graignes, La-Haye-du-Puits, Villiers-Fossard, St.-Sauveur-de-Pierrepont, La Chapelle-en-Juger—lovely names that American troops bastardized, as had been done a quarter-century earlier in saying "Wipers" for "Ypres."

"The whole battle," reported a German corps commander, "is one tremendous bloodbath, such as I have never seen in eleven years of war"[124]

Near midnight on July 15, Bradley's troops finally gained positions overlooking a road that Romans had built centuries before, leading northwestward out of St. Lô straight as a ruler to the town of Perriers. Bradley looked on the road as a line of departure for a sustained drive southward, designed to carry to the base of the Cotentin, whence he might turn the corner into Brittany. Yet before he could begin the drive, he had to have St. Lô itself and access to the roads that the provincial capital knits together.

The old part of St. Lô—what was left of it—stood on a rock bluff overlooking the little Vire River; its shops and houses were crowned by ancient ramparts, a tower, and the graceful spires of a fifteenth-century church. Beginning with D Day, St. Lô had felt the wrath of bombers as the Allies tried to turn it into a German roadblock. Almost eight hundred civilians had been buried beneath the rubble on D Day alone.

Even as others of Bradley's troops fought toward the St. Lô-Perrier road, two divisions on July 11 began to inch a painful way through the hedgerows and across the sunken lanes toward St. Lô. Nowhere did the Germans give way until forcibly rooted out. At one point American riflemen had to call on a bulldozer to bury alive three German paratroopers who refused to emerge from a dugout. At long last, late on July 18, the defense collapsed. A task force of the 29th Division entered the town, the men carrying with them as a symbol of their sacrifices a coffin containing the body of one of their number, Major Thomas D. Howie. St. Lô was smoking rubble, as lifeless as the still form the Americans bore, a macabre monument to all who had suffered and died in the battle of the hedgerows.

German departure from St. Lô reflected a growing independence on the part of the army group commander, Erwin Rommel. When on the seventeenth the new commander of the *Seventh Army*, Generaloberst Paul Hausser, had asked permission to pull out, Rommel had agreed without even bothering to broach the matter with the man who had succeeded

---

[124] Ibid., p. 182.

Rundstedt, the new Commander-in-Chief in the West, Field Marshal Guenther von Kluge, a former army group commander on the Russian front. "Take whatever measures you think are necessary," Rommel's Chief of Staff told Hausser. "Just report to us afterwards that the enemy penetrated your main line of resistance in several places and that you barely succeeded in re-establishing a new line to the rear."[125]

Not long after that exchange, Rommel was heading by car for the front when out of the sun flashed a covey of British fighter-bombers. In a strafing run the planes killed Rommel's driver. The car crashed, hurling Rommel onto the pavement. He lost consciousness, victim of a near-fatal skull fracture and concussion.

On the same day that St. Lô fell—July 18—the British-Canadian front around Caen again erupted—Montgomery's contribution to General Bradley's plan to launch a major thrust southward from the St. Lô-Perrier road. A big attack to seize the rest of Caen and in the process a sizable bridgehead across the Orne River, Montgomery reasoned, would hold the bulk of the German armor on that part of the front and thereby assist Bradley's drive.

Yet Montgomery's directive and his report on the plan to General Eisenhower were ambiguous. If Montgomery was planning only a supporting attack, why speak, as he did, of a "massive stroke," of a "whole eastern flank" that would "burst into flame"? Asking air support, he called for the "whole weight of air power" to bring about a "decisive victory."[126]

Both Eisenhower and his deputy, Air Chief Marshal Tedder, were enthusiastic. Tedder saw it as a "far-reaching and decisive plan" promising an end to the dearth of Allied airfields on the Continent. Eisenhower was "pepped up concerning the promise of this plan." He saw it as one prong of a two-pronged breakout ending the confinement in Normandy. "I would not be at all surprised," he wrote Montgomery, "to see you gaining a victory that will make some of the old classics' look like a skirmish between patrols."

The power Montgomery assembled to support his attack—labeled "Operation GOODWOOD"—reinforced that impression. In addition to

---

[125] Ibid., p. 169.

[126] All quotations related to Montgomery's attack of July 18, Ibid., pp. 190 and 194-95.

battleships off shore, more than three times the weight of heavy bombers used in the first attack on Caen participated in a preliminary bombardment—1,700 heavy bombers plus almost 400 mediums and fighter-bombers dropping more than 8,000 tons of bombs. To minimize the problem of craters, only fragmentation bombs were dropped in front of the main point of attack. That paid off, for 700 tanks followed the devastating blow closely and in little more than an hour advanced three miles.

Then trouble developed. In recognition of the lure of the open country beyond Caen, the Germans had dug a defense in depth, setting up a thick screen of tanks and anti-tank guns along ridgelines and in villages well behind the main line. As these came into play during the afternoon, the British armor paid dearly. On the first day alone the British lost 270 tanks. The next day and into July 20, British and Canadians continued to attack, but the going was tortuous—131 tanks the second day, 68 the third. When a thunderstorm drenched the countryside during the afternoon of the twentieth and spoiled the footing, Montgomery called in his surviving tanks.

Shocked disappointment reverberated through the Allied command. General Eisenhower, an aide recorded, "was mad."[127] Reflecting the dismay of airmen who yearned for the airfield country they had expected at last to realize, Tedder volunteered that the British Chiefs of Staff would support any recommendation Eisenhower cared to make with respect to Montgomery, presumably including relief. At Eisenhower's headquarters many officers, both British and American, urged Eisenhower to eliminate Montgomery's position as overall ground commander and take direct control himself.

The Supreme Commander flew to Normandy on July 20 and listened with obvious disappointment to Montgomery's explanation. Montgomery was convinced that Operation GOODWOOD had dealt a crippling blow to German armor and thereby made sure that the armor would not be employed when Bradley with the First U.S. Army dealt the annihilating attack that would break the confinement in Normandy. This result, Montgomery said, rather than any broad, general offensive which might dissipate Allied power, was what he had had in mind.

Whether Montgomery had in reality intended a "massive stroke" that

---

[127] Butcher, *My Three Years with Eisenhower*, p. 616. For an account by one taking Montgomery's side, see Wilmot, *The Struggle for Europe*, pp. 361-62.

would set aflame the eastern part of the line—another El Alamein—would forever remain uncertain. More likely than not, Operation GOODWOOD had developed much as Montgomery had planned, though he hardly would have expected such heavy tank losses, and he had failed to obtain all designated tactical objectives. His sin was in misleading his superiors with what turned out to be hyperbole and with failing to correct the erroneous impression as it developed. His failure to make the correction would indicate that in his own mind lived a hope that the operation well might produce a true explosion. If that happened, he wanted to be in a position to gain credit for having planned it from the start.

The situation on the German side gave reason to Montgomery's strategy. A combination of the attrition of almost six weeks of unrelenting battle, of the continuing ravages of Allied planes, and of two heavy blows at Caen had left the German army in Normandy hurt and bleeding, peculiarly susceptible to the heavy punch that General Bradley was preparing.

Only by skillful tactics had the Germans managed to survive in Normandy, to counter Allied superiority in materiel and equipment. In the face of Hitler's continuing expectation of a second Allied landing and of Allied aerial superiority, the Germans could do no better than match the Allied buildup in men. They could match it in tanks as well, but not in gasoline and ammunition. The inequality in the air was even more extreme. Allied planes, German soldiers remarked wryly, were painted silver; German planes were colorless and thus invisible.

To Field Marshal von Kluge—who upon Rommel's injury began to double as Commander-in-Chief and commander of *Army Group B*—the situation in Normandy was on the verge of becoming an *ungeheures Kladderadatsch*—an awful mess; and he wondered whether the high command appreciated how much the fight was costing. By the end of the first week in July the Germans had lost 250 tanks, 200 assault and anti-tank guns, and 200,000 men.

Whether as a result of Montgomery's strategy or of the simple logic of concentrating in defense of the open country leading to Paris—probably as a combination of the two—the Germans had assembled the bulk of their armor near Caen. Operation GOODWOOD prompted Kluge to increase that concentration, including an armored division that was to have been pulled into reserve near St. Lô and another that was en route to

St. Lô from the Pas de Calais. That made a total of seven panzer divisions and four heavy tank battalions near Caen, while only two panzer divisions and no separate heavy tank battalions opposed Bradley's First Army.

Allied commanders, for their part, had no way of knowing that the German front in Normandy was so brittle. Nor were they fully aware that it was so poorly aligned for countering the kind of blow Omar Bradley was getting ready to deliver.

Behind the German front other trouble was stirring. Since the early days of the war a clandestine but potentially powerful resistance to Hitler had festered, mainly among general officers of the army. The resistance revolved around Field Marshal Ludwig von Beck, who in protest had resigned as Chief of Staff at the time of the Munich crisis. As early as the fall of 1939 leaders of the conspiracy had attempted to act, and in the spring of 1943 they had placed a time bomb in the *Fuehrer*'s plane; but the bomb had failed to go off. They had hoped to try again in December of the same year when a young colonel, Count Klaus von Stauffenberg, was to plant a bomb in a briefcase at one of Hitler's conferences; but the conference was at the last minute canceled.

Through the spring of 1944 the conspirators had postponed action while awaiting the Allied invasion. If the Germans defeated the invasion, they reasoned, the Western Allies might be prepared to grant reasonable terms to a Germany that had rid itself of the blight of Nazism. Even should the invasion succeed and the war become irretrievably lost, they rationalized, they still might gain; for that would bring the conspiracy greater support from others in the army and from the people at large.

Since the second of these conditions had been met by early July, a plan was ready. Under the pretext of preparing to counter a civil emergency such as an uprising by foreign laborers, secret sealed orders already were in the hands of commanders of military districts throughout Germany. On receipt of a code word the commanders were to move swiftly to seize key installations in major cities. At that point news was to be flashed that Hitler was dead and the army empowered to form a new government.

Hitler's supporters themselves had played into the hands of the conspirators when in June they had assigned Count von Stauffenberg to a job that afforded him official *entrée* to the *Fuehrer*'s conferences. Although it would have been a simple matter at that point for Stauffenberg to assassinate

Hitler, so valuable had the young colonel become to the movement that the leaders deemed him essential for taking charge of the coup in Berlin. That meant devising a scheme that would enable Stauffenberg first to kill the *Fuehrer*, then to escape to play a second role. The plan they devised was for Stauffenberg to plant a time bomb in a briefcase, then on some excuse to leave the conference and escape before the bomb exploded.

The success of the Allied invasion afforded an opportunity to bring key field commanders fully into the conspiracy. As early as February a representative had approached Field Marshal Rommel in the hope that he might agree to become head of state—"a modern Hindenburg"; and again in May further discussions had evolved either with Rommel or his Chief of Staff. While sympathetic, Rommel had objected to killing Hitler, for that "would only make him a martyr."[128] Rommel thought at first that he should be arrested and brought to trial, but the invasion changed his thinking. Following the discouraging meeting with Hitler at Soissons on June 17, Rommel sent word to Field Marshal von Beck that the front in Normandy was about to collapse. It was time the conspirators moved, he said, whatever they intended to do with Hitler.

Despite both a long reputation as a resolute disciple of the *Fuehrer* and serious reservations because of the personal oath of loyalty Hitler had required from all of the officer corps, Field Marshal von Kluge also entered the conspiracy. Having hovered on the fringe for more than a year, he agreed to join only after he had seen at first hand the gravity of the situation in France. Yet unlike Rommel, Kluge stipulated that he would cooperate only if Hitler was dead.

If the conspirators were to act before the Allies achieved such a victory as to preclude any political advantage for Germany, they had to move soon. The first chance came on July 11 when Stauffenberg took the bomb to a conference at Berchtesgaden; but because Heinrich Himmler, head of the Nazi party's military arm, the *Waffen-SS*, and Hermann Goering, head of the *Luftwaffe*, were absent, he refrained from setting it off. Much the same happened at another conference on the fifteenth.

Before another opportunity arose, word came that the secret police were about to arrest one of the ringleaders in the plot. The news left Stauffenberg no choice but to act when on the twentieth he attended

---

[128] Wilmot, *The Struggle for Europe*, p. 369.

another conference, although again neither Himmler nor Goering was present, and the conference was held not in the usual concrete bunker—that was under repair—but in a frame wooden hut.

Arming the bomb before entering, Stauffenberg dutifully placed it beside a leg of the conference table, whispered to one of the conferees that he had to make a telephone call, and left. He was less than one hundred yards from the hut when the bomb went off. So powerful was the explosion that he had no doubt but that he had done his job well.

Despite Stauffenberg's report that the *Fuehrer* surely was dead, many in the conspiracy refrained from acting until they had proof. That was not to come.

The next day Hitler himself broadcast word of the attempt on his life. Four of the conferees had been killed, but because the frail wooden hut had failed to contain the force of the explosion, the *Fuehrer* had sustained only superficial wounds.

In the bloodbath that followed, as many as five thousand people may have been cut down, and another ten thousand sent to concentration camps. For the most hated of his enemies, Hitler reserved death by hanging from meat hooks, with the victims' agonies recorded on motion picture film.

Rommel, who was recuperating at home from the injury incurred in Normandy, was incriminated and given a choice of suicide or public disgrace and execution. When he had dutifully taken the cyanide capsule offered him, Hitler announced his death from wounds and afforded him a state funeral with all the trappings, including a eulogy from a presumably unsuspecting old soldier, Field Marshal von Rundstedt. Kluge, too, came under suspicion, but the denouement in his case was to come later.

The end result of the attempted *Putsch* was to strengthen the hold of the Nazi regime throughout Germany and its armed forces, to sharpen Hitler's distrust of his generals, and to tighten his control over the conduct of the battle on every front.

Chapter Eighteen – Breakout and Pursuit

The battle of the hedgerows, Omar Bradley in characteristic homespun voice told his assembled corps commanders, was "tough and costly, a slugger's match, too slow a process."[129] Since American troops had gained the St. Lô-Perrier highway and taken St. Lô, he revealed, he intended to break the battle open by laying a carpet of bombs along the highway in front of Joe Collins' VII Corps. As soon as infantry divisions traversed the carpet to achieve a penetration, he would send armor crashing through, first to stage an envelopment by driving to the west coast of the Cotentin near Coutances, fifteen miles southwest of St. Lô, then to forge on to Avranchcs for the turn into Brittany.[130]

Operation COBRA, Bradley called it—goodbye to the hedgerows.

Although Bradley set a target date of July 21, not until the twenty-fourth did the skies promise to clear enough for the strategic bombers to play their massive role. Even then the weather proved so doubtful that Air Chief Marshal Leigh-Mallory flew from England ahead of the bombers for a last-minute check of conditions. The sky was overcast, he found; low-lying clouds were too thick to risk bombardment by highflying aircraft that would be bombing in front of American troops with a safety margin of less than a mile.

Leigh-Mallory's message to call off the attack reached England only minutes before the first of the bombers was scheduled to strike. Although the word went out to turn back, it was too late for the first three waves of

---

[129] Blumenson, *Breakout and Pursuit*, p. 213.

[130] For this chapter, I have used extensively Blumenson's excellent accounts in *Breakout and Pursuit* and *The Duel for France*. See also Craven and Cate, eds., *ARGUMENT to V-E Day*; Wilmot, *The Struggle for Europe*; Davis, *Experience of War*; and (for the attempt on Hitler's life) William L. Shirer, *The Rise and Fall of the Third Reich* (New York, 1960).

planes. The first wave nevertheless failed to bomb because the bombardiers found visibility too poor. Most of the second wave also failed to release, but a third wave of more than three hundred planes found conditions improved. Most were on target; but one lead bombardier had trouble with his bomb release mechanism and inadvertently dropped his load short. Fifteen planes flying in his formation followed the lead.

On the ground, American troops who had already learned that the attack was postponed found it hard to comprehend why the planes went ahead with their runs. They were still pondering when the unmistakable sound of bombs descending—less a scream or screech than a terrifying rattle—made them realize with horror that something was shockingly amiss.

Where men of the 30th Division waited, the world turned suddenly upside down. When it was over, 131 men were wounded, 27 dead.

Bradley was furious. In the planning conference with the airmen, he had insisted that the bombers make their runs laterally along the front, not over the heads of the ground troops, so that any bombs falling short would hit other segments of the German line, not American positions. Yet the air commanders had found that unacceptable. To make a lateral run over a rectangular target three times wider than it was deep would mean that only narrow formations might strike together, thus precluding a quick, fierce bombardment. A lateral run also would expose one small formation of bombers after another to an alerted enemy's anti-aircraft fire over lengthy approaches and exits.

For all Bradley's ire, there was no time for recrimination. Since the premature strike would have alerted the Germans, reinforcements would soon be on their way to that part of the front. If COBRA was to retain any hope of the far-reaching success Bradley envisioned—if it was, in fact, to bid goodbye to the hedgerows—he would have to strike within at least twenty-four hours. That meant no time to alter the airmen's plan for a perpendicular rather than a lateral approach.

With prospects for good weather the next day, Bradley took the chance: despite the tragic mixup, COBRA was to start at 9:35 A.M. on July 25.

Again the planes came, waves of them in a "gigantic faraway surge of doomlike sound"[131]—2,500 in all, including more than 1,500 B-17's and B-24's. They bore in their bellies more than 4,000 tons of bombs, only

---

[131] Pyle, *Brave Men*, p. 434.

half as much as Montgomery had used in Operation GOODWOOD but enough nevertheless to assure ten big bombs per acre of target, a power never before concentrated in direct support of American troops.

Using the arrowlike St. Lô-Perrier highway as aiming point, the bombardiers in the leading waves dropped their loads with unerring accuracy. Observers on the ground watched in awe, cheered, clapped one another on the back. In the vernacular of the time, this was *it*. Nobody could withstand such a pounding. Yesterday's snafu clearly ensured today's success.

In mounting crescendo the big bombs exploded. The earth shook.

Yet at twelve thousand feet above the battlefield, succeeding waves of bombers were finding visibility increasingly difficult. Rising from the ground in answer to the fury of the early waves, great clouds of smoke and dust drifted high into the air, obscuring the black-topped ribbon that served as aiming point. To bombardiers who could not see the highway, the line of smoke and dust afforded at least a key to the target. They released their lethal loads on that line, unaware that a gentle but persistent wind had been shifting the smoke and dust gradually but inexorably northward, full onto the American soldiers who waited their turn at the battle.

Again the terrifying death rattle of bombs descending. Men who one minute had been cheering dived in terror the next for whatever cover they could find—foxhole, hedgerow, sunken lane, farmhouse basement. "I remember hitting the ground flat," wrote Ernie Pyle, "all spread out like the cartoons of people flattened by steam rollers, and then squirming like an eel to get under one of the heavy wagons in the shed."[132] Around about fell the loads of thirty-five heavy bombers and forty-two mediums.

In the second strike 490 men were wounded, and 111 killed; among the dead was the Chief of the Army Ground Forces, General McNair, who had come from England, where he was acting as commander of a fictitious army group to preserve the myth of impending invasion of the Pas de Calais. Hundreds of other men were so numbed that they wandered about like unthinking automatons. One company commander recalled:

The shock was awful. A lot of the men were sitting around in a complete daze. I called battalion and told them I was in no condition to move, that everything was completely disorganized and it would take me some time

---

[132] Pyle, *Brave Men*, p. 437.

to get my men back together...But battalion said no, push off, jump off immediately.[133]

The Germans meanwhile had absorbed infinitely greater punishment. Far from prompting them to revise and reinforce their defense, the first day's premature bombing actually had left them complacent. The powerful *Panzer Lehr Division*, they deduced, had frustrated the American attack. No need to strengthen the line; merely leave the tanks and grenadiers in place.

They were in place when the bombs started falling at 9:38 A.M. on the twenty-fifth. For two hours and forty-five minutes, observed the panzer division commander, Generalmajor Fritz Bayerlein:

The planes kept coming, as if on a conveyor belt...My flak had hardly opened its mouth when the batteries received direct hits which knocked out half the guns and silenced the rest. After an hour I had no communication with anybody, even by radio. By noon nothing was visible but dust and smoke. My front lines looked like the face of the moon and at least 70 percent of my troops were out of action—dead, wounded, crazed, or numbed.[134]

Yet to American infantrymen who followed in the wake of the bombardment, the effect on their adversary seemed hardly so devastating as that. Here and there some German positions had miraculously survived; and soldiers long conditioned to the slow pace and rampant death of the battle of the hedgerows had little inclination to rush the defenders. Disconsolate were many of the men after a second rain of death from their own planes, and so full of craters was the land that progress over it even on foot was difficult.

As twilight descended on the scarred landscape, Joe Collins' infantrymen still were short of their day's objectives, which left Collins in a quandary about what to do the next day. Were his troops, as one intelligence officer noted, at the point of a breakthrough with "nothing in back to stop us"? Or was it that the Germans, forewarned by the premature bombardment of July 24, had withdrawn their forward line after the manner of the French in front of Ludendorff in the summer of 1918? If the former, it behooved him to commit his armor immediately lest he afford the foe time to fashion a new line. If the latter, his armor would run immediately into armored counterattack. Either way it was a gamble.

---

[133] Blumenson, *Breakout and Pursuit*, p. 237, quoting the commander of Company B, 8th Infantry.

[134] Wilmot, *The Struggle for Europe*, p. 391, quoting Bayerlein.

Collins decided in favor of his tanks—a decision as wise as it was bold. Although infantry units the next day, July 26, found the going slow off the flanks of the rectangular bomb target, they already had served, in the remarkably mixed metaphor of Leland Hobbs of the 30th Division, as "the spearhead that broke the earners back." Parts of two armored divisions that Collins inserted in the center began to roll against little more than scattered artillery and anti-tank fire and an occasional defended hedgerow.

Field Marshal von Kluge reacted to the attack with dispatch, asking and receiving from his *Fuehrer* a free hand and gaining approval to transfer a panzer division from southern France and four infantry divisions from either southern France or the Pas de Calais—this despite Hitler's belief that an invasion of southern France was imminent. Yet Kluge still had eyes primarily for the sector around Caen, a concern heightened by a limited objective attack launched by the Canadians. When the commander of the *Seventh Army*, General Hausser, asked authority to withdraw to form a new line, which would include withdrawal from the vicinity of St. Lô, Kluge refused. That, he declared, would expose the flank of his forces in front of Caen.

The extent of the American victory began to appear on July 27 and 28. Although the German corps commander on the *Seventh Army's* threatened west wing pulled back all troops from along the coast to try to stop the American armor, he was too late. In full force Collins' two armored divisions drove south and southwest, at that point well behind the enemy's front line, rambling roughshod over rear installations, shooting up the landscape. American reconnaissance troops raced through a village unaware that in one of the houses Fritz Bayerlein was conferring with the surviving staff and the commanders of his neardefunct *Panzer Lehr Division*. A gunner in an American armored car took a shot at Hausser, the *Seventh Army's* commander. A patrol operating near the command post of the *2d SS Panzer Division* killed the division commander.

Apparently according to no pattern but remarkably ordered nevertheless, the armor advanced, each combat command with two or three columns moving down generally parallel roads. Overhead, in a sundrenched sky which dulled the memory of long days of rain earlier in July, flew fighter-bombers of the IX Tactical Air Command, constituting a fast-moving, far-ranging aerial artillery which pounced on anything German that moved. Roads soon were lined with wrecked and abandoned guns, tanks, wagons, command cars, and assorted flotsam and jetsam. While the leading tanks wore brightly colored fluorescent panels atop their decks, in each command tank rode an air support control officer in constant touch with the pilots by radio. In the months between Tunisia and Normandy close air support had come to mean something the world had never known before.

Coutances fell on July 28 to an armored division of Troy Middleton's VIII Corps, which was to have launched only a holding attack along the coast, but which plunged southward in reaction to the German withdrawal. Yet by that time armor of Collins' VII Corps was already far beyond Coutances at various points between the sea and the Vire River, twenty-two miles inland. Less than three days after the advance had begun, the start line along the St. Lô-Perrier road lay twenty-one miles behind. At and east of St. Lô, General Bradley's two remaining corps also had begun to advance, slowly but with a surencss designed to safeguard Collins' eastern flank by pinning German units in place and softening the angle between the deep penetration and the rest of the front.

On the German side Field Marshal von Kluge at last had begun to face up to the reality of the breach of his left wing. Since the Canadian attack had ground to a halt after only a day, and since nothing indicated that Montgomery intended anything more, Kluge pulled out two panzer divisions. During the night of the twenty-seventh he sent them on a forced march to strike the eastern flank of the American penetration.

Harried by air attacks, the panzer divisions arrived too late. Instead of hitting Joe Collins' rampaging armor, they ran into infantry of the XIX Corps driving southward from St. Lô. For four days the battle raged along the Vire River some ten miles south of St. Lô. Neither side could show much advantage in terms of ground gained, but the Americans could proclaim that by their fight they had left their comrades in the VII and VIII Corps free to exploit their penetration with sweeping stabs that removed almost all hope of the Germans' restoring their crumpled left wing between the Vire and the sea.

For there, as Collins' armor continued to plow southward, a new presence had become apparent. Presaging a reorganization of American forces soon to come, Bradley called in the man who earlier had maintained the myth of a second invasion, the man whose methods in matters other than the tactical had been partly responsible for Bradley's moving ahead of him up the ladder of command. To him Bradley gave general control of Middleton's VIII Corps in a command arrangement that was for the moment unofficial, yet that gave the attack a character that was "as visible as his shadow on the wall of the operations tent."[135]

The shadow was George Patton's.

Patton arrived on the scene as Middleton raised his sights from Coutances to Avranches at the base of the Cotentin peninsula, the gateway into Brittany. On July 29, with Patton in the background but unmistakably present, Middleton sent two armored divisions toward Avranches. When they failed to make striking gains, Patton railed and fumed. The next day both divisions broke loose, driving relentlessly forward under a lethal curtain maintained by P-47 Thunderbolts.

Just over three miles outside Avranches one column passed within a few hundred yards of the *Seventh Army's* command post, then unwittingly allowed General Hausser and his entourage to escape through meticulously regular intervals between vehicles in the column. On the fringe of Avranches leading tanks found highway bridges over a river intact. By nightfall of July 31, a week after B-17's and B-24's had appeared above the St. Lô-Perrier road, the door to Brittany stood ajar.

As Patton, on the first of August, swung the VIII Corps into Brittany along a single road in a remarkable feat of logistics, he did so not as unofficial overseer of the corps but as commander of a new force, the Third U.S. Army, created by taking a rib (the VIII Corps) from the First Army and adding another corps, newly operational. General Bradley in turn moved up to command another new American headquarters, the 12th Army Group, composed of the First and Third Armies. The new head of the First Army was Bradley's former deputy, Courtney H. Hodges, a calm, almost taciturn infantryman of fifty-seven, mustached, athletically trim, who looked more a businessman than a soldier.

Raising Bradley to command of an army group put him on a level with Montgomery, although for another month Montgomery would continue to serve as Eisenhower's overall ground commander. To flesh out Montgomery's 21st Army Group, the First Canadian Army under General Crerar already stood alongside Dempsey's Second British Army.

For the sweep into Brittany, Patton sent one armored division almost due south to reach the sea and cut off the peninsula, while another drove westward up the spine. Since the Germans had stripped Brittany of most

---

[135] Blumenson, *Duel for France*, pp. 136-37.

of their better units to fight in Normandy, it was much like the sweep to Palermo, this time helped by French forces—some thirty-one thousand Frenchmen armed with a potpourri of weapons and wearing armbands labeled "FFI."

The French irregulars, the American armor soon discovered, already controlled much of the high ground inland and were eager to assume the tasks of guiding American columns, mopping up bypassed Germans, and shepherding prisoners. It was as a direct result of the assistance that the FFI rendered in Brittany that Americans and British stepped up their delivery of arms and equipment to the maquis and to other Resistance forces elsewhere in France.

Patton's goal in Brittany was the ports—St. Malo, Brest, and on the south coast, Lorient, St. Nazaire, and the shores of Quiberon Bay, where the Allies intended to build a vast logistical complex deemed essential for the long fight to wrest the bulk of France from the conqueror once a solid lodgment had been established beyond the original beachhead. As events developed, Brittany as a logistical base proved too far behind the front, and the plan eventually was abandoned. It was just as well, for the Germans remaining in the peninsula gathered in the ports before American tanks arrived. St. Malo held out for two weeks, and it took a special attack mounted by three divisions in September to subdue Brest, which flattened the city in the process. Since Lorient and St. Nazaire had lost their real value as ports, the Allied command was content merely to contain the Germans in them until the war came to an end.

Events that would erase the importance of Brittany meanwhile had been fast developing in the region southeast of the original break-through line. There in countryside as verdant as any other in Normandy and marked by hills that French tourist brochures extravagantly call *la Suisse Normande*, the First U.S. Army under its new commander, Courtney Hodges, faced the bulk of Hausser's *Seventh Army*. The critical confrontation took place along an eighteen-mile arc extending from Vire, twenty-one miles from St. Lô, to Mortain, full in the hill country almost due east of Avranches.

The arena had begun to be prepared for a decisive action near Mortain as early as the second day of August, when it became apparent that Brittany might be left to only one American corps. With that in mind, Bradley told

Patton to send his newly operational XV Corps—under Major General Wade Hampton Haislip, a stocky, sandy-haired, ruddy man whose name revealed his Southern origin—not into Brittany but southeast and east. In three days Haislip's corps drove seventy-five miles, almost to the city of Le Mans, in open country, whence a swing to the northeast would lead directly to Paris.

Haislip's drive conformed to a plan that Montgomery as ground commander had been devising. Convinced that the American breakthrough had thoroughly unhinged the German left wing, he believed the only course open to the Germans was to withdraw behind the Seine River, downstream from Paris. They would be unable, he deduced, to maintain Caen as a pivot for their withdrawal and at the same time restore their crumbled left flank. Should they choose to hold before Caen, that would enable Bradley to swing full around their left and cut off their escape by a drive northeast toward Paris, thence down the left bank of the Seine. Should they choose instead to move troops from Caen to buttress their left, that would open to British and Canadians a quick, short route to the Seine.

On the theory that the Germans would concentrate on holding their pivot, Montgomery decided to unhinge it by a Canadian drive on Falaise, some twenty miles south of Caen, while the British coming up on the Canadian right cut even deeper into the pivot by driving on Argentan, another ten miles to the southeast. That accomplished, Canadians and British together would swing east to the Seine. In the meantime Bradley's 12th Army Group was to be making the main effort by thrusting rapidly east, then swinging northeast in a wide arc around the German left flank.

Bradley, for his part, was less convinced that the only choice open to the Germans was withdrawal. He sanctioned Haislip's thrust toward Le Mans and told Courtney Plodges to swing some of his troops southeast around Mortain to maintain contact with Haislip's flank; yet at the same time he looked warily at the corridor his forces had forged between Avranches and Mortain. Only twenty miles wide, that corridor, he believed, was too shallow for the Germans to ignore. By assembling a force heavy in armor near Mortain, they might strike through to the sea and cut off Patton's Third Army.

By all logic Montgomery rather than Bradley was right: the long weeks of attrition and Bradley's brilliant stroke with Operation COBRA had beaten the Germans in Normandy. Yet logic was not always a decisive factor in the tyrannical control that Adolf Hitler exercised over his field commanders.

When Hitler sent a representative to the field headquarters in France, Field Marshal von Kluge advised that the only rational policy was to withdraw behind the Seine. With a force of mobile divisions on his left flank, he might hold the Americans in check long enough to make a getaway, but that was all.

Hitler would have no part of it. On August 4 he issued a categorical order: Kluge was to attack with eight of the nine panzer divisions in Normandy. For the first time, restrictions on the divisions marking time in the Pas de Calais in anticipation of a second invasion were to be lifted to enable Kluge to free the armor. (Patton's appearance on the front probably had much to do with the decision.) With the panzer divisions Kluge was to drive between Vire and Mortain to the sea, whereupon all German troops in Normandy were to swing over to a grand offensive to plunge the Allies into the Channel.

To both Kluge and Hausser, Hitler's dictum was a stone sealing the sepulcher of the *Seventh Army*. Yet Kluge dared not protest, lest his *Fuehrer* seize upon his reluctance as evidence of complicity in the plot against his life.

Such a grandiose scheme as Hitler envisioned was patently impossible. Taking the time to bring together eight panzer divisions was to invite the Americans to encircle all German forces in Normandy, including those before Caen. At best there might be time to assemble four divisions—three to make a penetration, a fourth to drive through the hole to Avranches—thereby at least to re-establish a solid defensive line in Normandy.

Without notifying Hitler, Kluge planned the attack that way. In hope of surprise he ordered the strike to begin without artillery preparation after nightfall on August 6.

It was midnight before any portion of the attack got rolling, and then only in half the strength Kluge had specified. One division failed to move at all because the commander, Generalleutnant Gerhard Graf (Count) von Schwerin, declined to pass on the attack order to his subordinates. Schwerin was both dissatisfied with local arrangements for his part in the attack and disheartened that the conspiracy of July 20, in which he had been involved, had failed. The war, he believed, already was lost. Why expend more lives?

One panzer division nevertheless brushed aside American roadblocks on the fringes of Mortain to penetrate swiftly into the little town. Having moved into positions around Mortain only hours before the Germans struck, American troops were ill-prepared for the sudden onslaught. In the darkness three German columns plunged through the line to depths of from three to seven miles.

According to German meteorologists, a dense ground fog on the morning of August 7 was to afford the panzers several more hours of immunity from Allied fighter-bombers; but it did not develop that way. The day dawned bright and clear with visibility so perfect that men of a battalion of the 30th Division, surrounded on a height outside Mortain known as "Hill 317," could observe all about them, even to the sea twenty miles away. With unerring accuracy they called down concentration after concentration of artillery fire on the exposed German formations, while Allied fighter-bombers roared to the attack. Particularly deadly against German tanks were rocket-firing British Hurricanes and Typhoons. Some three hundred German planes that Hitler had promised would support the counterattack hardly got off their airfields before swarms of Allied planes engaged them in deadly dog fights. "Almost unbearable" was the way one German commander described the punishment.[136]

On the scene Joe Collins shifted combat commands of armor to strike the German columns, while fresh infantry units closed in to contain the flanks of the penetration. All through the day of the seventh the battle raged, but the Germans gained no more ground. So confident was General Bradley that his troops would hold that he made no move to call back any of the divisions that had passed beyond the Avranches corridor to the south and southeast.

The results of the first day's fighting convinced Kluge that the battle was lost. Hausser, too. And indications around Caen that the Canadians might be readying an attack did nothing to dispel the gloom. Yet a new order from Hitler droned like a broken record: "I command the attack be prosecuted daringly and recklessly to the sea…regardless of the risk… greatest daring, determination, and imagination."[137] On and on and on.

Behind another heavy aerial bombardment by one thousand planes,

---

[136] Wilmot, *The Struggle for Europe*, p. 402.

[137] Blumenson, *Breakout and Pursuit*, p. 464.

the First Canadian Army struck before daylight on August 8. By the time the sun rose, the Canadians had penetrated three miles. Despite increasing resistance they pushed on through that day and the next to gain five miles more, half the distance to Falaise. At the same time the British began a slow but inexorable advance to keep in touch with the Canadian right flank.

Although a Canadian breakthrough surely would trap German forces around Mortain, Kluge saw no alternative in view of Hitler's demands but to renew the attack at Mortain. He planned to begin the night of the ninth, but the Americans declined to break off the battle long enough to permit him to regroup.

The tenacity of the encircled battalion of the 30th Division on Hill 317 exemplified the nature of the American resistance. For five days the men of that battalion repulsed every German effort to carry their dominating position. Although an attempt to resupply them with drops from artillery liaison planes failed in the face of German anti-aircraft fire, C-47 transports managed to parachute a few items into the defensive perimeter, and French farmers shared chickens, eggs, and vegetables with the troops. To fill the most pressing need, artillerymen outside the perimeter loaded shell cases, normally used for propaganda leaflets, with medical supplies and fired them onto the hill.

At the end of five days three hundred men had been killed or wounded, but three hundred others walked off unharmed.

As late as August 11, with the Canadian drive slowed to a crawl, Kluge was still trying to devise some method of renewing the attack at Mortain. That was early in the day. Before night came, events on the American side abruptly changed his mind.

Omar Bradley saw the opportunity on the eighth. By counterattacking, Bradley believed, the Germans had invited their destruction. In the presence of General Eisenhower, who happened to be visiting the 12th Army Group's headquarters, Bradley telephoned Montgomery to propose a scheme. Instead of attacking from Le Mans eastward toward the Seine, Bradley suggested, why not a shorter envelopment by means of a 90-degree turn at Le Mans? While part of Hodges' First Army held fast around Vire and Mortain, the rest of the First Army and part of Patton's Third might drive around the German flank toward Argentan and Falaise to link with British and Canadians at the interarmy group boundary south of those towns. That would trap the entire *Seventh Army*, including the panzer forces Kluge had committed in what Americans knew as the "Mortain counterattack."

Montgomery agreed with alacrity. "Obviously," as he put it later in his formal directive, "if we can close the gap completely, we shall have put the enemy in the most awkward predicament."[138]

Having taken Le Mans on August 8, Wade Hampton Haislip's XV Corps began to attack northward on the tenth with two armored divisions—one American, one French—in the lead. Because Kluge already had pulled the only German armor from this sector to try to mount his new effort at Mortain, Haislip's divisions quickly plunged through makeshift defenses into the German rear.

As German service troops fled in disorder, the Allied armor raced through a countryside littered with vehicles destroyed by Allied planes. Before daylight on the twelfth, the French armor without a fight took Alençon, midway between Le Mans and Falaise, and the next day drew up on high ground south of Argentan. Although Argentan was beyond the interarmy group boundary, Haislip had no orders to halt at that line. When a French patrol in the afternoon entered the town and reached the main square without a fight, hope rose for quick conquest of Argentan and a drive on to Falaise.

The hope flickered only briefly. Even as civilians in Argentan cheered the French patrol, German tanks raced onto the scene. In response to the threat of envelopment Kluge had pulled out increments of three armored divisions from the fighting at Mortain. The total strength in tanks was no more than seventy, a force incapable of containing Haislip's armor-heavy corps for long; but this was something Haislip never had a chance to prove.

At the same time that Field Marshal von Kluge was at last gaining the courage to inform the German high command that all hope for renewed attack at Mortain had passed, orders from General Bradley reached Haislip, dictating a halt. To continue northward toward Falaise, Bradley believed, was to risk a head-on collision with the Canadians, who still were short of Falaise but were continuing to attack.

Although Patton fumed, Bradley refused to relent. Haislip's XV Corps was overextended, both flanks open. As Bradley put it later, he preferred "a

---

[138] Ibid., p. 495.

solid shoulder at Argentan to a broken neck at Falaise."[139] Altering the army group boundary to allow further American advance was Montgomery's province, not Bradley's; and neither Bradley nor Eisenhower made any overture to Montgomery to change it.

Bradley's decision left a twenty-five-mile gap between Americans and Canadians, which afforded the Germans no comfortable margin but an escape route nevertheless. Yet time remained for the Allies to seal the gap, either if the Canadians broke free or if Bradley arranged to revoke his order to Haislip; for the German commanders in Normandy still had no authority to withdraw, however perilous the pocket that had developed.

From a headquarters far from the scene in East Prussia, Hitler continued to insist on a new German attack, not again at Mortain but against the extended positions of the American XV Corps. Although Kluge tried to comply, he found on August 14, as he went from one command post to another, little to encourage him. Roads were clogged with dispirited troops, and everywhere were critical shortages—of tanks, gasoline, rations, ammunition. Worse still, the Canadians achieved a five- to six-mile gain toward Falaise, narrowing the escape gap to less than twenty miles.

Early the next day, August 15, as Kluge drove again from *Army Group B's* headquarters at La Roche-Guyon into the pocket, this time to confer with General Hausser, an Allied plane strafed his command car and knocked out his radio. Through much of the rest of the day Allied aircraft kept Kluge and his command party pinned to the ditches.

When Kluge at last made his way back after dark, he found awaiting him another order from Hitler demanding an attack to widen the gap; and once word of Kluge's return reached the *Fuehrer*, there came still another order directing him to stay out of the pocket. Unknown to Kluge, Hitler followed the second order the next morning with a summons to an ardent Nazi, Field Marshal Walter Model, to quit the Russian front and assume command in France. Kluge, Hitler believed, had spent the twelve hours when he was out of touch with his headquarters trying to arrange a rendezvous with the Allies in order to surrender German forces in France and go over himself to the enemy.

Unaware that he was already marked for relief, Kluge remained so concerned that Hitler might link him with the plot of July 20 that he still

---

[139] Bradley, *A Soldier's Story*, p. 377.

found it difficult to insist on withdrawal from Normandy, even though the situation in the pocket was fast becoming desperate. Not until noon of August 16, after he had learned that on the previous day the Allies had staged a second invasion in southern France, did he dare to make the point directly and emphatically. Kluge reported to OKW:

No matter how many orders are issued the troops cannot, are not able to, are not strong enough to defeat the enemy. It would be a fateful error to succumb to a hope that cannot be fulfilled, and no power in this world can accomplish its will simply by giving an order. That is the situation.[140]

Even before word of Hitler's approval arrived, Kluge issued the order to withdraw. The exodus would begin that night, the sixteenth, through a gap whose width had been reduced to no more than eleven miles.

Even as the Germans began to pull out, General Montgomery was despairing of sealing the gap along the direct route from Falaise to Argentan. Early on the seventeenth he ordered the Canadians to veer southeast from the vicinity of Falaise, the Americans to swing northeast from Argentan, the two to meet some ten miles east of the original gap.

The shift in direction enabled the Canadians to make swift progress, but the Americans were slow. Having waited at Argentan twenty-four hours with no authority for advance on Falaise forthcoming, General Bradley had turned most of Haislip's XV Corps eastward toward the Seine in quest of the deeper envelopment Montgomery originally had ordered. It took time to bring in more troops and a new corps headquarters for the drive northeast from Argentan.

Only after nightfall on August 18 was the pocket finally sealed. Even then a German panzer division managed to reopen a road for six hours.

Yet the panzer division's action was a desperation measure, for by then the situation in the pocket was utter carnage. Night and smoke, the latter forming a pall over the battlefield, provided the only relief from Allied planes. Not even these palliatives had much effect on Allied artillery, since gunners had but to aim their pieces into the constricted pocket to be assured of hitting something German. Everywhere a choked mass of smoking tanks, guns, trucks, field kitchens, horse-drawn wagons. Apathy, despair, terror strained at the fabric of German discipline. Abandoned horses still harnessed balked and reared in panic, often plunging into ravines, over river banks

---

[140] Blumenson, *Breakout and Pursuit*, pp. 522.

and dragging with them their wagons, their gun carriages, their loads. That a once-mighty German army was reduced to such dependence on horses came as a shock to many who viewed the pitiable debris of the battlefield.

The Allies took some 50,000 prisoners from the pocket. Another 10,000 Germans were killed. Yet perhaps as many as 35,000 escaped, including all but four of twenty corps and division commanders. Although seriously wounded by shellfire, the *Seventh Army* commander, General Hausser, also got away. The escapes cheated the Allies of a victory to compare with Stalingrad, but for the Germans it was a catastrophe of epic proportions nevertheless. Even the troops that survived left behind most of their equipment, including 500 tanks and assault guns strewn all the way from Mortain to Argentan.

The fact that the bag could have been bigger was for a long time a source of contention within the Allied command. Most of the criticism fell on Montgomery, probably justly so; for the Canadian drive lacked the vigor and elan that the occasion demanded, and Montgomery had failed to reinforce the Canadians, even though British divisions were available. At the same time the Second British Army had continued its attack against a side of the pocket with the effect—to use Bradley's metaphor—of squeezing toothpaste out of a tube.

Yet Bradley, too, could have done more to speed the closing of the pocket. The fact that he failed even to broach the subject with Montgomery of altering the interarmy group boundary revealed something less than intimacy in Allied command relationships. And for one concerned about maintaining "a solid shoulder at Argentan," he displayed considerable daring twenty-four hours later in sending much of Haislip's corps dashing off toward the Seine.

Faulty intelligence, which led Bradley to believe that sizable German formations already had escaped the trap even as Haislip first reached Argentan, probably had much to do with Bradley's decision. Yet if Bradley thought the Germans could react that quickly, it might have been better to eschew the shallow envelopment to Argentan in the first place, in favor of the deep envelopment all the way to the Seine which Montgomery had originally proposed.

Bradley tried for the deeper envelopment even as the fight in the Argentan-Falaise pocket continued. This time he did approach Montgomery for permission to cut across the British front. Although

Haislip sent an armored division dashing through the British sector down the left bank of the river, the Germans rallied to fight back at Elbeuf, some thirty-five miles from the sea, and the Canadians again were slow to close up to the lower reaches of the river. These events and rain and cloud which grounded Allied planes enabled the Germans to ferry thousands of troops across the river, though again they lost most of their remaining equipment. Of some twenty-three hundred German tanks and assault guns that had given battle in Normandy, just over one hundred got across the Seine, which ruled out any hope of a new defense on the north bank.

In the meantime the personal tragedy that the defeat in Normandy had become for Guenther von Kluge had drawn to an end. When Hitler's new choice to set things right in France, Field Marshal Model, assumed command on the night of August 18, Kluge departed by automobile for Germany, but not before first posting a letter to Hitler. After a long explanation of why the Germans had failed in Normandy, which he attributed primarily to the wealth of Allied material, weapons, and equipment, he begged the *Fuehrer* to bring the suffering of the German people to an end. He concluded:

You have made an honorable and tremendous fight. History will testify this for you. Show now that greatness that will be necessary if it comes to the point of ending a struggle which has become hopeless.[141]

Before Hitler read those words, Kluge was dead. On the way to Metz, not far from the *Canal de Mort Homme*, he bit on a capsule of potassium cyanide.

---

[141] Ibid., p. 536.

Chapter Nineteen – Southern France and Paris

Winston Churchill did more than drag his feet on Operation ANVIL, the invasion of southern France. He planted them firmly like a donkey and tugged the other way, almost up to the day of the landings.[142]

Even after the fall of Rome and Allied advance farther up the boot of Italy removed some of the rationale from British arguments for maintaining strength in the Mediterranean, Churchill and the British Chiefs of Staff continued to object to ANVIL. Churchill, at least, still was thinking of invading the Balkans to thwart Russian hegemony there—not now with an amphibious assault but overland from Italy through the incredibly difficult terrain of the Ljubljana Gap into Yugoslavia and thence to Vienna.

When the decision to postpone ANVIL until mid-August similarly weakened the American contention that ANVIL was essential to keep German forces away from Normandy, General Eisenhower emphasized another argument. He needed ANVIL, he said, to obtain a major port—Marseilles—for delivering more men and supplies essential to striking deep into the heart of Germany, not to mention eliminating the long southern flank which, without ANVIL, he would have to protect. Although it went unnoted, an added dividend would be final

---

[142] The U.S. Army's official account of the invasion of southern France is yet to be published, and no good, generally available account exists. For this chapter I have used the first of three volumes of *Seventh United States Army Report of Operations, France and Germany 1944-1945*, a creditable unit history published soon after the war in Germany. For the strategic argument underlying the invasion, see Matloff, *Strategic Planning, 1943-1944*; Churchill, *Closing the Ring*; Ehrman, *Grand Strategy*, Vol. V; and Maurice Matloff, "The ANVIL Decision: Crossroads of Strategy," in Greenfield, ed., *Command Decisions*. For the liberation of Paris, see Blumenson, *Breakout and Pursuit* and *Duel for France*; Willis Thornton, *The Liberation of Paris* (New York, 1962); Blake Ehrlich, *Resistance: France 1940-1945* (Boston, 1965); and Dominique Lapierre and Larry Collins, *Is Paris Burning?* (New York, 1965).

elimination of any German sea or air threat against Allied shipping in the western Mediterranean.

With the American Chiefs and President Roosevelt solidly behind Eisenhower, Churchill ostensibly acquiesced; but even after General Wilson—Allied commander in the Mediterranean—got his orders on July 2 to mount the invasion, Churchill continued to balk. Once American troops in the first days of August poured into Brittany, Churchill suggested landing the troops scheduled for southern France on Breton beaches. That, he argued, would avoid contested landings and eliminate any possibility of the Germans' containing a beachhead in the south. When he got nowhere with that ploy, he urged a shift to the Bay of Biscay where ports like St. Nazaire or even Bordeaux were closer to the main Allied force in northern France than was Marseilles.

It was August 10 before Churchill at last gave in, and General Wilson received the final signal to proceed. Rechristened Operation DRAGOON (Churchill said he had been "dragooned" into accepting it), the invasion was to begin five days later on August 15.

Behind a heavy air and naval bombardment witnessed by Churchill himself from a British destroyer, contingents of three American divisions and a French task force of armor began going ashore just after dawn on beaches between St. Tropez and Cannes, full on the renowned French Riviera. At the same time a task force of American and British airborne troops as large as a division landed by parachute and glider to cut roads and seize bridges ten to twenty miles inland. The overall commander was Lieutenant General Alexander M. Patch, an infantryman nicknamed "Sandy," who had fought earlier on Guadalcanal and now headed Patton's former command, the Seventh Army.

With only eleven divisions remaining in southern France to defend beaches in both the south and the southwest, the Germans had little hope of fighting off an invasion. Even before the landings OKW had considered ordering the commander in the south, Generaloberst Johannes Blaskowitz, heading *Army Group G*, to fall back to the north; but the defenders were still manning a thin line of bunkers and pillboxes when the Allies arrived.

Compared with Normandy, the invasion of southern France was no contest. Men died, others fell from wounds; but on the first day alone, 86,000 men, 12,000 vehicles, and 46,000 tons of supplies poured ashore, and before daylight faded contact with the airborne invaders was firm.

Although scattered in the drop and glider landings, the airborne troops encountered only scant opposition and with the aid of French Resistance fighters, who materialized as if by magic in the towns and countryside, rapidly seized all objectives. The next day French divisions staged a second landing and headed westward to invest the ports of Toulon and Marseilles.

On the third day, August 17, confronted with the crisis of the Argentan-Falaise pocket in Normandy, Hitler faced the reality of the situation. He ordered General Blaskowitz to leave troops behind to deny the major ports and to pull the bulk of his force back into the Vosges Mountains in northeastern France.

As the Germans retreated, Frenchmen of the Resistance, including organized units of the maquis, harried them at every turn. More than seventy thousand armed Frenchmen swarmed to the fight, along with thousands of others who played their roles without weapons. To the French fell the task and honor of liberating a vast quadrilateral in southwestern France, southward from the Loire River and westward from the Rhône. Only the fortified banks of the Gironde estuary, denying Allied use of the port of Bordeaux, remained to the Germans; and as in Brittany, the Allies were content to leave those Germans alone until overall victory neared.

The only serious fighting erupted in Toulon and Marseilles, but on August 28, two weeks after the first Allied landings, both ports fell to French divisions of what soon was to be designated the "First French Army" under General Jean de Lattre de Tassigny. On the same day American troops of the VI Corps, commanded by General Truscott—he who had succeeded Lucas at Anzio—took Montélimar, the nougat center of France, eighty-five miles up the valley of the Rhone.

They were too late at Montélimar to trap German forces retreating from southwestern France, but the overall gains of the first two weeks were impressive nevertheless. Having come ashore in a second major invasion, the Allies had taken two big ports and had seized 57,000 prisoners of war at a cost of 4,000 French and 2,700 American casualties; and in view of the German withdrawal, it could be but a matter of a few days before the troops from the south would link with General Eisenhower's columns streaming eastward from a beachhead in Normandy that had exploded.

It was just that in Normandy—an explosion.

Even as the intense drama of the Argentan-Falaise pocket unfolded,

George Patton sent two newly operational corps dashing eastward to deny a German defense of the Paris-Orléans gap south of Paris and to push on to the Seine upstream from the French capital. With a right flank anchored on the Loire River and protected by roving bands of FFI, one armored division drove 250 miles in thirty-four hours to reach, on August 16, the monument to Joan of Arc in the center of Orléans. At the same time another division raced across the great arable plain southwest of Paris to draw up to Chartres. Because several retreating German regiments had assembled at Chartres, and because American artillerymen exercised care to spare the historic old city and its incomparable cathedral, the Germans in Chartres were able to hold out until the eighteenth.

Elsewhere the Germans had only stragglers, service troops, remnants of combat units, an occasional anti-tank or anti-aircraft piece to bar the way. It was obvious to all that the Germans were powerless to stop the Allied armies, even at the Seine. Liberation of Paris—symbol of freedom to men everywhere—seemed close at hand.

General Eisenhower actually intended to bypass Paris on both sides and to enter the city only when the time appeared propitious. Not only did he seek to avoid a direct assault that might leave the capital in ruins, but he also wanted to avoid the diversion of transport and supplies from the continuing offensive which Allied responsibility for feeding the city's two million inhabitants would entail.

A political figure also cast a shadow over the question of taking Paris—Charles de Gaulle. Although the population of some towns in Normandy already had received de Gaulle enthusiastically, Eisenhower had no assurance that the rest of France shared the acclaim; nor could he ignore President Roosevelt's personal antipathy to the big Frenchman. Since Paris to the French is not only the seat of government but also the spiritual heart of France and the nexus of all transportation and communications, freeing the city and enabling de Gaulle to enter could impose on the French a government they might not want.

Yet all that was reckoning without Parisians themselves and their long tradition of response to the revolutionary cry: *Aux barricades!* Literally aching for freedom, craving revenge on the conqueror, longing for an active role in their own liberation, the Parisians grew more and more restless as Allied columns broke out of the Norman hedgerows. A long-smoldering feud between Communists and other factions in the Resistance for ultimate control of the government added to the tension.

Matters started to get out of hand on August 15 when railroad workers began a strike that soon spread to the police and other government employees. By the eighteenth, armed Resistance fighters were moving quite openly about some sections of the city. Resistance posters appeared calling for a general strike, for mobilization, for insurrection. So feeble was the German reaction that the next day small bands of FFI without central direction—indeed, in defiance of orders from de Gaulle to await Allied help—seized police stations, town halls, newspaper offices, and the seat of the municipal government, the Hôtel de Ville.

That was throwing down the gauntlet. The reaction of the German commander of Paris would determine the fate of the city.

The commander—Generalleutnant Dietrich von Choltitz, a rotund, bemonocled former corps commander whom Hitler had hurried to Paris when the front in Normandy began to disintegrate—had little enthusiasm for his assignment. He controlled some twenty thousand men west and south of the city, while inside he had another five thousand, a few tanks, and fifty pieces of artillery—scant strength for carrying out Hitler's orders to defend to the last, to destroy all bridges, and to ensure that "Paris must not fall into the hands of the enemy except as a field of ruins."[143]

Yet the French challenge, while serious, failed to awe Choltitz. He knew that few FFI in Paris and its environs were armed; and thus while they might appear in impressive numbers, they hardly could engage German soldiers in open warfare. Fighting of any sort in the city was nevertheless contrary to German interests, for Choltitz saw as his primary mission the blocking of Allied troops on the approaches to the city. When Resistance leaders, alarmed that their ranks were getting out of hand, arranged with the Swedish consul-general, Raoul Nordling, to negotiate an armistice, Choltitz agreed.

The truce failed to last: seeing a chance to seize control of the insurrection and eventually of the government, the Communists refused to honor it. As skirmishing and sniping continued, the German-controlled Paris radio broadcast a proclamation on the night of the twentieth: "Irresponsible

---

[143] This is found in a number of sources, including Blumenson, *Duel for France*, p. 337.

elements in Paris have taken up arms against the occupation authorities. The revolt will be rigorously suppressed."[144]

While the proclamation may have been issued primarily for Hitler's consumption, Resistance leaders considered it a breach of the armistice. The Resistance and hordes of unarmed civilians rushed to the barricades. They took over entire sections of the city, but in many places, such as the Ecole Militaire and along the arcades of the Rue de Rivoli near Choltitz's headquarters in the Hôtel Meurice, the Germans fought back with a fury. At other points, notably at the Hôtel de Ville, German tanks pounded French positions, raising doubts whether the French would be able to hold.

Outside Paris, radio reports of the uprising had so alarmed French leaders that on the twenty-first Charles de Gaulle hurriedly dispatched a letter to Eisenhower. If the Supreme Commander failed to send troops to Paris at once, de Gaulle wrote, he himself might have to do so. It was no idle threat: de Gaulle as head of the provisional French state might well order to Paris the armored division that Eisenhower had brought to France to assure French representation in the invasion and eventually to participate in liberating Paris.

Eisenhower was debating the issue when late in the day another Frenchman acted on his own to send a French force marching on Paris—Général de Division Jacques Philippe Leclerc, commander of the 2d French Armored Division. After trying unsuccessfully to persuade his American corps commander and Courtney Hodges of the First Army to allow his division to move from Argentan on Paris, Leclerc defied them and sent a reconnaissance force of 150 men marching toward the capital.

The next morning, August 22, an emissary from the Resistance reached General Bradley's command post. Exaggerating his colleagues' accomplishments, he claimed that the FFI controlled most of the city and all the bridges. He claimed, too, that only a few German roadblocks barred entrance into the city, and that Choltitz would surrender as soon as Allied troops gained the Hotel Meurice. If the Allies failed to arrive by noon of the twenty-third, when the poorly observed armistice was due to expire, the emissary warned, the Germans might move to wipe out the Resistance and destroy the city.

---

[144] Wilmot, *The Struggle for Europe*, p. 430.

Eisenhower already was weakening in his resolve when the word from inside the city reached him. He decided to reinforce the FFI in order, he noted later, to repay the Resistance for help that had been "of inestimable value in the campaign."[145] Although several American units were within twenty-five miles of Paris, and Leclerc's armor was a hundred miles away, he accommodated the French by ordering Leclerc's division to do the job.

Off the hook of disobedience, Leclerc hurried to his command post, ecstatic with the news.

For all Leclerc's enthusiasm, it was two days later, the morning of August 24, before his division could reach the outskirts of Paris and mount a full-scale attack. All that day his men fought. In some places jubilant crowds imposed greater delays than did the Germans, blocking the roads in their delirium and swarming over the tanks to press on the crews flowers, kisses, wine. Yet elsewhere it was the Germans, fighting back doggedly with tanks, anti-tank guns, cleverly positioned strong-points. As night came, Leclerc's men still were several miles from the center of the capital.

Exasperated American commanders found it hard to comprehend the delay. They could not wait, Bradley exclaimed, for the French "to dance their way into Paris." "To hell with prestige," he went on, and ordered an American infantry division, the 4th, to join the fight.[146]

Stung by this development, Leclerc decided to make one last try during the night. He ordered a small detachment to infiltrate through back streets into the heart of the city. As civilians pushed aside trees they had felled to hamper the Germans and repaved streets they had torn up to build barricades, the tanks and halftracks churned through the darkness. Making their way through the Porte de Gentilly, crossing the Seine at the Pont d'Austerlitz, driving down the quays of the right bank, they reached the Hôtel de Ville to relieve its besieged defenders shortly before midnight.

By the next morning, August 25, most German opposition had melted away. By noon a motorized regiment of the 4th Division stood in front of the cathedral of Notre Dame, while French troops gained the Arc de Triomphe, the Ecole Militaire, the Palais Bourbon. Sniping, occasional machine-gun fire, and sometimes a sharp engagement with Germans holed up in public buildings—as at the Quai d'Orsay, the Luxembourg Palace,

[145] Eisenhower, *Crusade in Europe*, p. 296.

[146] Bradley, A *Soldier's Story*, p. 392.

the Hôtel des Invalides—lent an air of incongruity to what was in the main a frenzied celebration. The crowds oh-ed and ah-ed at the exchanges, alternately pressing forward and falling back in response to the volume of fire.

The German commander, Choltitz, declined an ultimatium from the French to surrender. The end came only after French tanks in early afternoon surrounded the Hôtel Meurice and set German vehicles afire in the Rue de Rivoli.

A young French officer burst into Choltitz's room and shouted in excitement, "Do you speak German?"

"Probably better than you," Choltitz replied calmly, and rose to surrender.[147]

To his captors Choltitz revealed that, despite his orders from Hitler, he had consciously avoided destroying bridges and public buildings. Yet his motive appeared to be less respect for Paris and the French than recognition of the futility of it all. Probably also he lacked the means to create a field of ruins. In any event he was glad to be rid of his job.

All Paris not already in the streets moved into them later that afternoon as Charles de Gaulle appeared at the Hôtel de Ville. Far into the night the celebration continued and into the next day when de Gaulle staged a triumphal parade with part of Leclerc's division down the Champs d'Elysées. Despite American protests that the city still was unsafe for a parade, de Gaulle persisted: a formal ceremony of triumph was essential to cement his control over the factions of the Resistance and to assure the power of his provisional government.

Scattered sniping and the discoveiy of twenty-five hundred Germans in the Bois de Boulogne armed with artillery pieces failed to detract from the glory of the occasion. Three days later the populace turned out again to cheer Eisenhower and an American division that marched down the Champs d'Elysées on its way to the front.

---

[147] Blumenson, *Breakout and Pursuit*, p. 617.

Chapter Twenty – Pursuit to the Frontier

Failure of the Allied armies to pause at the Seine River concealed the fact that the Allied command had planned the campaign another way. Eisenhower and his pre-D Day planning Staff had intended to expand the original beachhead into what they called a "lodgment area," bounded on the north by the Seine, on the south by the Loire, and linked across the Paris-Orleans gap. Only after the ports of Brittany were open, supplies accumulated, airfields constructed, and a proper ratio of service to combat troops established was the final drive into Germany to begin.[148]

The final drive was to be a two-pronged thrust. Montgomery's 21st Army Group was to advance through Belgium along the most direct route to the Ruhr industrial area, a vast collection of coal mines and factories which was the basic source of German industrial strength; while Bradley's 12th Army Group passed south of the forested Ardennes region of Belgium and Luxembourg to seize a lesser industrial region, the Saar. Allied armies arriving from southern France were to provide support on Bradley's right.

The crushing defeat of the Germans in Normandy changed that.

Since pursuit of a defeated enemy is axiomatic, to decide to make no pause at the Seine required no serious debate within the Allied command. Why afford the Germans a chance to build a new position along any of several river lines that had served them all too well twenty-five years

---

[148] For this chapter I have used: Blumenson, *Breakout and Pursuit*; Cole, *The Lorraine Campaign*; Pogue, *The Supreme Command*; Ruppenthal, *Logistical Support*, Vol. I; Roland G. Ruppenthal, "Logistics and the Broad-Front Strategy," in Greenfield, ed., *Command Decisions*; MacDonald, *The Siegfried Line Campaign*; Wilmot, *The Struggle for Europe*; Christopher Hibbert, *The Battle of Arnhem* (New York, 1962); and Montgomery, *Normandy to the Baltic*. See also Cornells Bauer, *The Battle of Arnhem: The Betrayal Myth Refuted* (London, 1966); and Lieutenant General Lewis II. Brereton, *The Brereton Diaries* (New York, 1946).

before—the Somme, the Marne, the Aisne, the Meuse? The Allied goal at that point was the storied Rhine River, 250 miles away.

Whether Allied supporting troops could, without a stop for breath, keep the armies supplied with such vitals of war as food, gasoline, and ammunition as far as the Rhine was another matter, for the Allied logistical structure was jerry-built and shaky. When Eisenhower, on August 19, made the decision to jump the Seine, the only major port available was Cherbourg. Almost all supplies still were coming in over the invasion beaches, which autumn gales soon might close. Although the British and the Canadians might anticipate early easing of their supply problems by capture of Le Havre and other Channel ports lying along their route of advance, the Americans could foresee little immediate relief. As American armies plunged to the east, Brest and the other ports of Brittany soon lay far behind the front.

Yet the problem underlying Allied logistical difficulties was at the moment less a lack of ports and supplies than a shortage of transport. Ample supplies had reached Normandy, but the sudden surge from the beachhead had imposed a burden that service troops, with their cumbersome depots and limited numbers of trucks, found difficult to shoulder.

For long in the embattled beachhead, priority on buildup had been accorded combat units, and while trucks were adequate for the short distances in Normandy, they were too few for the long runs into northeastern France and Belgium. Moreover, the heavily bombed and sabotaged French rail network could assume little of the load. Despite a dramatic improvisation behind Bradley's troops of a one-way truck route called the "Red Ball Express," by the end of August the Allied armies were living a hand-to-mouth existence.

Because the Germans seldom were standing to fight, ammunition was no immediate concern; neither was food, since the troops could exist for weeks on concentrated emergency rations which took up little transport space, and on captured German stocks (two thousand cases of "liberated" champagne helped ease dietary monotony in the Third Army). The big problem was gasoline, the *sine qua non* of modern warfare. Without gasoline the mechanical mounts would falter and stop.

Yet for all the critical nature of the logistical problems, nobody advocated pause: the armies were to keep going as long and as far as they could, hopefully at least to the Rhine. The controversy that arose—perhaps the most acrimonious and persistent tactical argument to develop between British and Americans during the war—centered not on *whether* to continue the pursuit of the foe, but *how*.

Bradley's armies still were forging bridgeheads over the Seine, and Montgomery's forces had yet to begin to cross when, on August 23, General Montgomery proposed scrapping the plan for a two-pronged thrust into Germany. Montgomery wanted the 12th and the 21st Army Groups to stick together, driving northeast into Belgium as a "solid mass" of some forty divisions, "so strong that it need fear nothing."[149]

Eisenhower refused. To advance any great distance in one sector alone, Eisenhower believed, was to invite enemy riposte against the flanks. It also was to ignore the opportunity afforded by the plentiful roads of Western Europe for capitalizing on the great mobility of the Allied armies, and to have—as Eisenhower later put it—"more than one string to our bow."[150]

This was what later became known as Eisenhower's "broad front strategy." Yet just as Montgomery—contrary to his critics—was proposing no thin "knife-like" thrust, so Eisenhower was contemplating no gradual inching forward all along the front. Eisenhower was insisting instead on nothing more than the time-tested formula of advance in parallel columns; to stray from it even in the face of logistical difficulties seemed to him unsound.

While Eisenhower rejected Montgomery's proposal, he nevertheless saw compelling reasons for affording Montgomery some reinforcement and a short-term priority on supply, since there were objectives in Belgium worth the extra effort. A thrust into Belgium would eliminate the residue of the *Fifteenth Army* which had sat out the battle of the hedgerows while awaiting a second Allied invasion. It would erase the V-weapon launching sites from which the Germans were bombarding England. It also would secure airfields vital to continued advance, and, most important of all, it would assure early capture of the great port of Antwerp.

Although Eisenhower already had accorded Montgomery use of four airborne divisions banded together as the First Allied Airborne Army, so intent was he on securing the objectives in Belgium that he bowed further to Montgomery's demands. He told Bradley to send Courtney Hodges' First Army north of the Ardennes close along Montgomery's flank.

---

[149] Wilmot, *The Struggle for Europe*, p. 460.

[150] Pogue, *The Supreme Command*, p. 314.

Even though the First Army was to remain under Bradley's command, Eisenhower's decision had the effect of splitting the 12th Army Group by the inhospitable terrain of the Ardennes. American commanders reacted as if Montgomery had stolen their birthright.

To secure the objectives in the north, General Bradley insisted, Montgomery needed at most only one American corps. The rest of the 12th Army Group, he believed, should continue to the east in accord with a plan he and Patton had devised—a quick thrust south of the Ardennes to cross the Rhine from Mainz to Karlsruhe. Patton, for his part, insisted that with sufficient supplies the Third Army alone could drive eastward through Metz to cross the German border in ten days.

Bradley, Patton, and the usually taciturn Hodges protested to no avail. Although General Eisenhower had no doubt the 12th Army Group could reach the German border, he "saw no point in getting there until we are in a position to do something about it."[151] The drive into Belgium meanwhile would attain objectives—in particular, Antwerp—vital to a continued thrust into Germany.

To Montgomery's chagrin, Eisenhower nevertheless revealed that the priority on supply for the 21st Army Group and the First Army was to last only until Antwerp fell. He had no intention of stopping the Third Army indefinitely. As supplies became available, Patton was to resume a subsidiary thrust toward the Saar.

The gasoline crisis reached a climax during the first five days of September when the Third Army, fuel tanks dry, ground to a halt at the Meuse River at Verdun. Patton and his Staff cursed and flailed the air, directing much of their venom at the First Army and the priority Eisenhower had afforded General Hodges; yet so few were the trucks to haul the needed supplies and so great the distances that the priority was more a gesture than a reality. Hardly had the First Army crossed the Belgian frontier to capture or kill some thirty thousand Germans near Mons—part of the *Fifteenth Army* fleeing the Pas de Calais—when Hodges had to halt one of his corps for three days to get enough gasoline for the other two. Even in the two advancing corps the infantry divisions heading toward the German frontier had to move by alternately walking and shuttling in the few trucks for which there was fuel.

---

[151] Ibid., p. 251.

The British, too, had to halt one corps to keep the others moving. Even so, as the Canadians invested the Channel ports, the British on September 3 liberated a delirious Belgian capital and went on the next day to gain Antwerp, its extensive wharves and docks intact. Antwerp was the prize that might eliminate the supply problem, for such capacity had the port, and so close was it to the German border, that getting supplies to the front would pose little difficulty.

Yet that prize, once taken, lay unused, a jewel not to be worn for want of a setting. In one of the great tactical mistakes of the war, neither the commander of the Second British Army, General Dempsey, nor his superior, General Montgomery, sent anybody to sweep the banks of the Schelde estuary connecting Antwerp to the sea. So long as the Germans held those banks, no Allied ship could traverse the sixty miles of inland waterway to Antwerp.

In the midst of the supply crisis General Eisenhower himself arrived in France to assume personal command of the troops in the field. It had long been ordained that this would occur at some point after American strength on the Continent exceeded that of the British; it was unfortunate that it occurred just when it did, on the first day of September, when Allied columns needed a firm guiding hand. This Eisenhower was in no position to provide from a field headquarters four hundred miles behind the front which, newly opened, lacked radio and telephone links with forward units. The problem was compounded on September 2 when the Supreme Commander's plane made a forced landing, and Eisenhower wrenched his knee so painfully that he had to retire to bed.

How much the battle needed direction was apparent in the failure to clear the seaward approaches to Antwerp. It was apparent, too, in the way Courtney Hodges' First U.S. Army, beset by fuel shortages, headed for the German frontier.

The corps that General Hodges halted for three days for want of fuel was the corps on the left, linking Americans and British. This was the corps that should have had priority if the First Army was to fulfill its mission of assisting the Allied main effort being made by the British. Yet Hodges, at Bradley's direction, gave priority to his other two corps, ostensibly to strike swiftly to gain bridgeheads over the westward bulge of the Meuse River and deny a German reorganization behind the river line. On the other hand, it hardly could have escaped Bradley that by emphasizing these two corps, he would get the First and Third Armies moving together again to the east. So little priority did Bradley afford the corps on the left, the one linking Americans and British, that he withdrew one of its three divisions to reinforce the Third Army.

The two of Hodges' corps that had enough fuel to move at all were gaining bridgeheads over the Meuse at the same time—September 5—when Adolf Hitler was fixing upon a formula to set things right again on the western front.

Along the western frontier Hitler possessed an obstacle that he equated with the now-defunct Atlantic Wall, a band of concrete fortifications known to the Germans as the *Westwall* ("West Wall"), to the Allies as the "Siegfried Line"—after the German *Siegfriedstellung* of World War I and a tune popular in British music halls early in World War II, "Were Going to Hang Out the Washing on the Siegfried Line." Begun in 1938, the *Westwall* originally was a short belt of fortifications opposite France's Maginot Line, guarding the Saar, but Hitler later had extended it to run from the Swiss border to a point well north of Aachen along the Dutch frontier. Unlike the French Maginot Line, the *Westwall* was no thin line of *gros ouvrages* but a band, averaging three miles in depth, of hundreds of mutually supporting pillboxes, troop shelters, and command posts. Where no natural anti-tank obstacles existed, German engineers had constructed pyramidal concrete projections called "dragon's teeth," draped in parallel rows across hills and valleys like some endless, scaly-backed reptile.

Since the fortifications had lain in neglect following the victorious sweep through France and the Low Countries in 1940, few of the German troops or commanders in September 1944 saw the *Westwall* as much more than a Potemkin village. The only hope, most believed, was to withdraw farther, behind the broad moat of the Rhine.

That Hitler refused to sanction.

However outmoded the pillboxes, Hitler reckoned that concrete in any form lends impetus to the defense. He reckoned, too, on inhospitable terrain along the frontier which would restrict the Allies to narrowing corridors of advance: the Vosges Mountains in northeastern France and across the Rhine, the *Schwarzwald*, or Black Forest; the wooded hills of the Saar industrial region; the Ardennes and its contiguous region inside the frontier, the Eifel, with thick forests, deep chasms, and limited road network; and canal- and river-creased flatlands north of Aachen and in the Netherlands. When combined with the poor campaigning weather which comes early in northwestern Europe, the *Westwall* and the harsh terrain would be sufficient, Hitler believed, to slow and eventually to halt an Allied force already running short of supplies.

Defend as long as possible in front of the *Westwall*, Hitler decreed, then in the *Westwall* itself. Troops surrounded in the Channel ports were to fight to the death to deny the enemy port facilities close to the front. That part of the *Fifteenth Army* trapped against the coast by the swift British plunge to Antwerp was to cross the Schelde estuary by fishing boat or whatever means, while leaving behind a force sturdy enough to deny the banks of the Schelde and seaward access to Antwerp. A new headquarters, upgraded from a training command, the *First Parachute Army*, he rushed into the Netherlands to rally stragglers and retreating remnants and build a defensive line based on canals and rivers.

Except for the addition of the *First Parachute Army*, the German order of battle looked much as it had before the flight from France: in the north, the *First Parachute*, *Fifteenth*, and *Seventh Armies*, all under *Army Group B* with Walter Model, like the man he replaced, serving as both army group commander and Commander-in-Chief. South of the Ardennes, two armies—the *First* and *Nineteenth*—which had withdrawn from southern France, grouped under General Blaskowitz's *Army Group G*. Behind the German border, trying to assemble such armor as had survived the débâcle in France, was the *Fifth Panzer Army*, which was in reality the old *Panzer Group West* assuming the name of the force once feared in North Africa. Within these armies most corps and division headquarters had remained basically intact, so that a firm framework still existed on which to position reinforcements.

To the German grenadier, scurrying homeward past carcasses of tanks, trucks, half-tracked personnel carriers, horses, wagons, always under the eyes and guns of the *jabos*, neither that framework nor much of anything else that might set matters right was apparent. Yet in reality much still was on his side. Although thousand-plane Allied raids were commonplace, German industry still maintained a remarkably high rate of production. Indeed, not until late fall did German production reach its wartime peak. Hitler banked strongly on German industry and on a new secret weapon— jet-propelled aircraft—with which he hoped soon to redress the shocking imbalance between Allied and German forces in the skies.

Nor was this all. In five years of war the Germans had lost over 3,500,000 men, but they still had more than 10,000,000 in uniform, including 7,500,000 in the army and its Nazi party adjunct, the *Waffen*-SS. That many of those were of poor quality and that much of the army was on the elongated eastern front went without saying; but as the full extent of the defeat in France became apparent, Hitler ordered convalescents combed from hospitals, extended the age range for induction at both ends, converted sailors and fliers into infantrymen, and otherwise gleaned troops from the rear areas to create twenty-five new divisions that would reach the western front before winter set in. With a salaam to the national pride of the German people (*das Volk*), he called them *volks grenadier* divisions. As a stopgap measure to offset Allied numbers in tanks until panzer divisions could be refitted, he ordered quick formation of ten new panzer brigades.

Yet all were improvisations that could have effect only in weeks or even months. Hitler needed something that would have immediate impact, that would put new life into the dispirited formations falling back into the *Westwall*, behind the Moselle River in Lorraine, and into the Vosges Mountains in Alsace.

Hitler needed a symbol about which the troops might rally.

Almost instinctively he turned to the wizened old soldier to whom in July he had given simultaneously the oak leaf to the Knight's Cross and the kiss of relief, that one who irritated beyond belief because in private conversations, Hitler knew, he called the *Fuehrer* by his rank in the Great War—"the Corporal." Yet he was one who since his relief in France had demonstrated his loyalty by presiding over a Court of Honor to expel those officers associated with the July *Putsch* and who, whether he understood the implications or not, had delivered an impassioned oration at the false funeral staged for Rommel.

His name was Gerd von Rundstedt.

On September 5, Rundstedt returned as Commander-in-Chief in the west. Loyal Nazi Walter Model, who relinquished that post, stayed on as head of *Army Group B*. Rundstedt, Hitler charged, was to halt the Allies before the *Westwall*, on the Moselle, and in the Vosges until he could raise new forces.

If Rundstedt could hold until winter set in, Generaloberst Alfred Jodl, chief of OKW's planning Staff, told the *Fuehrer*, "fog, night, and snow"[152]

---

[152] Fragment 43 of the surviving record of the Fuehrer Conferences (copy in OCMPI). Wilmot in *The Struggle for Europe*" p. 478, mistakenly attributes the remark to Hitler.

would give the Germans an advantage. Jodl could not know it, but plans already were fermenting in the *Fuehrer*'s mind that would, in retrospect, afford Jodl's words a note of prophecy.

Rundstedt's most pressing task was to thwart the onrush of the First U.S. Army north of the Ardennes, where American patrols crossing the German frontier from eastern Belgium on September 11 struck fear in the hearts of feeble German defenders. The man charged with defending the border city of Aachen—to the Nazis a holy city, for there was the tomb of the Emperor Charlemagne, who in Hitler's interpretation of history had founded the First Reich (the Holy Roman Empire was the Second)—ordered the city abandoned without a fight. The man was Count von Schwerin, the panzer division commander who had refused to pass attack orders to his troops in the Mortain counterattack. Why submit German cities to further destruction, the German people to further suffering, reasoned Schwerin, when the war was lost?

Yet so overextended were General Hodges' formations, so fatigued were the troops from the long race across France and Belgium, and so reduced by wear and tear was their strength in tanks, that they were powerless to capitalize on Schwerin's apostasy. Unaware that Aachen was available for the taking, Joe Collins ordered his VII Corps to bypass the city to achieve the more important objective of breaching the *Westwall* before the Germans could man it in strength. Although the VII Corps achieved a minor penetration, the troops bogged down in the face of a fresh German infantry division that Hitler personally had ordered rushed by train from East Prussia. With one corps running far behind because of the gasoline shortage and the other already committed in the Ardennes, Courtney Hodges was powerless to help.

The First Army ground to a halt.

Having stopped the First Army, Rundstedt's next task, as dictated by Hitler, was to mount an ambitious counterattack. Promised three panzer grenadier divisions, three of the new panzer brigades, and, optimistically, the equivalent of four more divisions, the *Fifth Panzer Army* was to strike to deny juncture of Allied forces arriving from southern France with the Third U.S. Army. Following that, the panzer army was to cut north to destroy the divisions of the Third Army that had occupied the escarpment that is the west bank of the Meuse. Hitler even dallied with the idea of reinforcing the panzer army further for a drive northwest all the way to Antwerp.

In September, as it might not be in December, a thrust on Antwerp was nothing more than fancy, as the man Hitler brought from the Russian front to head the *Fifth Panzer Army* soon discovered. The new commander was General der Panzertruppen Hasso von Manteuffel, a small—even diminutive—dapper man, lacking in seniority but popular enough with his colleagues and—what was more important—apparently politically reliable.

Even before Manteuffel reached the scene, Patton got gasoline for his Third Army's tanks and began to advance from the Meuse toward the Moselle, pinning in place most of the German divisions earmarked for the counterattack and forcing commitment of one of the panzer brigades already on hand. American tanks quickly reduced the brigade to a cipher.

Next came juncture of Allied troops from southern France with the Third Army. Patrols met on September 11; four days later, with contact firm, General Eisenhower formally brought the forces from the south under his command. Composed of General Patch's Seventh U.S. Army and General de Lattre's First French Army, these forces were brigaded under the 6th Army Group, commanded by Lieutenant General Jacob L. Devers. An artilleryman whom Eisenhower personally knew only slightly, "Jakie" Devers had been "Jumbo" Wilson's deputy in the Mediterranean and came highly recommended by George Marshall. With youthful, almost cherubic face and winning smile, he could give Joe Collins competition for the title of "all-American boy."

By that time Patton's columns had not only reached the Moselle but had established substantial bridgeheads over the river. To General von Manteuffel and his superior at *Army Group G*, General Blaskowitz, a counterattack according to Hitler's original plan was impossible. The only way to communicate this to Hitler, Blaskowitz reasoned, was to submit an alternative, for in those troubled days not even Rundstedt would speak out flatly against one of the *Fuehrer*'s proposals. (He eventually reached the point, Rundstedt claimed later, where he personally could give orders only to the guards in front of his headquarters.)

Blaskowitz proposed to substitute for Hitler's major counterattack a smaller thrust up the east bank of the Moselle to eliminate the American bridgeheads. Surprisingly, Hitler agreed; but when the attack began on September 18, it was soon demonstrated that three panzer brigades, a lone panzer division (with but twenty-four tanks), and a panzer grenadier division were little more than pesky curs yipping at the carriage wheels of American strength. At Hitler's insistence the battle went on for ten days, but any genuine threat to Patton's flank had passed by the end of the second day. For the failure Blaskowitz paid with his command.

Those pesky curs, however ineffective, were nevertheless worrisome to a Third Army that needed rest, maintenance, repairs, replacements in men and equipment, vital gasoline and ammunition. Indications were rampant, for all Patton's bravado, that the Third Army, like Hodges' First, was nearing the end of its logistical tether. So rapid, too, had been the advance of the 6th Army Group from southern France that Devers' troops required a pause before testing the enemy in the Vosges.

The mammoth Allied war machine was creaking, coughing, sputtering. There remained, nevertheless, one hope for infusing new life into it.

"Had the pious teetotaling Montgomery wobbled into SHAEF with a hangover, I could not have been more astonished than I was by the daring adventure he proposed."[153] That was the reaction, as recalled later, of Omar Bradley to the scheme devised by his counterpart in the 21st Army Group in an effort to keep the pursuit going.

Using three divisions of the First Allied Airborne Army, Montgomery proposed to lay a carpet of airborne troops along a narrow corridor fifty miles deep into the Netherlands to jump three sprawling rivers, including the two downstream branches of the Rhine; whereupon the Second British Army was to drive up the corridor through the cities of Eindhoven, Nijmegen, and Arnhem and on to the Ijssel Meer (Zuider Zee), a total distance of ninety-nine miles. The object was to cut off the Germans in the western part of the Netherlands, outflank the *Westwall*, and put the Second Army in position to get at the Ruhr industrial region from the north, then perhaps to sweep on to Berlin. The code name for the airborne attack was MARKET; for the ground attack, GARDEN.

Promoted to field marshal, lest the stepdown from the job of overall ground commander be misinterpreted as a demotion, Montgomery broached the plan at a meeting in the Supreme Commanders plane at Brussels on September 10. Determined to use the occasion to dislodge

---

[153] Bradley, A *Soldier's Story*, p. 416.

Eisenhower from the concept of an advance on a broad front and win him to unqualified support for one thrust by the armies in the north, Montgomery opened the meeting on a note of acrimony.

So vehement was Montgomery's beginning tirade that Eisenhower leaned forward and put an admonishing hand on his colleague's knee. "Steady, Monty," Eisenhower cautioned. "You can't speak to me like that. I'm your boss."[154]

Montgomery altered the tone but not the content of his argument. To believe, as Eisenhower apparently did, that the Allies possessed enough steam to propel all their armies to the Rhine, getting the Saar industrial region in the process, then to jump the Rhine and seize the Ruhr, was to Montgomery fallacious. Only by halting the Third Army and the First Canadian Army, by affording them only the supplies necessary for maintaining defensive positions, and by putting their transport behind the British and the First Army was there any hope of continuing the offensive as far as the Ruhr. As the first step in the grand push he proposed the daring, unorthodox thrust of Operation MARKET-GARDEN.

Unmoved by the argument against a broad front advance, Eisenhower nevertheless listened sympathetically to the concept of MARKET-GARDEN. Ever since the breakout from Normandy he had sought an opportunity to use the idle airborne troops, only to see each projected operation canceled by the rapid strides of the men on the ground. General Marshall and the Chief of the Air Forces, General Arnold, were anxious, he knew, to see those troops tested in a strategic role. The airborne forces were, in effect, coins burning holes in the Allied command's pocket, which is often the way with elite formations.

A basic premise behind the plan for MARKET-GARDEN was that the long and hasty retreat had left the Germans thoroughly disorganized, that even though there were indications that reinforcements were arriving to take position behind canal and river lines, the incoming troops were few and ill trained. On the other hand, there were disturbing last-minute reports. Aerial reconnaissance noted heavy rail activity at Nijmegen and Arnhem, and the Dutch Resistance reported battered panzer formations arriving in the Netherlands to refit.

---

[154] Wilmot, *The Struggle for Europe*, p. 489.

Disturbing—but not enough to reverse a decision for an operation that many saw as the only hope of denying the Germans a chance to regroup and of continuing the pursuit and winning the war before 1944 ended. Yet how slender the resources underlying the hope: three light airborne divisions and one British armored and two infantry divisions. The latter represented all of the Second Army that had yet arrived in position to launch Operation GARDEN, the ground assault that had to succeed if contact—or rescue—of the airborne divisions was to be achieved.

The fact that the reports of increasing German strength actually were true further narrowed the chances of Allied success. The reinforcements digging in behind the canals and rivers were either paratrooper trainees and cadres arriving as the vanguard of the *First Parachute Army* or first contingents of the *Fifteenth Army* that had cheated Allied fighter-bombers by ferrying across the Schelde estuary by night in what was a minor Dunkirk. The rail activity and the word of arriving panzer formations portended the appearance near Arnhem of two SS panzer divisions under headquarters of the *II SS Panzer Corps*.

A fanciful story, which later gained some credence, had it that the Germans moved the panzer divisions in response to word of Allied plans provided by a Dutch traitor, a big man adept with the girls known as "King Kong" (after a gorilla in a motion picture of the same name).[155] It made a good spy story, but Field Marshal Model actually had ordered the divisions to the Netherlands on September 3, seven days before the Allies even decided on an airborne attack. One division was to remain near Arnhem, absorbing the tanks and equipment of the other while getting ready to move against the First U.S. Army at Aachen. The second was to prepare to move into Germany for full rehabilitation.

The early morning haze had cleared, and Sunday, September 17, 1944, turned into a lazy, beautiful, late summer day. Across the verdant flatlands of the Netherlands, the Dutch faithful, dressed in the drab, ill-fitting clothes that went with four years of German occupation, made their way home from church or sat down to a Sunday dinner short on meat, long

---

[155] The "King Kong" spy myth is perpetrated in Oresto Pinto, *Spy Catcher* (New York, 1952). With the help of material provided by the late Colonel Theodore A. Beerec of the Netherlands, I refuted the story in *The Siegfried Line Campaign*. See also Bauer, *The Battle of Arnhem*.

on potatoes. Here and there, at once a part of the crowd and yet isolated, strolled or bicycled German soldiers absorbing the sunshine and rest of a day away from their posts.

German commanders, too, for the most part, took their ease. An SS battalion commander was passing the day in his quarters with his Javanese mistress. At a desk in a commandeered country cottage a strikingly handsome General der Fallschirmtruppen Kurt Student was overwhelmed with the paper work incidental to the command of the *First Parachute Army*. In the serene park setting of suburban Hotel Tafelberg, west of Arnhem, bemonocled Field Marshal Model, commander of *Army Group B*, took aperitifs before sitting down to lunch in the glass-enclosed portico of the hotel. East of Arnhem the commander of the *II SS Panzer Corps* also spent the morning in his headquarters, absorbed in the logistical details of rebuilding one panzer division, shifting another to Germany.

Only the low-ranking commander of a depot battalion newly arrived from Germany suspected anything unusual about the day. Despite the clear skies, he noted, no waves of Allied bombers had passed overhead. What could that mean? Perturbed, the commander ordered his men confined to quarters on full alert and given a ration of gin.

"Mark my words," said an overage German soldier to the Dutchman who owned the country estate where the men were billeted, "something is up. They always give us gin when important things have to be done."[156]

In mid-morning that Sunday the air above southeastern England whirred with a tremendous drone as if a generation of outsized locusts had stirred to life. From twenty-two airfields, 1,545 troop-carrying aircraft and 478 thin-skinned gliders took to the air. The planes and gliders rendezvoused above the Channel and split into two great streams, one heading northeast across the Dutch coastal islands, the other east where at a point over Belgium it would turn north toward the Netherlands.

Inside the transports men sat "like grim steel-trap-jawed automatons, all softness, smiles, and good humor vanished from [their] faces."[157] Some pulled at cigarettes. Others ate K-rations. Many slept the consuming sleep that often overtakes men gripped with tension. For all the men,

---

[156] From material provided by Colonel Boeree

[157] Ross S. Carter, *Those Devils in Baggy Pants* (New York, 1951), p. 214, one of surprisingly few good memoirs at the fighting man's level.

newcomers and veterans of Sicily and Normandy alike, the operation ahead was to be a novel experience, for never before had Allied troops staged an airborne attack by day.

The question was, would the effort to avoid the dispersion of a night drop result in even heavier losses from enemy flak?

Over the Dutch islands flak was surprisingly light, meaning that fighters and bombers that had come first had done their job well. Only as the planes neared drop and landing zones did flak blossom in full fury. Deadly little black puffs of smoke bloomed to right and left, peppering the sides of the planes with a sound like hail hitting a tin roof.

One puff struck the right motor of Plane 332, bearing a "stick" of six men of the 101st Airborne Division, set the motor afire, and sent gasoline spraying along the side of the plane as a runway for the fire. Although the paratroopers, the crew chief, and the radio operator got out, the pilot and the co-pilot rode the doomed craft to their deaths. Two men who made it safely out of another crippled transport met death when the whirling propellers of a plummeting plane cut them to pieces. Another plane careened into a group of men who already had landed, and killed three of them. A heavy bundle of equipment fell on the head of another man and killed him.

For all these mishaps, the belt of flak was surprisingly thin. The British lost not a plane or a glider; the two American divisions lost thirty-five transports and thirteen gliders. For most men the countryside floating up to meet them could have been a parade ground in North Carolina or pastoral fields in Hampshire. The drop pattern was the most compact either British or Americans had ever staged, even in training.

Coming to earth farthest north, beyond the Neder (Lower) Rijn River west of Arnhem, men of the 1st British Airborne Division remarked great expanses of purple-blue heather contrasting sharply with the green of woods and the red-tiled roofs of ordered rows of cottages. Men of the 82d Airborne Division dropped southeast of Nijmegen on ground that rises only a few hundred feet above sea level but, in contrast to the lowlands everywhere else, seems almost mountainous. Those of the 101st Airborne Division, landing north of Eindhoven to form the south end of the airborne carpet, found themselves in flat countryside marked by tree-lined roads and dikes.

In minutes 16,500 Allied parachutists and 3,500 glidermen came to earth in the start of history's largest airborne attack. The air was full of white parachutes bearing men and of colored ones bearing equipment.

"What is it?" schoolboy Willem Haart, breathless from a race home on his bicycle, asked his grandfather.

"I don't know," said the old man, "but it looks like the end of the world."[158]

Success, once the men gathered on the ground, was in most cases swift. British drop and landing zones were six to eight miles from the primary British objective, a great highway span over the Neder Rijn at Arnhem; but Lieutenant Colonel J. D. Frost and some five hundred men nevertheless gained the north end of the bridge before dusk, though the Germans held firmly to the south end. Since men had dropped at both ends of another big highway bridge over the Maas (Meuse) River not far from Nijmegen, the 82d Airborne Division quickly took that objective. Along the lone northward-leading highway that British ground troops would have to take to reach Nijmegen and Arnhem ("Hell's Highway," the men christened it), paratroopers of the 101st secured all bridges over canals and small rivers except one. A canal bridge, closest to Eindhoven, the Germans blew in their faces; but the paratroopers secured the approaches, and the next day they would march almost unopposed into Eindhoven to the cheers of a populace that had festooned the city with orange, the national color.

As the first day of MARKET-GARDEN drew to an end, Allied commanders might have exulted in spectacular success except for three portentous developments. One occurred south of Eindhoven, another at Nijmegen, a third at Arnhem.

Attacking soon after the airborne troops had landed, ground troops of the Second British Army had found the resistance south of Eindhoven stronger than expected. Scheduled to be in Eindhoven before the day was out, they still were six miles short of the city when night fell.

At Nijmegen the 82d Airborne Division concentrated first on securing high ground southeast of the city before sending troops to seize a big highway span across the Waal River, a downstream branch of the Rhine. Although that was according to plan, it was regrettable. In the first hours after the landings only a few sentries stood between the paratroopers and

---

[158] Hibbert, *The Battle of Arnhem*, p. 53.

the bridge, but after dark, as a battalion at last began to move on the bridge, German reinforcements arrived by truck to begin a stalwart defense.

At Arnhem the most portentous development of all: there, despite Colonel Frost's success in reaching the bridge over the Neder Rijn, it became apparent all too swiftly that the reports from Dutch partisans had been right. Rushing from the Hotel Tafelberg (spilling a hastily packed suitcase in the process), Field Marshal Model personally ordered tanks and panzer grenadiers from the two SS panzer divisions that were refitting east of Arnhem to attack Frost's men and block the way between Frost and the drop and landing zones west of the city. Lightly armed airborne troops would in the long run be no match for armor.

As if those events were not misfortune enough for the Allied cause, a copy of the Allied operational order, taken from an American glider, was on General Student's desk within two hours after the first parachutes opened. The gods of war would scowl even more glumly the next day and for several days thereafter as inclement weather over England and the Continent delayed and in some cases precluded airborne resupply and reinforcement.

All those factors in the aggregate determined the outcome of Operation MARKET-GARDEN. Despite valor and sacrifice in such volume that the story might be told to the sound of trumpets, nothing the airborne troops could accomplish from then on would be enough to alter the pattern.

Not until near nightfall of the second day, September 18, did the British ground column fight a way into Eindhoven, and not until early the third morning was the destroyed bridge over the canal north of the city replaced. It was mid-morni ng of the third day before the ground column arrived at Nijmegen, there to find German defenders still holding the highway bridge over the Waal River.

Only late in the fourth day, September 20, after a hastily mounted assault crossing of the Waal's 1,200-foot width by paratroopers using flimsy little canvas assault craft, did the Germans relinquish the big span at Nijmegen. Even then diehard defenders clung like cockleburs in a dog's coat to superstructure and underpinnings of the bridge, so that not until near the end of the fifth day was even a small contingent of the British ground column able to cross the river and begin an attack to traverse a last ten miles and rescue the British paratroopers at Arnhem.

The British paratroopers—who called themselves "Red Devils" and wore jaunty maroon berets—were by then under a state of siege. Of Colonel

Frost's original five hundred men at the north end of the bridge over the Neder Rijn, only about fifty survived to try to escape individually or in small groups. None of the other "Red Devils" could rescue them, for the two German panzer divisions had driven the rest of the 1st Airborne Division into a cruelly confined little horseshoe-shaped position hinged on the Neder Rijn and the Hotel Tafelberg, which Field Marshal Model had fled the afternoon of September 17.

The British on the fifth day, the twenty-first, tried to reinforce the "Red Devils" by dropping a Polish parachute brigade south of the Neder Rijn, where the men were to cross into the perimeter by way of a ferry; but by the time the parachutists landed, German shells had sunk the ferry boat. The sole hope of reinforcing the perimeter lay with the assault boats arriving with the British ground column from Nijmegen.

How faint was that hope!

Most of the ground between the Waal and Neder Rijn rivers is polderland, too wet and soft to support the weight of tanks or even armored cars. To thwart the British attack, the Germans had but to block the main highway leading to Arnhem and a few secondary roads. Heavy German artillery fire on convoys plying Hell's Highway further south, culminating on the sixth day with ground attacks that temporarily cut the highway, stymied reinforcement and supply for the British troops.

Only on the seventh day, September 23, did the British in any strength reach the Neder Rijn across from the embattled "Red Devils." That night and the next they tried to go to the aid of the paratroopers, but treacherous mud along the banks and German shelling reduced the reinforcement to a trickle.

Finally forced to acknowledge defeat, British commanders on September 25 authorized the paratroopers to withdraw. Hungry, thirsty, red-eyed, the "Red Devils" wrapped their muddy boots in rags to muffle the sound of their footsteps and began after nightfall on the ninth day to run a gauntlet of German patrols to the water's edge. The night was mercifully dark. A heavy rain fell.

Patient despite nervousness, fatigue, the cold rain, the men queued for an empty boat. As dawn approached, many braved the swift current to swim across, but at daylight some three hundred remained on the north bank.

Of approximately 9,000 who had fought north of the Neder Rijn, only 2,400 made their way out. During the same period the two U.S. airborne divisions together had lost 3,500 men. Counting glider pilots and British ground troops, MARKET-GARDEN cost the Allies 11,850 casualties.

The operation accomplished some of what Field Marshal Montgomery had intended it to accomplish—an Allied corridor sixty-five miles deep into the Netherlands, including bridgeheads over the Maas and Waal rivers; but by the merciless logic of war, the operation was a failure. It had failed either to achieve a bridgehead over the last river, the Neder Rijn, or to split the Netherlands, or to outflank the *Westwall*, or to position the British for striking the Ruhr. Most important of all, it had failed to furnish the impetus to impel a supposedly tottering German command to collapse.

At first glance, much of the failure might be laid at the feet of Tyche, the goddess of chance: the location of the SS panzer divisions, Model's and Student's presence on the scene, the finding of the Allied operational order, the degenerating weather. Although intelligence had revealed some likelihood of German reserves near Arnhem, so worried were the British in early September with the start of the V-2 bombardment from bases in the Netherlands that it would have required considerably more information of enemy strength than was at hand to have deterred Field Marshal Montgomery from launching the attack. As for the weather, fog, mist, and rain are common in northwestern Europe in September; but the Allies, for all their wealth of resources, lacked sufficient planes and gliders to circumvent the weather by lifting all the airborne troops on the first day.

Those were cruel misfortunes. Yet despite them, Operation MARKET-GARDEN still might have succeeded had the British ground column attacked with greater *élan* south of Eindhoven and north of the Waal and had the commander of the 82d Airborne Division employed the verve and vigor expected of airborne troops and allotted at least a small force for a *coup de main* against the big bridge over the Waal at Nijmegen. That the American commander acted in accord with prior plan in no way erased the fact or the serious effect of the failure.

Chapter Twenty-One – The Fall Campaign

Whether a successful MARKET-GARDEN would have achieved the long-range effect many expected would forever remain unanswered; probably it would not have. Even though Hitler had no additional reserves to move immediately against the British, and even though the airborne landings whipped the *Fuehrer* into a lather of concern (what, he railed, if the Allies should drop airborne divisions to seize him and his Staff!), the Germans had displayed no evidence of panic, no inclination toward rout or mass desertion. Barring a complete German collapse, impoverished Allied armies which were still unable to use the port of Antwerp were incapable for the moment of accomplishing much more than they had already achieved.[159]

With the failure of MARKET-GARDEN and the stalling of other Allied forces before the *West wall* and in Lorraine and Alsace, another battle of buildup and attrition not unlike the battle of the hedgerows became inevitable. Although General Eisenhower at that point had some two million men and fifty-four divisions, eight of the divisions were immobilized either in Normandy or southern France for want of transport to keep them supplied at the front. The forty-six active divisions had to cover some six hundred miles from the North Sea to Switzerland—an average of more than twelve miles of front, not counting the twistings and turnings, per division—which made it not only difficult to concentrate for a powerful offensive but downright risky.

"Bradley's forces," the Supreme Commander noted as early as the last week of September, "are getting fearfully stretched" in the Ardennes and

---

[159] For this chapter, I have relied primarily on Cole, *The Lorraine Campaign*, and my own volume, *The Siegfried Line Campaign*. See also Craven and Cate, eds., *ARGUMENT to V-E Day*; Pogue, *The Supreme Command*; and *Seventh United States Army Report of Operations*, Vol. II.

"may get a nasty little 'Kasserine' if the enemy chooses the right place to concentrate his strength."[160]

Field Marshal von Rundstedt had theoretically approximately the same number of divisions, plus several of the new panzer brigades; but hardly one of the German units was anywhere near full strength. Rundstedt estimated that his forces were equivalent to about half those of Eisenhower. Allied superiority in artillery pieces was at least 2½ to 1, in tanks approximately 20 to 1, and in aircraft—overwhelming. Yet Rundstedt had shorter lines of communications, the fervor that defense of the homeland instilled in his troops, and an overextended foe who lacked adequate port facilities for long overseas supply routes.

For the Allies, opening Antwerp clearly was the key; yet Field Marshal Montgomery still resisted turning full strength to the assignment. While paying lip service to the need for Antwerp, he persisted in his argument that transport and supply concentrated behind his command still might gain the Ruhr before winter set in. Eisenhower, for his part, was slow to dictate otherwise, so that valuable weeks passed in tribute to meaningless semantics before the Supreme Commander, on October 13, finally spelled out in no uncertain terms the priority of Antwerp.

If after receiving his views Montgomery still classed them as "unsatisfactory," Eisenhower wrote, then an issue would exist that would have to be settled by "higher authority."[161] Only then did Montgomery, reluctant still, force his attention away from the enticing Ruhr to focus on the less glamorous task of providing a logistical base for operations to come.

The campaign that followed was bitter. The canal-creased countryside would have been one mammoth ooze of mud, in any case, as autumn rains fell; the Germans made it worse and turned it into a salt lake by opening the dikes that industrious Dutchmen through the years had erected to keep out an antagonistic North Sea. Plodding slowly forward, incurring thirteen thousand casualties in the process, the First Canadian Army bore the brunt of the onerous task. Not until November 8 were the last Germans cleared from the banks of the Schelde estuary, and not until November 28—almost three months after the British had taken Antwerp—was the channel swept of mines, and the first ship dropped anchor in the port.

---

[160] Butcher, *My Three Years with Eisenhower*, p. 676.

[161] MacDonald, *The Siegfried Line Campaign*, p. 215

Still smarting from supply shortages, the other Allied armies in the meantime also slogged slowly forward in a painful and conscious effort to afford their adversary no respite. Barring any untoward turn in the ratio of Allied to German casualties, General Eisenhower vetoed any idea of a winter pause in the fighting.

To the south French and Americans of General Devers' 6th Army Group—as short of supplies as anybody else, since it would take time to construct a 500-mile line of communications from Marseilles—fought in the rain across the tumbling streams and rolling forested terrain of the western foothills of the Vosges. Left behind were the swift armored drives up valleys already all but cleared of Germans by the maquis; gone were the jubilant hordes welcoming the liberator. It was a real war again, the kind that many of the troops had hoped they had left behind in Italy.

It was the kind of war that Devers' neighbor to the north, George Patton, detested. War in Patton's book was supposed to be slashing, smashing; yet there were times when war was grim infantry fighting which roar and rage could not drive away.

Before pushing on to the German border and the Saar industrial region, Patton deemed he had to have Metz, road hub and capital of Lorraine; but mammoth old forts, most dating from the Franco-Prussian War of 1870-1871, stood in the way. The fortifications were outmoded, adequate enough in their day to withstand Parrots and Napoleons and the *mitrailleuse*, but against napalm and the shells and bombs of 1944...?

Yet the thick masonry walls stood, and their underground labyrinths proved all but impervious to the weapons of a later generation. Only infantry could root the enemy out, dying in the process; and that kind of war took time. The month of October passed with Metz still in German hands.

Further north Courtney Hodges worked to concentrate his far-flung First Army in the vicinity of Aachen, where in the first week of October infantrymen using portable flamethrowers and supported by direct fire of tanks and self-propelled artillery etched a painful path through pillboxes of the *Westwall* north of the city. When linked with the penetration that Joe Collins' VII Corps had achieved in September, that served to encircle Aachen. After combat had raged from house to house, room to room, sewer to sewer, a city that in September might have been had simply for the occupying, finally surrendered on October 21.

That first major German city to fall, noted one American observer, was "as dead as a Roman ruin, but unlike a ruin it has none of the grace of gradual decay."[162]

For all the slowness of October's advances and for all the certainty that Antwerp was essential to victory, the optimism engendered by the race across France and Belguim dissipated only slowly. Meeting in Quebec in September on the eve of President Roosevelt's campaign for an unprecedented fourth term, the President, Prime Minister Churchill, and the Combined Chiefs of Staff had focused on the war in the Pacific, as if victory in Europe were already assured. Postwar occupation zones and a plan proposed by Secretary of the Treasury Henry Morgenthau to reduce Germany to an agricultural nation—grist for Hitler's propagandist, Joseph Goebbels—were the main topics affecting Europe. The leaders also shifted control of the strategic air forces from Eisenhower to the Combined Chiefs, a move Eisenhower deplored but one which, in view of command relationships already established, had no appreciable impact on the conduct of the war.

Meeting again a month later in Washington, the Combined Chiefs considered urging Eisenhower to institute extraordinary measures to assure victory before the year was out: use the supersecret proximity fuse against ground targets, employ all troops and stockpiles of supplies without regard to reserves, shift the air offensive from all but the most immediately remunerative targets.

Lacking Antwerp, Eisenhower felt impelled to scotch that kind of thinking, but even he saw sufficient improvement in the logistical situation to warrant a major offensive before winter came. It would be no overambitious *Friedensturm* ("peace offensive"), but instead an apparently realistic drive geared to available resources and aimed, if not at grabbing the Ruhr, at least at establishing bridgeheads over the Rhine.

With Montgomery preoccupied with the seaward approaches to Antwerp, Eisenhower designated Bradley's 12th Army Group and specifically Hodges' First Army to make the main effort. Attacking early in November, the First Army was to cross the Rhine south of Cologne, while Patton's Third Army drove northeast through the Saar to provide support

---

[162] Ibid., p. 320.

on the right. Devers' 6th Army Group meanwhile was to clear the west bank of the upper Rhine. A new force, the Ninth U.S. Army, which had first breathed operational life on the Brittany peninsula to conquer Brest, slipped into the line on the First Army's north flank, between Hodges' troops and the British. The Ninth Army was to join the First Army in crossing the Rhine and then in encircling the Ruhr.

The new Ninth Army was commanded by a tall, spare infantryman named William H. Simpson. "Big Bill," they called him, a man who kept a balding head cleanly shaven. Except for a kind crinkle at the corners of penetrating eyes, which softened an otherwise sharp face, Simpson's appearance might have matched the stereotype of the Prussian officer. He was a man, Eisenhower said later, who "never made a mistake."[163] Unlike the "noisy and bumptious" Third Army and the "temperamental" First, Bradley would note, Simpson's Ninth Army was "uncommonly normal."[164]

To most commanders and to many a common soldier alike, the projected offensive had all the trappings of a breakthrough on a grand scale. Replacements (by official order they were supposed to be called "reinforcements") had brought all units up to strength. Behind the lines artillery pieces stood in some places almost hub to hub, trucks churned to and fro, and word passed from man to man that the planes were coming—the big ones.

The men on the whole were rested, equipment and weapons cleaned and oiled, tanks and tank destroyers repaired or replaced. Foxholes were covered from the rain with tent tarpaulins or doors. A man had a chance to read *The Stars & Stripes*, to chuckle at the caustic cartoons by soldier artist Bill Mauldin, to ogle the pinup girls in *Yank*, or to peruse any number of dehydrated versions of home-front magazines. (Ernie Pyle was gone, headed for death on an obscure little Pacific isle. Another GI favorite, Glenn Miller, whose saxophone-heavy dance band was the era's most popular, also was to perish, on a cross-Channel flight in December.)

Whenever possible, divisions rotated battalions in the line, giving men a night or two in a dry place a few hundred yards behind the front. Regiments set up showers, run on the order of an assembly line, where a dirty man discarded his clothes at one end of a tent and emerged at the other with

---

[163] I rely here on a personal interview with General Eisenhower in 1967.

[164] Bradley, A *Soldier's Story*, p. 422.

fresh uniform, and clean. Division, corps, and army rest centers sprang up in towns beyond normal range of artillery fire. Although liquor and intimate female companionship were in short supply, blue-uniformed Red Cross girls smiled and smiled and smiled while dispensing doughnuts and coffee, and touring entertainers gave vaudeville a new lease on life. A few lucky men even got brief passes to Paris where, they assured everybody upon their return, liquor and women were no problem.

Most men had received winter clothing—long woolen underwear and heavy overcoats. Gone were the old canvas "leggings," a descendant of World War I's "puttees"; in their place, trim "combat boots," shoes with high leather uppers over which the men bulged their trousers as did paratroopers with their coveted jump boots. Partly because October was uncommonly cold and wet, but mainly because a man in a foxhole found it hard to exercise and keep his feet dry, the invidious enemy trench foot, which earlier had showed up in Italy, put in another appearance. Purple toes, gangrene, maybe amputation; in field hospitals row after row of men lay on cots with feet outside the covers, wads of cotton between discolored toes.

The big push began inauspiciously on the second day of November when a lone division, the 28th, wearing a red keystone shoulder patch denoting the Pennsylvania National Guard, attacked in a dense forest of towering fir trees southeast of Aachen. The goal was high ground near the town of Schmidt on which to anchor the First Army's right flank. Ten days later the men reeled back spent and bleeding, victims of one of the wars most costly divisional attacks and of a piece of wooded real estate that thousands would come to know by a name synonymous with dread: the Huertgen Forest.

What commanders in the 28th Division and their superiors as well had failed to appreciate was the importance of two big dams on upper reaches of the little Roer River commanded by the high ground at Schmidt. Downstream, where the First and Ninth Armies would have to cross the Roer on the way to the Rhine, the river flows through a low-lying plain. By demolishing the two dams or by releasing their waters in a calculated flow, the Germans could flood the valley, wash out tactical bridges, and trap any American force that had crossed the Roer.

The Germans were not about to give up such an ace without a fight. To oppose the 28th Division, they threw in a panzer division and two others. The 28th took over six thousand casualties, prompting some to rechristen the red keystone shoulder patch the "bloody bucket."

346

With the complex machinery of a big offensive already geared to other objectives, neither Hodges, Bradley, nor Eisenhower did anything immediately to counter the threat of the Roer River dams. It was as if, by refusing to face up to the reality, they hoped that the threatening dams would somehow disappear.

Because of harsh weather which day after day postponed a mammoth air strike in support of the First and Ninth Armies, the Third Army came to deal the first big blow of the offensive. Patton attacked in the rain on November 8 with two corps; but under grueling conditions of mud and flood it took eleven days before a pincers could close around Metz and another four days before the last Germans in the city and its forts died or surrendered. Not until near the end of the first week in December did the Third Army's troops batter their way thirty-five miles through one defended town after another and the forts of the Maginot Line to reach the German frontier and the pillboxes of the *Westwall* guarding the Saar.

Meanwhile, on November 13, in a snowstorm, General Devers' under-manned 6th Army Group to the south launched what was supposed to be a supporting attack, but it eventually achieved more than Patton's. On the sixteenth de Lattre's French broke through the Belfort Gap at the southern end of the Vosges, reached the Rhine four days later, and on the twenty-second captured Mulhouse before German defenses stiffened. Patch's Seventh Army at the same time penetrated the Saverne Gap between High and Low Vosges to afford General Leclerc's 2d French Armored Division the opportunity to capture Strasbourg, the picturesque Rhine city that long had been a pawn between warring French and Germans. (American scientists and top leaders breathed easier after a special intelligence mission discovered data in Strasbourg indicating that German scientists were lagging in their efforts to unlock the secret of the atom.)

Having reached the Rhine, General Devers wanted either to cross or to turn northward alongside the Third Army to help clear the Saar; otherwise the 6th Army Group would have to sit staring idly across the Rhine at the Black Forest. Since a crossing of the Rhine far from the critical objectives farther north had no part in the overall plan, Eisenhower instead sanctioned Devers' turning north, but only with the understanding that Devers also would clear all Germans from the west bank of the Rhine from Strasbourg to the Swiss border.

By mid-December a Seventh Army grown to a strength of seven divisions had conquered the mud of the Rhine plain and a succession of old Maginot forts to draw up to the *Westwall* where the German frontier meets the Rhine in the extreme northeastern corner of France. Yet to the south, between Strasbourg and Mulhouse, the enemy's *Nineteenth Army* still held a big, troublesome bridgehead on the Rhine's west bank, which became known as the "Colmar Pocket." De Lattre's manpower-short First French Army had failed to make good on Devers' promise to sweep the entire west bank in the 6th Army Group's zone.

In the north the weather in the meantime finally had cleared enough on November 16 to allow the main effort of the new offensive to begin in the wake of the war's heaviest air bombardment in direct support of ground troops. Known as Operation QUEEN, the bombardment was supposed to do again what the air strike in Normandy had done for Operation COBRA. On defenses that the Germans had erected around the penetrations of the *Westwall* generally east of Aachen, more than four thousand planes dropped over ten thousand tons of bombs.

It was a bombardment that struck awe in the hearts of those who witnessed it. Yet the effect was muted.[165]

In an effort to help both the First and Ninth Armies achieve quick penetrations, ground commanders had chosen targets covering too broad a range, and, in an effort to forestall a tragic short bombing like those that on successive days had marred COBRA, they had insisted on too great an interval between attacking troops and the bomb line. By the time American infantrymen could cross the two miles of ground between their line of departure and the bomb-scarred target, the German defenders had recovered. Operation QUEEN hurt the Germans, but not enough for a breakthrough.

The fighting that followed across an incredibly long eight miles of plain marked by ugly strip mines, fields of stock beets, and drab but stoutly built villages and through the dense evergreen jungle of the Huertgen Forest was, as fighting was everywhere during the late fall campaign, some of the most punishing of the war. It was the battle of the hedgerows all over again, only this time with the added misery of freezing rain, sleet, snow, flood, mud, pillboxes, and dense, dank

---

[165] David Irving, *The German Atomic Bomb* (New York, 1968).

woods straight out of frightening German folk tales. It was a depressing scene etched in gray where the Technicolor of exploding shells seemed strangely out of place.

Nowhere were the rigors and tribulations more pronounced than within the Huertgen Forest—the Argonne of World War II—where in the vain hope that one more attack, one more fresh division might break the German defense, General Hodges fed in unit after unit in brutal frontal attack—with shocking disregard for the fact that, as long as the Roer dams remained in German hands, nobody on the American side was free to cross the Roer downstream from them. With disregard, too, for the fact that had the Americans early seized the dams, the Germans would have been forced to withdraw or face the threat of a rampaging Roer at their backs.

Dawn reached slowly into the Huertgen Forest, as if reluctant to throw light on a stark tableau that it seemed only the devil himself could have created.[166] Once magnificent trees were now twisted, gashed, broken, their limbs and foilage forming a thick carpet on the floor of the forest. Some trees stood like gaunt, outsized toothpicks. Great jagged chunks of concrete and twisted reinforcing rods that together had been a pillbox. The mutilated carcass of a truck that had hit a mine. Everywhere discarded soldier equipment—gas masks, empty rations containers, helmets, rifles, here a field jacket with a sleeve rent, there a muddy overcoat with an ugly clotted dark stain on it. One man kicked a bloody shoe from his path, then shuddered to see that the shoe still had a foot in it.

It was misery unrelieved. So heavy were overcoats from rain and mud that men bowed under their weight. The constant moisture ate insidiously at radios and weapons. Here and there bodies of the dead lay about in grotesque positions, weather-soaked, bloated, the stench from them cloying. And everywhere hidden death in the form of buried mines. A man might blunder into a minefield, step on a mine, then in his agony set off others that killed him. Worst of all was the diabolical "Bouncing Betty," a three-pronged evil that leaped out of the ground and exploded in the air, as likely as not to catch a man between the legs and blast his sexual organs. The parade of men wounded by mines was constant

---

[166] The following sections are based on my volume, *The Battle of the Huertgen Forest* (Philadelphia, 1963). The indirect quote from Ernest Hemingway is from *Across the River and into the Trees* (New York, 1950).

and demoralizing, so that the fear of stepping on a mine—particularly a "Bouncing Betty"—was with a man at every turn. If not mines underfoot, then it was mortar and artillery shells dropping unheralded from the sky to crack with ear-splitting fury in the treetops and bathe the forest with jagged metal.

Passchendaele with tree bursts, Ernest Hemingway called it.

As November passed and a snow-drenched December neared its midpoint, most of the Huertgen Forest finally lay behind but at a cost of more than 24,000 Americans killed, missing, captured, or wounded, and of another 5,000 victims of trench foot, respiratory diseases, and combat fatigue. Eight divisions had entered the maw of the forest, and all had drawn back bloody.

On the plain to the north, the rest of the First Army and the Ninth at last drew up to the mud-slick western bank of the Roer River. All together the First and Ninth Armies lost 57,000 men to enemy shells, bullets, and mines in the fall battle, plus another 70,000 to the devil's helpers—fatigue, exposure, disease. In equipment the First Army alone lost 550 tanks, equivalent to the tank strength of almost four armored divisions.

And at the end of it American troops gazed not at the fabled Rhine but at an obscure, flood-threatened Roer, and were powerless to cross until somebody got around to concentrating on the Roer River dams.

The fact that Germans who in September had appeared beaten had fought back with such determination and relative success, Allied commanders attributed to German stubbornness, to blind faith in the *Fuehrer*, to devotion to the home soil. The abominable weather, the constricted terrain, the *Westwall*, some few continuing logistical problems on the Allied side—these had contributed to the outcome. The fall campaign had hurt the Germans nevertheless. The three armies in the south, for example, had inflicted on the Germans losses in prisoners alone of almost 72,000 men. Yet Passchendaele had hurt the Germans too, and they had still fought on.

Allied commanders and their intelligence experts failed to comprehend that the obstinate German defense in the rolling hills of Lorraine, in the Huertgen Forest, on the plain east of Aachen, and in the lowlands of the Netherlands might symbolize something more than determination in defense of the homeland. They did appreciate that Hitler had achieved remarkable rebuilding on the western front and had even managed to create a panzer reserve. Yet even though Field Marshal Montgomery deemed the failure of the November offensive to reach the Rhine a "strategic reverse"—confirmation of what he considered the error of failing to put overwhelming strength behind the 21st Army Group—and even though few looked for a sudden end of the war, nobody saw in the stalwart German stand any grand design that might threaten the integrity of the Allied armies.

Chapter Twenty-Two – Out of the Fog, Night, and Snow

Hitler on September 16 had revealed for the first time something that had been festering in his mind since at least mid-August. He did it following a daily situation conference in the Wolf's Lair, his spartan headquarters in East Prussia. Present were members of the household military staff, including the head of the Armed Forces High Command, Wilhelm Keitel, and the chief of the OKW planning Staff, General Jodl.[167]

"I have just made a momentous decision," the *Fuehrer* announced. "I shall go over to the counterattack, that is to say"—he gestured at a map unrolled before him—"here, out of the Ardennes, with the objective—Antwerp."[168]

As the *Fuehrer* began to outline his plan, his audience sat in stunned silence, shocked that their leader could yet see such hope in the adversity

---

[167] The definitive work on the counteroffensive is by my former colleague and mentor, Hugh M. Cole. I have drawn extensively on this official history: Cole, *The Ardennes: Battle of the Bulge*. See also Pogue, *The Supreme Command* (particularly for the intelligence failure); John Toland, *Battle: The Story of the Bulge* (New York, 1959); Robert Merriam, *Dark December* (Chicago, 1947), which was done quite early and thus must be used with care; Charles V. P. von Luttichau, "The German Counteroffensive in the Ardennes," in Greenfield, ed., *Command Decisions*; Craven and Cate, eds., *ARGUMENT to V-E Day*; S. L. A. Marshall, *Bastogne: The First Eight Days* (Washington, 1946); Fred MacKenzie, *The Men of Bastogne* (New York, 1968); Baldwin, *Battles Lost and Won*; and one of the best of the unofficial U.S. unit histories to emerge from the war, Leonard Rapport and Arthur Northwood, *Rendezvous with Destiny, A History of the 101st Airborne Division* (Washington, 1948). John S. D. Eisenhower's excellent work, *The Bitter Woods* (New York, 1969), appeared too late for me to use.

[168] Cole, *The Ardennes*, p. 2.

that pressed from all sides upon the Third Reich. The defeat in Normandy, the withdrawal from southern France, the retreat to the *Westwall*—these were but part of a broad pattern. In Italy the fighting centered in the northern Apennines, dangerously close to the entrance to the verdant Po valley. In the east, Russian armies had gained the frontier of East Prussia and crossed half of Poland. Rumania and Bulgaria had hastened to join the side of the victorious Red Army, necessitating German withdrawal from Greece, and Finland had pulled out of the war. The historical parallel with the defections that had helped speed the end in World War I was hardly to be missed.

To Hitler, the defections and the Allied and Soviet victories were but flitting scenes that had little to do with the climax to come. German industry was much alive, despite the mounting tonnage of Allied bombs; and morale on the home front was firm. The defeats, and the defections arising from them, were to be laid to high officers who, if not traitorous, were at least insufficiently devoted to the ideals of National Socialism. With those weaklings eliminated by the purge that followed the attack on the *Fuehrer*'s life, German troops might emulate the glorious victories of the past.

This belief drew support from juggled figures on production and manpower that the sycophants around Hitler constantly fed him, to his obvious delight. Had not Frederick the Great, whose portrait hung behind the desk in Hitler's study, faced superior forces converging on his kingdom in the Seven Years' War? And had not Frederick, by defeating his enemies in detail, hung on until the historical accident of the death of the Czarina had split the coalition opposing him? The coalition had failed to present a solid front in the face of defeats to individual members. Would the strange alliance of capitalism and bolshevism hold up any better?

Armed with the statistics he loved and unchallenged by a staff long housebroken, Hitler saw himself the head of a still powerful army which, if not strong enough to prevail simultaneously in the field against foes from east and west, still was sufficiently endowed to deal one or the other such a blow as to force both to question the utility of the alliance. Because the industry of the Ruhr was vital to the German war economy, because the Western Allies possessed no such vast numbers as did the Russians, and because the Western Alliance itself displayed some weaknesses at the seams, Hitler fixed his attention on the west.

As Hitler failed to consult his military leaders in choosing the west for his counterstroke, so he alone chose the Ardennes as the specific site. Yet he had justification other than intuition. Blows through the Ardennes had taken opposing armies by surprise in 1914 and again in 1940. So restrictive is the terrain that a few divisions can do the work of many, and the forested Eifel region adjoining the Ardennes afforded ideal concealment for German buildup.

More important, from the jumpoff line to a worthwhile strategic objective—the port of Antwerp—the distance was reasonable, just over one hundred miles as the Messerschmitt flies. A quick thrust to Antwerp would trap the entire troop commitment of one of the Allies, the British—a prize almost as alluring as that offered in the 1940 sweep to Dunkirk. Even if eliminating the 21st Army Group and those Americans located north of the point of penetration failed to bring disaster to the Western Alliance, it would at least erase the immediate threat to the Ruhr, whereupon the Germans might draw from the west to reinforce the east.

As in 1914 and 1940, so in 1944 secrecy was basic to the German plan. While Jodl and his planning staff drew up the plan, Gerd von Rundstedt, the man who would have to execute it, was left to believe as firmly as Allied intelligence officers in a general order issued by Keitel to the effect that no counteroffensive was possible, that all resources would have to be committed to passive defense of the fatherland. It was late in October, after Aachen had fallen, before the first word of Hitler's venture was released to Rundstedt, brought direct from the Wolf's Lair by Rundstedt's Chief of Staff, whom Hitler placed under penalty of death should word of the plan leak out.

The plan appalled Rundstedt. Although Hitler's promises were impressive—ample fuel and ammunition, 30 divisions, and 1,500 fighter planes, including 100 new jets—the plan seemed far too ambitious. Nine of the divisions, for example, would have to be drawn from the impoverished western front itself. To hold long enough along the frontier for the counterattacking troops to get ready was problem enough. Even if that problem was solved successfully, to expect to drive beyond the Meuse all the way to Antwerp without encountering an effective Allied riposte was to accord to Allied commanders a languor and a dearth of resources they had yet to exhibit. About all Hitler's plan could be expected to achieve was a salient or a bulge in the line—costly, indecisive, like those Ludendorff had created during the Great War.

Rundstedt was nevertheless in a poor position to remonstrate against his *Fuehrer*'s design. Although he had survived disfavor to return to high command, he received from Hitler and his entourage nothing more than the correct treatment due a venerable soldier. Relations between Rundstedt and his chief subordinate, the ardent Nazi, Field Marshal Model, whose *Army Group B* would be charged with the assault, were not much better. Model was considerably younger than Rundstedt and stood high in Hitler's fickle favor; his step down from top command in the west was attributable only to the *Fuehrer*'s desire to provide a figurehead around whom the troops might rally.

It was with considerable relief that Rundstedt learned that Model shared his misgivings about the plan. ("This damned thing hasn't a leg to stand on," said Model.[169]) While differing in detail, both commanders leaned toward a counteroffensive aimed at an objective considerably scaled down from the grand goal of Antwerp. Assuming the promised reinforcements, they deemed they would have the strength to cut off the fourteen American divisions that were attacking in the vicinity of Aachen, and would take in the process a growing American supply complex in eastern Belgium at Liège. That was all.

A modified plan as worked out by Rundstedt and Model drew some support at the top, from the head of the OKW planning staff, Jodl. To implement Hitler's grand plan, Jodl opined, divisions would have to be pulled from the eastern front, and the Third Reich turned into a fortress under total mobilization and martial law. Otherwise, what became known as the "Small Solution"—cutting off the American troops around Aachen—should prevail.

With a tact designed to avoid ruffling the *Fuehrer*, Jodl presented this view, but Hitler declined to face the issue. While unable to bring himself to order the stern measures that Jodl proposed, he saw no decision in the Small Solution and adhered stubbornly to the goal of Antwerp. Even as German troops were massing in the Eifel, Rundstedt and Model continued to argue in one form or another for the Small Solution, even eliciting support from two whom Hitler designated to lead the spearhead armies in the Ardennes: "Little" Manteuffel, the diminutive panzer general with the big reputation, and Gencraloberst der Waffen-SS Josef ("Sepp")

---

[169] Toland, *Battle: The Story of the Bulge*, p. 16.

Dietrich, an ardent Nazi who briefly had commanded *Panzer Group West* in France. To no avail.

In the final version of the operations order for the counteroffensive, the scope and ultimate objective remained just as Hitler had outlined them that day back in September when he had gestured at the map and first revealed his intentions:

"Here, out of the Ardennes, with the objective—Antwerp."

Hitler's final plan even retained the deceptive code name he had given it from the first: *WACHT AM RHEIN* ("Watch on the Rhine"). That fitted it neatly to a cover plan, also devised personally by the *Fuehrer*, to give verisimilitude to Keitel's general order for all German forces to stand on the defensive for the impending showdown in the west.

While the main buildup for the counteroffensive occurred amid the forests of the Eifel in strictest secrecy, panzer divisions under the *Sixth Panzer Army* staged a second buildup in the north, ostensibly aimed at countering the coming American drive eastward from Aachen. There the Germans intentionally bungled their security, parading their preparations before the hungry eyes of Allied intelligence. Only at the last minute would the panzer divisions slip away to join the true buildup in the Eifel. Lest some indication leak out of the assembly in the Eifel, the word was that a few depleted divisions were being readied there for use against the flank of the impending American penetration.

To conceal the preparations in the Eifel, the Germans displayed a mastery of the art of strategic surprise already demonstrated in 1870, in 1914, in the offensive against the Chemin des Dames in 1918, and again in 1940. For long weeks no one but Hitler's personal staff, plus Rundstedt, Model, and four officers from each of their staffs, was let in on the secret, while all others accepted as gospel the same cover arranged for Allied eyes. Orders and radio and telephone traffic reiterated details about the coming defensive battle, while the real exchanges dealing with preparations for the counteroffensive were passed by liaison officers who were closely tailed by Gestapo agents. Everyone admitted to the plan had to sign a sworn statement accepting the death penalty for any personal breach of security, a punishment none doubted that Hitler would exact on the slightest provocation.

Some generals got their briefing from Hitler himself under

humiliating security conditions. "We were all stripped of our weapons and briefcases..." recalled the panzer division commander Fritz Bayerlein, "[and] led between a double row of SS troops into a deep bunker."[170] While the *Fuehrer*, looking old and broken, his hand shaking, lectured them for two hours, an armed SS guard stood behind each chair, glowering with a ferocity that made Bayerlein fear to reach for his handkerchief.

In the Eifel nobody moved except by night. Special security detachments prowled in search of any who violated camouflage discipline. Patrolling on the existing front line was restricted to the most trusted soldiers. Alsatians and other foreigners serving in forward divisions were withdrawn lest some malcontent go over to the enemy with news of the buildup. No increase in artillery fires above the norm was permitted. Since it was impossible to conceal all necessary road improvements, troops in the false assembly area to the north staged even more extensive improvements. Not until a week before the target date were corps and division commanders told their assignments, and not until the night before the attack did the troops learn what they were about to do.

Bad weather for several days preceding the attack, to allow for the final concentration, was integral to the German plan. On the basis of meteorological prognostications Hitler first set November 25 as the target date, but that allowed far too little time for the formidable array of essential preparations—raising new divisions, refitting the old, strengthening rail bridges over the Rhine, keeping rail traffic moving despite Allied air attacks, shifting troops from as far away as East Prussia, moving and concealing thousands of tons of ammunition, fuel, other supplies.

Hitler next set the date for December 10, but that, too, was scrapped because preparations were incomplete. On the eleventh he designated December 15, then the next day changed it to the sixteenth. Barring the advent of good flying weather which would benefit Allied planes, that date would stand.

Rail movement of 13 infantry and 7 armored divisions scheduled for the initial assault had almost been completed by December 11, although reserve divisions that would eventually bring the total to 25 had yet to arrive. The armored divisions had about 970 tanks and armored assault

---

[170] Wilmot, *The Struggle for Europe*, pp. 577-78.

guns, with another 450 in reserve. Some 1,900 artillery pieces, including rocket launchers, stood in support.

However formidable the attacking force, it fell short by at least five divisions of what Hitler originally had envisioned. It was short, too, in aircraft, with 1,000 at most available at the start. It could not compare with the juggernauts the Germans had employed in earlier campaigns—2,500 tanks, for example, in the triumphant push to the sea in 1940. It was a force lacking in other ways as well—in motor transport, in spare parts, in signal and engineer equipment, in ammunition and fuel reserves. And the troops themselves, for all the enthusiasm that might seize them as they moved again to the offensive, were in no way equal to the men who had marched in 1940.

A final, rigidly controlled movement to assault positions began the night of December 13. Artillery and tanks crawled forward over roads strewn with straw to deaden the sound, while planes flew low to dull the ears of American listening posts. For all the bitter December cold, only charcoal fires were allowed.

Shortly before H hour, 5:30 A.M. on a dark, misty December 16, all on the German side was as ready as improvisation and the psychotic drive of Hitler could make it.

A few hundred yards to the west, American positions were comfortingly quiet.

On the sixty-mile front destined for assault, from the picturesque town of Monschau in the north—in pre-war years a haven for honeymooners—to the medieval streets of the Luxembourg town of Echternach in the south, only six American divisions held the line in what was at once the nursery and the old folks' home of the American command. There in beautiful but militarily difficult country Omar Bradley kept the line thin in order to free troops for the offensives under way to north and south. The units holding the line either were new to combat or needed a rest after rigorous fighting in places like the Huertgen Forest. Only in the extreme north, near Monschau, was there any appreciable concentration of troops. There on December 13 an infantry division had attacked through the snow-draped lines of another division in belated recognition of the importance of the Roer River dams.

The rest of the front was the responsibility of the VIII Corps under

Troy Middleton. It ran from the Losheim Gap, 15 miles southeast of Monschau—whence a panzer division commanded by Erwin Rommel had dashed in 1940 to the Meuse—southward along a dominant ridge-line inside the German frontier, the Schnee Eifel, thence behind the meandering little Our and Sauer rivers which mark the border between Germany and Luxembourg.

Held by two regiments of the 106th Infantry Division, newly arrived from the United States, the Schnee Eifel was a strong position but peculiarly susceptible because of passes at either end, especially the historic *débouché* at the north end, the Losheim Gap. Like other divisions on the elongated front, the 106th had to man more than twenty miles of twisting defensive lines, so that sometimes only scattered outposts were available to defend even critical sectors. Only an attached cavalry squadron, for example, equipped with feeble light tanks and armored cars, stood in the way of German egress from the Losheim Gap.

For all the vulnerability of the troops on the Schnee Eifel and of other thinly stretched units farther south, few on the American side saw any pressing danger. Through October, November, and the early days of December nothing had occurred to indicate that the Germans were any more anxious to disturb the relative quiet of the Ardennes than were their adversaries. American and British intelligence alike had nibbled with pleasure at the bait the Germans had dangled in the staged assembly of the *Sixth Panzer Army* north of the Ardennes. Although aerial reconnaissance had detected a growing buildup west of the Rhine, nobody saw it as anything more than a normal reaction to the American offensives north and south of the Ardennes. Such supplies and troops as showed up in the Eifel itself, intelligence officers deemed to be en route north or south to the threatened sectors. They "looked in a mirror for the enemy and [saw] there only the reflection of their own intentions."[171]

Even the tenacious defense the Germans mounted through the fall of 1944, the Allies discounted as a futile thing. "It is now certain," wrote the 12th Army Group's intelligence officer as late as December 12, "that attrition is steadily sapping the strength of German forces...and that the crust of defenses is thinner, more brittle and more vulnerable than

---

[171] Cole, *The Ardennes*, p. 63.

it appears on our G-2 maps or to the troops in the line."[172] Grandiose reports of destruction by the air forces reinforced the view. The fact that an experienced, rational soldier like Field Marshal von Rundstedt was again in command fed a belief that the defense would continue according to sane, accepted canons of the military art; that is, they would gradually fall back, with appropriate local counterattacks, to a final defense of the moat of the Rhine.

That was reckoning without the fact that the true commander was not Rundstedt but Adolf Hitler.

Some voices of caution were raised about the Ardennes. Eisenhower and Bradley themselves looked on the thinning of the line there as a "calculated risk."[173] Toward the end of November, General Eisenhower's Chief of Intelligence, the Britisher, General Strong, warned that the enemy might use his reforming *Fifth* and *Sixth Panzer Armies* for a spoiling attack in the Ardennes. In a report issued five days before the Germans were to strike, Courtney Hodges' G-2, Colonel Monk Dickson, noted some indication of buildup in the Eifel, high morale among recently captured prisoners, and a captured order asking German soldiers who spoke "the American dialect" to report for special training.[174]

Yet in neither case was the warning strong enough or backed with sufficient evidence to prompt American commanders to desist from their offensives and shift troops into the Ardennes. Dickson himself, for example, saw no reason to cancel a scheduled leave in Paris. To skitter and react with nervous defensive moves to every possibility open to the enemy was to surrender all initiative.

From the Ardennes itself during the last days two divisions reported noise of heavy vehicular traffic behind German lines; but one division discounted its own reports as evidence of no more than routine relief of units, and so inexperienced was the other, the 106th, that nobody attached particular import to its accounts. Four prisoners captured on

---

[172] Pogue, *The Supreme Command*, p. 369, quoting 12th Army Group Intelligence Summary of December 12, 1944.

[173] Dwight D. Eisenhower, *Report by the Supreme Commander to the Combined Chiefs of Staff on the Operations in Europe of the Allied Expeditionary Force, 6 June 1944 to 8 May 1945* (Washington, 1946), p. 75.

[174] Pogue, *The Supreme Command*, p. 367.

December 15 claimed that fresh troops were entering the line as prelude to a big attack to come, if not on December 16 or 17, then certainly before Christmas. Yet only one prisoner made any serious impression on his interrogators. Badly wounded, he was so drugged by morphine that additional questioning had to be postponed.

One final incident might have given away the elaborate German deception. On the fourteenth, a Luxembourg woman crossed into American lines from the Eifel. Telling of woods jammed with German vehicles and equipment, she so impressed her interrogators that they sent her on to headquarters of the First Army for further questioning.

She arrived there during the day of December 16. That was too late.

As finally evolved, Hitler's plan for the counteroffensive entrusted the main effort to the *Sixth Panzer Army*, commanded by "Sepp" Dietrich, whose four SS panzer divisions represented the steel heart of the attacking force. A hard-drinking crony of Hitler's since the days of the Munich *Putsch*, Dietrich possessed little other than his relationship with the *Fuehrer* to qualify him for military command—he was ex-sergeant, ex-butcher, ex-street brawler—but he had a capable Chief of Staff who spared him the more egregious errors. Dietrich was to plunge into the Ardennes generally between Monschau and St. Vith—the latter a Belgian road and rail center in the shadow of the Schnee Eifel—to cross the Meuse on both sides of Liège, and to wheel northeast to gain the Dutch-Belgian border east of Antwerp. The hope was that Dietrich's forces could reach the Meuse during the first twenty-four hours, or, at the latest, in forty-eight.

Attacking on Dietrich's left, through and south of St. Vith, Manteuffel's *Fifth Panzer Army* was to jump the Meuse on either side of the great bend of the river at Namur, and then drive on Brussels and Antwerp. Once past the Meuse, Manteuffel was to protect Dietrich's left flank. The job of flank protection in early stages up to the Meuse fell to the *Seventh Army*, resurrected from the Normandy débâcle and commanded by General der Panzertruppen Erich Brandenberger, a bald, bespectacled, pot-bellied officer who had demonstrated considerable dexterity through the fall campaign in shifting units to points of crisis.

The Germans were employing 200,000 men in the opening assault against perhaps 83,000 Americans, thus bringing to bear a superiority in manpower of about 3 to 1 all along the line, 6 to 1 at points of concentration. At the start they would possess a superiority in tanks of 2 to 1.

Nobody specified a plan of campaign once Antwerp fell, other than that the caretaker force on the Aachen front, the *Fifteenth Army*, was to mount a supporting attack; and Hitler spoke grandly of a complementary counteroffensive in Alsace. Rundstedt and his top subordinates, for their part, never really expected to get as far as Antwerp.

To take the place of the "fifth column" of Nazi sympathizers and pseudo-tourists who had spread havoc in the foe's ranks in the 1940 campaign, Hitler had ordered the creation of a special brigade under Otto Skorzeny, who had rescued Mussolini. The brigade was to have included only those soldiers who spoke "the American dialect," but in the end only 150 out of a total force of 2,000 so qualified. Although Hitler intended the entire force to be outfitted with captured American uniforms, weapons, and vehicles, that proved absurdly ambitious with the material on hand.

Skorzeny's brigade was supposed to speed the *Sixth Panzer Army* across the Meuse by seizing bridges with disguised raiding parties and by spreading confusion with sabotage and rumor. A battalion of paratroopers was to assist by dropping astride high marshland behind Monschau and blocking American reinforcement along a lone highway leading south through the marshes from Aachen.

As it turned out, only a handful of Skorzeny's disguised troops got behind American lines, there to do little damage other than to create an exaggerated impression of their numbers and to persuade American sentries that no one should pass without proper response to ridiculous queries on such Americana as baseball, Mickey Mouse, and the contemporary husbands of female film stars. As for the paratroopers, they were prevented from jumping the night of December 15 for the absurd reason that trucks assigned to carry them to war-weary *Junkers* transport planes lacked gasoline. Not until two nights later did even a small portion of the paratroopers execute a badly scattered jump; they were soon rounded up by American patrols—a pitiful farewell performance for a once-proud arm of the *Wehrmacht*.

Yet those and other German shortcomings were scarcely apparent along the extended American line in the Ardennes before dawn on December 16 when German artillery spoke with deep-throated rumble and searchlights bouncing their beams off low-hanging clouds turned the night to twilight.

Out of their bunks in sandbagged log huts or in cellars of requisitioned houses, American troops tumbled in startled disbelief.

It was bitter cold in the Ardennes that morning, the atmosphere thick with the wet breath of winter. Six inches of snow covered the ground. Artillery shells, irregularly but constantly, seemed to stir the tops of tall fir trees with their passing. Ugly black splotches in the snow told where shells had hit. High overhead occasional V-1 buzz bombs spat fire and sound from their tails with eerie effect. In holes dug painfully in frozen ground, men huddled for protection.

First came the German infantry, plowing, like men possessed, through the snow in gray-green greatcoats and duck-billed caps. The order had come from the *Fuehrer* himself: "Forward to and over the Meuse!"[175] Behind them the tanks, great, lumbering monsters which to the waiting Americans appeared to stick the muzzles of their big guns almost inside a man's foxhole before they fired. Everywhere the thick crump, crump of exploding artillery and mortars, the sputter of machine guns, the crack of rifles.

In the north, near Monschau, men of the 99th Infantry Division had held their overextended positions on the fringe of a dense fir forest along the boundary between Belgium and Germany for two months; but other than to repulse an occasional enemy patrol or to patrol themselves, they had seen no action. Yet their training had been good, and they had had time to dig deep, to ring foxholes and squad huts with barbed wire and mines, to coordinate machine guns, mortars, and artillery in final protective fires that could be quickly and systematically called down. Inexperienced, they looked on the sudden onslaught as merely predictable German response to the attack of the veteran 2d Division through the left portion of their lines toward the Roer River dams.

It was actually the main effort of the German counteroffensive—"Sepp" Dietrich's attempt to cross the Meuse on both sides of Liège. While an infantry corps secured the corner at Monschau, a panzer corps was to make the penetration a few miles to the south. In a doctrinal argument Field Marshal Model had insisted over Dietrich's objections that the infantry in the panzer corps make the actual breakthrough; only then were two SS

[175] Cole, *The Ardennes,* p. 75.

panzer divisions to add the weight of armor, followed in turn by a third corps with two more panzer divisions. Once past the American forward line along the international boundary, the troops had to get over or around the south flank of the Elsenborn Ridge, a stretch of high ground lying behind a former Belgian military training center near the border town of Elsenborn. From there, the prediction was for a swift drive along four major highways to the Meuse.

However they misinterpreted the goal of the German attack, the green but determined troops of the 99th Division did damage to the plan on the first day. So furious was their riposte that the panzer divisions in the rear early sent some of their tanks to try to get the infantry through. At a snow-encrusted crossroads, vital to the Germans for access to roads leading west, American infantry held despite depressing losses. Infantry companies pushed from their positions rallied around their battalion command posts. As an early winter twilight descended, the situation was desperate enough from the American viewpoint for the corps commander to order the attacking 2d Division to desist and send its reserve regiment to back up the 99th, but the Germans were still a long way from the Meuse.

The men of the 99th had held in a manner to elicit grudging admiration from their adversary, but weak cavalry squadrons screening a two-mile gap between the 99th and the 106th Division to the south had less success. Their thin line gave. As night came, a task force of the *1st SS Panzer Division* under Lieutenant-Colonel Joachim Peiper poured through. To American commanders yet unaware of the grand German design, it came as a sharp surprise that the German armor did not turn to the north to envelop the 2d and 99th Divisions but continued westward on roads bypassing the Elsenborn Ridge.

The fighting erupted with renewed fury the second day, December 17, so that by late afternoon the men of the 99th, for all their valiant stand, were routed. The Germans might have had free access to the Elsenborn Ridge and the other roads leading west had not Major General Walter Robertson moved to extricate his 2d Division from the attack on the Roer dams and re-formed it in front of the ridge. Robertson personally reconnoitered a trail and set his engineers to improving it to take the place of a division supply route that Joachim Peiper's tanks had cut.

Robertson's division executed a highly complex maneuver that probably few but an experienced division like the 2d could have pulled off.

Protected by the disintegrating screen of the 99th Division and its own reserve regiment, the 2d Division in the face of the enemy executed the child's maneuver of skinning the cat, by pulling its most advanced battalions from the attack on the Roer dams through others in the rear. Robertson himself, who at fifty-six was old for division command, was full on the scene, here nabbing a rifle company from a withdrawing column to meet a fresh German threat, there sending a platoon of tank destroyers to reinforce infantry about to be overrun by tanks. The battalions then wheeled from column to organize a defensive line in the darkness under intense enemy attack.

By that time some inkling, but not all, of the magnitude of the German attack was filtering through to higher American command. Robertson's orders were to hold in front of the Elsenborn Ridge while remnants of the 99th Division passed through; then he was to break away and re-form for defense of the ridge.

It was a do-or-die battle, for word spread early through the 2d Division—as only word can spread among soldiers—that SS troops were butchering American prisoners.

For two days and nights the fight raged in and around two villages barring access to the Elsenborn Ridge. German tanks broke through; American infantrymen hunted them down with bazookas. German infantrymen in their turn stalked American tanks and tank destroyers. In those few moments when snow clouds briefly cleared, German planes bombed and strafed—a rare experience for most of the American troops. Through it all the men of the 2d Division had to be alert for hundreds of the survivors of the 99th Division who were still trying to make their way into friendly lines. From house to house, from wall to wall, along muddy streets and down narrow alleys, the fight eddied. Artillery from both sides plowed the ground, demolished the houses.

As the fight progressed, message after message from higher German commanders ordered "Sepp" Dietrich, in terms often violent, to break through this troublesome mêlée, to get on with the main effort "to and over the Meuse." Poor Dietrich! He was using two *volks* grenadier divisions and an entire SS panzer division, yet it was futile, futile.

Even an attempt the night of December 18 to bypass the opposition to the south failed, for the Americans had rushed in a fresh regiment that had been resting behind the lines. After midnight of December 19 the men of the 2d Division executed a carefully planned withdrawal from the villages in front of the Elsenborn Ridge onto the ridge itself, there to find what was left of the 99th Division reorganized, plus two fresh infantry divisions and an impressive grouping of big corps artillery pieces.

Aided by a 99th Division that had refused to admit inexperience and the odds, men of the 2d Division had achieved much the same as had others wearing the big Indianhead shoulder patch a quarter-century before on the road from Château-Thierry to Paris: in a brutal four-day fight they had jammed the north shoulder of what would become known as the "bulge." They had denied the vital road network in the north. Together with the 99th, the 2d Division had incurred heavy casualties—probably a total of six thousand, including those sent to hospitals by trench foot and respiratory diseases in the bitter cold and snow. Yet in the process the two units had dealt heavy losses to three German divisions and made imperative a shift in the enemy's main effort. They had "knocked a part of Hitler's personal operations plan into a cocked hat."[176]

On the south shoulder of the German attacking force, Erich Brandenberger's *Seventh Army*, with a strength of but four infantry divisions, a smattering of tanks, and a handful of assault guns, played the role of poor country cousin. Even so, the Germans far outnumbered the American defenders: an infantry regiment each of the 4th and 28th Divisions, both severely mauled in the Huertgen Forest, and in between a battalion of armored infantrymen of General Middleton's corps reserve, the newly arrived 9th Armored Division, which was serving a brief stint in the line as part of a rotation plan to give the untested men battle experience under untrying conditions.

Opposite Echternach and north of the town, all four of Brandenbergers divisions were to make penetrations, then one by one to peel off and face southward to protect the flank of the counteroffensive. With a division on the attack confronting not quite two battalions on the defense, the assignment appeared relatively easy, for all Brandenbergers dearth of armor, shortage of bridging equipment, and dependence on the horse for drawing divisional artillery. It failed to turn out that way.

Getting across the river that marked the front line—in the north the Our, farther south the Sauer—was in itself difficult; for the rivers,

---

[176] Ibid., p. 135.

though small, run swift in the wet Ardennes winter, and American artillery commanded the crossing sites. Yet so thin was the American line—no more than company and platoon strong points in villages and farmhouses—that once across the river, even limited numbers of Germans could readily penetrate the open spaces in between.

Taking the strong points was another matter.

In a cluster of stone farm buildings twenty-one men from the 4th Division held out for four days against overwhelming odds. In a tourist hotel that in happier times advertised *confort moderne* in *situation isolée*, some sixty men resisted for five days, leaving at last only under orders and with regret on the part of the lieutenant in command that he had forbidden his men to sample the hotel's cache of wines and liquors. In Echternach, surrounded and cruelly besieged, a reinforced company also held for five days before the surviving 122 men, all efforts to rescue them having failed, at last surrendered.

The Germans of the *Seventh Army* made their most impressive gains in the north where General Brandenberger employed the bulk of such tanks and assault guns as he possessed against the regiment of the 28th Division behind the Our River. For two days men of the American regiment held their foe to minor gains, upsetting the German timetable; but on the night of the seventeenth German engineers at last put in a bridge across the Our, enabling tanks and assault guns to cross.

As darkness fell on the third day, the American commander reported only three choices open to him: to withdraw far to the west, to peel back to the southwest, or to stand and die. Afforded the choice himself, he elected to swing back to the southwest to tie in with the embattled armored infantrymen from the 9th Armored Division, who by that time had been reinforced by tanks to constitute a combat command. However reasonable the choice, it left the way open for Brandenberger's north wing to plunge on westward in the direction of the Meuse.

One reason for the American regiment's peril was the plight of the rest of the 28th Division, full in the path of the German *Fifth Panzer Army* a few miles farther north. Another was the general shortage of American reserves in the Ardennes and the priorities that determined where such as were available would be employed.

On December 17 a combat command of armor, sent scurrying northward from Patton's Third Army, arrived on the scene. Concerned lest the

Germans turn the southern prong of their penetration southward against Luxembourg City—not only the capital of Luxembourg but also site of the headquarters of the Ninth Air Force and of Bradley's 12th Army Group—General Middleton directed the armor to help the 4th Division around Echternach to stall the German south wing.

By nightfall of the nineteenth, the German south wing, like the north wing at Elsenborn Ridge, was jammed.

Forming the center of the German thrust, Hasso von Manteuffel's *Fifth Panzer Army* was to strike the inexperienced 106th Division on and south of the Schnee Eifel and the other two tired, depleted regiments of the 28th ("bloody bucket") Division farther south. Manteuffel had a lot else going for him, including six infantry and three panzer divisions.

On the way to the Meuse, Manteuffel's army, in spite of its status as second in importance to Dietrich's *Sixth*, anticipated two special prizes: the road and rail center of St. Vith, close behind the Schnee Eifel; and the town of Bastogne, twenty miles beyond the German frontier, almost in the geographical center of the Ardennes. Bastogne was important because it pulls together a number of good roads, then spits them out in various directions, including the northwest, the direction of Antwerp. Other than those roads in the north assigned to the *Sixth Panzer Army* and those controlled at Bastogne, the grain of the road network in the Ardennes tends southwest, where the Germans had gone in 1914 and 1940, but not where they wanted to go in 1944.

Manteuffel gained the same surprise as the others. Also like the others, he failed either to cross the Our or to go around the Schnee Eifel with the speed intended.

The northern pincers enveloping the Sehnee Eifel got through the Losheim Gap quickly enough, roughly pushing aside a lone American cavalry group which was capable of little more than raising the alarm, and then cut sharply south to come in on the service troops and artillery supporting the American regiments on the Schnce Eifel. Yet no sudden, deep thrust westward followed the penetration, as happened a scant two miles to the north where Peiper's tanks of the *1st SS Panzer Division* broke through; for Manteuffel had positioned no armor in this sector since the immediate goal was limited: to envelop the Schnee Eifel and take St. Vith.

The southern pincers had even less apparent success, failing to get much more than a mile beyond the line of departure; but that was enough to push in weak outposts that the Americans depended upon to maintain contact between the two regiments on the Schnee Eifel and a third farther south. Furthermore, Manteuffel had an entire *volks* grenadier division poised to exploit that thin seam early on the second day.

The 106th Division took comfort—undue comfort—from the fact that little ground other than that facing the Losheim Gap had changed hands during the day. A more experienced commander and staff might have better fathomed the depth of the threat facing them.

Having been told by General Middleton to use his discretion about withdrawing the regiments from the exposed Schnee Eifel, the 106th Division commander, Major General Alan W. Jones, elected to leave them in place. (His son was a platoon leader in one of the regiments.) Given a combat command of the corps reserve, Jones sent it not to the Losheim Gap but to the seam between regiments south of the Schnee Eifel, this on Middleton's word that a combat command of another armored division, the 7th, was to arrive from the Ninth Army early the next morning. Yet that combat command had to travel some sixty miles under blackout conditions, over snow-slick roads, and against a tide of fleeing refugees and rear echelon units—hospitals, corps artillery, ordnance shops, laundry companies, the chaff that inevitably clogs the roads when military reverse occurs. It would be not dawn but dark on the seventeenth before even the first vehicles of that combat command reached St. Vith.

The decisions by the inexperienced Jones doomed the two regiments on the Schnee Eifel and their supporting troops, altogether some eight thousand men. Two days later, on December 19, they surrendered—the most serious reverse incurred by American arms in the war against Germany.

In a saga of raw courage and determination, a quickly fashioned horse-shoe-shaped defense around St. Vith held out for another two days, until December 21, like the Elsenborn Ridge a major impediment in the path of the counteroffensive. Manteuffel had intended to take St. Vith with its vital roads by the afternoon of the second day. He did not get it until the fifth day.

A few miles to the south of the Schnee Eifel the *Fifth Panzer Army's* main force, composed of two panzer corps, struck two depleted regiments of the 28th Division. It should have been no contest, but the bone-weary American infantry refused to buckle under the weight of tanks or numbers.

Since no preliminary artillery preparation was directed against the northern regiment, the American infantrymen could only wonder what the pyrotechnics to the north and south meant. The coming of daylight revealed the answer: Manteuffel was borrowing a page from the "Hutier tactics" of World War I to sneak in behind widely spaced positions and get at bridges over the Our River, leaving others who came later to take out the strong points. Yet because even the Americans behind the line—artillerymen, anti-aircraft gunners, cooks, clerks—refused to panic, the stratagem faltered. As night fell on the first day, the men of the American regiment still held their original positions east of the Our, though with the certain knowledge born of experience that even rougher blows were in store. Those blows came and eventually forced the regiment to peel away from the rest of the 28th Division and move back to the north to form a part of the horseshoe defense of St. Vith; but the Germans paid dearly in the process.

The next of the 28th Division's regiments in line to the south held a sector even more skeletal than did the regiments to the north and further south. The positions were nothing more than company outposts in villages lying west of the Our astride a broad ridgeline topped by a highway that men familiar with the Virginia Appalachians had christened the "Skyline Drive." Behind the ridgeline the valley of the little Clerf River provided the Luxembourg version of the Shenandoah, while up to two miles of patrol-contested no-man's-land lay between the ridge-top road and the deep cut of the Our.

German infantry infiltrated into the no-man's-land before the big guns at 5:30 A.M. delivered their sudden thunder. All day long the fight raged in and around the villages, but it was primarily an infantry duel supported by artillery. The Germans had yet to put in bridges over the Our to add the weight of a panzer division, and it was early afternoon before the American commander, Major General Norman D. ("Dutch") Cota, could get his attached tank battalion forward from a depot where crewmen had been repairing damage incurred in the Huertgen Forest.

Against overwhelming odds Cota's infantry held the first day, even though often surrounded, but when German engineers threw bridges over the Our during the night, defeat in the villages astride the "Skyline Drive" became inevitable. So it was, too, for stragglers wearing the "bloody bucket" shoulder patch, who gathered around the regimental headquarters beside the Clerf River in the town of Clerf, there to give battle astride a main highway leading west to Bastogne.

No matter how inevitable the defeat at Clerf, the little cluster of Americans in the town refused all day and into the night of December 17 to accept it. From an ancient château commanding the town's main bridge and from close-packed masonry houses lining narrow, winding streets, they fought until German tanks arrived in strength not to be denied. After more than forty-eight hours of battle Manteuffel's left panzer corps was at last over the "Skyline Drive" and the Clerf, and the defending American regiment was all but destroyed, but the goal of Bastogne was still fifteen miles away.

Chapter Twenty-Three – The Drive for the Meuse

The battle for the Elsenborn Ridge did not decide the outcome of the counteroffensive in the Ardennes. Nor did the fights for the Schnee Eifel, for St. Vith, for the "Skyline Drive" and Clerf, for the Sauer River crossings and Echternach; but taken together those opening engagements—bitter, costly to both sides—drew much of the sting from the Germans' tactical and strategic surprise and denied Rundstedt the quick momentum he required.

The stand along the forward line in the Ardennes also afforded time for Troy Middleton to dispose his reserves, however meager, and contribute further to German delay. In addition to the combat command of the 9th Armored Division sent to St. Vith and another that already was in the line alongside the 4th Division, Middleton sent the third combat command to back up the center of the 28th Division behind Clerf and to bar the main highway to Bastogne. Also available were a few engineer battalions that Middleton turned from road building to reinforcing various threatened sectors.

There were other reserves, though not formally designated as such, that also had an impact: a kind of battlefield residue made up of head-quarters companies, supply and service troops, and stragglers filtering back from defeat. Here a handful of bedraggled infantrymen who tire of flight and at the fringe of a woods turn to set up a machine gun, open fire, and force a German column to deploy, to waste precious minutes, even hours. Elsewhere a group of ordnance mechanics manning a tank pulled from a repair shop holds up German tanks long enough for engineers to demolish a bridge. A sawmill company turns from its assigned task to fell a band of trees across a road. A major orders his men to pour gasoline into a deep cut in the road and set it aflame to deny German tanks access to a big gasoline depot. Trapped far behind German columns, a lieutenant constitutes himself a one-man guerrilla army to prey on German traffic until at last a German machine gun cuts him down. A captured nurse entices a *General der Panzertruppen* from his command responsibilities for a few hours.

In the heavily forested, sharply compartmented terrain of the Ardennes, those individuals or little bands of impromptu warriors had an effect out of proportion to their arms, their numbers. That is what happened, for example, at a collection of houses and shops called Stavelot, nestled in the picturesque valley of the Amblève River fifteen miles southwest of the Elsenborn Ridge, where at dusk on December 17, Joachim Peiper's tanks of the *1st SS Panzer Division* appeared.

Having rifled stocks of American gasoline in the rear of the 2d and 99th Divisions early on the seventeenth (massacring nineteen unarmed prisoners in the process), Peiper's SS troops shortly after midday shot up a passing American convoy near the town of Malmédy.[177] While Peiper's main body pushed on, others in the column rounded up more than one hundred captives, mowed them down with machine-gun fire, then sought out any who still moved or moaned and shot them through the head. A few men feigned death to escape. Eighty-six died.

When Peiper's tanks came up to a lone bridge over the Amblève at Stavelot, only a squad of engineers stood on the defense, but trucks of the First Army Quartermaster passing through the town on the way to evacuate gasoline from a nearby depot made it appear to the Germans that the town was alive with their foe. When after dark Peiper risked a dash for the bridge, an anti-tank mine crippled the lead tank. By the time Peiper mustered a genuine attack, a slender band of American reinforcements had arrived. It took Peiper most of the morning of the eighteenth to drive the Americans from Stavelot. It was then that the American major ordered gasoline poured into a road cut to deny access to gasoline stocks.

This delay alone would hardly prove fatal to Peiper, but little bands of diehard defenders were waiting at other spots as well. A lone towed anti-tank gun at the next town along the route delayed the tanks long enough for engineers to demolish two critical bridges. A brief break in the clouds

---

[177] For a detailed account of the Malmédy Massacre, see Richard Gallagher, *Malmédy Massaere* (New York, 1964).

afforded American fighter-bombers their first and only opportunity of the day, which they seized to knock out three tanks and seven halftracks.

It was much the same in the villages in front of Bastogne, both because of delays imposed by isolated groups at critical points of the terrain and because of Middleton's prescience in sending there the last remaining combat command of his reserve division. Yet without additional resources Middleton could only delay, but not reverse, the overwhelming tide that had surged into the Ardennes.

Full realization of what was happening in the Ardennes had been slow to come at headquarters of Courtney Hodges' First Army, located in the Hotel Britannique in the once fashionable watering place of Spa, the same hotel from which Hindenburg and Ludendorff had directed German armies in World War I. Because the opening artillery bombardment had knocked out most telephone lines to forward units, and because not all units resorted promptly to their radios, reports from some sectors were slow to come. Emanating mainly from the northernmost divisions, the first reports seemed to indicate only a local spoiling attack designed to upset the 2d Division's drive on the Roer dams. It took some argument for Leonard Gerow, whose V Corps was directing that attack, to obtain permission to call it off. In early afternoon a captured order at last revealed that an all-out counteroffensive was under way.

A spoiling attack was Omar Bradley's first reaction, too. He learned about it in late afternoon on December 16 while conferring with General Eisenhower at the Supreme Commander's main headquarters in Versailles.

Local attack or not, Eisenhower said, Middleton would have to have help to meet it.

That was what had started the 7th Armored Division moving south from Simpson's Ninth Army to St. Vith and the 10th Armored Division from Patton's Third Army northward, two combat commands of the latter to help around Echtemach, the third at Bastogne. At midnight Hodges himself sent a reserve infantry regiment marching for the Elsenborn Ridge, to be followed later by the rest of the regiment's parent division. He also alerted an armored division to begin pulling out of the line near Aachen for a shift south. A buddy of Hodges' since World War I, "Big Bill" Simpson volunteered to send another armored division and an infantry division, an offer Hodges accepted early the next day.

As more detailed reports on the 106th Divisions plight on the Schnee Eifel and on the awesome force thrown against the 28th Division reached Hodges on the morning of the seventeenth, he appealed for help from the Supreme Commanders reserve. Because Eisenhower had felt impelled to throw everything into the November offensives north and south of the Ardennes, the reserve consisted of only two divisions: the 82d and 101st Airborne Divisions which a scant three weeks before had drawn back bloody from the big air assault in the Netherlands.

On Bradley's recommendation Eisenhower agreed reluctantly to part with the airborne divisions. An alert to move reached them that evening. They were to head for Bastogne and for Houffalize, the latter ten miles northeast of Bastogne on a road the Germans might use to bypass Bastogne.

By midnight of December 17, the second day, some 60,000 men and 11,000 vehicles were on the way to reinforce Hodges' First Army in the Ardennes. In the next eight days three times those numbers would be on the move.

Almost instinctively everybody from Middleton and Gerow up to the Supreme Commander had begun to act in keeping with doctrine long taught in American service schools. The way to contain and eventually to erase a salient created by a major offensive—as demonstrated in World War I—was first to hold the shoulders of the penetration and thereby deny the enemy room for major commitments. Counterattack from the flanks then might eliminate a restricted penetration.

Recognition that the Germans would require the road network at Bastogne prompted a minor deviation from that doctrine, as did news of Peiper's armored column rampaging westward through Stavelot and passing little more than five miles south of the First Army's headquarters at Spa. When the commander of the 82d Airborne Division reported to Hodges, the First Army commander told him to take his division, not to Bastogne, as Eisenhower had directed, but to the vicinity of Werbomont, ten miles west of Stavelot, to block Peiper. The 101st, which was to have gone to Houffalize, was instead to stop at Bastogne for what was to become—as the men of the division later called it—a "rendezvous with destiny."

As the battle continued at the Elsenborn Ridge, at St. Vith, on the southern shoulder near Echternach, and on the approaches to Bastogne— where two combat commands of armor and a heterogeneous collection of artillerymen, engineers, and infantry stragglers were fighting desperately to keep the *Fifth Panzer Army* at arm's length—the two airborne divisions raced by truck through rain turning to snow to reach their appointed objectives. At the same time an infantry division arriving from the Ninth Army began to extend the northern shoulder westward from the Elsenborn Ridge along high ground north of the Amblève River, while to the Meuse rushed hastily formed teams of rear echelon troops to guard the bridges and prepare them for demolition.

Yet all those moves were makeshift to meet an immediate emergency in which the enemy still held the initiative. The broad, long-range decisions remained to be taken. How to stop the enemy short of the Meuse? How to bolster the southern shoulder? When and where to launch a counterattack?

On December 19, General Eisenhower sat down at a long table in a squad room of a venerable caserne in Verdun from which a glowing pot-bellied stove removed little of the damp chill. With him were Bradley, Devers, Patton, and key members of his staff. He wanted to see, Eisenhower said at the start, only cheerful faces.

A new infantry division, he revealed, had arrived in France and would be moved forward quickly. Three new divisions were to accelerate their shipping schedules from way stations in Britain, and he would ask that divisions alerted for early moves from the United States ship their infantry regiments in advance direct to French ports. He also would ask authority to use artillery shells equipped with the supersecret proximity (VT) fuze, heretofore employed only in anti-aircraft defense of shipping.

The American offensives north and south of the Ardennes, Eisenhower directed, were to be halted. (An obvious countermove—jumping the Roer and driving southeast into the German attack base in the Eifel—was impractical without control of the Roer River dams.) Both Bradley and Field Marshal Montgomery were to look to the possibility of limited withdrawals to gain reserves, but the Meuse River was to constitute the limit for withdrawal. Simpson's Ninth Army was to extend its positions southward to free divisions of the First Army around Aachen, while Devers' 6th Army Group extended northward to free the bulk of the Third Army.

Although the more obvious and desirable method of counterattack was to strike simultaneously from north and south close along the base of the German penetration, General Hodges was so preoccupied with trying to contain the penetration that only General Patton would be able to move swiftly. That being the case, Patton was to drive not along the base but on Bastogne, which might or might not be in American hands when he got there. From Bastogne he was to continue northeast to Houffalize, there—it was hoped—to meet Hodges' troops coming down from the north. While not eliminating the penetration, that at least would contain it.

As for the cheerful faces that Eisenhower asked, Patton gave him ebullience. "Hell," said Patton, "let's have the guts to let the sonsa-bitches go all the way to Paris." Then they could "cut 'em off and chew 'em up."[178]

When, Eisenhower asked, could George begin his counterattack? Patton responded with alacrity. "On the twenty-second."

That was just over forty-eight hours away, yet the same Patton who a few hours before had complained about releasing one armored division, was suddenly enthusiastic and determined that he could accomplish all that he promised. It had become a matter not of giving up a division but of turning the entire Third Army to the fray, absorbing Middleton's VIII Corps in the process, and affording Patton himself an opportunity for spectacular moves that would make Stonewall Jackson's maneuvers in the valley campaign in Virginia, or Gallieni's shift of troops in taxicabs to save Paris from the Kaiser, pale by comparison.

The meeting at Verdun had not long adjourned when Eisenhower's G-2, General Strong, remarked that the German thrust soon would so split the 12th Army Group that all forces north of the penetration should be transferred to Montgomery's command. An explosive suggestion, it nevertheless made sense—as even a shocked and hurt Omar Bradley would have to admit—for direct telephone communications already had been cut, long-range radio was no substitute for the telephone, and the penetration made travel between Bradley's headquarters in Luxembourg City and Hodges' circuitous at best. Since the counteroffensive opened, Bradley had met Hodges face to face only once; and confusion there was, not only from the streams of stragglers and refugees but from the command structure itself. Neither Hodges nor the corps commander, Middleton, could possibly maintain contact with all units on the broken, fluctuating front. If Bradley's headquarters moved out of Luxembourg City to a position west of the Meuse from which Bradley might control

[178] Eisenhower, *Crusade in Europe*, pp. 350-51.

the entire front, the civilian population was likely to panic, and possibly the morale of the troops would be damaged as well.

More important to Eisenhower—and it sweetened the pill for Bradley—giving Montgomery command north of the penetration would assure use of British reserves, which included an entire corps with four divisions and several armored brigades. It was a step that paid off as planned, for Montgomery promptly ordered his 30th Corps to move to reserve positions between Liège and Brussels, and he announced that the British would assume responsibility for the Meuse River bridges from Liège to the big bend at Namur.

Had Montgomery been an American, or even had he been less the assured, imperious Britisher, the shift in command would have been easier for American commanders to take. As it was, Montgomery strode into the First Army's headquarters on December 20 "like Christ come to cleanse the temple."[179] Ignoring the First Army's detailed operations map, he consulted a small one of his own, on which he had plotted information provided by British liaison officers. He also declined General Hodges' invitation to lunch, turning instead to eat alone from a lunch box and thermos. No matter that this was his usual dining practice; the Americans took it as an affront.

For all his apparently calculated rudeness, Montgomery approved the dispositions and measures Hodges already had taken. To his new chief, Hodges could report that an incoming 30th Division had cut Peiper's supply line by retaking Stavelot, that other troops of the 30th were battling Peiper at the tip of his penetration to cover assembly of the 82d Airborne Division, that a combat command of the 3d Armored Division was on the way, and that St. Vith was holding.

While approving those moves, Montgomery nevertheless urged withdrawal from St. Vith and the Elsenborn Ridge. It was a typical Montgomery maneuver, a step to "tidy the battlefield" by removing what by any standards was a perilous salient at St. Vith and to soften what was admittedly a sharp northern corner of the German salient at the Elsenborn Ridge. Yet when Hodges and his staff reacted as if he had proposed to strip them of their ranks, Montgomeiy desisted.

Having gone along with the American determination, Montgomery went farther and sanctioned a move already planned by Hodges to send

---

[179] Wilmot, *The Struggle for Europe*, p. 592, quoting one of Montgomery's staff officers.

the 82d Airborne Division to skirt the south flank of Peiper's finger-like penetration and push westward to the Salm River, which represented the rear of the St. Vith horseshoe. Except for Peiper's task force, which American reinforcements at last were effectively bottling up, tanks of the *Sixth Panzer Army* had yet to get over the Salm, so few were the roads available in the narrow corridor between St. Vith and the Elsenborn Ridge. To hold the Germans even temporarily at the Salm was to afford an avenue of escape for the troops in St. Vith while at the same time providing cover for assembling a force for counterattack.

Montgomery told Hodges that he wanted for counterattack the corps commander whom he deemed the First Army's most aggressive— "Lightning Joe" Collins. Pulled from the line near Aachen, Collins' VII Corps was to be fleshed out with two divisions each of infantry and armor and readied to hit the Germans once they had extended themselves in their quest for bridges over the Meuse.

As Montgomery took charge on the northern shoulder, combat commands of the 9th and 10th Armored Divisions were fighting a bitter delaying action in front of Bastogne. Their presence enabled the 101st Airborne Division to beat the Germans into the town, but from Bastogne all the way north to where the 82d Airborne Division was assembling near Werbomont, no American line existed, leaving a gap more than twenty miles wide which included the road center of Houffalize.

Having passed to the south of St. Vith, two of General von Manteuffel's crack panzer divisions—the *2d* and the *116th*—were hurtling almost without check into that gap. By nightfall of December 19 one column of the *116th Panzer* had reached Houffalize, while reconnaissance troops had pushed ten miles farther to the southwest toward a west branch of the Ourthe River. This branch joins the east-west main branch at a point west of Houffalize, where the Ourthe makes a turn to the northwest for an eventual swing to the north.

Fortunately for the American cause, the troops forming for the defense of Bastogne had pushed their perimeter out to the north as far as the town of Noville, almost half the distance to Houffalize, which left only one road leading west between Noville and Houffalize, that already taken by the *116th Panzer Division*. The position at Noville blocked passage of the *2d Panzer Division*.

Fortunately, too, General Middleton had rushed some of his conglomerate reserve—an engineer battalion, an independent tank destroyer battalion, even a Canadian forestry company—to destroy bridges and hold the west branch of the Ourthe. Before tanks of the *116th Panzer Division* could cross, the way was barred with outposts and demolished bridges.

Fortunately again, the *2d* and *116th Panzer Divisions* belonged to separate corps. Since the *116th* had been scheduled to swing northwest after getting across the west branch of the Ourthe, the corps commander deemed he had no choice in the absence of a bridge but to recall his troops to Houffalize and resume his advance along the north bank of the main branch. In the countermarch he lost twenty-four critical hours.

The *2d Panzer Division* meanwhile battered against the defenders of Noville and finally pushed the Americans aside during the afternoon of December 20. The German division belonged to the *XLVII Panzer Corps*, commanded by General der Panzertruppen Pleinrich Freiherr von Luettwitz, whose responsibility included Bastogne. Although Luettwitz was preoccupied with taking the town, he had other troops to do it with, including the *Panzer Lehr Division*. While the *Panzer Lehr* probed the Bastogne perimeter, encircling the town in the process, Luettwitz sent the *2d Panzer Division* pushing on to the west.

That night, the twentieth, the division's reconnaissance battalion reached the Ourthe at Ourtheville, where the troops found intact a bridge that men of the *116th Panzer Division* had neglected to storm in the belief the Americans would destroy it, as they had all others. Men of the *2d Panzer* made a run for it. The demolitions unaccountably failed, and the *2d Panzer Division* got across the Ourthe with dry feet.

From there the Meuse lay only twenty-three miles to the west, but—for a reason that seemed inexplicable at the time to the little bands of American defenders who still stood in the way—the *2d Panzer Division* ground to a halt.

In the north, in the meantime, the decision to send the 82d Airborne Division to push up to the Salm River behind the St. Vith horseshoe, had proved to be provident. Advancing without opposition, the airborne troops dropped off units along the way to face southward in the direction of Houffalize. That set up something of a blocking force in case the *116th Panzer Division* and accompanying infantry units swung northward. By the morning of December 21 the rest of the paratroopers were in position along the Salm, facing east, where during the day the Germans were finally to wrest the town of St. Vith from the 7th Armored Division and the mixed units that had held it for five days.

Not counting the two regiments of the 106th Division captured on the Schnee Eifel, the defenders of St. Vith had lost 6,000 out of some 22,000 men. After consulting with Hodges, Montgomery gave the kind of order that long ago had endeared him to the British Tommy: the heroic defenders of St. Vith were authorized to withdraw from the horseshoe "with all honor...They put up a wonderful show."[180]

Two days later, as the last survivor made his way to safety, a British corps provided additional warmth by sending to the 7th Armored Division a telegram that conveyed a camaraderie out of proportion to the number of words involved: "*A bas les Boche!*"[181]

As night fell on December 21, the battle from the American viewpoint was still going badly: St. Vith lost; its roads open to the foe. Peiper still dangerous even though trapped. The southern shoulder of the German penetration still fluid. The delaying forces in front of Bastogne all but destroyed, leaving the lightly armed 101st Airborne Division, encircled in Bastogne, to muster such support as could be salvaged to defend against an entire German corps. One German panzer division across the Ourthe twenty-three miles from the Meuse; another at Houffalize presumably preparing to resume the westward trek. Ever since the start of the German attack on the sixteenth, fog and low overcast denying all but the most daring (and usually unproductive) sorties by Allied fighter-bombers.

Yet, as is so often the case in battle, the other side saw the situation in quite another light. As early as the third day, December 18, the *Army Group B* commander, Field Marshal Model, had come to the conclusion that the counteroffensive had fallen short. That may have been merely an initial reaction of surprise and frustration attributable to the failure of the opening blows to penetrate the American line like water passing through a sieve. Yet even Hitler expressed at least tacit concern by canceling a projected supporting attack by the *Fifteenth Army* against thinned

---

[180] Cole, *The Ardennes*, p. 413.

[181] Baldwin, *Battles Lost and Won*, p. 344.

American lines near Aachen, although that was before the *2d Panzer Division* crossed the Ourthe, less than two hundred furlongs from the Meuse. So thrilled was the *Fuehrer* with this development that he afforded Field Marshal von Rundstedt two divisions from the general reserve to be employed as Rundstedt himself decided.

Problems enough remained nevertheless to justify Model's early pessimism. The American north shoulder at the Elsenborn Ridge continued to hold, a rock against which the *Sixth Panzer Army* could but batter futilely, restricting Dietrich's armor to only two of the four main roads intended for the advance westward; even one of those two roads was under heavy American artillery fire. That was why the remainder of the *1st SS Panzer Division* was so slow to follow Peiper's lead, and why Peiper was trapped. He eventually lost 39 tanks and all the rest of his transport and equipment, and only 800 out of his original 2,000 men at last returned to safety.

Dietrich's other three SS panzer divisions could not be brought to bear through the narrow passage. All efforts to do so forced traffic to spill over into the zone of the *Fifth Panzer Army* around St. Vith. At one point Field Marshal Model personally helped direct traffic near St. Vith and came upon General von Manteuffel doing the same thing. So critical was the jam that on the twenty-first Rundstedt ordered two of Dietrich's SS panzer divisions transferred southward to Manteuffel, whose *Fifth Panzer Army* from that point carried the banner of main effort. A shift southward of the boundary between the two armies, giving St. Vith to Dietrich, was part of the arrangement.

In spite of the success of the *2d* and *116th Panzer Divisions* in bypassing St. Vith to the south and streaming westward between St. Vith and Bastogne, the failure to capture the two road centers early in the fighting had sharply restricted Manteuffel's dash for the Meuse. Even after Panzer spearheads had drawn up to Bastogne on the nineteenth, General von Luettwitz had been slow to launch a full-blooded attack because thawing roads leading up from the river valleys behind him had slowed the arrival of supporting artillery.

Gasoline shortages crimped German operations everywhere. The shortages were attributable partly to German failure to capture appreciable American stocks, but also to mammoth traffic jams that developed on steep, twisting, icy roads behind the lines in the Eifel. One of Dietrich's panzer divisions used up its fuel battering against the Elsenborn Ridge. On December 21,

Rundstedt ordered two of Dietrich's divisions transferred to Manteuffel, but it took thirty-six hours to acquire enough gasoline for more than one division to move. As early as the nineteenth all Manteuffel's panzer divisions were crying for fuel. All that even as the weather denied American airmen an opportunity to take to the skies and compound the Germans' problems.

It was lack of gasoline that explained what Americans at the Ourthe River had been unable to fathom: why the *2d Panzer Division* abruptly stopped once it had crossed the river.

All the while German commanders had to keep looking over their left shoulders, for how long would it be before Patton threw the Third Army against their southern flank? How long, too, before fog and overcast parted to enable the deadly *jabos* to join the battle?

No one could have discerned it with any certainty at the time, but the day of December 22 saw the start of the climax in the battle in the Ardennes.

On that day, in a swirling snowstorm, General Patton made good on his promise to counterattack. While rushing an infantry division into the line northeast of Luxembourg City to bolster the American position at the southern base of the salient, he threw another infantry division and the veteran 4th Armored Division into a drive to break through to encircled Bastogne. The Third Army had withdrawn in the face of the enemy and begun a 90-degree shift in direction of attack with a speed unparalleled in military history.

"Drive like hell," Patton told his troops.[182]

On that day, too, the Germans surrounding Bastogne delivered a surrender ultimatum, only to be left to ponder the meaning of the reply that came back in American slang: "Nuts!"[183]

Also on the twenty-second the Germans launched what they hoped would be the last leg on the drive to the Meuse: the *2d Panzer Division* from its crossing of the Ourthe and the *116th Panzer Division* from Houffalize. Yet the Germans had lost too much time getting past Noville, waiting for fuel beyond the Ourthe, and countermarching to Houffalize to enjoy the same freewheeling they had experienced before.

---

[182] Cole, *The Ardennes*, p. 515.

[183] The most authoritative account is in Rapport and Northwood, *Rendezvous with Destiny*. Brigadier General Anthony C. McAuliffe, who gave the response, assured me in 1948 that "Nuts!" was the word he used.

Contrary to Field Marshal Montgomerys instructions, Courtney Hodges was not about to hold back the divisions scheduled to flesh out Joe Collins' VII Corps while the Germans dashed unimpeded to and over the Meuse. Hodges committed first a combat command of the 3d Armored Division astride the Houffalize-Liège highway to extend westward all the way to the Ourthe River the southward-facing positions assumed by the 82d Airborne Division between the Salm and the Ourthe. The 84th Infantry Division he assembled behind the Ourthe near the town of Marche, full in the projected path of the *2d Panzer Division.*

One final event on the twenty-second would have an authoritative impact on the continuing battle. As darkness fell, chill winds began to blow. Out of the the east emerged what weathermen call a "Russian high," which brought, in the wake of a heavy snowfall, sharply dropping temperatures that froze the ground, allowing tanks—both American and German—to maneuver freely, but which also brought weather that allowed aircraft to operate again.

Given the overwhelming Allied superiority in aircraft, the advantage of clear skies rested fully with the Allied side. As December 23 dawned, fighter-bombers and mediums were out in force, pummeling German columns that had been enjoying virtual immunity to punishment from the air. Out in force, too, were C-47 transport aircraft, looking like pregnant geese against the sky, to drop multihued parachutes bearing critical supplies to the troops in beleaguered Bastogne.

By midday of December 23, for all the assistance from the air, a hasty line thrown up by the 84th Division behind the Ourthe around Marche was close to breaking. So was the American line between the Salm and the Ourthe, where not only the *116th Panzer Division* but also the *2d SS Panzer Division*, at last come forward, attacked with a fury. This pulled into the fray another infantry division scheduled to join the VII Corps and left uncommitted only an armored division from the force Montgomery had intended for counterattack.

Crisis there was between the Salm and the Ourthe, but to American commanders the most serious was developing in the tip of the bulge where the *2d Panzer Division* bounced off a flank of the 84th Division and continued toward the Meuse. Not far off the German line of march the last remaining unit scheduled for Montgomery's counterattack was assembling: the American 2d Armored Division.

This development was to bring to a head an unspoken contest of wills that since the day Montgomery had assumed command on the northern shoulder had been running between him and Courtney Hodges. As demonstrated by his early wish to withdraw from St. Vith and the Elsenborn Ridge, the British commander believed in a policy of rolling with the punches; while the Americans, shocked at what a presumably defeated German army had done to them, were reluctant sometimes to the point of fault to give up any ground unless forced to do so, particularly ground that American soldiers had bought with blood.

Montgomery's theory was that, by holding the most economical line possible in the north and by amassing a reserve in the process, he might force the Germans to overextend themselves, whereupon he would strike with Joe Collins' VII Corps. Montgomery was relatively unconcerned about the Germans reaching or even crossing the Meuse, for by that time he had moved a British armored brigade to cover the critical bridges on either side of the big bend at Namur; and even should the Germans cross the river, he had the 30th Corps in position to annihilate them.

Possessed of no ready reserve, American commanders could hardly be so sanguine. As late as December 22 both Patton and Middleton still feared that the Germans might suddenly swing southwest in the direction of Sedan and the site of the triumph in 1940. Remembering 1914, 1918, and 1940, Paris had the jitters, and military police were enforcing a strict curfew in the French capital and guarding Eisenhower closely in case Otto Skorzeny's disguised raiders tried to assassinate the Supreme Commander. Hodges and the Staff of the First Army still thought that the Germans might turn north to take Liège and the supply depots in the environs. Even the British were not so unconcerned that they failed to station guards and erect roadblocks on the outskirts of Brussels.

Having had close personal experience with the power of the German drive, General Hodges remained most concerned of all. He saw the tip of the German striking force encompassing three panzer divisions and about to acquire a fourth—the *Panzer Lehr* from Bastogne. To withhold reserves when a force of such power was running amok—even in view of radio intercepts indicating that the Germans were growing short of fuel—was to flirt with disaster.

On December 23, without asking approval, Ernie Harmon, who had fought at Anzio, saw the emergency as so serious that he sent one of the combat commands of his 2d Armored Division to investigate reports of German tanks passing south of Marche. Yet word came back of no contact except with British armored patrols already working the area with no sign of the enemy.

Actually, the *2d Panzer Division* had found free passage even further south and was toiling toward the Meuse. (The only one of Skorzeny's disguised patrols to approach a Meuse bridge arrived before Dinant that night; the men were blown to bits when their jeep set off mines close to the bridge.) By mid-afternoon of December 24—Christmas Eve—Ernie Harmon was convinced that German tanks were present a few miles to the south in strength. He put in a call to General Collins, his corps commander, for authority to turn the 2d Armored Division to the attack.

Since Collins was away from his headquarters, his Chief of Staff relayed the request to the First Army. Hodges was torn. Although still under Montgomery's dictum to amass a reserve, and specifically to keep the 2d Armored Division from getting involved, Hodges' heart was with Harmon.

The word from Hodges was that Joe Collins was "authorized" to roll with the punches, to peel back to the northwest, to avoid a fight; but along with the failure specifically to order withdrawal, Hodges included no specific proviso forbidding attack. That was all the license General Collins—returned to his headquarters—needed. That night he and Harmon mapped out an attack, employing all the 2d Armored Division, to begin soon after dawn on Christmas Day.

"The bastards are in the bag!" roared Harmon. "In the bag!"[184]

Collins' decision marked the high-water mark of the German counteroffensive in the Ardennes. On Christmas Day, in conjunction with contingents of British armor and American fighter-bombers enjoying another day in the sun, the 2d Armored Division began to wipe out a *2d Panzer Division* that at the height of its achievement had run out of gasoline at the town of Celles, only four miles from the Meuse and not quite sixty miles from the starting line along the German frontier.

The Germans paid a price of more than eighty tanks and left not only their spearhead but their ambition broken in the snow.

---

[184] Toland, *Battle: The Story of the Bulge*, p. 245.

Chapter Twenty-Four – Victory in the Ardennes

For all the drama of the battle before the Meuse, it was clear to nobody on Christmas Day that the German counteroffensive had run its course. The specter of 1940 was an unwelcome guest that day at austere Christmas tables in Luxembourg City, Brussels, Paris. A solemnity close to gloom brooded over holiday celebrations in London and Washington, and was intensified by a mercurial press always quick to preach despair.[185]

On the scene in the Ardennes there were two other reasons beyond the success before the Meuse to encourage American optimism. The first was between the Salm and the Ourthe where the 3d Armored Division brought to a halt an all-out effort by the *2d* SS *Panzer Division* to break through to the northwest toward Namur, while on the west bank of the Ourthe other American units dealt harshly with the *116th Panzer Division*.

The second was at Bastogne. General von Manteuffel, who was obsessed with the idea that the panzer divisions were getting too far beyond their support, saw Bastogne as a cancer that had to be excised, or the counteroffensive would be totally disrupted by Patton's counterattack. He had ordered an all-out attack to take the town on Christmas Day, this time against a previously untested and presumably soft rear—or western—arc of the American perimeter. He might as well have stood in the snow singing *Tannenhaum! O, Tannenbaum! so* feeble were the chances of success. The paratroopers of the 101st with their potpourri of reinforcements (so diverse was one group that it was officially called "Task Force SNAFU")

---

[185] For the fighting in the Ardennes after January 2 (when Dr. Cole's work leaves off), I have relied in large measure on my own work for my forthcoming official volume, *The Last Offensive*.

either held or quickly sealed off every penetration. Once the Germans were beaten back, the men cheered their third straight day of resupply by waves of transport planes.

The next day, December 26, as dusk descended, an engineer battalion manning a portion of the southern fringe of the perimeter reported the approach of "three light tanks, believed friendly."[186] The 4th Armored Division had arrived.

The siege had ended.

On that day after Christmas the word reaching Hitler from Manteuffel, Model, and Rundstedt—to which Jodl nodded assent—was that no chance whatever remained of reaching Antwerp. The only hope of salvaging any sort of victory from the Ardennes was to turn the *Fifth* and *Sixth Panzer Armies* northward to cross the Meuse west of Liège and come in behind Aachen. Even that presupposed the capture of Bastogne and a secondary attack from the north to link with the panzer armies. If those prerequisites were to be met, Hitler would have to abandon the concept of a second counteroffensive in Alsace.

It was, in effect, a return to the Small Solution that the *Fuehrer* long ago had scorned. Again he rejected it. "We have had unexpected setbacks," he acknowledged, but that was "because my plan was not followed to the letter."[187]

Hitler believed that the Americans had become spread so thin in Alsace, in order to release Patton for counterattack, that a counterstroke there would force Patton to turn away from the Ardennes. Given the code name *NORDWIND*, the counteroffensive was to begin on New Year's Day.[188]

Neither would Hitler accept the contention that Antwerp lay beyond reach. While agreeing that once Bastogne was captured, the two panzer armies might turn northward, he intended no switch to the Small Solution

---

[186] Cole, *The Ardennes*, p. 480.

[187] Toland, *Battle: The Story of the Bulge*, p. 288.

[188] For the fight against Operation *NORDWIND* (pp. 394-98), I have relied primarily on *Seventh United States Army Report of Operations*, Vol. II. For the argument over Strasbourg, see also Eisenhower's memoirs; Marshal Jean de Lattre de Tassigny, *Histoire de la Premiere Armée Française* (Paris, 1949); and Dr. John W. Price, "The Strasbourg Incident," an unpublished manuscript in OCMH prepared by Dr. Price on two brief tours of duty as a reserve officer. The official U.S. Army history covering the action is unfinished.

but only a temporary diversion to trap the American divisions that had rushed to the north shoulder of the bulge. That would open a path for renewing the drive on Antwerp.

Since the German drive to the Meuse was apparently thwarted, first Bradley and then Eisenhower urged Field Marshal Montgomery to turn the First Army quickly to the offensive in order to take some of the pressure off Bastogne and the thin corridor into the town which Patton was trying to expand. Montgomery responded that he was awaiting an anticipated final German blow. Under some pressure from Eisenhower, he agreed that if the Germans failed to strike by the turn of the year, he would begin to attack by the third of January.

Montgomery's reluctance to attack provoked Bradley, Patton, and even Hodges; the latter was particularly annoyed because once Ernie Harmon's armor had blunted the tip of the German drive, the First Army wanted to get on with the job of erasing its apparent dishonor. Montgomery, all knew, had an entire British corps in reserve. Although neither Bradley, Hodges, nor Patton asked commitment of British troops, they deemed that so long as Montgomery had a reserve, he had no need to fear a further German thrust.

Another German blow in the north never came, primarily because Patton's troops in Bastogne and on either side of the relief corridor fought the *Fifth Panzer Army* to a standstill. In bitter cold and snow the combat was incredibly difficult and costly to both sides, a struggle for survival such as Bastogne had not known even in the critical days of encirclement.

The battle reached a climax on December 30 when Patton, his forces around Bastogne swollen to six divisions, tried to resume his attack northeastward on Houffalize. At almost precisely the same moment General von Manteuffel launched another major attempt to cut the corridor into Bastogne and take the town.

When, at Verdun on December 19, General Eisenhower had told General Devers to extend his lines to take over much of the Third Army's frontage, he recognized that he was handing the undermanned 6th Army Group a difficult assignment. Devers was to be prepared, Eisenhower said, to yield ground rather than to endanger the integrity of his forces.

The new arrangement charged General Patch's Seventh Army with

124 miles of front, most of it along the German frontier facing the Saar industrial region, and 40 miles of it along the Rhine, including the city of Strasbourg. From that point southward General de Lattre's First French Army took over, containing the Golmar Pocket, the German holdout west of the Rhine that loomed ever more worrisome in Eisenhower's mind as the Ardennes counteroffensive proceeded.

Occupying a right angle where the Franco-German border meets the Rhine in the extreme northeastern corner of France, several of General Patch's divisions were vulnerable should the Germans either launch converging thrusts against them or strike swiftly to deny the few passes through the Vosges Mountains behind them. Since little of strategic importance lay in the low plain between Vosges and Rhine, Eisenhower saw the region as one Patch might voluntarily relinquish so long as he held onto the critical passes through the Vosges.

To withdraw all the way to the Vosges would nevertheless involve? giving up Strasbourg, a city the French looked upon symbolically as the capital of Alsace and Lorraine, the provinces lost to the Germans from 1870 to 1918 and from 1940 to late 1944. And no Frenchman could forget that it was in Strasbourg in 1792 that Roger de Lisle had composed "La Marseillaise." And where was the French schoolchild who had not been moved to tears reading Alphonse Daudet's *La Dernière Leçon*, the touching short story about a schoolmaster's last French class before German authorities in 1871 take charge? To abandon Strasbourg was to expose thousands of Frenchmen to cruel German reprisal, but more than that: to abandon Strasbourg was to serve up a part of the soul of France.

Yet to defend 124 miles of front, including Strasbourg, the Seventh Army had only seven divisions, plus the infantry regiments of three new divisions, only recently arrived from the United States in response to Eisenhower's call for assistance at the start of the Ardennes counteroffensive. Also available as a last resort were two divisions that Elsenhower had managed to cull from the line to re-create a Supreme Headquarters reserve, but these might at any time have to be sent into the Ardennes. Thus, in the event of a major German attack, perhaps the only recourse was withdrawal.

That the Germans planned to attack around the turn of the war became clear to American commanders during the last week of December. Prisoners taken on the thirty-first revealed that the attack would come that night, an hour before the stroke of the New Year.

When Hitler had first proposed a counteroffensive in the south, Field Marshal von Rundstedt had suggested a powerful thrust from positions west of the Vosges to seize Metz, but that proved too ambitious for the forces available. Hitler rejected the plan, substituting instead his own Operation *NORDWIND*.

Attacking west of the Vosges, two divisions under the aegis of *Army Group G* (General Blaskowitz) were to make a penetration, whereupon two panzer divisions were to strike swiftly southward to seal from the rear the vital Saverne Gap, linking High Vosges and Low. At the same time three *volks* grenadier divisions were to push down the spine of the Low Vosges to cut all roads north of the Saverne Gap.

For a supporting effort Hitler called on the *Nineteenth Army*, which held the Colmar Pocket. In an odd command arrangement this army was under a special headquarters called *Army Group Oberrhein*, subject neither to *Army Group G* nor to the Commander-in-Chief in the west. Hitler had created *Army Group Oberrhein* to assuage the vanity and the desire for active field command of his crony and the head of the *Waffen-SS*, Heinrich Himmler.

Himmler's role in *NORDWIND* was first to establish a small Rhine bridgehead north of Strasbourg, then to attack northward from the Colmar Pocket to link both with that bridgehead and with *Army Group G*'s troops at the Saverne Gap. The effect would be to trap the equivalent of five American divisions east of the Low Vosges and those French forces guarding the northern periphery of the Colmar Pocket.

In comparison with the tempest in the Ardennes, Operation *NORDWIND* was but a gale. Yet however makeshift the German arrangements and however small the opening blow, it was to a defending force as stretched and as vulnerable as was the Seventh Army a storm to be met with every available resource. Once some indication of the strength of the attack reached General Eisenhower on New Year's Day, he promptly ordered General Devers to pull back to the Vosges from the northeastern salient, leaving only delaying forces on the Alsatian plain. That was as much as to say: abandon Strasbourg.

The head of the provisional French government, Charles de Gaulle, expressed his anxiety promptly. The next day he sent General Juin— serving as Chief of Staff of the Ministry of Defense—to Eisenhower's headquarters to protest. To prevent Hitler from obtaining *gratis* that bit of France that the *Fuehrer* claimed for the Reich—Juin announced furiously to Eisenhower's Chief of Staff, "Beetle" Smith—de Gaulle already had ordered General de Lattre to assume responsibility for defending Strasbourg.

As Smith well knew, this represented not only defiance of the Supreme Command but unilateral alteration of an interarmy boundary. Go through with it, the irascible Smith replied in cold anger, and not one more bullet, not one more gallon of gasoline would the French army receive.

In that case, Juin responded, the French might deny American use of the national railways. If Eisenhower should persist, de Gaulle was prepared to withdraw French troops from Eisenhower's command.

It sounded like an argument in a schoolyard. It was instead a clever maneuver. Juin could depart knowing that he had left General Smith visibly shaken and that the Chief of Staff would tell all to his chief. That would afford the Supreme Commander time to reconsider before he attended a requested meeting with General de Gaulle the next afternoon. Lest the stratagem miscarry, de Gaulle that night cabled President Roosevelt and Prime Minister Churchill for help. Roosevelt declined to intervene in what he labeled a military matter, while Churchill withheld judgment since he was scheduled to fly to Versailles on January 3 to lunch with Eisenhower.

Delayed by bumpy flying weather over the Channel, the Prime Minister arrived in Versailles well after the normal lunch hour, some time after 2 P.M. Word already had reached Jakie Devers almost an hour earlier that Eisenhower had changed his mind, a development that pleased Devers and Patch as well, for both had deemed the withdrawal order premature at best. The new order specified withdrawal only from the tip of the northeastern salient, back along successive lines some twenty miles to the little Moder River which cuts through the plain to enter the Rhine several miles north of Strasbourg. The boundary between French and Americans was to be adjusted northward to give responsibility for Strasbourg to the French.

Although the French later honored Churchill as the savior of Strasbourg, the credit belonged instead to the ploy practiced by Charles de Gaulle and Alphonse Juin. Or perhaps, more properly, to a Supreme Commander who in exercising coalition command saw resilience as a virtue.

In the fighting meanwhile, American troops west of the Vosges, with the help of the French 2d Armored Division, had almost brought the main effort of the German assault to a halt by nightfall of the second day, which may have had something to do with Eisenhower's decision on withdrawal. The secondary effort down the spine of the mountains made better progress, but near the town of Bitche, American defenders fighting in foot-deep snow, numbing cold, and a fog that denied air support reacted with the same determination their colleagues had exhibited in the Ardennes.

Although the Germans advanced half the distance to the Saverne Gap, swift counterattack drove them back. By nightfall of January 4, Hitler was despairing of getting the eastern exits of the Vosges and was looking instead to indications of imminent American withdrawal from the tip of the northeastern salient. Shift the attack, he ordered, eastward to the Wissembourg Gap, whence victorious Prussian columns had debouched in 1870.

It might have looked good on an operations map back in Berlin, but that signified nothing. Here American troops proved they could roll with the punches as well as anybody else. By January 20 the men in the tip of the northeastern salient were home safe on the line of the Moder.

More troublesome was Himmler's one-division assault across the Rhine between Strasbourg and the meeting of the Moder with the Rhine. There on January 5 inexperienced infantrymen, who had come to France ahead of their artillery and tanks, fell back. The Germans advanced to within seven miles of Strasbourg before commitment of a portion of General Eisenhower's reserve brought them to a halt. The *Nineteenth Army's* attack northward out of the Colmar Pocket got within thirteen miles of Strasbourg, but the French stopped it at the last bridge short of the city.

While Devers' 6th Army Group retained its integrity, Strasbourg stayed French. Having committed so much to the Ardennes, the Germans had simply been unequal to a second blow. A dying German effort to force the Moder River on January 25 ended Operation *NORDWIND* after only an inconsequential gain embracing nothing more than a short stretch of dull flat landscape. It cost the Germans 25,000 casualties; the Americans, 15,600.

As the Seventh Army was meeting the crisis in Alsace, the Germans produced two new blows in the Ardennes.

One came from the air, an extraordinary effort by the *Luftwaffe*. Early on New Year's Day, 700 German planes struck Allied airfields in Belgium and the Netherlands. For the Allies, another ugly surprise which cost them 156 planes, most of them destroyed on the ground, 36 of them American.

The second blow was aimed at the old objective of Bastogne, where General von Manteuffel had seen his offensive of December 30 collapse in the face of General Patton's renewed attack. Manteuffel himself wanted no new attack, at Bastogne or anywhere else. The time had come, he believed, to abandon all thought of further offensives in the Ardennes. Lest the troops in the tip of the bulge be trapped between Patton and an apparently impending attack by the First Army from the north, he appealed to Field Marshal Model, late on January 2, for permission to fall back to a line anchored on Houffalize.

Although both Model and Rundstedt gave their endorsement, Hitler refused. The counteroffensive under the original concept of taking Antwerp, Hitler at last admitted, no longer stood any chance of success; but he had arrived at definite ideas of how the bulge in the Ardennes might be turned to German advantage.

In creating the salient, Hitler reasoned, he had forced General Eisenhower to employ almost all his resources. Eisenhower's use of elite airborne divisions to do the brutal defensive work of infantry was proof of that. By holding the bulge, Hitler might keep the Allies spread thin while he pulled out some German units for spoiling attacks elsewhere—such as Operation *NORDWIND*. Thus he might prevent the Allies from concentrating their forces in the north for a renewed offensive against the Ruhr.

Yet even to pursue this strategy, the Germans required Bastogne. Hitler needed the town both to anchor the southern flank of the bulge and to deny its nexus of roads to his adversary.

To American troops, Manteuffer's final offensive at Bastogne, which ran its course on January 3 and 4, appeared less a concerted attack than reaction by counterattack to Patton's efforts to drive on to Houffalize. Furthermore, Manteuffel operated on borrowed time, for his attack opened on the same day that Field Marshal Montgomery at last released Hodges' First Army to attack from the north.

The pattern of the drive to eliminate the bulge had been set at the conference in Verdun on December 19 with the decision to send the Third Army to Bastogne. Once Bastogne was relieved, Patton insisted on shifting to the classic though venturesome maneuver for eliminating a salient—to cut it off at its base; but he found no support from either

Hodges or Bradley. They were concerned about the limited road net at the northern base and about the effect of winter weather in the more sharply compartmented terrain along the German border. Montgomery concurred, moving parts of two British divisions against the tip of the bulge to enable Joe Collins' VII Corps to shift slightly and take a shot at Houffalize from the northwest. Once the First and Third Armies met at Houffalize, both were to sweep, after the manner of synchronized windshield wipers, on to the German frontier.

The plan was—Field Marshal von Rundstedt would note later, not without a touch of irony—the Small Solution.

The snow was deeper than ever in the Ardennes, the temperatures were lower, the fog was thicker, the chill winds were more penetrating, when early on January 3, General Collins sent two armored divisions southeastward toward Houffalize across ground marked by stretches of high marshland, dense patches of fir trees, and deep-cut streambeds. Only three of "Sepp" Dietrich's badly damaged divisions barred the way, including fragments of a mauled *2d Panzer Division*, but that was enough along with the terrain and the weather to impose a crablike pace on the advance.

So murky was the atmosphere that not a single fighter-bomber could support the attack all day, and sorties by little observation aircraft were possible for no more than an hour during the entire day. It was a pattern that would undergo little change for a fortnight. On only three days were fighter-bombers able to take to the air at all. Much of the time the men advanced through snow flurries, followed on the fourth day by a heavy snowfall which piled drifts in places to a depth of several feet.

Tanks stalled on icy hillsides in long rows. Trucks towing anti-tank guns or artillery pieces skidded, jackknifed, collided, and blocked vital roads for hours. Two trucks towing 105-mm. howitzers plunged off a cliff. Bridges over streams everywhere were demolished, and the sites defended, forcing winter-weary infantrymen to march upstream or down to find an uncontested ford, then wade the icy stream to take the enemy in flank, often as not to find that the foe at the last moment had pulled out to fight again another day. The Germans occasionally counterattacked—a brace or so of tanks, a company or a battalion of infantry.

Under those conditions two miles a day was a major achievement.

Men of the Third Army had it as hard and worse, for the foe around

Bastogne represented the flint of German strength still left in the Ardennes. Bitterly cold, stung by biting winds and driven snow, nostrils frozen, lungs seared by the cold, Patton's troops saw little change in a pattern too long familiar. The names of German units were those of old and dreaded acquaintances: the *1st, 9th,* and *12th SS Panzer Divisions,* the *5th Parachute,* the *Panzer Lehr.* Familiar, too, were the place names, the same towns and villages where small clumps of infantrymen and tanks a fortnight before had thwarted the Germans in the race for Bastogne—but now less towns and villages than grotesque scars on a white landscape. Familiar, too, the tactics of attack followed by counterattack.

For all the bitterness of the fighting, the final crisis at Bastogne had passed. Late on January 4, Field Marshal Model tacitly admitted failure by ordering Manteuffel to release one of the SS panzer divisions to go to the aid of the *Sixth Panzer Army* in its hour of trial against the American First Army. The next day Manteuffel took it upon himself to pull another of the SS panzer divisions from the line to constitute a reserve. Three days later, on January 8, Hitler himself authorized withdrawal from the tip of the bulge—not all the way back to Houffalize as Manteuffel had asked, but to a line anchored on a great loop of the Ourthe River five miles west of Houffalize.

This was the *Fuehrer's* first grudging admission that the counterof-fensive in the Ardennes had failed utterly. Dietrich's *Sixth Panzer Army,* he directed, was gradually to relinquish control to Manteuffel of all but the SS panzer divisions, while these four divisions were to assemble in the rear near St. Vith. The SS divisions were ostensibly to guard against Allied attacks near the base of the bulge, but in reality they were executing the first step in quitting the Ardennes entirely for a shift to the east to oppose a burgeoning Russian offensive begun on January 12. The final order to depart came on January 22, and with it tacit admission not only that the great venture in the west was ended but that the eastern front had priority on resources.

Early on January 16, patrols of the First and Third U.S. Armies met at Houffalize. Rent apart by the counteroffensive, the two armies had joined hands at the waist of the bulge; but so measured had been the advance and such delays had the Germans and the weather imposed, that the foe had made good his escape from what was a sizable pocket. The junction at Houffalize nevertheless marked the end of the break in communications between American armies. Looking ahead to a renewed offensive toward the Ruhr, General Eisenhower elected to leave Simpson's Ninth Army under Field Marshal Montgomery's command; but the next day, the seventeenth, he let Hodges and the First Army go home, back to the open arms of Omar Bradley and the 12th Army Group.

It would take another eight days to push in what was left of the bulge—a slow contest against weather and long-proved German ingenuity on the defense. Back to St. Vith (the 7th Armored Division drew the honor of re-entry), back to Clerf, back to Echternach (several American soldiers, sustained for more than a month by Luxembourg civilians, emerged from hiding), back to the "Skyline Drive," back to many another place where at the start of the counteroffensive American soldiers, surprised, frightened, had delayed the Germans and gained a commodity called time.

On January 22 the clouds finally cleared. A brilliant sun came up to sparkle on a new snow cover. Pilots were early in the air, jubilant to find German vehicles stalled bumper to bumper waiting their turn to cross ice-encrusted bridges over the Our River. Astride the "Skyline Drive" infantrymen cheered to see the carnage that both air and artillery wrought.

Critically wounded, the beast that had misguidedly sprung, crept back, harried to the last. By January 28 the last vestige of the bulge in the Ardennes had disappeared.

The cost of this greatest pitched battle ever fought by American arms was on both sides enormous. Out of 600,000 Americans involved—more than three times the number that fought on both sides at Gettysburg—casualties totaled 81,000, of which probably 19,000 were killed, perhaps 15,000 captured (more than half from one unfortunate division). The British incurred 1,400 casualties, of which more than 200 were killed. Including wounded, the Germans probably had 100,000 casualties.

Both sides lost heavily in weapons and equipment, probably as many as 800 tanks on each side, and the Germans 1,000 aircraft. Yet the Americans could replace their losses in little more than a fortnight, while the Germans could no longer make theirs good. The Germans nevertheless had managed to extricate almost all they had taken into the Ardennes except what was destroyed in the fighting or by the Germans themselves at the end for want of gasoline. A combination of weather, German ingenuity, and American recourse to the Small Solution had seen to that.

Not only had the Germans failed to come close to achieving their objective of Antwerp; they had also fallen short of the interim objective of the Meuse. Although Eisenhower had issued an order of the day urging his troops to ever greater effort, he had never come close to proclaiming a "backs to the wall" order like that wrung from Sir Douglas Haig in 1918 during the German attempt to drive the British into the sea. This is not to say there had been 110 anxious moments. Hodges was for a while stunned by what had happened to his command; the First Army Staff had displayed a fleeting panic; and some at SHAEF (though not Eisenhower) had seen a goblin around every corner. Yet neither Patton, Bradley, Eisenhower, Montgomery, nor even Hodges—once the first brutal impact had passed—had indicated the slightest concern that matters would not be settled in their way in the end.

In deluding himself that the *Wehrmacht* of 1944 had the power to repeat the performance of 1940, Hitler had accomplished nothing more than to assure swift victory for a new Russian offensive and possibly to delay for a few weeks a renewed Allied drive. Whether he delayed the denouement was another matter. He was caught in the historic German dilemma of how to fight a two-front war and, for all the apparent rationale of his counteroffensive, may have attacked simply for the sake of the attack and in the process hastened the inevitable end.

The victor in the Ardennes was the American soldier—he who had given his allies some sharp concern almost two years before at Kasserine Pass, but who had come a long way since that first battle experience. Purportedly pampered, lacking motivation, he had met the test when it came, giving his commanders—for all their intelligence failure—time to bring their mobility and reserve power into play. Although Allied power would have told in the end in any case, the American soldier in the Ardennes made the outcome a certainty by his valor and determination at the Elsenborn Ridge, St. Vith, Echternach, Clerf, Stavelot, Bastogne, Celles, and countless other places.

An unfortunate footnote to the battle remained. Possibly as a reflection of agitation in the British press to revive the old issue of making Montgomery overall ground commander, the Field Marshal in a press conference on January 7—even as the fighting raged—indulged in undue exaggeration.

"As soon as I saw what was happening," Montgomery said, "I took certain steps myself to insure that if the Germans got to the Meuse they would certainly not get over that river."[189] He was "thinking ahead." When "the situation began to deteriorate...national considerations were thrown overboard," and "General Eisenhower placed me in command of the whole northern front." He had, he claimed, "employed the whole available power of the British Group of Armies," bringing it into play gradually and then finally "with a bang," so that "today British divisions are fighting hard on the right flank of the United States First Army." The operation was "one of the most interesting and tricky I have ever handled."

While Montgomery may not have intended to denigrate American commanders, the effect was much as if he had, particularly after the Germans broke in on a BBC wavelength to imitate a British broadcast and give a distorted version of Montgomery's remarks. So upset was General Bradley that he told Eisenhower that rather than serve under Montgomery he would ask to be relieved. Patton said that if Bradley went, so would he.

Bradley saw Montgomery's remarks as a reflection on his own ability as a commander, yet Eisenhower had called in Montgomery only because he hesitated to shift Bradley's headquarters from Luxembourg City to a point farther west, and because he wanted to ensure use of British reserves if needed. While those reserves had been conveniently at hand, few British resources had been employed—certainly no such force as Montgomery intimated in saying he had committed "with a bang" the "whole available power of the British Group of Armies." At most, an armored brigade and later parts of two British divisions had briefly entered the fight.

Montgomery's presence may have goaded Hodges to greater achievement at a time when the First Army commander was emotionally moved; but nothing existed in Hodges' background or record to indicate that he would not have recovered swiftly in any case. Since Montgomery had endorsed or gone along with all Hodges' early dispositions, and since Hodges had circumvented Montgomery's plan to keep the assembling divisions of the VII Corps from the line to form a reserve—in the process stopping the Germans short of the Meuse—what had Montgomery accomplished?

That Montgomery had withheld replacement-short British units purposely to save them for the coming offensive against the Ruhr was, in the American view, both understandable and justified. To withhold them and then boast that he had not was neither.

---

[189] Quotes from Montgomery's press conference are from Pogue, *The Supreme Command*, p. 388.

It remained for the splendid orator, Winston Churchill, to heal the wound. In an address before the House of Commons he paid full tribute to the American soldier and made abundantly clear that the Ardennes was an American battle and an American victory. It was, Churchill said, "the greatest American battle of the war and will, I believe, be regarded as an ever famous American victory."

Chapter Twenty-Five – The Drive to the Rhine

As *WACHT AM RHEIN* and *NORDWIND* came to inevitable ends, a force of awesome power stood along the German frontier: 4,000,000 men in three army groups, seven armies (an eighth, the Fifteenth U.S. Army, was forming), 21 corps, and 73 divisions, 20 of which were armored. Of the total, almost 3,000,000 of the men were Americans, along with two of the army groups, four of the armies, 14 of the corps, and 49 of the divisions. Of six tactical air commands, four were American, and of more than 17,500 combat aircraft in the Allied arsenal, 5,000 were U.S. fighter-bombers, and almost 7,000 were U.S. medium and heavy bombers.[191]

In command of this largest and most powerful American force ever put into battle was a close-knit team reflecting a camaraderie developed in the lean interwar years at West Point, at impoverished stateside posts, and at a few small overseas garrisons. The members displayed a unity of mind born of the branch schools and the Staff College at Fort Leavenworth.

At the top, Eisenhower, acknowledged master of coalition command and military diplomacy, who had begun to reveal a forcefulness and a decisiveness missing in the earlier days in North Africa, Sicily, Normandy, and even as late as the fall campaign of 1944. And Bradley, master tactician, who had made no effort to erase Missouri from speech, appearance, and bearing, yet who concealed behind that provincial front an uncommonly keen, perceptive mind. Hodges, an army commander of the first rank,

---

[191] Since published material on post-Ardennes American operations is limited, I have inevitably drawn heavily for this and all subsequent chapters on my work in preparing *The Last Offensive*. See also the memoirs of Eisenhower, Bradley, Patton, and Montgomery; Pogue, *The Supreme Command*; John Toland, *The Last 100 Days* (New York, 1966); Wilmot, *The Struggle for Europe*; and an excellent unit history, *Conquer: The Story of Ninth Army* (Washington, 1947). See also Stacey, *The Canadian Army*.

whose only fault, it appeared to Eisenhower, was that God had given him a face that always looked pessimistic, and "Big Bill" Simpson and "Sandy" Patch, like Hodges, sturdy, dependable, workmanlike, accomplished.[192] (Patch served under a double handicap: severe lung damage incurred in the great influenza epidemic of World War I, which eventually killed him; and the mental anguish over the death of his only son, an artillery captain, during the fall campaign while serving under Patch's own Seventh Army.)

Also, one whose flair for the spectacular attracted an attention from press, public, troops, and foe out of proportion to his proper position in the command structure, one for whom the adjective "charismatic" might have been created: George Patton. The intense emotion that Patton brought to war as to everything else served him well when breakthrough and pursuit were the order of the day, but the same characteristic worked against him when there was no alternative to grim, slugging warfare. That kind of fighting tore at Patton's thin patience, inducing despondency to a fault. In spite of his mask of self-confidence, he could be reduced to tears. Impetuous, he needed the sobriety of Bradley and Eisenhower to hold him in check.

One top American failed through no fault of his own to make the close-knit team. This was the other army group commander, Jakie Devers, who needed all the charm of winning smile, protruding ears, and boyish features to hold his own in a company where he lacked the full confidence of the chief. Somehow Devers' and Eisenhower's path had touched only tangentially. Devers was, instead, George Marshall's man, one whom Marshall had long used as a troubleshooter, first to head an embryonic armored force as the Army's expansion began, next as his personal observer in North Africa, then as caretaker of what became Eisenhower's command in England, and finally as deputy in the Mediterranean theater after Eisenhower departed for England.

Arriving by way of southern France rather than Normandy, Devers and his 6th Army Group were Johnnys-come-lately, poor relations from out of town, strangers to the established family. From the first Eisenhower, with his focus on a main effort in the north, planned for them only the minor role of protecting the south flank of the larger 12th Army Group.[193]

---

[192] I have relied on an interview with General Eisenhower in 1967.

[193] On the way Devers and Bradley ran their army groups, I have depended primarily on interviews with both generals in 1967.

When, after gaining Strasbourg in November, Devers' French charges had allowed the Germans to hold onto a bridgehead over the Rhine—the Colmar Pocket—it affected Eisenhower like a burr under a saddle. Eisenhower recognized that Devers had problems with the French—they lacked replacements and administrative and logistical support, and they had other responsibilities such as guarding German holdouts in southwestern France, manning an Alpine line along the Italian frontier, and shoring up de Gaulle's provisional government; yet he still remembered that he had approved Devers' swinging the Seventh Army northward only on the latter's promise that the French would swiftly clear the Rhine's west bank. Eisenhower's irritation was scarcely eased by the fact that Devers did not have enough troops through the fall and winter to accomplish all the tasks assigned him.

Furthermore, had it not been for the presence of Marshall's man Devers, Eisenhower would have been in a position early in the new year to recommend promoting to four-star rank not only Bradley but also Hodges and Patton. When the war ended, Eisenhower was still debating in his own mind Devers' rating in the hierarchy of generals, which may have been inevitable, since country cousins coming without patriarchal blessing seldom work their way fully into the family fold.

The fact that American experience provided no clearly prescribed guidelines for the conduct of an army group command may have had something to do with Devers' problem. There had never been a U.S. army group except in the closing days of World War I, when Pershing had established that command for himself. As that new level of command emerged, it was in essence a glorified corps command but without directly assigned troops and with an added logistical function. In exercising command at the new level, Devers and Bradley interpreted their assignments differently.

Devers played it loosely, informally. He left planning mainly to his army commanders, while he himself, using a little liaison plane in all but the most abominable weather, became a familiar figure at subordinate levels—army, corps, division. He authorized his Staff to operate accordingly. The Staff could seek first-hand information at lower levels and make changes on the spot; the only requirement was to notify Devers immediately. Under this arrangement Devers kept his headquarters small, altogether approximately six hundred men.

Bradley, on the other hand, played it closely and formally. Pic maintained

403

a Staff twice the size of Devers', engaged in intricate, detailed planning, and dealt in most cases only with his army commanders. On those, through liaison officers and the telephone, he held a close rein—something Patton, who often thought he was putting things over on Bradley and Eisenhower, failed to appreciate.

As the level of army group was new to the Americans, so the levels of corps and division were materially different from anything the U.S. Army had known before. This was a reflection of the ideas and influence of the man who had died in the short bombing near St. Lô, Lesley McNair, who as Chief of the Army Ground Forces had left a deep imprint on American conduct of the war. He had died too soon to see his ideas thoroughly proved.[194]

McNair's preoccupation had been to keep the army in the field lean and simple. Instead of the ponderous 28,000-man division that had fought in the trenches with Pershing, he advocated a division of just over 10,000, though he had to settle in the end for one with not quite 15,000. Yet McNair's theory had triumphed. If a division carried with it all the engineers, medical services, transport, fire power that it needed to meet any contingency, not only would it be outsized and difficult to control and maneuver, but many of the troops often would be idle while awaiting the conditions of battle for which they had been trained. Better to let infantrymen double as drivers, radio operators, mechanics, while heavy artillery, construction engineers, signals, transport, tank destroyers, and tanks (except those organic to armored divisions) could be organized in separate battalions and attached to divisions as needed. That in practice some of the attachments became quasi-permanent, as with tank and tank destroyer battalions, was less a contradiction of the principle than a recognition of the critical supporting role of armor to infantry under conditions of battle in Europe.

Similarly, the corps had no fixed composition but might be augmented with more armor, infantry, artillery, bridge-building equipment as needed. In the same vein, the corps had no supply function, for divisions could haul supplies with their own transport from army depots. The corps thus

---

[194] See Greenfield, et al., *The Organization of Ground Combat Troops*, and Palmer, *et al*, *The Procurement and Training of Ground Combat Troops*. Russell F. Weigley, *History of the United States Army* (New York, 1967), an excellent work, provides interesting analysis and observations.

emerged as a thin layer of command, able to focus full attention on the one critical factor of warfare: tactical conduct of the battle.

McNair had been wary, too, of overspecialization. While recognizing that the army would fight under varying conditions around the world, he believed that, when augmented by proper attachments, the standard infantry and armored divisions could do any job. With the exception of five airborne divisions, a "mountain" division that fought in Italy, and a cavalry division that fought on foot in the Pacific, that was the practice. Nor did the U.S. Army follow the German example of committing to battle an armored or any other specialized corps, except for an airborne corps that did most of its fighting as a normal ground formation. The usual corps contained one armored and two infantry divisions, and the infantry, rather than the armor, was normally given the role of penetration.

The American infantry division had three infantry regiments, three 105-mm. howitzer battalions for direct support, a 155-mm. howitzer battalion for general support, and small contingents of signal, engineer, quartermaster, and other supporting troops. Each regiment contained three battalions, each with three rifle companies and a heavy weapons company (81-mm. mortars and water-cooled .30-caliber machine guns), plus small groupings of anti-tank, reconnaissance, and headquarters troops. In practice one regiment and one artillery battalion usually worked together as the nucleus of a regimental combat team. The only "fat," as McNair would have put it, was a regimental cannon company equipped with short-nosed 105-mm. howitzers; so quick to provide fire was divisional artillery that regiments had no need to carry their own direct artillery support with them.

After a first rush to create a "heavy" armored division comparable to the early German panzer divisions, the U.S. Army had scaled down the medium tank strength in its armored divisions from 250 to 154 in order to accommodate additional infantry needed to provide staying power. With the new organization, out had gone the old armored and armored infantry regiments, leaving only battalions that could be grouped in various "mixes" under headquarters of three combat commands. While lacking some of the shock power of the old armored division (the 1st, 2d, and 3d), the new formation had proved capable of standing up to the German panzer division of 1944-1945.

The only real problem was the tank itself. The standard Sherman was, in comparison to the German Panther and Tiger, obsolescent, with little more going for it than speed and infrequency of major overhauls. The high-velocity 75-mm. gun on the Panther and the 88-mm. on the Tiger clearly outgunned the Sherman's short-nosed 75, and the 88 was even superior to a 76-mm. high-velocity piece that by the start of 1945 was appearing on some modified American tanks. A new medium tank, the Pershing, mounting a 90-mm. gun, was in production but reached Europe only in experimental quantities.

Except for the Pershing and a few 57-mm. and 75-mm. recoillcss rifles that arrived before the war ended, the weapons and equipment of each side were firmly established by early January. They were roughly equal qualitatively, but the effects of the long war had sharply cut quantities on the German side.

Against the GI's semiautomatic M-1 rifle, the German soldier carried a bolt-action 7.92-mm. piece. The Germans closed the gap in fire power by prolific issue of a machine pistol, a weapon that, because of an emetic sound produced by a high cyclic rate of fire, American troops called a "burp gun." The American squad had the additional fire power of a .30-caliber Browning Automatic Rifle, known as the "BAR."

Like the BAR, the American machine gun was a carryover from the latter days of World War I, the .30-caliber Browning available in both air-and water-cooled models. The slow putt-putt-putt sound of the Browning contrasted sharply with that of the German machine gun, an air-cooled 1942 model with a high cyclic rate of fire. Heard late at night along an otherwise quiet front, the German machine gun had the voice of an angry cougar.

The basic close-support mortar on both sides was an 81-mm. piece, although both also had a smaller mortar for use within the rifle company. The Americans employed a heavier mortar with deadly effect, a 4.2-inch piece designed primarily for firing chemicals but restricted, in view of an unwritten moratorium on poison gas, to high-explosive and white phosphorous shells. The Germans continued to employ the combination mortar-rocket launcher American troops had met in North Africa, the *Nebehcerfer*, or "Screaming Meemie." By late 1944 the Americans were firing rockets from a rack mounted on a Sherman tank, but like the *Nebelwerfer*, the rockets were more terrifying than accurate. (A German officer evaluated rockets in terms of a French proverb: *Faute de mieux, on se couche avec sa femme.*)

For close combat, the GI used a fragmentation hand grenade; his opponent, a "potato masher" concussion grenade. Although men on both sides carried the bayonet, they normally used it for nothing more damaging than opening ration tins. For close-in anti-tank defense, the Germans had developed their own version of the bazooka, a one-shot, shaped-charge piece called a *Panzerfaust*. American troops also employed a towed 57-mm. anti-tank gun, much improved over the old 37-mm., but the caliber still was so small and the gun so lacking in mobility that by early 1945 most divisions preferred to leave it behind. Although both combatants possessed similar anti-tank mines, the Germans scored a point in diabolical cleverness with their anti-personnel mines, the dreaded "Bouncing Betty" and a plastic *Schu* mine that defied electronic mine detectors.

Except that much German artillery was horse-drawn, artillery on both sides was generally equal. Since American guns were relatively free from air attack, they possessed a better supply system and thus could expend many more rounds than those of their foe. By means of a highly sophisticated fire-direction center with excellent communications down to forward observers with infantry companies, the Americans also could mass their fire quickly and make lightning adjustments that awed German artillerymen. An American practice called TOT—Time on Target, a means of timing the fire of a number of battalions to fall on a target simultaneously—was particularly terrifying (sometimes twenty battalions or more were put on a single target).

In the tank destroyer on the American side, the assault gun on the German, both sides had similar mobile pieces for supplementing the artillery with close fire support, although the Americans tended to use their destroyer less for infantry assault support than as an anti-tank weapon, leaving the support role to tanks. The German assault gun was the same used in North Africa, either a 75-mm. or 88-mm. high-velocity weapon. The Americans had an improved destroyer mounting a 3-inch piece. Although both the assault gun and the destroyer looked much like a tank, neither carried appreciable armor.

The two sides differed little in tactics, although as late as the Ardennes counteroffensive the Germans still displayed some predilection for breakthrough with armor rather than infantry. The Germans also showed allegiance to the dictum that counterattack invariably follows attack, from squad level up—a practice that consumed manpower in numbers the Germans could ill afford. Reflecting the new mobility and fire power, both sides employed open formations requiring far fewer men on a given sector of front than had the mass formations of World War I. Yet the same close infantry-artillery coordination of World War I still was essential if penetration was to be achieved. The basic difference between wars was the new means of exploitation made possible by the motor vehicle, the tank, improved radios (including frequency modulation—FM), and the fighter-bomber.

The one striking difference between German and American forces on the battlefield was the presence on the American side of the fighter-bomber. Except for its brief resurgence in the Ardennes, the *Luftwaffe* had almost ceased to exist as a tactical force. Although Hitler continued to conjure visions of great fleets of jet-propelled planes regaining mastery of the skies, it was owing to him that the jets would arrive too late to save Germany. As early as 1943, when shown the prototype of a Messerschmidt 262 jet fighter—125 miles per hour faster than any existing Allied plane—Hitler had insisted that it be modified to carry bombs. To hell with defense; he wanted to attack, to pay back the British for their destruction of German cities. The demand so set back development that by the fall of 1944 only thirty jets were available, and the war would end—for all the *Fuehrer*'s professed faith in jets as the salvation of the Reich—with few more than one hundred available at any one time.

American air, meanwhile, had achieved an intimate marriage with the troops on the ground which bore little resemblance to the indifferent association evident in North Africa. In every case American tactical air commands located their headquarters adjacent to the army headquarters they supported. Although monitored by an air officer at corps headquarters, requests for air support passed directly from division to an air operations officer at army for transmission to the tactical air command, which then ruled on the feasibility of the mission and assigned the proper number of aircraft to it. To handle targets of opportunity or to provide cover for armored columns in pursuit situations, a group often was assigned to a division or a corps and worked directly through the appropriate air support officer.

Like divisions attached to ground corps and armies, the number of fighter-bomber groups assigned to tactical air commands often varied, though the number usually was six. A group normally had three squadrons of twenty-five planes each—either P-38 Lightnings, P-47 Thunderbolts,

P-51 Mustangs, or, in the case of night fighter groups, P-61 Black Widows. Thunderbolts and Mustangs, the workhorses of tactical air support, carried six to eight wing-mounted .50-caliber machine guns, six 5-inch rockets, and up to two thousand pounds of bombs, which might be either fragmentation or deep-penetration types. A special bomb filled with Napalm—a kind of jellied gasoline—sometimes was employed against pillboxes or to set afire defended woods and villages.

The soldier on each side respected his counterpart, even though the man in the German ranks tended to ascribe the bulk of the American soldier's success to his wealth of arms, ammunition, and supplies. The *Ami*—as the German called the GI—was more effective in the German view on offense than defense, despite the demonstration of pertinacity in the Ardennes. The American early had nicknamed his foe "Jerry," a term borrowed from the British, but after the costly autumn and winter fighting he came to speak of him with some derision as a "Kraut." What impressed the GI most about the "Kraut" was his ability to keep up the fight despite constant defeat and overwhelming odds.

As American troops in late January were erasing the last of the bulge in the Ardennes, Omar Bradley was acutely conscious that the focus of Allied attack soon was to shift from his 12th Army Group. Through the course of the counteroffensive the Supreme Commander had never wavered in a determination to return eventually to the strategy he had been pursuing when the Germans launched their attack—a main effort in the north aimed at the Ruhr industrial region. Because of the realignment imposed on American troops by the counteroffensive, that meant the main effort would be invested in Montgomery's 21st Army Group. It meant, too, that Bradley would have to relinquish divisions to bolster Simpson's Ninth Army, which Eisenhower had left under Montgomery's command.

Releasing American units to Montgomery under any circumstances would have been objectionable to Bradley: having to do so just after Montgomery's baneful press conference was unthinkable. In Bradley's mind there were reasons enough, in any case, to justify his holding onto the twenty-nine divisions then comprising his First and Third Armies.

What could be more logical than to capitalize on the momentum generated by the elimination of the bulge and drive on through the Eifel, hoping to catch the Germans off balance while they were shifting troops northward in anticipation of renewed attack by Montgomery, and thereby gain the Rhine in a position to cut in behind the enemy facing Montgomery? Furthermore, such a move would enable Bradley's armies to bypass to the south the troublesome Roer River dams near Monschau. Although the matter went unspoken, was it not also logical to vest the principal role in the new offensive in an American command that had incurred a reverse?

The proposal was not incompatible with Eisenhower's own plan. While contemplating a main effort in the north, General Eisenhower still championed a "broad front strategy," which in current terms meant an advance generally all along the front as far as the Rhine before sending the main effort across the river to seize the Ruhr. Whether Montgomery or Bradley reached the Rhine first made little difference.

That fell considerably short of the British view. As early as the second week of January the British Chiefs of Staff had indicated their disagreement with Eisenhower's plan by asking a strategy review by the Combined Chiefs in advance of a forthcoming conference with the Russians at Yalta. The Allies lacked the strength, the British believed, for two major thrusts. Forces for the drive in the north, they insisted, should be assembled first and should include, they intimated, not only the Ninth U.S. Army but Hodges' First Army as well; whereupon whatever was left might advance as resources permitted toward the Rhine.

Eisenhower rejected the concept. In messages to General Marshall preceding the strategy conference, he reiterated his determination to hold an easily defended line along the Rhine before jumping the river in strength. Although he favored a main effort in the north, he also intended to send the First and Third Armies across the river south of the Ruhr in a secondary effort to link with the main effort north of the Ruhr.

While the British Chiefs of Staff had raised the issue, the argument was in essence the old question of who should prevail, Eisenhower or Montgomery. Since Marshall and the American Joint Chiefs had promised the Supreme Commander their support, Eisenhower told Bradley to get on with his drive through the Eifel, but he hedged the approval with a qualification stringent enough to reassure his British critics of his continued adherence to a main effort in the north. Nothing short of quick, decisive penetration of the frontier defenses of the *Westwall* and swift exploitation would spare Bradley from shifting divisions northward to the Ninth Army and assuming a supporting role.

Quick, decisive penetration, Bradley quickly discovered, would be hard to achieve. Although the Germans were, as expected, moving troops northward from the Eifel, the snow was too deep, the cold too bitter, the fatigue of American divisions too ingrained for success to come quickly. For five days, from January 28 through February 1, two corps of Hodges' First Army and one of Patton's Third tried to penetrate the frontier defenses northeast of St. Vith astride the Losheim Gap, but to little avail. Even when the enemy was nowhere in evidence, as was sometimes the case, infantrymen had to plough through snow piled in places in waist-high drifts, while tanks, artillery, and trucks piled up on icy roads in traffic jams that took hours to disentangle.

By the end of the first day of February the American divisions had accomplished little more than to draw up to the first pillboxes of the *Westwall*. That looked depressingly little like breakthrough.

Before the day was out, the Damoclean sword that had hung over the offensive from the start fell with a clatter. Eisenhower ordered Bradley to halt and begin transferring divisions to the Ninth Army. Although he afforded a few days' grace for securing the shoulders of the Losheim Gap to assist subsequent operations, the First Army was to move immediately to seize the Roer dams and then prepare to jump the Roer to protect the right flank of the Ninth Army in Montgomery's drive to the Rhine. Eisenhower also authorized Patton to nibble at the Eifel as resources permitted to gain a line of departure that might later prove useful.

The focus of Allied attack at that point shifted inevitably to the north. On February 8, from positions between the Maas and the Rhine gained in Operation MARKET-GARDEN, the First Canadian Army was to attack southeastward in an offensive called Operation VERITABLE. A day later—assuming the Roer dams were in hand—General Simpson's Ninth Army was to cross the Roer in Operation GRENADE, then swing northeast to link with the Canadians close along the Rhine.

In addition to taking the Roer dams, American forces faced two other assignments before they could be free to turn full attention to the drive to the Rhine. They had to clear a triangle embracing some one hundred square miles between the Saar and Moselle rivers south of their confluence near the old German border city of Trier; the base of the triangle was protected by a spur of the *Westwall* that the Germans called

Orscholz Sehnenstellung, or the Orscholz Switch. The Americans also had to eliminate, with French help, that irritating German bridgehead measuring some thirty by fifty miles on the Rhine's west bank south of Strasbourg—the Colmar Pocket.

The Germans had about 50,000 troops in the Colmar Pocket, constituting the bulk of the *Nineteenth Army*. Despite protests from Commander-in-Chief von Rundstedt that these men had served their purpose and should be withdrawn to fight again another day, Hitler, as usual, refused. As General Eisenhower reinforced General Devers' 6th Army Group with two American divisions—thereby enabling Devers for the first time to turn American forces to help the French—the task of reducing the pocket became a question only of hard fighting and time.

After some preliminary nibbling at the pocket by an American division and five French divisions of de Lattre's First French Army, an American corps that included five American divisions loaned from the Seventh Army joined the attack on January 29. With the French advancing from the south, the Americans from the north, the Allied forces split the pocket a week later, but by that time Rundstedt had at last wrung permission from Hitler to begin withdrawal. At a cost to French and Americans of 18,000 casualties and to the Germans of almost twice that number, by February 9 the west bank of the Rhine south of Strasbourg was finally free of Germans.

Eliminating the little Saar-Moselle triangle involved no such numbers, but in the cruel winter weather of late January and early February it was a harsh enough task for those involved in it. For almost a month, beginning late in January, the 94th Division picked at the pillboxes of the Orscholz Switch, then on February 19 launched an all-out attack. Three days later armored reinforcements erased the last Germans from the triangle, then went on to take Trier, where they found intact both the ancient *Kaiserbruecke* and the triumphal arch which link the city with the Romans and the earliest days of the Christian era.

The eyes of most Allied commanders had been focused in the meantime on another one-division attack designed finally to seize the Roer River dams. Unless the dams could be taken before February 9, General Simpson's Ninth Army would be delayed in launching the American portion of Montgomery's big drive to the Rhine.

The upstream dam, the Urft, fell quickly—a fact explained later when engineers discovered that the Germans already had destroyed discharge valves in a viaduct carrying waters of the Urft reservoir to a point downstream from the other dam, the Schwammenauel. Against the downstream dam, a relatively inexperienced 78th Division began to attack on February 5, but such strength did the Germans gain from pillboxes of the *Westwall* and from densely forested rollercoaster terrain that the Ninth Army's target date of February 9 passed with the Germans still in control of the dam.

It was just past midnight on the ninth when an American battalion at last gained the dam, and engineers entered a tunnel leading to the machinery controlling the discharge mechanism. Expecting the Germans to demolish the dam at any moment, the engineers crept slowly forward.

An explosion never came. The explanation was that the Germans already had done all the damage intended, destroying the control machinery and the discharge valves. That had precipitated no major cascade of water but instead a steady flow calculated to create a flood in the valley of the Roer downstream in front of the Ninth Army that lasted not for a few days but for more than two weeks. The Canadians in Operation VERITABLE had to fight alone while the Ninth Army waited impotently for the swollen Roer to subside.

Nowhere on the western front in World War II were the conditions of battle more trying than southeast of Nijmegaen in the low-lying countryside between the Maas and Rhine rivers in February 1945. Mud, flood, and cold would have been enemies enough in their own right. Because the Germans read the First Canadian Army's attack for what it was—the opening blow of the Allied drive to the Rhine—and took advantage of the protective moat of the flooded Roer River to rush every possible reserve to oppose the Canadians, the fight developed into as grim a contest as either side had yet known.

In the first two weeks the Canadians drew to their front three parachute divisions and such once-illustrious names as the *15th Panzer Grenadier* and the *116th Panzer* and *Panzer Lehr Divisions*. For the Canadians, however bitter the fight, there was the prospect of eventual victory; for the Germans, only a desperate gamble, for those units represented the last reserves in the west. Only if additional reserves somehow could be gathered from some part of the front before the waters of the Roer receded enough for the Americans to cross was there any hope of defeating the American drive.

Dismal was the picture that Field Marshal von Rundstedt portrayed to his superiors in Berlin: a picture that any reasonable mind would have interpreted as requiring withdrawal behind the Rhine. Each German battalion along the Roer, Rundstedt reported, faced the equivalent of an American division. All of *Army Group B*, he noted, had only the equivalent of six and one-half full divisions. What possible hope of holding the line of the Roer? Yet the *Fuehrer* would not even sanction local withdrawals to release a battalion here or there in order to gain some semblance of a local reserve.

As Rundstedt lamented his fate, General Simpson's Ninth Army was preparing a paralyzing blow that would turn out to be one of the last, but also one of the most powerful, setpiece attacks launched by an American force in World War II. Simpson had eleven divisions, a total of more than 300,000 men, plus another 75,000 of the First Army's VII Corps which was to launch a simultaneous Roer crossing on Simpson's southern flank; all that power was to attack from north of Linnich to south of Dueren, a front only about twenty miles wide. The supporting XXIX Tactical Air Command had 375 fighter-bombers. (In quest of surprise through night attack, Simpson was to eschew heavy bomber support.) More than two thousand artillery pieces—one for every ten yards of front—constituted one of the heaviest concentrations employed during the war. That was in addition to almost 1,400 tanks, plus tank destroyers, anti-tank guns, anti-aircraft guns, mortars, and infantry cannon. When it was so obviously expected, an attack had to depend upon power over subtlety, and power was what Simpson had.

The only question mark was the turbulent Roer River. In some places where the river is normally only 25 yards wide, it had swollen to as much as a mile, though more common were inundations of 300 to 400 yards. At Dueren, where the river tumbles through a gorge on its way out of the Eifel, the pace of the current was more than 10 miles an hour.

In setting a new target date for Operation GRENADE, General Simpson sought the first practicable moment when the river might be crossed with reasonable chance of success, rather than wait for it to return to normal and the Germans to come to full alert. That moment might come, his engineers advised him, on February 23, a day before the Roer reservoirs would be drained and just under a fortnight past the original target date for the attack.

* * *

As soon as it was dark on the twenty-second, thousands of men, voices hushed, began to stir. While infantrymen moved into cellars as close as possible to the waters edge, engineers transported cumbersome boats and bridging equipment to within hand-carrying distance of the water. Artillerymen were careful to fire no more than the usual night harassing missions, lest they give away the plot. As the night deepened, an occasional German plane passed overhead, its nationality revealed by the peculiar rhythmic throb of the motor. Incoming mortar and artillery shells were few. Here and there a nervous German sentry sent up a flare. A burp gun stuttered.

Beginning at 2:45 A.M. on the twenty-third, the mass of artillery suddenly thundered Armageddon, illuminating the night as if a host of giant lightning bugs were staging a carnival. Forty-five minutes later, infantrymen began in a variety of ways to cross the glistening black waters of the Roer. Some paddled across in twelve-man metal assault boats; others used motor-driven boats or LVT's (Landing Vehicle, Tank); still others pulled themselves across in rubber boats attached to a cable that a patrol operating under cover of the artillery preparation had anchored to the far bank. At some spots other patrols staked out small holdings so that engineers could follow in assault boats towing pre-assembled sections of duckboard footbridges mounted on assault boats; then infantrymen with weapons at high port raced across.

It was all carefully timed, carefully planned, but not all went according to time or plan. Almost everywhere the swift-running Roer pulled assault boats downstream—75, 100, 125 yards from planned points of touch-down—thus aggravating the problem of who was to attack what on the far bank and upsetting the schedules of followup companies that were to use the same boats. Sometimes the current manipulated a boat into careening circles and hurled it downstream to crash into some partially completed bridge like an amphibious bulldozer. A lucky hit by a German shell severed the cable supporting a footbridge, whereupon the current scattered sections of the bridge hither and yon. German mortar fire knocked out some boats, upset others, though life vests saved most of the men from drowning. Small-arms fire forced some boats to turn back.

As daylight came, at least some contingents of six divisions neverthe-less were on the east bank of the Roer. Yet the coming of day—drab as it was—introduced observed German artillery and mortar fire which smoke pots and white phosphorous shells could not eliminate entirely. Daylight brought German planes, too; not many—one, two, four at a time—but enough to do occasional damage to ponton bridges that engineers were struggling to construct to enable tanks and tank destroyers to cross. Strafing damaged one bridge; bombs knocked out another. Shells from German artillery eliminated other bridges. When night came again—as it does early in northwestern Europe in February—only three bridges serving men afoot and none serving vehicles spanned the swollen Roer.

Fortunate it was for the attackers that the Germans had little with which to strike back. After nightfall the commander of the *Fifteenth Army*, General der Infanterie Gustav von Zangen—a strong-willed man in the classic Teutonic mold—committed his only army reserve: two battalions of foot and thirty-six tanks and assault guns. That produced a flurry of concern at the local point of contact, prompting American infantry to retire to cellars and call down artillery fire on their own positions; but it had little impact on the overall course of events.

Early the next day the Americans finally put in their vehicular bridges, and as big guns, tanks, and reinforcements swarmed across the Roer, the Germans lost all chance of repulsing the assault. Crossing the Roer cost just over 1,400 casualties, including 158 men killed. For an attack on such a scale against a defended river line, the figures were comfortingly low.

As General Simpson, on the third and fourth days of Operation GRENADE, began to wheel his forces toward the north and northeast in keeping with the plan to link with the Canadians in Operation VERITABLE, German commanders saw the full implications of the situation. The north wing of Model's *Army Group B* and the south wing of *Army Group H* (a headquarters created before the Ardennes counteroffensive to manage units in the Netherlands and lessen Model's defensive responsibilities) were about to be crushed in a vise. That would mean the end of most of Zangen's *Fifteenth Army* and all of the *First Parachute Army* facing the Canadians, for neither *Army Groups B* nor *H* had any reserves left. That Hitler would continue to refuse withdrawal behind the Rhine went without saying.

It was with dismay that the German commanders watched on February 17 as General Simpson committed the first of his armored divisions to exploit the bridgehead over the Roer. On the last day of February and the first of March, there was nothing the Germans could do other than go through with a long-projected exchange of zones between headquarters of the *Fifteenth Army* and the *Fifth Panzer Army*, moved up from the Eifel. Designed to put a headquarters schooled in armored warfare in front of the American drive, the move was too late and involved too few resources. It accomplished about as much as shifting a flat tire from one wheel to another.

For the Americans it was everywhere a return at last to the halcyon days of August and early September of the preceding year. The weather was colder, damper; the landscape was more drab; the shop signs were in Old German script rather than French; but it was nonetheless pursuit warfare: goodbye to the slow, grim gains; hello to quick, tankspearheaded dashes. By nightfall of March 1, infantrymen riding tanks were in Venlo on the Maas River, only a mile or so from contact with the Canadians; and an armored division stood only seven miles from the Rhine.

The setting no longer even looked like a battlefield. In one town electric lights were on, trolleys were running. In many a village *Gasthaus*, beer was on tap. Tactical aircraft strafing fleeing German columns lent a kind of discordant note to the scene.

Yet the battle had been more shattered than ended. Here and there, meaningless in the larger picture, fragments hung on, real and bloody to the men unlucky enough to stumble onto them. After dashing forward nine miles one day, a company of the 84th Division on the next encountered a group of persistent German paratroopers defending a town west of Muenchen-Gladbach. Defeating them involved a determined assault over open ground with hand grenade and bayonet. Only two out of half a hundred Germans deigned to surrender. Then the next day the entire 84th Division broke away again.

With the German defense splintered, American commanders began to think in terms of seizing intact a bridge across the sprawling Rhine. Visiting General Simpson on both the first two days of March, the Supreme Commander himself displayed keen interest in the possibility.

Late on March 1 the 83d Division made a dash for Neuss, a Rhine city with three bridges, but found all destroyed. Undaunted, the division sent a task force marching through the night, bent on taking another bridge a few miles downstream at Oberkassel.

With Sherman tanks disguised to resemble German tanks and with

German-speaking soldiers riding the front of each tank to do any talking required, the column moved slowly through the darkness. At one point it passed along one side of the road while German soldiers marched in the opposite direction along the other. With incredible good fortune, the task force reached the outskirts of Oberkassel; but dawn was at hand. A German soldier on a bicycle in another passing column suddenly shouted the alarm.

Their identity discovered, the men riding the tanks turned their fire on the Germans while the tanks lurched forward. For all their verve, they were too late. The Oberkassel air raid siren blew a warning. Even as the lead tanks got astride the western end of the bridge, the Germans blew it.

Four times thwarted, the men of the Ninth Army tried again, this time for the Adolf Hitler Bridge farther downstream at Uerdingen; but there German paratroopers had arrived late on March 2 to form the southern anchor of a last-ditch bridgehead that German commanders planned to hold as long as possible west of the Rhine. Although a combat command of armor got tantalizingly close to the bridge, a big crater denied passage for the tanks, and intense mortar and small-arms fire stymied accompanying infantry.

After dark a six-man patrol led by an engineer captain slipped past the defenders, gained the bridge, crossed it and returned, cutting all visible demolition wires in the process. When German engineers later in the night tried to set off the explosives, they cursed harassing American artillery fire for having knocked out the wires. Although it was dawn before they could install new wiring, they succeeded in blowing the bridge.

After German demolitions had cheated another American division at road and rail bridges at Rheinhausen, not quite six miles downstream from the Adolf Hitler Bridge, no course apparently remained but to get on with reducing what was left of the German bridgehead. Yet General Simpson and an ambitious Ninth Army had other ideas. Why not exploit German failure to execute a timely withdrawal behind the Rhine with a quick surprise assault to cross the river?

Had Simpson been under American command, he would have done the job and asked approval later. As it was, he proposed to Field Marshal Montgomery a crossing south of Uerdingen, then a turn north to clear the east bank for further crossings and to gain relatively open country along the northern fringe of the Ruhr. Since Hitler's stubborn refusal to allow withdrawal had left his field commanders little with which to defend the Rhine and even what was left totally unready to counter a crossing, it was a stratagem that hardly could have failed.

Yet Montgomery said no. To cross near Uerdingen, the Field Marshal believed, was to become involved in the industrial wilderness of the Ruhr. A bitter Ninth Army Staff believed instead that the real reason for refusal was Montgomery's concern that an impromptu American crossing might detract from a grand assault that he himself was planning.

On the night of March 9 the Germans finally pulled back from the west bank of the Rhine, leaving only a few rear guards and stragglers to demolish the last two bridges at Wesel. In just over two weeks the Ninth Army had driven more than 50 diagonal miles from the Roer to the Rhine at Wesel and had cleared some 35 miles of the Rhine's west bank. In the process the army had captured 30,000 Germans and killed an estimated 6,000 while absorbing fewer than 8,000 casualties of its own. In the companion drive, the First Canadian Army had driven 40 miles with a loss of 15,600 men, while capturing over 22,000 Germans.

The Canadians' task had been the more difficult, because of both the flooded countryside and the delay the swollen Roer imposed on Operation GRENADE. Although Montgomery had not planned it so, the two operations had developed in a pattern already made familiar in Sicily and again in Normandy: Montgomery's troops attracted German reserves, while American troops broke through and rapidly exploited the gains.

From the standpoint of prestige Montgomery's refusal to allow a quick jump of the Rhine by Simpson's Ninth Army, however motivated, had in the meantime ceased to matter. Even as Montgomery had turned Simpson down, another American army had stolen a march on all others to jump the big obstacle without pause.

Chapter Twenty-Six – A Rhine Bridge at Remagen

As the VII Corps crossed the Roer to protect the Ninth Army's south flank, General Hodges prepared to put the rest of his First Army across the river. Rather than stage other assault crossings, Hodges evolved a plan whereby one division after another would use bridges of the adjacent division, then shift upstream to create other bridging sites. In that way the units of Major General John Millikin's III Corps were across the river with dry feet by the last day of February, while those of a third corps were getting ready to repeat the process.[195]

The maneuver was part of a new plan devised by General Bradley to carry his 12th Army Group to the Rhine. Called Operation LUMBERJACK, the plan called for the VII Corps to escort the Ninth Army all the way to the Rhine, then to turn and take Cologne—Germany's fifth largest city. The rest of the First Army meanwhile was to drive southeast toward the point where the Ahr River spills into the Rhine; there the units were to converge with a thrust by Patton's Third Army through the heart of the Eifel and create a pocket of trapped Germans in northern reaches of the Eifel.

Although General Bradley's army group had relinquished units to flesh out the Ninth Army, it was still a powerful force. Hodges had twelve divisions; Patton, ten. Furthermore, all through February, Patton had been taking good advantage of General Eisenhower's authorization to nibble at the Germans in the Eifel. One corps had already reached the Kyll River, almost twenty miles inside the German frontier.

By the first of March the Germans facing the First and the Third Armies

---

[195] Here I have relied extensively on Ken Hechler, *The Bridge at Remagen* (New York, 1957), which is based partially on interviews, partially on official records.

could do little but await the obviously impending American blow. On the north the *Fifteenth Army* (March 1 was the day Zangen's and Manteuffel's headquarters changed places) had been hit a glancing blow by the advance of the American VII Corps, while to the south Patton's probing attacks had left the *Seventh Army* almost shattered. A strike by Patton across the Kyll might trap most of the *Fifteenth Army* while finishing off the *Seventh Army* and all but eliminating Model's *Army Group B*. In pushing through the Eifel, Patton also would be clearing the north bank of the Moselle River and thus would imperil the rear of *Army Group G* in defense of the Saar industrial region south of the Moselle.

Hitler had relieved the *Seventh Army's* commander, General Brandenberger, for alleged defeatism. His successor, General der Infanterie Hans Felber, believed that the only hope for his troops and for *Army Group G* in the Saar as well was to give Patton free path to the Rhine and to withdraw the *Seventh Army* behind the Moselle to protect *Army Group G's* rear. Yet in view of continuing orders from Hitler to stand fast, nobody took Felber's proposal seriously. The only change was to transfer the faltering *Seventh Army* from *Army Group B* to *Army Group G*, which accomplished little other than to shift from one headquarters to another the dolorous task of presiding over the army's impending agony.

That agony was quick to come. It began on March 3 when a combat command of armor gained the Rhine north of Cologne, and Joe Collins turned the rest of his corps against the cathedral city. There for the first time a new German force appeared—the *Volkssturm*, a levy of ineffective old men and youths Hitler had ordered to rally to a final defense of the Reich. There, too, the Germans turned imposing 88- and 128- mm. anti-aircraft guns in fixed emplacements against American tanks, a practice Allied troops were to encounter frequently as they plunged deeper into Germany. Yet neither tactic prevented Collins' armor from breaking into Cologne on March 5 and plunging swiftly past the cathedral, still miraculously standing amid acres of bomb-blasted rubble, to reach the Rhine; but the Germans already had blasted the once-impressive Plohenzollern bridge into the river.

General Millikin's III Corps meanwhile was pushing eastward along Collins' south flank. Despite specific orders that the goal was not the Rhine but crossings of the Ahr River in order to link with the Third Army, Millikin and his division commanders still saw the fabled Rhine as the objective. Under Millikin's plan the III Corps was directing a main effort against the Rhine on either side of Bonn, with only one column of an armored division—the 9th—headed for the Ahr.

The emphasis on the Rhine around Bonn coincided with expectations of the *Army Group B* commander, Field Marshal Model. He made valiant but generally futile efforts to reinforce the city's defenses. His subordinate, Gustav von Zangen, saw it another way. The III Corps, Zangen remarked, had entered a terrain whose configuration resembled the cup of a funnel: its spout led southeastward to the Ahr and the nearby Rhine town of Remagen.

Remagen was important because of the location there of the Ludendorff Railroad Bridge, named for the First Quartermaster General of World War I. The bridge was even then being covered with a plank flooring to provide a vital supply artery—and escape route—for the *Fifteenth Army*. In hope of blocking the spout of the funnel leading to Remagen, Zangen begged permission to withdraw the two corps of his army that still were holding *Westwall* pillboxes in the Eifel. Without that permission the two corps soon would be trapped.

Model said no. Not a single pillbox, Hitler had decreed, was to be abandoned without a fight.

To Zangen and to other German commanders on the scene, probably including Model himself, the absurdity of further attempts to hold west of the Rhine was obvious. Yet the word of Hitler still exercised such a stranglehold at every level of command that nobody would authorize withdrawal. At division, at corps, at army, at army group, and even at the level of Rundstedt, commanders focused their General Staff-trained minds on issuing defense, assembly, and counterattack orders that looked as pretty as a war game on paper but made no sense in the stark reality of the situation in the Eifel and along the Rhine. In the process each protested to his next higher commander the idiocy of it all.

Just how desperate was the German situation was quickly demonstrated when, on March 3, Patton launched his attack in the Eifel. The most rapid gains were at the Kyll River, where the 5th Infantry Division, veteran of many a river crossing, sent patrols across in predawn darkness, then hurriedly put in footbridges. The only question remaining was when General Patton might choose to turn loose his veteran 4th Armored Division.

Patton had only one concern—the weather. Days of alternating snow and rain, freeze and thaw had wreaked havoc with the generally poor roads of the Eifel, and continued precipitation could severely crimp a plan for the armor to stick to the roads and leave the wooded ridges to artillery and fighter-bombers of the XIX Tactical Air Command.

Given a rapidly collapsing German defense, weather alone was hardly sufficient reason to delay the exploitation. At daylight on March 5 the armor began to move, cutting first to the north to trap German units still holding along the Kyll, then swinging northeast toward the Rhine. Although rain, snow flurries, and overcast denied air support, the attack quickly picked up momentum, so that reports back to the division headquarters soon began to read like a timetable. By nightfall the armor was twelve miles beyond the Kyll.

The first day did the Germans in. The next day, although fog and rain again denied air support, the tanks raced forward almost at will, clearing the Germans from the roads and villages and prompting them to stream from the hills and woods in great bunches to surrender. At one point a German corps commander saw so many German soldiers clustered about a group of tanks that he assumed it was a German unit. Too late he discovered that the tanks were American, the Germans prisoners.

"Where do you think you're going?" demanded an American lieutenant.

"It looks like," replied the German general, not without a touch of irony, "I'm going to the American rear."[196]

Despite crumbling roads and another day of rain and fog, the advance on the third day, March 7, became little more than a road march, as tank crewmen took no time to capture the Germans who tried to surrender, but instead signaled them to make their own way back to prisoner-of-war cages. Nightfall saw the armor coiling on the reverse slope of the last high ground short of the Rhine.

In just under three days the 4th Armored Division had driven 44 airline miles—much longer by road—and had taken five thousand prisoners, captured or destroyed volumes of equipment, and spread dismay through whatever cohesion remained in the German defense west of the Rhine and north of the Moselle. Everywhere irregular columns of German foot troops, interspersed with a confusion of motor and horse-drawn vehicles,

[196] George Dyer, *XII Corps — Spearhead of Patton's Third Army* (published in Germany, 1947), p. 330.

toiled toward the Rhine, hoping to find a barge, a ferry, perhaps a bridge still standing. Other Germans gave themselves up by the hundreds, while still others tried to slip behind the armored spearheads to escape southward across the Moselle. Abandoned equipment, vehicles, anti-tank guns, field pieces dotted the Eifel in macabre disarray.

As that spectacular advance developed, the First Army's General Hodges acted to remove any doubt that the goal of General Millikin's III Corps was not the Rhine but crossings over the Ahr to link with the Third Army. In response, the 9th Armored Division's commander, Major General John Leonard, directed the bulk of his division down the spout of the funnel toward the Ahr, but still left one small tank-infantry task force headed for the Rhine at Remagen.

The Germans could not so readily resolve their differences over how to defend against the multiple American thrusts. Indeed, order and efficiency had little part in preparations to hold the last great barrier protecting their homeland. Nowhere was this fact more apparent than at Remagen, where a small miscellany of troops operated under a variety of commands. A junior army officer commanded all army troops in the vicinity, but an engineer officer, Captain Karl Friesenhahn, was separately in charge of the railroad bridge. A *Luftwaffe* officer commanded an anti-aircraft detachment, while men of the *Volkssturm* were responsible to officials of the Nazi party.

The command situation at Remagen was destined for even further complication. To hold a bridgehead around Bonn and Remagen, Field Marshal Model set up a separate command responsible directly to Zangen's *Fifteenth Army*. The general in charge was just becoming familiar with the diverse command complex along the Rhine when Model pulled him out to take the place of the captured corps commander in the *Seventh Army*. Model viewed the shift as so urgent that he allowed no time for briefing the successor.

When General von Zangen learned of the change in command, he entertained new fears that the Americans would capture the bridge at Remagen. He ordered the crops commander whose sector included Remagen to send an officer to the town to check personally on the situation.

Before daylight on March 7 the corps adjutant, Major Hans Scheffer, headed for Remagen under blackout conditions over roads jammed with retreating troops. Not until an hour before noon did Scheller reach the railroad bridge—not in time, as events developed, to enable him to get a real grasp of the situation. Sounds of battle already were filtering down from hills to the west.

The American troops heading toward the Rhine had no specific plans for taking a bridge intact. Although the possibility intrigued their commanders all the way up to Eisenhower, so remote was the chance that the methodical Germans would neglect to demolish a bridge that nobody entertained any genuine belief that it could be accomplished.

That made it all the more astounding when an hour after midday on March 7, Second Lieutenant Emmet J. Burrows, commanding the leading infantry platoon with a tank-infantry task force of the 9th Armored Division, emerged from the woods on a bluff overlooking Remagen to see below him German troops streaming in retreat toward a railroad bridge on the southern fringe of the town. Incredibly it still stood—a Rhine bridge at Remagen.

Lieutenant Burrows quickly called to the scene his company commander, First Lieutenant Karl Timmerman. As excited by the discovery as his platoon leader, Timmerman called forward his task force commander, who ordered Timmerman to start moving with his infantry to seize the bridge. When the commander of Combat Command B, Brigadier General William Hoge, reached the bluff, he confirmed the order and directed a platoon of tanks—by coincidence, a platoon of the new, experimental Pershings—to plunge downhill to help.

In mid-afternoon Lieutenant Timmerman, his infantrymen, and the platoon of tanks neared two forbidding stone towers, black with grime, marking the west end of the bridge. As they approached, a volcano of rocks, dirt, and noise erupted. For a moment the men thought the explosion marked the end of the bridge, but it was instead a charge placed on the western approach designed to deny the bridge to tanks.

On the east bank, meanwhile, confusion piled upon confusion. The engineer commander, Captain Friesenhahn, whose responsibility it was to demolish the bridge, spent fifteen minutes on his face, knocked unconscious from the blast of an exploding shell. Even when he came to, he had to await a specific order from Major Scheller before turning the key to set off the prepared demolitions.

That order at last received, Friesenhahn turned the key. Nothing happened. He turned it again, and yet a third time. Still no response.

When Friesenhahn called for a volunteer to go onto the bridge and ignite the primer cord by hand, a sergeant responded. Crouching to avoid machine-gun bullets and shells fired by the American tanks on the west bank, the sergeant dashed onto the bridge, did his work quickly, then dashed back to safety.

Apparently endless moments passed before the anxious Germans heard at last a booming roar. Timbers flew into the air. The bridge lifted as if to rise from its foundations.

Cowering against the explosion, Captain Friesenhahn breathed a sigh of relief. The job was done.

Yet when he looked up again, the bridge was still there.

At the west end of the bridge Timmerman and his men were as surprised—and in some ways as disappointed—as the Germans when the explosion failed to demolish the bridge. Although Timmerman could see, as the dust cleared, that the blast had torn big holes in the planking over the railroad tracks, footpaths on either side of the tracks were intact. Calling for his platoon leaders, he signaled attack.

Bobbing and weaving, dashing from the cover of one metal girder to another, the men made their way across the bridge. Machine-gun fire from stone towers at the east end splattered about them, but return fire from the riflemen themselves and from the big tanks on the Remagen side silenced most of the German guns. Close behind the riflemen came engineers, cutting every wire they thought might lead to additional demolitions and shooting apart heavy cables with their carbines.

The first man to set foot beyond the Rhine was a shy, lanky sergeant, Alex Drabik. Timmerman and the rest of the company were close behind. Once on the east bank the men fanned out to capture cowering German soldiers hiding in a railroad tunnel, then began to climb a precipitous cliff commanding the countryside.

The First Army was across the Rhine.

The reaction of American commanders to the coup at Remagen was positive and swift. Despite the order to concentrate not on the Rhine but on crossing the Ahr, the 9th Armored Divisions commander, General Leonard, ordered reinforcements rushed to Remagen. At headquarters of the III Corps a little switchboard operator who handled the telephone

426

call bringing the news typified the reaction. "Hot damn!" he cried, tossing down his headpiece. "We got a bridge over the Rhine and we're crossing over!"[197]

When General Hodges got the word at headquarters of the First Army, he ordered engineers rushed to the bridge even before he passed on the news to General Bradley. The 12th Army Group commander was in turn equally stirred. "Hot dog, Courtney," Bradley exclaimed, "this will bust him wide open! Are you getting the stuff across?"[198]

General Eisenhower's reaction was much the same. Only the planners appeared to question whether to exploit the coup. Eisenhower's operations officer Major General Harold Bull, who arrived as a dinner guest just after the news reached Bradley's headquarters in Luxembourg City, mentioned the wooded, convoluted terrain eastward from Remagen and the limited road net. Remagen, he said, led nowhere, and "just doesn't fit into the overall plan."[199]

Yet Eisenhower sided with Bradley. Although he intended to stick with the plan of a main effort in the north, he deemed that Bradley had sufficient resources to employ five divisions to hold the bridgehead until it could be exploited later to tie in with a crossing farther south by Patton's Third Army.

Down at the bridge, engineers worked with a fervor to replace the damaged planking and enable the platoon of Pershing tanks that had supported Lieutenant Timmerman's assault to get across the Rhine. A Stygian darkness had descended when the five tanks of the platoon inched safely across; but the next vehicle to try, a tank destroyer, foundered in an unrepaired hole in the flooring. The destroyer appeared to teeter precariously over swirling black waters far below. For almost five hours every effort either to right the destroyer or to dump it into the river failed. Dawn was less than an hour away when engineers at last managed to tow the vehicle back off the bridge.

Reinforced by the five tanks, Lieutenant Timmerman and his men spent a troubled night holding their minuscule bridgehead. The Germans,

---

[197] Hechler, *The Bridge at Remagen*, p. viii.

[198] Bradley, A *Soldier's Story*, p. 510.

[199] Toland, *The Last 100 Days*, p. 214.

fortunately, mounted nothing more serious than platoon-sized counterattacks; but it was with considerable relief that soon after daylight the band of armored infantrymen greeted the arrival of additional infantry, tank destroyers, and more tanks, the vanguard of a host of reinforcements. In the twenty-four hours following seizure of the bridge, close to eight thousand men crossed the Rhine. They could note in the process the GI's penchant for advertising his feats, for a sign was soon up:

CROSS THE RHINE WITH DRY FEET
COURTESY OF THE 9TH ARM'D DIVISION.

So swift was the American buildup, and so confused and depleted were the German forces escaping to the east bank, that chances of dislodging the foothold were from the first almost nonexistent. Rundstedt, Model, Zangen—all three rushed every unit they could find to oppose the bridgehead; but even when they located a force of appreciable size, gasoline shortages and omnipresent Allied fighter-bombers slowed all movement. As regiments reached the front in driblets, local commanders felt impelled by the crisis to commit them piecemeal. Although the fighting was at times fierce enough for the troops involved, never was the integrity of the bridgehead threatened.

Hitler reacted to news of the débâcle with febrile intensity, ordering mock trials and swift executions for any officers who had been anywhere near the scene, including the major whom General von Zangen had ordered to the bridge, Hans Scheller. (The engineer officer, Captain Friesenhahn, was tried *in absentia*—he was in an American prisoner-of-war enclosure—and acquitted.) Hitler, too, for the second time, relieved his aging Commander-in-Chief, Field Marshal von Rundstedt. In retirement in his beloved Bavaria, the old man, unrecognized in civilian clothes, would grow increasingly irritated with shopgirls who snapped at him the German equivalent of "Don'tcha know there's a war on?"[200]

To take Rundstedt's place, Hitler brought from Italy Field Marshal Kesselring; but even the ever-optimistic "Smiling Albert" would find little in the situation along the Rhine to brighten an ever-increasing gloom. It was, Kesselring noted later, like being asked "to play a Beethoven sonata on an ancient, rickety, and out-of-tune instrument."

About all Kesselring could do was join the futile search for units powerful

---

[200] The German equivalent of "Don'tcha know there's a war on?" is a paraphrase of material found in Blumenson, *The Duel for France*, p. 407.

enough to have a decisive effect on the bridgehead—that and to order the *Luftwaffe* out of hiding to try to knock out the Ludendorff Bridge. For nine days the *Luftwaffe* tried, striking not only at the railroad bridge but also at the ferries and tactical bridges that the Americans quickly introduced. With no success.

The Germans tried to get the bridge in other ways as well: with V-2 rockets, eleven of which were fired at the bridge—the first and only tactical use of either of the V weapons; with a giant tank-mounted artillery piece reminiscent of the "Big Bertha" of World War I, the "Karl Howitzer," which fired a projectile of 4,400 pounds but had to be evacuated for repairs after expending a few errant rounds; and with swimmers (Otto Skorzeny in charge) carrying packets of plastic explosives. Using a new super secret development called, for deception purposes, "Canal Defense Light"—an infrared device whose source was undetectable—the Americans thwarted Skorzeny's effort.

As the first excitement over seizing a bridge passed, General Eisenhower reiterated his stipulation that General Hodges commit no more than five divisions to the bridgehead. Bradley in turn told Hodges to limit advances to one thousand yards a day, enough to keep the enemy from mining around the periphery. Once the troops reached the Ruhr-Frankfurt autobahn seven miles beyond the Rhine—one of the express highways with which Hitler had laced the country in order to speed military traffic—they were to hold in place until the Supreme Commander authorized a breakout.

General Hodges—eager to exploit the spectacular gain the little company of armored infantrymen had scored, and also sharply conscious that behind Eisenhower's restrictions lay the careful, ponderous assault to cross the Rhine which Field Marshal Montgomery was preparing—ceased to be his customarily placid self. (Montgomery had asked Eisenhower—some wag had it—to order the First Army to stage a diversion to help the 21st Army Group cross the Rhine; in compliance Hodges had jumped the river.) Despite Bradley's directive to limit daily advances, Hodges became increasingly irritated with what he considered slow, uninspired attacks by his corps commander, General Millikin. Neither Hodges nor anybody in his headquarters tried to conceal the fact that they all wished the bridge had been taken not by Millikin's troops but by "Lightning Joe" Collins' VII Corps. Joe Collins, many said, was Hodges' fair-haired boy.

It at last got through to Millikin what was troubling his superior. While

Millikin had been focusing on southeastward attacks in keeping with the theory of expanding the bridgehead eventually to link with a crossing by the Third Army, Hodges really wanted him to drive northward to clear a crossing site for Collins' VII Corps. By the time Millikin caught on, the Germans had strung their strongest barrier to the north for fear the Americans intended to drive in that direction on the Ruhr.

A steady, apparently capable but colorless commander, John Millikin had failed, while serving earlier with the Third Army, to work his way into George Patton's inner circle. Failing again with Hodges, he was in line for replacement.

During the afternoon of March 17, Hodges telephoned Millikin.

"I have some bad news for you," Hodges said, then went on to tell Millikin he was relieving him of his command.

Millikin waited until Hodges had finished.

"Sir," he said finally, "I have some bad news for you too. The railroad bridge has just collapsed."[201]

It happened when things were relatively quiet, no German planes about, German artillery silent. About two hundred American engineers with heavy equipment were working on the bridge.

The first indication that anything was wrong was a sharp report like the crack of a rifle. Then another. The deck of the bridge began to tremble, then to sway, as if moved by an earthquake. Dust rose from the planking.

It was suddenly every man for himself.

With a grinding roar of twisting, tearing steel, the Ludendorff Bridge slipped, sagged, and, with a convulsive twist, plunged into the Rhine, carrying twenty-eight American engineers to their deaths.

Nobody could say specifically why the bridge collapsed. Bombings dating from as far back as 1940, the weight of the heavy planking, fire of American tanks the day the bridge was taken, the German demolitions, the drumbeat of thousands of infantry feet and the heavy tread of military vehicles, the pounding of German artillery and near misses of German bombs, the constant reverberation of anti-aircraft guns emplaced nearby, the weight of heavy engineer equipment—all probably accumulated to send the Ludendorff Bridge crashing into the Rhine. Yet however dramatic,

---

[201] From a diary of General Hodges' activities kept by one of his aides, Major William C. Sylvan (copy in OCMH).

the event had no effect on operations in the bridgehead, since tactical ponton bridges already were handling the flow of traffic across the river.

As to why the German demolitions had failed—whether some errant shell from a Pershing had severed the primer cord or whether, as myth would have it, some impressed foreign laborer had cut it—the answer plunged into the Rhine with the bridge itself.

The capture of the Ludendorff Bridge was one of those *coups de théâtre* that sometimes happen in warfare and never fail to appeal to man's imagination. Just how much it speeded the end of the war was another matter. Since the bridgehead attracted such forces as the Germans could muster, it clearly weakened resistance to Rhine crossings elsewhere, and certainly the capture did considerable damage to German morale. On the other hand, so weak was the German army that the Allies would have gotten across the Rhine fairly readily in any case. Hitler's decision to fight it out west of the river and to launch a counteroffensive in the Ardennes had seen to that.

Chapter Twenty-Seven – Crossing the Rhine

For all the speed of the American thrusts to the Rhine (Bradley deemed it his most rewarding campaign), the bag of prisoners was disappointing—probably about thirty-five thousand. Many another German made his way ahead of or through the thin armored spearheads to cross the Rhine or to flee southward across the Moselle. Yet those Germans who escaped did so in disarray, with unit integrity in most cases gone, and left behind them small mountains of equipment, ammunition, weapons, vehicles.[202]

The German collapse meant, as General Felber had warned when anticipating demise of his *Seventh Army*, that the line of the Moselle, the rear of *Army Group G* in the Saar industrial region, would be virtually undefended. It was a situation hardly calculated to escape the practiced eye of a George Patton. Patton's 4th Armored Division had scarcely gained the Rhine before he was entreating Bradley and Eisenhower to let him turn swiftly southward across the Moselle to trap the Germans in the pillboxes of the *Westwall* in front of the American Seventh Army.

No German commander could have been unaware of the threat. Unless reinforcements could be found somewhere to bolster the remnants of the *Seventh Army* along the Moselle, warned a new commander of *Army Group G*, General Paul Hausser—he who had been wounded in the Argentan-Falaise pocket while commanding this same *Seventh Army*—envelopment and annihilation of both the *First Army* in the *Westwall* and the *Seventh Army* along the Moselle were inevitable.

Yet still Hitler reiterated with the maddening insistence of a broken record: Hold in place.

---

[202] See de Lattre, *Histoire de la Première Armée Française*; *Seventh United. States Army*, Vol. Ill; Craven and Cate, eds., *ARGUMENT to V-E Day*; and Morison, *The Invasion of France and Germany*.

The stage was set for the kind of driving, slashing attack Patton lived for. While "Sandy" Patch's Seventh Army, with a contingent of de Lattre's First French Army, assaulted the *Westwall* and pinned the German *First Army* in place, Patton turned his Third Army across the Moselle.

On March 12, Patton sent a corps eastward from Trier to attract any available German reserve. Signs of a disintegrating defense already were apparent in front of that corps when on the fourteenth another corps jumped the lower Moselle not far from the Rhine at Koblenz. That posed an obvious threat to cut off the entire *First* and *Seventh Armies* by a drive southward down the west bank of the Rhine. By the sixteenth the threat was distressingly real to the *Seventh Army* commander, General Felber, whom American fighter-bombers forced into an afternoon of hiding with his Chief of Staff in a forest while hostile armored columns rolled by. On the same day a third corps of the Third Army jumped the Moselle between the other two.

Stiffened by the pillboxes of the *Westwall*, the German *First Army* made a fight of it against Patch's divisions, yet how long the *First Army* might hold depended less on American pressure against the front of the pillboxes than on that against the rear. As spring weather afforded free rein to Mustangs and Thunderbolts, the trace of Patton's ground columns as depicted on a map looked, in the words of his colleague, Courtney Hodges, "like an intestinal tract."[203]

While *Army Group G's* Paul Hausser did what he could to rush in divisions from the near-defunct *Nineteenth Army*, only recently evacuated from the Colmar Pocket, he appealed time after time to the new Commander-in-Chief in the west, Field Marshal Kesselring, for authority to pull back across the Rhine. On March 17, Kesselring, who was as aware as Rundstedt had been of Hitler's long-standing and oft-repeated injunction against voluntary withdrawal, issued an ambiguous order. Hold your positions, he said in effect, but don't get trapped.

That was, in Hausser's mind, no authority for wholesale withdrawal, but it was enough to justify pulling out the most seriously threatened units. Division by division he began to peel them back from the westernmost positions of the *Westwall*.

By this time Patton's columns were dashing hither and yon, often

---

[203] See the Sylvan Diary cited in **Chapter Twenty-Six**.

overrunning the boundary between the Third and Seventh Armies before Patton and Patch could negotiate a new one. In the process the armored forays released the first large numbers of impressed laborers from countries the Germans had conquered—DP's, for "displaced persons," or slave laborers. A tattered mass of humanity talking in a babel of tongues, these people had been forced to serve the cruel ambition of National Socialism.

As the American columns appeared without warning, seemingly over every hill and around every curve, and as American planes staged a circus in the sky, hardly any semblance of organization remained in German ranks. Camouflage, dispersal—those were fancy terms from some other war, without meaning in the maelstrom of flight. Highways littered with wrecked and burning vehicles and the corpses of men and animals. Roadblocks built of logs sometimes halting the onrush of tanks and halftracks in defiles or at the entrances to towns and villages but only temporarily and, in the long run, to no point. Improvised white flags flying from almost every house and building to lend a final note of dejection to the scene.

It was less withdrawal than *sauve qui peut*.

Still denied authority to pull back behind the sacred Rhine, German commanders dutifully issued orders to build new lines, to shift units here and there, but those were for the most part war games played on paper. On March 20 the *Luftwaffe* came out of hiding again to stage some three hundred sorties, though to small avail. That same day word arrived at last for what was left of Felber's *Seventh Army* to cross the Rhine, while remnants of the *First Army* were reduced to trying to hold small enclaves around the west ends of three remaining Rhine bridges and were increasingly wary lest they touch off another Remagen.

In that way the Germans prevented a formal linking of the American Third and Seventh Armies until March 22. Approval finally came to withdraw across the Rhine the next day, by which time most Germans who were going to make it already had done so, with or without orders. By nightfall of the twenty-fourth only stragglers remained on the west bank.

As at Argentan-Falaise, the Germans had avoided total catastrophe, yet they had again been badly hurt. Just how many escaped from the Saar, and how much equipment they managed to take with them, would never be determined. Yet the losses obviously were severe. In prisoners alone the two American armies eliminated close to 100,000 Germans. They also cut off from the Reich vital coal and heavy industry in the Saar.

Most important, the west bank of the Rhine from the Swiss frontier to the Channel was at last free of the foe. While there might be no repetition of Remagen, that was hardly necessary in light of other ways, already demonstrated, by which the Allies could cross the Rhine.

As the Rhine maidens in Richard Wagner's opera guarded the gold stolen from the Nibelungs and hidden deep in the cool waters of the Rhine, so the Rhine guarded Germany from its traditional enemies to the west. There the fabled domain of legend, romance, and history—of Siegfried and Brunhild, of Vercingetorix, of Charlemagne, of the maiden Lorelei who sat on a huge rock near the town of St. Goar and with a wild melody lured boatsmen to destruction on rocks concealed in the waters below. There hills crowned by castles, once the strongholds of robber barons who exacted toll from passing boats. There, too, reminders of Julius Caesar and of Roman legions which for four hundred years controlled the west bank, using the river as a boundary between civilization and barbarism and leaving an indelible imprint on such cities as Strasbourg, Trier, Koblenz, Bonn, Cologne.

As George Patton—like Caesar and Napoleon before him (how Patton would have loved the comparison!)—saw his troops draw up to the Rhine, he wanted a quick, spectacular crossing. If for nothing else, he wanted it to produce newspaper headlines like those generated by the First Army's seizure of a bridge at Remagen. He wanted it for a variety of reasons, few of them altruistic; and most of all he wanted it in order to beat a certain British field marshal across the river.

The motive was not entirely selfish. Field Marshal Montgomery, Patton knew, had been pressing General Eisenhower for ten more American divisions to reinforce the 21st Army Group's main effort north of the Ruhr, which included a Rhine crossing that in the jargon of the musical stage would have been called a "production number." Although Eisenhower had denied any intention of relinquishing more American units to the British, Patton—and Bradley and Hodges as well—distrusted Montgomery's powers of persuasion.

They appeared unduly suspicious, for on March 19, Eisenhower had told Bradley that he could build up the First Army's Remagen bridgehead to nine divisions, which made allowance for headquarters of three corps. Once Montgomery crossed the Rhine, General Hodges was to be prepared to break out of the bridgehead and link with a crossing by the Third Army farther south, somewhere upstream from Koblenz. The wraps thus were about to be removed from the First Army, although Montgomery still controlled the timing of the unveiling.

Still dubious, Bradley arranged with his subordinates for the Third Army to jump the Rhine at the first opportunity. "Ike" had put no restrictions on that. Whereupon, once Montgomery made his crossing, Hodges was to break out of his bridgehead to link with Patton in the valley of the Lahn River, which in leading northeast toward Kassel forms a natural corridor, which the 12th Army Group could use to envelop the Ruhr from the south while at the same time getting into position for a continued drive eastward through the heart of Germany. The whole object—in Patton's mind, at least—was to get such a major force committed in a far-reaching campaign that Americans rather than British "could carry the ball."[204]

The man Patton picked to put his army across the Rhine was "Red" Irwin, who long ago had led a contingent of artillery on a forced march across North Africa to intervene decisively in the battle of the Kas-serine Pass. Under Irwin's command the 5th Infantry Division had conquered twenty-two rivers in France, Belgium, and Germany—the latest, the Kyll and the wine-scented Moselle. "Red" Irwin and men wearing the "Red Diamond" shoulder patch at that point were to challenge the really big one, the goal that in September 1944 had seemed so close but, in terms of men's lives and time, had proved to be so far: the Rhine.

They began to cross on the night of March 22, less than forty-eight hours after Patton had told them to, in assault boats rushed forward in a wild ride from stocks carefully maintained far behind the lines since the preceding fall. They did it silently, without advance artillery preparation, at the little town of Oppenheim, ten miles upstream from the Rhine city of Mainz, where the Main River flows into the Rhine. Patton himself chose the site on the theory that the Germans would anticipate no crossing there, since to expand the bridgehead would involve a second crossing operation at the Main.

Although the moon shone with disturbing brightness as boats carrying

---

[204] Patton, *War As I Knew It*, p. 264.

men of two battalions began to cross the thousand-foot width of the Rhine, no sign of protest arose at first from the opposite bank. As the first boat touched down, seven surprised Germans threw hands high in surrender; but a few yards away other Germans manning machine guns set up a clamor. Men in the boats approaching that part of the bank had no choice but to paddle straight into the teeth of the fire, but their losses were few. Altogether the crossing of the Rhine cost only twenty casualties.

By midnight an entire regiment was across, fanning out over canal-creased flatlands extending ten miles to the east; while, in disdain for German artillery, engineers began building bridges under the illumination of tank-mounted searchlights. Here and there the infantrymen ran into a fight that was sometimes disturbingly noisy but seldom costly in terms of casualties. Composed mostly of boys and old men, ill-organized German units exhibited a furious flurry of resistance or delivered a reckless charge, then quickly capitulated. Daylight came before any of the American infantry felt sufficiently pressed to call for artillery support.

On the German side the feeble resistance was readily explained. There stood General Felber's *Seventh Army*, authorized only two days before to pull back behind the Rhine. Charged with defending fifty miles of the east bank, Felber had only one corps headquarters and four divisions; the latter were no more than skeletons and were all positioned farther south, away from the crossing site the Americans had chosen. To man the hastily organized defenses opposite Oppenheim, the Germans had only rear-echelon security detachments, students and instructors of nearby training schools, convalescent companies, and the like.

By daylight on March 23 another regiment of the 5th Division was across the river, and when night came again, the entire division was over. So obvious was the success that the 4th Armored Division also started crossing to begin an immediate breakout from the bridgehead.

Elated, General Patton used the news of the crossing as a child taunts a playmate with a secret. Although he informed General Bradley of the coup early on the twenty-third, he enjoined him to guard the news until that evening. Montgomery's 21st Army Group, both men knew, was scheduled to jump the Rhine during the night only after an extensive aerial and artillery bombardment and with the help of an airborne assault. Patton wanted the world to learn of his impromptu crossing at a time calculated to take some of the luster from Montgomery's achievement.

Late that night, even as British troops were paddling across the Rhine, Bradley passed news of the 5th Division's feat to press and radio. American forces, he announced, could cross the Rhine at practically any point, without aerial bombardment and without airborne support. The Third Army, he went on, had crossed the night of March 22 without even so much as an artillery preparation.

Montgomery's big show, long in the planning and preparation, rivaled the invasion of Normandy in numbers and complexity. The British field marshal had a million and a quarter men under his command—nine divisions in the Second British Army, twelve in the Ninth U.S. Army, eight in the First Canadian Army, and two borrowed from the First Allied Airborne Army. Together the Second and Ninth Armies had stockpiled over 300,000 tons of supplies. The artillery alignment matched and even exceeded that of some of the big pushes in World War I—5,500 pieces. Artillerymen created dummy positions and massed many guns well south of the intended crossing sites in hope of deceiving the foe. Engineers erected elaborate camouflage nets, built dummy vehicle parks, carved new roads, sheered off the sides of buildings to make room for big landing craft to pass. Contingents of the U.S. and Royal Navies were on hand to operate landing craft. Civilians for several miles west of the Rhine were evacuated. Chemical troops for ten days maintained a mammoth smokescreen over the proceedings. In the Ninth Army, troops went so far as to borrow chemical heating pads from hospital units to wrap around motors of assault craft to assure ready starts in the early spring chill.

In broad preparation for the crossing, Allied air forces since mid-February had been executing an intensive bombardment to seal off the Ruhr industrial region by destroying rail bridges and viaducts and attacking canal traffic along a broad arc extending from the North Sea to the southern edge of the Ruhr. As Canadian and American ground troops drew up to the Rhine in early March, American and British tactical aircraft joined the campaign. In the last three days before the ground assault, British and American heavy bombers turned a special wrath against German airfields.

It was all exceedingly impressive, but was it necessary?

Already mortally wounded west of the Rhine, stabbed anew at Remagen and Oppenheim, the Germans in the west were, as the Chief of Staff of one German army group put it, no more than a "shadow of an army." Morale of the troops varied "from suspicion to callous resignation." The officer corps "lacked confidence and wondered just what were the demands of duty." This was an army, he noted, that "could only pretend to resist."[205]

The Germans nevertheless dutifully went about preparing to defend a Rhine already compromised, to fight a battle whose outcome was inevitable. Those standing on the lower Rhine opposite Montgomery's accumulated power had had longer than the others to prepare, but just over two weeks at that; and to hold the twenty-two-mile sector destined for assault, the commander of *Army Group H*, General Blaskowitz, whom Hitler had shifted from *Army Group G*, had only 85,000 men, which was some 35,000 less than the strength of the single American corps that was to be involved. A so-called panzer corps that Blaskowitz held in reserve had only a pitiable thirty-five tanks.

The land on both sides of the Rhine between the northwestern tip of the Ruhr and the Dutch border is low and flat, cut by creeks, canals, and drainage ditches. The average width of the river is about 1,200 feet. Flood-control dikes, sometimes standing well back from the main channel, provided a ready line of defense, as did a railroad built on fill. In winter and at the start of spring it is a drab, colorless landscape, a study in shades of gray, steeped in the musty, coal-tar smell of the nearby industry of the Ruhr.

The focal point of Montgomery's assault was the little city of Wesel, located where the Lippe River empties into the Rhine, for Wesel controls railroads and a spider's web of highways. While a corps of Simpson's Ninth Army jumped the Rhine along an eleven-mile stretch between the Lippe and the start of the urban complex of the Ruhr, then set up a screen against any German foray from the Ruhr, General Dempsey's Second Army was to take Wesel and, with a Canadian brigade participating, was to push downstream and clear crossing sites for the First Canadian Army.

In an airborne attack called "Operation VARSITY," which rivaled and in some ways exceeded the size of Operation MARKET, a division each of British and American airborne troops were to seize a lone stretch of wooded high ground near Wesel that afforded observation of the British crossing sites; they were also to seal off the city by

[205] See Generalmajor Carl Wagener, Chief of Staff, *Army Group B*, "Report of the Chief of Staff, 25 January–21 March 1945" (MS No. A-965), one of several hundred manuscripts written for the U.S. Army by captive German generals, which, along with captured German records, provide the basis for the German story in the official histories (copy in OCMH).

blocking highways entering Wesel from the north and northeast. Since the infantry needed darkness for the river crossing and the airborne troops preferred daylight for their operation, the airborne attack was to begin only after the British had established footholds beyond the river. That way, too, paratroopers and glidermen coming to earth little more than a mile from the river would meet no interference from a preliminary artillery bombardment.

Bridgeheads established, the Canadians were to push northward to the sea to seal off the Netherlands, while the British drove northeast toward Berlin, and the Americans formed the northern arm of a pincers enveloping the Ruhr. The armies, promised Montgomery, would "crack about in the plains of northern Germany, chasing the enemy from pillar to post."[206]

By mid-afternoon of March 23 all was ready for what was probably history's most elaborate river crossing operation. Following a last-minute consultation with the weather prophets, Montgomery passed the code words for the assault to begin. "Two if by sea." It was an old signal that to Americans had once meant that the British were coming.

Night had scarcely fallen when harassing Allied artillery fires began to build in intensity until they became an ear-pounding thunder. The assault opened in the left portion of the Second Army's zone, ten miles downstream from Wesel, at 9 P.M., then like a hungry flame ate its way up and down the river through much of the night. At 10 o'clock Commandos crossed close to Wesel, while at 1 A.M. a Scottish division made a third assault two miles downstream from the city. Against a continuing background of violence an American division (the 30th) slipped into the river at 2 A.M. a few hundred yards upstream from Wesel, while an hour later, a little farther upstream, a second American division (the 79th) launched the final assault crossing.

After all the buildup, all the planning and preparations, all the expectation, all the fury of the preliminary bombardment, it was like jumping into a vacuum. Here and there along the twenty-two miles of river line a few German riflemen, an occasional machine gunner, a mortar crew or so, dared to open fire; but for the most part the Germans cowered in their holes against the hell of an artillery fire that "completely stunned,

---

[206] See Montgomery's operational directive for the offensive (copy in OCMH).

440

scared and shook them." Their own artillery was silent, its eyes put out when Allied shelling disrupted all communications to forward observers.

"There was no real fight to it," noted a lieutenant in the 30th Division. "The artillery had done the job for us."[207]

Such Germans as dared emerge from their holes to engage the assault craft or the infantrymen stepping ashore found their vision blurred by low-lying fog and by smoke from the Allied screen blown in their faces by a west wind. So meager was the resistance that the two American divisions together incurred only thirty-one casualties.

It was not quite the same once the men began to push out from their footholds on the east bank. For the Americans, it was easy enough, since they had hit a weak scam linking *Army Groups B* and *H*; but the British were coming up against markedly understrength but still determined contingents of the *First Parachute Army*. Early the first morning General Blaskowitz committed a panzer grenadier division from his army group reserve against the British farthest downstream, and there, too, German paratroopers held onto a key town and a hillock overlooking the crossing site. For a full day and into the next the British had a fight on their hands until sufficient reinforcements could get across the river. At Wesel, too, the Commandos had to fight a full day to root Germans from the rubble that the little city had become.

It was not quite so easy either for the airborne troops, whose mammoth sky train began to emerge from the haze to the west shortly before 10 A.M. on the twenty-fourth with a steady, awesome drone of thousands of motors. Vast was the air armada: 889 escorting fighters; 1,696 transport planes, including the first combat use of a C-46 that had jump doors on both sides and was large enough to carry an entire platoon; and 1,348 gliders, bringing to the battlefield in one swoop 21,680 paratroopers and glider troops; followed closely by 240 bombers of the U.S. Eighth Air Force dropping tons of supplies. Another 2,153 fighter aircraft either maintained a protective umbrella over the target area or ranged far over Germany in search of any enemy plane that might risk a fight. At the same time 2,596 heavy bombers and 821 mediums attacked airfields, bridges, and railyards throughout Germany.

Inside the transports and gliders men of the 17th U.S. Airborne

---

[207] See my own work, *The Last Offensive*.

Division—who had fought before in the Ardennes but had yet to make a combat jump—and of the 6th British Airborne Division—also making a first combat jump—were even more apprehensive than are most men going into battle, for the word was that the Germans were lying in wait. Radio Berlin had boasted that German commanders knew the airborne troops were coming, and that the trap was set.

The Germans did know—or strongly suspected—yet not from any breach of intelligence but from the very logic of it. They knew the Allied resources in airborne troops—five divisions—and in carriers, and they knew Montgomery's thorough methods. Aware that Montgomery was bound to assault the Rhine somewhere between the Ruhr and the Dutch border, they expected an airborne attack some ten miles or so northeast of Wesel to help the Allies exploit their bridgehead. In that expectation they had moved all mobile anti-aircraft guns they could obtain from other portions of *Army Group H*'s front.

To many a paratrooper floating slowly earthward, a helpless target, and to many a glider infantryman or artilleryman bracing in a flak-rocked ship against the inevitable crash landing, the Germans appeared to have made good their boast. Anti-aircraft and machine-gun fire swept the skies.

Yet however frightening to the individual soldier, however shocking the carnage of wrecked gliders, of crippled aircraft plummeting earthward with black smoke trailing behind, the two airborne divisions hit the ground with most of their power intact. In a matter of hours they had seized all objectives, including the high ground near Wesel and bridges over rivers and canals north and northeast of Wesel that would be crucial in breaking out of the bridgehead.

It was nevertheless an expensive way to get across the Rhine. The 17th Airborne Division alone during the first day lost 159 men killed, 522 wounded, 240 missing. The IX U.S. Troop Carrier Command lost 41 killed, 153 wounded, 163 missing. While these figures might compare favorably with first-day losses in previous airborne attacks, they would bear no comparison with the casualties of the two American infantry divisions that jumped the Rhine by amphibious assault: for the first day, 41 killed, 450 wounded, 7 missing. The airborne assault also cost over 1,000 British casualties, and just over 50 gliders and 44 transport aircraft were destroyed, plus 15 of the bombers flying resupply.

Whether at that stage of the war elaborate preparation and support on the scale that Montgomery marshalled was justified for forcing the Rhine would forever remain conjecture. Simpson's Ninth Army, for example, had Montgomery but approved, might have done it all in one quick stroke back in the first week of March. Yet in the jubilation of success few but the most carping critics continued to labor the point.

"My dear General," Prime Minister Churchill had said to General Eisenhower as the two watched Allied power unleashed against the Rhine, "the German is whipped. We've got him. He is all through."[208]

To a man and to a nation that almost five long years before had known the nadir of Dunkirk, the pyrotechnics of March 23 and 24 were sweet and just and good and right.

As if to underscore the boast that American troops could cross the Rhine when and where they wanted, General Patton's Third Army was readying another crossing even as the 21st Army Group jumped the lower Rhine. It was a two-division assault to be launched over two days beginning before daylight on March 25. Patton actually had ordered it before the crossing at Oppenheim began. He wanted another crossing downstream from confluence of the Main with the Rhine, both as a logical move northward in the direction of the First Army and as insurance against a contested crossing of the Main River, which was the danger intrinsic in the original decision to go at Oppenheim.

The site Patton chose was the Rhine gorge a few miles upstream from Koblenz. There the river has sheared a canyon 300 to 400 feet below the top of adjacent highlands, leaving steep, cliff like sides; at some places the rock face is exposed, at others there is enough earth to support terraced vineyards clinging precariously to the slope. Between river and cliff is space usually for no more than highway and railroad, though here and there through the centuries industrious hands have erected picturesque towns and villages. So sharply restricted, the river flows swift and treacherous. This is the Rhine of the robber barons and of the Lorelei.

The Germans at this spot had had longer to prepare a defense than had those at Oppenheim. Here stood a corps that formerly belonged to the *Seventh Army* and had early fallen back across the river. Recognizing the split imposed on the *Seventh Army* by the Main River, Field Marshal

---

[208] Eisenhower, *Crusade in Europe*, p. 390.

Kesselring had transferred the corps to General von Zangen's *Fifteenth Army*. That made little real difference; Kesselring was merely following the form. So preoccupied was General von Zangen with the Remagen bridgehead that he could provide no help.

The Germans made a noisy show of it in the Rhine gorge, and they took some more lives; but the outcome was inevitable. Crossing first at midnight on March 24, the 87th Division had to abandon one regiment's crossing sites, so treacherous was the current, so damaging the enemy's fire, especially from 20-mm. anti-aircraft guns whose big slugs tore gaping holes in a man's flesh. Yet another regiment crossing nearby had little trouble.

It was much the same the next night when the 89th Division crossed. At one site flares and flames from a gasoline-soaked barge set afire in midstream by tracer bullets lit the entire gorge. Some boats sank; others swirled downstream, helpless in the swift waters. A round from one of the anti-aircraft guns exploded inside one assault boat, killing company commander and first sergeant at one blow; but other men got across, climbed like goats up the steep, terraced hillsides, fought their way through the storybook villages and up winding roads beyond. Somebody soon raised an American flag atop the Lorelei.

The next to challenge the Rhine was "Sandy" Patch's Seventh Army, upstream close by the Third Army's Oppenheim site on either side of Worms, where four centuries before Martin Luther had faced the judgment of the Imperial Diet. The plan at first was to use an airborne division to secure the hills and forests of the Odenwald, which command the flatlands bordering the Rhine; but rather than accept a week's delay while the paratroopers made ready, Patch decided to go without them. Although the main strength remaining in General Felber's *Seventh Army* stood at this location rather than at Oppenheim, Patch entertained no real concern about what the enemy might muster against him.

Foregoing artillery preparation in favor of surprise, two divisions began crossing some three hours before daylight on March 26. The 45th Division achieved surprise, but opposite the 3d Division vigilant German pickets detected the maneuver before the first assault craft entered the water. The Germans opened fire with mortars and with air bursts from fixed anti-aircraft guns located a little to the south in defense of the city of Mannheim.

With the chance for surprise lost, American artillery responded with a drumbeat of fire as if to set the east bank ablaze. In a little over half an hour the artillery expended 10,000 rounds. When men in power-driven assault boats slipped into the water, hardly a round of small-arms fire, scarcely a shell distracted them. In less than a minute the first boats were across, the occupants scrambling ashore with rifles and submachine guns at the ready. Tanks equipped with canvas floats like those the Allies had used on D Day followed the infantry quickly across.

As night came on the first day, supporting engineers were fast spanning the Rhine with tactical bridges, and the leading infantrymen already were beyond the Frankfurt-Mannheim autobahn, eight miles from the river. The day's losses were comparatively few—42 men killed, 150 wounded.

So ecstatic upon first crossing the Rhine was history-conscious George Patton that he dropped to the ground and scooped up dirt with his fingers after the manner of William the Conqueror come to England. (Disdainful, too; for on the way across he had stopped to urinate in the waters, as Churchill before him had done on the Siegfried Line.) Twice already men of Patton's command had conquered the river, but with one of his three corps still on the west bank, Patton had in mind yet another assault.

Patton wanted the 80th Division to cross from slips and docks along the waterfront in Mainz while other troops of the same division, having moved into the Oppenheim bridgehead, jumped the Main River three miles upstream from confluence with the Rhine. That way he might make quick work of linking his other two bridgeheads and open Mainz to the building of permanent rail and road bridges needed to speed his army's advance through Germany.

It was a noisy little war the 80th Division staged at Mainz and a few miles away on the Main River before daylight on March 28; but few—on the American side, at least—got hurt by it. Following a half-hour artillery preparation, men of one regiment pushed out from the Mainz waterfront amid a blaze of German fireworks, mainly small arms and 20-mm. anti-aircraft fire. Once the troops were ashore, the Germans mounted two small counterattacks, but like the fire on the river, they produced more tumult than effect. By the end of the day more than nine hundred Germans had surrendered, while the American regiment lost not a man killed and only five wounded. One of the more noteworthy events of the day was the finding of four thousand cases of champagne.

The regiment along the Main encountered less clamor but took a few more losses: three men killed, three missing, sixteen wounded; but there, too, it looked more like theatrics staged by *condottieri* than genuine battle. By early afternoon the regiment had linked its bridgehead with the Rhine crossing at Mainz, and bridge building was already under way.

One of the casualties of this and of the other Third Army crossings was the German *Seventh Army* commander, General Felber. Although anyone on the scene could have testified to the impossibility of Felber's task of holding the Rhine inviolate with the bits and pieces left to his command, that was no excuse to a demanding *Fuehrer*. As at Rema-gen, somebody had to pay. Hitler relieved Felber and put in his place a former interim commander of the *First Army*, General der Infanterie Hans von Obstfelder.

As darkness fell on March 28, Canadians were across the Rhine, also the British, and Americans in abundance—all the major allies except the French. A sensitive Charles de Gaulle was unprepared to accept that situation. The next day he sent a telegram to his field commander, General de Lattre.

"My dear General," wired de Gaulle, "you must cross the Rhine, even if the Americans do not agree and even if you have to cross it in rowboats. It is a matter of the greatest national interest."[209]

Something deeper than the mere glory of planting the tricolor on the Rhine's east bank was disturbing de Gaulle. In meeting the Russians at Yalta in February, British and Americans had agreed that for the postwar occupation of Germany, the French should be accorded a zone; but they had yet to do anything about it. De Gaulle was becoming increasingly troubled lest the other governments deny his nation's rightful role in administering the affairs of an enemy that had bled France so cruelly. If French troops crossed the Rhine and carved out their own share of Germany, that would erase the problem.

De Lattre actually was a step ahead of his chief of state. On the twenty-seventh the First French Army commander had gone to General Devers and arranged to extend the French sector northward to face a portion of the Rhine's east bank that was unguarded by pillboxes of the *Westwall*. In agreeing, Devers told de Lattre to prepare to cross the Rhine and turn

---

[209] De Lattre, *Histoire*, pp. 487-90.

south and southeast. Watching Patch's Seventh Army swiftly expand its bridgehead at Worms, de Lattre determined to get across fast lest rampaging American columns usurp his crossing site.

The way the French did it made even Patton's jump of the river at Oppenheim look like a deliberate, setpiece assault. Unable to put their hands on but one assault boat—and that one made of rubber—men of an Algerian division nevertheless began before dawn on March 31 to cross the Rhine, shuttling silently over, ten at a time. They had located four more rubber boats to speed the shuttle when shortly before daybreak the Germans awoke to the crossing and began to shell the site. The Germans were too late. A company already had made it, and the French were on the east bank to stay.

The crossing was at Speyer, ten miles upstream from Mannheim. A few miles farther upstream a more conventional crossing fared less well. Delayed in preparations for the assault, a Moroccan division began to cross only after daylight had come. Exposed to German observation, only three of twenty power-driven assault boats survived small-arms and mortar fire to make it to the east bank. While thirty men clung grimly to a foothold, French artillery encased them in fire until subsequent waves could bring reinforcements. Only when night produced relief from German observation was success of the bridgehead assured.

The crossings near Speyer in effect marked the end of the passage of all three Allied army groups to the east bank of the Rhine. The great river barrier remained a challenge only to those who followed the infantry to build the bridges.

Chapter Twenty-Eight – Reducing the Ruhr

As the month of April opened, a mighty Allied host grown to ninety divisions and almost four and one-half million men faced a tatterdemalion German army teetering on the brink of total defeat and a nation as nearly prostrate as had been any power in history while still continuing to resist. Cities devastated, the housing situation nearly desperate, the food supply only relatively less so, refugees numbering in the millions. In the west, all of the Rhineland lost, including the industry of the Saar; in the east, Poland, East Prussia, Rumania, Bulgaria, Greece, and much of Yugoslavia and Hungary. And the Russians held a bridgehead over the Oder River some thirty miles from Berlin.[210]

Yet the war went on. How and why was to many on the Allied side incredible, incomprehensible.

Many factors accounted for the Germans' stubborn resistance: the miracle that Hitler and National Socialism had wrought in years past by saving Germany from Marxist revolution; the place in the sun that Hitler had afforded a people commiserating with themselves over the presumed injustices of the Treaty of Versailles; the hatred and fear of bolshevism and international Jewry that Hitler and his propagandists had day in, day out pounded into German minds; the network of secret police that the Nazis had made integral to German life; the Wagnerian delight in cataclysm that was so much a part of the German psyche; finally, the personal magnetism

---

[210] In addition to my own work, *The Last Offensive*, see Pogue *The Supreme Command*; Toland, *The Last 100 Days*; *Conquer — The Story of Ninth Army*; Craven and Cate, eds., *ARGUMENT to V-E Day*; Churchill, *Triumph and Tragedy*; Smith, *Eisenhower's Six Great Decisions*; Forrest C. Pogue, "The Decision to Halt at the Elbe" in Greenfield, ed., *Command Decisions*; and Stephen Ambrose, *Eisenhower and Berlin, 1945 — The Decision to Halt at the Elbe* (New York, 1967).

of Hitler and his ability to transmit to others his own remarkable faith that the war somehow could be brought to a favorable end.

Given time, political *démarches*, dissent among the Allies, even continued conventional military efforts, Germany could anticipate eventual salvation. Given time alone, new miracle weapons could be developed and existing weapons improved so that the enemy still could be thwarted. Quit now, and all is lost; hold on, and something will happen to help; or in any case let us all perish together. That the reasoning was nihilistic mattered little.

Some, like the wife of the deputy chief of the Nazi party, put their faith in miracle. Gerda Bormann wrote to her husband:

In some ways, you know this reminds me of the "Twilight of the Gods" in the Edda. The giants and the dwarfs, the Fenris wolf and the snake of Mitgard, and all the forces of evil are in league against the gods; the majority have already fallen, and already the monsters are storming the bridge of the gods; the armies of the fallen heroes fight an invisible battle, the Valkyries join in, the citadel of the gods crumbles, and all seems lost; and then, suddenly, a new citadel rises, more beautiful than ever before, and Balder lives again.[211]

Yet there were others, some in high places, who recognized that no new citadel would rise, that Balder would have no second life. Men like Albert Speer, Reich Minister for Armament and War Production, who on the basis of his knowledge of a sadly flagging economy had realized the inevitable as early as two months before. Others, too; but like Ludendorff when, on the western front in the fall of 1918, he had recovered from a momentary lapse of nerve, they believed there were bargains to be struck at a time when Germany had nothing left to barter.

As early as mid-January the Reich Foreign Minister, Joachim von Ribbentrop, had sent secret emissaries to Sweden and Switzerland to try to contact Allied representatives to discuss a negotiated peace, but without success. In late January the Chief of the General Staff, Heinz Guderian, had urged on Hitler peace in the west, so that what was left of the German armies might concentrate against the bolshevik horde in the east; but it earned him only an accusation of "high treason"[212] from his *Fuehrer*. In February, Oberstgruppenfuehrer und General der Waffen-SS Karl Wolff, Hitler's SS chief in northern Italy, had gained a better reception

---

[211] H. R. Trevor-Roper, ed., *The Bormann Letters* (London, 1954), p. 177.

[212] Heinz Guderian, *Panzer Leader* (New York, 1952), pp. 401-2 and 404-5.

with an idea not dissimilar but couched in more positive terms. Pointing to a "natural difference between these unnatural allies"[213]—the United States, Britain, and the Soviet Union—Wolff suggested that the way to split the enemies of the Reich was to dicker with the Anglo-Americans. Although Hitler failed to say yes, he also failed to say no, which was to Wolff license to seek contacts in Switzerland.

Either in the bomb-damaged Reich Chancellery or, more often, in the *Fuehrerbunker* fifty feet under the garden of the Chancellery, Hitler himself trod a narrow path between acknowledging defeat and believing in miracle, between sanity and insanity. Only with difficulty had his subordinates in February talked him out of denouncing the Geneva Convention, ordering all captured airmen shot, and resorting to gas warfare. While his nation fell apart, he spent long, tedious hours arguing trivial details (promotion policy for officers, whether to cut down trees in the Tiergarten to make an aircraft landing strip) or, without regard for realities, raging at the presumed perversities of his underlings ("I am lied to on all sides. I can rely on no one. They all betray me"[214]).

On March 19, apparently having accepted the inevitability of defeat and determined to bring the entire German nation down with him, he ordered a "scorched earth" policy designed to turn Germany into a wasteland—an order circumvented only by the subterfuge of Albert Speer. On the first of April he called on all Germans to become "werewolves" to prey on Allied troops, Jews, and anybody who deigned to cooperate with Allied authorities. Even the long-expressed faith in miracle weapons had begun to pale.

Yet in the curious little world of delusion he had constructed for himself, the *Fuehrer* only a few days later could return enthusiastically to the belief that in the same way the death of the Czarina had saved Frederick the Great in 1762, some miracle would happen to drive the rabble from the temple of the Third Reich. Somehow the grand alliance between east and

---

[213] Toland, *The Last 100 Days*, p. 73.

[214] This and other quotations on the last days of Hitler are from the vast documentation available in a number of works, most of which have drawn on the surviving fragments of the Fuehrer Conferences. See Pogue, *The Supreme Command*; Shirer, *The Rise and Fall of the Third Reich*; Alan Bullock, *Hitler: A Study in Tyranny* (New York, n.d.); H. R. Trevor-Roper, *The Last Days of Hitler* (New York, 1947); Felix Gilbert, *Hitler Directs His War* (New York, 1950); Toland, *The Last 100 Days*; Cornelius Ryan, *The Last Battle* (New York, 1966); and Guderian, *Panzer Leader*.

west was going to fall apart, and the Western Allies would come obsequiously begging a magnanimous Germany to allow them to join the holy war against bolshevism.

The fighting, particularly in the west, was almost devoid of central direction. The old order to stand fast, nowhere to give ground, was still the order of the day, the only strategy. Such decisions as Hitler did make were usually based on the colored daily briefings of General Jodl, who had long since learned how to phrase his remarks to avoid inciting the *Fuehrer* to rage. In any event, the once powerful high command was reduced to pondering trivialities: when, for example, five assault guns, the only available reserve, might be moved against the bridgehead at Oppenheim.

Not even the new commander in the west, Field Marshal Kesselring, knew for sure how many troops remained. Since the start of the battle for the Rhineland in February, the Germans had lost more than 250,000 men as prisoners of war alone. Although Kesselring's operations map showed more than sixty divisions, some were no more than Staffs, others only small task forces, and none was anywhere near full strength. They represented, according to Allied estimates, the equivalent of only twenty-six complete divisions, in marked contrast to Eisenhower's ninety.

It was a dismal picture, in which few other than a megalomaniac like Hitler could have seen any hint of hope. Yet see it Hitler did—or he professed to do so. The battle then developing in the east against the Russians along the Oder and Neisse rivers, the Germans would win, Hitler insisted, if only the armies from the west could be held at arm's length for a few more weeks. If Kesselring could delay long enough, Hitler could form a reserve, mustered from all able-bodied manpower still uncommitted to the fight. To be assembled in the Harz Mountains of central Germany and known as the *Twelfth Army*, the reserve was to come to Kesselring's rescue by counterattacking through Model's *Army Group B* to split the Allied armies, to achieve what the Ardennes counteroffensive had failed to achieve with one hundred times the power.

It was as absurd, as futile, as a dog baying at the moon, yet infinitely more serious, for each new germ of an idea that emerged from the *Fuehrer*'s tortured mind cost more human lives, generated more human misery.

Some sane Allied minds were fairly adept at that business themselves.

To anybody who only slightly appreciated the situation, the strategic air war was long since won. Gone, obliterated, were any targets that mattered in the face of the overwhelming Allied strength on the ground. Yet men wearing airman's blue continued to draw big ovals with grease pencils on acetate overlays marking targets that they rationalized in one way or another as legitimate objectives but that were, in reality, people.

There were in particular some among top British air commanders, long wedded to the concept of area as opposed to precision bombing, who clung to the theory that air power might yet do the job that early exponents expected of it, and force German capitulation. As Germany neared military collapse, a series of powerful air raids against cities in eastern Germany that had yet to feel the true fury of strategic aerial bombardment, might precipitate surrender.

The idea attracted few supporters until after the Russians launched their big ground offensive in January. In light of apparently growing Russian suspicion of Allied motives, how better to demonstrate political solidarity than by military assistance? Raids on cities through which the Germans might be funneling reinforcements to the east would be a clear demonstration of a desire to help. Furthermore, the raids might increase the panic and confusion presumed to be present in cities full of refugees from Russian armies on the rampage and from the rape and murder that went with them.

The idea caught on. Churchill pressed it, and the Combined Chiefs in their meeting on Malta directed that it be done. At Yalta—that wake where the Russians picked at the carcass of Europe and demanded concessions of the next of kin—Stalin cooperated by going so far as to ask that it be done.

That gave the strategic air war a new lease on life. Berlin, Vienna, Magdeburg, Cottbus, Chemnitz, Dresden—the Allied air command responded nobly.

The worst of all was one of the first: Dresden, that city of such baroque architectural treasures that refugees had flocked there in belief that none but barbarians would desecrate it. The Allies, word had it, would spare Dresden in exchange for the *Luftwaffe's* having spared Oxford. Yet again, as at Hamburg, a fire storm, that scene out of Hell—only worse. Somewhere around 135,000 deaths. Nobody could ever be sure, but possibly more than the combined total of deaths in the atomic destruction of Hiroshima and Nagasaki, which was yet to come.[215]

---

[215] David Irving, *The Destruction of Dresden* (London, 1963).

The appetite of Allied air commanders was fortunately soon sated, partly because they feared that further bombing would complicate enormously the problem of reconstructing some rational existence out of the ruin. On April 7 the British called off further area strikes. Not quite a fortnight later General Spaatz, speaking for the Americans, declared the strategic air war won.

Cruel it had been right up to the last. But what of Rotterdam, of Coventry, of Lidice, of Oradour-sur-Glâne, of Klisoura, and of Warsaw? What of hostages executed summarily, people packed in freight cars and shipped away like so many cattle? And what of that unspeakable horror that the ground armies had begun to uncover even as the strategic air war ended—the concentration camp? The world might well ponder whether Hamburg, Dresden, and all the rest were punishment enough.

As the ground war surged beyond the Rhine, George Patton permitted himself an extravagance. Ecstatic when the 4th Armored Division seized crossings over the Main River beyond the Oppenheim bridgehead, Patton told the commander of his XII Corps, Major General Manton Eddy, to send an armored task force to liberate American officers from a prisoner-of-war camp outside the town of Hammelburg.

That meant a thrust sixty miles to the east at a time when the XII Corps was swinging northward to join the First Army for the sweep to encircle the Ruhr. Eddy protested vociferously. So did a new commander of the 4th Armored Division, General Hoge, who a few weeks earlier had led the combat command of the 9th Armored Division which had seized the bridge at Remagen.

Patton would listen to no one, displaying a fixation that puzzled Hoge until Patton's aide-de-camp explained confidentially what lay behind the assignment. Patton had reason to believe that one of the prisoners at Hammelburg was his thirty-nine-year-old son-in-law, John Waters, captured long months ago on a barren djebel behind the Faid Pass in Tunisia.

In the early morning darkness of March 26 a task force built around a company each of tanks and armored infantry under command of a lanky, red-haired New Yorker with a mustache, Captain Abraham J. Baum, began to roll. Patton's aide, Major Alexander Stiller, who as a sergeant had served with Patton in World War I, was along for the ride "looking for a thrill." He would get that and more.

Spraying doorways and windows with machine-gun fire, tanks and halftracks dashed through towns and villages, quickly picking up momentum. At one point they passed unknowingly within two miles of headquarters of the German *Seventh Army*, which spread the alarm that American armor—possibly an entire division—had broken loose. At Lohr, half the distance to Hammelburg, Baum's Shermans had to blast through a barricade, losing a tank to a *Panzerfaust* in the process. Shooting up locomotives, a flak train, a truck convoy, the column dashed on, but at another town the Germans blew a bridge, destroying two more tanks.

It was well into the afternoon before the task force approached Hammelburg and *Oflag XIIIB* three miles to the south.[216] Baum's tanks and halftracks were heading up a ridgeline toward the camp when a battalion of German assault guns that had arrived by chance only minutes before opened fire. As a full-scale engagement ensued, more than one thousand American and three thousand Yugoslav prisoners pressed to the windows of dull, drab prison barracks, jubilant in their approaching hour of liberation.

Losing three Shermans and seven halftracks, Task Force Baum at last beat off the assault guns and continued toward the barracks with some gunners still firing at uniformed Yugoslav prisoners they took for Germans. As bullets riddled the frail barracks, the German commandant excitedly agreed to surrender but asked an American volunteer to go under a white flag to stop the firing.

The main object of the battle (though he did not know it), John Waters, offered to go. With a German interpreter and two other volunteers, he marched forth, but he had not reached the task force when a lone German soldier fired a single shot from a rifle and struck him in the right thigh.

Darkness was falling when Baum's tanks at last crashed through enclosing wire fences and broke into the camp. As ebullient prisoners swarmed about, grasping the hands of their liberators, clutching at proffered cigarettes, Captain Baum was shocked to learn there were not 900 Americans, as Patton had said, but close to 1,300. Having already lost many of his tanks and other vehicles, he had no way of handling anywhere near that many for the hazardous return journey.

The revelation that Baum's force was no vanguard of Patton's army but

---

[216] Patton, *War as I Knew It*; Toland, *The Last 100 Days*; and unpublished material in OCMH on Task Force Baum. I have personally interviewed a number of the commanders involved.

only a small, exhausted raiding party persuaded many of the prisoners that their best chance lay in remaining in the camp. Still others—including Waters—were physically unfit for the ride. Some decided to try it on their own in small groups, among them Lieutenant Alexander R. Bolling, Jr., whose father commanded the 84th Division, and Lieutenant Alan Jones, Jr., who had been on the Schnee Eifel that day in December when his father, commanding the 106th Division, had elected to leave his two embattled regiments on the ridgeline. Still others found a perch on tanks, halftracks, and jeeps and cast their lot with Task Force Baum.

How grievous that lot was soon demonstrated. The task force had made only a few miles before a roadblock at the edge of a village erupted with one *Panzerfanst* rocket after another. The night blazed with exploding hand grenades, machine-gun fire. Amid the cries and moans of the wounded, Captain Baum ordered the column off the road to reorganize.

Out of 307 men who had originally composed Task Force Baum, a scant 100 in condition to fight remained, plus 65 of the liberated prisoners. With these Baum was getting ready to move out again just before daylight when a dozen German tanks and as many assault guns opened a deafening cannonade. Although the task force fought back, within a quarter of an hour every American vehicle was afire or smoldering. Baum deemed he had no choice but to order the men to break into small groups and try to make their way somehow across the sixty miles of hostile land to safety.

Baum himself went with Major Stiller and one of the liberated prisoners. For the better part of the day they successfully hid out, but as the hours passed the sound of baying bloodhounds drew closer. Just before dark a German sergeant spotted them. He fired, striking Baum in one leg. Baum scarcely had time to throw away his dog tags with the telltale "H" for "Hebrew" before the Germans were upon them.

The mission to Hammelburg—blessed from the first with little more than audacity—was over, a total failure. Over the next few days only fifteen men made their way back to American lines, plus a few of the liberated prisoners, including Lieutenants Bolling and Jones.

General Patton put up a brave show before newspaper correspondents, disclaiming any prior knowledge that his son-in-law was among the prisoners. He was probably technically correct, but on the basis of a report that had come by way of the Russians through Eisenhower's headquarters, he had strongly suspected it.

Privately Patton broke down, sometimes sobbing, distressed at what Bradley and Eisenhower might do to him.

As tragic and shocking as was the fate of Task Force Baum, it was but an incident in a ground war that fast was becoming a matter of how quickly the residue of a defeated foe could be swept aside.

The men, the commanders, the units doing the job were old hands, masters of a form of warfare called pursuit, fought less by specific orders than by SOP—Standard Operating Procedure. For the armored divisions, maintenance, resupply, task force organization, attack formations, coordination with covering planes, laagering for the night—these and myriad other functions and details all were second nature. In infantry divisions riflemen were long accustomed to cling to the backs of attached tanks and tank destroyers or to leap aboard two-and-one-half-ton trucks furnished by Quartermaster truck companies or borrowed from corps artillery whose big guns were seldom needed, then to spin forward along highways and side roads in wake of the armor or, when resistance developed, to lend their numbers to reopen the path. With attached weapons and motors, infantry divisions had become the equivalent of the enemy's once-powerful panzer grenadier divisions.

Long past were the gloomy days of rain-swept hedgerows bristling with German machine guns, of frozen, snow-drenched foxholes along the German frontier. Spring was at last more than a promise, while more often than not the war revolved about villages, towns, and cities, so that most men had a roof over their heads at night, and some a bed. Companies vied with battalions and regiments for a town's choicest villa to serve as a command post and dispatched the inhabitants with an unceremonious *heraus!* Sometimes electricity and water still functioned. Every platoon soon had a handsome radio set, which was often traded for a more elaborate model at the next night's stop.

A unit's front was usually no wider than the roads over which the columns passed, so that often only a few men and tanks at the tip saw anything of a fight. Others followed, sometimes bunching to long halts as forward troops cleared resistance, other times speeding to catch up as, accordionlike, the column began to move again. Going the other way were pathetic bunches of Frenchmen, Poles, Russians, Yugoslavs, Belgians,

Dutch, liberated slave laborers on the long march home, responding cheerfully to shouts of passing GI's with fingers raised in the "V" sign for "Victory." Harried military police at intersections grew accustomed to taunting shouts from men on the trucks: "You Frangais? You Belgique? You Rooskie?"[217]

From windows of homes and buildings draped with improvised white flags, German civilians watched apathetically. Others went about their business; here a farmer plowed his fields, there housewives queued for such food as local markets had for sale. Only in a few instances, mainly in cities, did civilians heed their *Fuehrer*'s call to join the fight. German children quickly learned the art of begging chewing gum and candy, and young women sometimes ignored, other times smiled at passing shouts: "*Fraulein, schlaffen mit?*" The soldiers newspaper *Stars & Stripes* and the weekly magazine *Yank* continued to reach the troops, though often several days late. Red Cross club-mobiles operated by blue-uniformed girls who had smiled their way indefatigably through Britain, France, and Belgium continued to dispense doughnuts and coffee. Free cigarettes there were, and an occasional Post Exchange ration, though little of the latter ever reached the tank crew or infantry squad by the time successive echelons had taken their pick. The only solace for the men doing the fighting lay in their getting first crack at the wars top souvenirs—Walther P-38 and Luger pistols.

A new factor was present in combat units with the first appearance of Negro troops in previously all-white regiments. As in World War I, the U.S. Army in World War II segregated Negroes either in service units, a few combat support battalions, or two divisions, but during the Ardennes crisis General Eisenhower had called for Negro volunteers to join the infantry. The first of fifty-three platoons of Negro troops, composed of men who often took reductions in grade to make the transfer, entered the fighting late in March. In the 12th Army Group the platoons were attached one to a regiment to serve under a white lieutenant and platoon sergeant as a fifth platoon in a rifle company. The 6th Army Group used them in provisional companies. In both cases, but particularly when serving in individual platoons, the men earned the appreciation and respect of their white associates, presaging a more rational use of Negro manpower

---

[217] Much of the material in this section are from my own "memoirs," *Company Commander* (current edition: New York, 1968).

in the years to come.

In contrast to the earlier pursuit across France and Belgium, shortages in critical items like gasoline, rations, and ammunition were few, since men of the supply echelon—the Communications Zone, or Com Z—had well learned the lessons of that earlier pursuit. Ports were no longer a problem: Antwerp, for example, was little more than one hundred miles behind the front. Engineers quickly laid fuel pipelines as far as the Rhine and spanned the river with fifty-seven road and rail bridges. A special supply train called the "Toot Sweet Express" (a play on the French phrase *tout de suite*) left Cherbourg every day for depots along the German border. One-way truck routes patterned after the "Red Ball Express" sped forward the most critical items. Since few transport aircraft were needed for airborne operations, almost all flew supplies forward and brought back casualties and liberated prisoners of war.

In the wake of the tank and infantry columns, military government units acted swiftly to establish control. "Passive," "lethargic," "negative," "disciplined"—those were some of the adjectives used to describe German civilians. Liberated slave laborers posed much the bigger problem. Their understandable exuberance sometimes led to tragic excesses, bringing them to inflict on German civilians and even among their own ranks many of the barbarisms they had suffered at the hands of the Germans. Some formed in organized bands to maraud and destroy.

Looting was a problem, too, with the American soldier himself. To many a man, anything in the nation that had plunged the world into war appeared fair game. Looting ranged from simple pilferage—appropriating china or glassware as a substitute for mess gear or taking some trinket as a souvenir (as likely as not, it was discarded another day when something more appealing caught the eye)—to outright theft of objects of genuine value—entire sets of silver and fine china, typewriters, cameras, jewelry, *objets d'art*. General Eisenhower early issued orders forbidding looting and specifying that only items clearly Nazi in origin— flags, armbands with swastika emblems, uniforms, weapons—might be taken as legitimate booty. That order sharply restricted the practice except in expendable's like wine and *schnapps* which could be made to disappear—with not unpleasant results—before some conscientious investigating officer could check on its source.

In order to preclude destruction of industrial facilities, banks, museums, art galleries, German records, special intelligence teams accompanied all Allied armies. Some were charged specifically with locating materials related to German research in supersonic rockets; others, with seeking information on German developments in nuclear fission—as at Strasbourg.

In effect was a directive from the Combined Chiefs of Staff, which General Eisenhower had passed down the preceding fall, forbidding all fraternizing with German civilians. By refusing to mingle with Germans "upon terms of friendliness, familiarity, or intimacy, individually or in groups in official or unofficial dealings,"[218] the Allied soldier was to demonstrate to the individual German his culpability in the carnage his nation had unleashed. Yet it was a policy that inevitably broke down, since it was antipathetic to the very nature of the young, healthy American—and Allied—soldier, particularly when children and women were involved.

Representing a cross-section of the American people, the soldier coming as conqueror was not always the epitome of virtue and discipline that ladies' clubs back home might believe. Aside from looting, some made small fortunes manipulating German and Allied military currency. Like some in every army since man first resorted to warfare, others committed crimes of desertion, misbehavior before the enemy, murder, rape. As pursuit warfare spread, cases of rape took a sharp upswing as more and more men came into direct contact with civilians, as officers lost some of the control they exercised in more static situations, and as soldiers recognized how swiftly they moved from one scene to the next. To many a man unaware of the terror Hitler's propaganda had instilled in German minds, it was difficult to separate fearful lack of resistance from seduction. In any case, did not woman everywhere always say no when meaning yes? Many there were, too, who suspected that crying rape was the German woman's way of getting back at the conqueror.

Yet for all the opportunity for misdemeanor and crime that wartime

[218] See a letter of instructions from Supreme Headquarters, Allied Expeditionary Force, September 12, 1944: subject: Policy, Relationship between Allied Occupation Troops and Inhabitants of Germany, in SHAEF files, The National Archives. Also of value for Allied dealings with the Germans are: Oliver J. Frederiksen, The American Military Occupation of Germany 1945-1953 (Historical Division, United States Army, Europe, 1953); Fraternization with the Germans in World War II (Historical Division, European Command, 1945); Walter Rundell, *Black Market Money* (Baton Rouge, 1964); and Franklin M. Davis, Jr., *Come as a Conqueror: The United States Army's Occupation of Germany 1945-1949* (New York, 1967).

conditions afforded, the number of serious incidents in relation to the tens of thousands of troops was few. The total of major crimes for the entire war, including the early years of buildup in Britain, involved only 53/100 of 1 per cent of the total number of Americans who served in Europe. Seventy were executed: one for desertion; the others for murder, rape, and rape associated with murder.

As seen on big operations maps at higher levels of command, the probing, fingerlike columns engaged in sweeping aside the defeated foe all along the front appeared to have little pattern other than to be moving east. That was an illusion, for in reality from each of the columns strings led, as from puppet to puppeteer, to General Eisenhower's supreme command. The fact that all Allied armies had so swiftly jumped the Rhine had violated the pattern Eisenhower had expected, but that was an exception to fit the circumstances. In keeping with long-contemplated plan, the thrusts of the First and Ninth Armies were eventually to join to seal off the Ruhr industrial region, while all others were for the moment but supporting drives.

What these columns were to do once the Ruhr was encircled was another matter.

General Eisenhower long months before had announced his intention to proceed from the Ruhr to Berlin, which had always been considered both theoretically and symbolically as the final objective in the war against Germany. He planned to vest the assignment in Montgomery's 21st Army Group, assisted by an American army. At the same time he had cautioned that if by the time Allied armies fanned out across Germany, the Russians already had taken Berlin, he might direct Montgomery against the north German ports, Bradley's 12th Army Group through central Germany to synthetic oil plants around Leipzig, and Devers' 6th Army Group to the industrial cities of southern Germany.

As Allied troops crossed the Rhine, the Russians had yet to take Berlin, but from their bridgehead over the Oder just over 30 miles from the capital, they apparently would get there long before Allied armies could negotiate the remaining 275 miles. With Berlin thus apparently out as an Allied objective, Eisenhower saw justification enough for shifting the main effort from Montgomery to Bradley. Since it was logical to return the Ninth Army to Bradley to assure unified command in reducing the Ruhr, that would make the 12th Army Group far the stronger force. Bradley also was in the logical position for driving through central Germany not only to seize the oil plants but also to link with the Red Army and split the Third Reich. Given Russian seizure of Berlin, that was the most worthwhile goal remaining.

In support of Bradley's main effort, Montgomery's 21st Army Group was to take the northern ports and drive to the Baltic coast to seal off the Jutland peninsula, thereby setting up conditions for clearing Denmark and eventually Norway, should the Germans in those two countries hold out. Devers' 6th Army Group was to push through southern Germany into the Bavarian and Austrian Alps to forestall a rumored last-ditch Nazi stand, a so-called National Redoubt.[219]

Aside from the Russian presence and considerations inherent in the assigned objectives, other matters affected the decision to forgo a drive on Berlin. Why expend Allied lives for an objective that had lost most military significance? Lateral German moves could be averted better by linking with the Russians in central Germany than by taking the roads and rails of the capital. And there was no guarantee that Hitler still was in Berlin. Why, also, force an objective the Germans obviously would fight for, only to relinquish it later to the Russians? General Eisenhower was aware that at Yalta, Churchill and Roosevelt had agreed with Stalin on zones of occupation, and the Russian zone encompassed not only Berlin but considerable territory to the west. There was the further consideration that a readily discernible line for meeting the Russians had to be chosen, to avoid a costly collision; and the most logical line appeared to be the Elbe River, some fifty miles west of Berlin.

Left unsaid but unquestionably a factor in Eisenhower's deliberation was the lingering effect of Montgomery's unfortunate press conference during the Ardennes counteroffensive. It was time American command, which furnished the bulk of Allied manpower, moved to the fore, particularly Courtney Hodges and Omar Bradley. Those two were in Eisenhower's opinion among the war's top tactical commanders, yet they had received precious little credit from a press and a public mesmerized by the flair of Patton and Montgomery.

Also unmentioned was the violence the change of plan did to Eisenhower's promise of main effort in the north, given to the Combined

---

[219] Rodney G. Minott, *The Fortress That Never Was* (New York, 1964).

Chiefs of Staff at late as February. That Eisenhower revealed his altered thinking only as Montgomery issued a new order directing the 21st Army Group and the Ninth Army to seize Berlin fanned the resentment the British were found to feel, not only about downgrading Montgomery's role but also about the larger issue: Berlin. When Eisenhower communicated his intentions directly to the Soviet dictator, Marshal Stalin, without going through the Combined Chiefs, who conceivably might have reversed his decision, the British were further incensed.

The British Chiefs of Staff protested both the decision and Eisenhower's communicating directly with the head of the Soviet state. They wanted the message to Stalin recalled until the Combined Chiefs could discuss the subject of Berlin.

The American Chiefs disagreed. To hold up Eisenhower's message would be to discredit or at least to disparage a highly successful field commander. The Supreme Commander was, they rationalized later, within his rights since the Soviet head of state was also head of the Soviet armed forces. (That was a fallacy: otherwise, why not bypass the American Chiefs and communicate directly with Roosevelt, Commander-in-Chief of American forces?) As for Berlin, the American Chiefs deemed that the war against Germany had reached a point where the commander on the scene was best qualified to judge questions of objective.

Dismayed, Prime Minister Churchill appealed personally to both Eisenhower and President Roosevelt: "I say quite frankly that Berlin remains of high strategic importance. Nothing will exert a psychological effect of despair upon all German forces…equal to that of the fall of Berlin. It will be the supreme signal of defeat to the German people."

It was the old argument: military versus political objectives. Churchill himself admitted as much: "The Russian armies will no doubt overrun all Austria and enter Vienna. If they also take Berlin, will not their impression that they have been the overwhelming contributor to our common victory be unduly imprinted in their minds, and may this not lead them into a mood which will raise grave and formidable difficulties in the future?"[220]

While regretting any misunderstanding, a tired President Roosevelt declined to intervene, and Eisenhower stuck by his decision. On the other hand, Eisenhower said, if by the time he had realized the other objectives,

[220] Churchill messages to Roosevelt, April 1, 1945, as quoted in Pogue, *The Supreme Command*, p443.

the Russians had yet to reach Berlin, he would consider moving on the capital; in that case he intended to share honors equally between British and American troops.

When Marshal Stalin predictably endorsed General Eisenhower's decision to head for Leipzig instead of Berlin, the British Chiefs saw in the unusual alacrity of the response Russian recognition of the importance of the capital and a delight that the Red Army was free to take it. The British again asked reconsideration. The American Chiefs again declined. Reaffirming his position, General Eisenhower added: "I am the first to admit that a war is waged in pursuance of political aims, and if the Combined Chiefs of Staff should decide that the Allied effort to take Berlin outweighs purely military considerations in this theater, I would cheerfully readjust my plans and my thinking so as to carry out such an operation."[221]

When the Combined Chiefs failed to take up the challenge, there the matter rested except for a request from Field Marshal Montgomery himself for loan of ten American divisions to help the 21st Army Group reach the Baltic coast and then take Berlin. Eisenhower responded with a light cuff to the car.

It was Montgomery's job, he said, to protect Bradley's north flank, not Bradley's job to protect the British south flank. Berlin, Eisenhower continued, would be taken only if a chance should develop to get it cheaply.

It was medicine laced with extra bitters for the British, for it was a reflection of the new balance within the Allied coalition which they had to accept. While America was mobilizing, the British had had their way in North Africa, Sicily, Italy, and to a certain extent Normandy—but no more. The Americans now provided the bulk of the men, the equipment, the weapons. That put the United States in a position of authority that Eisenhower, who had long nursed a Montgomery-instigated gall, was not about to relinquish.

Winston Churchill took it with his usual good grace. Already he had cabled the President: "*Amantium irae amoris integratio est.*"[222] Which the Pentagon translated as: Lovers' quarrels are a part of love.

* * *

---

[221] From an Eisenhower message to Marshall, April 7, 1915, as quoted in Pogue, *The Supreme Command*, p. 416.

[222] Pogue, p. 444.

So sure was Field Marshal Model that Courtney Hodges would strike straight for the Ruhr that he concentrated such strength as remained in the *Fifth Panzer* and *Fifteenth Armies* against the northern periphery of the Remagen bridgehead. That made it relatively easy when on March 26, having at last received approval for breaking out of the bridgehead, Hodges sent armored columns driving not north but east and southeast. The object was to link with the Third Army and then, with Patton protecting his right flank, to swing all the way around the Ruhr to Paderborn, there to join a Ninth Army enveloping the Ruhr from the north.

In two days the First Army's armor drove forty-five miles, much to Hodges' delight, for the gains gave the lie to newspaper correspondents who had been writing that Hodges had become overcautious in the Remagen bridgehead. One division alone took over twelve thousand prisoners in a day. The thrusts cut off General von Zangen and headquarters of his *Fifteenth Army* from all communication with Field Marshal Model and the rest of *Army Group B* in the Ruhr.

The armor was at that point roaming the enemy's rear echelon and everywhere surprising the Germans, who were not prepared to defend more than an occasional roadblock covered by a smattering of small-arms fire or perhaps by a *Panzerfaust* or a lone self-propelled gun, quickly put to flight. Only on the First Army's left flank, where infantry divisions brushed against the defenders of the southern periphery of the Ruhr, was there resistance worthy of the name. As the advance continued pell-mell on the twenty-eighth, the 3d Armored Division in the lead began to overrun hospitals and to take so many prisoners they had to be sent on their own toward the rear.

A swing northward the next day toward Paderborn made abundantly clear the American intention to encircle *Army Group B*. With the troops and supplies remaining, Field Marshal Model told Kesselring, he might be able to hold out until mid-April, just over a fortnight. The alternative to destruction was withdrawal, and at that stage withdrawal would entail attacking eastward to break the rapidly closing American pincers. That held no prospect of success unless Zangen's *Fifteenth Army*, which Model presumed had escaped to the east, could mount a converging attack to help open an escape route.

Attack, yes; withdraw, no, said Kesselring. Only the day before Hitler had reiterated the order against withdrawal upon pain of death. *Army Group B* would have to stand—and die as well, Model might have added—in the Ruhr.

The futility of counting on any help from Zangen's *Fifteenth Army* would soon be revealed. Tossed about helplessly like chaff in front of the American advance, General von Zangen and his staff discovered on March 29 that the First Army's armor had at last overtaken and passed them by. Herding his headquarters troops into a forest, Zangen watched warily through the day as tanks and other vehicles of the 3d Armored Division rolled past.

When sentries after nightfall reported large gaps in the blacked-out American column, Zangen divided his men and one hundred remaining vehicles into packets and threaded them one after another into the gaps. Rolling with the Americans for longer than an hour, the Germans at last reached a road junction where they turned out of the column westward into the Ruhr. Only one truckload of troops and a motorcyclist failed to make it. They committed the error of calling out in native tongue to the lead vehicle of an American serial that closed up on them from the rear.

Under orders to "just go like hell,"[223] a lead task force of the 3d Armored Division had plunged forward another forty-five miles that day, eager to gain Paderborn and beat the Ninth Army to the interarmy boundary. Crashing through some roadblocks, bypassing others, occasionally shooting up the landscape, the task force incurred its greatest delay when somebody just as night fell discovered a warehouse filled with champagne. That produced the only casualties of the day, but hangovers fortunately are temporary indispositions.

Still some twenty miles short of Paderborn, the armor the next day found the complexion of the battle changed abruptly. During the night a reinforced training and replacement regiment of SS troops from a nearby training camp had manned a defensive line reinforced by sixty Tiger and Panther tanks. The war—*sans* champagne—was on again, and Paderborn remained out of reach.

As Major General Maurice Rose—a man from the ranks, tall, crew-cut, tough—came forward that night to organize a new assault by his 3d Armored Division, four German tanks loomed out of the darkness. After a try at racing past the tanks was thwarted, Rose, his aide, and his driver were forced to surrender. Standing in front of one of the tanks, Rose

---

[223] Toland, *The Last 100 Days*, p. 309.

started either to unbuckle his pistol belt or to remove the pistol from its holster when a nervous German standing in the turret opened fire with a machine pistol. Esteemed by his superiors as one of the best division commanders in the business, esteemed, too, by his men, Maurice Rose pitched forward dead.

That same night Field Marshal Model tried to mount a drive eastward through the rear of the 3d Armored Division to avert *Army Group B's* entrapment. Any hope he might have entertained was dashed in advance by the speed with which the motorized American infantry divisions were following in the wake of their armor.

Of this nobody on either side could be certain as night came again on March 31. In doubt, Joe Collins of the First Army's VII Corps put in a telephone call to General Simpson, whose Ninth Army had broken from its Rhine bridgehead to streak eastward along the northern periphery of the Ruhr.

"Bill," said Collins, "I'm worried. I'm spread out so thin."[224]

His 3d Armored Division, Collins continued, had stirred up a fury of opposition from SS troops near Paderborn. It might take days to eliminate the resistance and continue north to establish contact with the Ninth Army and thereby seal off the Ruhr. If Simpson, on the other hand, could swing southward in a shorter encirclement, Collins thought he might bypass Paderborn to the west and establish contact.

Before daylight the next morning, the first of April—Easter Sunday—a task force from the Ninth Army's 2d Armored Division was on the way south, and another of the First Army's 3d Armored Division was en route north. The two met not long past noon amid cheers and ribald jokes to close the circle on the Ruhr. Trapped in a pocket measuring some thirty by seventy-five miles was all that remained of *Army Group B*, including headquarters of the *Fifteenth Army*, two corps of the *First Parachute Army* which General Simpson's advance had forced back into northern fringes of the Ruhr, and the entire *Fifth Panzer Army*.

However inevitable the outcome, it was no easy assignment to pierce the hasty defenses Field Marshal Model had erected around the Ruhr and clear

---

[224] Ibid., p. 331.

the welter of mines, factories, and cities in the industrial region. Buoyed by a wild promise from Hitler to send the inchoate *Twelfth Army* from the Harz Mountains to the rescue and, for a while, by a belief that pinning eighteen American divisions to the fight in the Ruhr would delay Allied advance to the east, the Germans in places fought with old-time fervor; but it was a spirit that was hard to sustain.

The advance overran hospitals, supply depots, thousands upon thousands of forced laborers, prisoner-of-war camps (in one housing Russians, prisoners had been dying at a rate of one hundred a day). Everywhere lay the rubble left by years of Allied bombing, but many mines and indusrial plants either were still functioning or were readily repairable.

On April 14 a battalion of the 8th Division reached the Ruhr River, serving as dividing line between First and Ninth Armies, there to greet men of the 79th Division on the north bank. That split the remaining enemy pocket into two and prepared the way for mass surrenders.

When and how to surrender had been a problem to German commanders and their Staffs ever since the American pincers closed. Although Model's Chief of Staff early urged him to ask Berlin for authority to surrender, the commander of *Army Group B* refused, for how was he to reconcile surrender with the demands he had put on subordinates through the years? Nervous, drawn, showing the effects of too much stress and too much alcohol, the heretofore self-confident Model struggled with his conscience for a solution.

Considering that every life saved was a life capable of taking up the struggle to rebuild Germany, Model decided at last simply to dissolve *Army Group B*. There could be no formal surrender of a command that had ceased to exist. All youths and older men, Model decreed on April 15, were to be discharged from the army and allowed to go home (an order—thousands were to discover—that lacked American concurrence). As of two days later, when ammunition and supplies presumably would be exhausted, all remaining noncombatant troops were to be free to surrender, while combat troops were either to fight on or to try to make their way out of the pocket.

Even before Model revealed his solution, many a German soldier had been finding his own answer. After the first ten days almost every American division had been taking at least two thousand prisoners a day, often more. Many a German walked mile after mile to find an American free enough of other duties to bother to accept his surrender. One American soldier started for the regimental stockade with sixty—eight prisoners and found upon arrival that he had twelve hundred.

General von Zangen surrendered with the staff of his *Fifteenth Army* on April 13; the commander and all that remained of the once mighty *Panzer Lehr Division* on the fifteenth. The next day an all-out rush to give up began. Handkerchiefs, bed sheets, table linen, anything white to denote surrender. While liberated slave laborers milled about, cheering, laughing, jeering, glum German civilians, incredulity stamped on their faces, watched silently or sought to ingratiate themselves with the conquerors by insisting they had never been Nazis. There were no Nazis, no Nazi sympathizers, not even any ex-Nazis anymore.

Young men, old men, arrogant SS troops, dejected infantrymen, paunchy reservists, female nurses and technicians, stiffly correct, monocle-wearing Prussians to gladden the heart of a Hollywood casting director, teen-age members of the Hitler Youth, corps commanders, division commanders, sergeants, privates, tall men, short men, round men, thin. In every conceivable manner they came: most plodding wearily on foot; some in civilian automobiles, assorted military vehicles, wagons, or on horseback; some pushing overloaded perambulators; one group riding bicycles in precise military formation; a horse-drawn artillery unit with reins taut, horses under faultless control; some carrying black bread and wine; others with musical instruments—accordions, guitars; some bringing wives or girlfriends.

Prisoner-of-war cages were nothing more than open fields hurriedly fenced with a few strands of barbed wire. There teeming masses of humanity lolled in the sun, sang sad soldier songs, stared at their captors, picked at lice. Some were in high spirits: others bedraggled, downcast. Some 317,000 there were in all, more than the Russians took at Stalingrad, more even than the total of Germans and Italians taken in Tunisia.

One missing was "Little" Manteuffel, commander of the *Fifth Panzer Army*, for Hitler had pulled him out before the pincers closed to command an army opposing the Russians. His successor was captured trying to sneak across a bridge over the Ruhr River to make his way to the Netherlands.

Missing, too, was Model.

To those who knew the field marshal intimately, it was a certainty that he would never surrender. He had long been critical of Field Marshal Friedrich Paulus for capitulating at Stalingrad. "A field marshal," Model had said then, "does not become a prisoner. Such a thing is just not possible."[225]

On one of the last days Model asked his Chief of Staff if they had done everything to justify their actions in the light of history. "What is there left," he went on, "to a commander in defeat?"

Pausing, Model answered his own question. "In ancient times," he said, "they took poison."[226]

The afternoon of April 21, Model drove with his aide to a forest near Duesseldorf. There he put a bullet through his head.

---

[225] From a letter from Major Ilansgeorg Model (the field marshal's son), March 29, 1966, to the U.S. Army Historical Office, Europe (copy in OCMH).

[226] Generalmajor Carl Wagoner, MS No. B — 583, "The Battles of *Army Group B* on the Rhine up to its dissolution, 22 March-17 April 1945" (copy in OCMH).

Chapter Twenty-Nine – Through the Heart of Germany

With *Army Group B* trapped, four Allied armies—the Second British and, from north to south, the Ninth, the First, and the Third U.S.—faced a gap that the Germans in their penury would find impossible to fill.[227]

It was not quite the same on the flanks.

In the north, General Crerars First Canadian Army still faced some hard fighting, not so much because of the caliber of the German troops but because in driving northward the Canadians encountered one canal and river line after another. One corps nevertheless reached the North Sea at the northeastern tip of the Netherlands on April 16, thereby making a pocket of the Germans in the Netherlands. A little farther to the west a second corps two days later strengthened the noose by gaining the Ijssel Meer, which long months before had been the goal of Operation MARKET-GARDEN.

Little reason remained for continuing the attack westward to clear the rest of the Netherlands, for that would invite the Germans to open dikes and impose more misery on a population already reduced to eating tulip bulbs to survive. A lull not unlike a truce settled over the lines while a representative from General Eisenhower's headquarters negotiated with the Germans to gain approval of relief food shipments to avoid a national catastrophe for the Dutch.

In the south, General Devers' 6th Army Group—and, in particular, General Patch's Seventh Army—also faced a stint of hard fighting as the Germans demonstrated again that they were masters of improvisation.

---

[227] Basic sources for this chapter were Pogue, *The Supreme Command*; Matloff, *Strategic Planning, 1043-1944*; Toland, *The Last 100 Days*; Ryan, *The Last Battle*; *Conquer — The Story of Ninth Army*; Davis, *The Experience of War*; and my forthcoming, *The Last Offensive*.

Along a crescent formed by the juncture of the Jagst and the Neckar rivers in wooded hill country near Heilbronn, where remnants of the German *First Army* rallied, fighting raged with a ferocity strangely out of place at this stage of the war.

When a combat command of the 10th Armored Division cut in behind the crescent and plunged twenty-five miles to the little city of Crailsheim, a conglomeration of small German units cut the roads behind the armor. The Americans had to call on transport aircraft to fly in supplies and evacuate wounded. Two days later, once the surprise and the speed essential to the attempt to turn the German line had been frustrated, the combat command fought its way out. That left the job of breaking the line along the crescent to infantrymen struggling to expand tiny bridgeheads. Only on the fourteenth, ten days after the battle was joined, did the Germans withdraw.

General Patch's left wing meanwhile had encountered no such determination on the part of remnants of the German *Seventh Army*. Driving generally eastward from what had once been the Third Army's bridgehead at Oppenheim, an armored division on April 6 had reached Hammelburg, there to liberate at last those who remained in *Oflag XIIIB*, mainly Yugoslavs. Following Task Force Baum's raid, the Germans had marched the American prisoners eastward, except for seventy-five who were seriously wounded. One of the wounded was Patton's son-in-law, Colonel Waters.

Having previously announced the decision to return General Simpson's Ninth Army to the 12th Army Group, General Eisenhower made the transfer official on April 4. That established Omar Bradley as the commander of four field armies (First, Third, Ninth, and Fifteenth), twelve corps, and forty-eight divisions, the largest exclusively American field command in the nation's history. Even after allotting eighteen divisions to the task of reducing the Ruhr, Bradley still had thirty for continuing through the heart of Germany.

With the British on the north and Patch's Seventh Army on the south protecting the flanks, Bradley's 12th Army Group was to launch the new Allied main effort aimed at splitting Germany by linking with the Russians. While the new Fifteenth Army held the Rhine's west bank facing the Ruhr and began occupation duties, Hodges' First Army was to make the main drive directly eastward on Leipzig. The Third Army was to head for Chemnitz, southeast of Leipzig, but was to be prepared to turn to help the 6th Army Group sweep into southern Germany and Austria. The Ninth Army was to aim for the Elbe River in the vicinity of Magdeburg, whence major highways led fifty-five miles or so to Berlin. Unaware of General Eisenhower's decision to make no drive on Berlin, General Simpson deemed the German capital to be the Ninth Army's objective. Did not Bradley's order read that once the Ninth Army had seized a bridgehead over the Elbe, Simpson was "to be prepared to continue the advance on Berlin or to the northeast"?[228]

As Bradley issued these instructions, part of the Ninth Army was drawing up to the broad Weser River, approximately midway between Rhine and Elbe and last major water obstacle short of the Elbe. The Third Army meanwhile had sent a flying column fifty miles beyond Kassel to the obscure town of Ohrdruf. Still short of the Weser, the First Army was regrouping after the drive to envelop the Ruhr.

Although General Bradley was eager to bring his three armies to the starting gate at the same time, he nevertheless allowed the Ninth Army to jump the Weser to deny the Germans time to build a defense at the river. Once bridgeheads were solidly established, Simpson was to pause to let the First Army catch up, while the Third Army marked time at Ohrdruf.

On the word of a German officer deserter that a big headquarters or communications center was to be found at Ohrdruf, Bradley had given Patton special dispensation to plunge ahead of the other armies. Taking the town on April 4, men of the 4th Armored Division discovered an immense underground communications center constructed as headquarters for OKW during the Czechoslovakian crisis in 1938, but never used.

They found something else at Ohrdruf. On the fringe of the town the first of the notorious concentration camps.

Small by the standards of others to be found later, the camp at Ohrdruf nevertheless contained enough horror to make the American soldier and even his Supreme Commander pale. Patton, when he saw it, vomited. After being forced by the Americans to tour the camp, the burgomaster of Ohrdruf and his wife went home and hanged themselves.

A few miles away, at the village of Merkers, other American troops found hidden in a salt mine almost all Germany's gold reserve, vast stores

---

[228] 12th Army Group Letter of Instructions No. 20, April 4, 1945 (copy in OCMH).

of German and foreign currency, and hundreds of priceless works of art looted from the conquered countries of Europe.

The dirty insides of the Third Reich were beginning to be exposed for a horrified world to see.

That portion of central Germany facing the 12th Army Group provides two main avenues eastward, one on either side of the Harz Mountains. North of the Harz, the Ninth Army was to advance across low, rolling country marked by several of Germany's bigger cities—Hanover, ancient seat of the Hanoverian kings, Brunswick, and Magdeburg. The First Army and the north wing of the Third were to utilize the wide Thueringen plain, while the Third Army's right wing would encounter more inhospitable terrain in the Thueringer Wald, a spinelike range of forested hills rising to more than three thousand feet. Having passed south of the headwaters of the Weser River, the Third Army faced no major water obstacles, while the First and Ninth Armies still had to get across the Weser.

In an effort to rally some force to defend this great stretch of central Germany, Hitler provided a hastily reconstituted headquarters of the *Eleventh Army*, whose troops had been lost on the eastern front. The *Eleventh Army* could only try to organize remnants of divisions that had escaped the Ruhr trap, students and cadre of training schools, a few local defense forces. In the larger cities a *Kampfkommandant* (combat commander) took control of anti-aircraft troops, training Staffs of the local *Wehrkreis* (military district), city police, stragglers, anybody else who showed up; but in most cases these conglomerate forces would be capable of holding for a few days at most.

Although Hitler had issued his fanciful order to form a new army, the *Twelfth*, to assemble in the Harz Mountains and drive to the relief of the Ruhr, most of the troops to fill the new divisions were in officer training schools and replacement centers east of the Elbe and had yet to head for the Harz. Not until April 6 did Hitler even settle on a commander for the new army, General der Panzertruppen Walter Wenck, a youthful, outspoken officer who was recuperating in a Bavarian resort from injuries incurred in an automobile accident.

The attack of the American armies was from the start a dash from one objective to the next, hardly a pursuit, for there was nothing really to pursue. It was more a race to prevent whatever German forces remained from gathering at strategic points and imposing delay.

Making the main effort in the center, the First Army got across the Weser late on April 6, and by nightfall the next day any concern that the Germans might have formed a solid position at any point along the river had passed. A day later, as Hodges' armored divisions assumed the lead, the Germans began to withdraw into the Harz, there to hold the wooded mountains as a fortress in keeping with the absurd notion that the *Twelfth Army* soon would arrive to set everything right again.

Bypassing the Harz to the south, the armor on April 11 swept into Nordhausen, there to discover concentration and slave labor camps that defied the capacity of the mind to comprehend.

A sergeant in a medical unit saw it this way:

Rows upon rows of skin-covered skeletons. Men lay as they had starved, discolored, and lying in indescribable human filth. Their striped coats and prison numbers hung to their frames. One girl in particular I noticed; I would say she was about seventeen years old. She lay there where she had fallen, gangrened and naked. In my own thoughts I choked up—couldn't quite understand how and why war could do these things. We went downstairs into a filth indescribable, accompanied by a horrible dead-rot stench. There in beds of crude wood I saw men too weak to move dead comrades from their side. One hunched-down French boy was huddled up against a dead comrade, as if to keep warm. There were others, in dark cellar rooms, lying in disease and filth, being eaten away by diarrhea and malnutrition. It was like stepping into the Dark Ages.[229]

Not far from the concentration camp were large underground factories, one for manufacturing V-2 rockets, and a slave labor camp with a capacity of 30,000. No worker ever left the camp alive. People too weak to work in the factory were left to die, 150 or more a day; and the Germans disposed of their remains in efficient crematory ovens.

On the same day troops of the Third Army uncovered their share of horror in a concentration camp near the capital of the short-lived Weimar Republic. This camp merited special notoriety because the commandant's wife, Ilse Koch, collected the tattooed skin of prisoners to make ornaments and lamp shades. This was Buchenwald.

---

[229] Leo A. Hoegh and Howard J. Doyle, *Timberwolf Tracks* (104th Division) (Washington, 1946), pp. 330-31.

On the 12th Army Group's north wing, General Simpson's divisions took the Weser on the run, including one crossing at Hamelin, the town that the Pied Piper reputedly rid of rats and children. By nightfall on the sixth the Weser lay behind.

Two of Simpson's divisions were operating with a special fervor, their eyes on bridgeheads over the Elbe and on Berlin. One was the 2d Armored Division, whose tempestuous commander, Major General I. D. White, had directed his operations officer to prepare a plan for marching on Berlin even before the division crossed the Rhine. The other was the 83d Infantry Division, whose men had added to their columns such a collection of captured German vehicles, military and civilian, that news correspondents called the division the "Rag Tag Circus." Sure of their ability to dash around the countryside as fast as anybody, the men preferred to call themselves the "83d Armored Division."

With the First Army coming abreast, Simpson was free on April 10 to turn the divisions loose. Despite an encounter with large-caliber antiaircraft guns protecting the Hermann Goering steelworks near Brunswick, the armored division made about twenty miles the first day; while the infantry division had to undergo a handicap, dropping off a regiment to guard against the Germans assembling in the Harz Mountains.

The next day, the eleventh, General White's armor was not to be denied. Overtaking fleeing Germans, sweeping aside the defenders of roadblocks with throaty blasts from tank guns, surprising *Volkssturm* defenders who could only throw down their newly acquired arms and gape in bewilderment, the lead combat command drove relentlessly eastward.

In late afternoon an attached contingent of the division's reconnaissance squadron raced into a suburb of Magdeburg, startling shoppers making the rounds of the stores. Just after dark a column of Sherman tanks made a run for a bridge across the Elbe a few miles southeast of Magdeburg, but the Germans demolished it.

Failing to get a bridge was a disappointment, but the men still were jubilant. Just over two weeks before they had been sitting on the west bank of the Rhine. Now they were 220 airline miles to the east, almost within spitting distance of the German capital. In the last day alone they had covered 73 miles.

The "Rag Tag Circus" was but a short distance behind. Late the next day, the twelfth, the 83d Division reached the Elbe a few miles upstream from the armor, only to see the front-running armor again steal a march. Soon after nightfall two battalions of armored infantrymen crossed the sprawling Elbe in DUKW's hastily brought forward. Not a shot sounded from the east bank.

The man who that same day sat for his portrait in a clapboard cottage in his favorite retreat at Warm Springs hardly seemed the same man who had stood, staunch and vigorous, on a platform in Charlottesville almost six years before and promised the resources of his powerful nation as an arsenal of democracy. His lips were drained of blood, his face ashen and thin, his hands shaky. He tired easily. Looking at his watch, he told the artist, "We've got just fifteen minutes more."[230]

Heaven knows there were reasons enough for the man to have aged. In those six years he had faced awesome tasks and responsibilities known to few before him. He had led his nation through the last steps of recovering from the debilitating depression, through a sluggish but sure beginning at rearmament, through the bitter opening defeats of war. He had set apparently unattainable goals and then had urged and prodded until at last the nation was a true arsenal of democracy and was also sending masses of its native sons marching down the long path toward military victory. In those six years he also had faced two more elections for unprecedented third and fourth terms that gave him a total of more than twelve years in office.

For one who relished his calling, there were rewards in shouldering the burdens, solving the tasks, leading his people toward victory in a just war that had to be won if mankind was to remain free. It was nevertheless at many times discouraging and over the long run enervating. The frustration and concern, for example, that had developed only in the last few weeks—since Yalta—as Soviet leaders had begun to display all the age-old Russian suspicions in a manner that put in jeopardy long and dedicated work aimed at establishing a postwar understanding that might spare the next generation the kind of holocaust that had overtaken the last two.

The specter of a postwar world divided between two giant powers posturing, glowering, threatening—perhaps each with the capacity to invoke total destruction of the other—was with him at every turn. At

---

[230] Toland, *The Last 100 Days*, p. 372. On Roosevelt's death, see also Bernard Asbell, *When FDR Died* (New York, 1961); William D. Hassell, *Off the Record with FDR* (New Brunswick, 1958); and Turnley Walker, *Roosevelt and the Warm Springs Story* (New York, 1953).

Yalta he thought he had sensed a burgeoning cooperation—or convinced himself that he had—that would lead to an end of Russian fears and establish that community of interests that had to exist if the world was to survive.

Then disillusion had set in, at each step imparting more and more verisimilitude to the concerns which his friend, Winston Churchill, had long voiced but which he in his fervor for essential solution had felt impelled to reject. Hardly were the principals back home from Yalta when the Russians did violence to a "Declaration on Liberated Europe" they had signed at Yalta to affirm the right of peoples everywhere to determine their own destiny through universal suffrage and secret ballot. First on Rumania, then on Poland, had the Russians imposed Communist governments with scarcely any pretense at broad representation. Yet these he might rationalize to some degree, for had not all at Yalta also proclaimed that governments in countries adjacent to Russia should be friendly to the Soviet Union?

An exchange that grew out of SS-General Karl Wolff's efforts to exploit the "natural difference between these unnatural allies" by entering negotiations in Switzerland was not so easily explained away. The aim— Wolff had told Hitler—was to end the war with the Western Allies while continuing to fight the Red Army. The goal was in reality to end the war in Italy so that in the impending German collapse Italian Communists, who were dominant in a powerful partisan movement, should not seize power.

After some preliminary contacts Wolff met with Allen Dulles, a senior representative of the Office of Strategic Services, in Switzerland early in March and again later in the month. When Wolff agreed to unconditional surrender, the negotiations showed some promise, only to falter when Hitler, in response to Remagen, transferred Field Marshal Kesselring from Italy to the western front. It was on the possible connivance of Kesselring that Wolff had hung his hopes for surrender.

The American Ambassador in Moscow, Averell Harriman, had kept the Russians informed of the talks from the start. Also from the start, the Russians had insisted on participating, for might not the surrender cause German divisions to depart from Italy for the east? Yet the surrender was actually to be nothing more than a military capitulation by a field commander on a strictly Anglo-American front, not unlike that of

Paulus at Stalingrad. To give in to Russian demands was, to Harriman, to establish dangerous precedent.

The Russians reacted with asperity. Demanding that the negotiations be broken off immediately, they accused the Allied governments of conniving with the Germans "behind the backs of the Soviet Union, which is bearing the brunt of the war against Germany."[231] As an exchange of messages continued, the Russian charge—from the pen of Stalin himself—became one of treachery and deceit. Despite American denials, Stalin stated, the negotiations had "ended in an agreement with the Germans, whereby the German commander on the western front, Marshal Kesselring, is to open the front to the Anglo-American troops and let them move east, while the British and Americans have promised, in exchange, to ease the armistice terms for the Germans."

It was a cruel blow to a man who saw hope for world peace in terms of eliminating Russia's historic distrust of foreigners and of thus gaining the cooperation of the eastern colossus. He saw no alternative but to send Stalin a firm, even aggressive message. He ended it with the admission that "I cannot avoid a feeling of bitter resentment toward your informers, whoever they are, for such vile misrepresentations of my actions or those of my trusted subordinates."[232]

That produced an apology of sorts from the Russian leader, but the blow to aspirations for future cooperation remained. It took on added weight from the fact that the exchange coincided with announcement that the Russian foreign minister would be missing from the Soviet delegation to the imminent opening conference of the United Nations in San Francisco. A man who had worked long to create a peacekeeping forum devoid of the impotence of the old League of Nations and to assure American participation, a man who was himself scheduled to open the conference and who knew that every other country was sending its top foreign officer, could interpret this only as a deliberate affront, a calculated downgrading of the world organization.

Disconcerting, even depressing—yet despair had no part in the character of the man. That morning of April 12, before he sat for his portrait, he cabled Churchill: "I would minimize the general Soviet problem as

---

[231] Toland, *The Last 100 Days*, p. 246.

[232] Ibid., p. 358.

much as possible because these problems, in one form or another, seem to arise every day and most of them straighten out...We must be firm, however, and our course thus far is correct."[233]

It was 1:15 P.M. He had just lit a cigarette in the accustomed long holder when he suddenly raised his left hand to his temple. The hand dropped. Closing his eyes, he whispered in a voice scarcely audible: "I have a terrible headache." Just over two hours later he was dead of a cerebral hemorrhage.

The next day's casualty list, carried in newspapers along with the names of next-of-kin and home addresses, included this notation:

ARMY-NAVY DEAD[234]

ROOSEVELT, *Franklin D., Commander-in-Chief; wife, Mrs. Anna Eleanor Roosevelt, the White House.*

As is customary among men in battle when one of their number falls, American soldiers in Europe continued to fight. It could still be quite a fight, as the men of the 2d Armored Division, who had crossed unopposed over the Elbe River, soon discovered, along with others at several points west of the Elbe. Men who had been engaged in an apparent end-the-war dash on Berlin suddenly found themselves facing a fanatical foe. It was combat as senseless as it was fierce. The Germans staging it could hope to accomplish nothing more than to ensure a warrior's death for more men on both sides and, by slowing the American drive, to expose more of their people and their land to the Russians whom they feared and dreaded.

The turn of events was attributable to a new force, the *Twelfth Army*. It was a force patently incapable of achieving the grand design of pushing through to relieve *Army Group B* in the Ruhr and gaining time while some nebulous thing happened to wrench victory from defeat in the east; it was a force even incapable of reaching its assigned assembly area in the Harz Mountains, but it could deal damaging blows to a little bridgehead that lacked adequate anti-tank defenses.

As the commander-designate, General Wenck, found upon reaching his new command post along the Elbe not far from where American troops had just crossed the river, the *Twelfth Army* was supposed to embrace nine divisions made up of young men from army schools, particularly officer

---

[233] Davis, *The Experience of War*, p. 616.

[234] *The Chicago Tribune*, April 12, 1945.

training schools, and from the Reich labor service. Short on tanks and assault guns, the divisions would have to depend primarily on the *élan* of spirited youths led by officers who had been instructors at the schools. Moreover, Wenck was never able to bring anywhere near nine divisions into the fight. Three were insufficiently organized for battle for more than a week, which was too late. Two others were assembling west of the Elbe in front of the British under orders to drive south to the Harz—they never made it—and another had been trapped in the Harz by the swift American advance. That left only three.

Even these three, Wenck soon realized, were already irretrievably committed, one to defense of the Elbe north of Magdeburg, the other two west of the Elbe against an onrushing First U.S. Army. All Wenck could put his hands on immediately was one regiment and a few tanks and assault guns from a nearby training school.

Wenck also had the fixed anti-aircraft guns protecting Magdeburg. These big guns, whose shells burst in the air and rained countless hot fragments, had from the first taken the 2d Armored Divisions crossing site under fire, making bridge building a task for the quick and the dead. So shallow was the water along both banks of the river that operating vehicular ferries proved impossible. Every call for fighter-bombers to strike the German flak positions went unanswered, for so far behind had airfields fallen in the race across Germany that the Elbe was beyond range of tactical aircraft bearing bombs.

Despite the shelling, hope rose in midday of April 13 when engineers advanced their pontons and treadway tracking to within twenty-five yards of the east bank. Then came a deluge of anti-aircraft shells that wrecked everything. The second night came and went with no more powerful anti-tank weapon in the little bridgehead than the individual infantry-man's bazooka.

As the darkness dissipated the next morning, the Germans struck. They rapidly cut off one American company, then began systematically to reduce the other defenders, foxhole by foxhole, with fire from tanks and assault guns. In the confusion a score of Americans surrendered. The Germans forced them to march at gunpoint in front of their tanks. By noon the bridgehead, held only by three battalions of infantry, had begun to break up.

The repulse was less painful than it might have been because of the determination of the men of the "Rag Tag Circus" to be in on the final drive to Berlin. Not to be outdone by the armor, a regiment of the 83d Division the preceding afternoon had crossed the Elbe in assault boats a few miles upstream, out of range of the deadly guns at Magdeburg. In the words of one man, it was "just like a Sunday afternoon picnic."

"Don't waste the opportunity of a lifetime," exhorted the regimental commander, racing up and down the west bank. "You're on your way to Berlin!"[235]

However misinformed that might turn out to be, the infantrymen quickly fanned out to establish a bridgehead. Before night fell a treadway bridge afforded passage for tanks and tank destroyers. They called the bridge the "Gateway to Berlin" and named it for their new Commander-in-Chief, Harry S Truman.

Nobody in either the 2d Armored Division or the 83d wanted to proceed with the drive on Berlin more than did the Ninth Army's commander, General Simpson. Having gained a bridgehead over the Elbe, Simpson was confident that, given two days to build up supplies, he could push through to the capital in another twenty-four hours, thereby beating the Russians, who had not yet renewed their offensive. The only real problem was tactical air support, so far behind that even the Elbe was beyond bombing range; but if the project was given priority, engineers could quickly put forward German airfields into shape.

The Ninth Army's Staff already had a plan for driving through to Berlin, couched behind the euphemism "to enlarge the Elbe River bridgehead to include Potsdam [a suburb of Berlin]."[236] On April 15, General Simpson flew to General Bradley's headquarters to present it. Although Bradley listened intently as General Simpson's operations officer disclosed the plan, he said he would have to telephone General Eisenhower for a decision.

Overhearing Bradley's end of the conversation, Simpson soon had his answer. "All right, Ike," Bradley said, "that's what I thought. I'll tell him. Goodbye." There was to be no drive on Berlin.

Eisenhower's decision took the climax out of the war for Simpson and

---

[235] In my own *The Last Offensive*.

[236] Ibid.

his Ninth Army and for much of the rest of the 12th Army Group. The war became primarily a matter of eliminating German holdouts and of building up along the Elbe River and the Mulde, a tributary of the Elbe, to await arrival of the Russians.

The brutality of the fighting that remained depended on the will of local German commanders.

After penetrating one of Europe's thickest belts of anti-aircraft guns— probably more than one thousand—the First Army's 2d Division entered Leipzig, Germany's sixth largest city, following nothing more than a skirmish on the outskirts and a night of negotiating between a rifle company commander and a *generalmajor der polizei* who wanted to spare the city further damage. At the same time the 69th Division ran into fierce combat in the historic old quarter of the city, where a German colonel, the city's official *Kampfkommandant*, holed up in the city hall and the Battle of the Nations monument commemorating Napoleon's defeat in 1813. When after a day of fighting the Americans captured the city hall, they found the mayor, his deputy, and their families dead by their own hands. It was well into the night before the colonel and 150 men inside the monument capitulated.

Nearby, at Halle, the 104th Division had a six-day fight against a diehard German general and about four thousand troops, including a sprinkling of the SS large enough to put starch into the defense. The absurdity of the battle was emphasized on April 16 when, in response to a demand for surrender, the German general refused but at the same time volunteered to evacuate major parts of the city to avoid damage to hospitals. Strange were the calls of honor and duty as a nation collapsed.

Northeast of Halle on the approaches to the Elbe, other divisions of the First Army had to sweep aside two of the newly formed divisions of Wenck's *Twelfth Army*. Short on mortars and artillery, the young Germans fired their *Panzerfaust* anti-tank rockets in battery as if they were mortars. Yet the resistance was from the first nothing but an exercise in futility, however costly in human life, a fleabite on a hide too toughened to feel it as much more than a ridiculous irritation.

It was the same north of the Harz Mountains, where two more of Wenck's fledgling divisions tried, to no avail, to break through rear echelons of the Ninth Army and get into the Harz. That scenic wooded sector itself reminded many a veteran in the First Army of the Huertgen Forest, but the

Germans—seventy thousand of them—this time lacked mines, mortars, artillery, and determination, not to mention the weather, to make of the Harz another Huertgen. By April 16 the prisoner bag was exceeding two thousand a day, and on the twentieth there were surrenders *en masse*.

The Germans themselves demonstrated that the war was over for most of the 12th Army Group, when on the twenty-third the *Twelfth Army* turned its back on the Americans. Seven days earlier, in response to a challenge from Stalin that the Allies were trying to beat the Red Army to Berlin, the Russians had completed their fastest redeployment of the war and opened their Berlin offensive. The city was virtually surrounded when in desperation Hitler ordered the *Twelfth Army* on a futile mission of rescue.

As the Germans turned, General Simpson and the Ninth Army could but watch in frustration. Given an affirmative nod from Eisenhower ten days earlier, the Ninth Army, Simpson believed, could have been on the fringe of the German capital even before the Russians launched their offensive. It was a theory hard to contradict.

What American capture of Berlin might have accomplished in terms of speeding the end of a war already tumbling pell-mell to a conclusion or of insuring a postwar world more favorable to Allied policies was a matter for more conjecture. The occupation zones and the four-power occupation status of Berlin with tenuous Allied communication routes to the city were already too well set to have been affected. All that could be said with any certainty was that the decision of the Supreme Allied Commander—not the Germans, not lack of supplies—halted the American armies at the Elbe.

Chapter Thirty – Götterdämmerung

As the First and Ninth Armies in mid-April approached the restraining line of the Elbe and the Mulde, General Eisenhower turned the Third Army southeastward to help the 6th Army Group sweep southern Germany and drive into Czechoslovakia and Austria. Swift occupation followed of historic old cities which had gained new notoriety from events of the war and association with the Nazis. Once B-24's had delivered a last lethal blow, infantrymen of the Seventh Army entered the rubble of Schweinfurt, that center of the German ball-bearing industry that had cost American airmen so dearly. A few days later men of the Third Army pushed through a ring of deadly anti-aircraft guns and in a punishing fight for one crumbling building after another, one more heap of rubble, one more cellar, cleared Nuremberg, scene of so many ritualistic goose-stepping orgies that to those who wore the swastika it had become a holy place.[237]

In the process the two American armies drove a wedge between the German *First* and *Seventh Armies*, whose commanders still went through the motions of issuing orders for defense, attack, counterattack, all the things that the staff schools said should be done but that long since had ceased really to matter. They even deluded themselves into hoarding gasoline for the nonexistent jet aircraft that presumably were to be the salvation of the dying Reich.

The German troops, meanwhile, displayed by their actions a gamut of emotions: here fighting like cornered gangsters, there throwing hands high in surrender at first sign of American presence. They often stole gasoline Nazi officials had reserved for themselves ("flight fuel," the soldiers called

---

[237] For this chapter, see Pogue, *The Supreme Command*; *Seventh United States Army Report*, Vol. III; de Lattre, *Histoire*; Toland, *The Last 100 Days*; Ryan, *The Last Battle*; Ziemke, *Stanlingrad to Berlin*; Jackson, *The Battle of Italy*; Starr, *From Salerno to the Alps*.

it), and they viewed with a mixture of dismay, incredulity, and frustrated anger vast warehouses stuffed with items like fur-lined boots which would have been heartily welcomed a few months earlier in the bitter cold of the Ardennes.

As the Americans rampaged, so did General de Lattre's French, who even staged another crossing of the Rhine, this time opposite Strasbourg to slice quickly through the middle of the Black Forest and for the first time in many months to release the Alsatian capital from artillery fire. Strasbourg rang its church bells in jubilant gratitude. The dashing thrust coincided with a swift drive by other French troops southward along the eastern edge of the forest to trap whatever forces of the enemy's *Nineteenth Army* remained in the northern half.

That accomplished, de Lattre turned some troops against the city of Stuttgart and launched a double envelopment of the southern half of the forest. This was all well and good, except that according to orders from General Devers at 6th Army Group, it was Patch's Seventh Army that was supposed to drive southward to the Swiss frontier to cut off the Black Forest. Since nothing succeeds like success, Devers sanctioned de Lattre's act after the event, but it proved to be only the start of a series of independent acts by the intractable French commander.

Ignoring Devers' plan for the Seventh Army to cut roads leading out of Stuttgart to southeast and south before the French attacked the city, de Lattre swiftly turned a corps against Stuttgart and gained entry the afternoon of April 21. A kind of delirium followed. Ecstatic in liberation, some fifty thousand slave laborers, including twenty thousand deportees from France, went on a drunken spree. Tales of wanton rape, murder, looting began to emerge, lent credence by the presence among French troops of colonials who reputedly countenanced the precedent in warfare established centuries before by Roman soldiers with Sabine women.

Aside from the damage to life and property, the reports seriously perturbed General Devers for other reasons. Playing accorded the French the honor of taking Stuttgart, he intended to give the Seventh Army's supply columns running rights on the city's main roads. Continued disorders would delay the process, plus another project Devers had in mind, highly secret.

Working temporarily with the 6th Army Group was a special intelligence mission known as ALSOS.[238] Composed of American scientists commanded by an Army officer, Colonel Boris Pash, ALSOS gathered information on German developments in nuclear fission. Word had it that important research had been taking place in a town about seventy miles southwest of Stuttgart, and Pash wanted to use the city as a sally port for sending the scientists and a motorized infantry battalion on a swift foray to seize the German scientists and their data before they fell into French hands.

On the twenty-second, to halt the disorders and assure American use of Stuttgart, General Devers ordered de Lattre to relinquish the city to the Seventh Army. To a sensitive de Lattrce, this was an unacceptable affront. While protesting to Devers, he appealed to his politico-military chief, General de Gaulle.

De Gaulle was still acutely conscious that at Yalta the Allies and the Russians had failed to assign the French a specific zone of occupation in Germany. Not only was the French First Army, he told de Lattre, to retain Stuttgart, but de Lattre was to inform the Americans that the French would hold and administer all territory they conquered until such time as agreement came on a French zone of occupation.

To Devers, at this point, Stuttgart ceased to be the issue. It was instead a direct violation of orders by a subordinate, a situation—he reported to General Eisenhower—that he found "intolerable." Reiterating the order to relinquish the city, Devers told an American infantry division to move in. As American troops entered, the French treated them amicably but again declined to evacuate the city.[239]

General Devers himself went into Stuttgart the next day. While disorders had been serious, he discovered, the number of incidents had been considerably fewer than reports had indicated. The city was too badly damaged anyway, he decided, to be of use to the Seventh Army. Furthermore, by skirting Stuttgart to the west, Boris Pash and his scientists had by this time already penetrated the French sector and come away with the German scientists and research data they sought. With a wry observation that the French were welcome to "the conditions there," Devers ordered the American division out.

---

[238] I have depended upon material provided me in 1968 by Colonel Boris Pash. See also Samuel A. Goudsmit, *ALSOS* (New York, 1947).

[239] See my *The Last Offensive*. On this incident, see also Pogue, *The Supreme Command*, pp. 459-61.

The Supreme Commander, in turn, protested officially to General de Gaulle. Issuing direct orders to the French First Army counter to operational orders given through the military chain of command, General Eisenhower said, violated the agreement under which the United States had armed and equipped French divisions. Because he was unwilling to do anything that might reduce the military effort against Germany, he himself would accept the situation, but he felt he had no choice but to refer the matter to the Combined Chiefs of Staff.

When the news reached Washington, President Truman was shocked. If the time had come, he wrote de Gaulle, when the French army was to be responsive only to the political wishes of the French government, then the command structure would have to be rearranged.

De Gaulle refused to back down. If the Allies, he replied, would consult the French on matters involving French interests, such incidents would not occur. There the matter rested, to be finally settled only on May 2 when British and Americans at last agreed on a French zone of occupation, carved mainly from the American zone, and afforded France a voice in the control machinery for administering a defeated Germany.

That prestige as much as a zone of occupation was at issue had been demonstrated in the meantime in a French drive on Ulm, fifty miles southeast of Stuttgart and scene of Napoleon Bonaparte's triumph over an Austrian Army in 1805. The fact that Ulm lay forty miles inside the American zone of advance bothered de Lattre not at all. "The Americans will perhaps dislodge us from it," he told his commanders, "but the French flag will have flown there."[240]

Crossing upper reaches of the Danube River, a French armored division drove rapidly down the rivers right bank. At one point the armor had to pass through an American bridgehead over the Danube, raising the danger of an inadvertent clash, but somehow the French got through without incident. Learning of the French presence, General Devers ordered de Lattre to withdraw his troops immediately; but de Lattre did not agree until after nightfall the next day, April 24, after two French battalions had participated in an American attack to capture Ulm. When the tricolor had flown above the city's historic fortress, as it had under Napoleon, the French pulled back.

240 De Lattre, *Histoire*, p. 560.

* * *

As division after division of the Third and Seventh Armies seized bridge-heads over the Danube, the Germans lost their last natural line of defense short of the Bavarian and Austrian Alps. Unable to hold anywhere along the Danube, the defenders in the south at last were as disorganized and impotent as those that had tried to stem the eastward surge of the 12th Army Group. Except for a headquarters, the *Nineteenth Army* had ceased to exist; its troops were all but annihilated after a French drive to Lake Constance and the Swiss border trapped them in the Black Forest. What was left of the *Seventh Army* recoiled eastward into Czechoslovakia, so that only the shattered formations of the *First Army* remained in southern Germany.

Armored divisions to the fore, infantry divisions in the followup, the Third and Seventh Armies spread in an irresistible flood through a pictur-esque Bavarian countryside ripe with spring. Daffodils bloomed, farmers tilled the land, cows grazed. Only in bomb-blasted cities did war seem to have any place; yet at the next hill, ridge, village, stream, wherever a group of Germans with a will to fight elected to stand, there still might occur a brief flurry of fighting. Everybody knew the war was over; but somehow, at one isolated spot or another, the war went on, real enough for the moment and sometimes deadly for those caught up in it.

Among villagers word spread that if they displayed white flags and no one fired, the war would pass them by. In some cases towns and cities, too, got the message. At Landsberg, site of another fearful concentration camp and of the prison where Hitler had written the bible of National Socialism, *Mein Kampf,* a garrison of Hungarian soldiers surrendered with parade-ground formality. At Augsburg a small underground resistance group, the first of only two to emerge in Germany, led an American patrol to surround headquarters of the city's combat commander. At Dachau some of the pitiful survivors of one of the most notorious concentration camps, overcome with joy in their liberation, rushed the electrically charged wire enclosing them and died. In Munich, capital of Bavaria and Germany's third city, a score or so of soldiers joined a civilian resistance group in an attempt to seize the city. They managed to gain the radio station before SS troops intervened; yet despite the intervention, on April 30, American troops entered some parts of the city to the cheers of citizens waving both white flags of surrender and Bavarian flags of celebration.

On April 26 a patrol from the Third Army crossed the Austrian frontier close by the Danube. A few days later, in early May, contingents of the Third and Seventh Armies vied to be first into Berchtesgaden, Hitler's mountain retreat. Feeble resistance there and at other Alpine passes made it clear that nobody need be concerned about any possibility of a last-ditch Nazi redoubt in the Alps.

General de Lattre, meanwhile, had hit upon another idea to bring glory to French arms. Since General Devers had adjusted the interarmy boundary to afford the French a pathway into Austria, de Lattre cast his eyes on the Oberjoch Pass, near the town of Fuessen. If French troops could get through the Oberjoch Pass before American troops seized the nearby Fern Pass, the French might push into Austria to the road center of Landeck. Although Devers had not yet assigned Landeck to either French or Americans, de Lattre resolved to take it, for it offered the only possible route for the French to continue south to the Italian frontier. De Lattre was determined to reach the frontier in order to attain the renown of linking with Allied armies in Italy.

On the last day of April the French got within eight miles of the Oberjoch Pass, only to learn, to de Lattre's dismay, that American troops had cleared the Fern Pass and wen' little more than a stone's throw from Landeck. Almost plaintively, de Lattre begged General Patch to promise him passage through Landeck and access to the Italian frontier, "just as I withdrew from Ulm," he said, "to leave you free passage in your sector."[241]

The matter was not Patch's to decide. Somebody at headquarters of the 6th Army Group—Devers had no knowledge of it—apparently decided to pay de Lattre back for his continued contumacy. An order went out to shift the interarmy boundary westward, denying the French First Army both the Oberjoch Pass and Landeck.

Determined to the end, de Lattre still saw a chance of beating the Americans to Landeck. Within his sector was a back road, blocked by snow, leading up to imposing Arlberg Pass and the town of St. Anton. From St. Anton, a main highway led to Landeck.

De Lattre hastily equipped a reinforced platoon with skis and sent the men on an arduous twenty-mile uphill trek through the snow. When the next day they reached the Arlberg Pass, the platoon leader placed a telephone call over the civilian network to Landeck. To the French officer's

---

[241] Seventh Army Diary, entry of April 20, 1945 (copy in OCMH).

chagrin, the voice that answered was American. Men of the 44th Division had reached the town late the day before.

Through those same spring days, marred by a siege of heavy rains, men of the First and Ninth Armies and part of the Third spent their time along the Elbe and Mulde rivers awaiting their Red allies from the east. Eager to go down in history as the unit first to establish contact, divisions vied with each other in devising stratagems to assure for themselves the honor, while news correspondents flitted like nervous butterflies from one headquarters to another, to whichever unit rumor named as the leading contender at any given time.

Ground rules for the meeting were few. General Eisenhower, who was acutely conscious of the damage that could result from a collision of two forces lacking liaison, notified the Russians of his intention to stop Allied armies on the Elbe-Mulde line, except in the north, where the British were to cross lower reaches of the Elbe and advance to the Baltic Sea at the base of the Jutland peninsula, and in the south, where American troops were to push down the valley of the Danube into Austria. The Russians agreed to these plans and noted that they intended to clear Czechoslovakia at least as far west as the capital of Prague. As the two forces came together, red rockets were to identify Russians, green rockets Allies. News of the first meeting was to be announced simultaneously in Washington, London, and Moscow. Although General Eisenhower permitted American units to retain small bridgeheads over the Elbe and the Mulde, he decreed that patrols were to venture no farther than five miles beyond the rivers.

As the days passed, excitement within the First and Ninth Armies mounted. Rumor piled upon rumor; one false report followed another. To many a unit, Russian radio traffic cutting in on American channels meant that contact was near. One division after another reported flares to the east and attached to them varied interpretations. Men of the 84th Division painted signs of welcome in Russian. The First Army's Staff readied a dressed-up jeep for presentation to the army commander of the first Russian troops encountered.

With the range of aerial flights sharply restricted, pilots of tactical aircraft nevertheless reported one sighting of Russian troops after another—all equally erroneous. Pilots of artillery observation planes worked overtime trying to spot Russian columns. One from the 104th Division was so sure he had located Russian troops that he landed, only to find a group of Germans with a few British prisoners heading west in hope of surrendering.

Few divisions there were that failed to violate the five-mile restriction on patrols, particularly those along the Mulde looking toward that part of the Elbe that lies some twenty miles farther east. One patrol from the 104th Division led by First Lieutenant Harlan W. Shank roamed all the way to the Elbe late on April 23, spent the night under occasional Russian artillery fire in the town of Torgau, then returned without seeing Russian troops. On April 25 another patrol under First Lieutenant Albert L. Kotzebue of the 69th Division kept going on to "just one more village" and then to "just one more," all the while encountering dispirited German soldiers eager to surrender, jubilant American and other Allied prisoners, exuberant and sometimes intoxicated foreign laborers.[242]

Entering the village of Leckwitz, less than two miles from the Elbe, Lieutenant Kotzebue and his men spotted an unusually dressed horseman just as he turned his mount into a courtyard and passed from view. Spinning forward in their jeeps, the men came to a halt at the entrance to the courtyard. Inside was the horseman. There could be no doubt. He was a Russian soldier.

The time was 11:30 A.M. on April 25, the setting was inauspicious, but the moment was historic. East had met West, or vice versa, but nobody would pay much attention.

Obviously suspicious, the Russian horseman exchanged only a few words before galloping away; but Kotzebue and his men, sure now that Russian units were nearby, continued to the Elbe. They commandeered a small boat and rowed across a few hundred yards north of the town of Strehla, there to establish contact with Lieutenant Colonel Alexander T. Gardiev, commander of the 175th Rifle Regiment.

Unfortunately for Lieutenant Kotzebue's proper niche in history, the map coordinates he sent back marking his location were in error. The 69th Division's operations officer, who wanted to confirm the contact before reporting the news, flew in an artillery observation plane to the coordinates Kotzebue had given. He encountered neither Lieutenant Kotzebue nor the Russians but a blast of German anti-aircraft fire.

Still another patrol from the 69th Division was out on the same day,

[242] Captain William J. Fox, "The Russian-American Linkup," unpublished narrative prepared from detailed interviews, The National Archives.

a four-man group headed by Second Lieutenant William D. Robertson. Although Robertson had no intention originally of going all the way to the Elbe, word from passing British prisoners that a number of Americans, some of them wounded, were in Torgau on the Elbe, prompted him to continue. Robertson found no large body of American prisoners in Torgau, but beyond the twisted girders of a destroyed highway bridge, on the east bank of the Elbe, he found something else—the Russians.

After fashioning a crude American flag from water paint and a bed sheet, Robertson and his men finally convinced those on the far bank that they were Americans. As they picked their way across the destroyed bridge, a Russian soldier began to climb toward them. Meeting over the swirling waters of the Elbe, neither Robertson nor the Russian could think of anything to say. They merely grinned and pounded each other exuberantly.

Although Robertson's contact came forty-five minutes after that of Lieutenant Kotzebue, Robertson had the foresight to take four Russians back with him as tangible proof of his accomplishment. The division commander, Major General Emil F. Reinhardt, was at first irate, shocked that his men had violated the five-mile restriction; but his anger soon dissolved with realization of the renown the feat would bring the 69th Division. Word of the meeting passed swiftly up the chain of command, while Reinhardt laid plans for a formal encounter with his Russian opposite the next day.

On the afternoon of May 26 General Reinhardt met Major General Vladimir Rusakov, commander of the 58th Guards Infantry Division, across the Elbe from Torgau. The order of the day included camaraderie, photographs, newsreel cameras, a hastily assembled feast with a main dish of fried eggs, dancing in the streets, and toast after toast after toast. Among those present was Lieutenant Shank of the 104th Division, who might have claimed the honor of first contact himself had he but stayed in Torgau another twenty-four hours.

Absent was Lieutenant Kotzebue, who with the men of his patrol still waited several miles upstream, perplexed at the lack of response to his historic first meeting with the Red Army.

The war was plainly careening to an end in Germany. It was careening to an end on another front as well—the forgotten front, in Italy.[243]

---

[243] As Alexander decried the failure to exploit the Italian campaign, so did Clark. See *Calculated Risk*.

Once the D Day landings in Normandy had cut short the glory of the capture of Rome, Allied commanders and men alike in Italy had recognized that Allied strategy had relegated their war to a backwater. The realization left the Allied army group commander, General Alexander, particularly perturbed; for unless some miracle happened, he soon would have to give up seven divisions, including all French troops, to the invasion of southern France. That would leave him, vis-à-vis German strength in Italy, in much the same fallible position as upon the fall of Sicily, when preparations for the invasion of Normandy had siphoned away seven divisions. The legacy of that earlier loss had been the slim margin of victory in the invasion at Salerno and the grueling, indecisive struggle through the winter of 1943-1944 in the Winter Line and at Anzio.

The pending cut in strength galled Alexander all the more because of the potentialities he believed inherent in the Italian campaign. Probably more than any other senior British commander, he endorsed Winston Churchill's view that the Allies were wrong in failing to provide enough forces in the Mediterranean for a thrust into the Balkans to get at the Germans through the back door. With vehemence Alexander argued the case for the primacy of Italy over southern France, but to no avail.

The decision taken, the Italian campaign lapsed into a struggle to build or at least to maintain Allied strength. At the same time, if the Germans were to be forced to hold appreciable strength in Italy, Alexander had to keep up the attack with forces that in number of divisions—though not in total strength—remained consistently below that of the foe.

Although sympathetic, the British Chiefs of Staff could provide no help. Before the year 1944 was out, dwindling manpower forced the British to cut their infantry battalions in Italy from four to three companies and to reduce a lone British armored division to cadre strength. After the Germans had evacuated Greece in the fall of 1944—their sole voluntary withdrawal of the war—the British had to send there first an Indian division, then as civil war raged, a British corps with two divisions. Only in the spring of 1945 did the units return to Italy.

Even though the American Chiefs of Staff believed Alexander had enough strength to contain the Germans in Italy, which was the extent of his mission, they had few resources to send there in any case. They did replace two of the three American divisions that had pulled out for southern France, but hardly with units of the same quality. In the fall they sent the 92d Infantry Division, one of two all-Negro divisions, whose generally shaky performance would be an argument in postwar years for breaking the U.S. Army's traditional segregation pattern; then in the winter they sent the light 10th Mountain Division, sole survivor other than the airborne of several specialized divisions formed before General McNair had had his way. A South American ally helped by contributing the division-size Brazilian Expeditionary Force.

Hardly had the American Chiefs committed these units when the Ardennes counteroffensive prompted them to join the British Chiefs in calling for reinforcements from Italy for the western front. Since the Canadians wanted to get all their force's together, Alexander elected to release his Canadian corps with three divisions, plus a British division.

Although the Germans during this time lost some of their better divisions to other fronts, Field Marshal Kesselring and his successor in March of 1945—General von Vietinghoff, former commander of the *Tenth Army*—still had up to the end five of the better German units: a panzer, two parachute, and two panzer grenadier divisions. Even when they lost mobile divisions, they received infantry divisions in return, and infantry was fully capable of stalwart defense from fixed positions in mountainous terrain.

When lack of strength forced a lull in Italy during the first quarter of 1945, Alexander worked diligently to raise additional forces while serving in a new rank as field marshal and a new role as theater commander (in November "Jumbo" Wilson had gone to Washington upon the death of Sir John Dill to become resident caretaker for the British Chiefs of Staff). The forces Alexander gained added even more of an international complexion to a command that formerly had included Canadian divisions and then included American, British, Polish, Brazilian, South African, New Zealand, and Indian divisions. The new units were a Jewish brigade from the Near East, the 442d Regimental Combat Team composed of Americans of Japanese descent, two new Polish brigades, five Italian combat groups, and two Italian partisan brigades.

Reflecting the lack of numbers, both Alexander and his successor as army group commander, Mark Clark, employed a stratagem that Alexander called a "one-two punch." In an effort to break the Gothic Line, the enemy's fortified position in the northern Apennines, General Leese's

Eighth Army struck first in late August 1944 and unhinged the line along the Adriatic coast. As German mobile divisions rushed to block the British drive, Clark's Fifth Army attacked north of Florence along two highways leading through the mountains to Bologna. For all the rugged nature of the German defenses in towering, craggy mountains, American infantrymen plodded inexorably forward behind powerful artillery support to score a penetration before German reserves could return to the scene.

Penetration but not breakthrough, for another twenty miles of inhospitable mountains still separated the Americans from Bologna and the beginning of the fertile open plains of the valley of the Po. In hopes of carrying the rest of the way, the Fifth Army in October delivered the first punch of a new drive; but when German reserves arrived from the front opposite the Eighth Army to give battle nine miles short of Bologna, the British in reclaimed lowlands along the Adriatic coast, creased by one river after another, lacked the power in the second punch to lure the German reserves back. That presaged another cold, bitter, dismal winter of misery and frustration not unlike that of 1943-1944.

For a few fleeting moments in early fall of 1944 a measure of hope did stir that the Allies might yet turn the campaign in Italy to some more positive advantage than merely containing German divisions. During the Quebec conference of mid-September, held in the climate of optimism that followed the dash of Eisenhower's armies across France and that of Alexander's to the Gothic Line, the Combined Chiefs at last sanctioned Alexander's planning an advance northeastward from Italy through the Ljubljana Gap into Austria. They even agreed to provide assault shipping for an amphibious strike into the Istrian peninsula to help Alexander's main thrust forward.

Yet these plans assumed that Allied troops would soon break through the Gothic Line with such verve as to threaten to split northern Italy in two by a drive to Lake Garda, forcing Kesselring to withdraw from northwestern Italy and to build a new line' north of the Po behind the Adige River. By the end of October the likelihood of that happening had become remote.

An enemy counteroffensive—promoted by Mussolini in attempted imitation of Hitler's blow in the Ardennes—threatened for a few days in late December to underscore Allied weakness. On the day after Christmas, employing two Italian divisions that had remained loyal to the *Duce*, and a German division, Axis forces struck the American 92d Division with the object of driving through to the Ligurian coast and taking the port of Leghorn. Although the Negro troops gave ground—in some cases precipitately—quick commitment of an Indian division and a shift of American units convinced Kesselling that surprise, and thus any hope of success, was lost. That ended Mussolini's last pathetic attempt to influence the outcome of the war.

Although Alexander continued to draw plans for entering the Balkans to exploit successes of Yugoslav partisans, they were paper exercises that even Churchill ceased to support. In the meeting of the Combined Chiefs on Malta at the end of January 1945, Churchill joined in the general agreement that several divisions should be transferred from Italy to Eisenhower's command. The new role of Allied troops in Italy was to contain the Germans with limited offensives but to seek no major advance unless Kesselring withdrew.

As exemplified by the efforts to raise new forces, neither Alexander, his army group commander, Mark Clark, nor two new army commanders—Lucian Truscott, brought from France to succeed Clark in command of the Fifth Army, and R. L. McCreery, who assumed command of the Eighth Army when General Leese left for assignment in Burma—accepted the deadening decree as final. Achieving some concentration by using the newly formed Italian units to hold quiet sectors, Clark employed Allied air power to pin Kesselring's divisions in place while readying another one-two punch.

By the end of March 1945 the Germans in Italy remained one of the most intact forces left to a crumbling Reich. General von Vietinghoff, the successor to Kesselring, still had twenty-three divisions, five of them elite. On the other hand, an elongated defensive line allowing for but two divisions in reserve stood, not on the forward face of a mountain massif, but along the last rim before the valley of the Po, which was not unlike fighting with a river at your back. Vietinghoff had no air support and little fuel for shifting reserves or withdrawing, and behind the lines Italian partisans were blowing bridges, derailing trains, ambushing columns, almost openly defying German authority.

On April 9 the Allied armies in Italy opened a final offensive with another one-two punch, this one started by the British Eighth Army close along the Adriatic. Employing intricately planned aerial bombardment by strategic, medium, and fighter-bombers and using a variety of amphibious vehicles to conquer the flooded lowlands, the British ground steadily forward. On the fourteenth, as General von Vietinghoff shifted reserves to oppose them, Truscott's Fifth Army struck for Bologna.

That same day, sensing the inevitable, Vietinghoff appealed in vain to Hitler for authority to pull back behind the Po. Six days later, on the twentieth, as the 10th Mountain Division broke into the Po valley to cut a main highway leading northeast out of Bologna, Vietinghoff realized he had no alternative but to fall back. Although the withdrawal began in good order, the columns soon began to disintegrate under attack from Allied planes which for the first time in the Italian campaign could strike their foe over vast stretches of open country rather than on sinuous mountain roads.

The same day that Vietinghoff defied his *Fuehrer* to order withdrawal, the SS general, Karl Wolff, returned from Berlin, where Hitler and Heinrich Himmler had summoned him to defend his surrender negotiations in Switzerland. Ostensibly blessed with authority to resume the talks, Wolff convinced Vietinghoff that in cooperation lay the only hope for the German armies in Italy. Three days later, on the twenty-third, as the American Fifth and British Eighth Armies linked on the south bank of the Po, Wolff and two emissaries representing Vietinghoff went to Switzerland to resume talks with Allen Dulles.

With dismay Wolff learned that the Allied governments had so despaired of Russian reaction to the talks and of Wolff's inability to produce that they had forbidden further discussions. Assured that General von Victinghoff was prepared to surrender, Dulles nevertheless agreed to contact the Combined Chiefs for authority to continue; but when no word had come by the twenty-sixth, Wolff deemed it imperative that he return to his headquarters.

As he discovered soon after crossing the border into Italy, Allied advances, German disintegration, and a general partisan uprising were rapidly eliminating any reason for surrender. Wolff himself was briefly a prisoner of the partisans before escaping to make his way to his headquarters, where on the twenty-seventh he received a telegram from Dulles. The Allied governments, the telegram revealed, had agreed to extend the talks and had asked the Russians to send representatives. General von Vietinghoff's emissaries were to leave immediately to confer with General Clark.

By this time Allied columns were across the Po and meeting scant resistance. The British had plunged on to jump the Adige and were heading for Venice and Trieste, while American units reached Lake Garda and fanned out to sever all roads leading into Austria by way of the Brenner Pass.

By this time, too, Benito Mussolini and his mistress, Claretta Petacci, were prisoners of the partisans. Mussolini was discovered in the back of a truck in a German convoy disguised in the greatcoat of a German soldier; he was docile, a sick shell of his former bombastic self. The next day, the twenty-eighth, a rival partisan band from Milan seized the two prisoners, shot them unceremoniously with a machine pistol, then transported their bodies to Milan. At a gasoline station, scene of an earlier murder of Italian partisans, a mob strung them up by their heels and spat on and reviled them.

With partisans roaming the countryside, with British and American columns racing from one town to another, with 120,000 Germans already captured, the German signing of surrender terms on April 29 at Clark's headquarters in Caserta was almost an anticlimax. As one million Germans laid down their arms, the holocaust was officially over in Italy at noon on the second day of May.

In the *Fuehrerbunker* beneath the ruined city of Berlin, the atmosphere in the last days of April ranged alternately from despair to blind hope.[244]

Visibly ill from the effect of drugs administered too freely by a personal physician, Adolf Hitler still commanded the obsequious loyalty of his military and political sycophants. Although the *Fuehrer* had intended to leave Berlin on April 20, his fifty-sixth birthday, to continue the fight from southern Germany, he procrastinated in the delusion that time remained, that his armies were about to achieve their greatest victory in defense of Berlin. He had constructed anti-tank defenses in such depth before the city, he told Karl Wolff, that every day 250 Russian tanks would be destroyed. Even the Red Army, he said, could not long be bled like that.

One moment Hitler railed that the German people had failed him, that they deserved the cruel fate they were about to suffer at the hands

---

[244] See in addition to works previously cited, Lev Bezymenski, *The Death of Adolf Hitler* (New York, 1968). The author, a Russian who cites evidence deduced from examining Hitler's remains, maintains that Hitler died not from a bullet but from a cyanide capsule, since, he says, a capsule was found in his mouth. The evidence to the contrary remains strong.

of the bloodthirsty conqueror from the east. The next moment it was his generals—incompetent, negligent, spineless; they were fools, fatheads. Yet the next moment he might seize upon some scheme for repairing in one swift move the long-crumbling walls of the Third Reich—previously uncommitted *Luftwaffe* and naval troops thrown into the line as infantry, a counterattack here, a shift of forces there.

The news of President Roosevelt's death produced a short-lived euphoria. Goebbels, the propagandist, reported it to Hitler by telephone while on air attack raged over the city. As it had been written in the stars, the miracle to save the Third Reich had come to pass. "My *Fuehrer*!" Goebbels exulted. "I congratulate you! Roosevelt is dead!"

Two days later Hitler used the news as basis for an order of the day. "At the moment when fate has removed the greatest war criminal of all time from the earth," he proclaimed, "the turning point of this war shall be decided."

As the military high command and the Nazi party hierarchy gathered in the bunker to pay obeisance on their leaders birthday, Hitler repeated over and over—as if repetition would make it so—that the Russians were about to incur their worst defeat in front of Berlin. Even though the generals warned that Russians and Western Allies soon would link to cut all escape routes to the south, he declined still to leave the capital. Should linkup occur, he decreed, the front was to be divided in two. Grossadmiral Doenitz, the naval chief, was to command in the north; somebody else in the south, possibly Kesselring or the *Luftwaffe's* Hermann Goering.

When Hitler observed magnanimously that others need not delay their departure from Berlin, many of the supposedly faithful scurried away. The SS chief, Himmler, headed north, to continue peace negotiations he had recently opened in secret with Count Folke Bernadotte, head of the Swedish Red Cross. Doenitz, too, headed north, while in a truck caravan loaded with luxuries the corpulent Goering turned south. Foreign Minister von Ribbentrop also got out, as did most of the staff officers and clerks of the high command, although Keitel and Jodl remained with a small Staff elsewhere in the city. The deputy head of the Nazi party, Martin Bormann, was among those staying on, and the faithful Goebbels moved with his wife and children into the bunker, where Hitler's mistress, Eva Braun, already had repaired.

Two days later, another slough of despond. At the daily situation conference Hitler staged what may have been the greatest of many notable rages. This was the end. Everybody had deserted him. Lies, corruption, cowardice, treason. They had left him no choice but to stand in Berlin and die.

Learning of this pronouncement the next day, Reichsmarshal Goering, whom Hitler long ago had designated to be his successor as head of state, deemed the time had come for him to take over and try to salvage something by peace negotiations. From Berchtesgaden, he radioed Hitler for instructions. If he had received no answer by late evening, he noted, he would assume that the *Fuehrer* had lost freedom of action; thereupon he would take control.

That same evening, in the north, Heinrich Himmler was usurping the powers of dictatorship without even asking. Himmler concluded his negotiations with Count Bernadotte and dispatched a letter to General Eisenhower. Germany, he wrote, was willing to surrender to the Western Allies while continuing to fight the Russians, until the Allies themselves were ready to assume responsibility for the campaign against bolshevism.

Goering's message threw Hitler into another rage. Accusing the Reichsmarshal of "high treason," Hitler demanded his resignation from the Nazi party and from command of the *Luftwaffe*. Before dawn the heir apparent of the Third Reich would find himself under arrest by the SS.

By this time an air of aimless resignation had descended over the bunker, relieved ever more rarely by some vain hope. It was common knowledge that Hitler intended suicide, as did Eva Braun. Late on April 26, Russian artillery fire began to fall in the garden of the Reich Chancellery above the bunker, reminder enough to any who still might doubt that the end was near.

Yet even though the *Fuehrer*'s military chiefs, Keitel and Jodl, had left the scene for a new headquarters in the north, they persisted in either coloring their reports on the military situation or refusing to face the facts themselves. The true picture, as General von Manteuffel insisted on telling them, was that Berlin had been surrounded since the twenty-third, that the Russians were pressing inexorably forward, that German troops were in profligate flight in company with the refugees, and that German officers who dared try to stop them took a bullet for their troubles.

On April 28 and 29 grim news poured into the bunker in a torrent. Word of American-Russian linkup; Italian partisans had arrested Mussolini;

distressing rumors of partisan insurrection and of army leaders in Italy negotiating surrender; an uprising in Munich. Then the news that the partisans had strung up Mussolini and his mistress by their heels. News, too, that the turnabout attack of General Wenck's *Twelfth Army* had failed, stalled seventeen miles short of the capital; and, by way of a broadcast by the BBC, that Himmler, like Goering, had turned traitor.

When a febrile reaction to Himmler's act had passed, Hitler drew a will and testament. He appointed Grossadmiral Doenitz as head of the German state and Supreme Commander of the Armed Forces, Goebbels as Chancellor of Germany, and Bormann as Nazi party minister. Then he married Eva Braun.

On the thirtieth Hitler spent much of the morning saying farewells to his household Staff; he was apparently unmoved by word that Russian troops were little more than a block away. In mid-afternoon he retired with Eva to his suite.

The newly wed Frau Hitler killed herself by biting on a cyanide capsule. The *Fuehrer* shot himself through the roof of his mouth with a pistol. SS guards, in accord with prior instructions, burned the bodies outside the bunker.

Chapter Thirty-One – Victory in Europe

News of Hitler's death was slow to emerge because Goebbels and Bormann delayed the announcement, the better to bargain over the surrender of Berlin in exchange for safe passage somewhere. When the Russians predictably declined to negotiate, word went out at last—more than twenty-four hours after the suicide—that Hitler was dead, even as Herr Doktor and Frau Goebbels were massacring their six children and arranging their own deaths at the hands of an SS guard. Other Nazis, including Martin Bormann, tried to make their way out of the city through the Russian encirclement; no one definitely made it, although Bormann may have.[245]

When Grossadmiral Doenitz announced the news of Hitler's death over the radio that evening, he resorted to the lie, the weak fabrication upon which the Third Reich had stood from the first. The *Fuehrer*, he told the German people, had died a hero's death at the head of his troops.

No matter how the *Fuehrer* had died, the word that he was gone all but eliminated the German soldier's resistance. It was as if some dreadful umbilical cord at last had been severed.

In the north, where the British with the help of an American corps with three divisions had crossed the Elbe and were driving toward the Baltic coast, resistance, which had been feeble all along, on May 2 collapsed entirely. The problem became one not of fighting but of advancing without running down pathetic masses of German soldiers and civilians who appeared to have but one goal: to get out of the way of the Russians.

While American units protected the right flank, a British division dashed all the way to the Baltic. The drive trapped German forces in the

---

[245] For this chapter, the basic sources were: Pogue, *The Supreme Command*, and my own work for *The Last Offensive*. See also those sources on the last days of Hitler listed under **Chapter Twenty-Eight**.

nation's northernmost province and barred Denmark to the Red Army. Only two hours later the first Russian troops appeared.

Resistance collapsed too, in the center, where two corps of the Third Army crossed into Czechoslovakia. What was left of a panzer division rolled into American lines under a white flag. On May 6, after filing past silent, undefended forts of Czechoslovakia's western fortifications, the "Little Maginot Line," American troops emerged abruptly from the disputed Sudetenland into a new world of frenzy and delight. It was Paris all over again, on a lesser scale and with a different flag and tongue but with the same jubilant faces, the same delrium of liberation. "*Nazdar!* *Nazdar!*" the people shouted.[246] War and non-fraternization lay behind.

American units penetrated approximately forty miles inside Czechoslovakia, entering Karlsbad and Pilzen and approaching Ceske Budejovice, along a line General Eisenhower had informed the Russians he intended to occupy. Although Churchill urged the gaining of political advantage by taking Prague, the Supreme Commander replied that he "would be loath to hazard American lives for purely political purposes."[247] Even after Czech partisans, beset by German tanks in Prague, appealed for help, Eisenhower stuck by his decision and passed on the request to the Russians, in whose sphere he deemed the Czechoslovakian capital to fall.

Resistance collapsed also in the south, where contingents of the Third Army took Linz and drew to a halt to await the Russians, and where the Seventh Army and the First French Army pushed into Austria's Alpine provinces. Seizing control of Innsbruck, Austrian "freedom fighters" delivered the city to the Seventh Army, whereupon, headlights blazing, a column of the 103d Division drove long into the night to take the Brenner Pass. A patrol continuing into Italy established contact the next morning, May 4, with the Fifth Army's 88th Division.

The new head of the German state and its armed forces had in the meantime begun to explore the possibilities of surrender. Although Doenitz knew that further resistance was futile, he wanted to save as many German soldiers and civilians as possible from the grasp of the Russians. Through information evolving out of Allied requests for German surrender in the Netherlands he knew that the Western Allies and the Soviet Union

[246] *Company Commander*, p. 308.

[247] Pogue, *The Supreme Command*, p. 468, quoting an Eisenhower message to Marshall.

were agreed to accept no overall surrender to east or west alone. The only chance of saving more Germans, he deduced, was to continue fighting in the east while arranging piecemeal surrenders in the west. Word went out late on May 2 to army group and army commanders that they were free to make local arrangements for surrender.

The first to do so was the commander of an army retreating before the Russians, who surrendered his command before night fell to an American airborne division that had participated in the British drive to the Baltic. A formal surrender was hardly necessary, for German officers and men—many with women and children in tow—already were falling over themselves to get into Allied prisoner-of-war enclosures. On this day and the next more than 150,000 gave up to the airborne troops; while on May 3, General von Manteuffel, who in the last weeks had commanded a panzer army opposing the Russians, surrendered with more than 200,000 men to an adjacent American infantry division.

On May 4, Field Marshal Montgomery accepted the unconditional surrender of all Germans in the Netherlands, the Frisian Islands, Heligoland and all other islands, northern Germany, and Denmark. Although he was unable, he said, to authorize withdrawal into Allied lines of German formations still fighting the Red Army, he could accept individual soldiers. Because the bulk of those opposing the Russians already had entered Allied lines in any case, the condition made little difference.

It was much the same for General Wenck's *Twelfth Army* and some 30,000 survivors of another army that had fought the Russians. These forces contacted General Simpson's Ninth U.S. Army and gained approval for individual soldiers to enter American lines, although civilians were excluded. In the event, nobody paid much attention to whether a refugee was soldier or civilian. By various means, including swimming, close to 100,000 Germans made their way into the lines of the Ninth Army.

In the south, what was left of the *Nineteenth Army*, commanded then by the former *Seventh Army* commander, General Brandenberger, surrendered at Innsbruck on May 5 to a corps of the U.S. Seventh Army. At the same time the current commander of the *First Army*, General der Infanterie Hermann Foertsch, was meeting at an estate near Munich with General Devers to arrange surrender of all of *Army Group G*.

It was no armistice but unconditional surrender, said General Devers. "Do you understand that?"

Foertsch stiffened. After nearly a minute, he responded. "I can assure you, sir," he said, "that no power is left at my disposal to prevent it."[248]

Foertsch's surrender included all German troops from the Swiss frontier to the Austro-Czechoslovakian border, thus marking surrender for the second time of the *Nineteenth Army* and providing the setting for General de Lattre of the First French Army to perform the final scene in his *opéra bouffe*.

In that part of Austria close to Switzerland, de Lattre's troops faced a shadow formation called the *Twenty-fourth Army*, which was no army at all but a collection of troops of less than divisional size that had long played a theatrical role along the Swiss frontier in an effort to convince the Allies that the Germans defended there in strength, and thus to discourage any Allied attempt to come at Germany by way of Switzerland. Subordinate to the *Nineteenth Army* and thus also to *Army Group* G, both of which had already surrendered all troops under their command, this so-called army by nightfall of May 5 had capitulated twice; but since the army's name had been mentioned specifically in the surrender of neither the *Nineteenth Army* nor *Army Group* G, de Lattre insisted on a formal surrender to the French.

The commander of the shadow army, General der Infanterie Hans Schmidt, declined to play the French game. He sent de Lattre a letter noting the broader surrender of *Army Group* G and suggesting that de Lattre discuss the matter with his superior, General Devers.

This "insolence" infuriated de Lattre. French troops, he insisted, would continue to fight until Schmidt gave in. Although General Devers sent a liaison officer to explain the situation to de Lattre and ordered a ceasefire, de Lattre remained adamant that Schmidt should be delivered to him for a formal ceremony of surrender.

There the matter rested while hostilities on the French front dwindled to an end, as the Germans ceased to fight back and as negotiations began for overall German surrender.

On May 5, still hoping to gain time to enable more soldiers and civilians to get inside Allied lines, Doenitz sent his successor in command of the German navy, Generaladmiral Hans Georg von Friedeburg, to Supreme Allied Headquarters to explain why total surrender was still impossible

---

[248] From the unpublished 6th Army Croup History (copy in OCMH).

and to explore the chance of more partial capitulations. When Friedeburg arrived at the headquarters in a red brick boys' school in Reims, he found the reception hostile.

That the Germans were stalling was hardly lost on General Eisenhower, and he intended to encourage it no more than he had encouraged Himmler to surrender only to the western powers. Eisenhower already had notified the Soviet Union that he intended to insist on simultaneous surrender on both fronts; the Russians had promptly agreed and had designated their senior liaison officer at Eisenhower's headquarters to represent Soviet interests.

Friedeburg had no choice but to notify Doenitz of the Allied stand. Shocked, Doenitz the next day sent General Jodl, strong opponent of surrender in the east, to try to find a way out. When it became clear early in the talks that Jodl, too, was stalling, General Eisenhower delivered an ultimatum. Either the Germans speedily agreed to unconditional surrender, he said, or he would "break off all negotiations and seal the western front, preventing by force any further westward movement of German soldiers and civilians."[249]

Convinced that the Supreme Commander meant what he said, Jodl telegraphed Doenitz for authority to make a final and complete surrender on all fronts. Since it was Jodl—only the day before he had strongly opposed surrender in the east—who insisted that this was the only course, Doenitz felt impelled to accede.

Jodl signed the surrender documents at 2:41 A.M. on May 7, to become effective at 11:01 P.M. the next day, May 8.

An Associated Press correspondent, Edward Kennedy—in violation of a pledge exacted of all correspondents to wait official pronouncement of the news—flashed word of the surrender to the United States soon after Jodl had signed. The news set off a wild celebration in New York's Times Square until Eisenhower's headquarters issued a statement that the story was unofficial. The formal announcement the next day from Washington and London designated that day, May 8, as V-E Day—Victory in Europe. The Russians waited to make their announcement until after a second surrender ceremony staged late on the eighth in Berlin with Keitel substituting for Jodl and "Beetle" Smith for Eisenhower.

[249] Pogue, *The Supreme Command*, p. 487.

In a kind of delirium people all over Europe ripped away blackout curtains. For the first time in almost six years house and street lights blazed. Military vehicles and such civilian automobiles as were abroad ran with headlights on. Soldiers lit cigarettes in the night without fear of drawing enemy fire. Seeing fireworks exploding in the sky above Pilsen, a young rifle company commander squeezed the hand of the Czechoslovakian girl with him and said the only word of her language he yet had learned: "*Dobri, dobri*" meaning "good."[250]

Jubilant were the celebrations—in Times Square, Piccadilly Circus, the Champs Elysées, Rome, Oslo, Copenhagen, Brussels, The Hague—but carried on with the knowledge, particularly in the United States, that the Pacific war still went on. For the troops in Europe the end brought a flush of relief, even though it was much like hearing of the death of an unmourned old man who had held grimly on until at long last the final dim spark of life had inevitably flowed out of him.

Myriad and taxing were the jobs remaining. Allied troops had to disarm and control German forces, many of them sizable, as in Denmark, Norway, and Czechoslovakia, and to discharge them quickly in order to reduce the strain on food stocks and facilities. They had to continue to evacuate Allied prisoners of war; control, feed, and eventually evacuate foreign laborers; assert authority over the Doenitz government. They had also to collect German records and documents; arrest those Germans who might be charged with war crimes; arrange for four-power occupation of Vienna and Berlin; and relocate troops in keeping with the agreed zones of occupation. The Americans had to begin deploying units for service in the war against Japan and to determine by a point system based on wounds, time in combat, and length of overseas service which men might go home first.

Even after the surrender became effective late on May 8, thousands of German soldiers and civilians still tried to find haven inside Allied lines. Since it was implicit in the surrender agreement that those still outside at the effective hour would have to surrender to the Russians, Allied troops had no choice but to turn the soldiers back. Pitiable were the scenes enacted, as many a German soldier murdered his wife and children, then killed himself, rather than submit to captivity in Russia. For some million

---

[250] *Company Commander*, p. 310.

and one quarter Germans who became prisoners of the Russians after the surrender, the way home—for those who made it—was long and toilsome.

The capitulation of other German troops to the Allies meanwhile produced few problems. The British took the surrender of units in Denmark and Norway; the Canadians, those in the Netherlands. A garrison that had held out on the French coast at Dunkirk surrendered on the ninth to a Czechoslovakian brigade that had besieged the port; the last holdouts in southwestern France fell to the French on the same day; those in the Channel Islands, to the British. The next day the Germans in two long-held ports in Brittany gave up to American troops.

As the war came to an end, General Eisenhower's command encompassed more than 4,500,000 troops including 91 divisions (61 of them American), 6 tactical air commands, and 2 strategic air forces. At peak strength Eisenhower's command had 28,000 combat aircraft, of which 14,845 were American. Between D Day and V-E Day, a cumulative total of almost 5,500,000 Allied troops had entered western Europe, along with 970,000 vehicles and over 18,000,000 tons of supplies The Allies at the same time had achieved victory in Italy with 18 divisions (7 of those present at the last were American), 2 tactical air commands, and 2 strategic air forces. Unlike World War I, when the United States had come late and had provided only the balance of power, the United States in World War II had provided well over half the forces leading to victory by the Western Allies in Europe. Yet for all the tremendous power at General Eisenhower's disposal, when V-E Day came, only one division—an American airborne division—remained uncommitted.

It was over. At long last it was over, man's most convulsive effort to destroy himself, all attributable in the long run to the demoniacal ambition of a twisted mind abetted by the docility, the indecision, the antipathy to sacrifice of saner minds, the incredible ability of free men to convince themselves that the bell tolls only for somebody else.

Appalling was the word for it. In North Africa and Europe, all told, on both sides, military and civilian, from 1939 to the end, there were probably more than 35,000,000 dead and a continent was in ruins.

In North Africa and Europe, including Italy, the U.S. Army and Army Air Forces incurred 765,694 casualties, including 177,062 dead. In the Mediterranean and the Atlantic, the U.S. Navy incurred 10,204 casualties, including 5,462 dead. The total for the war against Germany and Italy was 775,898 casualties; 182,524 dead.

However tremendous the contribution and sacrifice of the Soviet Union—particularly in human lives—that of the United States and the western powers was nevertheless immense. The peak strength of American armed forces alone, for example, nearly equaled that of the Russians (12,500,000 to 12,294,000). While fighting a multifront war over vast sea and land distances, the United States at the same time was contributing equipment and supplies to the other warring nations with a total value of more than $50,000,000,000. The Russians received more than 400,000 jeeps and trucks, more than 12,000 armored vehicles (including more than 7,000 tanks, enough to equip some 20-odd armored divisions), more than 14,000 aircraft, and close to 2,000,000 tons of food.

Although the Russian armies had absorbed the full fury of the German armed forces at the peak of their power and in the process so wore down the Germans that the Allied D Day was considerably less difficult than it might have been, it was nevertheless true that the Russians fought throughout a one-front ground war where space and distance meant considerably less than in Western Europe, while they contributed almost nothing to the strategic air war and even less to the war at sea, both integral parts of the victory. Nor were contributions to the ground war as weighted on the Soviet side as cursory appraisal might indicate. During the Ardennes counteroffensive, for example, the Germans had only two-thirds as many tanks on the entire eastern front as they had in the Ardennes. As the counteroffensive raged, only 125 German divisions were present on the eastern front, while 100 stood in the west and another 23 in Italy.

Some proponents of air power would try to maintain that the results of the strategic bombing had fulfilled the predictions of the theorists of the twenties and thirties that air power could do it all. Yet events had proved that the air weapon, while tremendously powerful, had not yet developed as the arm of decision. Despite the tremendous weight of bombs dropped on Germany, only at the end of 1944 had German production of essential military items dropped off sharply, and only in late January and early February of 1945 were indications of eventual collapse present in the German economy.

Had Allied airmen known from the start what they learned later— how persistent blasting of a select group of targets critical to the entire

509

economy may be more effective in less time than occasional strikes against a host of targets—the aerial campaign might have achieved a decision. As it was, the Allied and the Russian armies had broken the back of the German armies before the aerial bombardment could build to an intensity capable of decision in its own right. About all that could be said with any certainty about the aerial campaign was that American air commanders were right in insisting on precision as opposed to area bombing. The American way was more effective while at the same time it was relatively sparing of human life.

The Allied naval contribution was also an essential though not decisive element of the victory. Without success against the submarine, the Allied buildup in the United Kingdom, both for the strategic air campaign and for the ground invasion, well might have proved impossible.

World War II in Europe had demonstrated, as had all preceding wars, that decision comes in the clash of armies on the ground. Whether man's harnessing of the atom would change that remained to be seen.

Could the United States have stood clear of the war in Europe? Given the nation's cultural and economic ties to the Old World and the measure of the Axis threat, involvement was probably inevitable. Even though no literal peril to national security existed before Pearl Harbor, and even though there was no popular enthusiasm for intervention, the nation had drifted in a resigned but inevitable way into the war, as if unable to resist the world responsibilities it had first accepted in 1917. The changing attitudes of Roosevelt himself, ever sensitive to the mood of his people, reflected the pulse of the nation. The kind of involvement that Roosevelt practiced must almost always end in commitment.

Were American leaders right in resisting Churchill's peripheral strategy? What most American military men dealing with Churchill and the British Chiefs of Staff found hard to comprehend was the depth of concern the British felt for the ghosts of Passehendaelc, the Somme, and Dunkirk. The American Chiefs mistook trepidation for disaffection, delay for perfidy. While Churchill and his colleagues never doubted the necessity of an eventual cross-Channel attack, they did question its timing. The Americans were not, in fact, prepared for the direct invasion nearly so early as they thought; and without the peripheral diversions to which they reluctantly subscribed, they well might have failed in the direct blow.

As to Churchill's predilection for what he called the "soft underbelly" of Europe, those who saw in it a lack of dedication to an eventual cross-Channel attack misinterpreted the oratorical flourishes. Churchill wanted to go through the Balkans to Vienna to forestall the Red colossus, but he saw the move throughout as only another peripheral stab—albeit one capable of extending the utility of the forces in Italy and establishing a western beachhead against Communist expansion: a political awareness American leaders would have done well to emulate. Churchill never proposed—and not only the Combined Chiefs but the British Chiefs as well never considered—any substitution of a D Day in the Balkans for a D Day in Normandy. Who could have been more aware than the astute Churchill that it was less dangerous to have Communists in Belgrade and Bucharest than in Le Havre and Boulogne?

Even the invasion of North Africa, it might be argued, may have come too soon—frail landing craft, Grant tanks, 37-mm. anti-tank guns: these had no place in the warfare of 1942 and 1943. Yet the man who decreed North Africa, Franklin Roosevelt, had well calculated the mood of his people. There comes a time in the lives of free men and even of men who yearn to be free when, whatever the state of their preparation, they must act directly—even if impractically—against the foe. The various resistance movements, confronted with overwhelming odds and the necessity for appalling sacrifice, more than proved that point.

The campaigns in Sicily and Italy accomplished what Allied planners had expected of them. They knocked Italy and the cardboard *Duce* out of the war, and they tied down German divisions.

The question remained whether with justifiable risk the Allies might not have bypassed Sicily for Sardinia or Corsica and from one or the other have entered the Italian boot less painfully from north instead of south. That strategy might have obviated the harsh, grudging struggle up the length of the boot; yet it might have prompted the Germans to avoid what was in the end their egregious error in Italy: because of Hitler's obstinacy and Kesselring's ambition, they had stood in defense of Italy and thereby enabled the Allies to pin down twenty-odd German divisions which might have been used decisively elsewhere, notably in Normandy. Admiring as Hitler was of Frederick the Great, he had failed throughout to heed Frederick's dictum that he who holds all loses all.

The theory that Allied forces in Europe could have ended the war in the fall of 1944 had Eisenhower given Montgomery the support he asked, the Supreme Commander's logisticians had discounted at the time, labeling it a castle of theory built upon the sand of overambition. To have succeeded with one thrust, however powerful, the Allied armies would have required Antwerp as a working port, which, because of Montgomery's failure to clear the banks of the Schelde estuary, they had obtained only after another three months. They also would have had to have a line such as the Rhine that they might defend economically. Neither of these legitimate conditions had shown any signs of being met.

On the issue of Berlin, Eisenhower plainly was right. Why drive deeper into territory already allocated for Russian occupation merely for the sake of prestige? That General Simpson and his Ninth Army, with some help from Hodges' First Army, could have done the job was another matter. Given the inclination of German troops at that stage of the war to surrender to Allied forces, the Americans could have taken Berlin. Only Walter Wenck's *Twelfth Army* stood in the way, and that was an army of children, effective enough against a little bridgehead that had no anti-tank defense, but it would have collapsed in the face of the power of an entire American field army. On the other hand, given the direction and the force of Soviet intransigence, taking Berlin would have done nothing to forestall the problems that were later to arise over Allied access to the city. The pattern of four-power occupation of Berlin and tenuous Allied connections to the city already had been drawn.

Yet what of Prague? When Eisenhower first refused Churchill's overtures to go to the Czechoslovakian capital, he was right in view of the legitimate concern over possible Nazi holdouts in Denmark and Norway. Yet when, after V-E Day, Czechoslovak partisans cried for help under extreme duress, the matter became less political than humanitarian. After the way the Supreme Commander had been announcing his intentions and obtaining Russian approval in every case with alacrity, he easily could have notified the Russians that conditions in Prague demanded Allied entry. Partisans roaming the countryside made it clear that nothing stood in the way of a swift American move from Pilsen to Prague.

What such a move would have accomplished in terms of the postwar world is something else. As the Allies demonstrated by quick withdrawal from Pilsen and other sectors, they had no plan to stay long in Czechoslovakia. Furthermore, Czechoslovakia, for all its western orientation, had deep and abiding ties with the Slavic world that Allied armies taking Prague would have done little to sever.

In regard to both Berlin and Prague, General Eisenhower thus was innocent of the frequent charge that he failed to appreciate that politics is war's handmaiden if not its demanding mistress. In neither case was there anything to be gained politically by racing to beat the Russians to the scene.

On tactical matters Eisenhower and other Allied commanders were more vulnerable to criticism: the tactical dispositions and the intelligence failure that led to Kasserine; the way Allied naval and air forces allowed the Germans to escape from Sicily; Walker's methods at the Rapido, Lucas' at Anzio; Clark's decision to downgrade Valmontone and drive on Rome; the failure to seal the Argentan-Falaise pocket, owing equally to Montgomery's conservatism and Bradley's reluctance to press the issue; Montgomery's failure to clear the banks of the Schelde estuary; the costly and unimaginative campaign in the Huertgen Forest which might have been avoided by proper appreciation of the Roer River dams; the intelligence failure in the Ardennes; Montgomery's prideful refusal to allow Simpson's Ninth Army to jump the Rhine and his persistence in using airborne troops to cross the Rhine against a splintered foe; Patton's ill-advised and ill-starred foray to Hammelburg.

Yet in all cases except Hammelburg there were reasonable explanations and mitigating circumstances; and their effect on the conduct and outcome of the war was never marked. The Allied nations could be grateful that the challenge of the war in Europe had produced the imaginative, determined military leaders that the circumstances required, just as men like Roosevelt and Churchill and George Marshall had emerged to guide the war effort at the top. In no way were Allied leaders in Europe in World War II culpable in the manner of a Haig or a Joffre.

The Allied nations and the world could be grateful, too, that American leaders had made the decision: Europe First. Without that decision the Germans well might have attained the scientific advances they required for victory, and the world might have seen the first atomic bomb not in American hands, as dreadful as that turned out to be, but in the bloody hands of those who had ravaged European civilization.

Few who fought the fight could question the right of the cause, for the proof of the enemy's depravity, of the awful tyranny that man can practice on his fellow man, was there for all to see at Buchenwald, at Belsen, at Dachau, and at many another place, including little Ohrdruf. Elimination of those cruel monuments to evil was reason enough for the mighty endeavor that it was: from flaming ships in the Atlantic to plummeting aircraft over Germany; from embattled beaches in North Africa, Sicily, and Italy to bloody OMAHA; and on to a bridgehead to nowhere over the Elbe.

A Selected Bibliography

For all the vast amount of published material on World War II, the general works are few.

Several studies by distinguished historians emerged within a few years of the end of the war but were written before a broad selection of source material became available. They include Henry Steele Commager, *The Story of the Second World War* (Boston, 1945), which is basically a collection of contemporary writings with connective narrative; Harvey A. De Weerd and Roger Shugg, *World War II* (Washington, 1946); Cyril Falls, *The Second World War: A Short History* (London, 1948); J. F. C. Fuller, *The Second World War, 1939-1945: A Strategical and Tactical History* (New York, 1949); and Fletcher Pratt, *War for the World* (New Haven, 1950).

Among later works, Colonels T. Dodson Stamps and Vincent J. Esposito and other members of the faculty of the United States Military Academy produced A *Military History of World War II* (West Point, 1953) for the use of cadets studying tactics and strategy. Louis L. Snyder in *The War: A Concise History* (New York, 1960) depended too heavily on contemporary newspaper accounts and fell into unnecessary errors. Vincent J. Esposito, ed., A *Concise History of World War II* (New York, 1964), to which I contributed, is a collection of articles written originally for *The Encyclopedia Americana* and thus lacks cohesion and unity.

In the academic tradition, A. Russell Buchanan, *The United States and World War II* (two vols., New York, 1964) is comprehensive and generally accurate but lacks critical analysis. Kenneth S. Davis, *The Experience of War: The United States in World War II* (Garden City, 1965), is a highly readable account which, while impressionistic, deserves many readers; I have found it particularly helpful. Although Chester Wilmot, *The Struggle for Europe* (New York, 1952), deals primarily with the campaign on the European continent, it nevertheless provides a good summary of earlier events and remains the best one-volume work on the war in Europe from a British viewpoint. As I was completing my study, Barrie Pitt, ed., *History of the Second World War*, to which I contributed, began to appear as a weekly periodical in Britain and several other countries but, unfortunately, not in the United States. The issues contain much valuable material, particularly technical matter on weapons, planes, ships. C. L. Sulzberger and the editors of *American Heritage*, *The American Heritage Picture History of World War II* (New York, no date), is graphically impressive, but the text is not always accurate.

As with general works, the number of bibliographies also is limited, but four are so comprehensive and analytical that no real lacuna exists. They are: Louis Morton, *Writings on World War II* (American Historical Association, 1967); Professor Buchanan, *The United States and World War II*; Mr. Davis, *The Experience of War*; and Gordon Wright, *The Ordeal of Total War, 1939-1945* (New York, 1968). Professor Wright's work appeared as I completed my study and focuses on the war from the European viewpoint.

All four of the bibliographies note literature on subjects that I have been able either to touch upon only briefly or not at all. They embrace such topics as the background of the war in Europe, the early European campaigns, the war in Russia, espionage and intelligence operations, civil-military relations, economic, industrial, intellectual, and cultural aspects, science and technology, psychological warfare, the resistance movements, Nazi policy in occupied countries, politics and diplomacy, development of the atomic bomb, and others.

Since these excellent bibliographies exist, I have made no attempt to duplicate or supplement them. In general, I note under the appropriate chapter heading those works that have been of particular use to me, along with sources for direct quotations and special material.

Aside from the general works, a number of others have been of such broad value that they should be noted in relation to the entire volume. They include: two volumes written with Department of State cooperation by William L. Langer and S. Everett Gleason, *The Challenge to Isolation, 1937-1940* (New York, 1952) and *The Undeclared War, 1940-1941* (New York, 1953); Winston Churchill, *The Second World War* (6 vols., Boston, 1949-1953); and two volumes by Forrest C. Pogue in the authorized biography of George C. Marshall, *Education of a General, 1880-1939* (New York, 1963) and *Ordeal and Hope, 1939-1942* (New York, 1966).

They also include the official histories of the United States services, without which I could not have written this study. Having participated in the writing of the U.S. Army's volumes, I know the admirable conditions of access and objectivity under which the scholars who undertook the work labored, and I have no hesitation in making wide use of their material. The interpretations and opinions expressed nevertheless are mine and do not always agree with those of the other official historians.

Written by Samuel Eliot Morison but with research assistance by official naval historians and published commercially (Boston: Little, Brown, and Co.), the *History of the United States Naval Operations in World War II* is at least semi-official. Of eleven volumes, those of particular use were: Vol. I, *The Battle of the Atlantic* (1951); Vol. II, *Operations in North African Waters* (1950); Vol. IX, *Sicily—Salerno—Anzio* (1954); Vol. X, *The Atlantic Battle Won* (1956); and Vol. XI, *The Invasion of France and Germany* (1957). Professor Morison has also provided a two-volume summary of the series, *The Two-Ocean War* (Boston, 1963).

Also published outside of the government (The University of Chicago Press), *The Army Air Forces in World War II* is nevertheless fully official. Of seven volumes edited by Wesley Frank Craven and James Lea Cate, those of use for this work were: Vol. I, *Plans and Early Operations, January 1939 to August 1942* (1948); Vol. II, *Europe—TORCH to POINTBLANK* (1949); Vol. Ill, *Europe—ARGUMENT to V-E Day* (1951); and Vol. VI, *Men and Planes* (1955).

Of seventy published volumes out of some eighty projected in the series, *U.S. Army in World War II*, edited by Kent Roberts Greenfield and Stetson Conn and published by the Government Printing Office—the most comprehensive historical project ever undertaken—those that proved essential to my work were:

Martin Blumenson, *Breakout and Pursuit* (1961) and *Salerno to Cassino* (1969); Ray S. Cline, *Washington Command Post: The Operations Division* (1951); Hugh M. Cole, *The Lorraine Campaign* (1950) and *The Ardennes: Battle of the Bulge* (1965); Stetson Conn and Byron Fairchild, *The Framework of Hemisphere Defense* (1960) and, with Rose C. Engelman, *Guarding the United States and Its Outposts* (1964); Constance McLaughlin Green, Harry C. Thomson, and Peter C. Roots, *The Ordnance Department: Planning*

Munitions for War (1955); Kent Roberts Greenfield, Robert R. Palmer, and Bell I. Wiley, *The Organization of Ground Combat Troops* (1947).

Also, Gordon Harrison, *Cross-Channel Attack* (1951); George F. Howe, *Northwest Africa: Seizing the Initiative in the West* (1957); Ulysses Lee, *The Employment of Negro Troops* (1966); Richard M. Leighton and Robert W. Coakley, *Global Logistics and Strategy: 1940-1943* (1955); Charles B. MacDonald, *The Siegfried Line Campaign* (1963) and, with Sidney T. Mathews, *Three Battles: Arnaville, Altuzzo, and Schmidt* (1954); Maurice Matloff and Edwin M. Snell, *Strategic Planning for Coalition Warfare: 1941-1942* (1953); Maurice Matloff, *Strategic Planning for Coalition Warfare: 1943-1944* (1959); Lida Mayo, *The Ordnance Department: On Beachhead and Batdefront* (1968).

Also, Robert R. Palmer, Bell I. Wiley, and William R. Kcast, *The Procurement and Training of Ground Combat Troops* (1948); Forrest C. Pogue, *The Supreme Command* (1954); William F. Ross and Charles F. Romanus, *The Quartermaster Corps: Operations in the War Against Germany* (1965); Roland G. Ruppenthal, *Logistical Support of the Armies*, Vol. I (1953) and II (1959); R. Elberton Smith, *The Army and Economic Mobilization* (1959); Howard M. Smyth and Albert N. Garland, *Sicily and the Surrender of Italy* (1965); Marcel Vigneras, *Rearming the French* (1957); and Mark Skinner Watson, *Chief of Staff: Pre-war Plans and Preparations* (1950).

In addition, I have used three other of the Army's official works: Kent Roberts Greenfield, ed., *Command Decisions* (1960), a series of essays by Army historians; Earl F. Ziemke, *Stalingrad to Berlin: The German Defeat in the East* (1968); and my own manuscript now in the editorial process, *The Last Offensive.*

I have also used several of the official British histories: Sir Charles Webster and Noble Frankland, *The Strategic Air Offensive Against Germany, 1939-1945*, Vol. I, *Preparation* (London, 1961), Vol. II, *Endeavor* (1961), and Vol. III, *Victory* (1961); Capt. S. W. Roskill, *The War at Sea, 1939-1945*, Vol I, *The Defensive* (1954), Vol. II, *The Period of Balance* (1956), and Vol. III, *The Offensive* (1960); Maj. Gen. I. S. O. Playfair, *et al.*, *The Mediterranean and Middle East*, Vol. IV, *The Destruction of Axis Forces in Africa* (1966); J. M. A. Gwyer and J. R. M. Butler, *Grand Strategy*, Vol. Ill, *The Offensive* (1960); and John Ehrman, *Grand Strategy*, Vols. V and VI (1956).

The serious student of the war should also consult the appropriate volumes in the multi-volume documentary series published by the Department of State, *Foreign Relations of the United States*, and the related volumes on the various wartime conferences. The latest to be published is on the Casablanca conference.

In deciding to prepare this study in my off-duty time, I clearly had to confine most of my research to published materials; the documentation is too vast for one man in one lifetime to do otherwise, even as full-time labor. In order to avoid any problems of security clearance with original material that is still classified, I relied in all cases of classified documents on accounts previously published. Nevertheless, in the course of working for twenty years on the history of World War II with the Department of the Army's Office of the Chief of Military History (OCMH), writing two of the Army's official histories, co-authoring another, and supervising preparation of six more, I have examined much of the original material. In the case of documents from which I have quoted, I have in all cases examined the original.

Since I participated in the war in Europe, it is perhaps inevitable that some of my personal observations should emerge here and there. I also have had the privilege through the years of interviewing many of the leading characters in the story, including Generals Eisenhower, Bradley, Devers, Collins, Creighton W. Abrams, and Sir Frederick Morgan.

Acknowledgments

My gratitude to my colleagues in the Office of the Chief of Military History and to their counterparts in the historical offices of the Air Force and the Navy, whose prior work was essential to the writing of this history. For reading the manuscript and catching multiple errors, my appreciation to my friends, Forrest Pogue, official biographer of George C. Marshall; and Martin Blumenson, distinguished writer. Any errors that remain are my responsibility alone, and the views and opinions expressed bear no official endorsement by the Office of the Chief of Military History or any agency of the Department of Defense. My appreciation, also, to a patient editor, Sheldon Meyer, and an incomparable copy editor, Mrs. Norman Hoss. For help in selecting photographs, I thank Miss Ruth A. Phillips. A word, too, for my children, Moire and Bruce, whose understanding has sustained me through many travails.

Charles B. MacDonald

Portree

Oxon Hill, Maryland

Spring 1969

[NB Army units are italicised – ie. *First Army* – and some key operations and landings are capitalised ie. OMAHA.]

*